America's Top-Rated Cities: a Statistical Handbook

Volume III
Central Region

1998
6th Edition

Rhoda Garoogian, *Managing Editor*
Andrew Garoogian, *Research Editor*
Patrice Walsh Weingart, *Assistant Editor*

Universal Reference Publications

America's Top-Rated Cities: A Statistical Handbook 1998
ISBN 1-881220-38-7 (4 volume set)
ISBN 1-881220-40-0 (Vol. 1 - South)
ISBN 1-881220-41-9 (Vol. 2 - West)
ISBN 1-881220-42-7 (Vol. 3 - Central)
ISBN 1-881220-43-5 (Vol. 4 - East)

Printed and bound in the United States of America.

Preface

This revised and expanded 1998 edition of *America's Top-Rated Cities* is intended to provide the user with a current and concise statistical profile of 76 "top" U.S. cities with populations over 100,000, based on latest census data and/or current estimates. These cities, selected on the basis of their rankings in various surveys (*Money, Fortune, Entrepreneur, Home Office Computing, Site Selection* and others) were found to be the "best" for business and/or living, during 1997.

There are now four regional guides in the series: Southern, Western, Central and Eastern. Designed with ease of use in mind, each handbook is arranged alphabetically by city and divided into two sections: the business environment and the living environment. Rankings and evaluative comments follow a brief overview. Information is then presented under such topics as cost of living, finances, taxes, population, employment and earnings, commercial real estate, education, major employers, media, crime, climate and more. Where appropriate, comparisons with Metropolitan Statistical Areas (MSA) and U.S. figures are included.

There is also a section listing Chambers of Commerce, economic development groups, and State Departments of Labor/Employment Security, that the reader may wish to contact for further information.

In addition to material provided by public/private agencies/organizations, numerous library sources were also consulted. Also utilized were various web sites on the Internet. Tables and charts are properly cited with the appropriate reference to the source of the data. Those tables which are based on the 1990 Census of Population & Housing: Summary Tape File 3C contain sample data to represent the total population.

Although every effort has been made to gather the most current and most accurate information, discrepancies may occur due to the changing nature in the way private and governmental agencies compile and interpret statistical data.

Information in previous editions should not be compared with data in this edition since some historical and forecast data have been revised.

The *America's Top-Rated Cities* series has been compiled for individuals considering relocating, business persons, general and market researchers, real estate consultants, human resource personnel, urban planners as well as students and others who use public, school, academic and special libraries.

The editors wish to thank all of those individuals who responded to our requests for information. Especially helpful were the many Chambers of Commerce, economic development organizations, labor market information bureaus and city school districts. Their assistance is greatly appreciated.

The mission of Universal Reference Publications is to develop a series of comprehensive but reasonably priced statistical reference handbooks about America's "best" cities. Towards that end we have also published *America's Top-Rated Smaller Cities, Health & Environment in America's Top-Rated Cities* and *Crime in America's Top-Rated Cities*.

We welcome your comments and suggestions for improving the coverage and presentation of data in future editions of these handbooks.

The Editors

Table of Contents

Ann Arbor, Michigan

Chicago, Illinois

Des Moines, Iowa

Detroit, Michigan

Evansville, Indiana

Fort Wayne, Indiana

Grand Rapids, Michigan

Green Bay, Wisconsin

Indianapolis, Indiana

Kansas City, Missouri

Little Rock, Arkansas

Madison, Wisconsin

Milwaukee, Wisconsin

Minneapolis, Minnesota

Oklahoma City, Oklahoma

Saint Louis, Missouri

Saint Paul, Minnesota

Sioux Falls, South Dakota

Springfield, Missouri

Comparative Statistics

Ann Arbor, Michigan

Background

Located on the Huron River, 36 miles west of Detroit, Ann Arbor is the trading center for a rich agricultural area.

John Allen and Elisha W. Rumsey, two Eastern entrepreneurs, founded the community in 1824, which they named for their wives who were both called Ann, and for the community's location which was within natural groves.

Before the arrival of settlers, the Ojibwa tribe roamed the area, which they called Washtenaw, "the land beyond". The name now serves for the county of which Ann Arbor is the seat.

The original settlement developed as an agriculture trading center after the arrival of the Michigan Central Railroad in 1839. In 1837 the University of Michigan moved there and has since played a prominent role in Ann Arbor's development as a major Midwest center for aeronautical, space, nuclear, chemical and metallurgical research. The city's manufactures include machinery, tools, steel ball bearing, scientific instruments, doors and blinds, cameras and coil springs.

In 1851 Ann Arbor was chartered as a city.

Located in the humid continental climate zone, Ann Arbor's summers are hot, winters cold and there is an above-average occurrence of snow and rain. Because the city is near the Great Lakes extremes in both winter and summer temperatures are moderated, although it also causes high humidity and cloud cover two-thirds of the time.

General Rankings and Evaluative Comments

■ Ann Arbor was ranked #68 out of 300 cities by *Money's* 1997 "Survey of the Best Places to Live." Criteria used: health services, crime, economy, housing, education, transportation, weather, leisure and the arts. The city was ranked #5 in 1996 and #33 in 1995.
Money, July 1997; Money, September 1996; Money, September 1995

■ *Ladies Home Journal* ranked America's 200 largest cities based on the qualities women care about most. Ann Arbor ranked 10 out of 200. Criteria: low crime rate, good public schools, well-paying jobs, quality health and child care, the presence of women in government, proportion of women-owned businesses, size of the wage gap with men, local economy, divorce rates, the ratio of single men to single women, whether there are laws that require at least the same number of public toilets for women as men, and the probability of good hair days. *Ladies Home Journal, November 1997*

■ Ann Arbor is among "The Best Places to Raise a Family". Rank: 15 out of 301 metro areas. Criteria: low crime rate, low drug and alcohol abuse, good public schools, high-quality health care, a clean environment, affordable cost of living and strong economic growth. *Reader's Digest, April 1997*

■ Ann Arbor was ranked #8 out of 219 cities in terms of children's health, safety, and economic well-being. Criteria: total population, percent population change, birth rate, child immunization rate, infant mortality rate, percent low birth weight infants, percent of births to teens, physician-to-population ratio, student-to-teacher ratio, dropout rate, unemployment rate, median family income, percent of children in poverty, violent and property crime rates, number of juvenile arrests for violent crimes as a percent of the total crime index, number of days with pollution standard index (PSI) over 100, pounds toxic releases per 1,000 people and number of superfund sites. *Zero Population Growth, Children's Environmental Index 1997*

■ According to *Working Mother,* "Michigan increased its spending on child care by $44 million, which means that nearly 14,000 more kids will be served this year. Next year, child care funding is slated to reach $201 million, a $16 million boost over 1997 spending. One key part of the budget: a special program to recruit caregivers who want to specialize in infant care, since demand for such care is so great here.

In this state, as in so many others, there has been a raging controversy over how to expand child care options without diluting the quality of the programs. Governor John Engler had previously considered a radical approach to child care, which would have allowed parents to use state funds to pay unlicensed caregivers. Child care activists and providers managed to convince Engler that this was a bad idea, and it was never officially proposed. Another idea the governor floated—an elimination of background checks for caregivers—was also shelved." *Working Mother, July/August 1997*

Business Environment

STATE ECONOMY

State Economic Profile

"...retail sales growth and residential construction are below the national average, and bankruptcy filings have accelerated to 33% above one year ago.

Michigan will continue to nurture white-collar, auto-related operations. While international auto manufacturers have not located assembly plants in Michigan, they have located their research facilities in the state. Michigan is also a center for allied auto-related research activity, such as robotics and software development.

Michigan's population growth improved slightly last year to almost 0.6%, though it remains well below the national average. For the past two years, net migration has been positive in Michigan, a significant turnaround for the state. While net domestic migration remains stubbornly negative, many fewer people are leaving Michigan than earlier in the decade.

In the near term, Michigan's economy will continue to grow at about the national pace. Sizable auto industry bonuses will boost incomes and fatten the state treasury this year. Long term, substantial investments in auto-related production facilities will ensure that a significant portion of vehicle and parts manufacturing will remain in the state. However, Michigan's high cost of doing business, coupled with the high level of unionization, will continue to limit investment in the state. Michigan will be a below-average performer long term." *National Association of Realtors, Economic Profiles: The Fifty States, July 1997*

IMPORTS/EXPORTS

Total Export Sales

Area	1993 ($000)	1994 ($000)	1995 ($000)	1996 ($000)	% Chg. 1993-96	% Chg. 1995-96
MSA[1]	2,218,083	2,075,769	1,157,910	1,311,134	-40.9	13.2
U.S.	464,858,354	512,415,609	583,030,524	622,827,063	34.0	6.8

Note: (1) Metropolitan Statistical Area - see Appendix A for areas included
Source: U.S. Department of Commerce, International Trade Association, Metropolitan Area Exports: An Export Performance Report on Over 250 U.S. Cities, October 1997

Imports/Exports by Port

Type	Cargo Value			Share of U.S. Total	
	1995 (US$mil.)	1996 (US$mil.)	% Change 1995-1996	1995 (%)	1996 (%)
Imports	0	0	0	0	0
Exports	0	0	0	0	0

Source: Global Trade Information Services, WaterBorne Trade Atlas 1997

CITY FINANCES

City Government Finances

Component	FY92 ($000)	FY92 (per capita $)
Revenue	134,280	1,214.65
Expenditure	135,573	1,226.35
Debt Outstanding	96,769	875.34
Cash & Securities	207,034	1,872.76

Source: U.S. Bureau of the Census, City Government Finances: 1991-92

City Government Revenue by Source

Source	FY92 ($000)	FY92 (per capita $)	FY92 (%)
From Federal Government	8,252	74.64	6.1
From State Governments	21,084	190.72	15.7
From Local Governments	984	8.90	0.7
Property Taxes	41,831	378.39	31.2
General Sales Taxes	0	0.00	0.0
Selective Sales Taxes	0	0.00	0.0
Income Taxes	0	0.00	0.0
Current Charges	20,592	186.27	15.3
Utility/Liquor Store	11,119	100.58	8.3
Employee Retirement[1]	16,596	150.12	12.4
Other	13,822	125.03	10.3

Note: (1) Excludes "city contributions," classified as "nonrevenue," intragovernmental transfers.
Source: U.S. Bureau of the Census, City Government Finances: 1991-92

City Government Expenditures by Function

Function	FY92 ($000)	FY92 (per capita $)	FY92 (%)
Educational Services	0	0.00	0.0
Employee Retirement[1]	9,823	88.86	7.2
Environment/Housing	21,287	192.56	15.7
Government Administration	8,715	78.83	6.4
Interest on General Debt	4,120	37.27	3.0
Public Safety	19,628	177.55	14.5
Social Services	721	6.52	0.5
Transportation	13,888	125.63	10.2
Utility/Liquor Store	25,188	227.84	18.6
Other	32,203	291.30	23.8

Note: (1) Payments to beneficiaries including withdrawal of contributions.
Source: U.S. Bureau of the Census, City Government Finances: 1991-92

Municipal Bond Ratings

Area	Moody's	S & P
Ann Arbor	A1	n/a

Note: n/a not available; n/r not rated
Source: Moody's Bond Record, 2/98; Statistical Abstract of the U.S., 1997;
Governing Magazine, 9/97, 3/98

POPULATION

Population Growth

Area	1980	1990	% Chg. 1980-90	July 1996 Estimate	% Chg. 1990-96
City	107,960	109,592	1.5	108,758	-0.8
MSA[1]	264,740	282,937	6.9	529,898	87.3
U.S.	226,545,805	248,765,170	9.8	265,179,411	6.6

Note: (1) Metropolitan Statistical Area - see Appendix A for areas included
Source: 1980/1990 Census of Housing and Population, Summary Tape File 3C;
Census Bureau Population Estimates

Population Characteristics

Race	City 1980 Population	%	City 1990 Population	%	% Chg. 1980-90	MSA[1] 1990 Population	%
White	92,517	85.7	90,196	82.3	-2.5	237,109	83.8
Black	10,186	9.4	9,785	8.9	-3.9	31,468	11.1
Amer Indian/Esk/Aleut	240	0.2	263	0.2	9.6	851	0.3
Asian/Pacific Islander	4,062	3.8	8,513	7.8	109.6	11,764	4.2
Other	955	0.9	835	0.8	-12.6	1,745	0.6
Hispanic Origin[2]	2,096	1.9	2,629	2.4	25.4	5,526	2.0

Note: (1) Metropolitan Statistical Area - see Appendix A for areas included;
(2) people of Hispanic origin can be of any race
Source: 1980/1990 Census of Housing and Population, Summary Tape File 3C

Ancestry

Area	German	Irish	English	Italian	U.S.	French	Polish	Dutch
City	28.5	13.6	17.4	4.5	1.9	4.1	7.2	3.0
MSA[1]	31.5	14.8	16.7	3.9	3.2	5.0	6.8	3.3
U.S.	23.3	15.6	13.1	5.9	5.3	4.2	3.8	2.5

Note: Figures are percentages and include persons that reported multiple ancestry (eg. if a person reported being Irish and Italian, they were included in both columns); (1) Metropolitan Statistical Area - see Appendix A for areas included
Source: 1990 Census of Population and Housing, Summary Tape File 3C

Age

Area	Median Age (Years)	Under 5	Under 18	18-24	25-44	45-64	65+	80+
City	27.1	5.7	17.1	27.1	35.7	12.8	7.3	1.8
MSA[1]	29.2	6.7	21.5	19.4	36.1	15.5	7.5	1.7
U.S.	32.9	7.3	25.6	10.5	32.6	18.7	12.5	2.8

Note: (1) Metropolitan Statistical Area - see Appendix A for areas included
Source: 1990 Census of Population and Housing, Summary Tape File 3C

Male/Female Ratio

Area	Number of males per 100 females (all ages)	Number of males per 100 females (18 years old+)
City	97.4	96.2
MSA[1]	97.3	95.8
U.S.	95.0	91.9

Note: (1) Metropolitan Statistical Area - see Appendix A for areas included
Source: 1990 Census of Population, General Population Characteristics

INCOME

Per Capita/Median/Average Income

Area	Per Capita ($)	Median Household ($)	Average Household ($)
City	17,786	33,344	44,963
MSA[1]	17,115	36,307	45,105
U.S.	14,420	30,056	38,453

Note: all figures are for 1989; (1) Metropolitan Statistical Area - see Appendix A for areas included
Source: 1990 Census of Population and Housing, Summary Tape File 3C

Household Income Distribution by Race

Income ($)	City (%)					U.S. (%)				
	Total	White	Black	Other	Hisp.[1]	Total	White	Black	Other	Hisp.[1]
Less than 5,000	5.6	4.2	10.4	16.0	11.2	6.2	4.8	15.2	8.6	8.8
5,000 - 9,999	7.9	7.1	13.8	11.0	6.9	9.3	8.6	14.2	9.9	11.1
10,000 - 14,999	8.4	7.9	8.7	14.6	7.7	8.8	8.5	11.0	9.8	11.0
15,000 - 24,999	15.7	15.3	18.9	16.7	26.1	17.5	17.3	18.9	18.5	20.5
25,000 - 34,999	14.6	14.7	16.9	10.6	13.3	15.8	16.1	14.2	15.4	16.4
35,000 - 49,999	15.3	16.1	11.6	9.3	14.3	17.9	18.6	13.3	16.1	16.0
50,000 - 74,999	17.3	18.4	13.1	9.8	10.9	15.0	15.8	9.3	13.4	11.1
75,000 - 99,999	7.5	8.0	3.1	7.0	1.7	5.1	5.5	2.6	4.7	3.1
100,000+	7.8	8.4	3.5	4.9	7.7	4.4	4.8	1.3	3.7	1.9

Note: all figures are for 1989; (1) people of Hispanic origin can be of any race
Source: 1990 Census of Population and Housing, Summary Tape File 3C

Effective Buying Income

Area	Per Capita ($)	Median Household ($)	Average Household ($)
City	20,402	39,335	53,055
MSA[1]	18,945	44,359	52,666
U.S.	15,444	33,201	41,849

Note: data as of 1/1/97; (1) Metropolitan Statistical Area - see Appendix A for areas included
Source: Standard Rate & Data Service, Newspaper Advertising Source, 2/98

Effective Household Buying Income Distribution

Area	% of Households Earning						
	$10,000 -$19,999	$20,000 -$34,999	$35,000 -$49,999	$50,000 -$74,999	$75,000 -$99,000	$100,000 -$124,999	$125,000 and up
City	14.3	20.0	15.4	19.6	10.5	4.6	5.2
MSA[1]	11.7	19.0	17.9	24.1	11.5	4.2	3.8
U.S.	16.5	23.4	18.3	18.2	6.4	2.1	2.4

Note: data as of 1/1/97; (1) Metropolitan Statistical Area - see Appendix A for areas included
Source: Standard Rate & Data Service, Newspaper Advertising Source, 2/98

Poverty Rates by Race and Age

Area	Total (%)	By Race (%)				By Age (%)		
		White	Black	Other	Hisp.[2]	Under 5 years old	Under 18 years old	65 years and over
City	16.1	14.4	20.8	27.2	21.5	9.8	8.4	7.4
MSA[1]	12.2	10.0	23.0	25.8	18.9	12.6	10.8	8.0
U.S.	13.1	9.8	29.5	23.1	25.3	20.1	18.3	12.8

Note: figures show the percent of people living below the poverty line in 1989. The average poverty threshold was $12,674 for a family of four in 1989; (1) Metropolitan Statistical Area - see Appendix A for areas included; (2) people of Hispanic origin can be of any race
Source: 1990 Census of Population and Housing, Summary Tape File 3C

EMPLOYMENT

Labor Force and Employment

Area	Civilian Labor Force			Workers Employed		
	Dec. '95	Dec. '96	% Chg.	Dec. '95	Dec. '96	% Chg.
City	64,579	65,522	1.5	63,445	64,638	1.9
MSA[1]	282,399	285,916	1.2	275,064	280,236	1.9
U.S.	134,583,000	136,742,000	1.6	127,903,000	130,785,000	2.3

Note: Data is not seasonally adjusted and covers workers 16 years of age and older;
(1) Metropolitan Statistical Area - see Appendix A for areas included
Source: Bureau of Labor Statistics, http://stats.bls.gov

Unemployment Rate

Area	1997											
	Jan.	Feb.	Mar.	Apr.	May	Jun.	Jul.	Aug.	Sep.	Oct.	Nov.	Dec.
City	2.3	2.0	1.9	1.9	1.6	2.0	2.1	1.5	1.6	1.5	1.5	1.3
MSA[1]	3.6	3.1	2.9	2.7	2.2	2.6	3.1	2.1	2.2	1.9	2.0	2.0
U.S.	5.9	5.7	5.5	4.8	4.7	5.2	5.0	4.8	4.7	4.4	4.3	4.4

Note: Data is not seasonally adjusted and covers workers 16 years of age and older; All figures are percentages; (1) Metropolitan Statistical Area - see Appendix A for areas included
Source: Bureau of Labor Statistics, http://stats.bls.gov

Employment by Industry

Sector	MSA[1]		U.S.
	Number of Employees	Percent of Total	Percent of Total
Services	65,700	23.9	29.0
Retail Trade	47,300	17.2	18.5
Government	73,000	26.6	16.1
Manufacturing	53,200	19.4	15.0
Finance/Insurance/Real Estate	10,000	3.6	5.7
Wholesale Trade	8,900	3.2	5.4
Transportation/Public Utilities	6,600	2.4	5.3
Construction/Mining	10,100	3.7	5.0

Note: Figures cover non-farm employment as of 12/97 and are not seasonally adjusted;
(1) Metropolitan Statistical Area - see Appendix A for areas included
Source: Bureau of Labor Statistics, http://stats.bls.gov

Employment by Occupation

Occupation Category	City (%)	MSA[1] (%)	U.S. (%)
White Collar	79.3	68.1	58.1
Executive/Admin./Management	13.9	12.8	12.3
Professional	33.7	24.4	14.1
Technical & Related Support	7.6	5.8	3.7
Sales	9.7	10.0	11.8
Administrative Support/Clerical	14.3	15.2	16.3
Blue Collar	8.3	17.6	26.2
Precision Production/Craft/Repair	3.7	7.7	11.3
Machine Operators/Assem./Insp.	2.1	5.7	6.8
Transportation/Material Movers	1.1	2.1	4.1
Cleaners/Helpers/Laborers	1.4	2.1	3.9
Services	12.0	13.2	13.2
Farming/Forestry/Fishing	0.5	1.1	2.5

Note: figures cover employed persons 16 years old and over;
(1) Metropolitan Statistical Area - see Appendix A for areas included
Source: 1990 Census of Population and Housing, Summary Tape File 3C

Occupational Employment Projections: 1994 - 2005

High Demand Occupations (ranked by annual openings)	Fast-Growing Occupations (ranked by percent growth)
1. Cashiers	1. Home health aides
2. Salespersons, retail	2. Systems analysts
3. Waiters & waitresses	3. Computer engineers
4. General managers & top executives	4. Personal and home care aides
5. Registered nurses	5. First line supervisors, construction
6. Secretaries, except legal & medical	6. Dental hygienists
7. General office clerks	7. Medical assistants
8. Janitors/cleaners/maids, ex. priv. hshld.	8. Telemarketers/door-to-door sales
9. Marketing & sales, supervisors	9. Teachers, special education
10. Systems analysts	10. Food service and lodging managers

Projections cover Washtenaw County.
Source: Michigan Employment Security Commission, Annual Planning Information Report 1998, Washtenaw County MWA

Average Wages

Occupation	Wage	Occupation	Wage
Professional/Technical/Clerical	$/Week	**Health/Protective Services**	$/Week
Accountants III	-	Corrections Officers	-
Attorneys III	-	Firefighters	-
Budget Analysts III	-	Nurses, Licensed Practical II	-
Buyers/Contracting Specialists II	-	Nurses, Registered II	-
Clerks, Accounting III	421	Nursing Assistants II	-
Clerks, General III	-	Police Officers I	-
Computer Operators II	-	**Hourly Workers**	$/Hour
Computer Programmers II	-	Forklift Operators	15.43
Drafters II	-	General Maintenance Workers	8.94
Engineering Technicians III	-	Guards I	-
Engineering Technicians, Civil III	-	Janitors	8.83
Engineers III	-	Maintenance Electricians	21.28
Key Entry Operators I	-	Maintenance Electronics Techs II	-
Personnel Assistants III	-	Maintenance Machinists	18.11
Personnel Specialists III	-	Maintenance Mechanics, Machinery	20.68
Secretaries III	628	Material Handling Laborers	-
Switchboard Operator-Receptionist	352	Motor Vehicle Mechanics	20.47
Systems Analysts II	878	Shipping/Receiving Clerks	12.00
Systems Analysts Supervisor/Mgr II	-	Tool and Die Makers	20.31
Tax Collectors II	-	Truckdrivers, Tractor Trailer	-
Word Processors II	-	Warehouse Specialists	-

Note: Wage data includes full-time workers only for 7/95 and cover the Metropolitan Statistical Area (see Appendix A for areas included). Dashes indicate that data was not available.
Source: Bureau of Labor Statistics, Occupational Compensation Survey, 11/95

TAXES

Major State and Local Tax Rates

State Corp. Income (%)	State Personal Income (%)	Residential Property (effective rate per $100)	Sales & Use State (%)	Sales & Use Local (%)	State Gasoline (cents/ gallon)	State Cigarette (cents/ 20-pack)
2.3[a]	4.4	n/a	6.0	None	19	75

Note: Personal/corporate income tax rates as of 1/97. Sales, gasoline and cigarette tax rates as of 1/98; (a) Value added tax imposed on the sum of federal taxable income of the business, compensation paid to employees, dividends, interest, royalties paid and other items
Source: Federation of Tax Administrators, www.taxadmin.org; Washington D.C. Department of Finance and Revenue, Tax Rates and Tax Burdens in the District of Columbia: A Nationwide Comparison, June 1997; Chamber of Commerce

Total Taxes Per Capita and as a Percent of Income

Area	Per Capita Income ($)	Per Capita Taxes ($)			Taxes as Pct. of Income (%)		
		Total	Federal	State/ Local	Total	Federal	State/ Local
Michigan	26,934	9,533	6,409	3,124	35.4	23.8	11.6
U.S.	26,187	9,205	6,127	3,078	35.2	23.4	11.8

Note: Figures are for 1997
Source: Tax Foundation, Web Site, www.taxfoundation.org

COMMERCIAL REAL ESTATE

Data not available at time of publication.

COMMERCIAL UTILITIES

Typical Monthly Electric Bills

Area	Commercial Service ($/month)		Industrial Service ($/month)	
	12 kW demand 1,500 kWh	100 kW demand 30,000 kWh	1,000 kW demand 400,000 kWh	20,000 kW demand 10,000,000 kWh
City	n/a	n/a	n/a	n/a
U.S.	162	2,360	25,590	545,677

Note: Based on rates in effect July 1, 1997; n/a not available
Source: Edison Electric Institute, Typical Residential, Commercial and Industrial Bills, Summer 1997

TRANSPORTATION

Transportation Statistics

Avg. travel time to work (min.)	17.0
Interstate highways	I-94
Bus lines	
In-city	Ann Arbor Transportation Authority
Inter-city	4
Passenger air service	
Airport	Detroit-Wayne County Metropolitan Airport (25 miles east)
Airlines	14
Aircraft departures	n/a
Enplaned passengers	n/a
Rail service	Amtrak
Motor freight carriers	6
Major waterways/ports	None

Source: OAG, Business Travel Planner, Summer 1997; Editor & Publisher Market Guide, 1998; FAA Airport Activity Statistics, 1996; Amtrak National Time Table, Northeast Timetable, Fall/Winter 1997-98; 1990 Census of Population and Housing, STF 3C; Chamber of Commerce/Economic Development 1997; Jane's Urban Transport Systems 1997-98; Transit Fact Book 1997

Means of Transportation to Work

Area	Car/Truck/Van		Public Transportation			Bicycle	Walked	Other Means	Worked at Home
	Drove Alone	Car-pooled	Bus	Subway	Railroad				
City	61.8	9.2	5.4	0.0	0.0	2.1	17.1	0.5	3.9
MSA[1]	73.5	9.6	2.9	0.0	0.0	1.0	9.2	0.5	3.2
U.S.	73.2	13.4	3.0	1.5	0.5	0.4	3.9	1.2	3.0

Note: figures shown are percentages and only include workers 16 years old and over;
(1) Metropolitan Statistical Area - see Appendix A for areas included
Source: 1990 Census of Population and Housing, Summary Tape File 3C

BUSINESSES

Major Business Headquarters

Company Name	1997 Rankings	
	Fortune 500	Forbes 500
Domino's Pizza		200

Note: Companies listed are located in the city; Dashes indicate no ranking
Fortune 500: companies that produce a 10-K are ranked 1 - 500 based on 1996 revenue
Forbes 500: private companies are ranked 1 - 500 based on 1996 revenue
Source: Forbes 12/1/97; Fortune 4/28/97

Fast-Growing Businesses

Ann Arbor is home to one of *Business Week's* "hot growth" companies: Mechanical Dynamics. Criteria: sales and earnings, return on capital and stock price. *Business Week, 5/26/97*

Minority Business Opportunity

Ann Arbor is home to one company which is on the Black Enterprise Auto Dealer 100 list (largest based on gross sales): Jim Bradley Pontiac Cadillac GMC Truck Inc. (GM). Criteria: 1) operational in previous calendar year; 2) at least 51% black-owned. *Black Enterprise, June 1997*

One of the 500 largest Hispanic-owned companies in the U.S. are located in Ann Arbor. *Hispanic Business, June 1997*

HOTELS & MOTELS

Hotels/Motels

Area	Hotels/ Motels	Rooms	Luxury-Level Hotels/Motels		Average Minimum Rates ($)		
			◆◆◆◆	◆◆◆◆◆	◆◆	◆◆◆	◆◆◆◆
City	13	1,690	0	0	n/a	n/a	n/a
Airport	1	207	0	0	n/a	n/a	n/a
Suburbs	3	458	0	0	n/a	n/a	n/a
Total	17	2,355	0	0	n/a	n/a	n/a

Note: n/a not available; Classifications range from one diamond (budget properties with basic amenities) to five diamond (luxury properties with the finest service, rooms and facilities).
Source: OAG, Business Travel Planner, Summer 1997

CONVENTION CENTERS

Major Convention Centers

Center Name	Meeting Rooms	Exhibit Space (sf)

None listed in city
Source: Trade Shows Worldwide 1997

Living Environment

COST OF LIVING

Cost of Living Index

Composite Index	Housing	Utilities	Groceries	Health Care	Trans-portation	Misc. Goods/ Services
113.5	123.9	97.0	105.8	118.0	125.3	108.4

Note: U.S. = 100
Source: ACCRA, Cost of Living Index, 2nd Quarter 1996

HOUSING

Median Home Prices and Housing Affordability

Area	Median Price[2] 3rd Qtr. 1997 ($)	HOI[3] 3rd Qtr. 1997	Afford- ability Rank[4]
MSA[1]	146,000	57.5	159
U.S.	127,000	63.7	

Note: (1) Metropolitan Statistical Area - see Appendix A for areas included; (2) U.S. figures calculated from the sales of 625,000 new and existing homes in 195 markets; (3) Housing Opportunity Index - percent of homes sold that were within the reach of the median income household at the prevailing mortgage interest rate; (4) Rank is from 1-195 with 1 being most affordable
Source: National Association of Home Builders, Housing Opportunity Index, 3rd Quarter 1997

It is projected that the median price of existing single-family homes in the metro area will increase by 13.4% in 1998. Nationwide, home prices are projected to increase 6.6%.
Kiplinger's Personal Finance Magazine, January 1998

Average New Home Price

Area	Price ($)
City	155,000
U.S.	132,005

Note: Figures are based on a new home with 1,800 sq. ft. of living area on an 8,000 sq. ft. lot.
Source: ACCRA, Cost of Living Index, 2nd Quarter 1996

Average Apartment Rent

Area	Rent ($/mth)
City	807
U.S.	553

Note: Figures are based on an unfurnished two bedroom, 1-1/2 or 2 bath apartment, approximately 950 sq. ft. in size, excluding all utilities except water
Source: ACCRA, Cost of Living Index, 2nd Quarter 1996

RESIDENTIAL UTILITIES

Average Residential Utility Costs

Area	All Electric ($/mth)	Part Electric ($/mth)	Other Energy ($/mth)	Phone ($/mth)
City	–	57.85	39.99	22.53
U.S.	112.48	57.49	42.55	19.50

Source: ACCRA, Cost of Living Index, 2nd Quarter 1996

HEALTH CARE

Average Health Care Costs

Area	Hospital ($/day)	Doctor ($/visit)	Dentist ($/visit)
City	535.00	48.80	71.00
U.S.	378.47	45.86	57.32

Note: Hospital - based on a semi-private room. Doctor - based on a general practitioner's routine exam of an established patient. Dentist - based on adult teeth cleaning and periodic oral exam.
Source: ACCRA, Cost of Living Index, 2nd Quarter 1996

Distribution of Office-Based Physicians

Area	Family/Gen. Practitioners	Specialists		
		Medical	Surgical	Other
MSA[1]	111	499	320	520

Note: Data as of 12/31/96; (1) Metropolitan Statistical Area - see Appendix A for areas included
Source: American Medical Assn., Physician Characteristics & Distribution in the U.S., 1997-1998

Hospitals

Ann Arbor has 3 general medical and surgical hospitals. *AHA Guide to the Healthcare Field 1997-98*

According to *U.S. News and World Report,* Ann Arbor has 1 of the best hospitals in the U.S.: **University of Michigan Medical Center**, noted for AIDS, cancer, cardiology, endocrinology, gastroenterology, geriatrics, gynecology, neurology, orthopedics, otolaryngology, psychiatry, pulmonology, rehabilitation, rheumatology, urology; *U.S. News and World Report, "America's Best Hospitals", 7/28/97*

EDUCATION

Public School District Statistics

District Name	Num. Sch.	Enroll.	Classroom Teachers[1]	Pupils per Teacher	Minority Pupils (%)	Current Exp.[2] ($/pupil)
Ann Arbor Public Schools	33	15,255	845	18.1	n/a	n/a
Wash Isd-Honey Crk. Comm Sch	1	35	3	11.7	n/a	n/a

Note: Data covers the 1995-1996 school year unless otherwise noted; (1) Excludes teachers reported as working in school district offices rather than in schools; (2) Based on 1993-94 enrollment collected by the Census Bureau, not the enrollment figure shown in column 3; SD = School District; ISD = Independent School District; n/a not available
Source: National Center for Education Statistics, Common Core of Data Survey; Bureau of the Census

Educational Quality

School District	Education Quotient[1]	Graduate Outcome[2]	Community Index[3]	Resource Index[4]
Ann Arbor	142.0	146.0	147.0	134.0

Note: Nearly 1,000 secondary school districts were rated in terms of educational quality. The scores range from a low of 50 to a high of 150; (1) Average of the Graduate Outcome, Community and Resource indexes; (2) Based on graduation rates and college board scores (SAT/ACT); (3) Based on the surrounding community's average level of education and the area's average income level; (4) Based on teacher salaries, per-pupil expenditures and student-teacher ratios.
Source: Expansion Management, Ratings Issue 1997

Educational Attainment by Race

Area	High School Graduate (%)					Bachelor's Degree (%)				
	Total	White	Black	Other	Hisp.[2]	Total	White	Black	Other	Hisp.[2]
City	93.9	95.4	77.6	95.2	94.1	64.2	65.9	33.4	78.7	74.0
MSA[1]	87.2	88.5	74.3	92.1	82.0	41.9	43.0	21.5	67.0	44.9
U.S.	75.2	77.9	63.1	60.4	49.8	20.3	21.5	11.4	19.4	9.2

Note: figures shown cover persons 25 years old and over; (1) Metropolitan Statistical Area - see Appendix A for areas included; (2) people of Hispanic origin can be of any race
Source: 1990 Census of Population and Housing, Summary Tape File 3C

School Enrollment by Type

Area	Preprimary				Elementary/High School			
	Public		Private		Public		Private	
	Enrollment	%	Enrollment	%	Enrollment	%	Enrollment	%
City	1,151	55.4	928	44.6	9,948	88.5	1,299	11.5
MSA[1]	3,711	62.5	2,225	37.5	35,078	91.0	3,490	9.0
U.S.	2,679,029	59.5	1,824,256	40.5	38,379,689	90.2	4,187,099	9.8

Note: figures shown cover persons 3 years old and over;
(1) Metropolitan Statistical Area - see Appendix A for areas included
Source: 1990 Census of Population and Housing, Summary Tape File 3C

School Enrollment by Race

Area	Preprimary (%)				Elementary/High School (%)			
	White	Black	Other	Hisp.[1]	White	Black	Other	Hisp.[1]
City	82.9	9.4	7.7	3.6	72.4	17.0	10.6	2.5
MSA[2]	83.4	12.4	4.1	1.9	78.3	16.6	5.1	2.4
U.S.	80.4	12.5	7.1	7.8	74.1	15.6	10.3	12.5

Note: figures shown cover persons 3 years old and over; (1) people of Hispanic origin can be of any race; (2) Metropolitan Statistical Area - see Appendix A for areas included
Source: 1990 Census of Population and Housing, Summary Tape File 3C

SAT/ACT Scores

Area/District	1996 SAT				1996 ACT	
	Percent of Graduates Tested (%)	Average Math Score	Average Verbal Score	Average Combined Score	Percent of Graduates Tested (%)	Average Composite Score
Ann Arbor PS	58	584	572	1,156	69	23.7
State	11	565	557	1,122	64	21.1
U.S.	41	508	505	1,013	35	20.9

Note: Math and verbal SAT scores are out of a possible 800; ACT scores are out of a possible 36
Caution: Comparing or ranking states/cities on the basis of SAT/ACT scores alone is invalid and strongly discouraged by the The College Board and The American College Testing Program as students who take the tests are self-selected and do not represent the entire student population. 1996 SAT scores cannot be compared to previous years due to recentering.
Source: Ann Arbor Public Schools, Research Services, 1996; American College Testing Program, 1996; College Board, 1996

Classroom Teacher Salaries in Public Schools

District	B.A. Degree		M.A. Degree		Ph.D. Degree	
	Min. ($)	Max ($)	Min. ($)	Max. ($)	Min. ($)	Max. ($)
Ann Arbor	28,005	46,505	31,545	55,485	35,360	60,945
Average[1]	26,120	39,270	28,175	44,667	31,643	49,825

Note: Salaries are for 1996-1997; (1) Based on all school districts covered
Source: American Federation of Teachers (unpublished data)

Higher Education

Two-Year Colleges		Four-Year Colleges		Medical Schools	Law Schools	Voc/ Tech
Public	Private	Public	Private			
1	0	1	1	1	1	5

Source: College Blue Book, Occupational Education 1997; Medical School Admission Requirements, 1998-99; Peterson's Guide to Two-Year Colleges, 1997; Peterson's Guide to Four-Year Colleges, 1997; Barron's Guide to Law Schools 1997

MAJOR EMPLOYERS

Major Employers

Braun-Brumfield Inc. (book printing)	Edwards Brothers (book printing)
Environmental Research Institute of Michigan	Gelman Sciences (laboratory apparatus)
JAC Holding Corp. (plastics)	Malloy Lithographing
TISM Inc. (eating places)	Borders
Walden Book Co.	Townsend & Bottum (construction)

Note: companies listed are located in the city
Source: Dun's Business Rankings 1997; Ward's Business Directory, 1997

PUBLIC SAFETY

Crime Rate

Area	All Crimes	Violent Crimes				Property Crimes		
		Murder	Forcible Rape	Robbery	Aggrav. Assault	Burglary	Larceny -Theft	Motor Vehicle Theft
City	4,271.5	0.9	33.7	102.8	234.7	731.3	2,986.2	181.9
Suburbs[1]	4,109.9	2.2	52.5	78.1	228.3	709.9	2,690.7	348.3
MSA[2]	4,144.3	1.9	48.5	83.3	229.6	714.4	2,753.5	312.9
U.S.	5,078.9	7.4	36.1	202.4	388.2	943.0	2,975.9	525.9

Note: Crime rate is the number of crimes per 100,000 pop.; (1) defined as all areas within the MSA but located outside the central city; (2) Metropolitan Statistical Area - see Appendix A for areas incl.
Source: FBI Uniform Crime Reports 1996

RECREATION

Culture and Recreation

Museums	Symphony Orchestras	Opera Companies	Dance Companies	Professional Theatres	Zoos	Pro Sports Teams
15	1	1	3	1	0	0

Source: International Directory of the Performing Arts, 1996; Official Museum Directory, 1998; Chamber of Commerce/Economic Development 1997

Library System

The Ann Arbor District Library has three branches, holdings of 393,894 volumes and a budget of $5,605,931 (1995-1996). *American Library Directory, 1997-1998*

MEDIA

Newspapers

Name	Type	Freq.	Distribution	Circulation
The Ann Arbor News	n/a	7x/wk	Area	58,172
The Michigan Daily	n/a	5x/wk	Campus	community & alumni

Note: Includes newspapers with circulations of 500 or more located in the city; n/a not available
Source: Burrelle's Media Directory, 1998 Edition

AM Radio Stations

Call Letters	Freq. (kHz)	Target Audience	Station Format	Music Format
WWCM	990	General	M	Christian
WTKA	1050	n/a	N/S	n/a
WDEO	1290	General	M/T	Classic Rock
WSDS	1480	General	M/N/S	Country
WAAM	1600	General	M/N/S/T	Adult Standards

Note: Stations included broadcast in the Ann Arbor metro area; n/a not available
Station Format: E = Educational; M = Music; N = News; S = Sports; T = Talk
Source: Burrelle's Media Directory, 1998 Edition

FM Radio Stations

Call Letters	Freq. (mHz)	Target Audience	Station Format	Music Format
WCBN	88.3	n/a	M/N/S	Big Band/Classical/Country/Jazz/R&B/Urban Contemporary
WEMU	89.1	General	M/N	Jazz/R&B
WFUM	91.1	General	N/T	n/a
WUOM	91.7	General	N/T	n/a
WIQB	102.9	General	M	Alternative
WVGR	104.1	General	M/N/S	Classical/Jazz
WQKL	107.1	General	M/N	Oldies

Note: Stations included broadcast in the Ann Arbor metro area; n/a not available
Station Format: E = Educational; M = Music; N = News; S = Sports; T = Talk
Source: Burrelle's Media Directory, 1998 Edition

Television Stations

Name	Ch.	Affiliation	Type	Owner
WBSX	31	HSN	Commercial	Blackstar Communications, Inc.

Note: Stations included broadcast in the Ann Arbor metro area
Source: Burrelle's Media Directory, 1998 Edition

CLIMATE

Average and Extreme Temperatures

Temperature	Jan	Feb	Mar	Apr	May	Jun	Jul	Aug	Sep	Oct	Nov	Dec	Ann
Extreme High (°F)	62	65	81	89	93	104	102	100	98	91	77	68	104
Average High (°F)	30	33	44	58	70	79	83	81	74	61	48	35	58
Average Temp. (°F)	23	26	36	48	59	68	72	71	64	52	40	29	49
Average Low (°F)	16	18	27	37	47	56	61	60	53	41	32	21	39
Extreme Low (°F)	-21	-15	-4	10	25	36	41	38	29	17	9	-10	-21

Note: Figures cover the years 1958-1990
Source: National Climatic Data Center, International Station Meteorological Climate Summary, 3/95

Average Precipitation/Snowfall/Humidity

Precip./Humidity	Jan	Feb	Mar	Apr	May	Jun	Jul	Aug	Sep	Oct	Nov	Dec	Ann
Avg. Precip. (in.)	1.8	1.8	2.5	3.0	2.9	3.6	3.1	3.4	2.8	2.2	2.6	2.7	32.4
Avg. Snowfall (in.)	10	9	7	2	Tr	0	0	0	0	Tr	3	11	41
Avg. Rel. Hum. 7am (%)	80	79	79	78	78	79	82	86	87	84	82	81	81
Avg. Rel. Hum. 4pm (%)	67	63	59	53	51	52	52	54	55	55	64	70	58

Note: Figures cover the years 1958-1990; Tr = Trace amounts (<0.05 in. of rain; <0.5 in. of snow)
Source: National Climatic Data Center, International Station Meteorological Climate Summary, 3/95

Weather Conditions

Temperature			Daytime Sky			Precipitation		
5°F & below	32°F & below	90°F & above	Clear	Partly cloudy	Cloudy	0.01 inch or more precip.	0.1 inch or more snow/ice	Thunderstorms
15	136	12	74	134	157	135	38	32

Note: Figures are average number of days per year and covers the years 1958-1990
Source: National Climatic Data Center, International Station Meteorological Climate Summary, 3/95

AIR & WATER QUALITY

Maximum Pollutant Concentrations

	Particulate Matter (ug/m³)	Carbon Monoxide (ppm)	Sulfur Dioxide (ppm)	Nitrogen Dioxide (ppm)	Ozone (ppm)	Lead (ug/m³)
MSA[1] Level	n/a	n/a	n/a	n/a	0.10	n/a
NAAQS[2]	150	9	0.140	0.053	0.12	1.50
Met NAAQS?	n/a	n/a	n/a	n/a	Yes	n/a

Note: (1) Metropolitan Statistical Area - see Appendix A for areas included; (2) National Ambient Air Quality Standards; ppm = parts per million; ug/m³ = micrograms per cubic meter; n/a not available
Source: EPA, National Air Quality and Emissions Trends Report, 1996

Pollutant Standards Index

Data not available. *EPA, National Air Quality and Emissions Trends Report, 1996*

Drinking Water

Water System Name	Pop. Served	Primary Water Source Type	Number of Violations in Fiscal Year 1997	Type of Violation/ Contaminants
Ann Arbor	109,592	Surface	None	None

Note: Data as of January 16, 1998
Source: EPA, Office of Ground Water and Drinking Water, Safe Drinking Water Information System

Ann Arbor tap water is alkaline, soft and fluoridated.
Editor & Publisher Market Guide, 1998

Chicago, Illinois

Background

Chicago, from its very inception, has been colorful. It was a booming frontier trade town that welcomed the brawn of immigration from around the world to help build the city. Those workers lent themselves to the major industries of the times—steel and meat packing—that eventually provided fodder for Upton Sinclair's attack on the plants' labor abuses in his book "The Jungle".

If that were not enough, Chicago also witnessed the Haymarket Riot, wherein anarchists threw a bomb upon a congregation of policemen, in order to protest the city's unemployment rate.

However, Chicago continues to live up to its Native American namesake, Chicagou, meaning "strong" or "powerful". As the third most populous city in the United States, Chicago has no reason to slow down. The city is home to some of the best institutions of in the world. For example, if one enjoys art, one can visit the Art Institute of Chicago. If one wants to attend a fine university, one has a choice of the University of Chicago or Northwestern University, to name a few. If one wants to study architecture, one can have a first hand look at architectural wonders such as the Federal Center Plaza, designed by Mies Van Der Rohe, or the Robie House, designed by Frank Lloyd Wright.

Like most large cities, the wealthier suburbs do not want to involve themselves with the problems of the central city. However, Chicago still tries to fight urban decay, keeping social, economic, and physical perspectives in mind as relevant and interrelated factors of their policy-making.

Located along the southwest shore of Lake Michigan, Chicago is in a region of frequently changeable weather. Summers can be quite hot and winters are often quite cold. The nickname, "Windy City", is inappropriate as the average wind speed in Chicago is not greater than in many other areas of the country.

General Rankings and Evaluative Comments

- Chicago was ranked #201 out of 300 cities by *Money's* 1997 "Survey of the Best Places to Live." Criteria used: health services, crime, economy, housing, education, transportation, weather, leisure and the arts. The city was ranked #196 in 1996 and #183 in 1995. Money, July 1997; Money, September 1996; Money, September 1995

- *Ladies Home Journal* ranked America's 200 largest cities based on the qualities women care about most. Chicago ranked 135 out of 200. Criteria: low crime rate, good public schools, well-paying jobs, quality health and child care, the presence of women in government, proportion of women-owned businesses, size of the wage gap with men, local economy, divorce rates, the ratio of single men to single women, whether there are laws that require at least the same number of public toilets for women as men, and the probability of good hair days. Ladies Home Journal, November 1997

- Chicago was ranked #200 out of 219 cities in terms of children's health, safety, and economic well-being. Criteria: total population, percent population change, birth rate, child immunization rate, infant mortality rate, percent low birth weight infants, percent of births to teens, physician-to-population ratio, student-to-teacher ratio, dropout rate, unemployment rate, median family income, percent of children in poverty, violent and property crime rates, number of juvenile arrests for violent crimes as a percent of the total crime index, number of days with pollution standard index (PSI) over 100, pounds toxic releases per 1,000 people and number of superfund sites. *Zero Population Growth, Children's Environmental Index 1997*

- Cambridge at Carillon, located 37 miles southwest of Chicago, is among America's best retirement communities. Criteria: communities must have state-of-the-art facilities, newly built homes for sale, and give you the most value for your money in every price range. Communities must also welcome newcomers of all races and religions. *New Choices, July/August 1997*

- Chicago appeared on *Ebony's* list of the best cities for African-Americans Rank: 3 out of 4. The cities were selected based on a survey of the 100 Most Influential Black Americans. They were asked which city offered the best overall experience for African-Americans, and which dream city they would select if they could live anywhere they wanted to. *Ebony* also asked opinion-makers which cities offered the best cultural experiences, the best schools and the most diversity. *Ebony, 9/97*

- Chicago is among the 20 most livable cities for gay men and lesbians. The list was divided between 10 cities you might expect and 10 surprises. Chicago was on the cities you would expect list. Rank: 5 out of 10. Criteria: legal protection from antigay discrimination, an annual gay pride celebration, a community center, gay bookstores and publications, and an array of organizations, religious groups, and health care facilities that cater to the needs of the local gay community. *The Advocate, June 1997*

- Chicago appeared on *Travel & Leisure's* list of the world's best cities. Rank: 16 out of 25. Criteria: activities/attractions, culture/arts, people, restaurants/food, and value. Travel & Leisure, September 1997

- *Conde Nast Traveler* polled 37,000 readers in terms of travel satisfaction. Cities were ranked based on the following criteria: people/friendliness, environment/ambiance, cultural enrichment, restaurants and fun/energy. Chicago appeared in the top thirty, ranking number 14, with an overall rating of 66.1 out of 100 based on all the criteria. The cities were also ranked in each category separately. Chicago appeared in the top 10 based on cultural enrichment, ranking number 5 with a rating of 76.3 out of 100. Chicago appeared in the top 10 based on restaurants, ranking number 5 with a rating of 81.8 out of 100. *Conde Nast Traveler, Readers' Choice Poll 1997*

- *Yahoo! Internet Life* selected "America's 100 Most Wired Cities & Towns". 50 cities were large and 50 cities were small. Chicago ranked 9 out of 50 large cities. Criteria: Internet users per capita, number of networked computers, number of registered domain names, Internet backbone traffic, and the per-capita number of Web sites devoted to each city. *Yahoo! Internet Life, March 1998*

■ *Reader's Digest* non-scientifically ranked the 12 largest U.S. metropolitan areas in terms of having the worst drivers. The Chicago metro area ranked number 7. The areas were selected by asking approximately 1,200 readers on the *Reader's Digest* Web site and 200 interstate bus drivers and long-haul truckers which metro areas have the worst drivers. Their responses were factored in with fatality, insurance and rental-car rates to create the rankings. *Reader's Digest, March 1998*

■ Amoco Corp., Leo Burnett Co. Inc., First Chicago NBD Corp., Northern Trust Corp. and Sara Lee Corp., headquartered in Chicago, are among the "100 Best Companies for Working Mothers." Criteria: pay compared with competition, opportunities for women to advance, support for child care, flexible work schedules and family-friendly benefits. *Working Mother, October 1997*

■ According to *Working Mother,* "Illinois has made a serious commitment to early education, funding prekindergarten programs to the tune of $112 million, almost a 10 percent increase over last year. Some 3,500 more kids now attend pre-K. State officials approved another $40 million in child care subsidies, which will enable many moms with lower-paying jobs to stay in the work force. As we went to press, the state was also considering a proposal that would make workers earning 40 to 60 percent of the median income in the state eligible for new child care subsidies.

Illinois has also launched a new caregiver training program, modeled after the Teacher Education and Compensation Helps program (T.E.A.C.H.) in North Carolina. Under this initiative, caregivers can apply for scholarships to take courses in early education. Once they have completed the coursework, they are eligible for raises or bonuses.

There's still plenty of room for improvement in the child care picture in Illinois, as in other states, however. An important bill called 'Start Early,' which would have expanded the funding for prekindergarten programs, only made it as far as the House. This is the third year in a row lawmakers have failed to approve this initiative. This money would have gone toward, among other things, expanding pre-K from a half-day to a full-day program." *Working Mother, July/August 1997*

Business Environment

STATE ECONOMY

State Economic Profile

"The Illinois economy continues to expand at a moderate pace. Through December, the economy is creating jobs at a 1.4% annual pace, almost a percentage point below the national pace. Growth is trailing the nation in all industries, with the exception of manufacturing....

Manufacturing activity is expected to moderate this year as domestic demand weakens. Illinois' traditional manufacturing industries, such as heavy construction equipment, machine tools and steel, are currently being supported by commercial construction and auto sales. However, the growth in manufactured goods exports is far lower this year, with export growth of only 3% last year, compared with double-digit growth in previous years. Improved world demand should increase exports of Illinois' manufactured goods this year.

Illinois is hampered by the highest business costs in the Midwest. Labor costs are the fourth highest in the nation. In addition, Illinois has high energy costs and sales taxes. The state has enacted legislation including tort reform, the repeal of the Structural Work Act, and a decline in compensation insurance rates for high-risk workers, to improve its competitive advantage.

Population growth in Illinois remains among the weakest in the Midwest region due to the sustained outflow of an average 60,000 domestic migrants every year. However, the sizable and steady influx of international migrants, partially offsets the domestic population drain.

The Illinois economy is expected to continue expanding at a moderate pace this year. Longer term, Illinois' diversification into high-tech industries and the continued export penetration of its largest manufacturer by the well-developed distribution and transportation network, will support growth in the state's economy. However, relatively high business costs and poor demographic trends limit the prospects for the state's economy. Moreover, weak long-term employment growth will contribute to sustained out-migration of Illinois residents. Therefore, Illinois will remain a below-average performer over the forecast horizon." *National Association of Realtors, Economic Profiles: The Fifty States, July 1997*

IMPORTS/EXPORTS

Total Export Sales

Area	1993 ($000)	1994 ($000)	1995 ($000)	1996 ($000)	% Chg. 1993-96	% Chg. 1995-96
MSA[1]	14,446,576	17,333,603	21,083,418	22,030,068	52.5	4.5
U.S.	464,858,354	512,415,609	583,030,524	622,827,063	34.0	6.8

Note: (1) Metropolitan Statistical Area - see Appendix A for areas included
Source: U.S. Department of Commerce, International Trade Association, Metropolitan Area Exports: An Export Performance Report on Over 250 U.S. Cities, October 1997

Imports/Exports by Port

Type	Cargo Value			Share of U.S. Total	
	1995 (US$mil.)	1996 (US$mil.)	% Change 1995-1996	1995 (%)	1996 (%)
Imports	516	773	49.91	0.13	0.20
Exports	221	261	18.45	0.10	0.11

Source: Global Trade Information Services, WaterBorne Trade Atlas 1997

CITY FINANCES

City Government Finances

Component	FY94 ($000)	FY94 (per capita $)
Revenue	4,383,723	1,593.57
Expenditure	4,201,070	1,527.17
Debt Outstanding	6,965,521	2,532.11
Cash & Securities	9,655,076	3,509.81

Source: U.S. Bureau of the Census, City Government Finances: 1993-94

City Government Revenue by Source

Source	FY94 ($000)	FY94 (per capita $)	FY94 (%)
From Federal Government	242,316	88.09	5.5
From State Governments	707,812	257.30	16.1
From Local Governments	171	0.06	0.0
Property Taxes	624,252	226.93	14.2
General Sales Taxes	140,209	50.97	3.2
Selective Sales Taxes	634,223	230.55	14.5
Income Taxes	0	0.00	0.0
Current Charges	578,423	210.27	13.2
Utility/Liquor Store	260,214	94.59	5.9
Employee Retirement[1]	687,439	249.90	15.7
Other	508,664	184.91	11.6

Note: (1) Excludes "city contributions," classified as "nonrevenue," intragovernmental transfers.
Source: U.S. Bureau of the Census, City Government Finances: 1993-94

City Government Expenditures by Function

Function	FY94 ($000)	FY94 (per capita $)	FY94 (%)
Educational Services	56,630	20.59	1.3
Employee Retirement[1]	500,000	181.76	11.9
Environment/Housing	454,421	165.19	10.8
Government Administration	145,097	52.75	3.5
Interest on General Debt	395,997	143.95	9.4
Public Safety	1,004,058	365.00	23.9
Social Services	234,296	85.17	5.6
Transportation	716,944	260.62	17.1
Utility/Liquor Store	210,453	76.50	5.0
Other	483,174	175.64	11.5

Note: (1) Payments to beneficiaries including withdrawal of contributions.
Source: U.S. Bureau of the Census, City Government Finances: 1993-94

Municipal Bond Ratings

Area	Moody's	S & P
Chicago	A2	A

Note: n/a not available; n/r not rated
Source: Moody's Bond Record, 2/98; Statistical Abstract of the U.S., 1997; Governing Magazine, 9/97, 3/98

POPULATION

Population Growth

Area	1980	1990	% Chg. 1980-90	July 1996 Estimate	% Chg. 1990-96
City	3,005,072	2,783,726	-7.4	2,721,547	-2.2
MSA[1]	6,060,387	6,069,974	0.2	7,733,876	27.4
U.S.	226,545,805	248,765,170	9.8	265,179,411	6.6

Note: (1) Metropolitan Statistical Area - see Appendix A for areas included
Source: 1980/1990 Census of Housing and Population, Summary Tape File 3C; Census Bureau Population Estimates

Population Characteristics

Race	City				% Chg. 1980-90	MSA[1]	
	1980		1990			1990	
	Population	%	Population	%		Population	%
White	1,512,405	50.3	1,265,953	45.5	-16.3	4,102,292	67.6
Black	1,197,174	39.8	1,086,389	39.0	-9.3	1,330,636	21.9
Amer Indian/Esk/Aleut	6,804	0.2	6,761	0.2	-0.6	11,755	0.2
Asian/Pacific Islander	73,745	2.5	104,141	3.7	41.2	229,475	3.8
Other	214,944	7.2	320,482	11.5	49.1	395,816	6.5
Hispanic Origin[2]	422,063	14.0	535,315	19.2	26.8	716,644	11.8

Note: (1) Metropolitan Statistical Area - see Appendix A for areas included;
(2) people of Hispanic origin can be of any race
Source: 1980/1990 Census of Housing and Population, Summary Tape File 3C

Ancestry

Area	German	Irish	English	Italian	U.S.	French	Polish	Dutch
City	9.7	8.5	2.5	4.3	1.2	1.0	9.4	0.5
MSA[1]	20.2	14.1	5.9	8.1	1.3	2.0	12.2	1.5
U.S.	23.3	15.6	13.1	5.9	5.3	4.2	3.8	2.5

Note: Figures are percentages and include persons that reported multiple ancestry (eg. if a person reported being Irish and Italian, they were included in both columns); (1) Metropolitan Statistical Area - see Appendix A for areas included
Source: 1990 Census of Population and Housing, Summary Tape File 3C

Age

Area	Median Age (Years)	Age Distribution (%)						
		Under 5	Under 18	18-24	25-44	45-64	65+	80+
City	31.1	7.7	26.0	11.3	33.3	17.7	11.8	2.5
MSA[1]	32.5	7.5	25.4	10.2	33.7	18.9	11.8	2.5
U.S.	32.9	7.3	25.6	10.5	32.6	18.7	12.5	2.8

Note: (1) Metropolitan Statistical Area - see Appendix A for areas included
Source: 1990 Census of Population and Housing, Summary Tape File 3C

Male/Female Ratio

Area	Number of males per 100 females (all ages)	Number of males per 100 females (18 years old+)
City	91.8	88.4
MSA[1]	93.3	89.9
U.S.	95.0	91.9

Note: (1) Metropolitan Statistical Area - see Appendix A for areas included
Source: 1990 Census of Population, General Population Characteristics

INCOME

Per Capita/Median/Average Income

Area	Per Capita ($)	Median Household ($)	Average Household ($)
City	12,899	26,301	34,682
MSA[1]	16,447	35,265	44,583
U.S.	14,420	30,056	38,453

Note: all figures are for 1989; (1) Metropolitan Statistical Area - see Appendix A for areas included
Source: 1990 Census of Population and Housing, Summary Tape File 3C

Household Income Distribution by Race

Income ($)	City (%)					U.S. (%)				
	Total	White	Black	Other	Hisp.[1]	Total	White	Black	Other	Hisp.[1]
Less than 5,000	10.6	5.6	18.5	10.5	9.9	6.2	4.8	15.2	8.6	8.8
5,000 - 9,999	10.2	8.5	13.4	8.3	8.5	9.3	8.6	14.2	9.9	11.1
10,000 - 14,999	8.9	8.4	9.3	9.8	9.8	8.8	8.5	11.0	9.8	11.0
15,000 - 24,999	18.0	17.3	18.0	21.1	22.1	17.5	17.3	18.9	18.5	20.5
25,000 - 34,999	15.4	15.9	13.9	18.0	18.2	15.8	16.1	14.2	15.4	16.4
35,000 - 49,999	16.6	18.4	13.5	17.6	17.9	17.9	18.6	13.3	16.1	16.0
50,000 - 74,999	12.8	15.2	9.8	10.7	10.3	15.0	15.8	9.3	13.4	11.1
75,000 - 99,999	4.0	5.4	2.4	2.5	2.2	5.1	5.5	2.6	4.7	3.1
100,000+	3.5	5.4	1.2	1.5	1.1	4.4	4.8	1.3	3.7	1.9

Note: all figures are for 1989; (1) people of Hispanic origin can be of any race
Source: 1990 Census of Population and Housing, Summary Tape File 3C

Effective Buying Income

Area	Per Capita ($)	Median Household ($)	Average Household ($)
City	14,522	30,801	39,965
MSA[1]	19,019	43,449	53,209
U.S.	15,444	33,201	41,849

Note: data as of 1/1/97; (1) Metropolitan Statistical Area - see Appendix A for areas included
Source: Standard Rate & Data Service, Newspaper Advertising Source, 2/98

Effective Household Buying Income Distribution

Area	% of Households Earning						
	$10,000 -$19,999	$20,000 -$34,999	$35,000 -$49,999	$50,000 -$74,999	$75,000 -$99,000	$100,000 -$124,999	$125,000 and up
City	16.2	22.4	17.1	16.6	6.1	2.1	2.4
MSA[1]	11.3	18.8	18.1	23.1	10.6	4.1	4.6
U.S.	16.5	23.4	18.3	18.2	6.4	2.1	2.4

Note: data as of 1/1/97; (1) Metropolitan Statistical Area - see Appendix A for areas included
Source: Standard Rate & Data Service, Newspaper Advertising Source, 2/98

Poverty Rates by Race and Age

Area	Total (%)	By Race (%)				By Age (%)		
		White	Black	Other	Hisp.[2]	Under 5 years old	Under 18 years old	65 years and over
City	21.6	11.0	33.2	23.7	24.2	35.6	33.9	15.9
MSA[1]	12.4	5.8	30.0	18.4	20.7	19.9	19.1	10.5
U.S.	13.1	9.8	29.5	23.1	25.3	20.1	18.3	12.8

Note: figures show the percent of people living below the poverty line in 1989. The average poverty threshold was $12,674 for a family of four in 1989; (1) Metropolitan Statistical Area - see Appendix A for areas included; (2) people of Hispanic origin can be of any race
Source: 1990 Census of Population and Housing, Summary Tape File 3C

EMPLOYMENT

Labor Force and Employment

Area	Civilian Labor Force			Workers Employed		
	Dec. '95	Dec. '96	% Chg.	Dec. '95	Dec. '96	% Chg.
City	1,296,199	1,302,194	0.5	1,214,188	1,228,468	1.2
MSA[1]	4,075,063	4,103,252	0.7	3,879,369	3,924,995	1.2
U.S.	134,583,000	136,742,000	1.6	127,903,000	130,785,000	2.3

Note: Data is not seasonally adjusted and covers workers 16 years of age and older;
(1) Metropolitan Statistical Area - see Appendix A for areas included
Source: Bureau of Labor Statistics, http://stats.bls.gov

Unemployment Rate

Area	1997											
	Jan.	Feb.	Mar.	Apr.	May	Jun.	Jul.	Aug.	Sep.	Oct.	Nov.	Dec.
City	6.4	6.4	6.4	6.2	5.9	6.0	5.9	5.8	5.9	5.8	5.8	5.7
MSA[1]	5.2	5.2	5.1	4.7	4.2	4.3	4.3	4.2	4.1	4.0	4.1	4.3
U.S.	5.9	5.7	5.5	4.8	4.7	5.2	5.0	4.8	4.7	4.4	4.3	4.4

Note: Data is not seasonally adjusted and covers workers 16 years of age and older; All figures are percentages; (1) Metropolitan Statistical Area - see Appendix A for areas included
Source: Bureau of Labor Statistics, http://stats.bls.gov

Employment by Industry

Sector	MSA[1]		U.S.
	Number of Employees	Percent of Total	Percent of Total
Services	1,274,800	31.0	29.0
Retail Trade	683,900	16.6	18.5
Government	488,000	11.9	16.1
Manufacturing	662,200	16.1	15.0
Finance/Insurance/Real Estate	316,500	7.7	5.7
Wholesale Trade	271,500	6.6	5.4
Transportation/Public Utilities	254,100	6.2	5.3
Construction	161,400	3.9	4.5
Mining	1,600	0.0	0.5

Note: Figures cover non-farm employment as of 12/97 and are not seasonally adjusted;
(1) Metropolitan Statistical Area - see Appendix A for areas included
Source: Bureau of Labor Statistics, http://stats.bls.gov

Employment by Occupation

Occupation Category	City (%)	MSA[1] (%)	U.S. (%)
White Collar	57.9	64.0	58.1
Executive/Admin./Management	11.3	14.2	12.3
Professional	13.6	14.6	14.1
Technical & Related Support	3.2	3.5	3.7
Sales	10.1	12.5	11.8
Administrative Support/Clerical	19.7	19.2	16.3
Blue Collar	26.5	23.7	26.2
Precision Production/Craft/Repair	8.9	9.7	11.3
Machine Operators/Assem./Insp.	8.7	6.4	6.8
Transportation/Material Movers	4.0	3.6	4.1
Cleaners/Helpers/Laborers	4.9	4.0	3.9
Services	15.1	11.8	13.2
Farming/Forestry/Fishing	0.5	0.6	2.5

Note: figures cover employed persons 16 years old and over;
(1) Metropolitan Statistical Area - see Appendix A for areas included
Source: 1990 Census of Population and Housing, Summary Tape File 3C

Occupational Employment Projections: 1992 - 2005

Occupations Expected to have the Largest Job Growth (ranked by numerical growth)	Fast-Growing Occupations (ranked by percent growth)
1. Food preparation workers	1. Computer systems analysts
2. Managers & administrators, misc.	2. Securities, financial services sales
3. All other management support workers	3. Personal service occupations
4. Management support occupations	4. Therapists
5. Personal service occupations	5. Health services & related occupations
6. All other helper, laborer, mover	6. Travel agents
7. Protective service occupations	7. All other profess., paraprofess., tech.
8. Salespersons, retail	8. All other service workers
9. Cleaning/building svcs., exc. private	9. Engineers
10. Motor vehicle operators	10. Social workers, incl. med. & psych.

Projections cover Cook, DuPage, Kane, Lake, McHenry, Will, Grundy, Kendall and DeKalb Counties.
Source: State of Illinois Department of Employment Security, Occupational Employment (1992 and Projected 2005)

Average Wages

Occupation	Wage	Occupation	Wage
Professional/Technical/Clerical	$/Week	**Health/Protective Services**	$/Week
Accountants III	781	Corrections Officers	623
Attorneys III	1,281	Firefighters	-
Budget Analysts III	816	Nurses, Licensed Practical II	-
Buyers/Contracting Specialists II	693	Nurses, Registered II	-
Clerks, Accounting III	462	Nursing Assistants II	-
Clerks, General III	434	Police Officers I	816
Computer Operators II	473	**Hourly Workers**	$/Hour
Computer Programmers II	681	Forklift Operators	-
Drafters II	509	General Maintenance Workers	10.32
Engineering Technicians III	672	Guards I	6.84
Engineering Technicians, Civil III	627	Janitors	9.19
Engineers III	987	Maintenance Electricians	20.07
Key Entry Operators I	347	Maintenance Electronics Techs II	19.78
Personnel Assistants III	528	Maintenance Machinists	18.13
Personnel Specialists III	814	Maintenance Mechanics, Machinery	18.15
Secretaries III	593	Material Handling Laborers	9.01
Switchboard Operator-Receptionist	361	Motor Vehicle Mechanics	18.28
Systems Analysts II	969	Shipping/Receiving Clerks	10.15
Systems Analysts Supervisor/Mgr II	1,504	Tool and Die Makers	19.47
Tax Collectors II	-	Truckdrivers, Tractor Trailer	15.66
Word Processors II	538	Warehouse Specialists	-

Note: Wage data includes full-time workers only for 6/96 and cover the Metropolitan Statistical Area (see Appendix A for areas included). Dashes indicate that data was not available.
Source: Bureau of Labor Statistics, Occupational Compensation Survey, 12/96

TAXES

Major State and Local Tax Rates

State Corp. Income (%)	State Personal Income (%)	Residential Property (effective rate per $100)	Sales & Use State (%)	Sales & Use Local (%)	State Gasoline (cents/gallon)	State Cigarette (cents/20-pack)
7.3[a]	3.0	1.79	6.25	2.5	19.3[b]	58[c]

Note: Personal/corporate income tax rates as of 1/97. Sales, gasoline and cigarette tax rates as of 1/98; (a) Includes a 2.5% personal property replacement tax; (b) Rate is comprised of 19 cents excise and 0.3 cent motor carrier tax. Carriers pay an additional surcharge of 6.3 cents. Rate does not include a 5 cent local option tax in Chicago.; (c) Counties and cities may impose an additional tax of 10 - 15 cents per pack
Source: Federation of Tax Administrators, www.taxadmin.org; Washington D.C. Department of Finance and Revenue, Tax Rates and Tax Burdens in the District of Columbia: A Nationwide Comparison, June 1997; Chamber of Commerce

Total Taxes Per Capita and as a Percent of Income

Area	Per Capita Income ($)	Per Capita Taxes ($)			Taxes as Pct. of Income (%)		
		Total	Federal	State/Local	Total	Federal	State/Local
Illinois	28,390	10,271	7,042	3,229	36.2	24.8	11.4
U.S.	26,187	9,205	6,127	3,078	35.2	23.4	11.8

Note: Figures are for 1997
Source: Tax Foundation, Web Site, www.taxfoundation.org

Estimated Tax Burden

Area	State Income	Local Income	Property	Sales	Total
Chicago	1,830	0	4,725	796	7,351

Note: The numbers are estimates of taxes paid by a married couple with two kids and annual earnings of $65,000. Sales tax estimates assume they spend average amounts on food, clothing, household goods and gasoline. Property tax estimates assume they live in a $225,000 home.
Source: Kiplinger's Personal Finance Magazine, June 1997

COMMERCIAL REAL ESTATE

Office Market

Class/Location	Total Space (sq. ft.)	Vacant Space (sq. ft.)	Vac. Rate (%)	Under Constr. (sq. ft.)	Net Absorp. (sq. ft.)	Rental Rates ($/sq.ft./yr.)
Class A						
CBD	44,122,708	3,038,490	6.9	0	1,095,380	20.00-34.00
Outside CBD	23,741,901	1,606,160	6.8	n/a	496,491	22.50-27.00
Class B						
CBD	40,655,241	6,585,275	16.2	0	1,512,367	15.50-21.00
Outside CBD	n/a	n/a	n/a	n/a	n/a	16.00-22.00

Note: Data as of 10/97 and covers Chicago; CBD = Central Business District; n/a not available;
Source: Society of Industrial and Office Realtors, 1998 Comparative Statistics of Industrial and Office Real Estate Markets

"With shrinking Class 'A' vacancy rates, large users may need to resort to build-to-suits. More than 20 speculative office buildings are slated for construction in the quickly growing western suburbs. Downtown, it is likely that two buildings totaling 1.5 million sq. ft. will begin construction in 1998. SIOR's reporter has observed strong transactional activity during the past year. In addition, consolidation of developers is a current trend which is likely to continue at least in the short-term. The Chicago MSA is expected to grow at a slightly slower pace than the nation through the end of the decade. Short of a significant downturn in the national economy, local real estate markets should enjoy brisk activity during 1998." *Society of Industrial and Office Realtors, 1998 Comparative Statistics of Industrial and Office Real Estate Markets*

Industrial Market

Location	Total Space (sq. ft.)	Vacant Space (sq. ft.)	Vac. Rate (%)	Under Constr. (sq. ft.)	Net Absorp. (sq. ft.)	Net Lease ($/sq.ft./yr.)
Central City	217,400,000	15,435,165	7.1	0	1,191,835	1.42-6.88
Suburban	651,827,000	46,512,353	7.1	6,055,962	5,751,647	2.75-7.25

Note: Data as of 10/97 and covers Chicago; n/a not available
Source: Society of Industrial and Office Realtors, 1998 Comparative Statistics of Industrial and Office Real Estate Markets

"Strong export volumes form the foundation for steady growth and profits in Chicago's manufacturing sector. If exports from the region can maintain their pace in 1998, the Chicago area economy will continue to surpass economic activity in other parts of the country. This is largely predicated on stable economies in Canada, Mexico, South America, and the Far East. Another major facet of the local real estate market relates to securitization. Local REITs will continue to aggressively seek acquisition, spec development, and build-to-suit opportunities in this market. This trend toward securitization may be seriously tested if the Chicago area begins to slide next year. Lenders will continue to slow the flow of capital into speculative developments, recognizing the potential for overbuilding." *Society of Industrial and Office Realtors, 1998 Comparative Statistics of Industrial and Office Real Estate Markets*

Retail Market

Shopping Center Inventory (sq. ft.)	Shopping Center Construction (sq. ft.)	Construction as a Percent of Inventory (%)	Torto Wheaton Rent Index[1] ($/sq. ft.)
130,211,000	469,000	0.4	13.64

Note: Data as of 1997 and covers the Metropolitan Statistical Area - see Appendix A for areas included; (1) Index is based on a model that predicts what the average rent should be for leases with certain characteristics, in certain locations during certain years.
Source: National Association of Realtors, 1997-1998 Market Conditions Report

"Like the nation, economic growth in Chicago has slowed somewhat from the brisk pace set from 1994 through 1996. Per-capita income levels remain among the highest in the nation; however, sluggish population growth in the area continues to burden local retailers. The vacancy rate rose slightly last year, particularly due to a rise in vacancies in older, medium to large size shopping centers. Much of the new space under development is already pre-leased, with very little speculative development. Chicago's retail market is likely to remain flat over the next few years as the area's slowing economy struggles to fill the large supply of older space." *National Association of Realtors, 1997-1998 Market Conditions Report*

COMMERCIAL UTILITIES

Typical Monthly Electric Bills

Area	Commercial Service ($/month)		Industrial Service ($/month)	
	12 kW demand 1,500 kWh	100 kW demand 30,000 kWh	1,000 kW demand 400,000 kWh	20,000 kW demand 10,000,000 kWh
City	275	3,113	34,978	649,370
U.S.	162	2,360	25,590	545,677

Note: Based on rates in effect July 1, 1997
Source: Edison Electric Institute, Typical Residential, Commercial and Industrial Bills, Summer 1997

TRANSPORTATION

Transportation Statistics

Avg. travel time to work (min.)	31.5
Interstate highways	I-55; I-57; I-80; I-88; I-90
Bus lines	
In-city	Chicago TA, 2,040 vehicles
Inter-city	1
Passenger air service	
Airport	O'Hare International
Airlines	27
Aircraft departures	380,794 (1995)
Enplaned passengers	29,885,957 (1995)
Rail service	Amtrak; Metro; Commuter Rail
Motor freight carriers	750 (local trucking)
Major waterways/ports	Port of Chicago

Source: OAG, Business Travel Planner, Summer 1997; Editor & Publisher Market Guide, 1998; FAA Airport Activity Statistics, 1996; Amtrak National Time Table, Northeast Timetable, Fall/Winter 1997-98; 1990 Census of Population and Housing, STF 3C; Chamber of Commerce/Economic Development 1997; Jane's Urban Transport Systems 1997-98; Transit Fact Book 1997

A survey of 90,000 airline passengers during the first half of 1997 ranked most of the largest airports in the U.S. O'Hare International ranked #20 and Midway #29 out of 36. Criteria: cleanliness, quality of restaurants, attractiveness, speed of baggage delivery, ease of reaching gates, available ground transportation, ease of following signs and closeness of parking. *Plog Research Inc., First Half 1997*

Means of Transportation to Work

Area	Car/Truck/Van		Public Transportation			Bicycle	Walked	Other Means	Worked at Home
	Drove Alone	Car-pooled	Bus	Subway	Railroad				
City	46.3	14.8	19.3	7.9	1.5	0.3	6.4	1.7	1.7
MSA[1]	63.8	12.0	8.7	4.1	3.9	0.2	4.2	1.1	2.0
U.S.	73.2	13.4	3.0	1.5	0.5	0.4	3.9	1.2	3.0

Note: figures shown are percentages and only include workers 16 years old and over;
(1) Metropolitan Statistical Area - see Appendix A for areas included
Source: 1990 Census of Population and Housing, Summary Tape File 3C

BUSINESSES

Major Business Headquarters

Company Name	1997 Rankings	
	Fortune 500	Forbes 500
AON	324	-
Ameritech	77	-
Amoco	19	-
Amsted Industries	-	161
BDO Seidman	-	130
Baker & McKenzie	-	306
FMC	278	-
First Chicago NBD Corp.	139	-
General Instrument	486	-
Grant Thornton	-	116
H Group Holding	-	221
Inland Steel Industries	307	-
Leo Burnett	-	239
Marmon Group	-	23
Montgomery Ward & Co	-	17
Morton International	367	-
Navistar International	249	-
Pepper Cos	-	443
Quaker Oats	274	-
R.R. Donnelley & Sons	217	-
Sara Lee	57	-
Stone Container	275	-
USG	496	-
Unicom	209	-
Walsh Group	-	286
Wirtz	-	296

Note: Companies listed are located in the city; Dashes indicate no ranking
Fortune 500: companies that produce a 10-K are ranked 1 - 500 based on 1996 revenue
Forbes 500: private companies are ranked 1 - 500 based on 1996 revenue
Source: Forbes 12/1/97; Fortune 4/28/97

Fast-Growing Businesses

Chicago is home to three of *Business Week's* "hot growth" companies: Help at Home, SPSS and Whittman-Hart. Criteria: sales and earnings, return on capital and stock price. *Business Week, 5/26/97*

According to *Fortune*, Chicago is home to one of America's 100 fastest-growing companies: United States Cellular. Companies were ranked based on three years' earnings-per-share growth using least squares analysis to smooth out distortions. Criteria for inclusion: public companies with sales of least $50 million. Companies that lost money in the most recent quarter, or ended in the red for the past four quarters as a whole, were not eligible. Limited partnerships and REITs were also not considered. *Fortune, 9/29/97*

Chicago was ranked #13 out of 24 (#1 is best) in terms of the best-performing local stocks in 1996 according to the Money/Norby Cities Index. The index measures stocks of companies that have headquarters in 24 metro areas. *Money, 2/7/97*

Women-Owned Businesses: Number, Employment, Sales and Share

Area	Women-Owned Businesses in 1996				Share of Women-Owned Businesses in 1996	
	Number	Employment	Sales ($000)	Rank[2]	Percent (%)	Rank[3]
MSA[1]	225,100	706,000	96,222,200	3	36.5	30

Note: (1) Metropolitan Statistical Area - see Appendix A for areas included; (2) Calculated on an averaging of number of businesses, employment and sales and ranges from 1 to 50 where 1 is best; (3) Ranges from 1 to 50 where 1 is best
Source: The National Foundation for Women Business Owners, 1996 Facts on Women-Owned Businesses: Trends in the Top 50 Metropolitan Areas, March 26, 1997

Women-Owned Businesses: Growth

Area	Growth in Women-Owned Businesses (% change from 1987 to 1996)				Relative Growth in the Number of Women-Owned and All Businesses (% change from 1987 to 1996)			
	Num.	Empl.	Sales	Rank[2]	Women-Owned	All Firms	Absolute Difference	Relative Difference
MSA[1]	88.0	222.8	274.5	18	88.0	59.9	28.1	1.5:1

Note: (1) Metropolitan Statistical Area - see Appendix A for areas included; (2) Calculated on an averaging of the percent growth of number of businesses, employment and sales and ranges from 1 to 50 where 1 is best
Source: The National Foundation for Women Business Owners, 1996 Facts on Women-Owned Businesses: Trends in the Top 50 Metropolitan Areas, March 26, 1997

Minority Business Opportunity

Chicago is home to five companies which are on the Black Enterprise Industrial/Service 100 list (largest based on gross sales): Johnson Publishing Co. Inc. (publishing, broadcasting, TV prod., cosmetics, hair care); Burrell Communications Group Inc. (advertising, PR, consumer promotion, direct response mktg.); Soft Sheen Products Inc. (hair care products mfg.); Sayers Computer Source (value-added reseller of computers & related products); Luster Products Co. (hair care products mfg. and distrib.). Criteria: 1) operational in previous calendar year; 2) at least 51% black-owned; 3) manufactures/owns the product it sells or provides industrial or consumer services. Brokerages, real estate firms and firms that provide professional services are not eligible. *Black Enterprise, July 1997*

Chicago is home to two companies which are on the Black Enterprise Auto Dealer 100 list (largest based on gross sales): Chicago Truck Center Inc. (GM/Volvo); Southside Ford Truck Sales Inc. (Ford). Criteria: 1) operational in previous calendar year; 2) at least 51% black-owned. *Black Enterprise, June 1997*

Five of the 500 largest Hispanic-owned companies in the U.S. are located in Chicago. *Hispanic Business, June 1997*

Chicago is home to two companies which are on the Hispanic Business Fastest-Growing 100 list (greatest sales growth from 1992 to 1996): Suarez Electric Co. (electrical contracting) and David Gomez & Associates Inc. (executive search svcs.) *Hispanic Business, July/August 1997*

Chicago was listed among the top 25 metropolitan areas in terms of the number of Hispanic-owned companies. The city was ranked number 8 with 31,846 companies. *Hispanic Business, May 1997*

Small Business Opportunity

According to *Forbes*, Chicago is home to three of America's 200 best small companies: Duff & Phelps Credit Rating, SPSS, Whittman-Hart. Criteria: companies must be publicly traded, U.S.-based corporations with latest 12-month sales of between $5 and $350 million. Earnings must be at least $1 million for the 12-month period. Limited partnerships, REITs and closed-end mutual funds were not considered. Banks, S&Ls and electric utilities were not included. *Forbes, November 3, 1997*

HOTELS & MOTELS

Hotels/Motels

Area	Hotels/ Motels	Rooms	Luxury-Level Hotels/Motels		Average Minimum Rates ($)		
			♦♦♦♦	♦♦♦♦♦	♦♦	♦♦♦	♦♦♦♦
City	73	26,005	12	2	89	143	206
Airport	38	10,597	0	0	n/a	n/a	n/a
Suburbs	163	26,538	1	0	n/a	n/a	n/a
Total	274	63,140	13	2	n/a	n/a	n/a

Note: n/a not available; Classifications range from one diamond (budget properties with basic amenities) to five diamond (luxury properties with the finest service, rooms and facilities).
Source: OAG, Business Travel Planner, Summer 1997

Chicago is home to two of the top 100 hotels in the world according to *Travel & Leisure*: Four Seasons and Ritz-Carlton. Criteria: value, rooms/ambience, location, facilities/activities and service. *Travel & Leisure, September 1997*

CONVENTION CENTERS

Major Convention Centers

Center Name	Meeting Rooms	Exhibit Space (sf)
Chicago Hilton and Towers	43	120,000
Forum Hotel-Chicago	17	8,085
Hyatt Regency Chicago	87	180,000
McCormick Place on the Lake	51	1,300,000
Merchandise Mart Expocenter	14	105,000
Navy Pier	n/a	n/a
Inland Meeting & Exhibition Center	15	15,000
KPMG Center for Leadership Development	15	20,000

Note: n/a not available
Source: Trade Shows Worldwide 1997

Living Environment

COST OF LIVING

Cost of Living Index

Composite Index	Housing	Utilities	Groceries	Health Care	Trans-portation	Misc. Goods/ Services
n/a	n/a	n/a	n/a	n/a	n/a	n/a

Note: U.S. = 100; n/a not available
Source: ACCRA, Cost of Living Index, 3rd Quarter 1997

HOUSING

Median Home Prices and Housing Affordability

Area	Median Price[2] 3rd Qtr. 1997 ($)	HOI[3] 3rd Qtr. 1997	Afford-ability Rank[4]
MSA[1]	148,000	61.0	139
U.S.	127,000	63.7	–

Note: (1) Metropolitan Statistical Area - see Appendix A for areas included; (2) U.S. figures calculated from the sales of 625,000 new and existing homes in 195 markets; (3) Housing Opportunity Index - percent of homes sold that were within the reach of the median income household at the prevailing mortgage interest rate; (4) Rank is from 1-195 with 1 being most affordable
Source: National Association of Home Builders, Housing Opportunity Index, 3rd Quarter 1997

It is projected that the median price of existing single-family homes in the metro area will increase by 9.6% in 1998. Nationwide, home prices are projected to increase 6.6%.
Kiplinger's Personal Finance Magazine, January 1998

Average New Home Price

Area	Price ($)
City	n/a
U.S.	135,710

Note: n/a not available
Source: ACCRA, Cost of Living Index, 3rd Quarter 1997

Average Apartment Rent

Area	Rent ($/mth)
City	n/a
U.S.	569

Note: n/a not available
Source: ACCRA, Cost of Living Index, 3rd Quarter 1997

RESIDENTIAL UTILITIES

Average Residential Utility Costs

Area	All Electric ($/mth)	Part Electric ($/mth)	Other Energy ($/mth)	Phone ($/mth)
City	n/a	n/a	n/a	n/a
U.S.	109.40	55.25	43.64	19.48

Note: n/a not available
Source: ACCRA, Cost of Living Index, 3rd Quarter 1997

HEALTH CARE

Average Health Care Costs

Area	Hospital ($/day)	Doctor ($/visit)	Dentist ($/visit)
City	n/a	n/a	n/a
U.S.	392.91	48.76	60.84

Note: n/a not available
Source: ACCRA, Cost of Living Index, 3rd Quarter 1997

Distribution of Office-Based Physicians

Area	Family/Gen. Practitioners	Specialists		
		Medical	Surgical	Other
MSA[1]	1,621	5,664	3,539	3,923

Note: Data as of 12/31/96; (1) Metropolitan Statistical Area - see Appendix A for areas included
Source: American Medical Assn., Physician Characteristics & Distribution in the U.S., 1997-1998

Hospitals

Chicago has 40 general medical and surgical hospitals, 6 psychiatric, 2 rehabilitation, 1 children's general, 2 children's other specialty. *AHA Guide to the Healthcare Field 1997-98*

According to *U.S. News and World Report,* Chicago has 8 of the best hospitals in the U.S.: **Northwestern Memorial Hospital**, noted for AIDS, endocrinology, gastroenterology, geriatrics, gynecology, neurology, orthopedics, otolaryngology, pulmonology, urology; **Rush-Presbyterian-St. Luke's Medical Center**, noted for AIDS, cancer, cardiology, gastroenterology, geriatrics, gynecology, orthopedics, pulmonology; **Cook County Hospital**, noted for AIDS, endocrinology; **University of Chicago Hospital**, noted for AIDS, cancer, cardiology, endocrinology, gastroenterology, geriatrics, gynecology, neurology, orthopedics, otolaryngology, pulmonology, rheumatology, urology; **University of Illinois Hospital and Clinics**, noted for endocrinology, neurology, otolaryngology; **Children's Memorial Hospital**, noted for pediatrics; **Rehabilitation Institute of Chicago**, noted for rehabilitation; **Illinois Masonic Medical Center**, noted for endocrinology;   *U.S. News and World Report, "America's Best Hospitals", 7/28/97*

Northwestern Memorial Hospital is among the 100 best-run hospitals in the U.S. *Modern Healthcare, January 5, 1998*

EDUCATION

Public School District Statistics

District Name	Num. Sch.	Enroll.	Classroom Teachers[1]	Pupils per Teacher	Minority Pupils (%)	Current Exp.[2] ($/pupil)
Central Stickney Sch Dist 110	1	375	21	17.9	n/a	n/a
City of Chicago School Dist 29	555	412,921	22,918	18.0	89.2	5,613

Note: Data covers the 1995-1996 school year unless otherwise noted; (1) Excludes teachers reported as working in school district offices rather than in schools; (2) Based on 1993-94 enrollment collected by the Census Bureau, not the enrollment figure shown in column 3; SD = School District; ISD = Independent School District; n/a not available
Source: National Center for Education Statistics, Common Core of Data Survey; Bureau of the Census

Educational Quality

School District	Education Quotient[1]	Graduate Outcome[2]	Community Index[3]	Resource Index[4]
City of Chicago	98.0	53.0	95.0	147.0

Note: Nearly 1,000 secondary school districts were rated in terms of educational quality. The scores range from a low of 50 to a high of 150; (1) Average of the Graduate Outcome, Community and Resource indexes; (2) Based on graduation rates and college board scores (SAT/ACT); (3) Based on the surrounding community's average level of education and the area's average income level; (4) Based on teacher salaries, per-pupil expenditures and student-teacher ratios.
Source: Expansion Management, Ratings Issue 1997

Educational Attainment by Race

Area	High School Graduate (%)					Bachelor's Degree (%)				
	Total	White	Black	Other	Hisp.[2]	Total	White	Black	Other	Hisp.[2]
City	66.0	72.2	63.1	49.2	40.8	19.5	26.6	10.5	15.5	6.6
MSA[1]	75.7	80.5	65.6	58.0	44.2	24.4	27.9	11.8	24.0	8.0
U.S.	75.2	77.9	63.1	60.4	49.8	20.3	21.5	11.4	19.4	9.2

Note: figures shown cover persons 25 years old and over; (1) Metropolitan Statistical Area - see Appendix A for areas included; (2) people of Hispanic origin can be of any race
Source: 1990 Census of Population and Housing, Summary Tape File 3C

School Enrollment by Type

Area	Preprimary				Elementary/High School			
	Public		Private		Public		Private	
	Enrollment	%	Enrollment	%	Enrollment	%	Enrollment	%
City	27,249	61.1	17,333	38.9	391,046	79.5	101,138	20.5
MSA[1]	70,174	57.4	52,166	42.6	837,481	82.5	178,237	17.5
U.S.	2,679,029	59.5	1,824,256	40.5	38,379,689	90.2	4,187,099	9.8

Note: figures shown cover persons 3 years old and over;
(1) Metropolitan Statistical Area - see Appendix A for areas included
Source: 1990 Census of Population and Housing, Summary Tape File 3C

School Enrollment by Race

Area	Preprimary (%)				Elementary/High School (%)			
	White	Black	Other	Hisp.[1]	White	Black	Other	Hisp.[1]
City	36.1	50.5	13.5	17.5	30.7	48.4	20.9	27.8
MSA[2]	68.6	23.0	8.4	9.4	56.2	29.0	14.8	17.5
U.S.	80.4	12.5	7.1	7.8	74.1	15.6	10.3	12.5

Note: figures shown cover persons 3 years old and over; (1) people of Hispanic origin can be of any race; (2) Metropolitan Statistical Area - see Appendix A for areas included
Source: 1990 Census of Population and Housing, Summary Tape File 3C

SAT/ACT Scores

Area/District	1997 SAT				1997 ACT	
	Percent of Graduates Tested (%)	Average Math Score	Average Verbal Score	Average Combined Score	Percent of Graduates Tested (%)	Average Composite Score
Chicago PS	n/a	n/a	n/a	n/a	59	17.1
State	14	578	562	1,140	69	21.2
U.S.	42	511	505	1,016	36	21.0

Note: Math and verbal SAT scores are out of a possible 800; ACT scores are out of a possible 36
Caution: Comparing or ranking states/cities on the basis of SAT/ACT scores alone is invalid and strongly discouraged by the The College Board and The American College Testing Program as students who take the tests are self-selected and do not represent the entire student population.
Source: Chicago Public Schools, Department of Research, Assessment & Quality Reviews, 1997; American College Testing Program, 1997; College Board, 1997

Classroom Teacher Salaries in Public Schools

District	B.A. Degree		M.A. Degree		Ph.D. Degree	
	Min. ($)	Max. ($)	Min. ($)	Max. ($)	Min. ($)	Max. ($)
Chicago	29,604	46,521	31,655	48,572	35,756	52,673
Average[1]	26,120	39,270	28,175	44,667	31,643	49,825

Note: Salaries are for 1996-1997; (1) Based on all school districts covered
Source: American Federation of Teachers (unpublished data)

Higher Education

Two-Year Colleges		Four-Year Colleges		Medical Schools	Law Schools	Voc/ Tech
Public	Private	Public	Private			
7	5	3	22	5	6	33

Source: College Blue Book, Occupational Education 1997; Medical School Admission Requirements, 1998-99; Peterson's Guide to Two-Year Colleges, 1997; Peterson's Guide to Four-Year Colleges, 1997; Barron's Guide to Law Schools 1997

MAJOR EMPLOYERS

Major Employers

Amoco Corp.	Andersen Consulting
Chicago Tribune	Continental Casualty
First Chicago NBD Corp.	Harris Trust & Savings Bank
Healthcare Service Corp.	Illinois Bell Telephone
Illinois Masonic Medical Center	Leo Burnett Co. (advertising)
Northern Trust Co.	Rush-Presbyterian St. Lukes Medical Center
Stone-Consolidated Paper Sales Corp.	University of Chicago Hospitals
Children's Memorial Hospital	ComPsych Corp. (management consulting)
Gatorade Co.	Sun-Times Co.

Note: companies listed are located in the city
Source: Dun's Business Rankings 1997; Ward's Business Directory, 1997

PUBLIC SAFETY

Crime Rate

Area	All Crimes	Violent Crimes				Property Crimes		
		Murder	Forcible Rape	Robbery	Aggrav. Assault	Burglary	Larceny -Theft	Motor Vehicle Theft
City	0.0	28.6	0.0	975.3	1,347.0	1,469.6	4,338.7	1,237.8
Suburbs[1]	n/a	n/a	n/a	n/a	n/a	n/a	n/a	n/a
MSA[2]	n/a	n/a	n/a	n/a	n/a	n/a	n/a	n/a
U.S.	5,078.9	7.4	36.1	202.4	388.2	943.0	2,975.9	525.9

Note: Crime rate is the number of crimes per 100,000 pop.; (1) defined as all areas within the MSA but located outside the central city; (2) Metropolitan Statistical Area - see Appendix A for areas incl.
Source: FBI Uniform Crime Reports 1996

RECREATION

Culture and Recreation

Museums	Symphony Orchestras	Opera Companies	Dance Companies	Professional Theatres	Zoos	Pro Sports Teams
33	4	5	9	18	2	5

Source: International Directory of the Performing Arts, 1996; Official Museum Directory, 1998; Chamber of Commerce/Economic Development 1997

Library System

The Chicago Public Library has 81 branches, holdings of 11,463,011 volumes and a budget of $80,821,119 (1995). *American Library Directory, 1997-1998*

MEDIA

Newspapers

Name	Type	Freq.	Distribution	Circulation
Back of the Yards Journal and El Periodico	Hispanic	1x/wk	Local	44,000
Bridgeport News	General	1x/wk	Local	25,300
Brighton Park Life-McKinley Park Life	General	1x/wk	Local	30,500
The Calumet Herald	General	1x/wk	Local	62,000
Chatham Citizen	Black	1x/wk	Local	29,962
The Chicago Crusader	Black	1x/wk	Local	70,000
Chicago Defender	Black	6x/wk	Area	33,314
The Chicago Post	General	2x/mo	Area	38,000
Chicago Reader	General	1x/wk	Local	135,000
Chicago Shoreland News	Black	1x/wk	National	38,162
Chicago's Northwest Side Press	General	1x/wk	Area	40,500
Chicago Sun-Times	n/a	7x/wk	Area	491,143
Chicago Tribune	General	7x/wk	Area	664,584
Cicero/Berwyn Suburban Edition	n/a	2x/wk	Local	45,000
Clear-Ridge Reporter	n/a	1x/wk	Local	25,900
Connect-Time	General	1x/mo	n/a	7,000,000
Dziennik Chicagowski (Chicago Daily)	n/a	5x/wk	Local	40,000
Dziennik Zwiazkowy	n/a	5x/wk	Area	28,400
El Imparcial	Hispanic	1x/wk	Local	27,000
EXITO	Hispanic	1x/wk	Area	70,000
The Extra	Hispanic	1x/wk	Area	68,000
Independent Bulletin	Black	1x/wk	Area	61,000
Inside	General	1x/wk	Local	50,000
La Raza Newspaper	Hispanic	1x/wk	Local	150,000
Lawndale News/West Side Times	Hispanic	2x/wk	Local	88,976
New Metro News	Black	1x/wk	Area	80,000
Northside Express	Hispanic	2x/wk	Local	86,000
Northwest Leader	General	1x/wk	Local	25,000
Southeast Extra	Hispanic	1x/wk	Local	71,000
South End Citizen	Black	1x/wk	Local	28,707
South Suburban Standard	Black	1x/wk	Area	26,000
Southwest News-Herald	General	1x/wk	Area	25,000
Southwest Shopper	General	1x/wk	Local	52,000
Spotlight Chicago	General	2x/mo	Local	25,000
Tri-City Journal	Black	1x/wk	Local	50,000
Wicker Park/West Town Extra	Hispanic	1x/wk	Local	55,000

Note: Includes newspapers with circulations of 25,000 or more located in the city; n/a not available
Source: Burrelle's Media Directory, 1998 Edition

Television Stations

Name	Ch.	Affiliation	Type	Owner
WTTW	n/a	n/a	n/a	n/a
WBBM	2	CBS	Commercial	Westinghouse Broadcasting Company
WMAQ	5	NBC	Commercial	General Electric Company
WLS	7	ABC	Commercial	ABC Inc.
WGN	9	WB	Commercial	Tribune Company
WTTW	11	PBS	Public	Windows to the World Communications, Inc.
WYCC	20	PBS	Public	City Colleges of Chicago
WFBT	23	n/a	Commercial	Weigel Broadcasting Company
WCIU	26	n/a	Commercial	Weigel Broadcasting Company
WFLD	32	Fox	Commercial	Fox Television Stations Inc.
WCFC	38	Family Net	Commercial	Christian Communications of Chicago
WSNS	44	Telemundo	Commercial	Telemundo Group Inc.
WPWR	50	UPN	Commercial	Channel 50 TV Corporation
WEHS	60	HSN	Commercial	Silver King Communications Inc.
WJYS	62	HSN	Commercial	Jovon Broadcasting Corporation
WGBO	66	Univision	Commercial	Univision Inc.

Note: Stations included broadcast in the Chicago metro area
Source: Burrelle's Media Directory, 1998 Edition

AM Radio Stations

Call Letters	Freq. (kHz)	Target Audience	Station Format	Music Format
WIND	560	Hispanic	M	n/a
WMAQ	670	General	N/S/T	n/a
WGN	720	General	M/N/S/T	n/a
WBBM	780	General	N	n/a
WAIT	850	n/a	M	Easy Listening
WLS	890	General	N/T	n/a
WSPY	930	General	M	Oldies
WMVP	1000	General	S	n/a
WNVR	1030	General	M	n/a
WMBI	1110	Hisp/Relig	M	Christian
WSCR	1160	General	S	n/a
WSBC	1240	General	M	Christian
WTAQ	1300	Hispanic	M/N/S/T	n/a
WGCI	1390	General	M	Oldies/R&B/Urban Contemporary
WRMN	1410	General	N/T	n/a
WEEF	1430	General	M/N/S	n/a
WVON	1450	Black	M/N/S/T	Christian/R&B
WCFJ	1470	General	M/T	Christian
WPNA	1490	General	E/M/N/S/T	n/a
WJJG	1530	General	T	n/a
WBEE	1570	General	M/N	Christian/Jazz/R&B
WONX	1590	Hispanic	M/N/T	AOR/Christian/Spanish
WCGO	1600	General	M/T	Adult Standards

Note: Stations included broadcast in the Chicago metro area; n/a not available
Station Format: E = Educational; M = Music; N = News; S = Sports; T = Talk
Music Format: AOR = Album Oriented Rock; MOR = Middle-of-the-Road
Source: Burrelle's Media Directory, 1998 Edition

FM Radio Stations

Call Letters	Freq. (mHz)	Target Audience	Station Format	Music Format
WCRX	88.1	General	M	Urban Contemporary
WLTL	88.1	General	M/N/S	n/a
WNTH	88.1	n/a	E/M/N/S/T	n/a
WZRD	88.3	n/a	E/M/N	n/a
WHPK	88.5	General	E/M/T	n/a
WMWA	88.5	n/a	E/M	Christian
WHFH	88.5	n/a	E/M/N/S	n/a
WLUW	88.7	General	M/N/S/T	Contemporary Top 40
WRRG	88.9	n/a	M/N/S	Alternative
WARG	88.9	Hispanic	E/M/N/S	Alternative/Classical/Jazz
WOUI	88.9	n/a	M/N/S	n/a
WKKC	89.3	General	M	Urban Contemporary
WNUR	89.3	n/a	M/N/S	n/a
WMBI	90.1	General	M	Christian
WMTH	90.5	n/a	M/N/S	n/a
WRTE	90.5	Hispanic	M	Adult Contemporary/Spanish
WBEZ	91.5	General	M/N/T	Jazz
WCBR	92.7	General	M/T	AOR/Alternative
WXRT	93.1	General	M	Alternative
WLIT	93.9	General	M	Adult Contemporary
WJKL	94.3	General	M	Adult Contemporary
WKXK	94.7	General	N/T	n/a
WNUA	95.5	General	M	Jazz
WBBM	96.3	General	M	Contemporary Top 40
WNIB	97.1	General	M	Classical
WLUP	97.9	n/a	M/T	Classic Rock
WFMT	98.7	General	E/M/N	Classical
WSSD	99.3	General	M	Christian/R&B
WUSN	99.5	General	M	Country
WPNT	100.3	n/a	M/N	Adult Contemporary
WKQX	101.1	General	M	Alternative
WTMX	101.9	General	M	Easy Listening
WVAZ	102.7	Black	M	Urban Contemporary
WRCX	103.5	General	M	Adult Contemporary/Alternative/Classic Rock/ Hard Rock
WJMK	104.3	General	M	Oldies
WOJO	105.1	Hispanic	E/M/N/T	Adult Contemporary
WCKG	105.9	n/a	M/N/S	Classic Rock
WYLL	106.7	General	N/S/T	n/a
WGCI	107.5	n/a	M	Urban Contemporary
WYSY	107.9	Hispanic	M/N	Oldies

Note: Stations included broadcast in the Chicago metro area; n/a not available
Station Format: E = Educational; M = Music; N = News; S = Sports; T = Talk
Music Format: AOR = Album Oriented Rock; MOR = Middle-of-the-Road
Source: Burrelle's Media Directory, 1998 Edition

CLIMATE

Average and Extreme Temperatures

Temperature	Jan	Feb	Mar	Apr	May	Jun	Jul	Aug	Sep	Oct	Nov	Dec	Ann
Extreme High (°F)	65	71	88	91	93	104	102	100	99	91	78	71	104
Average High (°F)	29	33	45	59	70	79	84	82	75	63	48	34	59
Average Temp. (°F)	21	26	37	49	59	69	73	72	65	53	40	27	49
Average Low (°F)	13	17	28	39	48	57	63	62	54	42	32	19	40
Extreme Low (°F)	-27	-17	-8	7	24	36	40	41	28	17	1	-25	-27

Note: Figures cover the years 1958-1990
Source: National Climatic Data Center, International Station Meteorological Climate Summary, 3/95

Average Precipitation/Snowfall/Humidity

Precip./Humidity	Jan	Feb	Mar	Apr	May	Jun	Jul	Aug	Sep	Oct	Nov	Dec	Ann
Avg. Precip. (in.)	1.6	1.4	2.7	3.6	3.3	3.7	3.7	4.1	3.7	2.4	2.8	2.3	35.4
Avg. Snowfall (in.)	11	8	7	2	Tr	0	0	0	0	1	2	9	39
Avg. Rel. Hum. 6am (%)	76	77	79	77	77	78	82	85	85	82	80	80	80
Avg. Rel. Hum. 3pm (%)	65	63	59	53	51	52	54	55	55	53	61	68	57

Note: Figures cover the years 1958-1990; Tr = Trace amounts (<0.05 in. of rain; <0.5 in. of snow)
Source: National Climatic Data Center, International Station Meteorological Climate Summary, 3/95

Weather Conditions

Temperature			Daytime Sky			Precipitation		
5°F & below	32°F & below	90°F & above	Clear	Partly cloudy	Cloudy	0.01 inch or more precip.	0.1 inch or more snow/ice	Thunder-storms
21	132	17	83	136	146	125	31	38

Note: Figures are average number of days per year and covers the years 1958-1990
Source: National Climatic Data Center, International Station Meteorological Climate Summary, 3/95

AIR & WATER QUALITY

Maximum Pollutant Concentrations

	Particulate Matter (ug/m^3)	Carbon Monoxide (ppm)	Sulfur Dioxide (ppm)	Nitrogen Dioxide (ppm)	Ozone (ppm)	Lead (ug/m^3)
MSA[1] Level	122	5	0.032	0.032	0.13	0.06
NAAQS[2]	150	9	0.140	0.053	0.12	1.50
Met NAAQS?	Yes	Yes	Yes	Yes	No	Yes

Note: (1) Metropolitan Statistical Area - see Appendix A for areas included; (2) National Ambient Air Quality Standards; ppm = parts per million; ug/m^3 = micrograms per cubic meter; n/a not available
Source: EPA, National Air Quality and Emissions Trends Report, 1996

Pollutant Standards Index

In the Chicago MSA (see Appendix A for areas included), the Pollutant Standards Index (PSI) exceeded 100 on 4 days in 1996. A PSI value greater than 100 indicates that air quality would be in the unhealthful range on that day. *EPA, National Air Quality and Emissions Trends Report, 1996*

Drinking Water

Water System Name	Pop. Served	Primary Water Source Type	Number of Violations in Fiscal Year 1997	Type of Violation/ Contaminants
Chicago	3,000,000	Surface	None	None

Note: Data as of January 16, 1998
Source: EPA, Office of Ground Water and Drinking Water, Safe Drinking Water Information System

Chicago tap water is alkaline (Lake Michigan); fluoridated.
Editor & Publisher Market Guide, 1998

Des Moines, Iowa

Background

In 1843, Fort Des Moines was founded at the confluence of the Des Moines and Raccoon Rivers. Though the fort was initially established to protect local Native American populations, within two years the area was opened to white settlers. By 1857 the state capital was moved from Iowa City to Des Moines. Today Des Moines remains the capital of Iowa and is its largest city.

Des Moines is one of the top cities in the country for job seekers. Ranking third in the country for insurance activities, Des Moines has more than 50 insurance companies located in its environs. The city also has approximately 385 factories, producing a broad-based spectrum of goods ranging from grain drills to tires.

In addition to its great job market, Des Moines ranks high in areas such as education and the family. The city is known for its fine public school adult education program, as well as its concern for the family. Iowa Parent and Family Magazine, located in Des Moines, is one of the oldest Midwest parenting publications. The monthly newspaper provides valuable information for families in central Iowa reporting on summer camps, local parenting groups, kids activities and more.

One may not immediately think of Des Moines as progressive, but throughout the city one can see the evidence of Des Moines' progressive state of mind. The Des Moines Art Center was designed in 1944 by Eliel Saarinen, a Finnish architect and then President of the renown Cranbrook Academy of Art in Detroit. In 1968 I.M. Pei, architect of the John F. Kennedy International Airport in New York and the east wing of the National Gallery of Art in Washington DC, designed a gallery addition to the main Art Center structure. Finally, in 1985, Richard Meier, who had designed the Museum of Modern Art in Florence, Italy, designed an addition to the north wing. The Home Federal Savings and Loan Building was designed by Mies van der Rohe, of the famous German Bauhaus School of Design , and a sculpture called the Crusoe Umbrella designed by Pop artist Claes Oldenberg stands in the middle of Nollen Plaza, a wooded park and popular gathering place.

Another gathering place is The Des Moines Botanical Center which boasts a 150 foot wide and 80 foot tall tropical dome with gardens both inside and outside. The Botanical Center maintains a permanent collection of more than 15,000 plants and an ornamental plant collection that changes six times a year.

25 miles south west of Des Moines is the locale in the film Bridges of Madison County starring Clint Eastwood and Meryl Streep. In the film you can see Iowa's flat and fertile fields and how the land yielded easily to growing crops. Today, much of Des Moines' political and economic concerns still rally around agriculture.

Located in the heart of North America, Des Moines has a climate which is continental in character. This results in a marked seasonal contrast in both temperature and precipitation. The winter is a season of cold dry air, interrupted by occasional storms of short duration. The autumn is characteristically sunny with diminishing precipitation.

General Rankings and Evaluative Comments

■ Des Moines was ranked #218 out of 300 cities by *Money's* 1997 "Survey of the Best Places to Live." Criteria used: health services, crime, economy, housing, education, transportation, weather, leisure and the arts. The city was ranked #219 in 1996 and #229 in 1995.
Money, July 1997; Money, September 1996; Money, September 1995

■ *Ladies Home Journal* ranked America's 200 largest cities based on the qualities women care about most. Des Moines ranked 22 out of 200. Criteria: low crime rate, good public schools, well-paying jobs, quality health and child care, the presence of women in government, proportion of women-owned businesses, size of the wage gap with men, local economy, divorce rates, the ratio of single men to single women, whether there are laws that require at least the same number of public toilets for women as men, and the probability of good hair days. *Ladies Home Journal, November 1997*

■ Des Moines was ranked #56 out of 219 cities in terms of children's health, safety, and economic well-being. Criteria: total population, percent population change, birth rate, child immunization rate, infant mortality rate, percent low birth weight infants, percent of births to teens, physician-to-population ratio, student-to-teacher ratio, dropout rate, unemployment rate, median family income, percent of children in poverty, violent and property crime rates, number of juvenile arrests for violent crimes as a percent of the total crime index, number of days with pollution standard index (PSI) over 100, pounds toxic releases per 1,000 people and number of superfund sites. *Zero Population Growth, Children's Environmental Index 1997*

■ Des Moines appeared on *Sales & Marketing Management's* list of the 20 hottest domestic markets to do business in. Rank: 6 out of 20. America's 320 Metropolitan Statistical Areas were ranked based on the market's potential to buy products in certain industries like high-tech, manufacturing, office equipment and business services, as well as population and household income growth. The study had nine criteria in all.

"Iowa's capital is experiencing an economic renaissance thanks to some major construction projects currently under way. In addition to many corporate expansions and two new hotels in the city, the Des Moines International Airport is now undergoing a $30 million renovation." *Sales & Marketing Management, January 1998*

■ According to *Working Mother*, "State lawmakers have approved a $6 million increase in child care funding this past year, enough to create new slots for several thousand children across the state. A task force made up of state officials and advocates had recommended a $10 million infusion of state money to expand child care programs. So while the legislature didn't go the whole way, this is concrete progress.

Iowa also modestly improved training requirements for family child care providers—they must now learn CPR and basic first aid procedures.

Part of the reason Iowa keeps moving ahead in its efforts to improve child care is the number of lively and creative activists. In one recent campaign, for example, the Iowa Child Care Coalition and the state's resource and referral agency produced about 3,000 dolls and displayed them in the rotunda of the state Capitol. each doll had a note attached that described the needs of a real child in the state." *Working Mother, July/August 1997*

Business Environment

STATE ECONOMY

State Economic Profile

"As a result of the FAIR-96 Act, farmers had the option of planting almost any commodity that they wished last spring, and did not have to follow the production constraining set-aside acreage rules. As a result there were huge plantings of wheat, corn, and soybean. While prices have fallen more than expected, the fundamentals that have been supporting the grain industry's recent prosperity are still there. However, this year's farm earnings will not grow at last year's high pace because of smaller government payments moderating export growth to Russia and China. Longer term, export potential from other emerging industrial economies throughout the world contributes to the upbeat outlook for agriculture, and keep Iowa's farm land values appreciating.

Residential permits have remained relatively consistent with last year's level. Declining rural-to-urban migration and overall migration into the state will keep housing demand low. Constrained by slow population growth, residential permits will remain below 12,000 units per year through the forecast. The low costs of living and doing business in Iowa are the major catalysts of economic growth in the state.

As a regional agricultural supply and service center for the Great Plains, food processing, agricultural services, commodity brokerage, and farm equipment production are mainstays of the state's economy. Iowa's farm industry is back on sound footing, and will enjoy strong demand and good returns for its products in the next few years. Marginal labor force and household growth will keep the rest of Iowa's economy expanding at only a moderate pace. Over the long term, Iowa ranks above average for growth." *National Association of Realtors, Economic Profiles: The Fifty States, July 1997*

IMPORTS/EXPORTS

Total Export Sales

Area	1993 ($000)	1994 ($000)	1995 ($000)	1996 ($000)	% Chg. 1993-96	% Chg. 1995-96
MSA[1]	337,183	348,931	378,549	426,017	26.3	12.5
U.S.	464,858,354	512,415,609	583,030,524	622,827,063	34.0	6.8

Note: (1) Metropolitan Statistical Area - see Appendix A for areas included
Source: U.S. Department of Commerce, International Trade Association, Metropolitan Area Exports: An Export Performance Report on Over 250 U.S. Cities, October 1997

Imports/Exports by Port

Type	Cargo Value			Share of U.S. Total	
	1995 (US$mil.)	1996 (US$mil.)	% Change 1995-1996	1995 (%)	1996 (%)
Imports	0	0	0	0	0
Exports	0	0	0	0	0

Source: Global Trade Information Services, WaterBorne Trade Atlas 1997

CITY FINANCES

City Government Finances

Component	FY92 ($000)	FY92 (per capita $)
Revenue	214,189	1,097.84
Expenditure	241,536	1,238.00
Debt Outstanding	308,724	1,582.38
Cash & Securities	166,123	851.47

Source: U.S. Bureau of the Census, City Government Finances: 1991-92

City Government Revenue by Source

Source	FY92 ($000)	FY92 (per capita $)	FY92 (%)
From Federal Government	12,202	62.54	5.7
From State Governments	17,449	89.44	8.1
From Local Governments	113	0.58	0.1
Property Taxes	78,827	404.03	36.8
General Sales Taxes	0	0.00	0.0
Selective Sales Taxes	5,427	27.82	2.5
Income Taxes	0	0.00	0.0
Current Charges	42,098	215.78	19.7
Utility/Liquor Store	21,451	109.95	10.0
Employee Retirement[1]	0	0.00	0.0
Other	36,622	187.71	17.1

Note: (1) Excludes "city contributions," classified as "nonrevenue," intragovernmental transfers.
Source: U.S. Bureau of the Census, City Government Finances: 1991-92

City Government Expenditures by Function

Function	FY92 ($000)	FY92 (per capita $)	FY92 (%)
Educational Services	4,383	22.47	1.8
Employee Retirement[1]	0	0.00	0.0
Environment/Housing	80,109	410.60	33.2
Government Administration	10,751	55.10	4.5
Interest on General Debt	24,319	124.65	10.1
Public Safety	38,241	196.01	15.8
Social Services	5,146	26.38	2.1
Transportation	43,996	225.50	18.2
Utility/Liquor Store	22,732	116.51	9.4
Other	11,859	60.78	4.9

Note: (1) Payments to beneficiaries including withdrawal of contributions.
Source: U.S. Bureau of the Census, City Government Finances: 1991-92

Municipal Bond Ratings

Area	Moody's	S & P
Des Moines	Aa3	n/a

Note: n/a not available; n/r not rated
Source: Moody's Bond Record, 2/98; Statistical Abstract of the U.S., 1997;
Governing Magazine, 9/97, 3/98

POPULATION

Population Growth

Area	1980	1990	% Chg. 1980-90	July 1996 Estimate	% Chg. 1990-96
City	191,003	193,187	1.1	193,422	0.1
MSA[1]	367,561	392,928	6.9	427,436	8.8
U.S.	226,545,805	248,765,170	9.8	265,179,411	6.6

Note: (1) Metropolitan Statistical Area - see Appendix A for areas included
Source: 1980/1990 Census of Housing and Population, Summary Tape File 3C;
Census Bureau Population Estimates

Population Characteristics

Race	City				% Chg. 1980-90	MSA[1]	
	1980		1990			1990	
	Population	%	Population	%		Population	%
White	173,032	90.6	172,426	89.3	-0.4	368,765	93.9
Black	13,164	6.9	13,667	7.1	3.8	14,598	3.7
Amer Indian/Esk/Aleut	603	0.3	800	0.4	32.7	1,063	0.3
Asian/Pacific Islander	2,498	1.3	4,437	2.3	77.6	5,886	1.5
Other	1,706	0.9	1,857	1.0	8.9	2,616	0.7
Hispanic Origin[2]	3,523	1.8	4,550	2.4	29.2	6,892	1.8

Note: (1) Metropolitan Statistical Area - see Appendix A for areas included;
(2) people of Hispanic origin can be of any race
Source: 1980/1990 Census of Housing and Population, Summary Tape File 3C

Ancestry

Area	German	Irish	English	Italian	U.S.	French	Polish	Dutch
City	35.0	20.1	16.0	4.2	4.1	4.0	1.2	5.8
MSA[1]	39.5	20.2	17.7	3.6	3.8	4.2	1.4	6.1
U.S.	23.3	15.6	13.1	5.9	5.3	4.2	3.8	2.5

Note: Figures are percentages and include persons that reported multiple ancestry (eg. if a person reported being Irish and Italian, they were included in both columns); (1) Metropolitan Statistical Area - see Appendix A for areas included
Source: 1990 Census of Population and Housing, Summary Tape File 3C

Age

Area	Median Age (Years)	Age Distribution (%)						
		Under 5	Under 18	18-24	25-44	45-64	65+	80+
City	32.2	7.8	24.2	11.9	33.3	17.2	13.3	3.4
MSA[1]	32.5	7.5	25.5	10.7	33.8	18.4	11.7	2.9
U.S.	32.9	7.3	25.6	10.5	32.6	18.7	12.5	2.8

Note: (1) Metropolitan Statistical Area - see Appendix A for areas included
Source: 1990 Census of Population and Housing, Summary Tape File 3C

Male/Female Ratio

Area	Number of males per 100 females (all ages)	Number of males per 100 females (18 years old+)
City	89.0	85.0
MSA[1]	91.7	87.4
U.S.	95.0	91.9

Note: (1) Metropolitan Statistical Area - see Appendix A for areas included
Source: 1990 Census of Population, General Population Characteristics

INCOME

Per Capita/Median/Average Income

Area	Per Capita ($)	Median Household ($)	Average Household ($)
City	13,710	26,703	33,199
MSA[1]	14,972	31,182	37,958
U.S.	14,420	30,056	38,453

Note: all figures are for 1989; (1) Metropolitan Statistical Area - see Appendix A for areas included
Source: 1990 Census of Population and Housing, Summary Tape File 3C

Household Income Distribution by Race

Income ($)	City (%)					U.S. (%)				
	Total	White	Black	Other	Hisp.[1]	Total	White	Black	Other	Hisp.[1]
Less than 5,000	6.0	5.3	12.9	10.2	6.9	6.2	4.8	15.2	8.6	8.8
5,000 - 9,999	10.2	9.5	20.5	6.7	6.0	9.3	8.6	14.2	9.9	11.1
10,000 - 14,999	10.2	10.0	13.3	12.2	16.0	8.8	8.5	11.0	9.8	11.0
15,000 - 24,999	20.2	20.1	20.7	22.8	18.3	17.5	17.3	18.9	18.5	20.5
25,000 - 34,999	18.7	19.1	11.8	22.2	19.7	15.8	16.1	14.2	15.4	16.4
35,000 - 49,999	18.1	18.8	10.1	15.4	19.0	17.9	18.6	13.3	16.1	16.0
50,000 - 74,999	11.5	11.9	8.3	7.4	11.4	15.0	15.8	9.3	13.4	11.1
75,000 - 99,999	2.7	2.8	1.8	2.8	2.2	5.1	5.5	2.6	4.7	3.1
100,000+	2.3	2.5	0.7	0.2	0.5	4.4	4.8	1.3	3.7	1.9

Note: all figures are for 1989; (1) people of Hispanic origin can be of any race
Source: 1990 Census of Population and Housing, Summary Tape File 3C

Effective Buying Income

Area	Per Capita ($)	Median Household ($)	Average Household ($)
City	15,945	31,815	39,166
MSA[1]	17,860	38,151	45,650
U.S.	15,444	33,201	41,849

Note: data as of 1/1/97; (1) Metropolitan Statistical Area - see Appendix A for areas included
Source: Standard Rate & Data Service, Newspaper Advertising Source, 2/98

Effective Household Buying Income Distribution

Area	% of Households Earning						
	$10,000 -$19,999	$20,000 -$34,999	$35,000 -$49,999	$50,000 -$74,999	$75,000 -$99,000	$100,000 -$124,999	$125,000 and up
City	17.5	25.8	20.1	17.0	4.8	1.2	1.7
MSA[1]	13.9	23.1	20.4	21.8	7.6	2.4	2.4
U.S.	16.5	23.4	18.3	18.2	6.4	2.1	2.4

Note: data as of 1/1/97; (1) Metropolitan Statistical Area - see Appendix A for areas included
Source: Standard Rate & Data Service, Newspaper Advertising Source, 2/98

Poverty Rates by Race and Age

Area	Total (%)	By Race (%)				By Age (%)		
		White	Black	Other	Hisp.[2]	Under 5 years old	Under 18 years old	65 years and over
City	12.9	11.0	30.8	23.5	18.3	21.8	19.3	9.1
MSA[1]	8.8	7.7	29.6	19.9	14.3	14.4	11.7	8.5
U.S.	13.1	9.8	29.5	23.1	25.3	20.1	18.3	12.8

Note: figures show the percent of people living below the poverty line in 1989. The average poverty threshold was $12,674 for a family of four in 1989; (1) Metropolitan Statistical Area - see Appendix A for areas included; (2) people of Hispanic origin can be of any race
Source: 1990 Census of Population and Housing, Summary Tape File 3C

EMPLOYMENT

Labor Force and Employment

Area	Civilian Labor Force			Workers Employed		
	Dec. '95	Dec. '96	% Chg.	Dec. '95	Dec. '96	% Chg.
City	124,126	122,224	-1.5	119,030	118,815	-0.2
MSA[1]	260,007	257,079	-1.1	251,932	251,475	-0.2
U.S.	134,583,000	136,742,000	1.6	127,903,000	130,785,000	2.3

Note: Data is not seasonally adjusted and covers workers 16 years of age and older;
(1) Metropolitan Statistical Area - see Appendix A for areas included
Source: Bureau of Labor Statistics, http://stats.bls.gov

Unemployment Rate

Area	1997											
	Jan.	Feb.	Mar.	Apr.	May	Jun.	Jul.	Aug.	Sep.	Oct.	Nov.	Dec.
City	4.4	4.1	3.7	3.5	3.0	3.2	2.4	2.6	2.6	2.3	2.6	2.8
MSA[1]	3.4	3.2	2.9	2.7	2.3	2.4	1.8	2.0	2.0	1.8	2.0	2.2
U.S.	5.9	5.7	5.5	4.8	4.7	5.2	5.0	4.8	4.7	4.4	4.3	4.4

Note: Data is not seasonally adjusted and covers workers 16 years of age and older; All figures are percentages; (1) Metropolitan Statistical Area - see Appendix A for areas included
Source: Bureau of Labor Statistics, http://stats.bls.gov

Employment by Industry

Sector	MSA[1]		U.S.
	Number of Employees	Percent of Total	Percent of Total
Services	77,800	28.6	29.0
Retail Trade	50,600	18.6	18.5
Government	34,400	12.6	16.1
Manufacturing	25,200	9.3	15.0
Finance/Insurance/Real Estate	38,000	14.0	5.7
Wholesale Trade	21,300	7.8	5.4
Transportation/Public Utilities	13,700	5.0	5.3
Construction/Mining	11,000	4.0	5.0

Note: Figures cover non-farm employment as of 12/97 and are not seasonally adjusted; (1) Metropolitan Statistical Area - see Appendix A for areas included
Source: Bureau of Labor Statistics, http://stats.bls.gov

Employment by Occupation

Occupation Category	City (%)	MSA[1] (%)	U.S. (%)
White Collar	61.6	65.0	58.1
Executive/Admin./Management	11.3	13.5	12.3
Professional	12.1	13.2	14.1
Technical & Related Support	3.6	3.7	3.7
Sales	11.6	13.3	11.8
Administrative Support/Clerical	23.1	21.4	16.3
Blue Collar	22.9	20.5	26.2
Precision Production/Craft/Repair	9.2	8.6	11.3
Machine Operators/Assem./Insp.	5.9	4.8	6.8
Transportation/Material Movers	3.9	3.5	4.1
Cleaners/Helpers/Laborers	3.9	3.7	3.9
Services	14.8	12.8	13.2
Farming/Forestry/Fishing	0.7	1.7	2.5

Note: figures cover employed persons 16 years old and over; (1) Metropolitan Statistical Area - see Appendix A for areas included
Source: 1990 Census of Population and Housing, Summary Tape File 3C

Occupational Employment Projections: 1996 - 2005

Occupations Expected to have the Largest Job Growth (ranked by numerical growth)	Fast-Growing Occupations (ranked by percent growth)
1. General managers & top executives	1. Woodworkers, precision, all other
2. Salespersons, retail	2. Computer engineers
3. Cashiers	3. Computer systems analysts
4. All other profess., paraprofess., tech.	4. Human services workers
5. Waiters & waitresses	5. Home health aides
6. Marketing & sales, supervisors	6. Adjustment clerks
7. Computer systems analysts	7. Electrical/electronic techs.
8. Truck drivers, heavy	8. Teachers, special education
9. Adjustment clerks	9. Residential counselors
10. All other assemblers, fabricators	10. Medical assistants

Projections cover Audubon, Boone, Carroll, Dallas, Guthrie, Jasper, Madison, Marion, Polk, Story and Warren Counties.
Source: Iowa Workforce Development, Labor Market Information, Iowa Occupational Projections 1996-2005, I.W.D. Region 11

Average Wages

Occupation	Wage	Occupation	Wage
Professional/Technical/Clerical	$/Week	**Health/Protective Services**	$/Week
Accountants III	-	Corrections Officers	-
Attorneys III	-	Firefighters	-
Budget Analysts III	-	Nurses, Licensed Practical II	-
Buyers/Contracting Specialists II	-	Nurses, Registered II	-
Clerks, Accounting III	404	Nursing Assistants II	-
Clerks, General III	335	Police Officers I	-
Computer Operators II	421	**Hourly Workers**	$/Hour
Computer Programmers II	593	Forklift Operators	9.62
Drafters II	439	General Maintenance Workers	10.19
Engineering Technicians III	-	Guards I	5.90
Engineering Technicians, Civil III	-	Janitors	6.39
Engineers III	-	Maintenance Electricians	16.41
Key Entry Operators I	276	Maintenance Electronics Techs II	-
Personnel Assistants III	-	Maintenance Machinists	15.45
Personnel Specialists III	-	Maintenance Mechanics, Machinery	15.07
Secretaries III	507	Material Handling Laborers	-
Switchboard Operator-Receptionist	344	Motor Vehicle Mechanics	14.10
Systems Analysts II	876	Shipping/Receiving Clerks	9.28
Systems Analysts Supervisor/Mgr II	-	Tool and Die Makers	-
Tax Collectors II	-	Truckdrivers, Tractor Trailer	13.27
Word Processors II	396	Warehouse Specialists	9.31

Note: Wage data includes full-time workers only for 6/95 and cover the Metropolitan Statistical Area (see Appendix A for areas included). Dashes indicate that data was not available.
Source: Bureau of Labor Statistics, Occupational Compensation Survey, 8/95

TAXES

Major State and Local Tax Rates

State Corp. Income (%)	State Personal Income (%)	Residential Property (effective rate per $100)	Sales & Use		State Gasoline (cents/ gallon)	State Cigarette (cents/ 20-pack)
			State (%)	Local (%)		
6.0 - 12.0	0.4 - 9.98	2.95	5.0	None	20	36

Note: Personal/corporate income tax rates as of 1/97. Sales, gasoline and cigarette tax rates as of 1/98.
Source: Federation of Tax Administrators, www.taxadmin.org; Washington D.C. Department of Finance and Revenue, Tax Rates and Tax Burdens in the District of Columbia: A Nationwide Comparison, June 1997; Chamber of Commerce

Total Taxes Per Capita and as a Percent of Income

Area	Per Capita Income ($)	Per Capita Taxes ($)			Taxes as Pct. of Income (%)		
		Total	Federal	State/Local	Total	Federal	State/Local
Iowa	23,611	8,295	5,286	3,009	35.1	22.4	12.7
U.S.	26,187	9,205	6,127	3,078	35.2	23.4	11.8

Note: Figures are for 1997
Source: Tax Foundation, Web Site, www.taxfoundation.org

Estimated Tax Burden

Area	State Income	Local Income	Property	Sales	Total
Des Moines	3,330	0	6,075	510	9,915

Note: The numbers are estimates of taxes paid by a married couple with two kids and annual earnings of $65,000. Sales tax estimates assume they spend average amounts on food, clothing, household goods and gasoline. Property tax estimates assume they live in a $225,000 home.
Source: Kiplinger's Personal Finance Magazine, June 1997

COMMERCIAL REAL ESTATE

Office Market

Class/Location	Total Space (sq. ft.)	Vacant Space (sq. ft.)	Vac. Rate (%)	Under Constr. (sq. ft.)	Net Absorp. (sq. ft.)	Rental Rates ($/sq.ft./yr.)
Class A						
CBD	2,789,624	153,753	5.5	n/a	25,633	15.00-24.50
Outside CBD	2,921,137	232,978	8.0	150,000	-15,849	15.00-19.50
Class B						
CBD	1,508,572	406,164	26.9	n/a	-276,369	9.50-16.50
Outside CBD	1,274,482	109,059	8.6	n/a	10,508	9.00-16.50

Note: Data as of 10/97 and covers Des Moines; CBD = Central Business District; n/a not available;
Source: Society of Industrial and Office Realtors, 1998 Comparative Statistics of Industrial and Office Real Estate Markets

"Des Moines will experience continued growth in the financial services sector with strong ties to banking and other financial players. CBD Class 'B' space will slowly be absorbed by small users. The proliferation of single-story office/flex buildings is limiting the potential for speculative development. Our SIOR reporter does not anticipate any speculative construction for the next 24 months. Sales prices will increase up to 10 percent on the strength of improved occupancy. Continued low unemployment may limit further expansion in service-oriented businesses. Fulfillment centers will continue to grow, demanding large blocks of space. The profile suggests that build-to-suit developers will be active in 1998" *Society of Industrial and Office Realtors, 1998 Comparative Statistics of Industrial and Office Real Estate Markets*

Industrial Market

Location	Total Space (sq. ft.)	Vacant Space (sq. ft.)	Vac. Rate (%)	Under Constr. (sq. ft.)	Net Absorp. (sq. ft.)	Net Lease ($/sq.ft./yr.)
Central City	14,042,871	398,942	2.8	0	-20,166	2.75-5.00
Suburban	6,290,614	50,000	0.8	256,000	254,185	2.75-4.50

Note: Data as of 10/97 and covers Des Moines; n/a not available
Source: Society of Industrial and Office Realtors, 1998 Comparative Statistics of Industrial and Office Real Estate Markets

"Des Moines' low unemployment is predicted to limit economic growth. A slowdown in the population growth is likely to strain job expansion. The shortage of high cube space has caused lease prices to rise enough to promote new construction. Builders have broken ground on projects totaling more than 100,000 sq. ft. Des Moines will see more and more controlled projects with new building standards. Although the market is tight, construction is expected to increase for the warehouse/distribution sector only. Lease prices are not anticipated to increase

more than five percent. 1998 appears to be a year of steady, albeit unspectacular, progress."
Society of Industrial and Office Realtors, 1998 Comparative Statistics of Industrial and Office Real Estate Markets

COMMERCIAL UTILITIES

Typical Monthly Electric Bills

Area	Commercial Service ($/month)		Industrial Service ($/month)	
	12 kW demand 1,500 kWh	100 kW demand 30,000 kWh	1,000 kW demand 400,000 kWh	20,000 kW demand 10,000,000 kWh
City	n/a	n/a	n/a	n/a
U.S.	162	2,360	25,590	545,677

Note: Based on rates in effect July 1, 1997; n/a not available
Source: Edison Electric Institute, Typical Residential, Commercial and Industrial Bills, Summer 1997

TRANSPORTATION

Transportation Statistics

Avg. travel time to work (min.)	16.4
Interstate highways	I-35; I-80
Bus lines	
In-city	Des Moines Metropolitan TA
Inter-city	2
Passenger air service	
Airport	Des Moines Municipal
Airlines	12
Aircraft departures	16,336 (1995)
Enplaned passengers	710,535 (1885)
Rail service	No Amtrak Service
Motor freight carriers	82
Major waterways/ports	None

Source: OAG, Business Travel Planner, Summer 1997; Editor & Publisher Market Guide, 1998; FAA Airport Activity Statistics, 1996; Amtrak National Time Table, Northeast Timetable, Fall/Winter 1997-98; 1990 Census of Population and Housing, STF 3C; Chamber of Commerce/Economic Development 1997; Jane's Urban Transport Systems 1997-98; Transit Fact Book 1997

Means of Transportation to Work

Area	Car/Truck/Van		Public Transportation			Bicycle	Walked	Other Means	Worked at Home
	Drove Alone	Car-pooled	Bus	Subway	Railroad				
City	74.4	15.1	3.5	0.0	0.0	0.2	3.6	0.7	2.5
MSA[1]	77.3	13.7	2.1	0.0	0.0	0.1	2.9	0.6	3.4
U.S.	73.2	13.4	3.0	1.5	0.5	0.4	3.9	1.2	3.0

Note: figures shown are percentages and only include workers 16 years old and over;
(1) Metropolitan Statistical Area - see Appendix A for areas included
Source: 1990 Census of Population and Housing, Summary Tape File 3C

BUSINESSES

Major Business Headquarters

Company Name	1997 Rankings	
	Fortune 500	Forbes 500
Principal Mutual Life Insurance	157	-

Note: Companies listed are located in the city; Dashes indicate no ranking
Fortune 500: companies that produce a 10-K are ranked 1 - 500 based on 1996 revenue
Forbes 500: private companies are ranked 1 - 500 based on 1996 revenue
Source: Forbes 12/1/97; Fortune 4/28/97

Fast-Growing Businesses

According to *Inc.*, Des Moines is home to one of America's 100 fastest-growing private companies: Staffing Edge. Criteria for inclusion: must be an independent, privately-held, U.S.

corporation, proprietorship or partnership; sales of at least $200,000 in 1993; five-year operating/sales history; increase in 1997 sales over 1996 sales; holding companies, regulated banks, and utilities were excluded. *Inc. 500, 1997*

HOTELS & MOTELS

Hotels/Motels

Area	Hotels/ Motels	Rooms	Luxury-Level Hotels/Motels		Average Minimum Rates ($)		
			♦♦♦♦	♦♦♦♦♦	♦♦	♦♦♦	♦♦♦♦
City	18	2,723	0	0	48	80	n/a
Airport	5	636	0	0	n/a	n/a	n/a
Suburbs	23	2,661	0	0	n/a	n/a	n/a
Total	46	6,020	0	0	n/a	n/a	n/a

Note: n/a not available; Classifications range from one diamond (budget properties with basic amenities) to five diamond (luxury properties with the finest service, rooms and facilities).
Source: OAG, Business Travel Planner, Summer 1997

CONVENTION CENTERS

Major Convention Centers

Center Name	Meeting Rooms	Exhibit Space (sf)
Des Moines Convention Center	33	46,100
Veterans Memorial Auditorium	9	98,000

Source: Trade Shows Worldwide 1997

Living Environment

COST OF LIVING

Cost of Living Index

Composite Index	Housing	Utilities	Groceries	Health Care	Trans-portation	Misc. Goods/ Services
99.1	95.0	98.8	97.1	98.1	96.6	104.5

Note: U.S. = 100
Source: ACCRA, Cost of Living Index, 3rd Quarter 1997

HOUSING

Median Home Prices and Housing Affordability

Area	Median Price[2] 3rd Qtr. 1997 ($)	HOI[3] 3rd Qtr. 1997	Afford-ability Rank[4]
MSA[1]	93,000	81.2	18
U.S.	127,000	63.7	–

Note: (1) Metropolitan Statistical Area - see Appendix A for areas included; (2) U.S. figures calculated from the sales of 625,000 new and existing homes in 195 markets; (3) Housing Opportunity Index - percent of homes sold that were within the reach of the median income household at the prevailing mortgage interest rate; (4) Rank is from 1-195 with 1 being most affordable
Source: National Association of Home Builders, Housing Opportunity Index, 3rd Quarter 1997

It is projected that the median price of existing single-family homes in the metro area will increase by 9.7% in 1998. Nationwide, home prices are projected to increase 6.6%.
Kiplinger's Personal Finance Magazine, January 1998

Average New Home Price

Area	Price ($)
City	128,280
U.S.	135,710

Note: Figures are based on a new home with 1,800 sq. ft. of living area on an 8,000 sq. ft. lot.
Source: ACCRA, Cost of Living Index, 3rd Quarter 1997

Average Apartment Rent

Area	Rent ($/mth)
City	566
U.S.	569

Note: Figures are based on an unfurnished two bedroom, 1-1/2 or 2 bath apartment, approximately 950 sq. ft. in size, excluding all utilities except water
Source: ACCRA, Cost of Living Index, 3rd Quarter 1997

RESIDENTIAL UTILITIES

Average Residential Utility Costs

Area	All Electric ($/mth)	Part Electric ($/mth)	Other Energy ($/mth)	Phone ($/mth)
City	–	55.49	45.34	19.76
U.S.	109.40	55.25	43.64	19.48

Source: ACCRA, Cost of Living Index, 3rd Quarter 1997

HEALTH CARE

Average Health Care Costs

Area	Hospital ($/day)	Doctor ($/visit)	Dentist ($/visit)
City	407.75	43.83	60.33
U.S.	392.91	48.76	60.84

Note: Hospital - based on a semi-private room. Doctor - based on a general practitioner's routine exam of an established patient. Dentist - based on adult teeth cleaning and periodic oral exam.
Source: ACCRA, Cost of Living Index, 3rd Quarter 1997

Distribution of Office-Based Physicians

| Area | Family/Gen. Practitioners | Specialists | | |
		Medical	Surgical	Other
MSA[1]	81	173	175	171

Note: Data as of 12/31/96; (1) Metropolitan Statistical Area - see Appendix A for areas included
Source: American Medical Assn., Physician Characteristics & Distribution in the U.S., 1997-1998

Hospitals

Des Moines has 6 general medical and surgical hospitals. *AHA Guide to the Healthcare Field 1997-98*

EDUCATION

Public School District Statistics

District Name	Num. Sch.	Enroll.	Classroom Teachers1	Pupils per Teacher	Minority Pupils (%)	Current Exp.2 ($/pupil)
Des Moines Indep Comm Schs	65	32,414	2,106	15.4	23.7	5,363
Saydel Consolidated School Dis	4	1,440	113	12.7	n/a	n/a

Note: Data covers the 1995-1996 school year unless otherwise noted; (1) Excludes teachers reported as working in school district offices rather than in schools; (2) Based on 1993-94 enrollment collected by the Census Bureau, not the enrollment figure shown in column 3; SD = School District; ISD = Independent School District; n/a not available
Source: National Center for Education Statistics, Common Core of Data Survey; Bureau of the Census

Educational Quality

School District	Education Quotient[1]	Graduate Outcome[2]	Community Index[3]	Resource Index[4]
Des Moines	108.0	101.0	131.0	91.0

Note: Nearly 1,000 secondary school districts were rated in terms of educational quality. The scores range from a low of 50 to a high of 150; (1) Average of the Graduate Outcome, Community and Resource indexes; (2) Based on graduation rates and college board scores (SAT/ACT); (3) Based on the surrounding community's average level of education and the area's average income level; (4) Based on teacher salaries, per-pupil expenditures and student-teacher ratios.
Source: Expansion Management, Ratings Issue 1997

Educational Attainment by Race

| Area | High School Graduate (%) | | | | | Bachelor's Degree (%) | | | | |
	Total	White	Black	Other	Hisp.[2]	Total	White	Black	Other	Hisp.[2]
City	81.0	82.4	70.7	58.2	61.7	18.9	19.6	10.8	13.6	10.5
MSA[1]	85.4	86.2	71.7	66.8	68.9	22.6	23.0	12.1	21.9	12.6
U.S.	75.2	77.9	63.1	60.4	49.8	20.3	21.5	11.4	19.4	9.2

Note: figures shown cover persons 25 years old and over; (1) Metropolitan Statistical Area - see Appendix A for areas included; (2) people of Hispanic origin can be of any race
Source: 1990 Census of Population and Housing, Summary Tape File 3C

School Enrollment by Type

| Area | Preprimary | | | | Elementary/High School | | | |
| | Public | | Private | | Public | | Private | |
	Enrollment	%	Enrollment	%	Enrollment	%	Enrollment	%
City	2,441	67.2	1,194	32.8	26,321	91.6	2,402	8.4
MSA[1]	5,840	67.4	2,829	32.6	59,903	93.4	4,230	6.6
U.S.	2,679,029	59.5	1,824,256	40.5	38,379,689	90.2	4,187,099	9.8

Note: figures shown cover persons 3 years old and over; (1) Metropolitan Statistical Area - see Appendix A for areas included
Source: 1990 Census of Population and Housing, Summary Tape File 3C

School Enrollment by Race

Area	Preprimary (%)				Elementary/High School (%)			
	White	Black	Other	Hisp.[1]	White	Black	Other	Hisp.[1]
City	92.2	4.7	3.1	3.0	83.5	11.0	5.5	3.7
MSA[2]	95.8	2.2	2.1	1.7	91.2	5.3	3.5	2.7
U.S.	80.4	12.5	7.1	7.8	74.1	15.6	10.3	12.5

Note: figures shown cover persons 3 years old and over; (1) people of Hispanic origin can be of any race; (2) Metropolitan Statistical Area - see Appendix A for areas included
Source: 1990 Census of Population and Housing, Summary Tape File 3C

SAT/ACT Scores

Area/District	1997 SAT				1997 ACT	
	Percent of Graduates Tested (%)	Average Math Score	Average Verbal Score	Average Combined Score	Percent of Graduates Tested (%)	Average Composite Score
Des Moines ICSD	5	560	555	1,115	55	20.9
State	5	601	589	1,190	64	22.1
U.S.	42	511	505	1,016	36	21.0

Note: Math and verbal SAT scores are out of a possible 800; ACT scores are out of a possible 36
Caution: Comparing or ranking states/cities on the basis of SAT/ACT scores alone is invalid and strongly discouraged by the The College Board and The American College Testing Program as students who take the tests are self-selected and do not represent the entire student population.
Source: Des Moines Independent Community School District, School Improvement, 1997; American College Testing Program, 1997; College Board, 1997

Classroom Teacher Salaries in Public Schools

District	B.A. Degree		M.A. Degree		Ph.D. Degree	
	Min. ($)	Max ($)	Min. ($)	Max. ($)	Min. ($)	Max. ($)
Des Moines	21,700	36,727	23,870	41,827	27,040	45,973
Average[1]	26,120	39,270	28,175	44,667	31,643	49,825

Note: Salaries are for 1996-1997; (1) Based on all school districts covered; n/a not available
Source: American Federation of Teachers (unpublished data)

Higher Education

Two-Year Colleges		Four-Year Colleges		Medical Schools	Law Schools	Voc/ Tech
Public	Private	Public	Private			
0	1	0	3	0	1	8

Source: College Blue Book, Occupational Education 1997; Medical School Admission Requirements, 1998-99; Peterson's Guide to Two-Year Colleges, 1997; Peterson's Guide to Four-Year Colleges, 1997; Barron's Guide to Law Schools 1997

MAJOR EMPLOYERS

Major Employers

Principal Mutual Life Insurance
Central Iowa Health System Hospital Corp.
Communications Data Services
Des Moines Register & Tribune
Broadlawns Medical Center
T.L. Grantham & Assoc. (management consulting)
Titan Tire Corp.

Mercy Hospital Medical Center
IASD Health Services Corp.
Norwest Mortgage
Meredith Corp. (publishing)
Annett Holdings (trucking)
Allied Mutual Insurance

Note: companies listed are located in the city
Source: Dun's Business Rankings 1997; Ward's Business Directory, 1997

PUBLIC SAFETY

Crime Rate

Area	All Crimes	Violent Crimes				Property Crimes		
		Murder	Forcible Rape	Robbery	Aggrav. Assault	Burglary	Larceny -Theft	Motor Vehicle Theft
City	7,754.7	9.7	51.2	164.2	248.7	917.9	5,743.5	619.6
Suburbs[1]	3,460.3	0.0	8.0	21.4	126.2	568.4	2,550.5	185.9
MSA[2]	5,459.9	4.5	28.1	87.9	183.2	731.1	4,037.2	387.8
U.S.	5,078.9	7.4	36.1	202.4	388.2	943.0	2,975.9	525.9

Note: Crime rate is the number of crimes per 100,000 pop.; (1) defined as all areas within the MSA but located outside the central city; (2) Metropolitan Statistical Area - see Appendix A for areas incl.
Source: FBI Uniform Crime Reports 1996

RECREATION

Culture and Recreation

Museums	Symphony Orchestras	Opera Companies	Dance Companies	Professional Theatres	Zoos	Pro Sports Teams
6	1	1	1	2	1	0

Source: International Directory of the Performing Arts, 1996; Official Museum Directory, 1998; Chamber of Commerce/Economic Development 1997

Library System

The Public Library of Des Moines has five branches, holdings of 474,140 volumes and a budget of $4,504,075 (1995-1996). *American Library Directory, 1997-1998*

MEDIA

Newspapers

Name	Type	Freq.	Distribution	Circulation
Ankeny Press Citizen	General	1x/wk	Local	15,592
Central Shopper	n/a	1x/wk	Local	16,356
Cityview	General	1x/wk	Local	36,000
Community Shopper	General	1x/wk	Local	15,054
The Des Moines Register	General	7x/wk	Area	190,000
Lee Town Shopper	General	1x/wk	Local	14,172
North Central Shopper	General	1x/wk	Local	16,915
Northeast Shopper	General	1x/wk	Local	14,643
Northwest Shopper	General	1x/wk	Local	20,129
Southside Shopper	General	1x/wk	Local	16,506
Valley Shopper	General	1x/wk	Local	21,333

Note: Includes newspapers with circulations of 1,000 or more located in the city; n/a not available
Source: Burrelle's Media Directory, 1998 Edition

AM Radio Stations

Call Letters	Freq. (kHz)	Target Audience	Station Format	Music Format
KIOA	940	General	N/S/T	n/a
WHO	1040	General	N/T	n/a
KWKY	1150	Religious	M/N/S/T	Christian
KRNT	1350	General	M/S	n/a
KKSO	1390	n/a	E/M/N/T	n/a
KDMI	1460	Hisp/Relig	M/S/T	Christian/Spanish

Note: Stations included broadcast in the Des Moines metro area; n/a not available
Station Format: E = Educational; M = Music; N = News; S = Sports; T = Talk
Source: Burrelle's Media Directory, 1998 Edition

FM Radio Stations

Call Letters	Freq. (mHz)	Target Audience	Station Format	Music Format
KDPS	88.1	General	E/M/N/S	Adult Contemporary/Alternative/Classic Rock/Country/Contemporary Top 40/Oldies/R&B
KWDM	88.7	General	E/M/S	Alternative
KUCB	89.3	n/a	M/S	Christian/Jazz
KDFR	91.3	General	E/M/N/T	Christian
KJJY	92.5	n/a	E/M/N/S/T	Country
KIOA	93.3	General	M/N/S	Oldies
KGGO	94.9	n/a	M	Classic Rock
KHKI	97.3	n/a	M	Country
KZZQ	99.5	Religious	M	Christian
KLYF	100.3	General	M	Adult Contemporary
KSTZ	102.5	General	M	Adult Contemporary
KAZR	103.3	n/a	M	Classic Rock
KLTI	104.1	n/a	M	Adult Contemporary
KJJC	106.9	General	M/N/S	Country

Note: Stations included broadcast in the Des Moines metro area; n/a not available
Station Format: E = Educational; M = Music; N = News; S = Sports; T = Talk
Source: Burrelle's Media Directory, 1998 Edition

Television Stations

Name	Ch.	Affiliation	Type	Owner
WOI	5	ABC	Commercial	Citadel Communications Company Ltd.
KCCI	8	CBS	Commercial	Pulitzer Broadcasting Company
KDIN	11	PBS	Public	State of Iowa
KIIN	12	PBS	Public	State of Iowa
WHO	13	NBC	Commercial	The New York Times Co. Broadcast Group
KDSM	17	Fox	Commercial	Sinclair Broadcasting
KTIN	21	PBS	Public	State of Iowa
KYIN	24	PBS	Public	State of Iowa
KSIN	27	PBS	Public	State of Iowa
KBIN	32	PBS	Public	State of Iowa
KRIN	32	PBS	Public	State of Iowa
KHIN	36	PBS	Public	State of Iowa

Note: Stations included broadcast in the Des Moines metro area
Source: Burrelle's Media Directory, 1998 Edition

CLIMATE

Average and Extreme Temperatures

Temperature	Jan	Feb	Mar	Apr	May	Jun	Jul	Aug	Sep	Oct	Nov	Dec	Ann
Extreme High (°F)	65	70	91	93	98	103	105	108	99	95	76	69	108
Average High (°F)	29	34	45	61	72	82	86	84	76	65	48	33	60
Average Temp. (°F)	20	25	36	51	62	72	76	74	65	54	39	25	50
Average Low (°F)	11	16	27	40	51	61	66	64	54	43	29	17	40
Extreme Low (°F)	-24	-20	-22	9	28	42	47	40	28	14	-3	-22	-24

Note: Figures cover the years 1945-1990
Source: National Climatic Data Center, International Station Meteorological Climate Summary, 3/95

Average Precipitation/Snowfall/Humidity

Precip./Humidity	Jan	Feb	Mar	Apr	May	Jun	Jul	Aug	Sep	Oct	Nov	Dec	Ann
Avg. Precip. (in.)	1.1	1.1	2.3	3.1	3.8	4.4	3.5	3.9	3.1	2.4	1.7	1.2	31.8
Avg. Snowfall (in.)	8	7	7	2	Tr	0	0	0	Tr	Tr	3	7	33
Avg. Rel. Hum. 6am (%)	77	79	79	78	78	81	83	86	85	80	79	80	80
Avg. Rel. Hum. 3pm (%)	65	63	57	50	51	52	52	54	52	50	58	66	56

Note: Figures cover the years 1945-1990; Tr = Trace amounts (<0.05 in. of rain; <0.5 in. of snow)
Source: National Climatic Data Center, International Station Meteorological Climate Summary, 3/95

Weather Conditions

Temperature			Daytime Sky			Precipitation		
5°F & below	32°F & below	90°F & above	Clear	Partly cloudy	Cloudy	0.01 inch or more precip.	0.1 inch or more snow/ice	Thunder-storms
25	137	26	99	129	137	106	25	46

Note: Figures are average number of days per year and covers the years 1945-1990
Source: National Climatic Data Center, International Station Meteorological Climate Summary, 3/95

AIR & WATER QUALITY

Maximum Pollutant Concentrations

	Particulate Matter (ug/m^3)	Carbon Monoxide (ppm)	Sulfur Dioxide (ppm)	Nitrogen Dioxide (ppm)	Ozone (ppm)	Lead (ug/m^3)
MSA[1] Level	130	4	n/a	n/a	0.08	n/a
NAAQS[2]	150	9	0.140	0.053	0.12	1.50
Met NAAQS?	Yes	Yes	n/a	n/a	Yes	n/a

Note: (1) Metropolitan Statistical Area - see Appendix A for areas included; (2) National Ambient Air Quality Standards; ppm = parts per million; ug/m^3 = micrograms per cubic meter; n/a not available
Source: EPA, National Air Quality and Emissions Trends Report, 1996

Pollutant Standards Index

Data not available. *EPA, National Air Quality and Emissions Trends Report, 1996*

Drinking Water

Water System Name	Pop. Served	Primary Water Source Type	Number of Violations in Fiscal Year 1997	Type of Violation/ Contaminants
Des Moines Water Works	193,189	Surface	None	None

Note: Data as of January 16, 1998
Source: EPA, Office of Ground Water and Drinking Water, Safe Drinking Water Information System

Des Moines tap water is alkaline, soft and fluoridated.
Editor & Publisher Market Guide, 1998

Detroit, Michigan

Background

One may think of Los Angeles as a city based upon a car culture. One can say the same about Detroit, only it is based upon a car culture in a far different way.

Thanks to the power of advertising, we do not think twice about familiar names such as Ford, Pontiac, and Cadillac. They are the names of cars. However, it bears remembering that Henry Ford was the inventor of the Model T, the car that was "propelled by power generated from within itself"; Pontiac was an Ottawa Chieftain who led an attack against the British in 1763; and Antoine de la Mothe Cadillac was a French Colonial administrator who founded the city of Detroit with a flotilla of 25 canoes, 50 French soldiers, 50 artisans, and 100 friendly Native Americans.

When Detroit finally fell into American hands, the city's economy already showed the signs of what its industrial might was to become. During the 1820's, Detroit prospered in fur trading, shipbuilding, and flour and grain distribution. During the 1860's, the city added steam engine, railroad car, stove, and furnace manufacturing to its economy as well. Finally, at the turn of the twentieth century, Henry Ford, Ransom E. Olds, and John and Horace Dodge changed the nature of Detroit's economy forever. With a history of skilled and semi-skilled workers in its carriage bicycle industries, it was not hard for these industrialists to transfer the laborers' skills onto their products. Thus Detroit was allowed an early lead in the automobile market.

Despite the omnipresence of the automobile industry in Detroit, the city leads in inland river trade along the upper Great Lakes, steel, rubber products, and garden seeds.

Since 1994 when 18.35 square miles of Detroit was designated as an urban empowerment zone, nearly 30 companies have announced plans to spend over 2 billion opening, expanding or relocating their operations in the economic development area. Altogether the businesses will create thousands of new jobs paying anywhere from $6 to $18 an hour. The Big Three American Auto Makers, are the biggest investors expecting to spend over a billion dollars buying auto parts. Chrysler alone has about 20 minority-owned suppliers in the zone. *New York Times April 11, 1997*

On the international economic scene, Detroit has benefited greatly from increased trade activity. With annual increases in exports of more than 10% per annum since 1990, the area boasts the nation's third largest custom district behind Los Angeles and New York.

Detroit is undergoing a downtown housing boom with more than 360 building permits issued for single-family homes since 1990. Many of the buyers are black professionals who are moving into luxury homes in inner-city neighborhoods that were formerly areas of abandonment. *New York Times May 5, 1997*

Downtown Detroit got an economic boost last August (1996) when the Detroit Lions football team (owned by a branch of the Ford family) announced plans to move back to the city from the Silverdome in nearby Pontiac. The site of the new domed stadium will be near a new open-air baseball stadium planned by the Detroit Tigers. Together the two stadiums would form one of the largest entertainment complexes in the United States.

The climate of Detroit is influenced by its proximity to major storm tracks and to the Great Lakes. Winter storms can bring combinations of rain, freezing rain, sleet or snow with heavy snowfall accumulations possible at times. In summer, most storms pass to the north. Intervals of warm, humid, sunny skies with occasional thunderstorms are followed by days of mild, dry and fair weather.

General Rankings and Evaluative Comments

- Detroit was ranked #117 out of 300 cities by *Money's* 1997 "Survey of the Best Places to Live." Criteria used: health services, crime, economy, housing, education, transportation, weather, leisure and the arts. The city was ranked #86 in 1996 and #56 in 1995. *Money, July 1997; Money, September 1996; Money, September 1995*

- *Ladies Home Journal* ranked America's 200 largest cities based on the qualities women care about most. Detroit ranked 193 out of 200. Criteria: low crime rate, good public schools, well-paying jobs, quality health and child care, the presence of women in government, proportion of women-owned businesses, size of the wage gap with men, local economy, divorce rates, the ratio of single men to single women, whether there are laws that require at least the same number of public toilets for women as men, and the probability of good hair days. *Ladies Home Journal, November 1997*

- Detroit was ranked #218 out of 219 cities in terms of children's health, safety, and economic well-being. Criteria: total population, percent population change, birth rate, child immunization rate, infant mortality rate, percent low birth weight infants, percent of births to teens, physician-to-population ratio, student-to-teacher ratio, dropout rate, unemployment rate, median family income, percent of children in poverty, violent and property crime rates, number of juvenile arrests for violent crimes as a percent of the total crime index, number of days with pollution standard index (PSI) over 100, pounds toxic releases per 1,000 people and number of superfund sites. *Zero Population Growth, Children's Environmental Index 1997*

- Detroit is among the 20 most livable cities for gay men and lesbians. The list was divided between 10 cities you might expect and 10 surprises. Detroit was on the cities you wouldn't expect list. Rank: 7 out of 10. Criteria: legal protection from antigay discrimination, an annual gay pride celebration, a community center, gay bookstores and publications, and an array of organizations, religious groups, and health care facilities that cater to the needs of the local gay community. *The Advocate, June 1997*

- *Yahoo! Internet Life* selected "America's 100 Most Wired Cities & Towns". 50 cities were large and 50 cities were small. Detroit ranked 28 out of 50 large cities. Criteria: Internet users per capita, number of networked computers, number of registered domain names, Internet backbone traffic, and the per-capita number of Web sites devoted to each city. *Yahoo! Internet Life, March 1998*

- *Reader's Digest* non-scientifically ranked the 12 largest U.S. metropolitan areas in terms of having the worst drivers. The Detroit metro area ranked number 6. The areas were selected by asking approximately 1,200 readers on the *Reader's Digest* Web site and 200 interstate bus drivers and long-haul truckers which metro areas have the worst drivers. Their responses were factored in with fatality, insurance and rental-car rates to create the rankings. *Reader's Digest, March 1998*

- General Motors Corp., headquartered in Detroit, is among the "100 Best Companies for Working Mothers." Criteria: pay compared with competition, opportunities for women to advance, support for child care, flexible work schedules and family-friendly benefits. *Working Mother, October 1997*

- According to *Working Mother,* "Michigan increased its spending on child care by $44 million, which means that nearly 14,000 more kids will be served this year. Next year, child care funding is slated to reach $201 million, a $16 million boost over 1997 spending. One key part of the budget: a special program to recruit caregivers who want to specialize in infant care, since demand for such care is so great here.

  In this state, as in so many others, there has been a raging controversy over how to expand child care options without diluting the quality of the programs. Governor John Engler had previously considered a radical approach to child care, which would have allowed parents to use state funds to pay unlicensed caregivers. Child care activists and providers managed to convince Engler that this was a bad idea, and it was never officially proposed. Another idea the governor floated—an elimination of background checks for caregivers—was also shelved." *Working Mother, July/August 1997*

Business Environment

STATE ECONOMY

State Economic Profile

"...retail sales growth and residential construction are below the national average, and bankruptcy filings have accelerated to 33% above one year ago.

Michigan will continue to nurture white-collar, auto-related operations. While international auto manufacturers have not located assembly plants in Michigan, they have located their research facilities in the state. Michigan is also a center for allied auto-related research activity, such as robotics and software development.

Michigan's population growth improved slightly last year to almost 0.6%, though it remains well below the national average. For the past two years, net migration has been positive in Michigan, a significant turnaround for the state. While net domestic migration remains stubbornly negative, many fewer people are leaving Michigan than earlier in the decade.

In the near term, Michigan's economy will continue to grow at about the national pace. Sizable auto industry bonuses will boost incomes and fatten the state treasury this year. Long term, substantial investments in auto-related production facilities will ensure that a significant portion of vehicle and parts manufacturing will remain in the state. However, Michigan's high cost of doing business, coupled with the high level of unionization, will continue to limit investment in the state. Michigan will be a below-average performer long term." *National Association of Realtors, Economic Profiles: The Fifty States, July 1997*

IMPORTS/EXPORTS

Total Export Sales

Area	1993 ($000)	1994 ($000)	1995 ($000)	1996 ($000)	% Chg. 1993-96	% Chg. 1995-96
MSA[1]	16,780,889	27,469,655	27,314,657	27,531,231	64.1	0.8
U.S.	464,858,354	512,415,609	583,030,524	622,827,063	34.0	6.8

Note: (1) Metropolitan Statistical Area - see Appendix A for areas included
Source: U.S. Department of Commerce, International Trade Association, Metropolitan Area Exports: An Export Performance Report on Over 250 U.S. Cities, October 1997

Imports/Exports by Port

Type	Cargo Value			Share of U.S. Total	
	1995 (US$mil.)	1996 (US$mil.)	% Change 1995-1996	1995 (%)	1996 (%)
Imports	640	944	47.50	0.16	0.25
Exports	213	760	256.45	0.09	0.32

Source: Global Trade Information Services, WaterBorne Trade Atlas 1997

CITY FINANCES

City Government Finances

Component	FY94 ($000)	FY94 (per capita $)
Revenue	2,138,073	2,125.47
Expenditure	2,070,447	2,058.24
Debt Outstanding	2,016,123	2,004.24
Cash & Securities	5,383,564	5,351.82

Source: U.S. Bureau of the Census, City Government Finances: 1993-94

City Government Revenue by Source

Source	FY94 ($000)	FY94 (per capita $)	FY94 (%)
From Federal Government	150,859	149.97	7.1
From State Governments	509,528	506.52	23.8
From Local Governments	33,082	32.89	1.5
Property Taxes	226,435	225.10	10.6
General Sales Taxes	0	0.00	0.0
Selective Sales Taxes	53,255	52.94	2.5
Income Taxes	293,323	291.59	13.7
Current Charges	240,370	238.95	11.2
Utility/Liquor Store	169,766	168.77	7.9
Employee Retirement[1]	344,470	342.44	16.1
Other	116,985	116.30	5.5

Note: (1) Excludes "city contributions," classified as "nonrevenue," intragovernmental transfers.
Source: U.S. Bureau of the Census, City Government Finances: 1993-94

City Government Expenditures by Function

Function	FY94 ($000)	FY94 (per capita $)	FY94 (%)
Educational Services	27,925	27.76	1.3
Employee Retirement[1]	303,097	301.31	14.6
Environment/Housing	419,433	416.96	20.3
Government Administration	146,384	145.52	7.1
Interest on General Debt	90,885	90.35	4.4
Public Safety	393,217	390.90	19.0
Social Services	101,648	101.05	4.9
Transportation	94,056	93.50	4.5
Utility/Liquor Store	260,958	259.42	12.6
Other	232,844	231.47	11.2

Note: (1) Payments to beneficiaries including withdrawal of contributions.
Source: U.S. Bureau of the Census, City Government Finances: 1993-94

Municipal Bond Ratings

Area	Moody's	S & P
Detroit	Baa2	BBB

Note: n/a not available; n/r not rated
Source: Moody's Bond Record, 2/98; Statistical Abstract of the U.S., 1997;
Governing Magazine, 9/97, 3/98

POPULATION

Population Growth

Area	1980	1990	% Chg. 1980-90	July 1996 Estimate	% Chg. 1990-96
City	1,203,339	1,027,974	-14.6	1,000,272	-2.7
MSA[1]	4,488,072	4,382,299	-2.4	4,318,145	-1.5
U.S.	226,545,805	248,765,170	9.8	265,179,411	6.6

Note: (1) Metropolitan Statistical Area - see Appendix A for areas included
Source: 1980/1990 Census of Housing and Population, Summary Tape File 3C;
Census Bureau Population Estimates

Population Characteristics

Race	City				% Chg. 1980-90	MSA[1]	
	1980		1990			1990	
	Population	%	Population	%		Population	%
White	420,529	34.9	221,932	21.6	-47.2	3,334,082	76.1
Black	758,468	63.0	778,456	75.7	2.6	942,450	21.5
Amer Indian/Esk/Aleut	3,846	0.3	3,511	0.3	-8.7	18,480	0.4
Asian/Pacific Islander	7,614	0.6	8,354	0.8	9.7	56,122	1.3
Other	12,882	1.1	15,721	1.5	22.0	31,165	0.7
Hispanic Origin[2]	28,970	2.4	27,157	2.6	-6.3	79,389	1.8

Note: (1) Metropolitan Statistical Area - see Appendix A for areas included;
(2) people of Hispanic origin can be of any race
Source: 1980/1990 Census of Housing and Population, Summary Tape File 3C

Ancestry

Area	German	Irish	English	Italian	U.S.	French	Polish	Dutch
City	5.0	3.7	2.1	1.5	1.8	1.4	4.7	0.4
MSA[1]	24.3	13.9	11.6	6.4	2.9	6.4	12.3	1.9
U.S.	23.3	15.6	13.1	5.9	5.3	4.2	3.8	2.5

Note: Figures are percentages and include persons that reported multiple ancestry (eg. if a person
reported being Irish and Italian, they were included in both columns); (1) Metropolitan Statistical Area -
see Appendix A for areas included
Source: 1990 Census of Population and Housing, Summary Tape File 3C

Age

Area	Median Age (Years)	Age Distribution (%)						
		Under 5	Under 18	18-24	25-44	45-64	65+	80+
City	30.7	9.0	29.4	11.0	30.7	16.7	12.1	2.5
MSA[1]	33.0	7.6	26.1	9.8	33.0	19.2	11.8	2.4
U.S.	32.9	7.3	25.6	10.5	32.6	18.7	12.5	2.8

Note: (1) Metropolitan Statistical Area - see Appendix A for areas included
Source: 1990 Census of Population and Housing, Summary Tape File 3C

Male/Female Ratio

Area	Number of males per 100 females (all ages)	Number of males per 100 females (18 years old+)
City	86.3	80.7
MSA[1]	92.7	88.9
U.S.	95.0	91.9

Note: (1) Metropolitan Statistical Area - see Appendix A for areas included
Source: 1990 Census of Population, General Population Characteristics

INCOME

Per Capita/Median/Average Income

Area	Per Capita ($)	Median Household ($)	Average Household ($)
City	9,443	18,742	25,601
MSA[1]	15,694	34,612	42,218
U.S.	14,420	30,056	38,453

Note: all figures are for 1989; (1) Metropolitan Statistical Area - see Appendix A for areas included
Source: 1990 Census of Population and Housing, Summary Tape File 3C

Household Income Distribution by Race

Income ($)	City (%)					U.S. (%)				
	Total	White	Black	Other	Hisp.[1]	Total	White	Black	Other	Hisp.[1]
Less than 5,000	16.1	10.9	17.8	19.4	19.2	6.2	4.8	15.2	8.6	8.8
5,000 - 9,999	16.2	15.3	16.6	15.5	15.5	9.3	8.6	14.2	9.9	11.1
10,000 - 14,999	10.9	11.9	10.6	10.9	10.9	8.8	8.5	11.0	9.8	11.0
15,000 - 24,999	16.5	18.8	15.7	15.5	15.9	17.5	17.3	18.9	18.5	20.5
25,000 - 34,999	13.0	14.5	12.4	13.6	13.6	15.8	16.1	14.2	15.4	16.4
35,000 - 49,999	13.6	14.5	13.3	14.4	13.3	17.9	18.6	13.3	16.1	16.0
50,000 - 74,999	9.7	9.9	9.6	8.4	8.6	15.0	15.8	9.3	13.4	11.1
75,000 - 99,999	2.8	2.7	2.9	1.3	2.0	5.1	5.5	2.6	4.7	3.1
100,000+	1.2	1.5	1.2	1.0	1.0	4.4	4.8	1.3	3.7	1.9

Note: all figures are for 1989; (1) people of Hispanic origin can be of any race
Source: 1990 Census of Population and Housing, Summary Tape File 3C

Effective Buying Income

Area	Per Capita ($)	Median Household ($)	Average Household ($)
City	10,494	21,282	28,758
MSA[1]	17,547	39,473	46,927
U.S.	15,444	33,201	41,849

Note: data as of 1/1/97; (1) Metropolitan Statistical Area - see Appendix A for areas included
Source: Standard Rate & Data Service, Newspaper Advertising Source, 2/98

Effective Household Buying Income Distribution

Area	% of Households Earning						
	$10,000 -$19,999	$20,000 -$34,999	$35,000 -$49,999	$50,000 -$74,999	$75,000 -$99,000	$100,000 -$124,999	$125,000 and up
City	20.6	20.1	14.5	12.2	3.8	1.0	0.5
MSA[1]	13.5	19.1	17.7	22.0	9.6	3.2	3.0
U.S.	16.5	23.4	18.3	18.2	6.4	2.1	2.4

Note: data as of 1/1/97; (1) Metropolitan Statistical Area - see Appendix A for areas included
Source: Standard Rate & Data Service, Newspaper Advertising Source, 2/98

Poverty Rates by Race and Age

Area	Total (%)	By Race (%)				By Age (%)		
		White	Black	Other	Hisp.[2]	Under 5 years old	Under 18 years old	65 years and over
City	32.4	21.9	35.2	36.7	35.7	52.7	46.6	20.1
MSA[1]	12.9	7.1	33.0	17.7	20.6	22.9	19.6	10.5
U.S.	13.1	9.8	29.5	23.1	25.3	20.1	18.3	12.8

Note: figures show the percent of people living below the poverty line in 1989. The average poverty threshold was $12,674 for a family of four in 1989; (1) Metropolitan Statistical Area - see Appendix A for areas included; (2) people of Hispanic origin can be of any race
Source: 1990 Census of Population and Housing, Summary Tape File 3C

EMPLOYMENT

Labor Force and Employment

Area	Civilian Labor Force			Workers Employed		
	Dec. '95	Dec. '96	% Chg.	Dec. '95	Dec. '96	% Chg.
City	381,698	383,793	0.5	350,392	359,642	2.6
MSA[1]	2,172,045	2,211,680	1.8	2,088,728	2,143,873	2.6
U.S.	134,583,000	136,742,000	1.6	127,903,000	130,785,000	2.3

Note: Data is not seasonally adjusted and covers workers 16 years of age and older;
(1) Metropolitan Statistical Area - see Appendix A for areas included
Source: Bureau of Labor Statistics, http://stats.bls.gov

Unemployment Rate

Area	1997											
	Jan.	Feb.	Mar.	Apr.	May	Jun.	Jul.	Aug.	Sep.	Oct.	Nov.	Dec.
City	9.7	8.3	8.0	7.8	7.1	8.4	10.1	6.9	7.6	6.6	6.5	6.3
MSA[1]	4.9	4.3	4.1	3.8	3.4	4.0	4.9	3.3	3.6	3.2	3.2	3.1
U.S.	5.9	5.7	5.5	4.8	4.7	5.2	5.0	4.8	4.7	4.4	4.3	4.4

Note: Data is not seasonally adjusted and covers workers 16 years of age and older; All figures are percentages; (1) Metropolitan Statistical Area - see Appendix A for areas included
Source: Bureau of Labor Statistics, http://stats.bls.gov

Employment by Industry

Sector	MSA[1]		U.S.
	Number of Employees	Percent of Total	Percent of Total
Services	647,300	30.4	29.0
Retail Trade	382,600	18.0	18.5
Government	233,600	11.0	16.1
Manufacturing	447,600	21.0	15.0
Finance/Insurance/Real Estate	112,700	5.3	5.7
Wholesale Trade	128,000	6.0	5.4
Transportation/Public Utilities	96,400	4.5	5.3
Construction	81,900	3.8	4.5
Mining	800	0.0	0.5

Note: Figures cover non-farm employment as of 12/97 and are not seasonally adjusted; (1) Metropolitan Statistical Area - see Appendix A for areas included
Source: Bureau of Labor Statistics, http://stats.bls.gov

Employment by Occupation

Occupation Category	City (%)	MSA[1] (%)	U.S. (%)
White Collar	50.1	58.8	58.1
Executive/Admin./Management	7.8	12.0	12.3
Professional	11.0	14.1	14.1
Technical & Related Support	3.3	3.9	3.7
Sales	8.5	11.8	11.8
Administrative Support/Clerical	19.5	17.0	16.3
Blue Collar	29.3	27.6	26.2
Precision Production/Craft/Repair	8.8	11.9	11.3
Machine Operators/Assem./Insp.	11.5	8.5	6.8
Transportation/Material Movers	4.4	3.6	4.1
Cleaners/Helpers/Laborers	4.6	3.5	3.9
Services	20.0	12.9	13.2
Farming/Forestry/Fishing	0.5	0.8	2.5

Note: figures cover employed persons 16 years old and over; (1) Metropolitan Statistical Area - see Appendix A for areas included
Source: 1990 Census of Population and Housing, Summary Tape File 3C

Occupational Employment Projections: 1994 - 2005

High Demand Occupations (ranked by annual openings)	Fast-Growing Occupations (ranked by percent growth)
1. Cashiers	1. Computer engineers
2. Salespersons, retail	2. Systems analysts
3. Waiters & waitresses	3. Personal and home care aides
4. General managers & top executives	4. Home health aides
5. Systems analysts	5. Numerical control machine tool oper.
6. Engineers, mechanical	6. Designers, except interior designers
7. General office clerks	7. Aircraft pilots/flight engineers
8. Janitors/cleaners/maids, ex. priv. hshld.	8. Engineers, mechanical
9. Secretaries, except legal & medical	9. Construction managers
10. Hand packers & packagers	10. Combination machine tool setters

Projections cover the Detroit MSA - see Appendix A for areas included.
Source: Michigan Employment Security Commission, Annual Planning Information Report 1998, City of Detroit MWA

Average Wages

Occupation	Wage	Occupation	Wage
Professional/Technical/Clerical	$/Week	**Health/Protective Services**	$/Week
Accountants III	840	Corrections Officers	618
Attorneys III	1,357	Firefighters	672
Budget Analysts III	828	Nurses, Licensed Practical II	-
Buyers/Contracting Specialists II	734	Nurses, Registered II	-
Clerks, Accounting III	475	Nursing Assistants II	-
Clerks, General III	433	Police Officers I	698
Computer Operators II	470	**Hourly Workers**	$/Hour
Computer Programmers II	672	Forklift Operators	15.74
Drafters II	480	General Maintenance Workers	11.24
Engineering Technicians III	730	Guards I	6.75
Engineering Technicians, Civil III	632	Janitors	9.21
Engineers III	958	Maintenance Electricians	21.24
Key Entry Operators I	349	Maintenance Electronics Techs II	17.89
Personnel Assistants III	492	Maintenance Machinists	18.51
Personnel Specialists III	842	Maintenance Mechanics, Machinery	20.00
Secretaries III	620	Material Handling Laborers	14.34
Switchboard Operator-Receptionist	-	Motor Vehicle Mechanics	17.80
Systems Analysts II	940	Shipping/Receiving Clerks	13.05
Systems Analysts Supervisor/Mgr II	1,421	Tool and Die Makers	20.32
Tax Collectors II	-	Truckdrivers, Tractor Trailer	15.42
Word Processors II	480	Warehouse Specialists	-

Note: Wage data includes full-time workers only for 1/96 and cover the Metropolitan Statistical Area (see Appendix A for areas included). Dashes indicate that data was not available.
Source: Bureau of Labor Statistics, Occupational Compensation Survey, 7/96

TAXES

Major State and Local Tax Rates

State Corp. Income (%)	State Personal Income (%)	Residential Property (effective rate per $100)	Sales & Use		State Gasoline (cents/ gallon)	State Cigarette (cents/ 20-pack)
			State (%)	Local (%)		
2.3[a]	4.4	2.76	6.0	None	19	75

Note: Personal/corporate income tax rates as of 1/97. Sales, gasoline and cigarette tax rates as of 1/98; (a) Value added tax imposed on the sum of federal taxable income of the business, compensation paid to employees, dividends, interest, royalties paid and other items
Source: Federation of Tax Administrators, www.taxadmin.org; Washington D.C. Department of Finance and Revenue, Tax Rates and Tax Burdens in the District of Columbia: A Nationwide Comparison, June 1997; Chamber of Commerce

Total Taxes Per Capita and as a Percent of Income

Area	Per Capita Income ($)	Per Capita Taxes ($)			Taxes as Pct. of Income (%)		
		Total	Federal	State/Local	Total	Federal	State/Local
Michigan	26,934	9,533	6,409	3,124	35.4	23.8	11.6
U.S.	26,187	9,205	6,127	3,078	35.2	23.4	11.8

Note: Figures are for 1997
Source: Tax Foundation, Web Site, www.taxfoundation.org

Estimated Tax Burden

Area	State Income	Local Income	Property	Sales	Total
Detroit	2,438	1,878	4,500	510	9,326

Note: The numbers are estimates of taxes paid by a married couple with two kids and annual earnings of $65,000. Sales tax estimates assume they spend average amounts on food, clothing, household goods and gasoline. Property tax estimates assume they live in a $225,000 home.
Source: Kiplinger's Personal Finance Magazine, June 1997

COMMERCIAL REAL ESTATE

Office Market

Class/Location	Total Space (sq. ft.)	Vacant Space (sq. ft.)	Vac. Rate (%)	Under Constr. (sq. ft.)	Net Absorp. (sq. ft.)	Rental Rates ($/sq.ft./yr.)
Class A						
CBD	6,195,035	231,304	3.7	n/a	2,148,120	19.50-25.00
Outside CBD	18,040,152	892,999	5.0	n/a	254,556	18.00-24.00
Class B						
CBD	9,260,300	1,648,407	17.8	n/a	n/a	15.50-19.00
Outside CBD	25,716,074	1,949,866	7.6	n/a	n/a	16.00-22.00

Note: Data as of 10/97 and covers Detroit; CBD = Central Business District; n/a not available;
Source: Society of Industrial and Office Realtors, 1998 Comparative Statistics of Industrial and Office Real Estate Markets

"No new space is currently under construction, though Requests for Proposals are being solicited by national developers from the city for the Campus Martius project, a prospective multi-use development. Sales prices, already at over $100 per sq. ft. are expected to advance by another five to 10 percent. After consolidating at a record rate, lasting automotive suppliers plus auto-related research firms are generating demand due to expansions. Auto production in North America was up 2.8% in 1997. But the market's dependence on auto manufacturing leaves it captive to industry volatility. Investments in local casinos, the airport and new arenas should help diversify and contribute to the area's economic growth." *Society of Industrial and Office Realtors, 1998 Comparative Statistics of Industrial and Office Real Estate Markets*

Industrial Market

Location	Total Space (sq. ft.)	Vacant Space (sq. ft.)	Vac. Rate (%)	Under Constr. (sq. ft.)	Net Absorp. (sq. ft.)	Net Lease ($/sq.ft./yr.)
Central City	n/a	n/a	n/a	n/a	n/a	1.25-6.75
Suburban	217,930,707	12,177,091	5.6	4,900,000	7,316,702	3.75-6.75

Note: Data as of 10/97 and covers Detroit; n/a not available
Source: Society of Industrial and Office Realtors, 1998 Comparative Statistics of Industrial and Office Real Estate Markets

"Users will continue to purchase land to construct facilities in order to better serve their customer base. Nearly five million sq. ft. were under construction during the latter part of 1997 including almost 3.5 million sq. ft. of speculative construction. Most activity was along the I-75, I-96, and I-275 corridors. New industrial park development is in Shelby, Auburn Hills, Wixom and the airport areas. The concentration of automotive technology will continue to spur expansions of suppliers and research firms. The dollar volume of sales and leases is anticipated to grow by up to ten percent, following a number of major investment transactions in 1997.'' *Society of Industrial and Office Realtors, 1998 Comparative Statistics of Industrial and Office Real Estate Markets*

Retail Market

Shopping Center Inventory (sq. ft.)	Shopping Center Construction (sq. ft.)	Construction as a Percent of Inventory (%)	Torto Wheaton Rent Index[1] ($/sq. ft.)
51,996,000	302,000	0.6	14.30

Note: Data as of 1997 and covers the Metropolitan Statistical Area - see Appendix A for areas included; (1) Index is based on a model that predicts what the average rent should be for leases with certain characteristics, in certain locations during certain years.
Source: National Association of Realtors, 1997-1998 Market Conditions Report

"Manufacturing, particularly auto-related, accounts for over 21% of total non-farm employment in Detroit. The area's economy has been boosted by strong auto sales in recent years. Solid real personal income growth has buoyed the area's retail sector. The rent index has soared 41% over the past two years. Downtown revitalization efforts have spurred retail projects such as the 55,000 square foot Chene Square development, which opened this year. However, Detroit's retail sector is highly subject to the cyclical nature of the auto industry. The area's economy is expected to proceed at a much slower pace over the next five years. That, coupled with sluggish population growth, will dampen retail activity." *National Association of Realtors, 1997-1998 Market Conditions Report*

COMMERCIAL UTILITIES

Typical Monthly Electric Bills

Area	Commercial Service ($/month)		Industrial Service ($/month)	
	12 kW demand 1,500 kWh	100 kW demand 30,000 kWh	1,000 kW demand 400,000 kWh	20,000 kW demand 10,000,000 kWh
City	156	2,748	27,586	547,885
U.S.	162	2,360	25,590	545,677

Note: Based on rates in effect July 1, 1997
Source: Edison Electric Institute, Typical Residential, Commercial and Industrial Bills, Summer 1997

TRANSPORTATION

Transportation Statistics

Avg. travel time to work (min.)	24.7
Interstate highways	I-75; I-96; I-94
Bus lines	
In-city	D-DOT (Department of Transportation, City of Detroit), 487 vehicles; Suburban Mobile Authority for Regional Transportation, 401 vehicles
Inter-city	5
Passenger air service	
Airport	Detroit-Wayne County Metropolitan Airport
Airlines	19
Aircraft departures	165,711 (1995)
Enplaned passengers	13,293,568 (1995)
Rail service	Amtrak; Light Rail planned
Motor freight carriers	200
Major waterways/ports	Detroit River

Source: OAG, Business Travel Planner, Summer 1997; Editor & Publisher Market Guide, 1998; FAA Airport Activity Statistics, 1996; Amtrak National Time Table, Northeast Timetable, Fall/Winter 1997-98; 1990 Census of Population and Housing, STF 3C; Chamber of Commerce/Economic Development 1997; Jane's Urban Transport Systems 1997-98; Transit Fact Book 1997

A survey of 90,000 airline passengers during the first half of 1997 ranked most of the largest airports in the U.S. Detroit-Wayne County Metropolitan ranked number 36 out of 36. Criteria: cleanliness, quality of restaurants, attractiveness, speed of baggage delivery, ease of reaching gates, available ground transportation, ease of following signs and closeness of parking. *Plog Research Inc., First Half 1997*

Means of Transportation to Work

Area	Car/Truck/Van		Public Transportation			Bicycle	Walked	Other Means	Worked at Home
	Drove Alone	Car-pooled	Bus	Subway	Railroad				
City	67.8	16.1	10.2	0.0	0.0	0.1	3.4	1.3	1.1
MSA[1]	83.4	10.1	2.2	0.0	0.0	0.1	1.9	0.6	1.6
U.S.	73.2	13.4	3.0	1.5	0.5	0.4	3.9	1.2	3.0

Note: figures shown are percentages and only include workers 16 years old and over;
(1) Metropolitan Statistical Area - see Appendix A for areas included
Source: 1990 Census of Population and Housing, Summary Tape File 3C

BUSINESSES

Major Business Headquarters

Company Name	1997 Rankings	
	Fortune 500	Forbes 500
American Axle & Manufacturing	-	63
Comerica	444	-
DTE Energy	372	-
Flint Ink	-	245
General Motors	1	-
Little Caesar Enterprises	-	338
Penske	-	90
Sherwood Food Distributors	-	280
Stroh Brewery	-	121
Walbridge Aldinger	-	315

Note: Companies listed are located in the city; Dashes indicate no ranking
Fortune 500: companies that produce a 10-K are ranked 1 - 500 based on 1996 revenue
Forbes 500: private companies are ranked 1 - 500 based on 1996 revenue
Source: Forbes 12/1/97; Fortune 4/28/97

Fast-Growing Businesses

Detroit was ranked #21 out of 24 (#1 is best) in terms of the best-performing local stocks in 1996 according to the Money/Norby Cities Index. The index measures stocks of companies that have headquarters in 24 metro areas. *Money, 2/7/97*

Women-Owned Businesses: Number, Employment, Sales and Share

Area	Women-Owned Businesses in 1996				Share of Women-Owned Businesses in 1996	
	Number	Employment	Sales ($000)	Rank[2]	Percent (%)	Rank[3]
MSA[1]	108,300	256,600	32,112,700	9	36.0	32

Note: (1) Metropolitan Statistical Area - see Appendix A for areas included; (2) Calculated on an averaging of number of businesses, employment and sales and ranges from 1 to 50 where 1 is best; (3) Ranges from 1 to 50 where 1 is best
Source: The National Foundation for Women Business Owners, 1996 Facts on Women-Owned Businesses: Trends in the Top 50 Metropolitan Areas, March 26, 1997

Women-Owned Businesses: Growth

Area	Growth in Women-Owned Businesses (% change from 1987 to 1996)				Relative Growth in the Number of Women-Owned and All Businesses (% change from 1987 to 1996)			
	Num.	Empl.	Sales	Rank[2]	Women-Owned	All Firms	Absolute Difference	Relative Difference
MSA[1]	74.2	166.3	217.3	38	74.2	53.0	21.2	1.4:1

Note: (1) Metropolitan Statistical Area - see Appendix A for areas included; (2) Calculated on an averaging of the percent growth of number of businesses, employment and sales and ranges from 1 to 50 where 1 is best
Source: The National Foundation for Women Business Owners, 1996 Facts on Women-Owned Businesses: Trends in the Top 50 Metropolitan Areas, March 26, 1997

Minority Business Opportunity

Detroit is home to four companies which are on the Black Enterprise Industrial/Service 100 list (largest based on gross sales): The Bing Group (steel processing, metal stamping distribution); Barden Companies Inc. (radio broadcasting, real estate devel., casino gaming); Thomas Madison Inc. (automotive metal stamping, steel sales and processing); The O-J Group (transportation services). Criteria: 1) operational in previous calendar year; 2) at least 51% black-owned; 3) manufactures/owns the product it sells or provides industrial or consumer services. Brokerages, real estate firms and firms that provide professional services are not eligible. *Black Enterprise, July 1997*

Detroit is home to one company which is on the Black Enterprise Auto Dealer 100 list (largest based on gross sales): Conyers Riverside Ford Sales Inc. (Ford). Criteria: 1) operational in previous calendar year; 2) at least 51% black-owned. *Black Enterprise, June 1997*

One of the 500 largest Hispanic-owned companies in the U.S. are located in Detroit. *Hispanic Business, June 1997*

Small Business Opportunity

Detroit was included among *Entrepreneur* magazines listing of the "20 Best Cities for Small Business." It was ranked #11 among large metro areas. Criteria: risk of failure, business performance, economic growth, affordability and state attitude towards business. *Entrepreneur, 10/97*

HOTELS & MOTELS

Hotels/Motels

Area	Hotels/ Motels	Rooms	Luxury-Level Hotels/Motels		Average Minimum Rates ($)		
			◆◆◆◆	◆◆◆◆◆	◆◆	◆◆◆	◆◆◆◆
City	13	3,363	0	0	107	115	n/a
Airport	22	3,443	0	0	n/a	n/a	n/a
Suburbs	119	16,902	2	0	n/a	n/a	n/a
Total	154	23,708	2	0	n/a	n/a	n/a

Note: n/a not available; Classifications range from one diamond (budget properties with basic amenities) to five diamond (luxury properties with the finest service, rooms and facilities).
Source: OAG, Business Travel Planner, Summer 1997

CONVENTION CENTERS

Major Convention Centers

Center Name	Meeting Rooms	Exhibit Space (sf)
Cobo Conference and Exposition Center	84	700,000
Detroit Light Guard Armory	n/a	48,000
Joe Louis Arena	n/a	22,000
Michigan State Fair and Exposition Center	n/a	52,800
The Westin Hotel Renaissance Center	30	24,950

Note: n/a not available
Source: Trade Shows Worldwide 1997

Living Environment

COST OF LIVING

Cost of Living Index

Composite Index	Housing	Utilities	Groceries	Health Care	Trans-portation	Misc. Goods/ Services
108.1	117.6	107.5	106.1	118.8	104.7	100.1

Note: U.S. = 100
Source: ACCRA, Cost of Living Index, 1st Quarter 1997

HOUSING

Median Home Prices and Housing Affordability

Area	Median Price[2] 3rd Qtr. 1997 ($)	HOI[3] 3rd Qtr. 1997	Afford-ability Rank[4]
MSA[1]	120,000	62.8	132
U.S.	127,000	63.7	–

Note: (1) Metropolitan Statistical Area - see Appendix A for areas included; (2) U.S. figures calculated from the sales of 625,000 new and existing homes in 195 markets; (3) Housing Opportunity Index - percent of homes sold that were within the reach of the median income household at the prevailing mortgage interest rate; (4) Rank is from 1-195 with 1 being most affordable
Source: National Association of Home Builders, Housing Opportunity Index, 3rd Quarter 1997

It is projected that the median price of existing single-family homes in the metro area will increase by 10.3% in 1998. Nationwide, home prices are projected to increase 6.6%.
Kiplinger's Personal Finance Magazine, January 1998

Average New Home Price

Area	Price ($)
City	163,000
U.S.	133,782

Note: Figures are based on a new home with 1,800 sq. ft. of living area on an 8,000 sq. ft. lot.
Source: ACCRA, Cost of Living Index, 1st Quarter 1997

Average Apartment Rent

Area	Rent ($/mth)
City	709
U.S.	563

Note: Figures are based on an unfurnished two bedroom, 1-1/2 or 2 bath apartment, approximately 950 sq. ft. in size, excluding all utilities except water
Source: ACCRA, Cost of Living Index, 1st Quarter 1997

RESIDENTIAL UTILITIES

Average Residential Utility Costs

Area	All Electric ($/mth)	Part Electric ($/mth)	Other Energy ($/mth)	Phone ($/mth)
City	–	67.10	48.70	16.82
U.S.	110.19	56.83	45.14	19.36

Source: ACCRA, Cost of Living Index, 1st Quarter 1997

HEALTH CARE

Average Health Care Costs

Area	Hospital ($/day)	Doctor ($/visit)	Dentist ($/visit)
City	545.80	48.86	76.30
U.S.	385.60	47.34	59.26

Note: Hospital - based on a semi-private room. Doctor - based on a general practitioner's routine exam of an established patient. Dentist - based on adult teeth cleaning and periodic oral exam.
Source: ACCRA, Cost of Living Index, 1st Quarter 1997

Distribution of Office-Based Physicians

Area	Family/Gen. Practitioners	Specialists		
		Medical	Surgical	Other
MSA[1]	574	2,508	1,690	1,727

Note: Data as of 12/31/96; (1) Metropolitan Statistical Area - see Appendix A for areas included
Source: American Medical Assn., Physician Characteristics & Distribution in the U.S., 1997-1998

Hospitals

Detroit has 14 general medical and surgical hospitals, 1 psychiatric, 1 rehabilitation, 1 children's general, 1 children's psychiatric. *AHA Guide to the Healthcare Field 1997-98*

According to *U.S. News and World Report,* Detroit has 2 of the best hospitals in the U.S.: **Henry Ford Hospital**, noted for cardiology, orthopedics; **Hutzel Hospital**, noted for orthopedics;   *U.S. News and World Report, "America's Best Hospitals", 7/28/97*

EDUCATION

Public School District Statistics

District Name	Num. Sch.	Enroll.	Classroom Teachers[1]	Pupils per Teacher	Minority Pupils (%)	Current Exp.[2] ($/pupil)
Det Brd Ed-Web Dubois Prep	1	152	n/a	n/a	n/a	n/a
Detroit City School District	268	173,750	7,545	23.0	94.3	6,601
University Public Schools	n/a	398	n/a	n/a	n/a	n/a

Note: Data covers the 1995-1996 school year unless otherwise noted; (1) Excludes teachers reported as working in school district offices rather than in schools; (2) Based on 1993-94 enrollment collected by the Census Bureau, not the enrollment figure shown in column 3; SD = School District; ISD = Independent School District; n/a not available
Source: National Center for Education Statistics, Common Core of Data Survey; Bureau of the Census

Educational Quality

School District	Education Quotient[1]	Graduate Outcome[2]	Community Index[3]	Resource Index[4]
Detroit	78.0	53.0	58.0	123.0

Note: Nearly 1,000 secondary school districts were rated in terms of educational quality. The scores range from a low of 50 to a high of 150; (1) Average of the Graduate Outcome, Community and Resource indexes; (2) Based on graduation rates and college board scores (SAT/ACT); (3) Based on the surrounding community's average level of education and the area's average income level; (4) Based on teacher salaries, per-pupil expenditures and student-teacher ratios.
Source: Expansion Management, Ratings Issue 1997

Educational Attainment by Race

Area	High School Graduate (%)					Bachelor's Degree (%)				
	Total	White	Black	Other	Hisp.[2]	Total	White	Black	Other	Hisp.[2]
City	62.1	61.3	62.6	55.8	45.3	9.6	12.1	8.4	18.7	7.2
MSA[1]	75.7	78.5	64.4	73.2	62.9	17.7	19.2	9.9	34.1	13.1
U.S.	75.2	77.9	63.1	60.4	49.8	20.3	21.5	11.4	19.4	9.2

Note: figures shown cover persons 25 years old and over; (1) Metropolitan Statistical Area - see Appendix A for areas included; (2) people of Hispanic origin can be of any race
Source: 1990 Census of Population and Housing, Summary Tape File 3C

School Enrollment by Type

Area	Preprimary				Elementary/High School			
	Public		Private		Public		Private	
	Enrollment	%	Enrollment	%	Enrollment	%	Enrollment	%
City	13,196	72.4	5,027	27.6	180,245	87.3	26,179	12.7
MSA[1]	63,323	68.3	29,435	31.7	685,077	88.7	87,455	11.3
U.S.	2,679,029	59.5	1,824,256	40.5	38,379,689	90.2	4,187,099	9.8

Note: figures shown cover persons 3 years old and over;
(1) Metropolitan Statistical Area - see Appendix A for areas included
Source: 1990 Census of Population and Housing, Summary Tape File 3C

School Enrollment by Race

Area	Preprimary (%)				Elementary/High School (%)			
	White	Black	Other	Hisp.[1]	White	Black	Other	Hisp.[1]
City	18.1	78.5	3.4	3.5	13.5	83.3	3.1	3.3
MSA[2]	77.6	19.5	2.9	2.3	69.8	26.9	3.3	2.6
U.S.	80.4	12.5	7.1	7.8	74.1	15.6	10.3	12.5

Note: figures shown cover persons 3 years old and over; (1) people of Hispanic origin can be of any race; (2) Metropolitan Statistical Area - see Appendix A for areas included
Source: 1990 Census of Population and Housing, Summary Tape File 3C

SAT/ACT Scores

Area/District	1997 SAT				1997 ACT	
	Percent of Graduates Tested (%)	Average Math Score	Average Verbal Score	Average Combined Score	Percent of Graduates Tested (%)	Average Composite Score
Detroit PS	14	442	451	893	54	16.7
State	11	566	557	1,123	68	21.3
U.S.	42	511	505	1,016	36	21.0

Note: Math and verbal SAT scores are out of a possible 800; ACT scores are out of a possible 36
Caution: Comparing or ranking states/cities on the basis of SAT/ACT scores alone is invalid and strongly discouraged by the The College Board and The American College Testing Program as students who take the tests are self-selected and do not represent the entire student population.
Source: Detroit Public Schools, Research & Evaluation, 1997; American College Testing Program, 1997; College Board, 1997

Classroom Teacher Salaries in Public Schools

District	B.A. Degree		M.A. Degree		Ph.D. Degree	
	Min. ($)	Max. ($)	Min. ($)	Max. ($)	Min. ($)	Max. ($)
Detroit	30,537	48,289	33,755	55,408	34,355	56,408
Average[1]	26,120	39,270	28,175	44,667	31,643	49,825

Note: Salaries are for 1996-1997; (1) Based on all school districts covered
Source: American Federation of Teachers (unpublished data)

Higher Education

Two-Year Colleges		Four-Year Colleges		Medical Schools	Law Schools	Voc/Tech
Public	Private	Public	Private			
1	1	1	4	1	2	17

Source: College Blue Book, Occupational Education 1997; Medical School Admission Requirements, 1998-99; Peterson's Guide to Two-Year Colleges, 1997; Peterson's Guide to Four-Year Colleges, 1997; Barron's Guide to Law Schools 1997

MAJOR EMPLOYERS

Major Employers

American Axle & Manufacturing
Blue Cross & Blue Shield of Michigan
Chrysler Transport
Detroit Diesel Corp.
Detroit Newspapers
Grace Hospital
Michigan Consolidated Gas
St. John Hospital & Medical Ctr.
General Motors Acceptance Corp.

American Natural Resources Co.
Children's Hospital of Michigan
Westin Renaissance Co.
Detroit Edison
General Motors Corp.
Michigan Bell Telephone
Sinai Hospital
Holy Cross Hospital

Note: companies listed are located in the city
Source: Dun's Business Rankings 1997; Ward's Business Directory, 1997

PUBLIC SAFETY

Crime Rate

Area	All Crimes	Violent Crimes				Property Crimes		
		Murder	Forcible Rape	Robbery	Aggrav. Assault	Burglary	Larceny -Theft	Motor Vehicle Theft
City	11,991.2	42.7	111.6	948.2	1,216.0	2,144.2	4,109.9	3,418.6
Suburbs[1]	4,314.4	2.7	33.4	80.1	267.2	601.8	2,795.9	533.4
MSA[2]	6,081.7	11.9	51.4	280.0	485.6	956.9	3,098.4	1,197.6
U.S.	5,078.9	7.4	36.1	202.4	388.2	943.0	2,975.9	525.9

Note: Crime rate is the number of crimes per 100,000 pop.; (1) defined as all areas within the MSA but located outside the central city; (2) Metropolitan Statistical Area - see Appendix A for areas incl.
Source: FBI Uniform Crime Reports 1996

RECREATION

Culture and Recreation

Museums	Symphony Orchestras	Opera Companies	Dance Companies	Professional Theatres	Zoos	Pro Sports Teams
14	2	2	3	3	1	4

Source: International Directory of the Performing Arts, 1996; Official Museum Directory, 1998; Chamber of Commerce/Economic Development 1997

Library System

The Detroit Public Library has 24 branches, holdings of 2,746,571 volumes and a budget of $26,040,625 (1995-1996). *American Library Directory, 1997-1998*

MEDIA

Newspapers

Name	Type	Freq.	Distribution	Circulation
Detroit Free Press	General	7x/wk	State	638,083
The Detroit News	General	7x/wk	State	370,000
The Metro Times	n/a	1x/wk	Area	100,000
Michigan Catholic Newspaper	Religious	1x/wk	Area	29,000
Michigan Chronicle	Black	1x/wk	State	41,436
Michigan Chronicle-Pontiac Edition	General	1x/wk	State	37,618
Michigan Citizen	Black	1x/wk	State	48,000

Note: Includes newspapers with circulations of 25,000 or more located in the city; n/a not available
Source: Burrelle's Media Directory, 1998 Edition

AM Radio Stations

Call Letters	Freq. (kHz)	Target Audience	Station Format	Music Format
WJR	760	General	M/N/S/T	Adult Contemporary/MOR
WCAR	1090	n/a	E/M/N/S	Contemporary Top 40
WDFN	1130	n/a	S	n/a
WCHB	1200	General	N/S/T	n/a
WXYT	1270	General	T	n/a
WDOZ	1310	n/a	M	n/a
WQBH	1400	General	M/N/S	Christian/Jazz/Oldies/R&B
WPON	1460	General	M/T	Oldies

Note: Stations included broadcast in the Detroit metro area; n/a not available
Station Format: E = Educational; M = Music; N = News; S = Sports; T = Talk
Music Format: AOR = Album Oriented Rock; MOR = Middle-of-the-Road
Source: Burrelle's Media Directory, 1998 Edition

FM Radio Stations

Call Letters	Freq. (mHz)	Target Audience	Station Format	Music Format
WSDP	88.1	General	E/M/N/S	Alternative
WHPR	88.1	n/a	M	Jazz/R&B
WHFR	89.3	General	M/N/S	n/a
WDTR	90.9	General	E/M	n/a
WMXD	92.3	n/a	M	Adult Contemporary/Urban Contemporary
WDRQ	93.1	General	M/N	Adult Contemporary
WCSX	94.7	General	M	Classic Rock
WKQI	95.5	n/a	M	Adult Contemporary
WHYT	96.3	General	M	Alternative
WYST	97.1	Men	M	AOR
WJLB	97.9	Black	M	Christian/Urban Contemporary
WVMV	98.7	n/a	M	Adult Contemporary/Jazz/R&B
WYCD	99.5	General	M	n/a
WNIC	100.3	General	M/N/T	Adult Contemporary
WRIF	101.1	General	M	AOR
WDET	101.9	General	M/N	n/a
WMUZ	103.5	n/a	E/M/T	Christian
WQRS	105.1	General	M	Classical
WCHB	105.9	n/a	M	Urban Contemporary
WWWW	106.7	General	M	Country
WGPR	107.5	General	M/N/S/T	n/a

Note: Stations included broadcast in the Detroit metro area; n/a not available
Station Format: E = Educational; M = Music; N = News; S = Sports; T = Talk
Music Format: AOR = Album Oriented Rock; MOR = Middle-of-the-Road
Source: Burrelle's Media Directory, 1998 Edition

Television Stations

Name	Ch.	Affiliation	Type	Owner
WDIV	4	NBC	Commercial	Post-Newsweek Stations Inc.
WBZO	20	WB	Commercial	Granite Broadcasting Corporation
WTVS	56	PBS	Public	Detroit Educational Television Foundation
WWJ	62	CBS	Commercial	Westinghouse Broadcasting Company

Note: Stations included broadcast in the Detroit metro area
Source: Burrelle's Media Directory, 1998 Edition

CLIMATE

Average and Extreme Temperatures

Temperature	Jan	Feb	Mar	Apr	May	Jun	Jul	Aug	Sep	Oct	Nov	Dec	Ann
Extreme High (°F)	62	65	81	89	93	104	102	100	98	91	77	68	104
Average High (°F)	30	33	44	58	70	79	83	81	74	61	48	35	58
Average Temp. (°F)	23	26	36	48	59	68	72	71	64	52	40	29	49
Average Low (°F)	16	18	27	37	47	56	61	60	53	41	32	21	39
Extreme Low (°F)	-21	-15	-4	10	25	36	41	38	29	17	9	-10	-21

Note: Figures cover the years 1958-1990
Source: National Climatic Data Center, International Station Meteorological Climate Summary, 3/95

Average Precipitation/Snowfall/Humidity

Precip./Humidity	Jan	Feb	Mar	Apr	May	Jun	Jul	Aug	Sep	Oct	Nov	Dec	Ann
Avg. Precip. (in.)	1.8	1.8	2.5	3.0	2.9	3.6	3.1	3.4	2.8	2.2	2.6	2.7	32.4
Avg. Snowfall (in.)	10	9	7	2	Tr	0	0	0	0	Tr	3	11	41
Avg. Rel. Hum. 7am (%)	80	79	79	78	78	79	82	86	87	84	82	81	81
Avg. Rel. Hum. 4pm (%)	67	63	59	53	51	52	52	54	55	55	64	70	58

Note: Figures cover the years 1958-1990; Tr = Trace amounts (<0.05 in. of rain; <0.5 in. of snow)
Source: National Climatic Data Center, International Station Meteorological Climate Summary, 3/95

Weather Conditions

Temperature			Daytime Sky			Precipitation		
5°F & below	32°F & below	90°F & above	Clear	Partly cloudy	Cloudy	0.01 inch or more precip.	0.1 inch or more snow/ice	Thunder-storms
15	136	12	74	134	157	135	38	32

Note: Figures are average number of days per year and covers the years 1958-1990
Source: National Climatic Data Center, International Station Meteorological Climate Summary, 3/95

AIR & WATER QUALITY

Maximum Pollutant Concentrations

	Particulate Matter (ug/m³)	Carbon Monoxide (ppm)	Sulfur Dioxide (ppm)	Nitrogen Dioxide (ppm)	Ozone (ppm)	Lead (ug/m³)
MSA[1] Level	106	6	0.079	0.021	0.11	0.04
NAAQS[2]	150	9	0.140	0.053	0.12	1.50
Met NAAQS?	Yes	Yes	Yes	Yes	Yes	Yes

Note: (1) Metropolitan Statistical Area - see Appendix A for areas included; (2) National Ambient Air Quality Standards; ppm = parts per million; ug/m³ = micrograms per cubic meter; n/a not available
Source: EPA, National Air Quality and Emissions Trends Report, 1996

Pollutant Standards Index

In the Detroit MSA (see Appendix A for areas included), the Pollutant Standards Index (PSI) exceeded 100 on 3 days in 1996. A PSI value greater than 100 indicates that air quality would be in the unhealthful range on that day. *EPA, National Air Quality and Emissions Trends Report, 1996*

Drinking Water

Water System Name	Pop. Served	Primary Water Source Type	Number of Violations in Fiscal Year 1997	Type of Violation/ Contaminants
Detroit	1,027,974	Surface	None	None

Note: Data as of January 16, 1998
Source: EPA, Office of Ground Water and Drinking Water, Safe Drinking Water Information System

Detroit tap water is alkaline, soft.
Editor & Publisher Market Guide, 1998

Evansville, Indiana

Background

Evansville is the seat of Vanderburgh County in southwestern Indiana. Built on a large bend in the Ohio River, the city is the center of a metropolitan Tri-State area which includes part of western Kentucky and southeastern Illinois. Centrally located, Evansville is within a three-hour drive of Indianapolis, Nashville, Louisville, and St. Louis.

Founded in 1812 and named for Robert Evans, a Colonel in the militia and a member of the territorial legislature, Evansville grew rapidly with the coming of the steamboat. By 1822, steamboats had displaced the flatboats used in the past for river traffic. The discovery of coal and oil in the surrounding fertile farmland and the towns position on the Ohio River, which supplied hydropower, led to rapid growth of the small town. When the Wabash and Erie Canal was completed in 1843, it linked Lake Erie to the Ohio River. The canal's southern terminus was Evansville and the town's continued strong growth was assured.

With abundant hydropower and its links to the Great Lakes, via the Wabash and Erie Canal, and the Mississippi, via the Ohio River, it became a major transportation hub. Though the canal eventually failed, the city's industrial and transportation base grew. Today its modern river terminal acts as the exchange point for goods between river, truck and train traffic.

Evansville is a metropolitan center in southwestern Indiana and is joined to Henderson, Kentucky by a bridge spanning the Ohio River. Manufacturing in the Evansville-Henderson area includes pharmaceuticals, food products, agricultural tools, refrigeration and air-conditioning equipment, home appliances, and aluminum and rubber products. The large number of plastics-related companies have given the city the nickname of "Plastics Valley."

The Evansville Museum of Arts and Science provides a wide variety of art and science exhibits from around the world and includes the Koch Planetarium. For those who enjoy the theater, there are five theater groups in the city, in addition to the University of Evansville's Department of Theatre students, who provide plays throughout the year. Those who prefer symphonic music can attend the Evansville Philharmonic Orchestra.

If you are interested in outdoor pursuits, Mesker Park Zoo provides a great day out, as does the Wesselman Woods Nature Preserve. In nearby Henderson, Kentucky, John James Audubon, the artist-ornithologist who operated a general store in the town from 1810 to 1819, is commemorated by the Audubon Memorial Museum and State Park. The James C. Ellis Park and Audubon Raceway offer summer thoroughbred and harness racing. The nearby Angel Mounds State Historic Site is where archaeologists have found the remains of the area's earliest known inhabitants.

Throughout the summer and early fall, festivals enhance the warm seasons. There is the Ohio River Festival for the Arts; Thunder on the Ohio, a hydroplane race and festival; the Germania Maennerchor Volksfest, a Munich-style German food, music, regalia and beer festival; and the West Side Nut Club Fall Festival.

Geographically, Evansville lies in the path of moisture-bearing low pressure formations that move from the western Gulf region. Much of the precipitation results from these storm systems, especially in the cooler part of the year. There is considerable variation in seasonal and monthly temperature and precipitation from year to year. Severe storms are rather infrequent, but thunderstorms cause some wind damage each year. Evansville is in tornado alley with the most frequent occurrence in early spring and late fall.

General Rankings and Evaluative Comments

■ Evansville was ranked #177 out of 300 cities by *Money's* 1997 "Survey of the Best Places to Live." Criteria used: health services, crime, economy, housing, education, transportation, weather, leisure and the arts. The city was ranked #176 in 1996 and #277 in 1995. *Money, July 1997; Money, September 1996; Money, September 1995*

■ *Ladies Home Journal* ranked America's 200 largest cities based on the qualities women care about most. Evansville ranked 142 out of 200. Criteria: low crime rate, good public schools, well-paying jobs, quality health and child care, the presence of women in government, proportion of women-owned businesses, size of the wage gap with men, local economy, divorce rates, the ratio of single men to single women, whether there are laws that require at least the same number of public toilets for women as men, and the probability of good hair days. *Ladies Home Journal, November 1997*

■ Evansville was ranked #77 out of 219 cities in terms of children's health, safety, and economic well-being. Criteria: total population, percent population change, birth rate, child immunization rate, infant mortality rate, percent low birth weight infants, percent of births to teens, physician-to-population ratio, student-to-teacher ratio, dropout rate, unemployment rate, median family income, percent of children in poverty, violent and property crime rates, number of juvenile arrests for violent crimes as a percent of the total crime index, number of days with pollution standard index (PSI) over 100, pounds toxic releases per 1,000 people and number of superfund sites. *Zero Population Growth, Children's Environmental Index 1997*

■ According to *Working Mother*, "Indiana has come up with some innovative ways to tackle the tough issue of how to pay for child care. About two thirds of the state's 92 counties are now drawing up plans to expand and improve child care with help from private businesses. This new effort grew out of former governor Evan Bayh's Step Ahead initiative, which got all of Indiana's counties to draw up comprehensive plans for child care and other children's services. The program was developed in cooperation with the Child Care Action Campaign, a national advocacy group. Each county is now developing its own approach, with some interesting results....

At the same time, however, Indiana officials weakened rules for family child care, allowing providers to care for larger groups of children than in the past. Some caregivers can now take in as many as 16 kids at a time. State lawmakers also vetoed a proposal to require family child care providers to have six hours of annual training." *Working Mother, July/August 1997*

Business Environment

STATE ECONOMY

State Economic Profile

"Indiana's economy is well past its cyclical peak....retail sales growth trails the national pace, and the number of bankruptcy filings is at a record high.

Indiana is the nation's largest producer of steel, accounting for nearly one-quarter of the nation's output....

Indiana legislators reduced the auto excise tax last year. This revenue loss will be partly offset by revenues from Indiana's eleven casinos. Indiana has accumulated a $1.6 billion surplus by resisting pressures for additional tax cuts and spending increases. However, there are several initiatives under review at both the state and county levels to increase wage taxes from the current 3.4% to 5.4%. Another proposal would eliminate business inventory taxes.

Population growth weakened slightly in 1996 to under 0.8% as migration declined slightly, due in part to the closure of Fort Benjamin Harrison. However, Indiana still enjoys strong, positive domestic net in-migration, in contrast to its three Great Lakes neighbors. Indiana's relatively optimistic economic outlook should provide for long-run population growth just short of the national average. This will support expansion of the state's local and population-dependent industries, such as retail trade and housing.

...Compared with neighboring manufacturing states, Indiana enjoys a significant comparative advantage in low costs. Combined with generous tax incentives, Indiana's low costs will enable the state to attract firms relocating from higher cost states or seeking to expand. However, the state is at risk due to its high dependence on traditional durable manufacturing industries, particularly steel and autos. Indiana will be an average performer long term."
National Association of Realtors, Economic Profiles: The Fifty States, July 1997

IMPORTS/EXPORTS

Total Export Sales

Area	1993 ($000)	1994 ($000)	1995 ($000)	1996 ($000)	% Chg. 1993-96	% Chg. 1995-96
MSA[1]	448,534	487,403	525,072	545,088	21.5	3.8
U.S.	464,858,354	512,415,609	583,030,524	622,827,063	34.0	6.8

Note: (1) Metropolitan Statistical Area - see Appendix A for areas included
Source: U.S. Department of Commerce, International Trade Association, Metropolitan Area Exports: An Export Performance Report on Over 250 U.S. Cities, October 1997

Imports/Exports by Port

Type	Cargo Value			Share of U.S. Total	
	1995 (US$mil.)	1996 (US$mil.)	% Change 1995-1996	1995 (%)	1996 (%)
Imports	0	0	0	0	0
Exports	0	0	0	0	0

Source: Global Trade Information Services, WaterBorne Trade Atlas 1997

CITY FINANCES

City Government Finances

Component	FY92 ($000)	FY92 (per capita $)
Revenue	88,775	705.26
Expenditure	98,441	782.05
Debt Outstanding	62,064	493.06
Cash & Securities	34,311	272.58

Source: U.S. Bureau of the Census, City Government Finances: 1991-92

City Government Revenue by Source

Source	FY92 ($000)	FY92 (per capita $)	FY92 (%)
From Federal Government	11,148	88.56	12.6
From State Governments	13,965	110.94	15.7
From Local Governments	2,527	20.08	2.8
Property Taxes	22,450	178.35	25.3
General Sales Taxes	0	0.00	0.0
Selective Sales Taxes	0	0.00	0.0
Income Taxes	0	0.00	0.0
Current Charges	20,069	159.44	22.6
Utility/Liquor Store	8,892	70.64	10.0
Employee Retirement[1]	3,220	25.58	3.6
Other	6,504	51.67	7.3

Note: (1) Excludes "city contributions," classified as "nonrevenue," intragovernmental transfers.
Source: U.S. Bureau of the Census, City Government Finances: 1991-92

City Government Expenditures by Function

Function	FY92 ($000)	FY92 (per capita $)	FY92 (%)
Educational Services	0	0.00	0.0
Employee Retirement[1]	5,873	46.66	6.0
Environment/Housing	35,943	285.55	36.5
Government Administration	2,141	17.01	2.2
Interest on General Debt	3,900	30.98	4.0
Public Safety	20,582	163.51	20.9
Social Services	1,788	14.20	1.8
Transportation	7,411	58.88	7.5
Utility/Liquor Store	13,629	108.27	13.8
Other	7,174	56.99	7.3

Note: (1) Payments to beneficiaries including withdrawal of contributions.
Source: U.S. Bureau of the Census, City Government Finances: 1991-92

Municipal Bond Ratings

Area	Moody's	S & P
Evansville	n/r	n/a

Note: n/a not available; n/r not rated
Source: Moody's Bond Record, 2/98; Statistical Abstract of the U.S., 1997;
Governing Magazine, 9/97, 3/98

POPULATION

Population Growth

Area	1980	1990	% Chg. 1980-90	July 1996 Estimate	% Chg. 1990-96
City	130,496	126,272	-3.2	123,456	-2.2
MSA[1]	276,252	278,990	1.0	288,735	3.5
U.S.	226,545,805	248,765,170	9.8	265,179,411	6.6

Note: (1) Metropolitan Statistical Area - see Appendix A for areas included
Source: 1980/1990 Census of Housing and Population, Summary Tape File 3C;
Census Bureau Population Estimates

Population Characteristics

Race	City 1980 Population	%	City 1990 Population	%	% Chg. 1980-90	MSA[1] 1990 Population	%
White	118,020	90.4	112,956	89.5	-4.3	260,788	93.5
Black	11,652	8.9	12,043	9.5	3.4	16,080	5.8
Amer Indian/Esk/Aleut	263	0.2	256	0.2	-2.7	592	0.2
Asian/Pacific Islander	478	0.4	814	0.6	70.3	1,289	0.5
Other	83	0.1	203	0.2	144.6	241	0.1
Hispanic Origin[2]	611	0.5	552	0.4	-9.7	1,195	0.4

Note: (1) Metropolitan Statistical Area - see Appendix A for areas included;
(2) people of Hispanic origin can be of any race
Source: 1980/1990 Census of Housing and Population, Summary Tape File 3C

Ancestry

Area	German	Irish	English	Italian	U.S.	French	Polish	Dutch
City	42.5	18.3	15.1	1.4	6.4	3.8	0.7	2.0
MSA[1]	43.7	18.9	15.8	1.4	7.7	3.7	0.8	2.1
U.S.	23.3	15.6	13.1	5.9	5.3	4.2	3.8	2.5

Note: Figures are percentages and include persons that reported multiple ancestry (eg. if a person
reported being Irish and Italian, they were included in both columns); (1) Metropolitan Statistical Area -
see Appendix A for areas included
Source: 1990 Census of Population and Housing, Summary Tape File 3C

Age

Area	Median Age (Years)	Age Distribution (%) Under 5	Under 18	18-24	25-44	45-64	65+	80+
City	34.5	6.9	23.0	10.3	30.9	18.7	17.1	4.2
MSA[1]	34.0	7.0	25.4	9.5	31.8	19.3	14.0	3.2
U.S.	32.9	7.3	25.6	10.5	32.6	18.7	12.5	2.8

Note: (1) Metropolitan Statistical Area - see Appendix A for areas included
Source: 1990 Census of Population and Housing, Summary Tape File 3C

Male/Female Ratio

Area	Number of males per 100 females (all ages)	Number of males per 100 females (18 years old+)
City	86.6	82.2
MSA[1]	91.5	87.3
U.S.	95.0	91.9

Note: (1) Metropolitan Statistical Area - see Appendix A for areas included
Source: 1990 Census of Population, General Population Characteristics

INCOME

Per Capita/Median/Average Income

Area	Per Capita ($)	Median Household ($)	Average Household ($)
City	12,564	22,936	29,445
MSA[1]	13,265	27,229	33,710
U.S.	14,420	30,056	38,453

Note: all figures are for 1989; (1) Metropolitan Statistical Area - see Appendix A for areas included
Source: 1990 Census of Population and Housing, Summary Tape File 3C

Household Income Distribution by Race

Income ($)	City (%)					U.S. (%)				
	Total	White	Black	Other	Hisp.[1]	Total	White	Black	Other	Hisp.[1]
Less than 5,000	8.3	7.0	20.9	14.5	11.3	6.2	4.8	15.2	8.6	8.8
5,000 - 9,999	13.0	12.4	19.8	9.0	28.4	9.3	8.6	14.2	9.9	11.1
10,000 - 14,999	11.3	11.2	11.9	17.0	8.3	8.8	8.5	11.0	9.8	11.0
15,000 - 24,999	21.1	21.4	18.9	14.9	16.2	17.5	17.3	18.9	18.5	20.5
25,000 - 34,999	16.9	17.5	10.7	13.8	20.1	15.8	16.1	14.2	15.4	16.4
35,000 - 49,999	16.3	16.9	9.6	11.5	6.4	17.9	18.6	13.3	16.1	16.0
50,000 - 74,999	9.1	9.4	6.2	7.9	5.4	15.0	15.8	9.3	13.4	11.1
75,000 - 99,999	1.9	1.9	1.4	4.8	3.9	5.1	5.5	2.6	4.7	3.1
100,000+	2.2	2.3	0.6	6.6	0.0	4.4	4.8	1.3	3.7	1.9

Note: all figures are for 1989; (1) people of Hispanic origin can be of any race
Source: 1990 Census of Population and Housing, Summary Tape File 3C

Effective Buying Income

Area	Per Capita ($)	Median Household ($)	Average Household ($)
City	14,699	26,934	34,510
MSA[1]	15,956	33,145	40,460
U.S.	15,444	33,201	41,849

Note: data as of 1/1/97; (1) Metropolitan Statistical Area - see Appendix A for areas included
Source: Standard Rate & Data Service, Newspaper Advertising Source, 2/98

Effective Household Buying Income Distribution

Area	% of Households Earning						
	$10,000 -$19,999	$20,000 -$34,999	$35,000 -$49,999	$50,000 -$74,999	$75,000 -$99,000	$100,000 -$124,999	$125,000 and up
City	20.5	25.9	17.5	14.1	3.1	1.0	1.6
MSA[1]	16.8	23.5	18.6	19.6	5.6	1.8	1.8
U.S.	16.5	23.4	18.3	18.2	6.4	2.1	2.4

Note: data as of 1/1/97; (1) Metropolitan Statistical Area - see Appendix A for areas included
Source: Standard Rate & Data Service, Newspaper Advertising Source, 2/98

Poverty Rates by Race and Age

Area	Total (%)	By Race (%)				By Age (%)		
		White	Black	Other	Hisp.[2]	Under 5 years old	Under 18 years old	65 years and over
City	14.6	12.1	37.4	21.8	15.7	25.5	21.7	12.5
MSA[1]	11.4	9.8	36.6	14.8	16.8	18.3	15.0	12.4
U.S.	13.1	9.8	29.5	23.1	25.3	20.1	18.3	12.8

Note: figures show the percent of people living below the poverty line in 1989. The average poverty threshold was $12,674 for a family of four in 1989; (1) Metropolitan Statistical Area - see Appendix A for areas included; (2) people of Hispanic origin can be of any race
Source: 1990 Census of Population and Housing, Summary Tape File 3C

EMPLOYMENT

Labor Force and Employment

Area	Civilian Labor Force			Workers Employed		
	Dec. '95	Dec. '96	% Chg.	Dec. '95	Dec. '96	% Chg.
City	66,141	67,551	2.1	63,615	64,767	1.8
MSA[1]	152,268	155,119	1.9	146,505	149,547	2.1
U.S.	134,583,000	136,742,000	1.6	127,903,000	130,785,000	2.3

Note: Data is not seasonally adjusted and covers workers 16 years of age and older;
(1) Metropolitan Statistical Area - see Appendix A for areas included
Source: Bureau of Labor Statistics, http://stats.bls.gov

Unemployment Rate

Area	1997											
	Jan.	Feb.	Mar.	Apr.	May	Jun.	Jul.	Aug.	Sep.	Oct.	Nov.	Dec.
City	4.7	4.5	4.8	4.9	4.4	4.4	4.9	4.5	4.3	4.9	4.3	4.1
MSA[1]	4.5	4.2	4.5	4.3	3.9	4.1	4.8	4.0	3.8	4.1	3.7	3.6
U.S.	5.9	5.7	5.5	4.8	4.7	5.2	5.0	4.8	4.7	4.4	4.3	4.4

Note: Data is not seasonally adjusted and covers workers 16 years of age and older; All figures are percentages; (1) Metropolitan Statistical Area - see Appendix A for areas included
Source: Bureau of Labor Statistics, http://stats.bls.gov

Employment by Industry

Sector	MSA[1]		U.S.
	Number of Employees	Percent of Total	Percent of Total
Services	43,500	28.1	29.0
Retail Trade	31,100	20.1	18.5
Government	14,300	9.2	16.1
Manufacturing	31,900	20.6	15.0
Finance/Insurance/Real Estate	7,500	4.9	5.7
Wholesale Trade	8,500	5.5	5.4
Transportation/Public Utilities	7,000	4.5	5.3
Construction	9,500	6.1	4.5
Mining	1,300	0.8	0.5

Note: Figures cover non-farm employment as of 12/97 and are not seasonally adjusted;
(1) Metropolitan Statistical Area - see Appendix A for areas included
Source: Bureau of Labor Statistics, http://stats.bls.gov

Employment by Occupation

Occupation Category	City (%)	MSA[1] (%)	U.S. (%)
White Collar	54.5	53.4	58.1
Executive/Admin./Management	9.9	10.2	12.3
Professional	12.0	12.0	14.1
Technical & Related Support	4.0	4.0	3.7
Sales	13.0	12.1	11.8
Administrative Support/Clerical	15.7	15.0	16.3
Blue Collar	28.5	31.3	26.2
Precision Production/Craft/Repair	10.3	12.6	11.3
Machine Operators/Assem./Insp.	9.0	9.2	6.8
Transportation/Material Movers	4.6	4.8	4.1
Cleaners/Helpers/Laborers	4.6	4.6	3.9
Services	16.2	13.7	13.2
Farming/Forestry/Fishing	0.8	1.6	2.5

Note: figures cover employed persons 16 years old and over;
(1) Metropolitan Statistical Area - see Appendix A for areas included
Source: 1990 Census of Population and Housing, Summary Tape File 3C

Occupational Employment Projections: 1994 - 2005

Projections not available at time of publication.

Average Wages

Occupation	Wage	Occupation	Wage
Professional/Technical/Clerical	$/Week	**Health/Protective Services**	$/Week
Accountants III	837	Corrections Officers	378
Attorneys III	-	Firefighters	542
Budget Analysts III	-	Nurses, Licensed Practical II	418
Buyers/Contracting Specialists II	592	Nurses, Registered II	588
Clerks, Accounting III	351	Nursing Assistants II	297
Clerks, General III	337	Police Officers I	519
Computer Operators II	356	**Hourly Workers**	$/Hour
Computer Programmers II	521	Forklift Operators	9.38
Drafters II	522	General Maintenance Workers	8.76
Engineering Technicians III	-	Guards I	-
Engineering Technicians, Civil III	-	Janitors	6.67
Engineers III	-	Maintenance Electricians	14.89
Key Entry Operators I	258	Maintenance Electronics Techs II	18.36
Personnel Assistants III	-	Maintenance Machinists	15.26
Personnel Specialists III	736	Maintenance Mechanics, Machinery	18.08
Secretaries III	530	Material Handling Laborers	-
Switchboard Operator-Receptionist	292	Motor Vehicle Mechanics	11.55
Systems Analysts II	903	Shipping/Receiving Clerks	9.95
Systems Analysts Supervisor/Mgr II	-	Tool and Die Makers	-
Tax Collectors II	-	Truckdrivers, Tractor Trailer	15.33
Word Processors II	-	Warehouse Specialists	10.59

Note: Wage data includes full-time workers only for 8/94 and cover the Metropolitan Statistical Area (see Appendix A for areas included). Dashes indicate that data was not available.
Source: Bureau of Labor Statistics, Occupational Compensation Survey

TAXES

Major State and Local Tax Rates

State Corp. Income (%)	State Personal Income (%)	Residential Property (effective rate per $100)	Sales & Use		State Gasoline (cents/ gallon)	State Cigarette (cents/ 20-pack)
			State (%)	Local (%)		
7.9[a]	3.4	n/a	5.0	None	15	15.5

Note: Personal/corporate income tax rates as of 1/97. Sales, gasoline and cigarette tax rates as of 1/98; (a) Consists of 3.4% on income from sources within the state plus a 4.5% supplemental income tax
Source: Federation of Tax Administrators, www.taxadmin.org; Washington D.C. Department of Finance and Revenue, Tax Rates and Tax Burdens in the District of Columbia: A Nationwide Comparison, June 1997; Chamber of Commerce

Total Taxes Per Capita and as a Percent of Income

Area	Per Capita Income ($)	Per Capita Taxes ($)			Taxes as Pct. of Income (%)		
		Total	Federal	State/ Local	Total	Federal	State/ Local
Indiana	24,003	8,243	5,717	2,526	34.3	23.8	10.5
U.S.	26,187	9,205	6,127	3,078	35.2	23.4	11.8

Note: Figures are for 1997
Source: Tax Foundation, Web Site, www.taxfoundation.org

COMMERCIAL REAL ESTATE

Data not available at time of publication.

COMMERCIAL UTILITIES

Typical Monthly Electric Bills

Area	Commercial Service ($/month)		Industrial Service ($/month)	
	12 kW demand 1,500 kWh	100 kW demand 30,000 kWh	1,000 kW demand 400,000 kWh	20,000 kW demand 10,000,000 kWh
City	131	1,627	17,891	404,412
U.S.	162	2,360	25,590	545,677

Note: Based on rates in effect July 1, 1997
Source: Edison Electric Institute, Typical Residential, Commercial and Industrial Bills, Summer 1997

TRANSPORTATION

Transportation Statistics

Avg. travel time to work (min.)	15.9
Interstate highways	I-164 connecting with I-64
Bus lines	
In-city	Metropolitan Evanvsille Transit System
Inter-city	6
Passenger air service	
Airport	Evansville Regional
Airlines	8
Aircraft departures	n/a
Enplaned passengers	n/a
Rail service	No Amtrak Service
Motor freight carriers	50
Major waterways/ports	Ohio River

Source: OAG, Business Travel Planner, Summer 1997; Editor & Publisher Market Guide, 1998; FAA Airport Activity Statistics, 1996; Amtrak National Time Table, Northeast Timetable, Fall/Winter 1997-98; 1990 Census of Population and Housing, STF 3C; Chamber of Commerce/Economic Development 1997; Jane's Urban Transport Systems 1997-98; Transit Fact Book 1997

Means of Transportation to Work

Area	Car/Truck/Van		Public Transportation			Bicycle	Walked	Other Means	Worked at Home
	Drove Alone	Car-pooled	Bus	Subway	Railroad				
City	80.7	11.3	1.6	0.0	0.0	0.4	3.7	0.7	1.6
MSA[1]	82.3	11.3	0.8	0.0	0.0	0.2	2.6	0.6	2.0
U.S.	73.2	13.4	3.0	1.5	0.5	0.4	3.9	1.2	3.0

Note: figures shown are percentages and only include workers 16 years old and over; (1) Metropolitan Statistical Area - see Appendix A for areas included
Source: 1990 Census of Population and Housing, Summary Tape File 3C

BUSINESSES

Major Business Headquarters

Company Name	1997 Rankings	
	Fortune 500	Forbes 500
Atlas World Group	-	450

Note: Companies listed are located in the city; Dashes indicate no ranking
Fortune 500: companies that produce a 10-K are ranked 1 - 500 based on 1996 revenue
Forbes 500: private companies are ranked 1 - 500 based on 1996 revenue
Source: Forbes 12/1/97; Fortune 4/28/97

HOTELS & MOTELS

Hotels/Motels

Area	Hotels/ Motels	Rooms	Luxury-Level Hotels/Motels		Average Minimum Rates ($)		
			♦♦♦♦	♦♦♦♦♦	♦♦	♦♦♦	♦♦♦♦
City	12	1,648	0	0	n/a	n/a	n/a
Airport	2	348	0	0	n/a	n/a	n/a
Total	14	1,996	0	0	n/a	n/a	n/a

Note: n/a not available; Classifications range from one diamond (budget properties with basic amenities) to five diamond (luxury properties with the finest service, rooms and facilities).
Source: OAG, Business Travel Planner, Summer 1997

CONVENTION CENTERS

Major Convention Centers

Center Name	Meeting Rooms	Exhibit Space (sf)
National Guard Armory	n/a	15,000

Note: n/a not available
Source: Trade Shows Worldwide 1997

Living Environment

COST OF LIVING

Cost of Living Index

Composite Index	Housing	Utilities	Groceries	Health Care	Trans- portation	Misc. Goods/ Services
97.5	97.8	91.5	102.8	91.6	96.3	97.6

Note: U.S. = 100
Source: ACCRA, Cost of Living Index, 3rd Quarter 1997

HOUSING

Median Home Prices and Housing Affordability

Area	Median Price[2] 3rd Qtr. 1997 ($)	HOI[3] 3rd Qtr. 1997	Afford- ability Rank[4]
MSA[1]	n/a	n/a	n/a
U.S.	127,000	63.7	--

Note: (1) Metropolitan Statistical Area - see Appendix A for areas included; (2) U.S. figures calculated from the sales of 625,000 new and existing homes in 195 markets; (3) Housing Opportunity Index - percent of homes sold that were within the reach of the median income household at the prevailing mortgage interest rate; (4) Rank is from 1-195 with 1 being most affordable; n/a not available
Source: National Association of Home Builders, Housing Opportunity Index, 3rd Quarter 1997

Average New Home Price

Area	Price ($)
City	136,150
U.S.	135,710

Note: Figures are based on a new home with 1,800 sq. ft. of living area on an 8,000 sq. ft. lot.
Source: ACCRA, Cost of Living Index, 3rd Quarter 1997

Average Apartment Rent

Area	Rent ($/mth)
City	440
U.S.	569

Note: Figures are based on an unfurnished two bedroom, 1-1/2 or 2 bath apartment, approximately 950 sq. ft. in size, excluding all utilities except water
Source: ACCRA, Cost of Living Index, 3rd Quarter 1997

RESIDENTIAL UTILITIES

Average Residential Utility Costs

Area	All Electric ($/mth)	Part Electric ($/mth)	Other Energy ($/mth)	Phone ($/mth)
City	--	52.15	38.68	21.36
U.S.	109.40	55.25	43.64	19.48

Source: ACCRA, Cost of Living Index, 3rd Quarter 1997

HEALTH CARE

Average Health Care Costs

Area	Hospital ($/day)	Doctor ($/visit)	Dentist ($/visit)
City	374.67	44.20	54.20
U.S.	392.91	48.76	60.84

Note: Hospital - based on a semi-private room. Doctor - based on a general practitioner's routine exam of an established patient. Dentist - based on adult teeth cleaning and periodic oral exam.
Source: ACCRA, Cost of Living Index, 3rd Quarter 1997

Distribution of Office-Based Physicians

Area	Family/Gen. Practitioners	Specialists		
		Medical	Surgical	Other
MSA[1]	104	145	145	131

Note: Data as of 12/31/96; (1) Metropolitan Statistical Area - see Appendix A for areas included
Source: American Medical Assn., Physician Characteristics & Distribution in the U.S., 1997-1998

Hospitals

Evansville has 3 general medical and surgical hospitals, 1 psychiatric, 1 rehabilitation. *AHA Guide to the Healthcare Field 1997-98*

EDUCATION

Public School District Statistics

District Name	Num. Sch.	Enroll.	Classroom Teachers[1]	Pupils per Teacher	Minority Pupils (%)	Current Exp.[2] ($/pupil)
Evansville-Vanderburgh Sch Cor	40	23,713	1,408	16.8	15.3	5,975

Note: Data covers the 1995-1996 school year unless otherwise noted; (1) Excludes teachers reported as working in school district offices rather than in schools; (2) Based on 1993-94 enrollment collected by the Census Bureau, not the enrollment figure shown in column 3; SD = School District; ISD = Independent School District; n/a not available
Source: National Center for Education Statistics, Common Core of Data Survey; Bureau of the Census

Educational Quality

School District	Education Quotient[1]	Graduate Outcome[2]	Community Index[3]	Resource Index[4]
Evansville-Vanderburgh	105.0	94.0	86.0	134.0

Note: Nearly 1,000 secondary school districts were rated in terms of educational quality. The scores range from a low of 50 to a high of 150; (1) Average of the Graduate Outcome, Community and Resource indexes; (2) Based on graduation rates and college board scores (SAT/ACT); (3) Based on the surrounding community's average level of education and the area's average income level; (4) Based on teacher salaries, per-pupil expenditures and student-teacher ratios.
Source: Expansion Management, Ratings Issue 1997

Educational Attainment by Race

Area	High School Graduate (%)					Bachelor's Degree (%)				
	Total	White	Black	Other	Hisp.[2]	Total	White	Black	Other	Hisp.[2]
City	72.4	73.3	61.3	73.6	61.4	14.6	15.1	7.0	34.0	13.9
MSA[1]	75.1	75.8	61.1	77.4	72.3	14.8	15.1	7.5	37.0	20.2
U.S.	75.2	77.9	63.1	60.4	49.8	20.3	21.5	11.4	19.4	9.2

Note: figures shown cover persons 25 years old and over; (1) Metropolitan Statistical Area - see Appendix A for areas included; (2) people of Hispanic origin can be of any race
Source: 1990 Census of Population and Housing, Summary Tape File 3C

School Enrollment by Type

Area	Preprimary				Elementary/High School			
	Public		Private		Public		Private	
	Enrollment	%	Enrollment	%	Enrollment	%	Enrollment	%
City	1,110	52.2	1,017	47.8	16,003	85.9	2,621	14.1
MSA[1]	2,844	55.3	2,299	44.7	41,082	86.9	6,197	13.1
U.S.	2,679,029	59.5	1,824,256	40.5	38,379,689	90.2	4,187,099	9.8

Note: figures shown cover persons 3 years old and over;
(1) Metropolitan Statistical Area - see Appendix A for areas included
Source: 1990 Census of Population and Housing, Summary Tape File 3C

School Enrollment by Race

Area	Preprimary (%)				Elementary/High School (%)			
	White	Black	Other	Hisp.[1]	White	Black	Other	Hisp.[1]
City	83.7	14.2	2.0	1.1	83.5	14.9	1.6	0.5
MSA[2]	90.8	7.7	1.5	0.9	91.1	7.8	1.2	0.5
U.S.	80.4	12.5	7.1	7.8	74.1	15.6	10.3	12.5

Note: figures shown cover persons 3 years old and over; (1) people of Hispanic origin can be of any race; (2) Metropolitan Statistical Area - see Appendix A for areas included
Source: 1990 Census of Population and Housing, Summary Tape File 3C

SAT/ACT Scores

Area/District	1997 SAT				1997 ACT	
	Percent of Graduates Tested (%)	Average Math Score	Average Verbal Score	Average Combined Score	Percent of Graduates Tested (%)	Average Composite Score
Evansville-Vanderburgh SD	34	519	509	1,028	50	20.5
State	57	497	494	991	19	21.2
U.S.	42	511	505	1,016	36	21.0

Note: Math and verbal SAT scores are out of a possible 800; ACT scores are out of a possible 36
Caution: Comparing or ranking states/cities on the basis of SAT/ACT scores alone is invalid and strongly discouraged by the The College Board and The American College Testing Program as students who take the tests are self-selected and do not represent the entire student population.
Source: Evansville-Vanderburgh School Corporation, Psychological Services & Testing, 1997; American College Testing Program, 1997; College Board, 1997

Classroom Teacher Salaries in Public Schools

District	B.A. Degree		M.A. Degree		Ph.D. Degree	
	Min. ($)	Max ($)	Min. ($)	Max. ($)	Min. ($)	Max. ($)
Evansville	25,292	34,782	26,184	47,423	28,630	49,869
Average[1]	26,120	39,270	28,175	44,667	31,643	49,825

Note: Salaries are for 1996-1997; (1) Based on all school districts covered
Source: American Federation of Teachers (unpublished data)

Higher Education

Two-Year Colleges		Four-Year Colleges		Medical Schools	Law Schools	Voc/ Tech
Public	Private	Public	Private			
1	1	1	1	0	0	10

Source: College Blue Book, Occupational Education 1997; Medical School Admission Requirements, 1998-99; Peterson's Guide to Two-Year Colleges, 1997; Peterson's Guide to Four-Year Colleges, 1997; Barron's Guide to Law Schools 1997

MAJOR EMPLOYERS

Major Employers

Mead Johnson & Co.	Deaconess Hospital
St. Mary's Medical Center	Welborn Memorial Baptist Hospital
Welborn Clinic	BPC Holding Corp. (plastics)
American General Finance	Berry Plastics Corp.
CNB Bancshares	Guardian Automotive Trim
Keller-Crescent Co. (advertising)	Anchor Industries (canvas products)
Evansville Courier	Ira E. Clark Detective Agency

Note: companies listed are located in the city
Source: Dun's Business Rankings 1997; Ward's Business Directory, 1997

PUBLIC SAFETY

Crime Rate

Area	All Crimes	Violent Crimes				Property Crimes		
		Murder	Forcible Rape	Robbery	Aggrav. Assault	Burglary	Larceny -Theft	Motor Vehicle Theft
City	5,633.1	5.3	31.2	126.3	430.6	1,094.7	3,600.5	344.6
Suburbs[1]	n/a	n/a	n/a	n/a	n/a	n/a	n/a	n/a
MSA[2]	n/a	n/a	n/a	n/a	n/a	n/a	n/a	n/a
U.S.	5,078.9	7.4	36.1	202.4	388.2	943.0	2,975.9	525.9

Note: Crime rate is the number of crimes per 100,000 pop.; (1) defined as all areas within the MSA but located outside the central city; (2) Metropolitan Statistical Area - see Appendix A for areas incl.
Source: FBI Uniform Crime Reports 1996

RECREATION

Culture and Recreation

Museums	Symphony Orchestras	Opera Companies	Dance Companies	Professional Theatres	Zoos	Pro Sports Teams
4	2	0	1	1	1	0

Source: International Directory of the Performing Arts, 1996; Official Museum Directory, 1998; Chamber of Commerce/Economic Development 1997

Library System

The Evansville-Vanderburgh County Public Library has seven branches, holdings of 767,947 volumes and a budget of $5,707,447 (1995). *American Library Directory, 1997-1998*

MEDIA

Newspapers

Name	Type	Freq.	Distribution	Circulation
The Evansville Courier	n/a	7x/wk	Area	64,500
The Evansville Press	n/a	6x/wk	Local	28,073
Message	Religious	1x/wk	Area	7,500

Note: Includes newspapers with circulations of 500 or more located in the city; n/a not available
Source: Burrelle's Media Directory, 1998 Edition

AM Radio Stations

Call Letters	Freq. (kHz)	Target Audience	Station Format	Music Format
WSWI	820	General	M/N/S	Alternative/Big Band
WGBF	1280	General	S	n/a
WVHI	1330	n/a	M/N	Christian
WJPS	1400	n/a	M	Oldies

Note: Stations included broadcast in the Evansville metro area; n/a not available
Station Format: E = Educational; M = Music; N = News; S = Sports; T = Talk
Source: Burrelle's Media Directory, 1998 Edition

FM Radio Stations

Call Letters	Freq. (mHz)	Target Audience	Station Format	Music Format
WNIN	88.3	n/a	M/N	Classical
WPSR	90.7	General	E/M/S	n/a
WUEV	91.5	n/a	M/N/S/T	n/a
WJPS	93.5	General	M/N/S	Oldies
WIKY	104.1	General	M/N/S	Adult Contemporary
WYNG	105.3	General	M	Country

Note: Stations included broadcast in the Evansville metro area; n/a not available
Station Format: E = Educational; M = Music; N = News; S = Sports; T = Talk
Source: Burrelle's Media Directory, 1998 Edition

Television Stations

Name	Ch.	Affiliation	Type	Owner
WTVW	7	Fox	Commercial	Petracom Inc.
WNIN	9	PBS	Non-Commercial	Tri-State Public Teleplex Inc.
WFIE	14	NBC	Commercial	Cosmos Broadcasting Corporation
WEHT	25	ABC	Commercial	Gilmore Broadcasting Corporation
WEVV	44	CBS	Commercial	WEVV Inc.
WAZ	52	UPN/WB	Commercial	South Central Communications Corp.

Note: Stations included broadcast in the Evansville metro area
Source: Burrelle's Media Directory, 1998 Edition

CLIMATE

Average and Extreme Temperatures

Temperature	Jan	Feb	Mar	Apr	May	Jun	Jul	Aug	Sep	Oct	Nov	Dec	Ann
Extreme High (°F)	71	72	85	89	93	102	104	102	100	90	81	74	104
Average High (°F)	35	39	50	63	73	82	85	84	78	66	51	39	62
Average Temp. (°F)	27	31	41	52	63	72	76	73	67	55	43	31	53
Average Low (°F)	18	22	31	41	52	61	65	63	55	44	33	23	42
Extreme Low (°F)	-22	-21	-7	18	28	39	48	41	34	20	-2	-23	-23

Note: Figures cover the years 1948-1990
Source: National Climatic Data Center, International Station Meteorological Climate Summary, 3/95

Average Precipitation/Snowfall/Humidity

Precip./Humidity	Jan	Feb	Mar	Apr	May	Jun	Jul	Aug	Sep	Oct	Nov	Dec	Ann
Avg. Precip. (in.)	2.8	2.5	3.6	3.6	4.0	3.9	4.3	3.4	2.9	2.6	3.3	3.3	40.2
Avg. Snowfall (in.)	7	6	4	1	Tr	0	0	0	0	Tr	2	5	25
Avg. Rel. Hum. 7am (%)	81	81	79	77	79	80	84	87	87	85	83	83	82
Avg. Rel. Hum. 4pm (%)	68	64	59	53	53	53	56	56	53	53	63	70	59

Note: Figures cover the years 1948-1990; Tr = Trace amounts (<0.05 in. of rain; <0.5 in. of snow)
Source: National Climatic Data Center, International Station Meteorological Climate Summary, 3/95

Weather Conditions

Temperature			Daytime Sky			Precipitation		
10°F & below	32°F & below	90°F & above	Clear	Partly cloudy	Cloudy	0.01 inch or more precip.	0.1 inch or more snow/ice	Thunder-storms
19	119	19	83	128	154	127	24	43

Note: Figures are average number of days per year and covers the years 1948-1990
Source: National Climatic Data Center, International Station Meteorological Climate Summary, 3/95

AIR & WATER QUALITY

Maximum Pollutant Concentrations

	Particulate Matter (ug/m^3)	Carbon Monoxide (ppm)	Sulfur Dioxide (ppm)	Nitrogen Dioxide (ppm)	Ozone (ppm)	Lead (ug/m^3)
MSA[1] Level	59	4	0.097	0.017	0.12	n/a
NAAQS[2]	150	9	0.140	0.053	0.12	1.50
Met NAAQS?	Yes	Yes	Yes	Yes	Yes	n/a

Note: (1) Metropolitan Statistical Area - see Appendix A for areas included; (2) National Ambient Air Quality Standards; ppm = parts per million; ug/m^3 = micrograms per cubic meter; n/a not available
Source: EPA, National Air Quality and Emissions Trends Report, 1996

Pollutant Standards Index

Data not available. *EPA, National Air Quality and Emissions Trends Report, 1996*

Drinking Water

Water System Name	Pop. Served	Primary Water Source Type	Number of Violations in Fiscal Year 1997	Type of Violation/ Contaminants
Evansville Water Dept	150,000	Purchased surface	None	None

Note: Data as of January 16, 1998
Source: EPA, Office of Ground Water and Drinking Water, Safe Drinking Water Information System

Evansville tap water is alkaline, hard and fluoridated.
Editor & Publisher Market Guide, 1998

Fort Wayne, Indiana

Background

115 miles northeast of Indianapolis at the confluence of the St. Marys and St. Joseph Rivers which form the Maumee River lies Fort Wayne. The waters, spanned by 21 bridges, divide the town into three parts.

Once the stronghold of the Miami tribe, the place was prominent in frontier history. The Miami Native Americans ruled the lower peninsula region, fighting against the Iroquois who had been armed by the English colonists. Later, the tribe established itself in the Wabash Valley and built a village at the Lakeside district in Fort Wayne. They continued to side with the British during the American Revolution. After the revolution, President Washington ordered armies into the center of the Miami Territory to stop the Miami War Parties, which had been encouraged to attack the new nation by the British. After Chief Little Turtle, one of the most feared and respected tribal leaders, defeated the army of General Arthur St. Clair, Washington sought the help of General "Mad" Anthony Wayne who succeeded in defeating the rebellious tribes. Wayne marched on Miamitown and built the first American fort there. When the fort was turned over to Colonel John Hamtramck on October 21, 1794, the Colonel immediately changed the name to Fort Wayne.

Fort Wayne's industrial growth began with the building of the Wabash and Erie Canal in the 1830's and was further stimulated in the 1850s when the railway came.

Although the city is in a rich dairy and farming area which raises cattle and poultry, it is primarily a diversified industrial center. Heavy truck, copper wire and diamond dies are its primary manufactures. Its manufacturing fortunes have benefited from a General Motors Truck & Bus group plant, with more than 2,000 employes. It has attracted manufacturers of fans, piston, gas pumps and weatherstripping for autos.

The land surrounding the city is generally level to the south and east. To the west and southwest, the terrain is somewhat rolling, while to the north and northwest of the city, it becomes quite hilly.

The climate is influenced to a certain extent by the Great Lakes. It does not differ greatly from the climates of other midwestern cities on the same general latitude.

The distribution of rain is fairly constant throughout the warmer months, with somewhat larger amounts falling in late spring and early summer. Damaging hailstorms occur approximately twice a year. Severe flooding has also occurred in the area and snow generally covers the ground for about 30 days during the winter months. Heavy snowstorms are infrequent. With the exception of considerable cloudiness during the winter, Fort Wayne enjoys a good Midwestern average for sunshine.

General Rankings and Evaluative Comments

■ Fort Wayne was ranked #75 out of 300 cities by *Money's* 1997 "Survey of the Best Places to Live." Criteria used: health services, crime, economy, housing, education, transportation, weather, leisure and the arts. The city was ranked #125 in 1996 and #134 in 1995. *Money, July 1997; Money, September 1996; Money, September 1995*

■ *Ladies Home Journal* ranked America's 200 largest cities based on the qualities women care about most. Fort Wayne ranked 99 out of 200. Criteria: low crime rate, good public schools, well-paying jobs, quality health and child care, the presence of women in government, proportion of women-owned businesses, size of the wage gap with men, local economy, divorce rates, the ratio of single men to single women, whether there are laws that require at least the same number of public toilets for women as men, and the probability of good hair days. *Ladies Home Journal, November 1997*

■ Fort Wayne was ranked #88 out of 219 cities in terms of children's health, safety, and economic well-being. Criteria: total population, percent population change, birth rate, child immunization rate, infant mortality rate, percent low birth weight infants, percent of births to teens, physician-to-population ratio, student-to-teacher ratio, dropout rate, unemployment rate, median family income, percent of children in poverty, violent and property crime rates, number of juvenile arrests for violent crimes as a percent of the total crime index, number of days with pollution standard index (PSI) over 100, pounds toxic releases per 1,000 people and number of superfund sites. *Zero Population Growth, Children's Environmental Index 1997*

■ Lincoln National Corp., headquartered in Fort Wayne, is among the "100 Best Companies for Working Mothers." Criteria: pay compared with competition, opportunities for women to advance, support for child care, flexible work schedules and family-friendly benefits. *Working Mother, October 1997*

■ According to *Working Mother,* "Indiana has come up with some innovative ways to tackle the tough issue of how to pay for child care. About two thirds of the state's 92 counties are now drawing up plans to expand and improve child care with help from private businesses. This new effort grew out of former governor Evan Bayh's Step Ahead initiative, which got all of Indiana's counties to draw up comprehensive plans for child care and other children's services. The program was developed in cooperation with the Child Care Action Campaign, a national advocacy group. Each county is now developing its own approach, with some interesting results....

At the same time, however, Indiana officials weakened rules for family child care, allowing providers to care for larger groups of children than in the past. Some caregivers can now take in as many as 16 kids at a time. State lawmakers also vetoed a proposal to require family child care providers to have six hours of annual training." *Working Mother, July/August 1997*

Business Environment

STATE ECONOMY

State Economic Profile

"Indiana's economy is well past its cyclical peak....retail sales growth trails the national pace, and the number of bankruptcy filings is at a record high.

Indiana is the nation's largest producer of steel, accounting for nearly one-quarter of the nation's output....

Indiana legislators reduced the auto excise tax last year. This revenue loss will be partly offset by revenues from Indiana's eleven casinos. Indiana has accumulated a $1.6 billion surplus by resisting pressures for additional tax cuts and spending increases. However, there are several initiatives under review at both the state and county levels to increase wage taxes from the current 3.4% to 5.4%. Another proposal would eliminate business inventory taxes.

Population growth weakened slightly in 1996 to under 0.8% as migration declined slightly, due in part to the closure of Fort Benjamin Harrison. However, Indiana still enjoys strong, positive domestic net in-migration, in contrast to its three Great Lakes neighbors. Indiana's relatively optimistic economic outlook should provide for long-run population growth just short of the national average. This will support expansion of the state's local and population-dependent industries, such as retail trade and housing.

...Compared with neighboring manufacturing states, Indiana enjoys a significant comparative advantage in low costs. Combined with generous tax incentives, Indiana's low costs will enable the state to attract firms relocating from higher cost states or seeking to expand. However, the state is at risk due to its high dependence on traditional durable manufacturing industries, particularly steel and autos. Indiana will be an average performer long term."
National Association of Realtors, Economic Profiles: The Fifty States, July 1997

IMPORTS/EXPORTS

Total Export Sales

Area	1993 ($000)	1994 ($000)	1995 ($000)	1996 ($000)	% Chg. 1993-96	% Chg. 1995-96
MSA[1]	640,584	770,882	1,029,423	991,375	54.8	-3.7
U.S.	464,858,354	512,415,609	583,030,524	622,827,063	34.0	6.8

Note: (1) Metropolitan Statistical Area - see Appendix A for areas included
Source: U.S. Department of Commerce, International Trade Association, Metropolitan Area Exports: An Export Performance Report on Over 250 U.S. Cities, October 1997

Imports/Exports by Port

Type	Cargo Value 1995 (US$mil.)	1996 (US$mil.)	% Change 1995-1996	Share of U.S. Total 1995 (%)	1996 (%)
Imports	0	0	0	0	0
Exports	0	0	0	0	0

Source: Global Trade Information Services, WaterBorne Trade Atlas 1997

CITY FINANCES

City Government Finances

Component	FY92 ($000)	FY92 (per capita $)
Revenue	112,214	589.57
Expenditure	113,447	596.04
Debt Outstanding	80,260	421.68
Cash & Securities	34,599	181.78

Source: U.S. Bureau of the Census, City Government Finances: 1991-92

City Government Revenue by Source

Source	FY92 ($000)	FY92 (per capita $)	FY92 (%)
From Federal Government	2,470	12.98	2.2
From State Governments	16,001	84.07	14.3
From Local Governments	1,219	6.40	1.1
Property Taxes	39,478	207.42	35.2
General Sales Taxes	0	0.00	0.0
Selective Sales Taxes	0	0.00	0.0
Income Taxes	4,655	24.46	4.1
Current Charges	16,945	89.03	15.1
Utility/Liquor Store	19,482	102.36	17.4
Employee Retirement[1]	4,633	24.34	4.1
Other	7,331	38.52	6.5

Note: (1) Excludes "city contributions," classified as "nonrevenue," intragovernmental transfers.
Source: U.S. Bureau of the Census, City Government Finances: 1991-92

City Government Expenditures by Function

Function	FY92 ($000)	FY92 (per capita $)	FY92 (%)
Educational Services	0	0.00	0.0
Employee Retirement[1]	8,217	43.17	7.2
Environment/Housing	23,909	125.62	21.1
Government Administration	5,149	27.05	4.5
Interest on General Debt	4,048	21.27	3.6
Public Safety	23,407	122.98	20.6
Social Services	777	4.08	0.7
Transportation	11,888	62.46	10.5
Utility/Liquor Store	13,296	69.86	11.7
Other	22,756	119.56	20.1

Note: (1) Payments to beneficiaries including withdrawal of contributions.
Source: U.S. Bureau of the Census, City Government Finances: 1991-92

Municipal Bond Ratings

Area	Moody's	S & P
Fort Wayne	Aa2	AA-

Note: n/a not available; n/r not rated
Source: Moody's Bond Record, 2/98; Statistical Abstract of the U.S., 1997;
Governing Magazine, 9/97, 3/98

POPULATION

Population Growth

Area	1980	1990	% Chg. 1980-90	July 1996 Estimate	% Chg. 1990-96
City	172,196	173,072	0.5	184,783	6.8
MSA[1]	354,156	363,811	2.7	475,299	30.6
U.S.	226,545,805	248,765,170	9.8	265,179,411	6.6

Note: (1) Metropolitan Statistical Area - see Appendix A for areas included
Source: 1980/1990 Census of Housing and Population, Summary Tape File 3C;
Census Bureau Population Estimates

Population Characteristics

Race	City 1980 Population	%	City 1990 Population	%	% Chg. 1980-90	MSA[1] 1990 Population	%
White	144,255	83.8	139,005	80.3	-3.6	326,568	89.8
Black	24,644	14.3	28,915	16.7	17.3	30,141	8.3
Amer Indian/Esk/Aleut	431	0.3	665	0.4	54.3	1,133	0.3
Asian/Pacific Islander	1,158	0.7	1,733	1.0	49.7	2,640	0.7
Other	1,708	1.0	2,754	1.6	61.2	3,329	0.9
Hispanic Origin[2]	3,506	2.0	4,394	2.5	25.3	6,105	1.7

Note: (1) Metropolitan Statistical Area - see Appendix A for areas included;
(2) people of Hispanic origin can be of any race
Source: 1980/1990 Census of Housing and Population, Summary Tape File 3C

Ancestry

Area	German	Irish	English	Italian	U.S.	French	Polish	Dutch
City	43.7	14.5	11.6	2.4	3.9	5.8	1.9	2.9
MSA[1]	50.6	15.0	12.7	2.4	4.1	6.3	2.3	3.1
U.S.	23.3	15.6	13.1	5.9	5.3	4.2	3.8	2.5

Note: Figures are percentages and include persons that reported multiple ancestry (eg. if a person reported being Irish and Italian, they were included in both columns); (1) Metropolitan Statistical Area - see Appendix A for areas included
Source: 1990 Census of Population and Housing, Summary Tape File 3C

Age

Area	Median Age (Years)	Age Distribution (%) Under 5	Under 18	18-24	25-44	45-64	65+	80+
City	31.5	8.0	26.4	10.9	33.1	16.2	13.4	3.4
MSA[1]	32.1	7.8	27.9	9.7	33.2	17.6	11.6	2.6
U.S.	32.9	7.3	25.6	10.5	32.6	18.7	12.5	2.8

Note: (1) Metropolitan Statistical Area - see Appendix A for areas included
Source: 1990 Census of Population and Housing, Summary Tape File 3C

Male/Female Ratio

Area	Number of males per 100 females (all ages)	Number of males per 100 females (18 years old+)
City	91.2	86.3
MSA[1]	94.6	90.7
U.S.	95.0	91.9

Note: (1) Metropolitan Statistical Area - see Appendix A for areas included
Source: 1990 Census of Population, General Population Characteristics

INCOME

Per Capita/Median/Average Income

Area	Per Capita ($)	Median Household ($)	Average Household ($)
City	12,726	26,344	31,336
MSA[1]	14,287	31,689	37,952
U.S.	14,420	30,056	38,453

Note: all figures are for 1989; (1) Metropolitan Statistical Area - see Appendix A for areas included
Source: 1990 Census of Population and Housing, Summary Tape File 3C

Household Income Distribution by Race

Income ($)	City (%)					U.S. (%)				
	Total	White	Black	Other	Hisp.[1]	Total	White	Black	Other	Hisp.[1]
Less than 5,000	5.0	4.0	11.1	5.9	6.3	6.2	4.8	15.2	8.6	8.8
5,000 - 9,999	9.9	9.3	13.7	9.0	11.8	9.3	8.6	14.2	9.9	11.1
10,000 - 14,999	10.1	10.0	11.0	9.0	11.3	8.8	8.5	11.0	9.8	11.0
15,000 - 24,999	22.1	21.9	23.0	22.8	23.6	17.5	17.3	18.9	18.5	20.5
25,000 - 34,999	18.6	19.2	14.5	21.0	17.5	15.8	16.1	14.2	15.4	16.4
35,000 - 49,999	18.9	19.4	15.3	21.1	18.6	17.9	18.6	13.3	16.1	16.0
50,000 - 74,999	11.5	12.0	9.1	7.3	8.7	15.0	15.8	9.3	13.4	11.1
75,000 - 99,999	2.3	2.4	2.0	2.6	1.3	5.1	5.5	2.6	4.7	3.1
100,000+	1.5	1.7	0.2	1.3	0.7	4.4	4.8	1.3	3.7	1.9

Note: all figures are for 1989; (1) people of Hispanic origin can be of any race
Source: 1990 Census of Population and Housing, Summary Tape File 3C

Effective Buying Income

Area	Per Capita ($)	Median Household ($)	Average Household ($)
City	14,788	30,705	36,481
MSA[1]	16,451	37,274	43,762
U.S.	15,444	33,201	41,849

Note: data as of 1/1/97; (1) Metropolitan Statistical Area - see Appendix A for areas included
Source: Standard Rate & Data Service, Newspaper Advertising Source, 2/98

Effective Household Buying Income Distribution

Area	% of Households Earning						
	$10,000 -$19,999	$20,000 -$34,999	$35,000 -$49,999	$50,000 -$74,999	$75,000 -$99,000	$100,000 -$124,999	$125,000 and up
City	18.3	27.5	20.3	16.5	4.2	1.0	1.0
MSA[1]	14.2	24.3	21.2	21.8	6.7	1.9	1.8
U.S.	16.5	23.4	18.3	18.2	6.4	2.1	2.4

Note: data as of 1/1/97; (1) Metropolitan Statistical Area - see Appendix A for areas included
Source: Standard Rate & Data Service, Newspaper Advertising Source, 2/98

Poverty Rates by Race and Age

Area	Total (%)	By Race (%)				By Age (%)		
		White	Black	Other	Hisp.[2]	Under 5 years old	Under 18 years old	65 years and over
City	11.5	8.4	25.8	16.4	11.9	18.6	16.5	9.0
MSA[1]	7.6	5.8	24.9	15.7	10.6	12.3	10.0	8.3
U.S.	13.1	9.8	29.5	23.1	25.3	20.1	18.3	12.8

Note: figures show the percent of people living below the poverty line in 1989. The average poverty threshold was $12,674 for a family of four in 1989; (1) Metropolitan Statistical Area - see Appendix A for areas included; (2) people of Hispanic origin can be of any race
Source: 1990 Census of Population and Housing, Summary Tape File 3C

EMPLOYMENT

Labor Force and Employment

Area	Civilian Labor Force			Workers Employed		
	Dec. '95	Dec. '96	% Chg.	Dec. '95	Dec. '96	% Chg.
City	96,729	98,230	1.6	93,186	95,064	2.0
MSA[1]	259,607	264,256	1.8	252,228	257,310	2.0
U.S.	134,583,000	136,742,000	1.6	127,903,000	130,785,000	2.3

Note: Data is not seasonally adjusted and covers workers 16 years of age and older;
(1) Metropolitan Statistical Area - see Appendix A for areas included
Source: Bureau of Labor Statistics, http://stats.bls.gov

Unemployment Rate

Area	1997											
	Jan.	Feb.	Mar.	Apr.	May	Jun.	Jul.	Aug.	Sep.	Oct.	Nov.	Dec.
City	3.6	3.4	3.6	3.4	3.1	3.4	3.4	3.6	3.4	3.7	3.2	3.2
MSA[1]	2.8	2.7	3.0	2.8	2.6	2.7	2.9	2.8	2.7	2.9	2.5	2.6
U.S.	5.9	5.7	5.5	4.8	4.7	5.2	5.0	4.8	4.7	4.4	4.3	4.4

Note: Data is not seasonally adjusted and covers workers 16 years of age and older; All figures are percentages; (1) Metropolitan Statistical Area - see Appendix A for areas included
Source: Bureau of Labor Statistics, http://stats.bls.gov

Employment by Industry

Sector	MSA[1]		U.S.
	Number of Employees	Percent of Total	Percent of Total
Services	61,800	22.7	29.0
Retail Trade	50,700	18.6	18.5
Government	27,800	10.2	16.1
Manufacturing	75,000	27.6	15.0
Finance/Insurance/Real Estate	14,900	5.5	5.7
Wholesale Trade	16,000	5.9	5.4
Transportation/Public Utilities	12,900	4.7	5.3
Construction/Mining	13,100	4.8	5.0

Note: Figures cover non-farm employment as of 12/97 and are not seasonally adjusted;
(1) Metropolitan Statistical Area - see Appendix A for areas included
Source: Bureau of Labor Statistics, http://stats.bls.gov

Employment by Occupation

Occupation Category	City (%)	MSA[1] (%)	U.S. (%)
White Collar	56.0	55.6	58.1
Executive/Admin./Management	10.7	11.7	12.3
Professional	12.4	12.8	14.1
Technical & Related Support	3.7	3.4	3.7
Sales	12.1	11.9	11.8
Administrative Support/Clerical	17.1	15.9	16.3
Blue Collar	29.1	31.1	26.2
Precision Production/Craft/Repair	10.9	12.1	11.3
Machine Operators/Assem./Insp.	9.6	10.1	6.8
Transportation/Material Movers	4.1	4.4	4.1
Cleaners/Helpers/Laborers	4.5	4.5	3.9
Services	14.5	12.1	13.2
Farming/Forestry/Fishing	0.5	1.2	2.5

Note: figures cover employed persons 16 years old and over;
(1) Metropolitan Statistical Area - see Appendix A for areas included
Source: 1990 Census of Population and Housing, Summary Tape File 3C

Occupational Employment Projections: 1994 - 2005

Projections not available at time of publication.

Average Wages

Occupation	Wage	Occupation	Wage
Professional/Technical/Clerical	$/Week	**Health/Protective Services**	$/Week
Accountants III	-	Corrections Officers	-
Attorneys III	-	Firefighters	-
Budget Analysts III	-	Nurses, Licensed Practical II	-
Buyers/Contracting Specialists II	-	Nurses, Registered II	602
Clerks, Accounting III	427	Nursing Assistants II	-
Clerks, General III	346	Police Officers I	-
Computer Operators II	407	**Hourly Workers**	$/Hour
Computer Programmers II	633	Forklift Operators	11.38
Drafters II	-	General Maintenance Workers	10.04
Engineering Technicians III	544	Guards I	7.25
Engineering Technicians, Civil III	-	Janitors	7.44
Engineers III	-	Maintenance Electricians	16.59
Key Entry Operators I	310	Maintenance Electronics Techs II	15.48
Personnel Assistants III	-	Maintenance Machinists	16.79
Personnel Specialists III	-	Maintenance Mechanics, Machinery	14.76
Secretaries III	486	Material Handling Laborers	8.24
Switchboard Operator-Receptionist	293	Motor Vehicle Mechanics	15.64
Systems Analysts II	823	Shipping/Receiving Clerks	9.87
Systems Analysts Supervisor/Mgr II	-	Tool and Die Makers	14.75
Tax Collectors II	-	Truckdrivers, Tractor Trailer	13.72
Word Processors II	-	Warehouse Specialists	9.67

Note: Wage data includes full-time workers only for 2/94 and cover the Metropolitan Statistical Area (see Appendix A for areas included). Dashes indicate that data was not available.
Source: Bureau of Labor Statistics, Occupational Compensation Survey

TAXES

Major State and Local Tax Rates

State Corp. Income (%)	State Personal Income (%)	Residential Property (effective rate per $100)	Sales & Use State (%)	Sales & Use Local (%)	State Gasoline (cents/ gallon)	State Cigarette (cents/ 20-pack)
7.9[a]	3.4	n/a	5.0	None	15	15.5

Note: Personal/corporate income tax rates as of 1/97. Sales, gasoline and cigarette tax rates as of 1/98; (a) Consists of 3.4% on income from sources within the state plus a 4.5% supplemental income tax
Source: Federation of Tax Administrators, www.taxadmin.org; Washington D.C. Department of Finance and Revenue, Tax Rates and Tax Burdens in the District of Columbia: A Nationwide Comparison, June 1997; Chamber of Commerce

Total Taxes Per Capita and as a Percent of Income

Area	Per Capita Income ($)	Per Capita Taxes ($) Total	Per Capita Taxes ($) Federal	Per Capita Taxes ($) State/ Local	Taxes as Pct. of Income (%) Total	Taxes as Pct. of Income (%) Federal	Taxes as Pct. of Income (%) State/ Local
Indiana	24,003	8,243	5,717	2,526	34.3	23.8	10.5
U.S.	26,187	9,205	6,127	3,078	35.2	23.4	11.8

Note: Figures are for 1997
Source: Tax Foundation, Web Site, www.taxfoundation.org

Estimated Tax Burden

Area	State Income	Local Income	Property	Sales	Total
Fort Wayne	2,074	244	4,950	425	7,693

Note: The numbers are estimates of taxes paid by a married couple with two kids and annual earnings of $65,000. Sales tax estimates assume they spend average amounts on food, clothing, household goods and gasoline. Property tax estimates assume they live in a $225,000 home.
Source: Kiplinger's Personal Finance Magazine, June 1997

COMMERCIAL REAL ESTATE

Office Market

Class/ Location	Total Space (sq. ft.)	Vacant Space (sq. ft.)	Vac. Rate (%)	Under Constr. (sq. ft.)	Net Absorp. (sq. ft.)	Rental Rates ($/sq.ft./yr.)
Class A						
CBD	1,803,173	69,106	3.8	0	-18,808	13.75-18.00
Outside CBD	1,960,000	46,515	2.4	0	159,699	13.50-16.50
Class B						
CBD	670,110	123,624	18.4	0	30,604	11.00-13.00
Outside CBD	993,517	148,174	14.9	0	51,785	11.00-12.75

Note: Data as of 10/97 and covers Fort Wayne; CBD = Central Business District; n/a not available;
Source: Society of Industrial and Office Realtors, 1998 Comparative Statistics of Industrial and Office Real Estate Markets

"With virtually no suburban Class 'A' space available, expect strong leasing of Class 'B' product as well as new development. Several speculative buildings have been proposed for the southwest submarket along I-69 near the airport. Despite a rather healthy economy, the lack of properly zoned commercial and industrial land will continue to restrict the area's growth potential as does the shortage of skilled labor. These factors will not, however, prevent investors and developers from constructing new buildings. SIOR's reporter is predicting office construction to pick up. With its very low cost of doing business, the Fort Wayne metropolitan area should continue to attract call-center operations and companies supporting the large automobile manufacturers." *Society of Industrial and Office Realtors, 1998 Comparative Statistics of Industrial and Office Real Estate Markets*

Industrial Market

Location	Total Space (sq. ft.)	Vacant Space (sq. ft.)	Vac. Rate (%)	Under Constr. (sq. ft.)	Net Absorp. (sq. ft.)	Net Lease ($/sq.ft./yr.)
Central City	n/a	n/a	n/a	n/a	n/a	1.50-4.00
Suburban	33,765,000	2,490,000	7.4	150,000	135,000	2.00-4.50

Note: Data as of 10/97 and covers Fort Wayne; n/a not available
Source: Society of Industrial and Office Realtors, 1998 Comparative Statistics of Industrial and Office Real Estate Markets

"Besides the recent renovation of its local plant, GM is also building a new sheet metal plant in Fort Wayne and plans to hire 300 more employees. Strength in the automotive industry is also sparking the development of a new steel plant and expansion of a second. Parts manufacturers including Autoliv (steering wheels) and Xolox (disc drives) are expanding in the MSA and plan to be fully operational within the next two-to three years. Navistar, a truck and bus manufacturer plans to hire more than 150 engineers and technicians in the near future. On the down side, the fate of Hughes Aircraft's local facility is uncertain and will not be known until a potential take-over by Raytheon is either completed or cast aside. Despite a slowing national economy and a tight supply of labor, the local economy is expected to expand modestly in 1998." *Society of Industrial and Office Realtors, 1998 Comparative Statistics of Industrial and Office Real Estate Markets*

COMMERCIAL UTILITIES

Typical Monthly Electric Bills

Area	Commercial Service ($/month)		Industrial Service ($/month)	
	12 kW demand 1,500 kWh	100 kW demand 30,000 kWh	1,000 kW demand 400,000 kWh	20,000 kW demand 10,000,000 kWh
City	145	1,850	21,679	449,656
U.S.	162	2,360	25,590	545,677

Note: Based on rates in effect July 1, 1997
Source: Edison Electric Institute, Typical Residential, Commercial and Industrial Bills, Summer 1997

TRANSPORTATION

Transportation Statistics

Avg. travel time to work (min.)	18.0
Interstate highways	I-69
Bus lines	
In-city	Ft. Wayne Public Transportation Commission
Inter-city	7
Passenger air service	
Airport	Ft. Wayne International
Airlines	7
Aircraft departures	8,987 (1995)
Enplaned passengers	263,075 (1995)
Rail service	No Amtrak service
Motor freight carriers	73
Major waterways/ports	None

Source: OAG, Business Travel Planner, Summer 1997; Editor & Publisher Market Guide, 1998; FAA Airport Activity Statistics, 1996; Amtrak National Time Table, Northeast Timetable, Fall/Winter 1997-98; 1990 Census of Population and Housing, STF 3C; Chamber of Commerce/Economic Development 1997; Jane's Urban Transport Systems 1997-98; Transit Fact Book 1997

Means of Transportation to Work

Area	Car/Truck/Van		Public Transportation			Bicycle	Walked	Other Means	Worked at Home
	Drove Alone	Car-pooled	Bus	Subway	Railroad				
City	79.9	12.1	2.0	0.0	0.0	0.3	3.1	0.7	1.8
MSA[1]	82.3	11.0	1.1	0.0	0.0	0.2	2.3	0.6	2.5
U.S.	73.2	13.4	3.0	1.5	0.5	0.4	3.9	1.2	3.0

Note: figures shown are percentages and only include workers 16 years old and over;
(1) Metropolitan Statistical Area - see Appendix A for areas included
Source: 1990 Census of Population and Housing, Summary Tape File 3C

BUSINESSES

Major Business Headquarters

Company Name	1997 Rankings	
	Fortune 500	Forbes 500
Essex Group	-	129
Kelley Automotive Group	-	279
Lincoln National	211	-
OmniSource	-	360

Note: Companies listed are located in the city; Dashes indicate no ranking
Fortune 500: companies that produce a 10-K are ranked 1 - 500 based on 1996 revenue
Forbes 500: private companies are ranked 1 - 500 based on 1996 revenue
Source: Forbes 12/1/97; Fortune 4/28/97

HOTELS & MOTELS

Hotels/Motels

Area	Hotels/ Motels	Rooms	Luxury-Level Hotels/Motels		Average Minimum Rates ($)		
			♦♦♦♦	♦♦♦♦♦	♦♦	♦♦♦	♦♦♦♦
City	20	2,332	0	0	58	78	n/a
Airport	2	221	0	0	n/a	n/a	n/a
Suburbs	1	223	0	0	n/a	n/a	n/a
Total	23	2,776	0	0	n/a	n/a	n/a

Note: n/a not available; Classifications range from one diamond (budget properties with basic amenities) to five diamond (luxury properties with the finest service, rooms and facilities).
Source: OAG, Business Travel Planner, Summer 1997

CONVENTION CENTERS

Major Convention Centers

Center Name	Meeting Rooms	Exhibit Space (sf)
Allen Co. War Memorial Coliseum & Expo Ctr.	11	180,000
Grand Wayne Center	7	25,000

Source: Trade Shows Worldwide 1997

Living Environment

COST OF LIVING

Cost of Living Index

Composite Index	Housing	Utilities	Groceries	Health Care	Trans-portation	Misc. Goods/ Services
91.9	84.0	96.7	100.3	90.6	94.1	93.1

Note: U.S. = 100; Figures are for Fort Wayne/Allen County
Source: ACCRA, Cost of Living Index, 3rd Quarter 1997

HOUSING

Median Home Prices and Housing Affordability

Area	Median Price[2] 3rd Qtr. 1997 ($)	HOI[3] 3rd Qtr. 1997	Afford-ability Rank[4]
MSA[1]	n/a	n/a	n/a
U.S.	127,000	63.7	–

Note: (1) Metropolitan Statistical Area - see Appendix A for areas included; (2) U.S. figures calculated from the sales of 625,000 new and existing homes in 195 markets; (3) Housing Opportunity Index - percent of homes sold that were within the reach of the median income household at the prevailing mortgage interest rate; (4) Rank is from 1-195 with 1 being most affordable; n/a not available
Source: National Association of Home Builders, Housing Opportunity Index, 3rd Quarter 1997

It is projected that the median price of existing single-family homes in the metro area will increase by 5.1% in 1998. Nationwide, home prices are projected to increase 6.6%.
Kiplinger's Personal Finance Magazine, January 1998

Average New Home Price

Area	Price ($)
City[1]	110,240
U.S.	135,710

Note: Figures are based on a new home with 1,800 sq. ft. of living area on an 8,000 sq. ft. lot; (1) Fort Wayne/Allen County
Source: ACCRA, Cost of Living Index, 3rd Quarter 1997

Average Apartment Rent

Area	Rent ($/mth)
City[1]	509
U.S.	569

Note: Figures are based on an unfurnished two bedroom, 1-1/2 or 2 bath apartment, approximately 950 sq. ft. in size, excluding all utilities except water; (1) Fort Wayne/Allen County
Source: ACCRA, Cost of Living Index, 3rd Quarter 1997

RESIDENTIAL UTILITIES

Average Residential Utility Costs

Area	All Electric ($/mth)	Part Electric ($/mth)	Other Energy ($/mth)	Phone ($/mth)
City[1]	–	45.80	49.22	23.83
U.S.	109.40	55.25	43.64	19.48

Note: (1) Fort Wayne/Allen County
Source: ACCRA, Cost of Living Index, 3rd Quarter 1997

HEALTH CARE

Average Health Care Costs

Area	Hospital ($/day)	Doctor ($/visit)	Dentist ($/visit)
City[1]	450.67	41.40	52.00
U.S.	392.91	48.76	60.84

Note: Hospital - based on a semi-private room. Doctor - based on a general practitioner's routine exam of an established patient. Dentist - based on adult teeth cleaning and periodic oral exam; (1) (1) Fort Wayne/Allen County
Source: ACCRA, Cost of Living Index, 3rd Quarter 1997

Distribution of Office-Based Physicians

Area	Family/Gen. Practitioners	Specialists		
		Medical	Surgical	Other
MSA[1]	151	162	190	183

Note: Data as of 12/31/96; (1) Metropolitan Statistical Area - see Appendix A for areas included
Source: American Medical Assn., Physician Characteristics & Distribution in the U.S., 1997-1998

Hospitals

Fort Wayne has 3 general medical and surgical hospitals, 2 psychiatric. AHA Guide to the Healthcare Field 1997-98

EDUCATION

Public School District Statistics

District Name	Num. Sch.	Enroll.	Classroom Teachers[1]	Pupils per Teacher	Minority Pupils (%)	Current Exp.[2] ($/pupil)
Fort Wayne Community Schools	53	31,748	1,708	18.6	29.9	5,500
M S D Southwest Allen County	9	5,215	304	17.2	n/a	n/a
Northwest Allen County Schools	7	3,497	182	19.2	n/a	n/a

Note: Data covers the 1995-1996 school year unless otherwise noted; (1) Excludes teachers reported as working in school district offices rather than in schools; (2) Based on 1993-94 enrollment collected by the Census Bureau, not the enrollment figure shown in column 3; SD = School District; ISD = Independent School District; n/a not available
Source: National Center for Education Statistics, Common Core of Data Survey; Bureau of the Census

Educational Quality

School District	Education Quotient[1]	Graduate Outcome[2]	Community Index[3]	Resource Index[4]
Fort Wayne	112.0	79.0	121.0	137.0

Note: Nearly 1,000 secondary school districts were rated in terms of educational quality. The scores range from a low of 50 to a high of 150; (1) Average of the Graduate Outcome, Community and Resource indexes; (2) Based on graduation rates and college board scores (SAT/ACT); (3) Based on the surrounding community's average level of education and the area's average income level; (4) Based on teacher salaries, per-pupil expenditures and student-teacher ratios.
Source: Expansion Management, Ratings Issue 1997

Educational Attainment by Race

Area	High School Graduate (%)					Bachelor's Degree (%)				
	Total	White	Black	Other	Hisp.[2]	Total	White	Black	Other	Hisp.[2]
City	77.1	79.6	64.4	61.4	60.0	15.7	17.1	6.9	15.3	7.2
MSA[1]	80.6	82.0	65.6	65.5	63.0	17.3	18.0	8.0	17.7	9.3
U.S.	75.2	77.9	63.1	60.4	49.8	20.3	21.5	11.4	19.4	9.2

Note: figures shown cover persons 25 years old and over; (1) Metropolitan Statistical Area - see Appendix A for areas included; (2) people of Hispanic origin can be of any race
Source: 1990 Census of Population and Housing, Summary Tape File 3C

School Enrollment by Type

Area	Preprimary				Elementary/High School			
	Public		Private		Public		Private	
	Enrollment	%	Enrollment	%	Enrollment	%	Enrollment	%
City	1,880	53.2	1,652	46.8	24,519	83.7	4,783	16.3
MSA[1]	4,397	54.1	3,726	45.9	56,218	84.7	10,137	15.3
U.S.	2,679,029	59.5	1,824,256	40.5	38,379,689	90.2	4,187,099	9.8

Note: figures shown cover persons 3 years old and over;
(1) Metropolitan Statistical Area - see Appendix A for areas included
Source: 1990 Census of Population and Housing, Summary Tape File 3C

School Enrollment by Race

Area	Preprimary (%)				Elementary/High School (%)			
	White	Black	Other	Hisp.[1]	White	Black	Other	Hisp.[1]
City	74.6	21.5	3.9	3.4	69.8	26.0	4.2	4.3
MSA[2]	88.1	9.6	2.3	2.4	85.5	11.9	2.6	2.7
U.S.	80.4	12.5	7.1	7.8	74.1	15.6	10.3	12.5

Note: figures shown cover persons 3 years old and over; (1) people of Hispanic origin can be of any race; (2) Metropolitan Statistical Area - see Appendix A for areas included
Source: 1990 Census of Population and Housing, Summary Tape File 3C

SAT/ACT Scores

Area/District	1997 SAT				1997 ACT	
	Percent of Graduates Tested (%)	Average Math Score	Average Verbal Score	Average Combined Score	Percent of Graduates Tested (%)	Average Composite Score
Fort Wayne CS	54	499	491	990	14	21.3
State	57	497	494	991	19	21.2
U.S.	42	511	505	1,016	36	21.0

Note: Math and verbal SAT scores are out of a possible 800; ACT scores are out of a possible 36
Caution: Comparing or ranking states/cities on the basis of SAT/ACT scores alone is invalid and strongly discouraged by the The College Board and The American College Testing Program as students who take the tests are self-selected and do not represent the entire student population.
Source: Ft. Wayne Community Schools, 1997; American College Testing Program, 1997; College Board, 1997

Classroom Teacher Salaries in Public Schools

District	B.A. Degree		M.A. Degree		Ph.D. Degree	
	Min. ($)	Max. ($)	Min. ($)	Max. ($)	Min. ($)	Max. ($)
Fort Wayne	24,425	41,034	26,868	45,919	30,532	49,583
Average[1]	26,120	39,270	28,175	44,667	31,643	49,825

Note: Salaries are for 1996-1997; (1) Based on all school districts covered
Source: American Federation of Teachers (unpublished data)

Higher Education

Two-Year Colleges		Four-Year Colleges		Medical Schools	Law Schools	Voc/ Tech
Public	Private	Public	Private			
1	1	1	5	0	0	8

Source: College Blue Book, Occupational Education 1997; Medical School Admission Requirements, 1998-99; Peterson's Guide to Two-Year Colleges, 1997; Peterson's Guide to Four-Year Colleges, 1997; Barron's Guide to Law Schools 1997

MAJOR EMPLOYERS

Major Employers

BCP/Essex Holdings (metals)	Ft. Wayne Newspapers
Lutheran Hospital of Indiana	North American Van Lines
Parkview Memorial Hospital	Seyfert Foods
Slater Steels Corp.	St. Joseph Medical Center of Ft. Wayne
Zollner Co. (auto parts)	

Note: companies listed are located in the city
Source: Dun's Business Rankings 1997; Ward's Business Directory, 1997

PUBLIC SAFETY

Crime Rate

Area	All Crimes	Violent Crimes				Property Crimes		
		Murder	Forcible Rape	Robbery	Aggrav. Assault	Burglary	Larceny -Theft	Motor Vehicle Theft
City	7,500.7	7.0	65.0	268.0	234.2	1,034.9	5,052.2	839.4
Suburbs[1]	2,463.5	1.0	17.2	23.1	166.8	438.8	1,631.8	184.8
MSA[2]	4,432.6	3.4	35.9	118.8	193.2	671.8	2,968.9	440.7
U.S.	5,078.9	7.4	36.1	202.4	388.2	943.0	2,975.9	525.9

Note: Crime rate is the number of crimes per 100,000 pop.; (1) defined as all areas within the MSA but located outside the central city; (2) Metropolitan Statistical Area - see Appendix A for areas incl.
Source: FBI Uniform Crime Reports 1996

RECREATION

Culture and Recreation

Museums	Symphony Orchestras	Opera Companies	Dance Companies	Professional Theatres	Zoos	Pro Sports Teams
4	1	0	2	1	1	0

Source: International Directory of the Performing Arts, 1996; Official Museum Directory, 1998; Chamber of Commerce/Economic Development 1997

Library System

The Allen County Public Library has 13 branches, holdings of 2,477,541 volumes and a budget of $15,981,583 (1995). *American Library Directory, 1997-1998*

MEDIA

Newspapers

Name	Type	Freq.	Distribution	Circulation
Frost Illustrated	Black	1x/wk	Local	9,000
The Journal Gazette	General	7x/wk	Local	62,000
The News-Sentinel	n/a	6x/wk	Local	55,000
Today's Catholic	Religious	1x/wk	Area	15,600

Note: Includes newspapers with circulations of 1,000 or more located in the city; n/a not available
Source: Burrelle's Media Directory, 1998 Edition

AM Radio Stations

Call Letters	Freq. (kHz)	Target Audience	Station Format	Music Format
WFCV	1090	Religious	N/T	n/a
WOWO	1190	n/a	N/T	n/a
WGL	1250	General	T	n/a
WPDJ	1300	General	M/N/S	n/a
WHWD	1380	n/a	M	Big Band

Note: Stations included broadcast in the Fort Wayne metro area; n/a not available
Station Format: E = Educational; M = Music; N = News; S = Sports; T = Talk
Source: Burrelle's Media Directory, 1998 Edition

FM Radio Stations

Call Letters	Freq. (mHz)	Target Audience	Station Format	Music Format
WLAB	88.3	Religious	M	Christian
WBNI	89.1	General	M/N	Classical/Jazz
WBCL	90.3	General	M	Christian
WFWI	92.3	General	M/N/S	Classic Rock/Oldies
WBTU	93.3	General	M	Country
WAJI	95.1	General	M	Adult Contemporary
WEJE	96.3	General	M	Alternative
WMEE	97.3	n/a	M	Contemporary Top 40
WBYR	98.9	General	M	AOR
WLDE	101.7	General	M/N/S	Oldies
WEXI	102.9	n/a	M	AOR/Classic Rock
WXKE	103.9	n/a	M/S	AOR
WQHK	105.1	n/a	M	Country
WJFX	107.9	General	M	R&B/Urban Contemporary

Note: Stations included broadcast in the Fort Wayne metro area; n/a not available
Station Format: E = Educational; M = Music; N = News; S = Sports; T = Talk
Music Format: AOR = Album Oriented Rock; MOR = Middle-of-the-Road
Source: Burrelle's Media Directory, 1998 Edition

Television Stations

Name	Ch.	Affiliation	Type	Owner
WANE	15	CBS	Commercial	LIN Television Corporation
WPTA	21	ABC	Commercial	Granite Broadcasting Corporation
WKJG	33	NBC	Commercial	Corporation for General Trade
WFWA	39	PBS	Public	Fort Wayne Public Television
WFFT	55	Fox/UPN	Commercial	Great Trails Broadcasting Co.

Note: Stations included broadcast in the Fort Wayne metro area
Source: Burrelle's Media Directory, 1998 Edition

CLIMATE

Average and Extreme Temperatures

Temperature	Jan	Feb	Mar	Apr	May	Jun	Jul	Aug	Sep	Oct	Nov	Dec	Ann
Extreme High (°F)	69	69	82	88	94	106	103	101	100	90	79	71	106
Average High (°F)	31	35	46	60	71	81	84	82	76	64	49	36	60
Average Temp. (°F)	24	27	37	49	60	70	74	72	65	53	41	29	50
Average Low (°F)	16	19	28	39	49	59	63	61	53	42	32	22	40
Extreme Low (°F)	-22	-18	-10	7	27	38	44	38	29	19	-1	-18	-22

Note: Figures cover the years 1948-1990
Source: National Climatic Data Center, International Station Meteorological Climate Summary, 3/95

Average Precipitation/Snowfall/Humidity

Precip./Humidity	Jan	Feb	Mar	Apr	May	Jun	Jul	Aug	Sep	Oct	Nov	Dec	Ann
Avg. Precip. (in.)	2.3	2.1	2.9	3.4	3.6	3.8	3.6	3.4	2.6	2.7	2.8	2.7	35.9
Avg. Snowfall (in.)	8	8	5	2	Tr	0	0	0	0	Tr	3	7	33
Avg. Rel. Hum. 7am (%)	81	81	80	77	76	78	81	86	86	84	83	83	81
Avg. Rel. Hum. 4pm (%)	71	68	62	54	52	52	53	55	53	55	67	74	59

Note: Figures cover the years 1948-1990; Tr = Trace amounts (<0.05 in. of rain; <0.5 in. of snow)
Source: National Climatic Data Center, International Station Meteorological Climate Summary, 3/95

Weather Conditions

Temperature			Daytime Sky			Precipitation		
5°F & below	32°F & below	90°F & above	Clear	Partly cloudy	Cloudy	0.01 inch or more precip.	0.1 inch or more snow/ice	Thunder-storms
16	131	16	75	140	150	131	31	39

Note: Figures are average number of days per year and covers the years 1948-1990
Source: National Climatic Data Center, International Station Meteorological Climate Summary, 3/95

AIR & WATER QUALITY

Maximum Pollutant Concentrations

	Particulate Matter (ug/m³)	Carbon Monoxide (ppm)	Sulfur Dioxide (ppm)	Nitrogen Dioxide (ppm)	Ozone (ppm)	Lead (ug/m³)
MSA[1] Level	80	3	0.010	0.007	0.11	0.02
NAAQS[2]	150	9	0.140	0.053	0.12	1.50
Met NAAQS?	Yes	Yes	Yes	Yes	Yes	Yes

Note: (1) Metropolitan Statistical Area - see Appendix A for areas included; (2) National Ambient Air Quality Standards; ppm = parts per million; ug/m³ = micrograms per cubic meter; n/a not available
Source: EPA, National Air Quality and Emissions Trends Report, 1996

Pollutant Standards Index

Data not available. *EPA, National Air Quality and Emissions Trends Report, 1996*

Drinking Water

Water System Name	Pop. Served	Primary Water Source Type	Number of Violations in Fiscal Year 1997	Type of Violation/ Contaminants
Ft. Wayne-3 Rivers Filtration Plant	180,000	Surface	None	None

Note: Data as of January 16, 1998
Source: EPA, Office of Ground Water and Drinking Water, Safe Drinking Water Information System

Fort Wayne tap water is alkaline, hard and fluoridated.
Editor & Publisher Market Guide, 1998

Grand Rapids, Michigan

Background

The city of Grand Rapids, Michigan is perhaps best known for its fine furniture making. The presence of an abundant forest, as well as the hydropower and trade afforded by a powerful river, contributed to the reputation of an industry that is known worldwide.

However, before Grand Rapids became involved in making seats for churches, buses, and schools, the site was a Native American settlement of the Ottawa, Chippewa, and Potawatomi tribes. The earliest white presence in the area were fur traders who bought furs from the Native American tribes in the early 19th century. One by one, more white settlers found their way into the area on the rapids of the Grand River. A Baptist Mission was established in 1825, and a year after that, Louis Campau erected a trading post. 1833 saw its first permanent white settlement, led under the guidance of Samuel Dexter, of Herkimer County, New York.

The Grand Rapids metro area was cited in a study as the only one in the midwest to recover all of the manufacturing jobs it lost in the recessions of the early 1980s. Its 2,200 manufacturers employ nearly 15 percent more than they did in 1990 according to the Grand Rapids Areas Chamber of Commerce. The main industries are office furniture, auto components, fabricated metals, and food processing. *Industry Week 4/7/97*

Grand Rapids is located in the westcentral part of Kent County in the picturesque Grand River Valley about 30 miles east of Lake Michigan. It is under the natural climatic influence of the lake.

Fall is a very colorful time of year in western Michigan, perhaps compensating for the late spring. During the winter, excessive cloudiness and numerous snow flurries occur with strong westerly winds. Lake Michigan has a tempering effect on cold waves coming in from the west in the winter. Prolonged severe cold waves with temperatures below zero are infrequent.

Summer days are pleasantly warm and most summer nights are quite comfortable. There may only be three weeks of hot, humid weather during most summers.

The snowfall season extends from mid-November to mid-March and some winters have had continuous snow cover throughout this period.

General Rankings and Evaluative Comments

- Grand Rapids was ranked #150 out of 300 cities by *Money's* 1997 "Survey of the Best Places to Live." Criteria used: health services, crime, economy, housing, education, transportation, weather, leisure and the arts. The city was ranked #71 in 1996 and #122 in 1995. *Money, July 1997; Money, September 1996; Money, September 1995*

- *Ladies Home Journal* ranked America's 200 largest cities based on the qualities women care about most. Grand Rapids ranked 131 out of 200. Criteria: low crime rate, good public schools, well-paying jobs, quality health and child care, the presence of women in government, proportion of women-owned businesses, size of the wage gap with men, local economy, divorce rates, the ratio of single men to single women, whether there are laws that require at least the same number of public toilets for women as men, and the probability of good hair days. *Ladies Home Journal, November 1997*

- Grand Rapids was ranked #173 out of 219 cities in terms of children's health, safety, and economic well-being. Criteria: total population, percent population change, birth rate, child immunization rate, infant mortality rate, percent low birth weight infants, percent of births to teens, physician-to-population ratio, student-to-teacher ratio, dropout rate, unemployment rate, median family income, percent of children in poverty, violent and property crime rates, number of juvenile arrests for violent crimes as a percent of the total crime index, number of days with pollution standard index (PSI) over 100, pounds toxic releases per 1,000 people and number of superfund sites. *Zero Population Growth, Children's Environmental Index 1997*

- Steelcase (office-furniture manufacturer), headquartered in Grand Rapids, is among the "100 Best Companies to Work for in America." Criteria: trust in management, pride in work/company, camaraderie, company responses to the Hewitt People Practices Inventory, and employee responses to their Great Place to Work survey. The companies also had to be at least 10 years old and have a minimum of 500 employees. *Fortune, January 12, 1998*

- According to *Working Mother,* "Michigan increased its spending on child care by $44 million, which means that nearly 14,000 more kids will be served this year. Next year, child care funding is slated to reach $201 million, a $16 million boost over 1997 spending. One key part of the budget: a special program to recruit caregivers who want to specialize in infant care, since demand for such care is so great here.

  In this state, as in so many others, there has been a raging controversy over how to expand child care options without diluting the quality of the programs. Governor John Engler had previously considered a radical approach to child care, which would have allowed parents to use state funds to pay unlicensed caregivers. Child care activists and providers managed to convince Engler that this was a bad idea, and it was never officially proposed. Another idea the governor floated—an elimination of background checks for caregivers—was also shelved." *Working Mother, July/August 1997*

Business Environment

STATE ECONOMY

State Economic Profile

"...retail sales growth and residential construction are below the national average, and bankruptcy filings have accelerated to 33% above one year ago.

Michigan will continue to nurture white-collar, auto-related operations. While international auto manufacturers have not located assembly plants in Michigan, they have located their research facilities in the state. Michigan is also a center for allied auto-related research activity, such as robotics and software development.

Michigan's population growth improved slightly last year to almost 0.6%, though it remains well below the national average. For the past two years, net migration has been positive in Michigan, a significant turnaround for the state. While net domestic migration remains stubbornly negative, many fewer people are leaving Michigan than earlier in the decade.

In the near term, Michigan's economy will continue to grow at about the national pace. Sizable auto industry bonuses will boost incomes and fatten the state treasury this year. Long term, substantial investments in auto-related production facilities will ensure that a significant portion of vehicle and parts manufacturing will remain in the state. However, Michigan's high cost of doing business, coupled with the high level of unionization, will continue to limit investment in the state. Michigan will be a below-average performer long term." *National Association of Realtors, Economic Profiles: The Fifty States, July 1997*

IMPORTS/EXPORTS

Total Export Sales

Area	1993 ($000)	1994 ($000)	1995 ($000)	1996 ($000)	% Chg. 1993-96	% Chg. 1995-96
MSA[1]	1,704,960	1,993,494	2,304,077	2,656,497	55.8	15.3
U.S.	464,858,354	512,415,609	583,030,524	622,827,063	34.0	6.8

Note: (1) Metropolitan Statistical Area - see Appendix A for areas included
Source: U.S. Department of Commerce, International Trade Association, Metropolitan Area Exports: An Export Performance Report on Over 250 U.S. Cities, October 1997

Imports/Exports by Port

Type	Cargo Value			Share of U.S. Total	
	1995 (US$mil.)	1996 (US$mil.)	% Change 1995-1996	1995 (%)	1996 (%)
Imports	0	0	0	0	0
Exports	0	0	0	0	0

Source: Global Trade Information Services, WaterBorne Trade Atlas 1997

CITY FINANCES

City Government Finances

Component	FY92 ($000)	FY92 (per capita $)
Revenue	222,109	1,178.01
Expenditure	247,324	1,311.74
Debt Outstanding	278,306	1,476.06
Cash & Securities	472,958	2,508.45

Source: U.S. Bureau of the Census, City Government Finances: 1991-92

City Government Revenue by Source

Source	FY92 ($000)	FY92 (per capita $)	FY92 (%)
From Federal Government	14,665	77.78	6.6
From State Governments	28,235	149.75	12.7
From Local Governments	5,053	26.80	2.3
Property Taxes	29,312	155.46	13.2
General Sales Taxes	0	0.00	0.0
Selective Sales Taxes	0	0.00	0.0
Income Taxes	26,525	140.68	11.9
Current Charges	42,878	227.41	19.3
Utility/Liquor Store	31,240	165.69	14.1
Employee Retirement[1]	26,161	138.75	11.8
Other	18,040	95.68	8.1

Note: (1) Excludes "city contributions," classified as "nonrevenue," intragovernmental transfers.
Source: U.S. Bureau of the Census, City Government Finances: 1991-92

City Government Expenditures by Function

Function	FY92 ($000)	FY92 (per capita $)	FY92 (%)
Educational Services	3,808	20.20	1.5
Employee Retirement[1]	11,611	61.58	4.7
Environment/Housing	64,149	340.23	25.9
Government Administration	14,885	78.95	6.0
Interest on General Debt	5,232	27.75	2.1
Public Safety	36,264	192.34	14.7
Social Services	0	0.00	0.0
Transportation	22,447	119.05	9.1
Utility/Liquor Store	71,654	380.03	29.0
Other	17,274	91.62	7.0

Note: (1) Payments to beneficiaries including withdrawal of contributions.
Source: U.S. Bureau of the Census, City Government Finances: 1991-92

Municipal Bond Ratings

Area	Moody's	S & P
Grand Rapids	n/r	n/a

Note: n/a not available; n/r not rated
Source: Moody's Bond Record, 2/98; Statistical Abstract of the U.S., 1997;
Governing Magazine, 9/97, 3/98

POPULATION

Population Growth

Area	1980	1990	% Chg. 1980-90	July 1996 Estimate	% Chg. 1990-96
City	181,843	189,126	4.0	188,242	-0.5
MSA[1]	601,680	688,399	14.4	1,015,099	47.5
U.S.	226,545,805	248,765,170	9.8	265,179,411	6.6

Note: (1) Metropolitan Statistical Area - see Appendix A for areas included
Source: 1980/1990 Census of Housing and Population, Summary Tape File 3C;
Census Bureau Population Estimates

Population Characteristics

Race	City 1980 Population	%	City 1990 Population	%	% Chg. 1980-90	MSA[1] 1990 Population	%
White	147,220	81.0	145,123	76.7	-1.4	624,739	90.8
Black	28,811	15.8	35,134	18.6	21.9	40,858	5.9
Amer Indian/Esk/Aleut	1,346	0.7	1,501	0.8	11.5	3,555	0.5
Asian/Pacific Islander	1,415	0.8	1,968	1.0	39.1	7,509	1.1
Other	3,051	1.7	5,400	2.9	77.0	11,738	1.7
Hispanic Origin[2]	5,751	3.2	8,447	4.5	46.9	21,151	3.1

Note: (1) Metropolitan Statistical Area - see Appendix A for areas included;
(2) people of Hispanic origin can be of any race
Source: 1980/1990 Census of Housing and Population, Summary Tape File 3C

Ancestry

Area	German	Irish	English	Italian	U.S.	French	Polish	Dutch
City	21.4	12.3	10.4	2.5	2.2	4.5	10.4	21.4
MSA[1]	27.5	13.2	13.5	2.5	2.8	5.0	7.9	30.5
U.S.	23.3	15.6	13.1	5.9	5.3	4.2	3.8	2.5

Note: Figures are percentages and include persons that reported multiple ancestry (eg. if a person reported being Irish and Italian, they were included in both columns); (1) Metropolitan Statistical Area - see Appendix A for areas included
Source: 1990 Census of Population and Housing, Summary Tape File 3C

Age

Area	Median Age (Years)	Age Distribution (%) Under 5	Under 18	18-24	25-44	45-64	65+	80+
City	29.8	9.4	27.6	12.5	32.9	14.0	13.0	3.8
MSA[1]	30.6	8.7	28.6	11.0	33.3	16.6	10.5	2.6
U.S.	32.9	7.3	25.6	10.5	32.6	18.7	12.5	2.8

Note: (1) Metropolitan Statistical Area - see Appendix A for areas included
Source: 1990 Census of Population and Housing, Summary Tape File 3C

Male/Female Ratio

Area	Number of males per 100 females (all ages)	Number of males per 100 females (18 years old+)
City	90.2	85.6
MSA[1]	94.8	91.1
U.S.	95.0	91.9

Note: (1) Metropolitan Statistical Area - see Appendix A for areas included
Source: 1990 Census of Population, General Population Characteristics

INCOME

Per Capita/Median/Average Income

Area	Per Capita ($)	Median Household ($)	Average Household ($)
City	12,070	26,809	32,106
MSA[1]	14,370	33,515	39,827
U.S.	14,420	30,056	38,453

Note: all figures are for 1989; (1) Metropolitan Statistical Area - see Appendix A for areas included
Source: 1990 Census of Population and Housing, Summary Tape File 3C

Household Income Distribution by Race

Income ($)	City (%)					U.S. (%)				
	Total	White	Black	Other	Hisp.[1]	Total	White	Black	Other	Hisp.[1]
Less than 5,000	6.1	4.4	13.8	9.5	6.8	6.2	4.8	15.2	8.6	8.8
5,000 - 9,999	11.2	9.7	18.1	16.7	17.6	9.3	8.6	14.2	9.9	11.1
10,000 - 14,999	10.0	9.2	13.3	12.6	14.4	8.8	8.5	11.0	9.8	11.0
15,000 - 24,999	19.3	19.2	18.8	23.4	19.0	17.5	17.3	18.9	18.5	20.5
25,000 - 34,999	17.9	19.2	12.1	13.2	17.5	15.8	16.1	14.2	15.4	16.4
35,000 - 49,999	18.4	19.8	12.3	14.7	13.1	17.9	18.6	13.3	16.1	16.0
50,000 - 74,999	12.4	13.1	9.1	8.5	7.3	15.0	15.8	9.3	13.4	11.1
75,000 - 99,999	2.9	3.2	1.9	1.5	3.1	5.1	5.5	2.6	4.7	3.1
100,000+	1.9	2.3	0.6	0.0	1.1	4.4	4.8	1.3	3.7	1.9

Note: all figures are for 1989; (1) people of Hispanic origin can be of any race
Source: 1990 Census of Population and Housing, Summary Tape File 3C

Effective Buying Income

Area	Per Capita ($)	Median Household ($)	Average Household ($)
City	14,498	32,240	39,150
MSA[1]	16,479	38,944	45,860
U.S.	15,444	33,201	41,849

Note: data as of 1/1/97; (1) Metropolitan Statistical Area - see Appendix A for areas included
Source: Standard Rate & Data Service, Newspaper Advertising Source, 2/98

Effective Household Buying Income Distribution

Area	% of Households Earning						
	$10,000 -$19,999	$20,000 -$34,999	$35,000 -$49,999	$50,000 -$74,999	$75,000 -$99,000	$100,000 -$124,999	$125,000 and up
City	17.4	24.4	19.5	18.2	5.2	1.5	1.3
MSA[1]	13.6	22.2	20.7	22.9	7.5	2.3	2.3
U.S.	16.5	23.4	18.3	18.2	6.4	2.1	2.4

Note: data as of 1/1/97; (1) Metropolitan Statistical Area - see Appendix A for areas included
Source: Standard Rate & Data Service, Newspaper Advertising Source, 2/98

Poverty Rates by Race and Age

Area	Total (%)	By Race (%)				By Age (%)		
		White	Black	Other	Hisp.[2]	Under 5 years old	Under 18 years old	65 years and over
City	16.1	10.8	33.8	31.1	33.3	24.6	23.2	10.0
MSA[1]	8.3	6.4	31.4	20.0	22.9	12.5	10.7	8.1
U.S.	13.1	9.8	29.5	23.1	25.3	20.1	18.3	12.8

Note: figures show the percent of people living below the poverty line in 1989. The average poverty threshold was $12,674 for a family of four in 1989; (1) Metropolitan Statistical Area - see Appendix A for areas included; (2) people of Hispanic origin can be of any race
Source: 1990 Census of Population and Housing, Summary Tape File 3C

EMPLOYMENT

Labor Force and Employment

Area	Civilian Labor Force			Workers Employed		
	Dec. '95	Dec. '96	% Chg.	Dec. '95	Dec. '96	% Chg.
City	106,407	108,997	2.4	101,567	104,958	3.3
MSA[1]	560,545	575,496	2.7	541,647	559,732	3.3
U.S.	134,583,000	136,742,000	1.6	127,903,000	130,785,000	2.3

Note: Data is not seasonally adjusted and covers workers 16 years of age and older;
(1) Metropolitan Statistical Area - see Appendix A for areas included
Source: Bureau of Labor Statistics, http://stats.bls.gov

Unemployment Rate

Area	1997											
	Jan.	Feb.	Mar.	Apr.	May	Jun.	Jul.	Aug.	Sep.	Oct.	Nov.	Dec.
City	5.6	5.2	4.9	4.1	4.2	5.2	5.1	4.1	4.1	3.7	3.9	3.7
MSA[1]	4.5	4.1	3.7	3.1	3.0	3.7	3.5	2.9	3.0	2.8	2.9	2.7
U.S.	5.9	5.7	5.5	4.8	4.7	5.2	5.0	4.8	4.7	4.4	4.3	4.4

Note: Data is not seasonally adjusted and covers workers 16 years of age and older; All figures are percentages; (1) Metropolitan Statistical Area - see Appendix A for areas included
Source: Bureau of Labor Statistics, http://stats.bls.gov

Employment by Industry

	MSA[1]		U.S.
Sector	Number of Employees	Percent of Total	Percent of Total
Services	146,400	25.8	29.0
Retail Trade	105,000	18.5	18.5
Government	56,300	9.9	16.1
Manufacturing	157,200	27.7	15.0
Finance/Insurance/Real Estate	22,700	4.0	5.7
Wholesale Trade	36,400	6.4	5.4
Transportation/Public Utilities	19,100	3.4	5.3
Construction/Mining	23,700	4.2	5.0

Note: Figures cover non-farm employment as of 12/97 and are not seasonally adjusted;
(1) Metropolitan Statistical Area - see Appendix A for areas included
Source: Bureau of Labor Statistics, http://stats.bls.gov

Employment by Occupation

Occupation Category	City (%)	MSA[1] (%)	U.S. (%)
White Collar	54.8	54.9	58.1
Executive/Admin./Management	10.2	11.7	12.3
Professional	14.0	12.4	14.1
Technical & Related Support	3.0	3.0	3.7
Sales	11.6	12.3	11.8
Administrative Support/Clerical	16.0	15.5	16.3
Blue Collar	28.6	30.9	26.2
Precision Production/Craft/Repair	9.6	11.7	11.3
Machine Operators/Assem./Insp.	10.9	10.8	6.8
Transportation/Material Movers	3.3	4.1	4.1
Cleaners/Helpers/Laborers	4.8	4.4	3.9
Services	15.7	12.6	13.2
Farming/Forestry/Fishing	0.9	1.6	2.5

Note: figures cover employed persons 16 years old and over;
(1) Metropolitan Statistical Area - see Appendix A for areas included
Source: 1990 Census of Population and Housing, Summary Tape File 3C

Occupational Employment Projections: 1994 - 2005

High Demand Occupations (ranked by annual openings)	Fast-Growing Occupations (ranked by percent growth)
1. Cashiers	1. Computer engineers
2. Waiters & waitresses	2. Systems analysts
3. Salespersons, retail	3. Home health aides
4. General managers & top executives	4. Residential counselors
5. Truck drivers, heavy	5. Engineers, other
6. Hand packers & packagers	6. Engineers, mechanical
7. Secretaries, except legal & medical	7. Plastic molding/casting mach. oper.
8. General office clerks	8. Designers, except interior designers
9. Janitors/cleaners/maids, ex. priv. hshld.	9. Combination machine tool setters
10. Clerical supervisors	10. Waiters & waitresses

Projections cover Kent and Allegan Counties.
Source: Michigan Employment Security Commission, Annual Planning Information Report 1998, Kent-Allegan MWA

Average Wages

Occupation	Wage	Occupation	Wage
Professional/Technical/Clerical	$/Week	**Health/Protective Services**	$/Week
Accountants III	-	Corrections Officers	-
Attorneys III	-	Firefighters	-
Budget Analysts III	-	Nurses, Licensed Practical II	-
Buyers/Contracting Specialists II	-	Nurses, Registered II	672
Clerks, Accounting III	463	Nursing Assistants II	-
Clerks, General III	388	Police Officers I	-
Computer Operators II	-	**Hourly Workers**	$/Hour
Computer Programmers II	-	Forklift Operators	12.51
Drafters II	513	General Maintenance Workers	9.47
Engineering Technicians III	614	Guards I	5.94
Engineering Technicians, Civil III	-	Janitors	7.92
Engineers III	-	Maintenance Electricians	18.22
Key Entry Operators I	-	Maintenance Electronics Techs II	-
Personnel Assistants III	-	Maintenance Machinists	-
Personnel Specialists III	-	Maintenance Mechanics, Machinery	19.67
Secretaries III	600	Material Handling Laborers	-
Switchboard Operator-Receptionist	330	Motor Vehicle Mechanics	17.65
Systems Analysts II	-	Shipping/Receiving Clerks	11.62
Systems Analysts Supervisor/Mgr II	-	Tool and Die Makers	-
Tax Collectors II	-	Truckdrivers, Tractor Trailer	14.74
Word Processors II	-	Warehouse Specialists	-

Note: Wage data includes full-time workers only for 5/95 and cover the nearby metro area of Kalamazoo-Battle Creek, MI. Dashes indicate that data was not available.
Source: Bureau of Labor Statistics, Occupational Compensation Survey

TAXES

Major State and Local Tax Rates

State Corp. Income (%)	State Personal Income (%)	Residential Property (effective rate per $100)	Sales & Use State (%)	Local (%)	State Gasoline (cents/gallon)	State Cigarette (cents/20-pack)
2.3[a]	4.4	n/a	6.0	None	19	75

Note: Personal/corporate income tax rates as of 1/97. Sales, gasoline and cigarette tax rates as of 1/98; (a) Value added tax imposed on the sum of federal taxable income of the business, compensation paid to employees, dividends, interest, royalties paid and other items
Source: Federation of Tax Administrators, www.taxadmin.org; Washington D.C. Department of Finance and Revenue, Tax Rates and Tax Burdens in the District of Columbia: A Nationwide Comparison, June 1997; Chamber of Commerce

Total Taxes Per Capita and as a Percent of Income

Area	Per Capita Income ($)	Per Capita Taxes ($)			Taxes as Pct. of Income (%)		
		Total	Federal	State/Local	Total	Federal	State/Local
Michigan	26,934	9,533	6,409	3,124	35.4	23.8	11.6
U.S.	26,187	9,205	6,127	3,078	35.2	23.4	11.8

Note: Figures are for 1997
Source: Tax Foundation, Web Site, www.taxfoundation.org

COMMERCIAL REAL ESTATE

Office Market

Class/Location	Total Space (sq. ft.)	Vacant Space (sq. ft.)	Vac. Rate (%)	Under Constr. (sq. ft.)	Net Absorp. (sq. ft.)	Rental Rates ($/sq.ft./yr.)
Class A						
CBD	1,795,000	51,400	2.9	0	74,200	15.50-22.50
Outside CBD	3,697,300	138,900	3.8	140,000	303,900	12.00-18.50
Class B						
CBD	1,947,100	196,400	10.1	295,000	186,600	10.00-17.00
Outside CBD	1,823,500	92,080	5.0	0	35,520	8.00-14.50

Note: Data as of 10/97 and covers Grand Rapids; CBD = Central Business District; n/a not available;
Source: Society of Industrial and Office Realtors, 1998 Comparative Statistics of Industrial and Office Real Estate Markets

"With vacancies at such low levels, interest in new development is likely to increase. Most new office properties are located in the southeast submarket, which could see another 300,000 sq. ft. of speculative development in the coming year. Another 200,000 sq. ft. of spec space is planned for the central business district. Despite slowing national trends, Grand Rapids will probably experience another year of strong economic growth, thanks to the relative strength of its local industries. Local unemployment is below the national level and is expected to stabilize in the mid-to-upper-three percent range through the turn of the century." *Society of Industrial and Office Realtors, 1998 Comparative Statistics of Industrial and Office Real Estate Markets*

Industrial Market

Location	Total Space (sq. ft.)	Vacant Space (sq. ft.)	Vac. Rate (%)	Under Constr. (sq. ft.)	Net Absorp. (sq. ft.)	Net Lease ($/sq.ft./yr.)
Central City	77,400,000	3,200,000	4.1	1,750,000	2,200,000	1.50-4.60
Suburban	n/a	n/a	n/a	n/a	n/a	2.50-4.50

Note: Data as of 10/97 and covers Grand Rapids (including Kent and Ottawa counties). Inventory figures for central city and suburbs are combined.; n/a not available
Source: Society of Industrial and Office Realtors, 1998 Comparative Statistics of Industrial and Office Real Estate Markets

"Newly established 'tax free' renaissance zones are revitalizing development in the older areas of downtown. The MSA's economy is expected to grow at a quicker pace than the nation as a whole, though slower than in recent years. Population and employment trends in Grand Rapids are very strong. Unemployment is low, though not at levels that would indicate a shortage of qualified labor. In addition, the anticipated slowdown in employment growth should stabilize unemployment between 3.5 and four percent through the end of the decade. Limits to growth include potential consolidations in the medical services and automotive industries, and cyclical changes in the national economy." *Society of Industrial and Office Realtors, 1998 Comparative Statistics of Industrial and Office Real Estate Markets*

COMMERCIAL UTILITIES

Typical Monthly Electric Bills

Area	Commercial Service ($/month)		Industrial Service ($/month)	
	12 kW demand 1,500 kWh	100 kW demand 30,000 kWh	1,000 kW demand 400,000 kWh	20,000 kW demand 10,000,000 kWh
City	152	2,065	23,321	535,840
U.S.	162	2,360	25,590	545,677

Note: Based on rates in effect July 1, 1997
Source: Edison Electric Institute, Typical Residential, Commercial and Industrial Bills, Summer 1997

TRANSPORTATION

Transportation Statistics

Avg. travel time to work (min.)	16.7
Interstate highways	I-96
Bus lines	
In-city	Grand Rapids Area TA
Inter-city	2
Passenger air service	
Airport	Kent County International
Airlines	7
Aircraft departures	17,367 (1995)
Enplaned passengers	737,610 (1995)
Rail service	Amtrak
Motor freight carriers	32
Major waterways/ports	Grand River

Source: OAG, Business Travel Planner, Summer 1997; Editor & Publisher Market Guide, 1998; FAA Airport Activity Statistics, 1996; Amtrak National Time Table, Northeast Timetable, Fall/Winter 1997-98; 1990 Census of Population and Housing, STF 3C; Chamber of Commerce/Economic Development 1997; Jane's Urban Transport Systems 1997-98; Transit Fact Book 1997

Means of Transportation to Work

Area	Car/Truck/Van		Public Transportation			Bicycle	Walked	Other Means	Worked at Home
	Drove Alone	Car-pooled	Bus	Subway	Railroad				
City	76.8	11.7	3.2	0.0	0.0	0.3	4.3	1.0	2.7
MSA[1]	82.7	9.8	1.1	0.0	0.0	0.2	2.8	0.6	2.8
U.S.	73.2	13.4	3.0	1.5	0.5	0.4	3.9	1.2	3.0

Note: figures shown are percentages and only include workers 16 years old and over;
(1) Metropolitan Statistical Area - see Appendix A for areas included
Source: 1990 Census of Population and Housing, Summary Tape File 3C

BUSINESSES

Major Business Headquarters

Company Name	1997 Rankings	
	Fortune 500	Forbes 500
Bissell	-	492
Gordon Food Service	-	105
Meijer	-	15
Steelcase	-	46
Transnational Motors	-	485

Note: Companies listed are located in the city; Dashes indicate no ranking
Fortune 500: companies that produce a 10-K are ranked 1 - 500 based on 1996 revenue
Forbes 500: private companies are ranked 1 - 500 based on 1996 revenue
Source: Forbes 12/1/97; Fortune 4/28/97

HOTELS & MOTELS

Hotels/Motels

Area	Hotels/ Motels	Rooms	Luxury-Level Hotels/Motels		Average Minimum Rates ($)		
			♦♦♦♦	♦♦♦♦♦	♦♦	♦♦♦	♦♦♦♦
City	10	1,875	1	0	n/a	n/a	n/a
Airport	14	1,839	0	0	n/a	n/a	n/a
Suburbs	6	281	0	0	n/a	n/a	n/a
Total	30	3,995	1	0	n/a	n/a	n/a

Note: n/a not available; Classifications range from one diamond (budget properties with basic amenities) to five diamond (luxury properties with the finest service, rooms and facilities).
Source: OAG, Business Travel Planner, Summer 1997

CONVENTION CENTERS

Major Convention Centers

Center Name	Meeting Rooms	Exhibit Space (sf)
Amway Grand Plaza Hotel	52	155,000
Grand Center	7	118,518

Source: Trade Shows Worldwide 1997

Living Environment

COST OF LIVING

Cost of Living Index

Composite Index	Housing	Utilities	Groceries	Health Care	Trans- portation	Misc. Goods/ Services
107.8	112.7	95.3	107.3	104.5	105.9	107.9

Note: U.S. = 100
Source: ACCRA, Cost of Living Index, 2nd Quarter 1997

HOUSING

Median Home Prices and Housing Affordability

Area	Median Price[2] 3rd Qtr. 1997 ($)	HOI[3] 3rd Qtr. 1997	Afford- ability Rank[4]
MSA[1]	96,000	73.1	65
U.S.	127,000	63.7	–

Note: (1) Metropolitan Statistical Area - see Appendix A for areas included; (2) U.S. figures calculated from the sales of 625,000 new and existing homes in 195 markets; (3) Housing Opportunity Index - percent of homes sold that were within the reach of the median income household at the prevailing mortgage interest rate; (4) Rank is from 1-195 with 1 being most affordable
Source: National Association of Home Builders, Housing Opportunity Index, 3rd Quarter 1997

It is projected that the median price of existing single-family homes in the metro area will increase by 9.1% in 1998. Nationwide, home prices are projected to increase 6.6%.
Kiplinger's Personal Finance Magazine, January 1998

Average New Home Price

Area	Price ($)
City	153,399
U.S.	135,150

Note: Figures are based on a new home with 1,800 sq. ft. of living area on an 8,000 sq. ft. lot.
Source: ACCRA, Cost of Living Index, 2nd Quarter 1997

Average Apartment Rent

Area	Rent ($/mth)
City	586
U.S.	575

Note: Figures are based on an unfurnished two bedroom, 1-1/2 or 2 bath apartment, approximately 950 sq. ft. in size, excluding all utilities except water
Source: ACCRA, Cost of Living Index, 2nd Quarter 1997

RESIDENTIAL UTILITIES

Average Residential Utility Costs

Area	All Electric ($/mth)	Part Electric ($/mth)	Other Energy ($/mth)	Phone ($/mth)
City	–	52.43	44.10	21.00
U.S.	108.38	56.32	44.12	19.66

Source: ACCRA, Cost of Living Index, 2nd Quarter 1997

HEALTH CARE

Average Health Care Costs

Area	Hospital ($/day)	Doctor ($/visit)	Dentist ($/visit)
City	414.00	52.25	60.20
U.S.	390.32	48.32	60.14

Note: Hospital - based on a semi-private room. Doctor - based on a general practitioner's routine exam of an established patient. Dentist - based on adult teeth cleaning and periodic oral exam.
Source: ACCRA, Cost of Living Index, 2nd Quarter 1997

Distribution of Office-Based Physicians

Area	Family/Gen. Practitioners	Specialists		
		Medical	Surgical	Other
MSA[1]	200	384	347	346

Note: Data as of 12/31/96; (1) Metropolitan Statistical Area - see Appendix A for areas included
Source: American Medical Assn., Physician Characteristics & Distribution in the U.S., 1997-1998

Hospitals

Grand Rapids has 4 general medical and surgical hospitals, 2 psychiatric, 1 rehabilitation, 2 children's other specialty. *AHA Guide to the Healthcare Field 1997-98*

Blodgett Memorial Medical Center is among the 100 best-run hospitals in the U.S. *Modern Healthcare, January 5, 1998*

EDUCATION

Public School District Statistics

District Name	Num. Sch.	Enroll.	Classroom Teachers[1]	Pupils per Teacher	Minority Pupils (%)	Current Exp.[2] ($/pupil)
Forest Hills Public Schools	10	6,902	402	17.2	n/a	n/a
Grand Rapids City School Dist	94	27,087	1,337	20.3	56.2	6,976
Kelloggsville Public Schools	6	2,186	109	20.1	n/a	n/a
Kenowa Hills Public Schools	7	3,041	138	22.0	n/a	n/a
Northview Public School Dist	7	3,164	162	19.5	n/a	n/a

Note: Data covers the 1995-1996 school year unless otherwise noted; (1) Excludes teachers reported as working in school district offices rather than in schools; (2) Based on 1993-94 enrollment collected by the Census Bureau, not the enrollment figure shown in column 3; SD = School District; ISD = Independent School District; n/a not available
Source: National Center for Education Statistics, Common Core of Data Survey; Bureau of the Census

Educational Quality

School District	Education Quotient[1]	Graduate Outcome[2]	Community Index[3]	Resource Index[4]
Grand Rapids	n/a	n/a	n/a	n/a

Note: Nearly 1,000 secondary school districts were rated in terms of educational quality. The scores range from a low of 50 to a high of 150; (1) Average of the Graduate Outcome, Community and Resource indexes; (2) Based on graduation rates and college board scores (SAT/ACT); (3) Based on the surrounding community's average level of education and the area's average income level; (4) Based on teacher salaries, per-pupil expenditures and student-teacher ratios.
Source: Expansion Management, Ratings Issue 1997

Educational Attainment by Race

Area	High School Graduate (%)					Bachelor's Degree (%)				
	Total	White	Black	Other	Hisp.[2]	Total	White	Black	Other	Hisp.[2]
City	76.4	80.0	63.8	46.9	41.0	20.8	23.7	7.7	10.7	8.2
MSA[1]	80.2	81.6	65.9	54.1	48.0	20.2	21.0	8.4	12.4	7.7
U.S.	75.2	77.9	63.1	60.4	49.8	20.3	21.5	11.4	19.4	9.2

Note: figures shown cover persons 25 years old and over; (1) Metropolitan Statistical Area - see Appendix A for areas included; (2) people of Hispanic origin can be of any race
Source: 1990 Census of Population and Housing, Summary Tape File 3C

School Enrollment by Type

Area	Preprimary				Elementary/High School			
	Public		Private		Public		Private	
	Enrollment	%	Enrollment	%	Enrollment	%	Enrollment	%
City	3,105	60.8	2,004	39.2	24,319	76.0	7,660	24.0
MSA[1]	12,129	66.4	6,136	33.6	103,726	81.8	23,081	18.2
U.S.	2,679,029	59.5	1,824,256	40.5	38,379,689	90.2	4,187,099	9.8

Note: figures shown cover persons 3 years old and over;
(1) Metropolitan Statistical Area - see Appendix A for areas included
Source: 1990 Census of Population and Housing, Summary Tape File 3C

School Enrollment by Race

Area	Preprimary (%)				Elementary/High School (%)			
	White	Black	Other	Hisp.[1]	White	Black	Other	Hisp.[1]
City	73.4	20.5	6.1	5.5	62.8	29.6	7.6	7.3
MSA[2]	89.6	6.5	3.9	2.6	86.5	8.4	5.1	4.5
U.S.	80.4	12.5	7.1	7.8	74.1	15.6	10.3	12.5

Note: figures shown cover persons 3 years old and over; (1) people of Hispanic origin can be of any race; (2) Metropolitan Statistical Area - see Appendix A for areas included
Source: 1990 Census of Population and Housing, Summary Tape File 3C

SAT/ACT Scores

Area/District	1997 SAT				1997 ACT	
	Percent of Graduates Tested (%)	Average Math Score	Average Verbal Score	Average Combined Score	Percent of Graduates Tested (%)	Average Composite Score
Grand Rapids PS	4	562	531	1,093	52	19.7
State	11	566	557	1,123	68	21.3
U.S.	42	511	505	1,016	36	21.0

Note: Math and verbal SAT scores are out of a possible 800; ACT scores are out of a possible 36
Caution: Comparing or ranking states/cities on the basis of SAT/ACT scores alone is invalid and strongly discouraged by the The College Board and The American College Testing Program as students who take the tests are self-selected and do not represent the entire student population.
Source: Grand Rapids Public Schools, Research & Evaluation, 1997; American College Testing Program, 1997; College Board, 1997

Classroom Teacher Salaries in Public Schools

District	B.A. Degree		M.A. Degree		Ph.D. Degree	
	Min. ($)	Max. ($)	Min. ($)	Max. ($)	Min. ($)	Max. ($)
Grand Rapids	28,037	43,136	31,005	49,875	32,417	51,287
Average[1]	26,120	39,270	28,175	44,667	31,643	49,825

Note: Salaries are for 1996-1997; (1) Based on all school districts covered; n/a not available
Source: American Federation of Teachers (unpublished data)

Higher Education

Two-Year Colleges		Four-Year Colleges		Medical Schools	Law Schools	Voc/ Tech
Public	Private	Public	Private			
1	0	0	7	0	0	5

Source: College Blue Book, Occupational Education 1997; Medical School Admission Requirements, 1998-99; Peterson's Guide to Two-Year Colleges, 1997; Peterson's Guide to Four-Year Colleges, 1997; Barron's Guide to Law Schools 1997

MAJOR EMPLOYERS

Major Employers

Autodie International	Bissell
Blodgett Memorial Medical Center	Gordon Food Service
Diesel Technology (auto parts)	Kent Community Hospital
Knape & Vogt Manufacturing (store fixtures)	LG Cook Distributors (hardware)
Meijer Companies (department stores)	Metropolitan Hospital
Old Kent Financial Corp.	Spartan Stores
Steelcase	Butterworth Hospital
Rapistan Demag Corp. (conveyors)	Amway Hotel Corp.

Note: companies listed are located in the city
Source: Dun's Business Rankings 1997; Ward's Business Directory, 1997

PUBLIC SAFETY

Crime Rate

Area	All Crimes	Violent Crimes				Property Crimes		
		Murder	Forcible Rape	Robbery	Aggrav. Assault	Burglary	Larceny -Theft	Motor Vehicle Theft
City	7,590.0	10.4	52.5	350.9	856.2	1,576.7	4,185.4	557.8
Suburbs[1]	3,886.2	2.2	42.9	46.7	211.1	699.1	2,658.1	226.1
MSA[2]	4,602.2	3.8	44.7	105.5	335.8	868.7	2,953.3	290.2
U.S.	5,078.9	7.4	36.1	202.4	388.2	943.0	2,975.9	525.9

Note: Crime rate is the number of crimes per 100,000 pop.; (1) defined as all areas within the MSA but located outside the central city; (2) Metropolitan Statistical Area - see Appendix A for areas incl.
Source: FBI Uniform Crime Reports 1996

RECREATION

Culture and Recreation

Museums	Symphony Orchestras	Opera Companies	Dance Companies	Professional Theatres	Zoos	Pro Sports Teams
4	1	1	1	0	1	0

Source: International Directory of the Performing Arts, 1996; Official Museum Directory, 1998; Chamber of Commerce/Economic Development 1997

Library System

The Grand Rapids Public Library has six branches, holdings of 634,520 volumes and a budget of $6,736,339 (1994-1995). The Kent District Library has 19 branches, holdings of 761,808 volumes and a budget of $4,595,822 (1995). *American Library Directory, 1997-1998*

MEDIA

Newspapers

Name	Type	Freq.	Distribution	Circulation
The Grand Rapids Press	n/a	7x/wk	Area	153,061
Grand Rapids Times	Black	1x/wk	Local	6,000

Note: Includes newspapers with circulations of 1,000 or more located in the city; n/a not available
Source: Burrelle's Media Directory, 1998 Edition

AM Radio Stations

Call Letters	Freq. (kHz)	Target Audience	Station Format	Music Format
WMFN	640	Men	S	n/a
WMJH	810	n/a	M/N	Big Band
WKWM	1140	n/a	M/N/S	Urban Contemporary
WTKG	1230	General	M/N	Country
WOOD	1300	General	N/S/T	n/a
WBBL	1340	Men	S	n/a
WRCV	1410	General	M/N/S	Country
WGVU	1480	General	M/N/T	Jazz/R&B
WYGR	1530	Hispanic	M	Big Band
WFUR	1570	General	M/N/S	Christian

Note: Stations included broadcast in the Grand Rapids metro area; n/a not available
Station Format: E = Educational; M = Music; N = News; S = Sports; T = Talk
Source: Burrelle's Media Directory, 1998 Edition

FM Radio Stations

Call Letters	Freq. (mHz)	Target Audience	Station Format	Music Format
WYCE	88.1	General	M	AOR/Jazz/R&B
WGVU	88.5	General	M	Jazz
WCSG	91.3	General	M/N/S	Christian
WBCT	93.7	General	M	Country
WKLQ	94.5	General	M	Alternative
WLHT	95.7	General	M/N/S	Adult Contemporary
WVTI	96.1	n/a	M	Adult Contemporary
WLAV	96.9	General	M	Classic Rock
WGRD	97.9	General	M	Alternative
WCUZ	101.3	General	M	Country
WFUR	102.9	Religious	M/N/S	Christian/MOR
WSNX	104.5	General	M	Contemporary Top 40
WOOD	105.7	General	M	Adult Contemporary
WODJ	107.3	General	M/N	Oldies

Note: Stations included broadcast in the Grand Rapids metro area; n/a not available
Station Format: E = Educational; M = Music; N = News; S = Sports; T = Talk
Music Format: AOR = Album Oriented Rock; MOR = Middle-of-the-Road
Source: Burrelle's Media Directory, 1998 Edition

Television Stations

Name	Ch.	Affiliation	Type	Owner
WOOD	8	NBC	Commercial	LCH Communications, Inc.
WZZM	13	ABC	Commercial	Gannett Broadcasting
WXMI	17	Fox	Commercial	TV-17 Unlimited Inc.
WGVU	35	PBS	Public	Grand Valley State University
WGVK	52	PBS	Public	Grand Valley State University
WTLJ	54	TBN	Commercial	Tri-State Christian TV Inc.

Note: Stations included broadcast in the Grand Rapids metro area
Source: Burrelle's Media Directory, 1998 Edition

CLIMATE

Average and Extreme Temperatures

Temperature	Jan	Feb	Mar	Apr	May	Jun	Jul	Aug	Sep	Oct	Nov	Dec	Ann
Extreme High (°F)	66	67	80	88	92	102	100	100	97	87	81	67	102
Average High (°F)	30	32	42	57	69	79	83	81	73	61	46	34	57
Average Temp. (°F)	23	25	34	47	58	67	72	70	62	51	39	28	48
Average Low (°F)	15	16	25	36	46	56	60	59	51	41	31	21	38
Extreme Low (°F)	-22	-19	-8	3	22	33	41	39	28	18	-10	-18	-22

Note: Figures cover the years 1948-1990
Source: National Climatic Data Center, International Station Meteorological Climate Summary, 3/95

Average Precipitation/Snowfall/Humidity

Precip./Humidity	Jan	Feb	Mar	Apr	May	Jun	Jul	Aug	Sep	Oct	Nov	Dec	Ann
Avg. Precip. (in.)	1.9	1.6	2.6	3.5	3.0	3.5	3.2	3.2	3.7	2.7	3.1	2.7	34.7
Avg. Snowfall (in.)	21	12	11	3	Tr	0	0	0	Tr	1	8	18	73
Avg. Rel. Hum. 7am (%)	81	80	80	79	79	81	84	88	89	85	83	83	83
Avg. Rel. Hum. 4pm (%)	71	66	61	54	50	52	52	55	58	60	68	74	60

Note: Figures cover the years 1948-1990; Tr = Trace amounts (<0.05 in. of rain; <0.5 in. of snow)
Source: National Climatic Data Center, International Station Meteorological Climate Summary, 3/95

Weather Conditions

Temperature			Daytime Sky			Precipitation		
5°F & below	32°F & below	90°F & above	Clear	Partly cloudy	Cloudy	0.01 inch or more precip.	0.1 inch or more snow/ice	Thunder-storms
15	146	11	67	119	179	142	57	34

Note: Figures are average number of days per year and covers the years 1948-1990
Source: National Climatic Data Center, International Station Meteorological Climate Summary, 3/95

AIR & WATER QUALITY

Maximum Pollutant Concentrations

	Particulate Matter (ug/m^3)	Carbon Monoxide (ppm)	Sulfur Dioxide (ppm)	Nitrogen Dioxide (ppm)	Ozone (ppm)	Lead (ug/m^3)
MSA[1] Level	71	3	0.011	0.009	0.13	0.01
NAAQS[2]	150	9	0.140	0.053	0.12	1.50
Met NAAQS?	Yes	Yes	Yes	Yes	No	Yes

Note: (1) Metropolitan Statistical Area - see Appendix A for areas included; (2) National Ambient Air Quality Standards; ppm = parts per million; ug/m^3 = micrograms per cubic meter; n/a not available
Source: EPA, National Air Quality and Emissions Trends Report, 1996

Pollutant Standards Index

In the Grand Rapids MSA (see Appendix A for areas included), the Pollutant Standards Index (PSI) exceeded 100 on 4 days in 1996. A PSI value greater than 100 indicates that air quality would be in the unhealthful range on that day. *EPA, National Air Quality and Emissions Trends Report, 1996*

Drinking Water

Water System Name	Pop. Served	Primary Water Source Type	Number of Violations in Fiscal Year 1997	Type of Violation/ Contaminants
Grand Rapids	197,649	Surface	None	None

Note: Data as of January 16, 1998
Source: EPA, Office of Ground Water and Drinking Water, Safe Drinking Water Information System

Grand Rapids tap water is alkaline, hard and fluoridated.
Editor & Publisher Market Guide, 1998

Green Bay, Wisconsin

Background

Green Bay is Wisconsin's oldest settlement. In 1634 the French-Canadian explorer Jean Nicolet founded a trading post near Green Bay, an inlet of Lake Michigan. In 1671 a French missionary settlement called La Baye was established and in 1717 the French built a fort. The area soon became the center of an active fur trade. After the French and Indian War, British traders moved into the region and changed the name to Green Bay. In 1825, as a result of the opening of the Erie Canal, the city developed as an agricultural and lumbering center. The city was incorporated in 1854.

Today Green Bay's main products are wood pulp, paper, machinery and cheese. The city is home to the largest meat packing center east of the Mississippi and is a Great Lakes port of entry for vessels that use the St. Lawrence Seaway. A major distribution center, Green Bay lies at the head of Lake Michigan and at the mouth of the Fox River, 112 miles north of Milwaukee.

Green Bay has more to offer than just its famous NFL football team, the Green Bay Packers. The University of Wisconsin - Green Bay Campus, St. Norbert College and the Northeast Wisconsin Technical College offer educational opportunities for both college students and the Green Bay community. The arts also thrive in Green Bay which boasts of an opera company, two symphony orchestras and several local theaters. Located on the University of Wisconsin - Green Bay campus, the Weidner Center for the Performing Arts provides a wide range of cultural events from Broadway touring companies to Chinese acrobatic troupes.

The city's climate is modified by the Bay of Green Bay, Lakes Michigan and Superior, and to a lesser extent the Fox River Valley. This modified continental climate is reflected in the few occurrences of 90 degree temperatures in summer or subzero temperatures in winter.

General Rankings and Evaluative Comments

■ Green Bay was ranked #108 out of 300 cities by *Money's* 1997 "Survey of the Best Places to Live." Criteria used: health services, crime, economy, housing, education, transportation, weather, leisure and the arts. The city was ranked #119 in 1996 and #190 in 1995. *Money, July 1997; Money, September 1996; Money, September 1995*

■ Green Bay is among "The Best Places to Raise a Family". Rank: 47 out of 301 metro areas. Criteria: low crime rate, low drug and alcohol abuse, good public schools, high-quality health care, a clean environment, affordable cost of living and strong economic growth. *Reader's Digest, April 1997*

■ Green Bay was ranked #30 out of 219 cities in terms of children's health, safety, and economic well-being. Criteria: total population, percent population change, birth rate, child immunization rate, infant mortality rate, percent low birth weight infants, percent of births to teens, physician-to-population ratio, student-to-teacher ratio, dropout rate, unemployment rate, median family income, percent of children in poverty, violent and property crime rates, number of juvenile arrests for violent crimes as a percent of the total crime index, number of days with pollution standard index (PSI) over 100, pounds toxic releases per 1,000 people and number of superfund sites. *Zero Population Growth, Children's Environmental Index 1997*

■ According to *Working Mother*, "Governor Tommy Thompson's welfare reform effort, 'Wisconsin Works,' included sweeping changes in the state's child care rules and funding. On the positive side, state funding is increasing by $36 million this year alone, which means all families on the waiting list for child care subsidies have now received them. In 1996-97, the state pumped $89 million in new state money into child care. By 1998, the number of children receiving aid will zoom from the current 17,000 to 60,000. This is a remarkable achievement.

The state also gave a big one-time boost to efforts to increase supply and quality to the tune of $5 million. That money will translate into more staff for licensing, improved resource and referral services and more grants for caregiver training.

At the same time, however, Wisconsin has created a new class of providers, known as 'provision' caregivers. These providers will not be required to have any training and the state will reimburse them at half the rate it pays those who are certified and have credentials in early education. Many advocates are worried that these policies—paying caregivers less and lowering training standards—could hurt the quality of child care in Wisconsin. (Wisconsin is among the 10 best states for child care.)" *Working Mother, July/August 1997*

Business Environment

STATE ECONOMY

State Economic Profile

"Wisconsin's economy in general, and manufacturing and wholesale trade in particular, continue to lag the nation....

Slow population growth is taking a serious toll on Wisconsin's labor market. Wisconsin is experiencing its tightest labor market since the late 1970's. Just as in other parts of the Midwest, skilled workers, such as machinists, are in short supply. Also, acute shortages are being felt in many entry-level distribution and retail trade jobs. The more industrialized southeastern MSAs of Wisconsin face tighter labor markets than the rest of Wisconsin. Slower household growth will erode demand for residential construction, eventually stifling the strong job growth that has characterized the construction industry of late.

Wisconsin is making a concerted effort to lighten the residential property tax burden, because differences in Wisconsin's and Minnesota's tax systems encourage people to locate their businesses in Wisconsin and commute from Minnesota. Another popular approach to economic development that Wisconsin is now employing is the use of enterprise development zones.

The outlook for Wisconsin is for moderate growth. Positive demographic trends will support service growth and retail and residential construction over the longer term....Wisconsin will be an average performer through the forecast." *National Association of Realtors, Economic Profiles: The Fifty States, July 1997*

IMPORTS/EXPORTS

Total Export Sales

Area	1993 ($000)	1994 ($000)	1995 ($000)	1996 ($000)	% Chg. 1993-96	% Chg. 1995-96
MSA[1]	134,097	187,290	212,672	188,950	40.9	-11.2
U.S.	464,858,354	512,415,609	583,030,524	622,827,063	34.0	6.8

Note: (1) Metropolitan Statistical Area - see Appendix A for areas included
Source: U.S. Department of Commerce, International Trade Association, Metropolitan Area Exports: An Export Performance Report on Over 250 U.S. Cities, October 1997

Imports/Exports by Port

Type	Cargo Value			Share of U.S. Total	
	1995 (US$mil.)	1996 (US$mil.)	% Change 1995-1996	1995 (%)	1996 (%)
Imports	10	18	84.02	0.00	0.00
Exports	17	7	-58.11	0.00	0.00

Source: Global Trade Information Services, WaterBorne Trade Atlas 1997

CITY FINANCES

City Government Finances

Component	FY92 ($000)	FY92 (per capita $)
Revenue	91,804	926.17
Expenditure	100,814	1,017.07
Debt Outstanding	141,791	1,430.47
Cash & Securities	129,380	1,305.26

Source: U.S. Bureau of the Census, City Government Finances: 1991-92

City Government Revenue by Source

Source	FY92 ($000)	FY92 (per capita $)	FY92 (%)
From Federal Government	990	9.99	1.1
From State Governments	33,966	342.67	37.0
From Local Governments	743	7.50	0.8
Property Taxes	18,556	187.20	20.2
General Sales Taxes	1	0.01	0.0
Selective Sales Taxes	495	4.99	0.5
Income Taxes	0	0.00	0.0
Current Charges	18,244	184.06	19.9
Utility/Liquor Store	6,699	67.58	7.3
Employee Retirement[1]	0	0.00	0.0
Other	12,110	122.17	13.2

Note: (1) Excludes "city contributions," classified as "nonrevenue," intragovernmental transfers.
Source: U.S. Bureau of the Census, City Government Finances: 1991-92

City Government Expenditures by Function

Function	FY92 ($000)	FY92 (per capita $)	FY92 (%)
Educational Services	0	0.00	0.0
Employee Retirement[1]	0	0.00	0.0
Environment/Housing	26,936	271.75	26.7
Government Administration	3,188	32.16	3.2
Interest on General Debt	10,594	106.88	10.5
Public Safety	28,348	285.99	28.1
Social Services	1,502	15.15	1.5
Transportation	20,520	207.02	20.4
Utility/Liquor Store	9,487	95.71	9.4
Other	239	2.41	0.2

Note: (1) Payments to beneficiaries including withdrawal of contributions.
Source: U.S. Bureau of the Census, City Government Finances: 1991-92

Municipal Bond Ratings

Area	Moody's	S & P
Green Bay	Aa2	n/a

Note: n/a not available; n/r not rated
Source: Moody's Bond Record, 2/98; Statistical Abstract of the U.S., 1997;
Governing Magazine, 9/97, 3/98

POPULATION

Population Growth

Area	1980	1990	% Chg. 1980-90	July 1996 Estimate	% Chg. 1990-96
City	87,899	96,466	9.7	102,076	5.8
MSA[1]	175,280	194,594	11.0	213,072	9.5
U.S.	226,545,805	248,765,170	9.8	265,179,411	6.6

Note: (1) Metropolitan Statistical Area - see Appendix A for areas included
Source: 1980/1990 Census of Housing and Population, Summary Tape File 3C;
Census Bureau Population Estimates

Population Characteristics

Race	City					MSA[1]	
	1980		1990		% Chg. 1980-90	1990	
	Population	%	Population	%		Population	%
White	85,064	96.8	91,040	94.4	7.0	186,901	96.0
Black	216	0.2	536	0.6	148.1	1,028	0.5
Amer Indian/Esk/Aleut	1,705	1.9	2,230	2.3	30.8	3,590	1.8
Asian/Pacific Islander	697	0.8	2,288	2.4	228.3	2,587	1.3
Other	217	0.2	372	0.4	71.4	488	0.3
Hispanic Origin[2]	641	0.7	1,061	1.1	65.5	1,465	0.8

Note: (1) Metropolitan Statistical Area - see Appendix A for areas included;
(2) people of Hispanic origin can be of any race
Source: 1980/1990 Census of Housing and Population, Summary Tape File 3C

Ancestry

Area	German	Irish	English	Italian	U.S.	French	Polish	Dutch
City	48.0	12.8	6.0	2.1	1.5	9.6	12.1	6.7
MSA[1]	50.2	13.3	5.8	2.0	1.4	9.3	12.8	9.0
U.S.	23.3	15.6	13.1	5.9	5.3	4.2	3.8	2.5

Note: Figures are percentages and include persons that reported multiple ancestry (eg. if a person reported being Irish and Italian, they were included in both columns); (1) Metropolitan Statistical Area - see Appendix A for areas included
Source: 1990 Census of Population and Housing, Summary Tape File 3C

Age

Area	Median Age (Years)	Age Distribution (%)						
		Under 5	Under 18	18-24	25-44	45-64	65+	80+
City	31.3	8.1	25.9	11.2	34.3	16.0	12.7	3.2
MSA[1]	31.4	7.8	27.0	11.0	34.2	17.0	10.8	2.6
U.S.	32.9	7.3	25.6	10.5	32.6	18.7	12.5	2.8

Note: (1) Met·politan Statistical Area - see Appendix A for areas included
Source: 1990 Census of Population and Housing, Summary Tape File 3C

Male/Female Ratio

Area	Number of males per 100 females (all ages)	Number of males per 100 females (18 years old+)
City	91.8	87.4
MSA[1]	95.4	92.1
U.S.	95.0	91.9

Note: (1) Metropolitan Statistical Area - see Appendix A for areas included
Source: 1990 Census of Population, General Population Characteristics

INCOME

Per Capita/Median/Average Income

Area	Per Capita ($)	Median Household ($)	Average Household ($)
City	12,969	26,770	32,080
MSA[1]	13,906	31,303	36,923
U.S.	14,420	30,056	38,453

Note: all figures are for 1989; (1) Metropolitan Statistical Area - see Appendix A for areas included
Source: 1990 Census of Population and Housing, Summary Tape File 3C

Household Income Distribution by Race

Income ($)	City (%)					U.S. (%)				
	Total	White	Black	Other	Hisp.[1]	Total	White	Black	Other	Hisp.[1]
Less than 5,000	4.2	3.9	1.2	14.1	0.0	6.2	4.8	15.2	8.6	8.8
5,000 - 9,999	12.4	11.9	12.0	28.0	15.9	9.3	8.6	14.2	9.9	11.1
10,000 - 14,999	10.7	10.4	3.6	19.3	22.4	8.8	8.5	11.0	9.8	11.0
15,000 - 24,999	19.6	19.6	21.6	17.8	30.9	17.5	17.3	18.9	18.5	20.5
25,000 - 34,999	17.8	18.1	12.6	10.0	11.0	15.8	16.1	14.2	15.4	16.4
35,000 - 49,999	19.5	19.8	34.7	7.7	15.0	17.9	18.6	13.3	16.1	16.0
50,000 - 74,999	11.5	11.9	4.8	1.7	3.7	15.0	15.8	9.3	13.4	11.1
75,000 - 99,999	2.5	2.6	6.0	0.8	1.2	5.1	5.5	2.6	4.7	3.1
100,000+	1.8	1.8	3.6	0.5	0.0	4.4	4.8	1.3	3.7	1.9

Note: all figures are for 1989; (1) people of Hispanic origin can be of any race
Source: 1990 Census of Population and Housing, Summary Tape File 3C

Effective Buying Income

Area	Per Capita ($)	Median Household ($)	Average Household ($)
City	15,258	31,437	37,873
MSA[1]	16,720	38,117	44,484
U.S.	15,444	33,201	41,849

Note: data as of 1/1/97; (1) Metropolitan Statistical Area - see Appendix A for areas included
Source: Standard Rate & Data Service, Newspaper Advertising Source, 2/98

Effective Household Buying Income Distribution

Area	% of Households Earning						
	$10,000 -$19,999	$20,000 -$34,999	$35,000 -$49,999	$50,000 -$74,999	$75,000 -$99,000	$100,000 -$124,999	$125,000 and up
City	19.1	25.0	20.3	17.3	4.4	1.1	1.2
MSA[1]	14.8	22.4	21.6	22.2	7.0	1.8	2.0
U.S.	16.5	23.4	18.3	18.2	6.4	2.1	2.4

Note: data as of 1/1/97; (1) Metropolitan Statistical Area - see Appendix A for areas included
Source: Standard Rate & Data Service, Newspaper Advertising Source, 2/98

Poverty Rates by Race and Age

Area	Total (%)	By Race (%)				By Age (%)		
		White	Black	Other	Hisp.[2]	Under 5 years old	Under 18 years old	65 years and over
City	13.4	11.1	17.4	56.7	34.2	25.1	19.2	9.9
MSA[1]	9.2	7.8	14.6	47.9	27.1	16.7	12.1	8.5
U.S.	13.1	9.8	29.5	23.1	25.3	20.1	18.3	12.8

Note: figures show the percent of people living below the poverty line in 1989. The average poverty threshold was $12,674 for a family of four in 1989; (1) Metropolitan Statistical Area - see Appendix A for areas included; (2) people of Hispanic origin can be of any race
Source: 1990 Census of Population and Housing, Summary Tape File 3C

EMPLOYMENT

Labor Force and Employment

Area	Civilian Labor Force			Workers Employed		
	Dec. '95	Dec. '96	% Chg.	Dec. '95	Dec. '96	% Chg.
City	63,099	63,098	-0.0	60,850	60,859	0.0
MSA[1]	130,906	130,951	0.0	127,679	127,699	0.0
U.S.	134,583,000	136,742,000	1.6	127,903,000	130,785,000	2.3

Note: Data is not seasonally adjusted and covers workers 16 years of age and older;
(1) Metropolitan Statistical Area - see Appendix A for areas included
Source: Bureau of Labor Statistics, http://stats.bls.gov

Unemployment Rate

Area	1997											
	Jan.	Feb.	Mar.	Apr.	May	Jun.	Jul.	Aug.	Sep.	Oct.	Nov.	Dec.
City	4.9	5.0	4.9	4.5	4.2	5.1	4.7	4.2	4.3	3.8	3.9	3.5
MSA[1]	3.5	3.6	3.5	3.2	3.0	3.5	3.2	2.9	2.9	2.6	2.7	2.5
U.S.	5.9	5.7	5.5	4.8	4.7	5.2	5.0	4.8	4.7	4.4	4.3	4.4

Note: Data is not seasonally adjusted and covers workers 16 years of age and older; All figures are percentages; (1) Metropolitan Statistical Area - see Appendix A for areas included
Source: Bureau of Labor Statistics, http://stats.bls.gov

Employment by Industry

Sector	MSA[1]		U.S.
	Number of Employees	Percent of Total	Percent of Total
Services	33,400	24.5	29.0
Retail Trade	25,400	18.6	18.5
Government	16,100	11.8	16.1
Manufacturing	28,500	20.9	15.0
Finance/Insurance/Real Estate	9,500	7.0	5.7
Wholesale Trade	6,900	5.1	5.4
Transportation/Public Utilities	9,900	7.3	5.3
Construction/Mining	6,600	4.8	5.0

Note: Figures cover non-farm employment as of 12/97 and are not seasonally adjusted; (1) Metropolitan Statistical Area - see Appendix A for areas included
Source: Bureau of Labor Statistics, http://stats.bls.gov

Employment by Occupation

Occupation Category	City (%)	MSA[1] (%)	U.S. (%)
White Collar	54.7	55.2	58.1
Executive/Admin./Management	10.1	11.0	12.3
Professional	11.6	12.3	14.1
Technical & Related Support	3.2	3.2	3.7
Sales	13.3	12.6	11.8
Administrative Support/Clerical	16.4	15.9	16.3
Blue Collar	28.6	29.2	26.2
Precision Production/Craft/Repair	10.7	11.2	11.3
Machine Operators/Assem./Insp.	8.4	8.7	6.8
Transportation/Material Movers	4.3	4.6	4.1
Cleaners/Helpers/Laborers	5.2	4.6	3.9
Services	16.0	13.6	13.2
Farming/Forestry/Fishing	0.6	2.1	2.5

Note: figures cover employed persons 16 years old and over; (1) Metropolitan Statistical Area - see Appendix A for areas included
Source: 1990 Census of Population and Housing, Summary Tape File 3C

Occupational Employment Projections: 1994 - 2005

Occupations Expected to have the Largest Job Growth (ranked by numerical growth)	Fast-Growing Occupations (ranked by percent growth)
1. Waiters & waitresses	1. Computer engineers
2. General managers & top executives	2. Systems analysts
3. Cashiers	3. Electronic pagination systems workers
4. Salespersons, retail	4. Personal and home care aides
5. Janitors/cleaners/maids, ex. priv. hshld.	5. Manicurists
6. Truck drivers, heavy & light	6. Credit authorizers
7. Systems analysts	7. Computer scientists
8. Teachers, secondary school	8. Pressers, hand
9. Marketing & sales, supervisors	9. Geologists/geophysicists/oceanographers
10. Registered nurses	10. Home health aides

Projections cover Wisconsin.
Source: U.S. Department of Labor, Employment and Training Administration, America's Labor Market Information System (ALMIS)

Average Wages

Occupation	Wage	Occupation	Wage
Professional/Technical/Clerical	$/Week	**Health/Protective Services**	$/Week
Accountants III	-	Corrections Officers	-
Attorneys III	-	Firefighters	-
Budget Analysts III	-	Nurses, Licensed Practical II	-
Buyers/Contracting Specialists II	-	Nurses, Registered II	-
Clerks, Accounting III	406	Nursing Assistants II	-
Clerks, General III	378	Police Officers I	-
Computer Operators II	403	**Hourly Workers**	$/Hour
Computer Programmers II	569	Forklift Operators	12.04
Drafters II	451	General Maintenance Workers	9.37
Engineering Technicians III	552	Guards I	6.24
Engineering Technicians, Civil III	-	Janitors	6.17
Engineers III	-	Maintenance Electricians	16.37
Key Entry Operators I	257	Maintenance Electronics Techs II	17.15
Personnel Assistants III	-	Maintenance Machinists	15.86
Personnel Specialists III	-	Maintenance Mechanics, Machinery	15.42
Secretaries III	476	Material Handling Laborers	8.81
Switchboard Operator-Receptionist	300	Motor Vehicle Mechanics	15.00
Systems Analysts II	823	Shipping/Receiving Clerks	10.00
Systems Analysts Supervisor/Mgr II	-	Tool and Die Makers	15.32
Tax Collectors II	-	Truckdrivers, Tractor Trailer	12.44
Word Processors II	-	Warehouse Specialists	12.29

Note: Wage data includes full-time workers only for 5/94 and cover the Appleton-Oshkosh-Neenah-Green Bay metro area. Dashes indicate that data was not available.
Source: Bureau of Labor Statistics, Occupational Compensation Survey

TAXES

Major State and Local Tax Rates

State Corp. Income (%)	State Personal Income (%)	Residential Property (effective rate per $100)	Sales & Use		State Gasoline (cents/ gallon)	State Cigarette (cents/ 20-pack)
			State (%)	Local (%)		
7.9[a]	4.9 - 6.93	n/a	5.0	None	24.8	59

Note: Personal/corporate income tax rates as of 1/97. Sales, gasoline and cigarette tax rates as of 1/98; (a) Plus a surtax set annually by the Dept. of Revenue to finance a special recycling fund
Source: Federation of Tax Administrators, www.taxadmin.org; Washington D.C. Department of Finance and Revenue, Tax Rates and Tax Burdens in the District of Columbia: A Nationwide Comparison, June 1997; Chamber of Commerce

Total Taxes Per Capita and as a Percent of Income

Area	Per Capita Income ($)	Per Capita Taxes ($)			Taxes as Pct. of Income (%)		
		Total	Federal	State/Local	Total	Federal	State/Local
Wisconsin	25,105	9,165	5,825	3,340	36.5	23.2	13.3
U.S.	26,187	9,205	6,127	3,078	35.2	23.4	11.8

Note: Figures are for 1997
Source: Tax Foundation, Web Site, www.taxfoundation.org

COMMERCIAL REAL ESTATE

Data not available at time of publication.

COMMERCIAL UTILITIES

Typical Monthly Electric Bills

Area	Commercial Service ($/month)		Industrial Service ($/month)	
	12 kW demand 1,500 kWh	100 kW demand 30,000 kWh	1,000 kW demand 400,000 kWh	20,000 kW demand 10,000,000 kWh
City	90	1,319	14,574	325,238
U.S.	162	2,360	25,590	545,677

Note: Based on rates in effect July 1, 1997
Source: Edison Electric Institute, Typical Residential, Commercial and Industrial Bills, Summer 1997

TRANSPORTATION

Transportation Statistics

Avg. travel time to work (min.)	15.7
Interstate highways	I-43
Bus lines	
In-city	Green Bay Transit
Inter-city	3
Passenger air service	
Airport	Austin Straubel International
Airlines	7
Aircraft departures	6,876 (1995)
Enplaned passengers	267,939 (1995)
Rail service	No Amtrak Service
Motor freight carriers	49
Major waterways/ports	Green Bay

Source: OAG, Business Travel Planner, Summer 1997; Editor & Publisher Market Guide, 1998; FAA Airport Activity Statistics, 1996; Amtrak National Time Table, Northeast Timetable, Fall/Winter 1997-98; 1990 Census of Population and Housing, STF 3C; Chamber of Commerce/Economic Development 1997; Jane's Urban Transport Systems 1997-98; Transit Fact Book 1997

Means of Transportation to Work

Area	Car/Truck/Van		Public Transportation			Bicycle	Walked	Other Means	Worked at Home
	Drove Alone	Car-pooled	Bus	Subway	Railroad				
City	80.4	9.7	2.1	0.0	0.0	0.5	4.8	0.6	2.0
MSA[1]	81.5	8.8	1.3	0.0	0.0	0.4	4.2	0.5	3.3
U.S.	73.2	13.4	3.0	1.5	0.5	0.4	3.9	1.2	3.0

Note: figures shown are percentages and only include workers 16 years old and over;
(1) Metropolitan Statistical Area - see Appendix A for areas included
Source: 1990 Census of Population and Housing, Summary Tape File 3C

BUSINESSES

Major Business Headquarters

Company Name	1997 Rankings	
	Fortune 500	Forbes 500

No companies listed.

Note: Companies listed are located in the city; Dashes indicate no ranking
Fortune 500: companies that produce a 10-K are ranked 1 - 500 based on 1996 revenue
Forbes 500: private companies are ranked 1 - 500 based on 1996 revenue
Source: Forbes 12/1/97; Fortune 4/28/97

Minority Business Opportunity

Green Bay is home to one company which is on the Black Enterprise Auto Dealer 100 list (largest based on gross sales): Bay City Chrysler-Plymouth Inc. (Chrysler). Criteria: 1) operational in previous calendar year; 2) at least 51% black-owned. *Black Enterprise, June 1997*

HOTELS & MOTELS

Hotels/Motels

Area	Hotels/ Motels	Rooms	Luxury-Level Hotels/Motels		Average Minimum Rates ($)		
			♦♦♦♦	♦♦♦♦♦	♦♦	♦♦♦	♦♦♦♦
City	10	1,054	0	0	61	89	n/a
Airport	7	937	0	0	n/a	n/a	n/a
Suburbs	5	422	0	0	n/a	n/a	n/a
Total	22	2,413	0	0	n/a	n/a	n/a

Note: n/a not available; Classifications range from one diamond (budget properties with basic amenities) to five diamond (luxury properties with the finest service, rooms and facilities).
Source: OAG, Business Travel Planner, Summer 1997

CONVENTION CENTERS

Major Convention Centers

Center Name	Meeting Rooms	Exhibit Space (sf)
Brown County Veterans Memorial Arena	5	70,000
Embassy Suites Regency Conference Center	18	20,815

Source: Trade Shows Worldwide 1997

Living Environment

COST OF LIVING

Cost of Living Index

Composite Index	Housing	Utilities	Groceries	Health Care	Trans-portation	Misc. Goods/ Services
98.2	100.6	85.4	95.4	105.2	99.6	98.9

Note: U.S. = 100
Source: ACCRA, Cost of Living Index, 3rd Quarter 1997

HOUSING

Median Home Prices and Housing Affordability

Area	Median Price[2] 3rd Qtr. 1997 ($)	HOI[3] 3rd Qtr. 1997	Afford-ability Rank[4]
MSA[1]	100,000	72.5	73
U.S.	127,000	63.7	–

Note: (1) Metropolitan Statistical Area - see Appendix A for areas included; (2) U.S. figures calculated from the sales of 625,000 new and existing homes in 195 markets; (3) Housing Opportunity Index - percent of homes sold that were within the reach of the median income household at the prevailing mortgage interest rate; (4) Rank is from 1-195 with 1 being most affordable
Source: National Association of Home Builders, Housing Opportunity Index, 3rd Quarter 1997

Average New Home Price

Area	Price ($)
City	136,900
U.S.	135,710

Note: Figures are based on a new home with 1,800 sq. ft. of living area on an 8,000 sq. ft. lot.
Source: ACCRA, Cost of Living Index, 3rd Quarter 1997

Average Apartment Rent

Area	Rent ($/mth)
City	536
U.S.	569

Note: Figures are based on an unfurnished two bedroom, 1-1/2 or 2 bath apartment, approximately 950 sq. ft. in size, excluding all utilities except water
Source: ACCRA, Cost of Living Index, 3rd Quarter 1997

RESIDENTIAL UTILITIES

Average Residential Utility Costs

Area	All Electric ($/mth)	Part Electric ($/mth)	Other Energy ($/mth)	Phone ($/mth)
City	–	38.87	49.14	15.94
U.S.	109.40	55.25	43.64	19.48

Source: ACCRA, Cost of Living Index, 3rd Quarter 1997

HEALTH CARE

Average Health Care Costs

Area	Hospital ($/day)	Doctor ($/visit)	Dentist ($/visit)
City	343.67	56.10	65.60
U.S.	392.91	48.76	60.84

Note: Hospital - based on a semi-private room. Doctor - based on a general practitioner's routine exam of an established patient. Dentist - based on adult teeth cleaning and periodic oral exam.
Source: ACCRA, Cost of Living Index, 3rd Quarter 1997

Distribution of Office-Based Physicians

Area	Family/Gen. Practitioners	Specialists		
		Medical	Surgical	Other
MSA[1]	43	102	96	99

Note: Data as of 12/31/96; (1) Metropolitan Statistical Area - see Appendix A for areas included
Source: American Medical Assn., Physician Characteristics & Distribution in the U.S., 1997-1998

Hospitals

Green Bay has 3 general medical and surgical hospitals, 2 psychiatric. *AHA Guide to the Healthcare Field 1997-98*

EDUCATION

Public School District Statistics

District Name	Num. Sch.	Enroll.	Classroom Teachers[1]	Pupils per Teacher	Minority Pupils (%)	Current Exp.[2] ($/pupil)
Ashwaubenon Sch Dist	5	3,110	185	16.8	n/a	n/a
Green Bay Area Sch Dist	35	19,618	1,191	16.5	n/a	n/a
Howard-Suamico Sch Dist	6	3,582	209	17.1	n/a	n/a

Note: Data covers the 1995-1996 school year unless otherwise noted; (1) Excludes teachers reported as working in school district offices rather than in schools; (2) Based on 1993-94 enrollment collected by the Census Bureau, not the enrollment figure shown in column 3; SD = School District; ISD = Independent School District; n/a not available
Source: National Center for Education Statistics, Common Core of Data Survey; Bureau of the Census

Educational Quality

School District	Education Quotient[1]	Graduate Outcome[2]	Community Index[3]	Resource Index[4]
Green Bay	124.0	139.0	122.0	110.0

Note: Nearly 1,000 secondary school districts were rated in terms of educational quality. The scores range from a low of 50 to a high of 150; (1) Average of the Graduate Outcome, Community and Resource indexes; (2) Based on graduation rates and college board scores (SAT/ACT); (3) Based on the surrounding community's average level of education and the area's average income level; (4) Based on teacher salaries, per-pupil expenditures and student-teacher ratios.
Source: Expansion Management, Ratings Issue 1997

Educational Attainment by Race

Area	High School Graduate (%)					Bachelor's Degree (%)				
	Total	White	Black	Other	Hisp.[2]	Total	White	Black	Other	Hisp.[2]
City	80.9	81.8	78.8	54.5	53.0	16.7	17.0	25.9	4.7	6.2
MSA[1]	82.6	83.2	71.3	60.9	59.0	17.7	17.9	18.0	8.1	8.1
U.S.	75.2	77.9	63.1	60.4	49.8	20.3	21.5	11.4	19.4	9.2

Note: figures shown cover persons 25 years old and over; (1) Metropolitan Statistical Area - see Appendix A for areas included; (2) people of Hispanic origin can be of any race
Source: 1990 Census of Population and Housing, Summary Tape File 3C

School Enrollment by Type

Area	Preprimary				Elementary/High School			
	Public		Private		Public		Private	
	Enrollment	%	Enrollment	%	Enrollment	%	Enrollment	%
City	1,213	61.8	751	38.2	12,907	82.0	2,831	18.0
MSA[1]	2,488	59.7	1,679	40.3	27,918	81.3	6,414	18.7
U.S.	2,679,029	59.5	1,824,256	40.5	38,379,689	90.2	4,187,099	9.8

Note: figures shown cover persons 3 years old and over;
(1) Metropolitan Statistical Area - see Appendix A for areas included
Source: 1990 Census of Population and Housing, Summary Tape File 3C

School Enrollment by Race

Area	Preprimary (%)				Elementary/High School (%)			
	White	Black	Other	Hisp.[1]	White	Black	Other	Hisp.[1]
City	90.0	2.4	7.6	2.5	89.7	0.7	9.5	1.7
MSA[2]	93.4	1.2	5.4	1.2	93.7	0.7	5.6	1.1
U.S.	80.4	12.5	7.1	7.8	74.1	15.6	10.3	12.5

Note: figures shown cover persons 3 years old and over; (1) people of Hispanic origin can be of any race; (2) Metropolitan Statistical Area - see Appendix A for areas included
Source: 1990 Census of Population and Housing, Summary Tape File 3C

SAT/ACT Scores

Area/District	1997 SAT				1997 ACT	
	Percent of Graduates Tested (%)	Average Math Score	Average Verbal Score	Average Combined Score	Percent of Graduates Tested (%)	Average Composite Score
Green Bay Area PS	n/a	n/a	n/a	n/a	68	22.6
State	7	590	579	1,169	64	22.3
U.S.	42	511	505	1,016	36	21.0

Note: Math and verbal SAT scores are out of a possible 800; ACT scores are out of a possible 36
Caution: Comparing or ranking states/cities on the basis of SAT/ACT scores alone is invalid and strongly discouraged by the The College Board and The American College Testing Program as students who take the tests are self-selected and do not represent the entire student population.
Source: Green Bay Area Public Schools, 1997; American College Testing Program, 1997; College Board, 1997

Classroom Teacher Salaries in Public Schools

District	B.A. Degree		M.A. Degree		Ph.D. Degree	
	Min. ($)	Max ($)	Min. ($)	Max. ($)	Min. ($)	Max. ($)
Green Bay	n/a	n/a	n/a	n/a	n/a	n/a
Average[1]	26,120	39,270	28,175	44,667	31,643	49,825

Note: Salaries are for 1996-1997; (1) Based on all school districts covered; n/a not available
Source: American Federation of Teachers (unpublished data)

Higher Education

Two-Year Colleges		Four-Year Colleges		Medical Schools	Law Schools	Voc/ Tech
Public	Private	Public	Private			
1	0	1	1	0	0	5

Source: College Blue Book, Occupational Education 1997; Medical School Admission Requirements, 1998-99; Peterson's Guide to Two-Year Colleges, 1997; Peterson's Guide to Four-Year Colleges, 1997; Barron's Guide to Law Schools 1997

MAJOR EMPLOYERS

Major Employers

Fort Howard Corp. (paper mills)
St. Vincent Hospital
Bellin Memorial Hospital
Wisconsin Public Service Corp.
Shopko Stores (department stores)
Schreiber Foods

Schneider National (trucking)
Employers Health Insurance
Packerland Holdings (meat packing)
Krueger International (office furniture)
Paper Converting Machine Co.

Note: companies listed are located in the city
Source: Dun's Business Rankings 1997; Ward's Business Directory, 1997

PUBLIC SAFETY

Crime Rate

Area	All Crimes	Violent Crimes				Property Crimes		
		Murder	Forcible Rape	Robbery	Aggrav. Assault	Burglary	Larceny -Theft	Motor Vehicle Theft
City	4,486.8	2.9	37.4	65.2	268.5	560.0	3,338.0	214.8
Suburbs[1]	3,134.8	0.0	17.0	11.3	42.4	446.5	2,480.2	137.5
MSA[2]	3,804.8	1.4	27.1	38.0	154.4	502.7	2,905.3	175.8
U.S.	5,078.9	7.4	36.1	202.4	388.2	943.0	2,975.9	525.9

Note: Crime rate is the number of crimes per 100,000 pop.; (1) defined as all areas within the MSA but located outside the central city; (2) Metropolitan Statistical Area - see Appendix A for areas incl.
Source: FBI Uniform Crime Reports 1996

RECREATION

Culture and Recreation

Museums	Symphony Orchestras	Opera Companies	Dance Companies	Professional Theatres	Zoos	Pro Sports Teams
5	2	1	0	1	0	1

Source: International Directory of the Performing Arts, 1996; Official Museum Directory, 1998; Chamber of Commerce/Economic Development 1997

Library System

The Brown County Library has eight branches, holdings of 388,236 volumes and a budget of $4,453,180 (1995). *American Library Directory, 1997-1998*

MEDIA

Newspapers

Name	Type	Freq.	Distribution	Circulation
The Green Bay News-Chronicle	General	6x/wk	Area	9,110
Green Bay Press-Gazette	n/a	7x/wk	Area	58,000

Note: Includes newspapers with circulations of 500 or more located in the city; n/a not available
Source: Burrelle's Media Directory, 1998 Edition

AM Radio Stations

Call Letters	Freq. (kHz)	Target Audience	Station Format	Music Format
WGEE	1360	General	M/N/T	Country
WDUZ	1400	Men	S	n/a
WNFL	1440	General	N/S/T	n/a

Note: Stations included broadcast in the Green Bay metro area; n/a not available
Station Format: E = Educational; M = Music; N = News; S = Sports; T = Talk
Source: Burrelle's Media Directory, 1998 Edition

FM Radio Stations

Call Letters	Freq. (mHz)	Target Audience	Station Format	Music Format
WPNE	89.3	n/a	E/M	Classical
WGBW	91.5	General	E/T	n/a
WQLH	98.5	General	M	Christian
WIXX	101.1	General	M/N/S	Contemporary Top 40
WOGB	103.1	n/a	M	Oldies
WPCK	104.9	General	M/N/S	Country
WJLW	106.7	General	E/M/N/S/T	Country
WEZR	107.5	General	M	Jazz

Note: Stations included broadcast in the Green Bay metro area; n/a not available
Station Format: E = Educational; M = Music; N = News; S = Sports; T = Talk
Source: Burrelle's Media Directory, 1998 Edition

Television Stations

Name	Ch.	Affiliation	Type	Owner
WBAY	2	ABC	Commercial	Young Broadcasting Inc.
WJMN	3	CBS	Commercial	Westinghouse Broadcasting Company
WFRV	5	CBS	Commercial	Westinghouse Broadcasting Company
WLUK	11	Fox	Commercial	SF Broadcasting
WGBA	26	NBC	Commercial	Aries Telecommunications Corp.
WACY	32	UPN	Commercial	Ace TV Inc.

Note: Stations included broadcast in the Green Bay metro area
Source: Burrelle's Media Directory, 1998 Edition

CLIMATE

Average and Extreme Temperatures

Temperature	Jan	Feb	Mar	Apr	May	Jun	Jul	Aug	Sep	Oct	Nov	Dec	Ann
Extreme High (°F)	50	55	77	89	91	98	99	99	95	88	72	62	99
Average High (°F)	23	27	38	54	67	76	81	78	70	58	42	28	54
Average Temp. (°F)	15	19	29	44	55	65	70	68	59	48	34	21	44
Average Low (°F)	6	10	21	34	44	53	58	56	48	38	26	13	34
Extreme Low (°F)	-31	-26	-29	7	21	32	40	38	24	15	-9	-27	-31

Note: Figures cover the years 1949-1990
Source: National Climatic Data Center, International Station Meteorological Climate Summary, 3/95

Average Precipitation/Snowfall/Humidity

Precip./Humidity	Jan	Feb	Mar	Apr	May	Jun	Jul	Aug	Sep	Oct	Nov	Dec	Ann
Avg. Precip. (in.)	1.1	1.1	1.9	2.6	2.9	3.2	3.3	3.3	3.2	2.2	2.0	1.4	28.3
Avg. Snowfall (in.)	11	8	9	2	Tr	0	0	0	Tr	Tr	5	11	46
Avg. Rel. Hum. 6am (%)	77	79	81	79	79	82	86	90	89	85	82	80	83
Avg. Rel. Hum. 3pm (%)	68	65	63	54	52	55	55	58	59	59	67	71	60

Note: Figures cover the years 1949-1990; Tr = Trace amounts (<0.05 in. of rain; <0.5 in. of snow)
Source: National Climatic Data Center, International Station Meteorological Climate Summary, 3/95

Weather Conditions

Temperature			Daytime Sky			Precipitation		
5°F & below	32°F & below	90°F & above	Clear	Partly cloudy	Cloudy	0.01 inch or more precip.	0.1 inch or more snow/ice	Thunder-storms
39	163	7	86	125	154	120	40	33

Note: Figures are average number of days per year and covers the years 1949-1990
Source: National Climatic Data Center, International Station Meteorological Climate Summary, 3/95

AIR & WATER QUALITY

Maximum Pollutant Concentrations

	Particulate Matter (ug/m³)	Carbon Monoxide (ppm)	Sulfur Dioxide (ppm)	Nitrogen Dioxide (ppm)	Ozone (ppm)	Lead (ug/m³)
MSA[1] Level	n/a	n/a	0.011	n/a	0.11	n/a
NAAQS[2]	150	9	0.140	0.053	0.12	1.50
Met NAAQS?	n/a	n/a	Yes	n/a	Yes	n/a

Note: (1) Metropolitan Statistical Area - see Appendix A for areas included; (2) National Ambient Air Quality Standards; ppm = parts per million; ug/m³ = micrograms per cubic meter; n/a not available
Source: EPA, National Air Quality and Emissions Trends Report, 1996

Pollutant Standards Index

Data not available. *EPA, National Air Quality and Emissions Trends Report, 1996*

Drinking Water

Water System Name	Pop. Served	Primary Water Source Type	Number of Violations in Fiscal Year 1997	Type of Violation/ Contaminants
Green Bay Waterworks	96,466	Surface	None	None

Note: Data as of January 16, 1998
Source: EPA, Office of Ground Water and Drinking Water, Safe Drinking Water Information System

Green Bay tap water is alkaline, hard and fluoridated and comes from Lake Michigan.
Editor & Publisher Market Guide, 1998

Indianapolis, Indiana

Background

Indianapolis sits within the boundaries of the Northern manufacturing belt and the Midwestern corn belt. For that reason, the economy reflects its two-fold nature. On one side of the spectrum lies Indianapolis' industrial colors: transportation, airplane and truck parts, paper and rubber products, and computer software. This sector of approximately 1,400 firms employs one-fourth of the total Indianapolis workforce. On the other side of the spectrum lies Indianapolis's agricultural colors. Indianapolis is a leading grain market, as well as the largest meat processing center outside of Chicago.

All this economic activity, however, led to pollution and other problems of urban decay. In the 1960's, the city was rated one of the dirtiest cities in America. The city experienced a rise in its population of African-Americans, while many whites chose to abandon the city for cleaner and safer living environments.

During the 1970's Unigov, a city and county agency, and the Indiana Redevelopment Commission, sought to actively combat urban blight. Today Indianapolis can boast of one of the lowest crime rates for a major U.S. city, usually indicative of equitable living standards and wages.

Since 1995 there have been several recent and major business expansions in Indianapolis. As part of its downtown revitalization, Circle Centre a $319 million retail and entertainment complex opened in September of 1995. United Airlines is investing nearly $1 billion for a 7,500-employee maintenance center and Federal Express is expanding its sorting capabilities at the Indianapolis hub, a $250 million investment creating 1,000 jobs. Indianapolis is also a national leader in saving costs through the privatization of services previously done by the public sector, namely the Indianapolis International Airport and the city's wastewater treatment plants. *Site Selection April/May 1997*

In addition to trying to improve its living conditions, the city tries to promote an active cultural recreational, and educational scene. Indianapolis possesses one of the finest children's museums in the United States. The city's 85 parks accommodate a number of people's outdoor interests, and the Indianapolis 500 draws thousands of spectators towards its race track. Finally, the city's university quarter, housing divisions of Indiana and Purdue Universities, make for a lively learning center.

Indianapolis has a temperate climate, with very warm summers and without a dry season. Very cold winter weather may be produced by the invasion of continental polar air from northern latitudes. In the summer the arrival of tropical air from the Gulf of Mexico brings warm temperatures and moderate humidity.

General Rankings and Evaluative Comments

■ Indianapolis was ranked #141 out of 300 cities by *Money's* 1997 "Survey of the Best Places to Live." Criteria used: health services, crime, economy, housing, education, transportation, weather, leisure and the arts. The city was ranked #72 in 1996 and #199 in 1995.
Money, July 1997; Money, September 1996; Money, September 1995

■ Indianapolis appeared on *Fortune's* list of "North America's Most Improved Cities" Rank: 7 out of 10. The selected cities satisfied basic business-location needs and also demonstrated improvement over a five- to ten-year period in a number of business and quality-of-life measures.

"There was a time when most of the world thought of Indianapolis as a bland Midwestern city without much going for it—except an exceptionally popular car race. Things have changed. Today Indy boasts a turned-around downtown, a healthy city government, and a new role as one of America's sports capitals.

Over the past ten years the city has seen an impressive influx of public and private funds that have fundamentally altered its appearance. The makeover campaign has been led by a group of business and civic leaders who created the Indian Sports Corp., dedicated to using sports to put Indy on the national radar screen...In May the NCAA announced it was relocating its headquarters from Kansas City to Indy.

To spur innovation in city government through privatization, the current mayor, Stephen Goldsmith, has opened up certain city services to competitive bidding. The Indianapolis International Airport, for example, is now operated by the Briish Airport Authority, with a projected savings to the city of $105 million over ten years....

...since 1992 the city has generated over 25,000 new jobs and retained more than 100,000 existing ones resulting in a drop in the unemployment rate...the lowest in three decades. The availability of work has attracted people from all over, creating for the first time, a diverse ethnic community...." *Fortune, 11/24/97*

■ *Ladies Home Journal* ranked America's 200 largest cities based on the qualities women care about most. Indianapolis ranked 157 out of 200. Criteria: low crime rate, good public schools, well-paying jobs, quality health and child care, the presence of women in government, proportion of women-owned businesses, size of the wage gap with men, local economy, divorce rates, the ratio of single men to single women, whether there are laws that require at least the same number of public toilets for women as men, and the probability of good hair days. *Ladies Home Journal, November 1997*

■ Indianapolis was ranked #112 out of 219 cities in terms of children's health, safety, and economic well-being. Criteria: total population, percent population change, birth rate, child immunization rate, infant mortality rate, percent low birth weight infants, percent of births to teens, physician-to-population ratio, student-to-teacher ratio, dropout rate, unemployment rate, median family income, percent of children in poverty, violent and property crime rates, number of juvenile arrests for violent crimes as a percent of the total crime index, number of days with pollution standard index (PSI) over 100, pounds toxic releases per 1,000 people and number of superfund sites. *Zero Population Growth, Children's Environmental Index 1997*

■ *Yahoo! Internet Life* selected "America's 100 Most Wired Cities & Towns". 50 cities were large and 50 cities were small. Indianapolis ranked 21 out of 50 large cities. Criteria: Internet users per capita, number of networked computers, number of registered domain names, Internet backbone traffic, and the per-capita number of Web sites devoted to each city. *Yahoo! Internet Life, March 1998*

■ Eli Lily and USA Group Inc., headquartered in Indianapolis, are among the "100 Best Companies for Working Mothers." Criteria: pay compared with competition, opportunities for women to advance, support for child care, flexible work schedules and family-friendly benefits. *Working Mother, October 1997*

■ According to *Working Mother,* "Indiana has come up with some innovative ways to tackle the tough issue of how to pay for child care. About two thirds of the state's 92 counties are now drawing up plans to expand and improve child care with help from private businesses. This new effort grew out of former governor Evan Bayh's Step Ahead initiative, which got all of Indiana's counties to draw up comprehensive plans for child care and other children's services. The program was developed in cooperation with the Child Care Action Campaign, a national advocacy group. Each county is now developing its own approach, with some interesting results....

At the same time, however, Indiana officials weakened rules for family child care, allowing providers to care for larger groups of children than in the past. Some caregivers can now take in as many as 16 kids at a time. State lawmakers also vetoed a proposal to require family child care providers to have six hours of annual training." *Working Mother, July/August 1997*

Business Environment

STATE ECONOMY

State Economic Profile

"Indiana's economy is well past its cyclical peak....retail sales growth trails the national pace, and the number of bankruptcy filings is at a record high.

Indiana is the nation's largest producer of steel, accounting for nearly one-quarter of the nation's output....

Indiana legislators reduced the auto excise tax last year. This revenue loss will be partly offset by revenues from Indiana's eleven casinos. Indiana has accumulated a $1.6 billion surplus by resisting pressures for additional tax cuts and spending increases. However, there are several initiatives under review at both the state and county levels to increase wage taxes from the current 3.4% to 5.4%. Another proposal would eliminate business inventory taxes.

Population growth weakened slightly in 1996 to under 0.8% as migration declined slightly, due in part to the closure of Fort Benjamin Harrison. However, Indiana still enjoys strong, positive domestic net in-migration, in contrast to its three Great Lakes neighbors. Indiana's relatively optimistic economic outlook should provide for long-run population growth just short of the national average. This will support expansion of the state's local and population-dependent industries, such as retail trade and housing.

...Compared with neighboring manufacturing states, Indiana enjoys a significant comparative advantage in low costs. Combined with generous tax incentives, Indiana's low costs will enable the state to attract firms relocating from higher cost states or seeking to expand. However, the state is at risk due to its high dependence on traditional durable manufacturing industries, particularly steel and autos. Indiana will be an average performer long term."
National Association of Realtors, Economic Profiles: The Fifty States, July 1997

IMPORTS/EXPORTS

Total Export Sales

Area	1993 ($000)	1994 ($000)	1995 ($000)	1996 ($000)	% Chg. 1993-96	% Chg. 1995-96
MSA[1]	2,626,626	3,003,834	3,555,925	4,012,775	52.8	12.8
U.S.	464,858,354	512,415,609	583,030,524	622,827,063	34.0	6.8

Note: (1) Metropolitan Statistical Area - see Appendix A for areas included
Source: U.S. Department of Commerce, International Trade Association, Metropolitan Area Exports: An Export Performance Report on Over 250 U.S. Cities, October 1997

Imports/Exports by Port

Type	Cargo Value			Share of U.S. Total	
	1995 (US$mil.)	1996 (US$mil.)	% Change 1995-1996	1995 (%)	1996 (%)
Imports	0	0	0	0	0
Exports	0	0	0	0	0

Source: Global Trade Information Services, WaterBorne Trade Atlas 1997

CITY FINANCES

City Government Finances

Component	FY94 ($000)	FY94 (per capita $)
Revenue	1,068,586	1,429.97
Expenditure	1,316,567	1,761.81
Debt Outstanding	1,559,942	2,087.49
Cash & Securities	972,527	1,301.42

Source: U.S. Bureau of the Census, City Government Finances: 1993-94

City Government Revenue by Source

Source	FY94 ($000)	FY94 (per capita $)	FY94 (%)
From Federal Government	51,854	69.39	4.9
From State Governments	250,916	335.77	23.5
From Local Governments	1,468	1.96	0.1
Property Taxes	413,336	553.12	38.7
General Sales Taxes	0	0.00	0.0
Selective Sales Taxes	22,423	30.01	2.1
Income Taxes	53,875	72.09	5.0
Current Charges	191,303	256.00	17.9
Utility/Liquor Store	6,652	8.90	0.6
Employee Retirement[1]	26,068	34.88	2.4
Other	50,691	67.83	4.7

Note: (1) Excludes "city contributions," classified as "nonrevenue," intragovernmental transfers.
Source: U.S. Bureau of the Census, City Government Finances: 1993-94

City Government Expenditures by Function

Function	FY94 ($000)	FY94 (per capita $)	FY94 (%)
Educational Services	738	0.99	0.1
Employee Retirement[1]	35,459	47.45	2.7
Environment/Housing	424,340	567.85	32.2
Government Administration	95,941	128.39	7.3
Interest on General Debt	58,963	78.90	4.5
Public Safety	166,244	222.47	12.6
Social Services	286,385	383.24	21.8
Transportation	128,907	172.50	9.8
Utility/Liquor Store	24,022	32.15	1.8
Other	95,568	127.89	7.3

Note: (1) Payments to beneficiaries including withdrawal of contributions.
Source: U.S. Bureau of the Census, City Government Finances: 1993-94

Municipal Bond Ratings

Area	Moody's	S & P
Indianapolis	Aaa	n/r

Note: n/a not available; n/r not rated
Source: Moody's Bond Record, 2/98; Statistical Abstract of the U.S., 1997; Governing Magazine, 9/97, 3/98

POPULATION

Population Growth

Area	1980	1990	% Chg. 1980-90	July 1996 Estimate	% Chg. 1990-96
City	700,807	731,321	4.4	746,737	2.1
MSA[1]	1,166,575	1,249,822	7.1	1,492,297	19.4
U.S.	226,545,805	248,765,170	9.8	265,179,411	6.6

Note: (1) Metropolitan Statistical Area - see Appendix A for areas included
Source: 1980/1990 Census of Housing and Population, Summary Tape File 3C; Census Bureau Population Estimates

Population Characteristics

Race	City 1980 Population	City 1980 %	City 1990 Population	City 1990 %	% Chg. 1980-90	MSA[1] 1990 Population	MSA[1] 1990 %
White	540,584	77.1	555,216	75.9	2.7	1,061,822	85.0
Black	152,590	21.8	164,861	22.5	8.0	171,545	13.7
Amer Indian/Esk/Aleut	1,356	0.2	1,758	0.2	29.6	2,695	0.2
Asian/Pacific Islander	4,539	0.6	6,656	0.9	46.6	10,001	0.8
Other	1,738	0.2	2,830	0.4	62.8	3,759	0.3
Hispanic Origin[2]	6,143	0.9	7,463	1.0	21.5	11,114	0.9

Note: (1) Metropolitan Statistical Area - see Appendix A for areas included;
(2) people of Hispanic origin can be of any race
Source: 1980/1990 Census of Housing and Population, Summary Tape File 3C

Ancestry

Area	German	Irish	English	Italian	U.S.	French	Polish	Dutch
City	28.7	15.9	12.8	2.3	6.7	3.1	1.4	2.4
MSA[1]	32.5	17.5	15.2	2.3	7.5	3.4	1.5	3.0
U.S.	23.3	15.6	13.1	5.9	5.3	4.2	3.8	2.5

Note: Figures are percentages and include persons that reported multiple ancestry (eg. if a person reported being Irish and Italian, they were included in both columns); (1) Metropolitan Statistical Area - see Appendix A for areas included
Source: 1990 Census of Population and Housing, Summary Tape File 3C

Age

Area	Median Age (Years)	Age Distribution (%) Under 5	Under 18	18-24	25-44	45-64	65+	80+
City	31.6	8.0	25.6	10.4	34.9	17.6	11.4	2.6
MSA[1]	32.3	7.7	26.4	9.8	34.4	18.4	11.1	2.5
U.S.	32.9	7.3	25.6	10.5	32.6	18.7	12.5	2.8

Note: (1) Metropolitan Statistical Area - see Appendix A for areas included
Source: 1990 Census of Population and Housing, Summary Tape File 3C

Male/Female Ratio

Area	Number of males per 100 females (all ages)	Number of males per 100 females (18 years old+)
City	90.4	86.1
MSA[1]	92.4	88.4
U.S.	95.0	91.9

Note: (1) Metropolitan Statistical Area - see Appendix A for areas included
Source: 1990 Census of Population, General Population Characteristics

INCOME

Per Capita/Median/Average Income

Area	Per Capita ($)	Median Household ($)	Average Household ($)
City	14,478	29,006	35,946
MSA[1]	15,159	31,655	39,103
U.S.	14,420	30,056	38,453

Note: all figures are for 1989; (1) Metropolitan Statistical Area - see Appendix A for areas included
Source: 1990 Census of Population and Housing, Summary Tape File 3C

Household Income Distribution by Race

Income ($)	City (%)					U.S. (%)				
	Total	White	Black	Other	Hisp.[1]	Total	White	Black	Other	Hisp.[1]
Less than 5,000	5.9	3.8	13.7	8.1	8.3	6.2	4.8	15.2	8.6	8.8
5,000 - 9,999	8.6	7.3	13.9	7.3	7.9	9.3	8.6	14.2	9.9	11.1
10,000 - 14,999	9.0	8.2	12.0	9.9	13.4	8.8	8.5	11.0	9.8	11.0
15,000 - 24,999	19.1	18.9	20.1	17.6	21.3	17.5	17.3	18.9	18.5	20.5
25,000 - 34,999	17.0	17.7	14.3	15.2	17.8	15.8	16.1	14.2	15.4	16.4
35,000 - 49,999	18.8	20.1	13.9	17.6	19.5	17.9	18.6	13.3	16.1	16.0
50,000 - 74,999	14.4	15.8	8.8	16.5	6.8	15.0	15.8	9.3	13.4	11.1
75,000 - 99,999	4.0	4.5	2.5	3.2	2.5	5.1	5.5	2.6	4.7	3.1
100,000+	3.2	3.7	0.9	4.7	2.6	4.4	4.8	1.3	3.7	1.9

Note: all figures are for 1989; (1) people of Hispanic origin can be of any race
Source: 1990 Census of Population and Housing, Summary Tape File 3C

Effective Buying Income

Area	Per Capita ($)	Median Household ($)	Average Household ($)
City	16,864	34,180	41,684
MSA[1]	18,101	38,688	46,658
U.S.	15,444	33,201	41,849

Note: data as of 1/1/97; (1) Metropolitan Statistical Area - see Appendix A for areas included
Source: Standard Rate & Data Service, Newspaper Advertising Source, 2/98

Effective Household Buying Income Distribution

Area	% of Households Earning						
	$10,000 -$19,999	$20,000 -$34,999	$35,000 -$49,999	$50,000 -$74,999	$75,000 -$99,000	$100,000 -$124,999	$125,000 and up
City	15.8	24.2	19.0	19.0	6.6	2.0	2.1
MSA[1]	13.8	22.3	18.9	21.9	8.7	2.7	2.7
U.S.	16.5	23.4	18.3	18.2	6.4	2.1	2.4

Note: data as of 1/1/97; (1) Metropolitan Statistical Area - see Appendix A for areas included
Source: Standard Rate & Data Service, Newspaper Advertising Source, 2/98

Poverty Rates by Race and Age

Area	Total (%)	By Race (%)				By Age (%)		
		White	Black	Other	Hisp.[2]	Under 5 years old	Under 18 years old	65 years and over
City	12.5	8.4	26.4	13.8	13.0	20.1	18.9	11.7
MSA[1]	9.6	6.9	26.2	12.1	11.5	15.1	13.7	10.3
U.S.	13.1	9.8	29.5	23.1	25.3	20.1	18.3	12.8

Note: figures show the percent of people living below the poverty line in 1989. The average poverty threshold was $12,674 for a family of four in 1989; (1) Metropolitan Statistical Area - see Appendix A for areas included; (2) people of Hispanic origin can be of any race
Source: 1990 Census of Population and Housing, Summary Tape File 3C

EMPLOYMENT

Labor Force and Employment

Area	Civilian Labor Force			Workers Employed		
	Dec. '95	Dec. '96	% Chg.	Dec. '95	Dec. '96	% Chg.
City	412,855	422,096	2.2	400,442	408,340	2.0
MSA[1]	809,267	826,621	2.1	788,116	803,660	2.0
U.S.	134,583,000	136,742,000	1.6	127,903,000	130,785,000	2.3

Note: Data is not seasonally adjusted and covers workers 16 years of age and older;
(1) Metropolitan Statistical Area - see Appendix A for areas included
Source: Bureau of Labor Statistics, http://stats.bls.gov

Unemployment Rate

Area	1997											
	Jan.	Feb.	Mar.	Apr.	May	Jun.	Jul.	Aug.	Sep.	Oct.	Nov.	Dec.
City	2.9	2.8	3.0	3.1	2.9	3.0	2.9	3.0	3.1	3.4	3.0	3.3
MSA[1]	2.6	2.6	2.7	2.6	2.5	2.6	2.6	2.6	2.6	2.9	2.6	2.8
U.S.	5.9	5.7	5.5	4.8	4.7	5.2	5.0	4.8	4.7	4.4	4.3	4.4

Note: Data is not seasonally adjusted and covers workers 16 years of age and older; All figures are percentages; (1) Metropolitan Statistical Area - see Appendix A for areas included
Source: Bureau of Labor Statistics, http://stats.bls.gov

Employment by Industry

Sector	MSA[1]		U.S.
	Number of Employees	Percent of Total	Percent of Total
Services	227,200	26.8	29.0
Retail Trade	168,400	19.9	18.5
Government	103,800	12.3	16.1
Manufacturing	128,100	15.1	15.0
Finance/Insurance/Real Estate	63,500	7.5	5.7
Wholesale Trade	55,500	6.6	5.4
Transportation/Public Utilities	51,800	6.1	5.3
Construction	47,100	5.6	4.5
Mining	800	0.1	0.5

Note: Figures cover non-farm employment as of 12/97 and are not seasonally adjusted;
(1) Metropolitan Statistical Area - see Appendix A for areas included
Source: Bureau of Labor Statistics, http://stats.bls.gov

Employment by Occupation

Occupation Category	City (%)	MSA[1] (%)	U.S. (%)
White Collar	62.1	60.9	58.1
Executive/Admin./Management	12.7	12.9	12.3
Professional	14.4	13.6	14.1
Technical & Related Support	3.9	3.8	3.7
Sales	12.5	12.8	11.8
Administrative Support/Clerical	18.6	17.8	16.3
Blue Collar	23.6	25.4	26.2
Precision Production/Craft/Repair	9.8	11.2	11.3
Machine Operators/Assem./Insp.	5.9	6.3	6.8
Transportation/Material Movers	3.9	4.0	4.1
Cleaners/Helpers/Laborers	4.0	3.9	3.9
Services	13.6	12.5	13.2
Farming/Forestry/Fishing	0.7	1.3	2.5

Note: figures cover employed persons 16 years old and over;
(1) Metropolitan Statistical Area - see Appendix A for areas included
Source: 1990 Census of Population and Housing, Summary Tape File 3C

Occupational Employment Projections: 1994 - 2005

Projections not available at time of publication.

Average Wages

Occupation	Wage	Occupation	Wage
Professional/Technical/Clerical	$/Week	**Health/Protective Services**	$/Week
Accountants III	785	Corrections Officers	401
Attorneys III	1,385	Firefighters	639
Budget Analysts III	-	Nurses, Licensed Practical II	-
Buyers/Contracting Specialists II	630	Nurses, Registered II	-
Clerks, Accounting III	445	Nursing Assistants II	-
Clerks, General III	377	Police Officers I	645
Computer Operators II	467	**Hourly Workers**	$/Hour
Computer Programmers II	606	Forklift Operators	14.06
Drafters II	490	General Maintenance Workers	10.18
Engineering Technicians III	642	Guards I	6.98
Engineering Technicians, Civil III	490	Janitors	8.03
Engineers III	908	Maintenance Electricians	20.14
Key Entry Operators I	326	Maintenance Electronics Techs II	19.16
Personnel Assistants III	-	Maintenance Machinists	16.36
Personnel Specialists III	806	Maintenance Mechanics, Machinery	18.89
Secretaries III	491	Material Handling Laborers	14.66
Switchboard Operator-Receptionist	363	Motor Vehicle Mechanics	16.83
Systems Analysts II	918	Shipping/Receiving Clerks	-
Systems Analysts Supervisor/Mgr II	-	Tool and Die Makers	20.55
Tax Collectors II	-	Truckdrivers, Tractor Trailer	-
Word Processors II	424	Warehouse Specialists	12.79

Note: Wage data includes full-time workers only for 8/96 and cover the Metropolitan Statistical Area (see Appendix A for areas included). Dashes indicate that data was not available.
Source: Bureau of Labor Statistics, Occupational Compensation Survey, 12/96

TAXES

Major State and Local Tax Rates

State Corp. Income (%)	State Personal Income (%)	Residential Property (effective rate per $100)	Sales & Use		State Gasoline (cents/ gallon)	State Cigarette (cents/ 20-pack)
			State (%)	Local (%)		
7.9[a]	3.4	1.93	5.0	None	15	15.5

Note: Personal/corporate income tax rates as of 1/97. Sales, gasoline and cigarette tax rates as of 1/98; (a) Consists of 3.4% on income from sources within the state plus a 4.5% supplemental income tax
Source: Federation of Tax Administrators, www.taxadmin.org; Washington D.C. Department of Finance and Revenue, Tax Rates and Tax Burdens in the District of Columbia: A Nationwide Comparison, June 1997; Chamber of Commerce

Total Taxes Per Capita and as a Percent of Income

Area	Per Capita Income ($)	Per Capita Taxes ($)			Taxes as Pct. of Income (%)		
		Total	Federal	State/ Local	Total	Federal	State/ Local
Indiana	24,003	8,243	5,717	2,526	34.3	23.8	10.5
U.S.	26,187	9,205	6,127	3,078	35.2	23.4	11.8

Note: Figures are for 1997
Source: Tax Foundation, Web Site, www.taxfoundation.org

Estimated Tax Burden

Area	State Income	Local Income	Property	Sales	Total
Indianapolis	2,074	427	2,250	425	5,176

Note: The numbers are estimates of taxes paid by a married couple with two kids and annual earnings of $65,000. Sales tax estimates assume they spend average amounts on food, clothing, household goods and gasoline. Property tax estimates assume they live in a $225,000 home.
Source: Kiplinger's Personal Finance Magazine, June 1997

**COMMERCIAL
REAL ESTATE**

Office Market

Class/ Location	Total Space (sq. ft.)	Vacant Space (sq. ft.)	Vac. Rate (%)	Under Constr. (sq. ft.)	Net Absorp. (sq. ft.)	Rental Rates ($/sq.ft./yr.)
Class A						
CBD	6,886,154	886,551	12.9	125,000	-14,856	12.75-22.00
Outside CBD	4,336,368	302,906	7.0	457,000	-16,232	14.00-21.00
Class B						
CBD	2,261,440	397,933	17.6	0	122,054	10.00-20.00
Outside CBD	5,352,093	624,861	11.7	250,000	-452,284	8.00-18.25

Note: Data as of 10/97 and covers Indianapolis; CBD = Central Business District; n/a not available; Source: Society of Industrial and Office Realtors, 1998 Comparative Statistics of Industrial and Office Real Estate Markets

"Growth for the Indianapolis area is anticipated during 1998, though at a slower pace than in recent years. Strong population trends will continue to place this MSA above most Midwestern metros in overall growth. Nonetheless, changes in the national economy as well as the auto industry may cause some instability. Potential labor shortages may slow expansion and the possibility of over-building in the office market still exists. The likelihood of a major downturn, however, is small. The area's well-diversified industrial base and standing as a key distribution and warehousing center will serve to protect the area from drastic cyclical changes in the short-term." *Society of Industrial and Office Realtors, 1998 Comparative Statistics of Industrial and Office Real Estate Markets*

Industrial Market

Location	Total Space (sq. ft.)	Vacant Space (sq. ft.)	Vac. Rate (%)	Under Constr. (sq. ft.)	Net Absorp. (sq. ft.)	Gross Lease ($/sq.ft./yr.)
Central City	176,865,000	12,677,505	7.2	2,400,000	5,600,000	3.35-5.50
Suburban	n/a	n/a	n/a	n/a	n/a	3.35-5.50

Note: Data as of 10/97 and covers Indianapolis. Central city and suburban figures are combined.; n/a not available
Source: Society of Industrial and Office Realtors, 1998 Comparative Statistics of Industrial and Office Real Estate Markets

"The industrial market in Indianapolis continues to thrive. Many companies are looking to expand their distribution facilities. The construction of new speculative space will be warehouse for mid-size and bulk. Though spec construction may slow from 1997's pace, this will still be an active development market. One of the ongoing concerns for manufacturing and distribution companies is the availability of labor, much the same as most midwestern marketplaces. Overall, the industrial market will continue to see significant growth and absorption." *Society of Industrial and Office Realtors, 1998 Comparative Statistics of Industrial and Office Real Estate Markets*

Retail Market

Shopping Center Inventory (sq. ft.)	Shopping Center Construction (sq. ft.)	Construction as a Percent of Inventory (%)	Torto Wheaton Rent Index[1] ($/sq. ft.)
31,989,000	1,109,000	3.5	9.69

Note: Data as of 1997 and covers the Metropolitan Statistical Area - see Appendix A for areas included; (1) Index is based on a model that predicts what the average rent should be for leases with certain characteristics, in certain locations during certain years.
Source: National Association of Realtors, 1997-1998 Market Conditions Report

"The Indianapolis area has experienced healthy economic growth throughout the 90s. Its population has grown faster than the national average, while real income growth has consistently been strong. The retail rent index has risen steadily over the past four years, including 1.9% in 1997. Indianapolis' success has many national retailers considering it as a favorable place for expansion. However, like elsewhere in the nation many small, independent retailers have fallen prey to the large, national chains. Indianapolis' current labor shortage should improve over the next few years. Retail rents in the area are expected to remain relatively steady." National Association of Realtors, 1997-1998 Market Conditions Report

COMMERCIAL UTILITIES

Typical Monthly Electric Bills

Area	Commercial Service ($/month)		Industrial Service ($/month)	
	12 kW demand 1,500 kWh	100 kW demand 30,000 kWh	1,000 kW demand 400,000 kWh	20,000 kW demand 10,000,000 kWh
City	121	1,941	19,590	413,851
U.S.	162	2,360	25,590	545,677

Note: Based on rates in effect July 1, 1997
Source: Edison Electric Institute, Typical Residential, Commercial and Industrial Bills, Summer 1997

TRANSPORTATION

Transportation Statistics

Avg. travel time to work (min.)	20.8
Interstate highways	I-65; I-69; I-70; I-74
Bus lines	
In-city	Indianapolis Public Transportation Corp. (METRO), 209 vehicles
Inter-city	2
Passenger air service	
Airport	Indianapolis International
Airlines	16
Aircraft departures	61,168 (1995)
Enplaned passengers	2,968,300 (1995)
Rail service	Amtrak
Motor freight carriers	n/a
Major waterways/ports	White River

Source: OAG, Business Travel Planner, Summer 1997; Editor & Publisher Market Guide, 1998; FAA Airport Activity Statistics, 1996; Amtrak National Time Table, Northeast Timetable, Fall/Winter 1997-98; 1990 Census of Population and Housing, STF 3C; Chamber of Commerce/Economic Development 1997; Jane's Urban Transport Systems 1997-98; Transit Fact Book 1997

Means of Transportation to Work

Area	Car/Truck/Van		Public Transportation			Bicycle	Walked	Other Means	Worked at Home
	Drove Alone	Car-pooled	Bus	Subway	Railroad				
City	78.0	13.4	3.1	0.0	0.0	0.2	2.4	0.8	2.0
MSA[1]	79.7	12.9	1.9	0.0	0.0	0.1	2.2	0.7	2.4
U.S.	73.2	13.4	3.0	1.5	0.5	0.4	3.9	1.2	3.0

Note: figures shown are percentages and only include workers 16 years old and over;
(1) Metropolitan Statistical Area - see Appendix A for areas included
Source: 1990 Census of Population and Housing, Summary Tape File 3C

BUSINESSES

Major Business Headquarters

Company Name	1997 Rankings	
	Fortune 500	Forbes 500
Anthem Insurance	231	-
Bindley Western	268	-
Eli Lilly	194	-
Huber Hunt & Nichols	-	199
LDI	-	300
National Wine & Spirits	-	445

Note: Companies listed are located in the city; Dashes indicate no ranking
Fortune 500: companies that produce a 10-K are ranked 1 - 500 based on 1996 revenue
Forbes 500: private companies are ranked 1 - 500 based on 1996 revenue
Source: Forbes 12/1/97; Fortune 4/28/97

Fast-Growing Businesses

According to *Inc.*, Indianapolis is home to one of America's 100 fastest-growing private companies: Support Net. Criteria for inclusion: must be an independent, privately-held, U.S. corporation, proprietorship or partnership; sales of at least $200,000 in 1993; five-year operating/sales history; increase in 1997 sales over 1996 sales; holding companies, regulated banks, and utilities were excluded. *Inc. 500, 1997*

Women-Owned Businesses: Number, Employment, Sales and Share

Area	Women-Owned Businesses in 1996				Share of Women-Owned Businesses in 1996	
	Number	Employment	Sales ($000)	Rank[2]	Percent (%)	Rank[3]
MSA[1]	48,000	153,400	16,667,000	31	37.2	22

Note: (1) Metropolitan Statistical Area - see Appendix A for areas included; (2) Calculated on an averaging of number of businesses, employment and sales and ranges from 1 to 50 where 1 is best; (3) Ranges from 1 to 50 where 1 is best
Source: The National Foundation for Women Business Owners, 1996 Facts on Women-Owned Businesses: Trends in the Top 50 Metropolitan Areas, March 26, 1997

Women-Owned Businesses: Growth

Area	Growth in Women-Owned Businesses (% change from 1987 to 1996)				Relative Growth in the Number of Women-Owned and All Businesses (% change from 1987 to 1996)			
	Num.	Empl.	Sales	Rank[2]	Women-Owned	All Firms	Absolute Difference	Relative Difference
MSA[1]	82.1	150.9	215.2	37	82.1	53.7	28.4	1.5:1

Note: (1) Metropolitan Statistical Area - see Appendix A for areas included; (2) Calculated on an averaging of the percent growth of number of businesses, employment and sales and ranges from 1 to 50 where 1 is best
Source: The National Foundation for Women Business Owners, 1996 Facts on Women-Owned Businesses: Trends in the Top 50 Metropolitan Areas, March 26, 1997

Minority Business Opportunity

Indianapolis is home to one company which is on the Black Enterprise Industrial/Service 100 list (largest based on gross sales): Mays Chemical Co. Inc. (industrial chemical distributor). Criteria: 1) operational in previous calendar year; 2) at least 51% black-owned; 3) manufactures/owns the product it sells or provides industrial or consumer services. Brokerages, real estate firms and firms that provide professional services are not eligible. *Black Enterprise, July 1997*

Two of the 500 largest Hispanic-owned companies in the U.S. are located in Indianapolis. *Hispanic Business, June 1997*

Indianapolis is home to three companies which are on the Hispanic Business Fastest-Growing 100 list (greatest sales growth from 1992 to 1996): GSC Industries Inc. (auto parts machining), Communications Products Inc. (telecom. svcs.), and GM Construction Inc. (construction mgmt. and general contracting) *Hispanic Business, July/August 1997*

Small Business Opportunity

According to *Forbes*, Indianapolis is home to three of America's 200 best small companies: Consolidated Products, Crossmann Communities, Software Artistry. Criteria: companies must be publicly traded, U.S.-based corporations with latest 12-month sales of between $5 and $350 million. Earnings must be at least $1 million for the 12-month period. Limited partnerships, REITs and closed-end mutual funds were not considered. Banks, S&Ls and electric utilities were not included. *Forbes, November 3, 1997*

HOTELS & MOTELS

Hotels/Motels

Area	Hotels/ Motels	Rooms	Luxury-Level Hotels/Motels		Average Minimum Rates ($)		
			◆◆◆◆	◆◆◆◆◆	◆◆	◆◆◆	◆◆◆◆
City	67	11,511	1	0	62	108	180
Airport	9	1,822	0	0	n/a	n/a	n/a
Suburbs	16	1,306	0	0	n/a	n/a	n/a
Total	92	14,639	1	0	n/a	n/a	n/a

Note: n/a not available; Classifications range from one diamond (budget properties with basic amenities) to five diamond (luxury properties with the finest service, rooms and facilities).
Source: OAG, Business Travel Planner, Summer 1997

CONVENTION CENTERS

Major Convention Centers

Center Name	Meeting Rooms	Exhibit Space (sf)
Indiana Convention Center and RCA Dome	55	300,000
Indiana State Fairgrounds Event Center	15	1,000,000
University Place Conference Center and Hotel	30	n/a

Note: n/a nct available
Source: Trade Shows Worldwide 1997

Living Environment

COST OF LIVING

Cost of Living Index

Composite Index	Housing	Utilities	Groceries	Health Care	Trans- portation	Misc. Goods/ Services
98.3	92.8	94.2	104.5	98.5	99.3	100.5

Note: U.S. = 100
Source: ACCRA, Cost of Living Index, 3rd Quarter 1997

HOUSING

Median Home Prices and Housing Affordability

Area	Median Price[2] 3rd Qtr. 1997 ($)	HOI[3] 3rd Qtr. 1997	Afford- ability Rank[4]
MSA[1]	125,000	68.9	100
U.S.	127,000	63.7	–

Note: (1) Metropolitan Statistical Area - see Appendix A for areas included; (2) U.S. figures calculated from the sales of 625,000 new and existing homes in 195 markets; (3) Housing Opportunity Index - percent of homes sold that were within the reach of the median income household at the prevailing mortgage interest rate; (4) Rank is from 1-195 with 1 being most affordable
Source: National Association of Home Builders, Housing Opportunity Index, 3rd Quarter 1997

It is projected that the median price of existing single-family homes in the metro area will increase by 5.0% in 1998. Nationwide, home prices are projected to increase 6.6%.
Kiplinger's Personal Finance Magazine, January 1998

Average New Home Price

Area	Price ($)
City	124,111
U.S.	135,710

Note: Figures are based on a new home with 1,800 sq. ft. of living area on an 8,000 sq. ft. lot.
Source: ACCRA, Cost of Living Index, 3rd Quarter 1997

Average Apartment Rent

Area	Rent ($/mth)
City	600
U.S.	569

Note: Figures are based on an unfurnished two bedroom, 1-1/2 or 2 bath apartment, approximately 950 sq. ft. in size, excluding all utilities except water
Source: ACCRA, Cost of Living Index, 3rd Quarter 1997

RESIDENTIAL UTILITIES

Average Residential Utility Costs

Area	All Electric ($/mth)	Part Electric ($/mth)	Other Energy ($/mth)	Phone ($/mth)
City	–	48.01	47.39	19.66
U.S.	109.40	55.25	43.64	19.48

Source: ACCRA, Cost of Living Index, 3rd Quarter 1997

HEALTH CARE

Average Health Care Costs

Area	Hospital ($/day)	Doctor ($/visit)	Dentist ($/visit)
City	396.25	47.80	59.20
U.S.	392.91	48.76	60.84

Note: Hospital - based on a semi-private room. Doctor - based on a general practitioner's routine exam of an established patient. Dentist - based on adult teeth cleaning and periodic oral exam.
Source: ACCRA, Cost of Living Index, 3rd Quarter 1997

Distribution of Office-Based Physicians

Area	Family/Gen. Practitioners	Specialists		
		Medical	Surgical	Other
MSA[1]	455	939	752	845

Note: Data as of 12/31/96; (1) Metropolitan Statistical Area - see Appendix A for areas included
Source: American Medical Assn., Physician Characteristics & Distribution in the U.S., 1997-1998

Hospitals

Indianapolis has 10 general medical and surgical hospitals, 2 psychiatric, 1 rehabilitation, 1 alcoholism and other chemical dependency. *AHA Guide to the Healthcare Field 1997-98*

According to *U.S. News and World Report,* Indianapolis has 2 of the best hospitals in the U.S.: **Indiana University Medical Center**, noted for cancer, cardiology, gastroenterology, gynecology, neurology, otolaryngology, rheumatology, urology; **Methodist Hospital of Indiana**, noted for otolaryngology, urology;   *U.S. News and World Report, "America's Best Hospitals", 7/28/97*

EDUCATION

Public School District Statistics

District Name	Num. Sch.	Enroll.	Classroom Teachers[1]	Pupils per Teacher	Minority Pupils (%)	Current Exp.[2] ($/pupil)
Franklin Township Com Sch Corp	7	4,896	236	20.7	n/a	n/a
IN Department of Mental Health	1	42	8	5.3	n/a	n/a
IN State Department of Health	4	640	160	4.0	n/a	n/a
Indianapolis Public Schools	95	44,896	2,491	18.0	59.4	6,324
M S D Decatur Township	6	5,014	249	20.1	n/a	n/a
M S D Lawrence Township	15	13,685	778	17.6	n/a	n/a
M S D Perry Township	15	11,802	642	18.4	n/a	n/a
M S D Pike Township	11	6,980	392	17.8	n/a	n/a
M S D Warren Township	17	9,777	613	15.9	n/a	n/a
M S D Washington Township	14	10,190	554	18.4	n/a	n/a
M S D Wayne Township	15	12,694	716	17.7	n/a	n/a

Note: Data covers the 1995-1996 school year unless otherwise noted; (1) Excludes teachers reported as working in school district offices rather than in schools; (2) Based on 1993-94 enrollment collected by the Census Bureau, not the enrollment figure shown in column 3; SD = School District; ISD = Independent School District; n/a not available
Source: National Center for Education Statistics, Common Core of Data Survey; Bureau of the Census

Educational Quality

School District	Education Quotient[1]	Graduate Outcome[2]	Community Index[3]	Resource Index[4]
Indianapolis	76.0	51.0	105.0	73.0

Note: Nearly 1,000 secondary school districts were rated in terms of educational quality. The scores range from a low of 50 to a high of 150; (1) Average of the Graduate Outcome, Community and Resource indexes; (2) Based on graduation rates and college board scores (SAT/ACT); (3) Based on the surrounding community's average level of education and the area's average income level; (4) Based on teacher salaries, per-pupil expenditures and student-teacher ratios.
Source: Expansion Management, Ratings Issue 1997

Educational Attainment by Race

Area	High School Graduate (%)					Bachelor's Degree (%)				
	Total	White	Black	Other	Hisp.[2]	Total	White	Black	Other	Hisp.[2]
City	76.4	79.2	65.2	79.8	75.2	21.7	24.5	9.6	39.4	20.2
MSA[1]	78.6	80.4	65.6	79.9	76.3	21.1	22.4	9.9	37.9	21.6
U.S.	75.2	77.9	63.1	60.4	49.8	20.3	21.5	11.4	19.4	9.2

Note: figures shown cover persons 25 years old and over; (1) Metropolitan Statistical Area - see Appendix A for areas included; (2) people of Hispanic origin can be of any race
Source: 1990 Census of Population and Housing, Summary Tape File 3C

School Enrollment by Type

Area	Preprimary				Elementary/High School			
	Public		Private		Public		Private	
	Enrollment	%	Enrollment	%	Enrollment	%	Enrollment	%
City	6,699	51.1	6,414	48.9	101,922	87.2	14,951	12.8
MSA[1]	12,635	53.2	11,125	46.8	191,105	90.0	21,252	10.0
U.S.	2,679,029	59.5	1,824,256	40.5	38,379,689	90.2	4,187,099	9.8

Note: figures shown cover persons 3 years old and over;
(1) Metropolitan Statistical Area - see Appendix A for areas included
Source: 1990 Census of Population and Housing, Summary Tape File 3C

School Enrollment by Race

Area	Preprimary (%)				Elementary/High School (%)			
	White	Black	Other	Hisp.[1]	White	Black	Other	Hisp.[1]
City	76.0	22.5	1.5	1.2	67.8	30.4	1.8	1.3
MSA[2]	85.9	12.8	1.4	1.1	81.0	17.5	1.5	1.2
U.S.	80.4	12.5	7.1	7.8	74.1	15.6	10.3	12.5

Note: figures shown cover persons 3 years old and over; (1) people of Hispanic origin can be of any race; (2) Metropolitan Statistical Area - see Appendix A for areas included
Source: 1990 Census of Population and Housing, Summary Tape File 3C

SAT/ACT Scores

Area/District	1996 SAT				1996 ACT	
	Percent of Graduates Tested (%)	Average Math Score	Average Verbal Score	Average Combined Score	Percent of Graduates Tested (%)	Average Composite Score
Indianapolis PS	44	423	443	866	17	18.2
State	57	494	494	988	19	21.3
U.S.	41	508	505	1,013	35	20.9

Note: Math and verbal SAT scores are out of a possible 800; ACT scores are out of a possible 36
Caution: Comparing or ranking states/cities on the basis of SAT/ACT scores alone is invalid and strongly discouraged by the The College Board and The American College Testing Program as students who take the tests are self-selected and do not represent the entire student population. 1996 SAT scores cannot be compared to previous years due to recentering.
Source: Indianapolis Public Schools, Research, Evaluation & Assessment, 1995-96; American College Testing Program, 1996; College Board, 1996

Classroom Teacher Salaries in Public Schools

District	B.A. Degree		M.A. Degree		Ph.D. Degree	
	Min. ($)	Max. ($)	Min. ($)	Max. ($)	Min. ($)	Max. ($)
Indianapolis	24,247	39,842	25,914	46,978	29,091	50,166
Average[1]	26,120	39,270	28,175	44,667	31,643	49,825

Note: Salaries are for 1996-1997; (1) Based on all school districts covered
Source: American Federation of Teachers (unpublished data)

Higher Education

Two-Year Colleges		Four-Year Colleges		Medical Schools	Law Schools	Voc/ Tech
Public	Private	Public	Private			
1	2	1	5	1	1	17

Source: College Blue Book, Occupational Education 1997; Medical School Admission Requirements, 1998-99; Peterson's Guide to Two-Year Colleges, 1997; Peterson's Guide to Four-Year Colleges, 1997; Barron's Guide to Law Schools 1997

MAJOR EMPLOYERS

Major Employers

Allison Engine Co.	American Trans Air
American United Life Insurance	BankOne Indianapolis
Boehringer Manheim Corp. (laboratory instruments)	Celadon Trucking Services
Dowelanco (pesticides)	Eli Lilly & Co.
Indiana Bell Telephone	Methodist Hospital
Resort Condominiums International	Simon Property Group
St. Vincent Hospital & Health Care Center	Bridgeport Brass Corp.
Indiana Insurance	American Health Network

Note: companies listed are located in the city
Source: Dun's Business Rankings 1997; Ward's Business Directory, 1997

PUBLIC SAFETY

Crime Rate

Area	All Crimes	Violent Crimes				Property Crimes		
		Murder	Forcible Rape	Robbery	Aggrav. Assault	Burglary	Larceny -Theft	Motor Vehicle Theft
City	4,877.0	14.7	54.5	334.4	550.5	1,002.9	2,166.3	753.7
Suburbs[1]	5,974.8	4.8	41.3	125.4	304.8	960.7	4,007.0	530.9
MSA[2]	5,400.0	10.0	48.2	234.8	433.4	982.8	3,043.2	647.6
U.S.	5,078.9	7.4	36.1	202.4	388.2	943.0	2,975.9	525.9

Note: Crime rate is the number of crimes per 100,000 pop.; (1) defined as all areas within the MSA but located outside the central city; (2) Metropolitan Statistical Area - see Appendix A for areas incl.
Source: FBI Uniform Crime Reports 1996

RECREATION

Culture and Recreation

Museums	Symphony Orchestras	Opera Companies	Dance Companies	Professional Theatres	Zoos	Pro Sports Teams
14	2	2	2	3	1	2

Source: International Directory of the Performing Arts, 1996; Official Museum Directory, 1998; Chamber of Commerce/Economic Development 1997

Library System

The Indianapolis-Marion County Public Library has 21 branches, holdings of 1,951,804 volumes and a budget of $26,742,241 (1994). *American Library Directory, 1997-1998*

MEDIA

Newspapers

Name	Type	Freq.	Distribution	Circulation
The Criterion	Religious	1x/wk	Area	71,800
East Side Herald	General	1x/wk	Local	19,000
Greenwood Gazette	General	1x/wk	Local	20,000
Indiana Herald	Black	1x/wk	Local	25,000
The Indianapolis News	General	6x/wk	Area	54,423
Indianapolis Recorder	Black	1x/wk	Area	20,000
The Indianapolis Star	General	7x/wk	Local	230,932
National Jewish Post and Opinion	n/a	1x/wk	National	24,000
Northeast Reporter	General	1x/wk	Local	15,000
Nuvo	General	1x/wk	Area	50,000
The Spotlight	General	1x/wk	Local	25,000
White River Gazette	n/a	1x/wk	Local	10,000

Note: Includes newspapers with circulations of 10,000 or more located in the city; n/a not available
Source: Burrelle's Media Directory, 1998 Edition

AM Radio Stations

Call Letters	Freq. (kHz)	Target Audience	Station Format	Music Format
WSYW	810	n/a	E/M	n/a
WXLW	950	Religious	M/N/S/T	Christian
WIBC	1070	General	N/S/T	n/a
WNDE	1260	General	S	n/a
WTLC	1310	Black	M/N/S	Jazz/Oldies/R&B
WBAT	1400	General	M/N/S	Adult Contemporary
WMYS	1430	n/a	n/a	n/a
WBRI	1500	Religious	M/N/T	Christian
WNTS	1590	Religious	M/T	Christian

Note: Stations included broadcast in the Indianapolis metro area; n/a not available
Station Format: E = Educational; M = Music; N = News; S = Sports; T = Talk
Source: Burrelle's Media Directory, 1998 Edition

FM Radio Stations

Call Letters	Freq. (mHz)	Target Audience	Station Format	Music Format
WFBQ	n/a	n/a	n/a	n/a
WICR	88.7	General	M/N/S	Alternative/Big Band/Classical/Jazz
WJEL	89.3	n/a	M/N/S	Classic Rock/Contemporary Top 40/Urban Contemporary
WFYI	90.1	n/a	M/N/T	Adult Contemporary/Classical/Contemporary Top 40/Jazz/Oldies/R&B/Urban Contemporary
WBDG	90.9	n/a	M/N/S	AOR/Adult Contemporary/Alternative/Contemporary Top 40/R&B/Urban Contemporary
WEDM	91.1	General	M/N/S	Contemporary Top 40
WRFT	91.5	General	E/M/N/S	Adult Contemporary/Alternative/Classic Rock/Contemporary Top 40/Urban Contemporary
WNAP	93.1	General	M	Classic Rock
WGLD	93.9	General	M	Adult Contemporary/Jazz
WFBQ	94.7	General	M/N	AOR
WFMS	95.5	General	M	Country
WHHH	96.3	General	M	Contemporary Top 40/Urban Contemporary
WENS	97.1	n/a	M	Adult Contemporary
WXIR	98.3	Religious	M	Adult Contemporary/Christian
WCJC	99.3	General	M/N/S	Country
WZPL	99.5	General	M	Contemporary Top 40
WQFE	101.9	General	M	Oldies
WRZX	103.3	General	M	Alternative
WGRL	104.5	n/a	M	Country
WTLC	105.7	General	M/N/S	Urban Contemporary
WGGR	106.7	n/a	M/N	Oldies
WMRI	106.9	General	M/N	Easy Listening
WSYW	107.1	n/a	M	Classical
WTPI	107.9	General	M	Adult Contemporary/Jazz

Note: Stations included broadcast in the Indianapolis metro area; n/a not available
Station Format: E = Educational; M = Music; N = News; S = Sports; T = Talk
Music Format: AOR = Album Oriented Rock; MOR = Middle-of-the-Road
Source: Burrelle's Media Directory, 1998 Edition

Television Stations

Name	Ch.	Affiliation	Type	Owner
WTTV	4	UPN	Commercial	River City Broadcasting
WRTV	6	ABC	Commercial	McGraw-Hill
WISH	8	CBS	Commercial	LIN Television
WTHR	13	NBC	Commercial	Dispatch Printing Company/VideoIndiana Inc.
WFYI	20	PBS	Public	Metropolitan Indianapolis Public Broadcasting
WNDY	23	WB	Commercial	Wabash Valley Broadcasting Corp.
WHMB	40	n/a	n/a	Le Sea Broadcasting Corporation
WXIN	59	Fox	Commercial	Renaissance Communications Corp.
WTBU	69	PBS	Public	Butler University

Note: Stations included broadcast in the Indianapolis metro area
Source: Burrelle's Media Directory, 1998 Edition

CLIMATE

Average and Extreme Temperatures

Temperature	Jan	Feb	Mar	Apr	May	Jun	Jul	Aug	Sep	Oct	Nov	Dec	Ann
Extreme High (°F)	71	72	85	89	93	102	104	102	100	90	81	74	104
Average High (°F)	35	39	50	63	73	82	85	84	78	66	51	39	62
Average Temp. (°F)	27	31	41	52	63	72	76	73	67	55	43	31	53
Average Low (°F)	18	22	31	41	52	61	65	63	55	44	33	23	42
Extreme Low (°F)	-22	-21	-7	18	28	39	48	41	34	20	-2	-23	-23

Note: Figures cover the years 1948-1990
Source: National Climatic Data Center, International Station Meteorological Climate Summary, 3/95

Average Precipitation/Snowfall/Humidity

Precip./Humidity	Jan	Feb	Mar	Apr	May	Jun	Jul	Aug	Sep	Oct	Nov	Dec	Ann
Avg. Precip. (in.)	2.8	2.5	3.6	3.6	4.0	3.9	4.3	3.4	2.9	2.6	3.3	3.3	40.2
Avg. Snowfall (in.)	7	6	4	1	Tr	0	0	0	0	Tr	2	5	25
Avg. Rel. Hum. 7am (%)	81	81	79	77	79	80	84	87	87	85	83	83	82
Avg. Rel. Hum. 4pm (%)	68	64	59	53	53	53	56	56	53	53	63	70	59

Note: Figures cover the years 1948-1990; Tr = Trace amounts (<0.05 in. of rain; <0.5 in. of snow)
Source: National Climatic Data Center, International Station Meteorological Climate Summary, 3/95

Weather Conditions

Temperature			Daytime Sky			Precipitation		
10°F & below	32°F & below	90°F & above	Clear	Partly cloudy	Cloudy	0.01 inch or more precip.	0.1 inch or more snow/ice	Thunder-storms
19	119	19	83	128	154	127	24	43

Note: Figures are average number of days per year and covers the years 1948-1990
Source: National Climatic Data Center, International Station Meteorological Climate Summary, 3/95

AIR & WATER QUALITY

Maximum Pollutant Concentrations

	Particulate Matter (ug/m³)	Carbon Monoxide (ppm)	Sulfur Dioxide (ppm)	Nitrogen Dioxide (ppm)	Ozone (ppm)	Lead (ug/m³)
MSA[1] Level	71	3	0.041	0.018	0.12	0.07
NAAQS[2]	150	9	0.140	0.053	0.12	1.50
Met NAAQS?	Yes	Yes	Yes	Yes	Yes	Yes

Note: (1) Metropolitan Statistical Area - see Appendix A for areas included; (2) National Ambient Air Quality Standards; ppm = parts per million; ug/m³ = micrograms per cubic meter; n/a not available
Source: EPA, National Air Quality and Emissions Trends Report, 1996

Pollutant Standards Index

In the Indianapolis MSA (see Appendix A for areas included), the Pollutant Standards Index (PSI) exceeded 100 on 5 days in 1996. A PSI value greater than 100 indicates that air quality would be in the unhealthful range on that day. *EPA, National Air Quality and Emissions Trends Report, 1996*

Drinking Water

Water System Name	Pop. Served	Primary Water Source Type	Number of Violations in Fiscal Year 1997	Type of Violation/ Contaminants
Indianapolis Water Company	801,000	Surface	None	None

Note: Data as of January 16, 1998
Source: EPA, Office of Ground Water and Drinking Water, Safe Drinking Water Information System

Indianapolis tap water is alkaline, hard and fluoridated. Three separate systems with separate sources and purification plants.
Editor & Publisher Market Guide, 1998

Kansas City, Missouri

Background

Kansas City, Missouri lies on the western boundary of the state. With its sister city of the same name on the other side of the Kansas/Missouri border, both Kansas Cities make up the greater Kansas City metropolitan area.

As one might expect from the "Heart of America", Kansas City's major industries are hard wheat and cattle. However, do not be lulled into painting this picture for all of Kansas City. Kansas City is the largest city in Missouri. As such, the city is a modern urban institution with over 100 parks and playgrounds; suburban areas with an above average living standard; European statues that line wide stretching boulevards; and a foreign trade zone where foreign countries can store their goods free of import duties.

Downtown Kansas City is in the midst of a major renovation/restoration project which is transforming the landscape by blending 19th century buildings with modern skyscrapers. In addition, planned, completed or under construction will be the new corporate headquarters for DST Systems, a fast-growing processor of mutual fund accounts, a new Federal Court complex and an AMC entertainment center with a 30-screen movie theater. Historic Union Station is presently undergoing a $234 million major renovation which will eventually restore the grand hall with its 95-foot ceilings, but will also be home to the new Science City Museum. The completion date is November 1999 and the station renovation is seen as vital to the revitalization of downtown. *New York Times 2/8/98*

The territory of the Kansa (or Kaw), tribe received intermittent visits from white settlers during the 18th and 19th centuries. In 1724, Etienne Venyard, Sieur de Bougmont built a fort in the general vicinity, and in 1804, Meriwether Lewis and William Clark explored the area on behalf of President Jefferson for the Louisiana Purchase. In 1821, the site was a trading post established by Francois Chouteau.

A combination of gold prospectors passing through on their way to California; steamboat, rail, and overland trade; and the migration of would be settlers to California and the Southwest stimulated economic activity in Kansas City during the 1800's.

It was in this solid Midwestern city that the jazz clubs on 18th Street and Vine gave birth to the careers of Charlie Parker and Count Basie.

The National Weather Service office at Kansas City is very near the geographical center of the United States. The gently rolling terrain with no topographic impediments allows for the free sweep of air from all directions. There is often conflict between the warm moist air from the Gulf of Mexico and the cold polar air from the north. The summer season is characterized by warm days, mild nights and moderate humidity. Winters are not severely cold and snowfalls of 10 inches or more are comparatively rare.

General Rankings and Evaluative Comments

- Kansas City was ranked #221 out of 300 cities by *Money's* 1997 "Survey of the Best Places to Live." Criteria used: health services, crime, economy, housing, education, transportation, weather, leisure and the arts. The city was ranked #172 in 1996 and #209 in 1995. *Money, July 1997; Money, September 1996; Money, September 1995*

- *Ladies Home Journal* ranked America's 200 largest cities based on the qualities women care about most. Kansas City ranked 138 out of 200. Criteria: low crime rate, good public schools, well-paying jobs, quality health and child care, the presence of women in government, proportion of women-owned businesses, size of the wage gap with men, local economy, divorce rates, the ratio of single men to single women, whether there are laws that require at least the same number of public toilets for women as men, and the probability of good hair days. *Ladies Home Journal, November 1997*

- Kansas City was ranked #147 out of 219 cities in terms of children's health, safety, and economic well-being. Criteria: total population, percent population change, birth rate, child immunization rate, infant mortality rate, percent low birth weight infants, percent of births to teens, physician-to-population ratio, student-to-teacher ratio, dropout rate, unemployment rate, median family income, percent of children in poverty, violent and property crime rates, number of juvenile arrests for violent crimes as a percent of the total crime index, number of days with pollution standard index (PSI) over 100, pounds toxic releases per 1,000 people and number of superfund sites. *Zero Population Growth, Children's Environmental Index 1997*

- *Yahoo! Internet Life* selected "America's 100 Most Wired Cities & Towns". 50 cities were large and 50 cities were small. Kansas City ranked 31 out of 50 large cities. Criteria: Internet users per capita, number of networked computers, number of registered domain names, Internet backbone traffic, and the per-capita number of Web sites devoted to each city. *Yahoo! Internet Life, March 1998*

- Hallmark Cards, headquartered in Kansas City, is among the "100 Best Companies to Work for in America." Criteria: trust in management, pride in work/company, camaraderie, company responses to the Hewitt People Practices Inventory, and employee responses to their Great Place to Work survey. The companies also had to be at least 10 years old and have a minimum of 500 employees. *Fortune, January 12, 1998*

- Hallmark Cards and VCW Inc., headquartered in Kansas City, are among the "100 Best Companies for Working Mothers." Criteria: pay compared with competition, opportunities for women to advance, support for child care, flexible work schedules and family-friendly benefits. *Working Mother, October 1997*

- According to *Working Mother*, "More and more school-age programs in Missouri are earning state accreditation, under a grants program developed three years ago by the state department of education. Happily, the Missouri Center for Accreditation reports it is now swamped with applications for accreditation, which means school-age programs are meeting higher standards. These new rules are not the same as those required for NAEYC accreditation, but they are far better than having no standards at all.

  Advocates here managed to beat back a bill in the state legislature that would have hurt many family child care providers by requiring them to be in compliance with all local business zoning laws—a problem that plagues many child care providers across the county.

  Child care programs in religious institutions are now subject to inspection, and state officials have asked for funding to hire more inspectors to visit these centers." *Working Mother, July/August 1997*

Business Environment

STATE ECONOMY

State Economic Profile

"...The housing industry improved upon its performance in 1993, but fell well short of the number of permits issued during the industry's peak in 1994.

Missouri's largest employer, McDonnell Douglas Corp. is attempting to merge with Being. The combined companies promise as much as $1 billion in savings per year, making job cuts in Missouri likely. Since McDonnell Douglas is more active in defense contracting than Boeing, much of the St. Louis manufacturing workforce and facilities will likely remain intact, while cutbacks are more likely at commercial aircraft facilities.

Bank mergers will begin to have a dampening effect on the state's economy..., Mercantile bank purchased Mark Twain Bancshares and Roosevelt Financial Group, while NationsBank purchased Boatmen's Banchsares. There will be considerable branch consolidation.

TWA continues to look like a bigger risk to the Missouri economy as time goes on. Already on shaky financial footing, TWA has yet to recover from the fallout of the Flight 800 explosion....

Missouri's economy will recover as the year goes on and will eventually shadow the national economy through the forecast. St. Louis will continue to be a drag on Missouri's growth, but faster growing Kansas City, Columbia, and Springfield will help pick up the slack. Sizable exposure to a few large employers is a downside risk in the overall outlook. Moderate population growth will keep Missouri on track to be an average performer through the forecast." *National Association of Realtors, Economic Profiles: The Fifty States, July 1997*

IMPORTS/EXPORTS

Total Export Sales

Area	1993 ($000)	1994 ($000)	1995 ($000)	1996 ($000)	% Chg. 1993-96	% Chg. 1995-96
MSA[1]	2,225,901	2,578,560	3,350,170	3,985,073	79.0	19.0
U.S.	464,858,354	512,415,609	583,030,524	622,827,063	34.0	6.8

Note: (1) Metropolitan Statistical Area - see Appendix A for areas included
Source: U.S. Department of Commerce, International Trade Association, Metropolitan Area Exports: An Export Performance Report on Over 250 U.S. Cities, October 1997

Imports/Exports by Port

Type	Cargo Value			Share of U.S. Total	
	1995 (US$mil.)	1996 (US$mil.)	% Change 1995-1996	1995 (%)	1996 (%)
Imports	0	0	0	0	0
Exports	0	0	0	0	0

Source: Global Trade Information Services, WaterBorne Trade Atlas 1997

CITY FINANCES

City Government Finances

Component	FY92 ($000)	FY92 (per capita $)
Revenue	670,837	1,542.36
Expenditure	662,313	1,522.76
Debt Outstanding	905,332	2,081.50
Cash & Securities	1,542,753	3,547.02

Source: U.S. Bureau of the Census, City Government Finances: 1991-92

City Government Revenue by Source

Source	FY92 ($000)	FY92 (per capita $)	FY92 (%)
From Federal Government	27,663	63.60	4.1
From State Governments	24,249	55.75	3.6
From Local Governments	4,657	10.71	0.7
Property Taxes	62,233	143.08	9.3
General Sales Taxes	69,121	158.92	10.3
Selective Sales Taxes	77,908	179.12	11.6
Income Taxes	103,750	238.54	15.5
Current Charges	83,447	191.86	12.4
Utility/Liquor Store	46,960	107.97	7.0
Employee Retirement[1]	82,514	189.71	12.3
Other	88,335	203.10	13.2

Note: (1) Excludes "city contributions," classified as "nonrevenue," intragovernmental transfers.
Source: U.S. Bureau of the Census, City Government Finances: 1991-92

City Government Expenditures by Function

Function	FY92 ($000)	FY92 (per capita $)	FY92 (%)
Educational Services	23,559	54.17	3.6
Employee Retirement[1]	30,310	69.69	4.6
Environment/Housing	128,522	295.49	19.4
Government Administration	40,484	93.08	6.1
Interest on General Debt	45,672	105.01	6.9
Public Safety	125,914	289.50	19.0
Social Services	41,212	94.75	6.2
Transportation	132,189	303.92	20.0
Utility/Liquor Store	62,030	142.62	9.4
Other	32,421	74.54	4.9

Note: (1) Payments to beneficiaries including withdrawal of contributions.
Source: U.S. Bureau of the Census, City Government Finances: 1991-92

Municipal Bond Ratings

Area	Moody's	S & P
Kansas City	Aa3	AA

Note: n/a not available; n/r not rated
Source: Moody's Bond Record, 2/98; Statistical Abstract of the U.S., 1997; Governing Magazine, 9/97, 3/98

POPULATION

Population Growth

Area	1980	1990	% Chg. 1980-90	July 1996 Estimate	% Chg. 1990-96
City	448,159	435,141	-2.9	441,259	1.4
MSA[1]	1,433,458	1,566,280	9.3	1,690,343	7.9
U.S.	226,545,805	248,765,170	9.8	265,179,411	6.6

Note: (1) Metropolitan Statistical Area - see Appendix A for areas included
Source: 1980/1990 Census of Housing and Population, Summary Tape File 3C; Census Bureau Population Estimates

Population Characteristics

Race	City 1980 Population	%	City 1990 Population	%	% Chg. 1980-90	MSA[1] 1990 Population	%
White	313,840	70.0	290,898	66.9	-7.3	1,321,680	84.4
Black	122,336	27.3	128,843	29.6	5.3	200,436	12.8
Amer Indian/Esk/Aleut	2,115	0.5	2,240	0.5	5.9	8,178	0.5
Asian/Pacific Islander	3,591	0.8	4,903	1.1	36.5	15,908	1.0
Other	6,277	1.4	8,257	1.9	31.5	20,078	1.3
Hispanic Origin[2]	14,703	3.3	16,819	3.9	14.4	45,092	2.9

Note: (1) Metropolitan Statistical Area - see Appendix A for areas included;
(2) people of Hispanic origin can be of any race
Source: 1980/1990 Census of Housing and Population, Summary Tape File 3C

Ancestry

Area	German	Irish	English	Italian	U.S.	French	Polish	Dutch
City	23.9	16.6	12.5	3.6	3.7	3.4	1.4	2.3
MSA[1]	32.3	19.7	16.4	3.1	4.9	4.3	1.9	3.2
U.S.	23.3	15.6	13.1	5.9	5.3	4.2	3.8	2.5

Note: Figures are percentages and include persons that reported multiple ancestry (eg. if a person reported being Irish and Italian, they were included in both columns); (1) Metropolitan Statistical Area - see Appendix A for areas included
Source: 1990 Census of Population and Housing, Summary Tape File 3C

Age

Area	Median Age (Years)	Under 5	Under 18	18-24	25-44	45-64	65+	80+
City	32.7	7.7	24.7	9.8	34.2	18.4	12.9	3.2
MSA[1]	32.9	7.7	26.4	9.1	34.2	18.7	11.6	2.8
U.S.	32.9	7.3	25.6	10.5	32.6	18.7	12.5	2.8

Note: (1) Metropolitan Statistical Area - see Appendix A for areas included
Source: 1990 Census of Population and Housing, Summary Tape File 3C

Male/Female Ratio

Area	Number of males per 100 females (all ages)	Number of males per 100 females (18 years old+)
City	90.3	86.6
MSA[1]	93.5	89.9
U.S.	95.0	91.9

Note: (1) Metropolitan Statistical Area - see Appendix A for areas included
Source: 1990 Census of Population, General Population Characteristics

INCOME

Per Capita/Median/Average Income

Area	Per Capita ($)	Median Household ($)	Average Household ($)
City	13,799	26,713	33,510
MSA[1]	15,067	31,613	38,701
U.S.	14,420	30,056	38,453

Note: all figures are for 1989; (1) Metropolitan Statistical Area - see Appendix A for areas included
Source: 1990 Census of Population and Housing, Summary Tape File 3C

Household Income Distribution by Race

Income ($)	City (%)					U.S. (%)				
	Total	White	Black	Other	Hisp.[1]	Total	White	Black	Other	Hisp.[1]
Less than 5,000	8.4	5.0	17.4	11.2	7.5	6.2	4.8	15.2	8.6	8.8
5,000 - 9,999	9.5	7.7	14.0	12.3	10.8	9.3	8.6	14.2	9.9	11.1
10,000 - 14,999	9.5	8.7	11.9	7.5	8.6	8.8	8.5	11.0	9.8	11.0
15,000 - 24,999	19.2	18.9	20.0	19.8	20.6	17.5	17.3	18.9	18.5	20.5
25,000 - 34,999	16.8	17.6	14.6	19.2	18.5	15.8	16.1	14.2	15.4	16.4
35,000 - 49,999	17.3	19.1	12.3	16.4	17.9	17.9	18.6	13.3	16.1	16.0
50,000 - 74,999	12.9	14.9	7.8	9.8	14.1	15.0	15.8	9.3	13.4	11.1
75,000 - 99,999	3.5	4.4	1.3	2.4	1.5	5.1	5.5	2.6	4.7	3.1
100,000+	2.9	3.7	0.8	1.4	0.5	4.4	4.8	1.3	3.7	1.9

Note: all figures are for 1989; (1) people of Hispanic origin can be of any race
Source: 1990 Census of Population and Housing, Summary Tape File 3C

Effective Buying Income

Area	Per Capita ($)	Median Household ($)	Average Household ($)
City	15,668	31,151	38,554
MSA[1]	17,469	37,630	45,369
U.S.	15,444	33,201	41,849

Note: data as of 1/1/97; (1) Metropolitan Statistical Area - see Appendix A for areas included
Source: Standard Rate & Data Service, Newspaper Advertising Source, 2/98

Effective Household Buying Income Distribution

Area	% of Households Earning						
	$10,000 -$19,999	$20,000 -$34,999	$35,000 -$49,999	$50,000 -$74,999	$75,000 -$99,000	$100,000 -$124,999	$125,000 and up
City	17.0	24.2	18.2	17.0	5.5	1.7	1.8
MSA[1]	13.9	22.7	19.6	21.1	7.9	2.5	2.6
U.S.	16.5	23.4	18.3	18.2	6.4	2.1	2.4

Note: data as of 1/1/97; (1) Metropolitan Statistical Area - see Appendix A for areas included
Source: Standard Rate & Data Service, Newspaper Advertising Source, 2/98

Poverty Rates by Race and Age

Area	Total (%)	By Race (%)				By Age (%)		
		White	Black	Other	Hisp.[2]	Under 5 years old	Under 18 years old	65 years and over
City	15.3	8.7	29.6	21.8	18.4	26.2	22.8	14.6
MSA[1]	9.8	6.9	28.1	16.1	14.9	15.9	13.7	11.2
U.S.	13.1	9.8	29.5	23.1	25.3	20.1	18.3	12.8

Note: figures show the percent of people living below the poverty line in 1989. The average poverty threshold was $12,674 for a family of four in 1989; (1) Metropolitan Statistical Area - see Appendix A for areas included; (2) people of Hispanic origin can be of any race
Source: 1990 Census of Population and Housing, Summary Tape File 3C

EMPLOYMENT

Labor Force and Employment

Area	Civilian Labor Force			Workers Employed		
	Dec. '95	Dec. '96	% Chg.	Dec. '95	Dec. '96	% Chg.
City	260,223	257,747	-1.0	247,614	247,479	-0.1
MSA[1]	953,956	962,004	0.8	916,305	930,387	1.5
U.S.	134,583,000	136,742,000	1.6	127,903,000	130,785,000	2.3

Note: Data is not seasonally adjusted and covers workers 16 years of age and older;
(1) Metropolitan Statistical Area - see Appendix A for areas included
Source: Bureau of Labor Statistics, http://stats.bls.gov

Unemployment Rate

Area	1997											
	Jan.	Feb.	Mar.	Apr.	May	Jun.	Jul.	Aug.	Sep.	Oct.	Nov.	Dec.
City	4.5	4.5	4.2	5.2	4.3	4.5	4.2	4.4	4.6	4.2	4.0	4.0
MSA[1]	4.0	3.9	3.6	4.1	3.5	3.6	3.4	3.4	3.6	3.4	3.3	3.3
U.S.	5.9	5.7	5.5	4.8	4.7	5.2	5.0	4.8	4.7	4.4	4.3	4.4

Note: Data is not seasonally adjusted and covers workers 16 years of age and older; All figures are percentages; (1) Metropolitan Statistical Area - see Appendix A for areas included
Source: Bureau of Labor Statistics, http://stats.bls.gov

Employment by Industry

Sector	MSA[1]		U.S.
	Number of Employees	Percent of Total	Percent of Total
Services	272,700	29.1	29.0
Retail Trade	168,900	18.0	18.5
Government	134,700	14.4	16.1
Manufacturing	107,500	11.5	15.0
Finance/Insurance/Real Estate	65,900	7.0	5.7
Wholesale Trade	65,000	6.9	5.4
Transportation/Public Utilities	77,400	8.2	5.3
Construction/Mining	46,400	4.9	5.0

Note: Figures cover non-farm employment as of 12/97 and are not seasonally adjusted;
(1) Metropolitan Statistical Area - see Appendix A for areas included
Source: Bureau of Labor Statistics, http://stats.bls.gov

Employment by Occupation

Occupation Category	City (%)	MSA[1] (%)	U.S. (%)
White Collar	62.0	63.0	58.1
Executive/Admin./Management	12.2	13.2	12.3
Professional	14.3	14.1	14.1
Technical & Related Support	3.9	3.9	3.7
Sales	11.3	12.8	11.8
Administrative Support/Clerical	20.3	19.0	16.3
Blue Collar	22.1	23.4	26.2
Precision Production/Craft/Repair	8.5	10.0	11.3
Machine Operators/Assem./Insp.	5.8	5.6	6.8
Transportation/Material Movers	3.8	3.9	4.1
Cleaners/Helpers/Laborers	4.1	3.9	3.9
Services	15.1	12.4	13.2
Farming/Forestry/Fishing	0.7	1.3	2.5

Note: figures cover employed persons 16 years old and over;
(1) Metropolitan Statistical Area - see Appendix A for areas included
Source: 1990 Census of Population and Housing, Summary Tape File 3C

Occupational Employment Projections: 1994 - 2005

Occupations Expected to have the Largest Job Growth (ranked by numerical growth)	Fast-Growing Occupations[1] (ranked by percent growth)
1. General managers & top executives	1. Electronic pagination systems workers
2. Salespersons, retail	2. Amusement and recreation attendants
3. Waiters & waitresses	3. Computer engineers
4. Janitors/cleaners/maids, ex. priv. hshld.	4. Home health aides
5. Marketing & sales, supervisors	5. Systems analysts
6. Systems analysts	6. Database administrators
7. Teachers, secondary school	7. Occupational therapy assistants
8. Cashiers	8. Computer support specialists
9. Nursing aides/orderlies/attendants	9. Occupational therapists
10. Truck drivers, heavy	10. Manicurists

Projections cover the Kansas City MSA - see Appendix A for areas included.
Note: (1) Excludes occupations with employment less than 100 in 1994
Source: Missouri Dept. of Labor and Industrial Relations, Kansas City MSA Employment Outlook, Projections to 2005 for Industries and Occupations

Average Wages

Occupation	Wage	Occupation	Wage
Professional/Technical/Clerical	$/Week	**Health/Protective Services**	$/Week
Accountants III	805	Corrections Officers	424
Attorneys III	1,285	Firefighters	605
Budget Analysts III	782	Nurses, Licensed Practical II	-
Buyers/Contracting Specialists II	655	Nurses, Registered II	-
Clerks, Accounting III	436	Nursing Assistants II	-
Clerks, General III	381	Police Officers I	616
Computer Operators II	430	**Hourly Workers**	$/Hour
Computer Programmers II	677	Forklift Operators	11.61
Drafters II	499	General Maintenance Workers	9.27
Engineering Technicians III	676	Guards I	6.56
Engineering Technicians, Civil III	537	Janitors	7.68
Engineers III	900	Maintenance Electricians	19.67
Key Entry Operators I	312	Maintenance Electronics Techs II	18.36
Personnel Assistants III	474	Maintenance Machinists	16.51
Personnel Specialists III	816	Maintenance Mechanics, Machinery	15.36
Secretaries III	538	Material Handling Laborers	9.57
Switchboard Operator-Receptionist	353	Motor Vehicle Mechanics	-
Systems Analysts II	958	Shipping/Receiving Clerks	9.80
Systems Analysts Supervisor/Mgr II	1,400	Tool and Die Makers	20.83
Tax Collectors II	492	Truckdrivers, Tractor Trailer	14.95
Word Processors II	456	Warehouse Specialists	13.67

Note: Wage data includes full-time workers only for 9/96 and cover the Metropolitan Statistical Area (see Appendix A for areas included). Dashes indicate that data was not available.
Source: Bureau of Labor Statistics, Occupational Compensation Survey, 2/97

TAXES

Major State and Local Tax Rates

State Corp. Income (%)	State Personal Income (%)	Residential Property (effective rate per $100)	Sales & Use		State Gasoline (cents/ gallon)	State Cigarette (cents/ 20-pack)
			State (%)	Local (%)		
6.25	1.5 - 6.0	1.20	4.225	2.375	17.05[a]	17[b]

Note: Personal/corporate income tax rates as of 1/97. Sales, gasoline and cigarette tax rates as of 1/98; (a) Rate is comprised of 17 cents excise and 0.05 cents motor carrier tax; (b) Counties and cities may impose an additional tax of 4 - 7 cents per pack
Source: Federation of Tax Administrators, www.taxadmin.org; Washington D.C. Department of Finance and Revenue, Tax Rates and Tax Burdens in the District of Columbia: A Nationwide Comparison, June 1997; Chamber of Commerce

Total Taxes Per Capita and as a Percent of Income

Area	Per Capita Income ($)	Per Capita Taxes ($)			Taxes as Pct. of Income (%)		
		Total	Federal	State/Local	Total	Federal	State/Local
Missouri	24,554	8,421	5,674	2,747	34.3	23.1	11.2
U.S.	26,187	9,205	6,127	3,078	35.2	23.4	11.8

Note: Figures are for 1997
Source: Tax Foundation, Web Site, www.taxfoundation.org

Estimated Tax Burden

Area	State Income	Local Income	Property	Sales	Total
Kansas City	2,193	650	1,800	921	5,564

Note: The numbers are estimates of taxes paid by a married couple with two kids and annual earnings of $65,000. Sales tax estimates assume they spend average amounts on food, clothing, household goods and gasoline. Property tax estimates assume they live in a $225,000 home.
Source: Kiplinger's Personal Finance Magazine, June 1997

COMMERCIAL REAL ESTATE

Office Market

Class/Location	Total Space (sq. ft.)	Vacant Space (sq. ft.)	Vac. Rate (%)	Under Constr. (sq. ft.)	Net Absorp. (sq. ft.)	Rental Rates ($/sq.ft./yr.)
Class A						
CBD	5,481,014	427,369	7.8	n/a	1,526	16.75-22.50
Outside CBD	8,373,374	318,398	3.8	240,000	131,000	17.50-23.50
Class B						
CBD	4,362,115	634,290	14.5	n/a	70,954	11.00-16.25
Outside CBD	14,373,554	1,006,579	7.0	300,000	457,579	14.25-18.25

Note: Data as of 10/97 and covers Kansas City, Missouri and Kansas City, Kansas; CBD = Central Business District; n/a not available;
Source: Society of Industrial and Office Realtors, 1998 Comparative Statistics of Industrial and Office Real Estate Markets

"Kansas City's diversified economy is in top shape, with excellent job growth and demographic trends. Even with the risk of downsizing industries, Kansas City will continue to prosper. New development is focused in the southern suburban markets. There will be much construction especially of Class 'B' space. Sprint occupies more than three million sq. ft. of leased space at present. Construction of the New Sprint Campus, another three million sq. ft. of leased space at present. Construction of the New Sprint Campus, another three million sq. ft. is to be completed in phases over the next six years. Less than 300,000 sq. ft. of speculative space is planned for 1998. SIOR's reporters indicate a slow down in investment sales. There will be a 20-25 percent increase in lead prices for prime office sites." *Society of Industrial and Office Realtors, 1998 Comparative Statistics of Industrial and Office Real Estate Markets*

Industrial Market

Location	Total Space (sq. ft.)	Vacant Space (sq. ft.)	Vac. Rate (%)	Under Constr. (sq. ft.)	Net Absorp. (sq. ft.)	Gross Lease ($/sq.ft./yr.)
Central City	87,473,073	5,006,866	5.7	600,000	4,287,016	3.75-5.00
Suburban	45,098,870	2,523,276	5.6	1,600,000	1,771,246	5.00-9.00

Note: Data as of 10/97 and covers Kansas City, Missouri and Kansas City, Kansas; n/a not available
Source: Society of Industrial and Office Realtors, 1998 Comparative Statistics of Industrial and Office Real Estate Markets

"Moderate growth is expected in 1998 across the board. Currently, there are 840,000 sq. ft. of bulk space under construction coming on line in the spring of 1998. A large chunk of space, 420,000 sq. ft., will be complete in late 1998. There is concern that this new space will stay on the market for a few years based on absorption trends. Since there has been a shortage of new space on the market, absorption trends could reflect a lack of appropriate space as opposed to a lack of demand. Therefore we may see a rise in absorption. New development has traditionally been slow to start due to the market's strong commitment to local developers and a slow acceptance of outside developers. Developed sites are few and far between." *Society of Industrial and Office Realtors, 1998 Comparative Statistics of Industrial and Office Real Estate Markets*

Retail Market

Shopping Center Inventory (sq. ft.)	Shopping Center Construction (sq. ft.)	Construction as a Percent of Inventory (%)	Torto Wheaton Rent Index[1] ($/sq. ft.)
35,751,000	1,083,000	3.0	11.19

Note: Data as of 1997 and covers the Metropolitan Statistical Area - see Appendix A for areas included; (1) Index is based on a model that predicts what the average rent should be for leases with certain characteristics, in certain locations during certain years.
Source: National Association of Realtors, 1997-1998 Market Conditions Report

"Population growth in Kansas City has exceeded the national average during the past two years. That, combined with solid personal income growth, has helped expand the area's retail sector. The retail rent index erased a sharp decline in 1995, rising 18.3% in 1996 and 2.6% last year. Kansas City's suburban areas have experienced robust growth. Strong demographics and increased traffic activity near Independence Center have set off a restaurant boom. While the majority of stores are doing well, some local analysts feel the market may be reaching a saturation point. Shopping center completions are expected to slow substantially over the next two years." *National Association of Realtors, 1997-1998 Market Conditions Report*

COMMERCIAL UTILITIES

Typical Monthly Electric Bills

Area	Commercial Service ($/month)		Industrial Service ($/month)	
	12 kW demand 1,500 kWh	100 kW demand 30,000 kWh	1,000 kW demand 400,000 kWh	20,000 kW demand 10,000,000 kWh
City	186	2,539	25,794	490,025
U.S.	162	2,360	25,590	545,677

Note: Based on rates in effect July 1, 1997
Source: Edison Electric Institute, Typical Residential, Commercial and Industrial Bills, Summer 1997

TRANSPORTATION

Transportation Statistics

Avg. travel time to work (min.)	20.5
Interstate highways	I-29; I-35; I-70
Bus lines	
In-city	Kansas City Area TA, 277 vehicles
Inter-city	2
Passenger air service	
Airport	Kansas City International
Airlines	14
Aircraft departures	66,299 (1995)
Enplaned passengers	4,533,185 (1995)
Rail service	Amtrak; Light Rail planned
Motor freight carriers	225
Major waterways/ports	Kansas/Missouri Rivers

Source: OAG, Business Travel Planner, Summer 1997; Editor & Publisher Market Guide, 1998; FAA Airport Activity Statistics, 1996; Amtrak National Time Table, Northeast Timetable, Fall/Winter 1997-98; 1990 Census of Population and Housing, STF 3C; Chamber of Commerce/Economic Development 1997; Jane's Urban Transport Systems 1997-98; Transit Fact Book 1997

A survey of 90,000 airline passengers during the first half of 1997 ranked most of the largest airports in the U.S. Kansas City International ranked number 12 out of 36. Criteria: cleanliness, quality of restaurants, attractiveness, speed of baggage delivery, ease of reaching gates, available ground transportation, ease of following signs and closeness of parking. *Plog Research Inc., First Half 1997*

Means of Transportation to Work

Area	Car/Truck/Van		Public Transportation			Bicycle	Walked	Other Means	Worked at Home
	Drove Alone	Car-pooled	Bus	Subway	Railroad				
City	74.7	13.6	5.6	0.0	0.0	0.1	2.8	1.0	2.2
MSA[1]	79.9	12.5	2.0	0.0	0.0	0.1	1.9	0.8	2.8
U.S.	73.2	13.4	3.0	1.5	0.5	0.4	3.9	1.2	3.0

Note: figures shown are percentages and only include workers 16 years old and over;
(1) Metropolitan Statistical Area - see Appendix A for areas included
Source: 1990 Census of Population and Housing, Summary Tape File 3C

BUSINESSES

Major Business Headquarters

Company Name	1997 Rankings	
	Fortune 500	Forbes 500
American Century Cos.	-	406
Bartlett and Co	-	236
Black & Veatch	-	118
DeBruce Grain	-	237
Dunn Industries	-	329
Farmland Industries	151	-
Hallmark Cards	-	40
Interstate Bakeries	464	-
Payless Cashways	490	-
Russel Stover Candies	-	494
Sutherland Lumber	-	202
Utilicorp United	316	-

Note: Companies listed are located in the city; Dashes indicate no ranking
Fortune 500: companies that produce a 10-K are ranked 1 - 500 based on 1996 revenue
Forbes 500: private companies are ranked 1 - 500 based on 1996 revenue
Source: Forbes 12/1/97; Fortune 4/28/97

Women-Owned Businesses: Number, Employment, Sales and Share

Area	Women-Owned Businesses in 1996				Share of Women-Owned Businesses in 1996	
	Number	Employment	Sales ($000)	Rank[2]	Percent (%)	Rank[3]
MSA[1]	52,200	92,300	16,421,900	33	37.0	24

Note: (1) Metropolitan Statistical Area - see Appendix A for areas included; (2) Calculated on an averaging of number of businesses, employment and sales and ranges from 1 to 50 where 1 is best; (3) Ranges from 1 to 50 where 1 is best
Source: The National Foundation for Women Business Owners, 1996 Facts on Women-Owned Businesses: Trends in the Top 50 Metropolitan Areas, March 26, 1997

Women-Owned Businesses: Growth

Area	Growth in Women-Owned Businesses (% change from 1987 to 1996)				Relative Growth in the Number of Women-Owned and All Businesses (% change from 1987 to 1996)			
	Num.	Empl.	Sales	Rank[2]	Women-Owned	All Firms	Absolute Difference	Relative Difference
MSA[1]	57.1	118.4	230.1	46	57.1	37.5	19.6	1.5:1

Note: (1) Metropolitan Statistical Area - see Appendix A for areas included; (2) Calculated on an averaging of the percent growth of number of businesses, employment and sales and ranges from 1 to 50 where 1 is best
Source: The National Foundation for Women Business Owners, 1996 Facts on Women-Owned Businesses: Trends in the Top 50 Metropolitan Areas, March 26, 1997

Minority Business Opportunity

Kansas City is home to one company which is on the Black Enterprise Industrial/Service 100 list (largest based on gross sales): Perfection Industrial Distributors (distributor of medical & industrial supplies). Criteria: 1) operational in previous calendar year; 2) at least 51%

black-owned; 3) manufactures/owns the product it sells or provides industrial or consumer services. Brokerages, real estate firms and firms that provide professional services are not eligible. *Black Enterprise, July 1997*

One of the 500 largest Hispanic-owned companies in the U.S. are located in Kansas City. *Hispanic Business, June 1997*

Kansas City is home to one company which is on the Hispanic Business Fastest-Growing 100 list (greatest sales growth from 1992 to 1996): Rafael Architects Inc. (architecture, design and planning svcs.) *Hispanic Business, July/August 1997*

Small Business Opportunity

Kansas City was included among *Entrepreneur* magazines listing of the "20 Best Cities for Small Business." It was ranked #10 among large metro areas. Criteria: risk of failure, business performance, economic growth, affordability and state attitude towards business. *Entrepreneur, 10/97*

HOTELS & MOTELS

Hotels/Motels

Area	Hotels/ Motels	Rooms	Luxury-Level Hotels/Motels		Average Minimum Rates ($)		
			◆◆◆◆	◆◆◆◆◆	◆◆	◆◆◆	◆◆◆◆
City	37	7,978	3	0	73	100	153
Airport	13	2,205	0	0	n/a	n/a	n/a
Suburbs	52	5,999	0	0	n/a	n/a	n/a
Total	102	16,182	3	0	n/a	n/a	n/a

Note: n/a not available; Classifications range from one diamond (budget properties with basic amenities) to five diamond (luxury properties with the finest service, rooms and facilities).
Source: OAG, Business Travel Planner, Summer 1997

CONVENTION CENTERS

Major Convention Centers

Center Name	Meeting Rooms	Exhibit Space (sf)
American Royal Center	2	372,000
Kansas City Convention Center	58	388,000
Kansas City Market Center/Convention Center	20	59,000
Kansas City Marriott Downtown	23	22,380
Park Place Hotel	n/a	15,108
The Ritz-Carlton, Kansas City	n/a	19,250
Westin Crown Center	25	16,000
Hyatt Regency Crown Center	21	n/a
Radisson Suites-Kansas City	9	n/a

Note: n/a not available
Source: Trade Shows Worldwide 1997

Living Environment

COST OF LIVING

Cost of Living Index

Composite Index	Housing	Utilities	Groceries	Health Care	Trans- portation	Misc. Goods/ Services
95.8	90.4	81.9	96.2	103.3	97.5	101.6

Note: U.S. = 100; Figures are for the Metropolitan Statistical Area - see Appendix A for areas included
Source: ACCRA, Cost of Living Index, 3rd Quarter 1997

HOUSING

Median Home Prices and Housing Affordability

Area	Median Price[2] 3rd Qtr. 1997 ($)	HOI[3] 3rd Qtr. 1997	Afford- ability Rank[4]
MSA[1]	98,000	83.3	11
U.S.	127,000	63.7	–

Note: (1) Metropolitan Statistical Area - see Appendix A for areas included; (2) U.S. figures calculated from the sales of 625,000 new and existing homes in 195 markets; (3) Housing Opportunity Index - percent of homes sold that were within the reach of the median income household at the prevailing mortgage interest rate; (4) Rank is from 1-195 with 1 being most affordable
Source: National Association of Home Builders, Housing Opportunity Index, 3rd Quarter 1997

It is projected that the median price of existing single-family homes in the metro area will decrease by -3.2% in 1998. Nationwide, home prices are projected to increase 6.6%.
Kiplinger's Personal Finance Magazine, January 1998

Average New Home Price

Area	Price ($)
MSA[1]	119,370
U.S.	135,710

Note: Figures are based on a new home with 1,800 sq. ft. of living area on an 8,000 sq. ft. lot; (1) Metropolitan Statistical Area - see Appendix A for areas included
Source: ACCRA, Cost of Living Index, 3rd Quarter 1997

Average Apartment Rent

Area	Rent ($/mth)
MSA[1]	578
U.S.	569

Note: Figures are based on an unfurnished two bedroom, 1-1/2 or 2 bath apartment, approximately 950 sq. ft. in size, excluding all utilities except water; (1) Metropolitan Statistical Area - see Appendix A for areas included
Source: ACCRA, Cost of Living Index, 3rd Quarter 1997

RESIDENTIAL UTILITIES

Average Residential Utility Costs

Area	All Electric ($/mth)	Part Electric ($/mth)	Other Energy ($/mth)	Phone ($/mth)
MSA[1]	–	55.17	26.96	18.13
U.S.	109.40	55.25	43.64	19.48

Note: (1) (1) Metropolitan Statistical Area - see Appendix A for areas included
Source: ACCRA, Cost of Living Index, 3rd Quarter 1997

HEALTH CARE

Average Health Care Costs

Area	Hospital ($/day)	Doctor ($/visit)	Dentist ($/visit)
MSA[1]	505.49	48.71	57.75
U.S.	392.91	48.76	60.84

Note: Hospital - based on a semi-private room. Doctor - based on a general practitioner's routine exam of an established patient. Dentist - based on adult teeth cleaning and periodic oral exam; (1) Metropolitan Statistical Area - see Appendix A for areas included
Source: ACCRA, Cost of Living Index, 3rd Quarter 1997

Distribution of Office-Based Physicians

Area	Family/Gen. Practitioners	Specialists		
		Medical	Surgical	Other
MSA[1]	169	511	427	360

Note: Data as of 12/31/96; (1) Metropolitan Statistical Area - see Appendix A for areas included
Source: American Medical Assn., Physician Characteristics & Distribution in the U.S., 1997-1998

Hospitals

Kansas City has 11 general medical and surgical hospitals, 4 psychiatric, 1 rehabilitation, 1 children's general, 1 children's psychiatric. *AHA Guide to the Healthcare Field 1997-98*

EDUCATION

Public School District Statistics

District Name	Num. Sch.	Enroll.	Classroom Teachers[1]	Pupils per Teacher	Minority Pupils (%)	Current Exp.[2] ($/pupil)
Center 58	7	2,645	178	14.9	n/a	n/a
Hickman Mills C-1	14	7,084	450	15.7	n/a	n/a
Kansas City 33	83	36,515	2,841	12.9	78.1	8,788
North Kansas City 74	28	16,569	1,049	15.8	n/a	n/a
Park Hill	11	8,220	477	17.2	n/a	n/a

Note: Data covers the 1995-1996 school year unless otherwise noted; (1) Excludes teachers reported as working in school district offices rather than in schools; (2) Based on 1993-94 enrollment collected by the Census Bureau, not the enrollment figure shown in column 3; SD = School District; ISD = Independent School District; n/a not available
Source: National Center for Education Statistics, Common Core of Data Survey; Bureau of the Census

Educational Quality

School District	Education Quotient[1]	Graduate Outcome[2]	Community Index[3]	Resource Index[4]
Kansas City	96.0	58.0	102.0	129.0

Note: Nearly 1,000 secondary school districts were rated in terms of educational quality. The scores range from a low of 50 to a high of 150; (1) Average of the Graduate Outcome, Community and Resource indexes; (2) Based on graduation rates and college board scores (SAT/ACT); (3) Based on the surrounding community's average level of education and the area's average income level; (4) Based on teacher salaries, per-pupil expenditures and student-teacher ratios.
Source: Expansion Management, Ratings Issue 1997

Educational Attainment by Race

Area	High School Graduate (%)					Bachelor's Degree (%)				
	Total	White	Black	Other	Hisp.[2]	Total	White	Black	Other	Hisp.[2]
City	78.8	82.9	68.5	68.6	62.4	22.0	26.5	10.0	18.5	11.4
MSA[1]	82.3	84.2	70.3	71.8	67.3	23.4	24.9	11.7	22.0	13.3
U.S.	75.2	77.9	63.1	60.4	49.8	20.3	21.5	11.4	19.4	9.2

Note: figures shown cover persons 25 years old and over; (1) Metropolitan Statistical Area - see Appendix A for areas included; (2) people of Hispanic origin can be of any race
Source: 1990 Census of Population and Housing, Summary Tape File 3C

School Enrollment by Type

| Area | Preprimary | | | | Elementary/High School | | | |
| | Public | | Private | | Public | | Private | |
	Enrollment	%	Enrollment	%	Enrollment	%	Enrollment	%
City	4,496	55.5	3,601	44.5	57,590	85.6	9,712	14.4
MSA[1]	18,724	56.8	14,261	43.2	236,921	89.4	28,033	10.6
U.S.	2,679,029	59.5	1,824,256	40.5	38,379,689	90.2	4,187,099	9.8

Note: figures shown cover persons 3 years old and over;
(1) Metropolitan Statistical Area - see Appendix A for areas included
Source: 1990 Census of Population and Housing, Summary Tape File 3C

School Enrollment by Race

| Area | Preprimary (%) | | | | Elementary/High School (%) | | | |
	White	Black	Other	Hisp.[1]	White	Black	Other	Hisp.[1]
City	65.3	31.4	3.3	4.2	55.4	40.0	4.6	5.5
MSA[2]	85.4	12.3	2.3	3.3	80.0	16.3	3.7	4.0
U.S.	80.4	12.5	7.1	7.8	74.1	15.6	10.3	12.5

Note: figures shown cover persons 3 years old and over; (1) people of Hispanic origin can be of any race; (2) Metropolitan Statistical Area - see Appendix A for areas included
Source: 1990 Census of Population and Housing, Summary Tape File 3C

SAT/ACT Scores

| Area/District | 1997 SAT | | | | 1997 ACT | |
	Percent of Graduates Tested (%)	Average Math Score	Average Verbal Score	Average Combined Score	Percent of Graduates Tested (%)	Average Composite Score
Kansas City SD	n/a	n/a	n/a	n/a	40	18.1
State	9	568	567	1,135	64	21.5
U.S.	42	511	505	1,016	36	21.0

Note: Math and verbal SAT scores are out of a possible 800; ACT scores are out of a possible 36
Caution: Comparing or ranking states/cities on the basis of SAT/ACT scores alone is invalid and strongly discouraged by the The College Board and The American College Testing Program as students who take the tests are self-selected and do not represent the entire student population.
Source: Kansas City Missouri School District, Assessment Office, 1997; American College Testing Program, 1997; College Board, 1997

Classroom Teacher Salaries in Public Schools

| District | B.A. Degree | | M.A. Degree | | Ph.D. Degree | |
	Min. ($)	Max. ($)	Min. ($)	Max. ($)	Min. ($)	Max. ($)
Kansas City	24,539	33,816	27,069	41,402	29,599	46,457
Average[1]	26,120	39,270	28,175	44,667	31,643	49,825

Note: Salaries are for 1996-1997; (1) Based on all school districts covered; n/a not available
Source: American Federation of Teachers (unpublished data)

Higher Education

| Two-Year Colleges | | Four-Year Colleges | | Medical Schools | Law Schools | Voc/ Tech |
Public	Private	Public	Private			
2	0	1	8	1	1	17

Source: College Blue Book, Occupational Education 1997; Medical School Admission Requirements, 1998-99; Peterson's Guide to Two-Year Colleges, 1997; Peterson's Guide to Four-Year Colleges, 1997; Barron's Guide to Law Schools 1997

MAJOR EMPLOYERS

Major Employers

Farmland Industries	BGM Industries (building cleaning services)
Black & Veatch (engineering)	Children's Mercy Hospital
DST Systems (accounting services)	Hallmark Cards
Kansas City Star	Research Medical Center
Sprint Communications	St. Joseph Health Center
St. Lukes Hospital	Trinity Lutheran Hospital
Truman Medical Center	UMB Bank
Boyd Kansas City (gaming)	Missouri Gaming
Blue Cross & Blue Shield of KC	

Note: companies listed are located in the city
Source: Dun's Business Rankings 1997; Ward's Business Directory, 1997

PUBLIC SAFETY

Crime Rate

Area	All Crimes	Violent Crimes				Property Crimes		
		Murder	Forcible Rape	Robbery	Aggrav. Assault	Burglary	Larceny -Theft	Motor Vehicle Theft
City	11,661.8	23.2	91.9	642.4	1,223.7	1,995.0	6,271.0	1,414.6
Suburbs[1]	n/a	n/a	n/a	n/a	n/a	n/a	n/a	n/a
MSA[2]	n/a	n/a	n/a	n/a	n/a	n/a	n/a	n/a
U.S.	5,078.9	7.4	36.1	202.4	388.2	943.0	2,975.9	525.9

Note: Crime rate is the number of crimes per 100,000 pop.; (1) defined as all areas within the MSA but located outside the central city; (2) Metropolitan Statistical Area - see Appendix A for areas incl.
Source: FBI Uniform Crime Reports 1996

RECREATION

Culture and Recreation

Museums	Symphony Orchestras	Opera Companies	Dance Companies	Professional Theatres	Zoos	Pro Sports Teams
9	2	1	2	3	1	2

Source: International Directory of the Performing Arts, 1996; Official Museum Directory, 1998; Chamber of Commerce/Economic Development 1997

Library System

The Kansas City Public Library has eight branches, holdings of 1,895,264 volumes and a budget of $10,314,502 (1995-1996). *American Library Directory, 1997-1998*

MEDIA

Newspapers

Name	Type	Freq.	Distribution	Circulation
The Call	Black	1x/wk	Local	17,999
The Catholic Key	Religious	1x/wk	Area	17,500
Clay Sun Chronicle	n/a	1x/wk	Local	9,400
Dos Mundos	Hispanic	2x/mo	Local	20,000
East Side News	General	1x/wk	Area	19,000
Gladstone Sun Chronicle	n/a	1x/wk	Local	15,500
Kansas City Globe	Black	1x/wk	Local	10,500
The Kansas City Star	n/a	7x/wk	Regional	297,041
Liberty Sun Chronicle	General	1x/wk	Local	9,000
Missouri State Post	n/a	1x/wk	State	30,600
Mr. Pennypincher	General	1x/wk	Local	10,000
The New Times	Alternative	1x/wk	Regional	40,000
The Northeast News	General	1x/wk	Local	15,000
North Kansas City Sun Chronicle	n/a	1x/wk	Local	8,100
Penny Shopper	General	1x/wk	Local	3,000
Pitch Weekly	General	1x/wk	Regional	100,000
Press Dispatch-Tribune	General	2x/wk	Area	49,720
Wednesday Magazine	General	1x/wk	Local	33,723

Note: Includes newspapers with circulations of 1,000 or more located in the city; n/a not available
Source: Burrelle's Media Directory, 1998 Edition

AM Radio Stations

Call Letters	Freq. (kHz)	Target Audience	Station Format	Music Format
WDAF	610	General	M	Country
WHB	810	n/a	M/N/S/T	Country
KUGT	1170	General	M	Adult Contemporary/Christian
KCTE	1510	General	S	n/a
KPRT	1590	Religious	M/T	Christian

Note: Stations included broadcast in the Kansas City metro area; n/a not available
Station Format: E = Educational; M = Music; N = News; S = Sports; T = Talk
Source: Burrelle's Media Directory, 1998 Edition

FM Radio Stations

Call Letters	Freq. (mHz)	Target Audience	Station Format	Music Format
KLJC	88.5	Religious	E/M	Christian
KCUR	89.3	General	M/N/T	Big Band/Jazz/Spanish
KWJC	91.9	Religious	M/N/S	Adult Contemporary/Christian/Classic Rock
KMXV	93.3	n/a	M	Contemporary Top 40
KFKF	94.1	General	M	Country
KXTR	96.5	General	M/N/T	Classical
KUDL	98.1	n/a	M	Adult Contemporary
KCFX	101.1	General	M	Classic Rock
KYYS	102.1	n/a	M	AOR
KPRS	103.3	General	E/M/N/S/T	Urban Contemporary
KBEQ	104.3	General	M	Country
KCIY	106.5	General	M	Jazz
KISF	107.3	General	M/N/S	Alternative

Note: Stations included broadcast in the Kansas City metro area; n/a not available
Station Format: E = Educational; M = Music; N = News; S = Sports; T = Talk
Music Format: AOR = Album Oriented Rock; MOR = Middle-of-the-Road
Source: Burrelle's Media Directory, 1998 Edition

Television Stations

Name	Ch.	Affiliation	Type	Owner
WDAF	4	Fox	Commercial	New World Communications
KMBC	9	ABC	Commercial	Hearst Broadcasting Stations
KCPT	19	PBS	Public	Public Television 19, Inc.
KSHB	41	NBC	Commercial	Scripps Howard Broadcasting

Note: Stations included broadcast in the Kansas City metro area
Source: Burrelle's Media Directory, 1998 Edition

CLIMATE

Average and Extreme Temperatures

Temperature	Jan	Feb	Mar	Apr	May	Jun	Jul	Aug	Sep	Oct	Nov	Dec	Ann
Extreme High (°F)	69	76	86	93	92	105	107	109	102	92	82	70	109
Average High (°F)	35	40	54	65	74	84	90	87	79	66	52	39	64
Average Temp. (°F)	26	31	44	55	64	74	79	77	68	56	43	30	54
Average Low (°F)	17	22	34	44	54	63	69	66	58	45	34	21	44
Extreme Low (°F)	-17	-19	-10	12	30	42	54	43	33	21	1	-23	-23

Note: Figures cover the years 1972-1990
Source: National Climatic Data Center, International Station Meteorological Climate Summary, 3/95

Average Precipitation/Snowfall/Humidity

Precip./Humidity	Jan	Feb	Mar	Apr	May	Jun	Jul	Aug	Sep	Oct	Nov	Dec	Ann
Avg. Precip. (in.)	1.1	1.2	2.8	3.0	5.5	4.1	3.8	4.1	4.9	3.6	2.1	1.6	38.1
Avg. Snowfall (in.)	6	5	3	1	0	0	0	0	0	Tr	1	5	21
Avg. Rel. Hum. 6am (%)	76	77	78	77	82	84	84	86	86	80	79	78	80
Avg. Rel. Hum. 3pm (%)	58	59	54	50	54	54	51	53	53	51	57	60	54

Note: Figures cover the years 1972-1990; Tr = Trace amounts (<0.05 in. of rain; <0.5 in. of snow)
Source: National Climatic Data Center, International Station Meteorological Climate Summary, 3/95

Weather Conditions

Temperature			Daytime Sky			Precipitation		
10°F & below	32°F & below	90°F & above	Clear	Partly cloudy	Cloudy	0.01 inch or more precip.	0.1 inch or more snow/ice	Thunder-storms
22	110	39	112	134	119	103	17	51

Note: Figures are average number of days per year and covers the years 1972-1990
Source: National Climatic Data Center, International Station Meteorological Climate Summary, 3/95

AIR & WATER QUALITY

Maximum Pollutant Concentrations

	Particulate Matter (ug/m³)	Carbon Monoxide (ppm)	Sulfur Dioxide (ppm)	Nitrogen Dioxide (ppm)	Ozone (ppm)	Lead (ug/m³)
MSA[1] Level	120	4	0.057	0.022	0.11	0.07
NAAQS[2]	150	9	0.140	0.053	0.12	1.50
Met NAAQS?	Yes	Yes	Yes	Yes	Yes	Yes

Note: (1) Metropolitan Statistical Area - see Appendix A for areas included; (2) National Ambient Air Quality Standards; ppm = parts per million; ug/m³ = micrograms per cubic meter; n/a not available
Source: EPA, National Air Quality and Emissions Trends Report, 1996

Pollutant Standards Index

In the Kansas City MSA (see Appendix A for areas included), the Pollutant Standards Index (PSI) exceeded 100 on 3 days in 1996. A PSI value greater than 100 indicates that air quality would be in the unhealthful range on that day. *EPA, National Air Quality and Emissions Trends Report, 1996*

Drinking Water

Water System Name	Pop. Served	Primary Water Source Type	Number of Violations in Fiscal Year 1997	Type of Violation/ Contaminants
Kansas City	450,000	Surface	None	None

Note: Data as of January 16, 1998
Source: EPA, Office of Ground Water and Drinking Water, Safe Drinking Water Information System

Kansas City tap water is neutral, soft and fluoridated.
Editor & Publisher Market Guide, 1998

Little Rock, Arkansas

Background

In 1722, Bernard de la Harpe paddled his canoe along what would become known as the Arkansas River. On the southern bank of the river, near the site of an Akansa tribal village and a mossy boulder which de la Harpe called La Petit Roche - Little Rock, he built a trading post. 90 years later a trapper by the name of William Lewis built his home at the "little rock." In 1819 Arkansas became a territory, and in 1821 Little Rock was chosen as the territorial capital. The river became the lifeline of the town and steamboats docked to load bales of cotton and other products of the Arkansas land.

In 1861 Arkansas withdrew from the Union. But by 1863 it became the second Confederate capital to fall to the Yankees, who occupied the city for the remainder of the war. The post-war period was a time of rapid growth for the town. By 1888 Little Rock had telephones, waterworks, electric trolleys and streetlights.

By the 1890's, Little Rock had become an important transportation center with the expansion of the railways. Industry in the metropolitan area grew rapidly due to nearby oil, gas, coal timber and bauxite reserves. In 1969, the city became a river port with the opening of locks on the Arkansas River. The city remains the chief market for the surrounding agricultural region.

In 1957, the city became the center of attention for the Civil Rights Movement when the Arkansas governor ordered the state militia to prevent nine black students from being the first to integrate a local high school. U.S. President Dwight D. Eisenhower sent federal troops to maintain order and the black students began to attend classes. Within ten years, all of the Little Rock schools were desegregated.

Today the city's higher education institutions include; the University of Arkansas at Little Rock, Philander Smith College, the University of Arkansas for Medical Sciences, Arkansas Baptist College, and the state schools for the blind and deaf.

Little Rock is one of the most agreeable cities in the South. The town has lovingly restored the original Pulaski County Courthouse from Little Rock's earliest years, as well as the Old State House, which now serves as an Arkansas state history museum. The oldest part of Little Rock is called the Quapaw Quarter, a neighborhood of shady trees and beautifully restored Victorian homes. The nearby MacArthur Park reminds the city of one of it's most famous sons, General Douglas MacArthur. The General was born in the Old Arsenal in Little Rock, where his father was the commanding officer. That 1836 building now houses the Museum of Science and History, which looks across the park to Arkansas Art Center. Of course, another famous son of Little Rock is the 42nd President of the United States, Bill Clinton.

Little Rock is located on the Arkansas River near the geographical center of the state. The modified continental climate includes exposure to all of the North American air mass types. However, with its proximity to the Gulf of Mexico, the summer season is marked by prolonged periods of warm and humid weather. Precipitation is fairly well distributed throughout the year. Snow is almost negligible. Glaze and ice storms, although infrequent, are at times severe.

General Rankings and Evaluative Comments

- Little Rock was ranked #142 out of 300 cities by *Money's* 1997 "Survey of the Best Places to Live." Criteria used: health services, crime, economy, housing, education, transportation, weather, leisure and the arts. The city was ranked #195 in 1996 and #176 in 1995. *Money, July 1997; Money, September 1996; Money, September 1995*

- *Ladies Home Journal* ranked America's 200 largest cities based on the qualities women care about most. Little Rock ranked 77 out of 200. Criteria: low crime rate, good public schools, well-paying jobs, quality health and child care, the presence of women in government, proportion of women-owned businesses, size of the wage gap with men, local economy, divorce rates, the ratio of single men to single women, whether there are laws that require at least the same number of public toilets for women as men, and the probability of good hair days. *Ladies Home Journal, November 1997*

- Little Rock was ranked #106 out of 219 cities in terms of children's health, safety, and economic well-being. Criteria: total population, percent population change, birth rate, child immunization rate, infant mortality rate, percent low birth weight infants, percent of births to teens, physician-to-population ratio, student-to-teacher ratio, dropout rate, unemployment rate, median family income, percent of children in poverty, violent and property crime rates, number of juvenile arrests for violent crimes as a percent of the total crime index, number of days with pollution standard index (PSI) over 100, pounds toxic releases per 1,000 people and number of superfund sites. *Zero Population Growth, Children's Environmental Index 1997*

- According to *Working Mother,* "Arkansas made some encouraging progress in helping centers get accredited and getting caregivers to seek more education. With state aid and technical assistance, the number of state-accredited centers grew tenfold in the past year and a half, from 27 to 270. (The state's accreditation standards are not quite as demanding as NAEYC's, but this is still an initiative that boosts quality.) Parents who use accredited centers can double the state tax credit they take for child care. The state also used $400,000 in federal funds to award scholarships to 300 caregivers who wanted to work toward a Child Development Associate degree.

  State legislators agreed to upgrade adult-to-child ratios in programs for school-age kids, a positive step. There must now be one adult on hand for every 20 kids, instead of 25. State lawmakers also upheld quality in child care by refusing to pass a bill that would have gutted training requirements for caregivers—a smart move, since so many studies show that caregivers do a better job when they have some training. Finally, a bill that requires all kids to have their hepatitis shots before they enter a child care program passed this year." *Working Mother, July/August 1997*

Business Environment

STATE ECONOMY

State Economic Profile

"The Arkansas economy is neutral. The decline in the manufacturing industries is offsetting increases in construction employment. The unemployment rate has dipped below the national rate..., despite continued labor force growth. Arkansas is experiencing a sharp rise in personal bankruptcies, up by 43% over the last year, as the weakened economy is straining consumers.

Early March tornadoes ripped through Arkansas destroying buildings throughout the state. Although such a tragedy will slow trade in 1997, the influx of insurance money and the need to rebuild the destroyed homes and businesses will provide a small boon to the state....

Arkansas's slowdown has caused net migration to fall below 17,000 migrants per year, after averaging 21,000 over the previous three years. Longer term, net-migration into Arkansas will benefit from retirees who continue to leave the colder, more expensive states and settle in the more temperate climates of the South.

The Arkansas economy continues to tread water. A re-acceleration of the economy is near, however, as the state's low cost structure, especially in the form of low wages, and right to work environment will continue to attract firms. With numerous construction projects slated for the next couple of years, the economy is well-positioned for solid growth. Longer term, Arkansas is expected to benefit from the surge in retirees. The greatest risk for Arkansas is that manufacturers will shun this low-cost state for even less expensive foreign locations. Arkansas will be an above-average performer over the forecast horizon." *National Association of Realtors, Economic Profiles: The Fifty States, July 1997*

IMPORTS/EXPORTS

Total Export Sales

Area	1993 ($000)	1994 ($000)	1995 ($000)	1996 ($000)	% Chg. 1993-96	% Chg. 1995-96
MSA[1]	200,140	218,994	193,609	210,392	5.1	8.7
U.S.	464,858,354	512,415,609	583,030,524	622,827,063	34.0	6.8

Note: (1) Metropolitan Statistical Area - see Appendix A for areas included
Source: U.S. Department of Commerce, International Trade Association, Metropolitan Area Exports: An Export Performance Report on Over 250 U.S. Cities, October 1997

Imports/Exports by Port

Type	Cargo Value 1995 (US$mil.)	Cargo Value 1996 (US$mil.)	% Change 1995-1996	Share of U.S. Total 1995 (%)	Share of U.S. Total 1996 (%)
Imports	0	0	0	0	0
Exports	0	0	0	0	0

Source: Global Trade Information Services, WaterBorne Trade Atlas 1997

CITY FINANCES

City Government Finances

Component	FY92 ($000)	FY92 (per capita $)
Revenue	159,689	902.64
Expenditure	159,085	899.23
Debt Outstanding	295,176	1,668.48
Cash & Securities	337,306	1,906.62

Source: U.S. Bureau of the Census, City Government Finances: 1991-92

City Government Revenue by Source

Source	FY92 ($000)	FY92 (per capita $)	FY92 (%)
From Federal Government	5,315	30.04	3.3
From State Governments	11,338	64.09	7.1
From Local Governments	19,425	109.80	12.2
Property Taxes	12,960	73.26	8.1
General Sales Taxes	0	0.00	0.0
Selective Sales Taxes	15,971	90.28	10.0
Income Taxes	0	0.00	0.0
Current Charges	43,749	247.29	27.4
Utility/Liquor Store	16,377	92.57	10.3
Employee Retirement[1]	5,872	33.19	3.7
Other	28,682	162.12	18.0

Note: (1) Excludes "city contributions," classified as "nonrevenue," intragovernmental transfers.
Source: U.S. Bureau of the Census, City Government Finances: 1991-92

City Government Expenditures by Function

Function	FY92 ($000)	FY92 (per capita $)	FY92 (%)
Educational Services	3,820	21.59	2.4
Employee Retirement[1]	3,503	19.80	2.2
Environment/Housing	27,615	156.09	17.4
Government Administration	8,908	50.35	5.6
Interest on General Debt	19,551	110.51	12.3
Public Safety	34,094	192.72	21.4
Social Services	4,462	25.22	2.8
Transportation	32,689	184.77	20.5
Utility/Liquor Store	12,862	72.70	8.1
Other	11,581	65.46	7.3

Note: (1) Payments to beneficiaries including withdrawal of contributions.
Source: U.S. Bureau of the Census, City Government Finances: 1991-92

Municipal Bond Ratings

Area	Moody's	S & P
Little Rock	Aa	n/a

Note: n/a not available; n/r not rated
Source: Moody's Bond Record, 2/98; Statistical Abstract of the U.S., 1997;
Governing Magazine, 9/97, 3/98

POPULATION

Population Growth

Area	1980	1990	% Chg. 1980-90	July 1996 Estimate	% Chg. 1990-96
City	158,461	175,781	10.9	175,752	-0.0
MSA[1]	474,464	513,117	8.1	548,352	6.9
U.S.	226,545,805	248,765,170	9.8	265,179,411	6.6

Note: (1) Metropolitan Statistical Area - see Appendix A for areas included
Source: 1980/1990 Census of Housing and Population, Summary Tape File 3C;
Census Bureau Population Estimates

Population Characteristics

Race	City 1980 Population	%	City 1990 Population	%	% Chg. 1980-90	MSA[1] 1990 Population	%
White	105,504	66.6	113,723	64.7	7.8	404,696	78.9
Black	51,093	32.2	59,864	34.1	17.2	101,877	19.9
Amer Indian/Esk/Aleut	379	0.2	460	0.3	21.4	2,048	0.4
Asian/Pacific Islander	1,099	0.7	1,475	0.8	34.2	3,176	0.6
Other	386	0.2	259	0.1	-32.9	1,320	0.3
Hispanic Origin[2]	1,331	0.8	1,427	0.8	7.2	4,741	0.9

Note: (1) Metropolitan Statistical Area - see Appendix A for areas included;
(2) people of Hispanic origin can be of any race
Source: 1980/1990 Census of Housing and Population, Summary Tape File 3C

Ancestry

Area	German	Irish	English	Italian	U.S.	French	Polish	Dutch
City	15.6	14.5	14.2	1.4	6.3	3.5	1.1	1.9
MSA[1]	18.0	18.3	13.6	1.5	10.2	3.5	1.1	2.6
U.S.	23.3	15.6	13.1	5.9	5.3	4.2	3.8	2.5

Note: Figures are percentages and include persons that reported multiple ancestry (eg. if a person reported being Irish and Italian, they were included in both columns); (1) Metropolitan Statistical Area - see Appendix A for areas included
Source: 1990 Census of Population and Housing, Summary Tape File 3C

Age

Area	Median Age (Years)	Age Distribution (%) Under 5	Under 18	18-24	25-44	45-64	65+	80+
City	32.7	7.3	24.9	10.3	34.9	17.4	12.5	3.1
MSA[1]	32.2	7.3	26.5	10.5	33.4	18.2	11.3	2.6
U.S.	32.9	7.3	25.6	10.5	32.6	18.7	12.5	2.8

Note: (1) Metropolitan Statistical Area - see Appendix A for areas included
Source: 1990 Census of Population and Housing, Summary Tape File 3C

Male/Female Ratio

Area	Number of males per 100 females (all ages)	Number of males per 100 females (18 years old+)
City	85.3	81.6
MSA[1]	92.0	88.2
U.S.	95.0	91.9

Note: (1) Metropolitan Statistical Area - see Appendix A for areas included
Source: 1990 Census of Population, General Population Characteristics

INCOME

Per Capita/Median/Average Income

Area	Per Capita ($)	Median Household ($)	Average Household ($)
City	15,307	26,889	36,897
MSA[1]	12,809	26,501	33,336
U.S.	14,420	30,056	38,453

Note: all figures are for 1989; (1) Metropolitan Statistical Area - see Appendix A for areas included
Source: 1990 Census of Population and Housing, Summary Tape File 3C

Household Income Distribution by Race

Income ($)	City (%)					U.S. (%)				
	Total	White	Black	Other	Hisp.[1]	Total	White	Black	Other	Hisp.[1]
Less than 5,000	7.1	4.4	13.9	9.5	5.7	6.2	4.8	15.2	8.6	8.8
5,000 - 9,999	9.7	7.7	14.9	6.8	12.2	9.3	8.6	14.2	9.9	11.1
10,000 - 14,999	10.1	8.3	14.6	12.8	11.5	8.8	8.5	11.0	9.8	11.0
15,000 - 24,999	19.3	18.8	21.0	8.0	12.0	17.5	17.3	18.9	18.5	20.5
25,000 - 34,999	16.0	16.7	14.2	18.2	22.0	15.8	16.1	14.2	15.4	16.4
35,000 - 49,999	15.6	16.9	12.1	18.7	15.9	17.9	18.6	13.3	16.1	16.0
50,000 - 74,999	13.7	16.1	7.5	15.8	19.3	15.0	15.8	9.3	13.4	11.1
75,000 - 99,999	4.1	5.1	1.3	5.2	1.3	5.1	5.5	2.6	4.7	3.1
100,000+	4.4	6.0	0.4	5.0	0.0	4.4	4.8	1.3	3.7	1.9

Note: all figures are for 1989; (1) people of Hispanic origin can be of any race
Source: 1990 Census of Population and Housing, Summary Tape File 3C

Effective Buying Income

Area	Per Capita ($)	Median Household ($)	Average Household ($)
City	19,056	34,656	46,227
MSA[1]	16,504	34,959	43,421
U.S.	15,444	33,201	41,849

Note: data as of 1/1/97; (1) Metropolitan Statistical Area - see Appendix A for areas included
Source: Standard Rate & Data Service, Newspaper Advertising Source, 2/98

Effective Household Buying Income Distribution

Area	% of Households Earning						
	$10,000 -$19,999	$20,000 -$34,999	$35,000 -$49,999	$50,000 -$74,999	$75,000 -$99,000	$100,000 -$124,999	$125,000 and up
City	15.8	23.1	16.7	18.3	7.8	2.8	3.8
MSA[1]	15.2	23.6	18.4	19.4	7.3	2.3	2.5
U.S.	16.5	23.4	18.3	18.2	6.4	2.1	2.4

Note: data as of 1/1/97; (1) Metropolitan Statistical Area - see Appendix A for areas included
Source: Standard Rate & Data Service, Newspaper Advertising Source, 2/98

Poverty Rates by Race and Age

Area	Total (%)	By Race (%)				By Age (%)		
		White	Black	Other	Hisp.[2]	Under 5 years old	Under 18 years old	65 years and over
City	14.6	7.2	28.9	12.4	19.8	23.6	21.7	13.5
MSA[1]	13.5	9.2	30.8	12.2	17.4	19.8	18.2	16.8
U.S.	13.1	9.8	29.5	23.1	25.3	20.1	18.3	12.8

Note: figures show the percent of people living below the poverty line in 1989. The average poverty threshold was $12,674 for a family of four in 1989; (1) Metropolitan Statistical Area - see Appendix A for areas included; (2) people of Hispanic origin can be of any race
Source: 1990 Census of Population and Housing, Summary Tape File 3C

EMPLOYMENT

Labor Force and Employment

Area	Civilian Labor Force			Workers Employed		
	Dec. '95	Dec. '96	% Chg.	Dec. '95	Dec. '96	% Chg.
City	102,342	102,286	-0.1	98,638	98,814	0.2
MSA[1]	297,598	297,812	0.1	286,356	286,868	0.2
U.S.	134,583,000	136,742,000	1.6	127,903,000	130,785,000	2.3

Note: Data is not seasonally adjusted and covers workers 16 years of age and older;
(1) Metropolitan Statistical Area - see Appendix A for areas included
Source: Bureau of Labor Statistics, http://stats.bls.gov

Unemployment Rate

Area	1997											
	Jan.	Feb.	Mar.	Apr.	May	Jun.	Jul.	Aug.	Sep.	Oct.	Nov.	Dec.
City	3.7	3.9	3.7	3.3	3.4	4.2	4.4	4.3	3.8	3.4	3.0	3.4
MSA[1]	4.1	4.3	4.0	3.4	3.4	4.1	4.4	4.2	3.8	3.5	3.3	3.7
U.S.	5.9	5.7	5.5	4.8	4.7	5.2	5.0	4.8	4.7	4.4	4.3	4.4

Note: Data is not seasonally adjusted and covers workers 16 years of age and older; All figures are percentages; (1) Metropolitan Statistical Area - see Appendix A for areas included
Source: Bureau of Labor Statistics, http://stats.bls.gov

Employment by Industry

Sector	MSA[1]		U.S.
	Number of Employees	Percent of Total	Percent of Total
Services	89,500	29.1	29.0
Retail Trade	54,400	17.7	18.5
Government	59,700	19.4	16.1
Manufacturing	33,400	10.9	15.0
Finance/Insurance/Real Estate	17,500	5.7	5.7
Wholesale Trade	17,400	5.7	5.4
Transportation/Public Utilities	21,400	7.0	5.3
Construction/Mining	14,100	4.6	5.0

Note: Figures cover non-farm employment as of 12/97 and are not seasonally adjusted; (1) Metropolitan Statistical Area - see Appendix A for areas included
Source: Bureau of Labor Statistics, http://stats.bls.gov

Employment by Occupation

Occupation Category	City (%)	MSA[1] (%)	U.S. (%)
White Collar	69.6	60.7	58.1
Executive/Admin./Management	14.8	12.3	12.3
Professional	18.9	14.1	14.1
Technical & Related Support	4.0	3.6	3.7
Sales	14.2	13.6	11.8
Administrative Support/Clerical	17.7	17.1	16.3
Blue Collar	17.0	25.3	26.2
Precision Production/Craft/Repair	6.5	10.6	11.3
Machine Operators/Assem./Insp.	4.2	6.2	6.8
Transportation/Material Movers	3.1	4.6	4.1
Cleaners/Helpers/Laborers	3.1	3.9	3.9
Services	12.6	12.4	13.2
Farming/Forestry/Fishing	0.8	1.5	2.5

Note: figures cover employed persons 16 years old and over; (1) Metropolitan Statistical Area - see Appendix A for areas included
Source: 1990 Census of Population and Housing, Summary Tape File 3C

Occupational Employment Projections: 1994 - 2005

Occupations Expected to have the Largest Job Growth (ranked by numerical growth)	Fast-Growing Occupations (ranked by percent growth)
1. Truck drivers, heavy & light	1. Residential counselors
2. Cashiers	2. Personal and home care aides
3. Nursing aides/orderlies/attendants	3. Occupational therapy assistants
4. Salespersons, retail	4. Systems analysts
5. Registered nurses	5. Electronic pagination systems workers
6. General managers & top executives	6. Occupational therapists
7. Marketing & sales, supervisors	7. Medical records technicians
8. Licensed practical nurses	8. Computer engineers
9. Janitors/cleaners/maids, ex. priv. hshld.	9. Psychiatric aides
10. Waiters & waitresses	10. Physical therapists

Projections cover Arkansas.
Source: U.S. Department of Labor, Employment and Training Administration, America's Labor Market Information System (ALMIS)

Average Wages

Occupation	Wage	Occupation	Wage
Professional/Technical/Clerical	$/Week	**Health/Protective Services**	$/Week
Accountants III	649	Corrections Officers	375
Attorneys III	1,022	Firefighters	446
Budget Analysts III	792	Nurses, Licensed Practical II	372
Buyers/Contracting Specialists II	522	Nurses, Registered II	629
Clerks, Accounting III	382	Nursing Assistants II	218
Clerks, General III	484	Police Officers I	405
Computer Operators II	331	**Hourly Workers**	$/Hour
Computer Programmers II	473	Forklift Operators	9.09
Drafters II	514	General Maintenance Workers	7.40
Engineering Technicians III	-	Guards I	6.86
Engineering Technicians, Civil III	506	Janitors	5.09
Engineers III	-	Maintenance Electricians	15.77
Key Entry Operators I	279	Maintenance Electronics Techs II	10.88
Personnel Assistants III	367	Maintenance Machinists	-
Personnel Specialists III	690	Maintenance Mechanics, Machinery	11.75
Secretaries III	429	Material Handling Laborers	7.12
Switchboard Operator-Receptionist	257	Motor Vehicle Mechanics	16.35
Systems Analysts II	741	Shipping/Receiving Clerks	7.54
Systems Analysts Supervisor/Mgr II	-	Tool and Die Makers	-
Tax Collectors II	423	Truckdrivers, Tractor Trailer	15.33
Word Processors II	-	Warehouse Specialists	11.42

Note: Wage data includes full-time workers only for 12/94 and cover the Metropolitan Statistical Area (see Appendix A for areas included). Dashes indicate that data was not available.
Source: Bureau of Labor Statistics, Occupational Compensation Survey

TAXES

Major State and Local Tax Rates

State Corp. Income (%)	State Personal Income (%)	Residential Property (effective rate per $100)	Sales & Use		State Gasoline (cents/ gallon)	State Cigarette (cents/ 20-pack)
			State (%)	Local (%)		
1.0 - 6.5	1.0 - 7.0[a]	1.25	4.625	1.5	18.7[b]	31.5

Note: Personal/corporate income tax rates as of 1/97. Sales, gasoline and cigarette tax rates as of 1/98; (a) A special tax table is available for low income taxpayers reducing their tax payments; (b) Rate is comprised of 18.5 cents excise plus 0.2 cent motor carrier tax
Source: Federation of Tax Administrators, www.taxadmin.org; Washington D.C. Department of Finance and Revenue, Tax Rates and Tax Burdens in the District of Columbia: A Nationwide Comparison, June 1997; Chamber of Commerce

Total Taxes Per Capita and as a Percent of Income

Area	Per Capita Income ($)	Per Capita Taxes ($)			Taxes as Pct. of Income (%)		
		Total	Federal	State/Local	Total	Federal	State/Local
Arkansas	20,766	6,780	4,523	2,257	32.6	21.8	10.9
U.S.	26,187	9,205	6,127	3,078	35.2	23.4	11.8

Note: Figures are for 1997
Source: Tax Foundation, Web Site, www.taxfoundation.org

Estimated Tax Burden

Area	State Income	Local Income	Property	Sales	Total
Little Rock	3,072	0	2,475	839	6,386

Note: The numbers are estimates of taxes paid by a married couple with two kids and annual earnings of $65,000. Sales tax estimates assume they spend average amounts on food, clothing, household goods and gasoline. Property tax estimates assume they live in a $225,000 home.
Source: Kiplinger's Personal Finance Magazine, June 1997

COMMERCIAL REAL ESTATE

Office Market

Class/Location	Total Space (sq. ft.)	Vacant Space (sq. ft.)	Vac. Rate (%)	Under Constr. (sq. ft.)	Net Absorp. (sq. ft.)	Rental Rates ($/sq.ft./yr.)
Class A						
CBD	2,297,771	360,073	15.7	n/a	-79,073	9.90-15.00
Outside CBD	2,569,142	106,079	4.1	40,000	149,163	14.30-16.75
Class B						
CBD	2,425,510	260,061	10.7	n/a	25,939	7.00-11.00
Outside CBD	2,974,471	316,971	10.7	35,000	29,679	7.50-12.50

Note: Data as of 10/97 and covers Little Rock; CBD = Central Business District; n/a not available;
Source: Society of Industrial and Office Realtors, 1998 Comparative Statistics of Industrial and Office Real Estate Markets

"Two Class 'A' office developments are planned for 1998 in the west suburban market. Additionally, 35,000 sq. ft. of Class 'B' space is under construction in the suburbs. Little Rock's CBD office market should register inventory increases with several rehab projects, and the anticipated announcement of the Presidential library. Net absorption is expected to remain on par with last year, still ahead of supply additions, pushing the vacancy rate down. Rental rates and sales prices are projected to remain the same in the coming year. Long-term, Little Rock's central location and favorable cost structure should promote a solid office-using business services sector." *Society of Industrial and Office Realtors, 1998 Comparative Statistics of Industrial and Office Real Estate Markets*

Industrial Market

Location	Total Space (sq. ft.)	Vacant Space (sq. ft.)	Vac. Rate (%)	Under Constr. (sq. ft.)	Net Absorp. (sq. ft.)	Gross Lease ($/sq.ft./yr.)
Central City	8,835,000	582,291	6.6	0	-238,715	1.25-3.50
Suburban	21,947,700	945,397	4.3	0	-58,653	2.00-5.00

Note: Data as of 10/97 and covers Greater Little Rock; n/a not available
Source: Society of Industrial and Office Realtors, 1998 Comparative Statistics of Industrial and Office Real Estate Markets

"Lease prices are expected to remain steady in 1998 for warehouse/distribution, and manufacturing. A significant shortage of high-tech/R&D space will curtail absorption in this sector and trigger a modest uptick in lease prices. Overall, demand levels should be back on track. SIOR's reporter expects much of the space left behind by GE, Kroger, and Handleman to be leased during the upcoming year. Vacancy levels should drop. No new construction is anticipated in the Little Rock industrial market during 1998. Sales prices are expected to remain steady for all property segments. Long term, Little Rock's economy will be supported by a diversified industrial base with below average employment volatility." *Society of Industrial and Office Realtors, 1998 Comparative Statistics of Industrial and Office Real Estate Markets*

COMMERCIAL UTILITIES

Typical Monthly Electric Bills

Area	Commercial Service ($/month)		Industrial Service ($/month)	
	12 kW demand 1,500 kWh	100 kW demand 30,000 kWh	1,000 kW demand 400,000 kWh	20,000 kW demand 10,000,000 kWh
City	159	2,655	29,478	620,440
U.S.	162	2,360	25,590	545,677

Note: Based on rates in effect July 1, 1997
Source: Edison Electric Institute, Typical Residential, Commercial and Industrial Bills, Summer 1997

TRANSPORTATION

Transportation Statistics

Avg. travel time to work (min.)	17.1
Interstate highways	I-30; I-40
Bus lines	
In-city	Central Arkansas Transit, 49 vehicles
Inter-city	2
Passenger air service	
Airport	Little Rock National Airport
Airlines	7
Aircraft departures	22,166 (1995)
Enplaned passengers	342,913 (1995)
Rail service	Amtrak
Motor freight carriers	70
Major waterways/ports	Arkansas River

Source: OAG, Business Travel Planner, Summer 1997; Editor & Publisher Market Guide, 1998; FAA Airport Activity Statistics, 1996; Amtrak National Time Table, Northeast Timetable, Fall/Winter 1997-98; 1990 Census of Population and Housing, STF 3C; Chamber of Commerce/Economic Development 1997; Jane's Urban Transport Systems 1997-98; Transit Fact Book 1997

Means of Transportation to Work

Area	Car/Truck/Van		Public Transportation			Bicycle	Walked	Other Means	Worked at Home
	Drove Alone	Car-pooled	Bus	Subway	Railroad				
City	80.5	13.5	1.4	0.0	0.0	0.1	1.9	1.0	1.7
MSA[1]	79.8	14.4	0.8	0.0	0.0	0.1	1.9	1.0	2.0
U.S.	73.2	13.4	3.0	1.5	0.5	0.4	3.9	1.2	3.0

Note: figures shown are percentages and only include workers 16 years old and over;
(1) Metropolitan Statistical Area - see Appendix A for areas included
Source: 1990 Census of Population and Housing, Summary Tape File 3C

BUSINESSES

Major Business Headquarters

Company Name	1997 Rankings	
	Fortune 500	Forbes 500
Alltel	423	-
Dillard Dept. Stores	225	-

Note: Companies listed are located in the city; Dashes indicate no ranking
Fortune 500: companies that produce a 10-K are ranked 1 - 500 based on 1996 revenue
Forbes 500: private companies are ranked 1 - 500 based on 1996 revenue
Source: Forbes 12/1/97; Fortune 4/28/97

HOTELS & MOTELS

Hotels/Motels

Area	Hotels/ Motels	Rooms	Luxury-Level Hotels/Motels		Average Minimum Rates ($)		
			♦♦♦♦	♦♦♦♦♦	♦♦	♦♦♦	♦♦♦♦
City	23	3,410	0	0	55	85	n/a
Airport	4	624	0	0	n/a	n/a	n/a
Suburbs	16	1,704	0	0	n/a	n/a	n/a
Total	43	5,738	0	0	n/a	n/a	n/a

Note: n/a not available; Classifications range from one diamond (budget properties with basic amenities) to five diamond (luxury properties with the finest service, rooms and facilities).
Source: OAG, Business Travel Planner, Summer 1997

CONVENTION CENTERS

Major Convention Centers

Center Name	Meeting Rooms	Exhibit Space (sf)
Arkansas State Fair Grounds	5	86,000
Camelot Hotel	9	8,720
Statehouse Convention Center	8	62,125
University Conference Center	9	11,000

Source: Trade Shows Worldwide 1997

Living Environment

COST OF LIVING

Cost of Living Index

Composite Index	Housing	Utilities	Groceries	Health Care	Trans- portation	Misc. Goods/ Services
86.7	79.0	107.6	95.5	70.8	92.8	85.2

Note: U.S. = 100; Figures are for Little Rock-North Little Rock
Source: ACCRA, Cost of Living Index, 1st Quarter 1997

HOUSING

Median Home Prices and Housing Affordability

Area	Median Price[2] 3rd Qtr. 1997 ($)	HOI[3] 3rd Qtr. 1997	Afford- ability Rank[4]
MSA[1]	100,000	67.9	106
U.S.	127,000	63.7	–

Note: (1) Metropolitan Statistical Area - see Appendix A for areas included; (2) U.S. figures calculated from the sales of 625,000 new and existing homes in 195 markets; (3) Housing Opportunity Index - percent of homes sold that were within the reach of the median income household at the prevailing mortgage interest rate; (4) Rank is from 1-195 with 1 being most affordable
Source: National Association of Home Builders, Housing Opportunity Index, 3rd Quarter 1997

It is projected that the median price of existing single-family homes in the metro area will increase by 9.6% in 1998. Nationwide, home prices are projected to increase 6.6%.
Kiplinger's Personal Finance Magazine, January 1998

Average New Home Price

Area	Price ($)
City[1]	109,000
U.S.	133,782

Note: Figures are based on a new home with 1,800 sq. ft. of living area on an 8,000 sq. ft. lot;
(1) Little Rock-North Little Rock
Source: ACCRA, Cost of Living Index, 1st Quarter 1997

Average Apartment Rent

Area	Rent ($/mth)
City[1]	436
U.S.	563

Note: Figures are based on an unfurnished two bedroom, 1-1/2 or 2 bath apartment, approximately 950 sq. ft. in size, excluding all utilities except water; (1) Little Rock-North Little Rock
Source: ACCRA, Cost of Living Index, 1st Quarter 1997

RESIDENTIAL UTILITIES

Average Residential Utility Costs

Area	All Electric ($/mth)	Part Electric ($/mth)	Other Energy ($/mth)	Phone ($/mth)
City[1]	–	71.03	39.19	23.63
U.S.	110.19	56.83	45.14	19.36

Note: (1) Little Rock-North Little Rock
Source: ACCRA, Cost of Living Index, 1st Quarter 1997

HEALTH CARE

Average Health Care Costs

Area	Hospital ($/day)	Doctor ($/visit)	Dentist ($/visit)
City[1]	221.80	35.20	39.40
U.S.	385.60	47.34	59.26

Note: Hospital - based on a semi-private room. Doctor - based on a general practitioner's routine exam of an established patient. Dentist - based on adult teeth cleaning and periodic oral exam; (1) (1) Little Rock-North Little Rock
Source: ACCRA, Cost of Living Index, 1st Quarter 1997

Distribution of Office-Based Physicians

Area	Family/Gen. Practitioners	Specialists		
		Medical	Surgical	Other
MSA[1]	190	404	356	411

Note: Data as of 12/31/96; (1) Metropolitan Statistical Area - see Appendix A for areas included
Source: American Medical Assn., Physician Characteristics & Distribution in the U.S., 1997-1998

Hospitals

Little Rock has 6 general medical and surgical hospitals, 2 psychiatric, 1 rehabilitation, 1 children's general. *AHA Guide to the Healthcare Field 1997-98*

EDUCATION

Public School District Statistics

District Name	Num. Sch.	Enroll.	Classroom Teachers[1]	Pupils per Teacher	Minority Pupils (%)	Current Exp.[2] ($/pupil)
Ark. School For The Blind	2	108	33	3.3	n/a	n/a
Ark. School For The Deaf	2	206	44	4.7	n/a	n/a
Ark. Youth Servs. School Syst.	1	93	17	5.5	n/a	n/a
Little Rock School District	48	24,901	1,613	15.4	68.7	5,477
Pulaski Co. Spec. School Dist.	37	20,534	1,192	17.2	33.4	4,786

Note: Data covers the 1995-1996 school year unless otherwise noted; (1) Excludes teachers reported as working in school district offices rather than in schools; (2) Based on 1993-94 enrollment collected by the Census Bureau, not the enrollment figure shown in column 3; SD = School District; ISD = Independent School District; n/a not available
Source: National Center for Education Statistics, Common Core of Data Survey; Bureau of the Census

Educational Quality

School District	Education Quotient[1]	Graduate Outcome[2]	Community Index[3]	Resource Index[4]
Little Rock	110.0	75.0	112.0	142.0

Note: Nearly 1,000 secondary school districts were rated in terms of educational quality. The scores range from a low of 50 to a high of 150; (1) Average of the Graduate Outcome, Community and Resource indexes; (2) Based on graduation rates and college board scores (SAT/ACT); (3) Based on the surrounding community's average level of education and the area's average income level; (4) Based on teacher salaries, per-pupil expenditures and student-teacher ratios.
Source: Expansion Management, Ratings Issue 1997

Educational Attainment by Race

Area	High School Graduate (%)					Bachelor's Degree (%)				
	Total	White	Black	Other	Hisp.[2]	Total	White	Black	Other	Hisp.[2]
City	82.0	87.0	68.9	80.5	78.6	30.3	35.4	16.5	45.5	34.7
MSA[1]	76.6	79.0	64.8	74.8	76.0	20.4	21.8	13.1	24.7	19.3
U.S.	75.2	77.9	63.1	60.4	49.8	20.3	21.5	11.4	19.4	9.2

Note: figures shown cover persons 25 years old and over; (1) Metropolitan Statistical Area - see Appendix A for areas included; (2) people of Hispanic origin can be of any race
Source: 1990 Census of Population and Housing, Summary Tape File 3C

School Enrollment by Type

Area	Preprimary				Elementary/High School			
	Public		Private		Public		Private	
	Enrollment	%	Enrollment	%	Enrollment	%	Enrollment	%
City	1,427	40.4	2,108	59.6	22,873	79.7	5,818	20.3
MSA[1]	4,862	53.5	4,231	46.5	80,860	88.7	10,321	11.3
U.S.	2,679,029	59.5	1,824,256	40.5	38,379,689	90.2	4,187,099	9.8

Note: figures shown cover persons 3 years old and over;
(1) Metropolitan Statistical Area - see Appendix A for areas included
Source: 1990 Census of Population and Housing, Summary Tape File 3C

School Enrollment by Race

Area	Preprimary (%)				Elementary/High School (%)			
	White	Black	Other	Hisp.[1]	White	Black	Other	Hisp.[1]
City	65.5	34.1	0.4	1.0	45.6	53.0	1.4	0.6
MSA[2]	77.6	21.9	0.5	1.1	69.4	29.0	1.6	1.3
U.S.	80.4	12.5	7.1	7.8	74.1	15.6	10.3	12.5

Note: figures shown cover persons 3 years old and over; (1) people of Hispanic origin can be of any
race; (2) Metropolitan Statistical Area - see Appendix A for areas included
Source: 1990 Census of Population and Housing, Summary Tape File 3C

SAT/ACT Scores

Area/District	1997 SAT				1997 ACT	
	Percent of Graduates Tested (%)	Average Math Score	Average Verbal Score	Average Combined Score	Percent of Graduates Tested (%)	Average Composite Score
Little Rock SD	n/a	n/a	n/a	n/a	68	19.9
State	6	558	567	1,125	66	20.3
U.S.	42	511	505	1,016	36	21.0

Note: Math and verbal SAT scores are out of a possible 800; ACT scores are out of a possible 36
Caution: Comparing or ranking states/cities on the basis of SAT/ACT scores alone is invalid and
strongly discouraged by the The College Board and The American College Testing Program as
students who take the tests are self-selected and do not represent the entire student population.
Source: Little Rock School District, Office of Communication, 1997; American College Testing
Program, 1997; College Board, 1997

Classroom Teacher Salaries in Public Schools

District	B.A. Degree		M.A. Degree		Ph.D. Degree	
	Min. ($)	Max. ($)	Min. ($)	Max. ($)	Min. ($)	Max. ($)
Little Rock	20,760	33,216	24,019	38,136	26,782	42,560
Average[1]	26,120	39,270	28,175	44,667	31,643	49,825

Note: Salaries are for 1996-1997; (1) Based on all school districts covered; n/a not available
Source: American Federation of Teachers (unpublished data)

Higher Education

Two-Year Colleges		Four-Year Colleges		Medical Schools	Law Schools	Voc/ Tech
Public	Private	Public	Private			
0	1	2	1	1	1	20

Source: College Blue Book, Occupational Education 1997; Medical School Admission Requirements,
1998-99; Peterson's Guide to Two-Year Colleges, 1997; Peterson's Guide to Four-Year Colleges,
1997; Barron's Guide to Law Schools 1997

MAJOR EMPLOYERS

Major Employers

Alltel Information Services (computer processing)	Baptist Health
Arkansas Children's Hospital	Arkansas Blue Cross & Blue Shield
HCA Health Services	Little Rock Newspapers
CareNetwork (help supply services)	Stephens Inc. (security brokers)
Affiliated Foods Southwest	Alltel Corp. (telephone communications)
Dillard Department Stores	Entergy Arkansas (electric services)
Cal-Ark (trucking)	Quality Foods

Note: companies listed are located in the city
Source: Dun's Business Rankings 1997; Ward's Business Directory, 1997

PUBLIC SAFETY

Crime Rate

Area	All Crimes	Violent Crimes				Property Crimes		
		Murder	Forcible Rape	Robbery	Aggrav. Assault	Burglary	Larceny -Theft	Motor Vehicle Theft
City	11,496.8	15.9	90.8	457.9	943.7	1,850.1	7,250.0	888.4
Suburbs[1]	5,150.1	7.9	59.6	122.6	288.2	955.3	3,370.8	345.6
MSA[2]	7,257.4	10.5	69.9	234.0	505.9	1,252.4	4,658.9	525.8
U.S.	5,078.9	7.4	36.1	202.4	388.2	943.0	2,975.9	525.9

Note: Crime rate is the number of crimes per 100,000 pop.; (1) defined as all areas within the MSA but located outside the central city; (2) Metropolitan Statistical Area - see Appendix A for areas incl.
Source: FBI Uniform Crime Reports 1996

RECREATION

Culture and Recreation

Museums	Symphony Orchestras	Opera Companies	Dance Companies	Professional Theatres	Zoos	Pro Sports Teams
4	1	1	1	2	1	0

Source: International Directory of the Performing Arts, 1996; Official Museum Directory, 1998; Chamber of Commerce/Economic Development 1997

Library System

The Central Arkansas Library System has six branches, holdings of 494,573 volumes and a budget of $n/a (1995-1996). Note: n/a means not available. *American Library Directory, 1997-1998*

MEDIA

Newspapers

Name	Type	Freq.	Distribution	Circulation
Arkansas Catholic	Religious	48x/yr	State	7,000
Arkansas Democrat-Gazette	n/a	7x/wk	State	176,683
Arkansas State Press	Black	1x/wk	Local	5,000
Arkansas Times	General	1x/wk	Local	43,000
The Arkansas Tribune	Black	1x/wk	State	3,000
The Daily Record	n/a	5x/wk	Local	6,000
Good News Reporter	n/a	1x/mo	Local	20,000
Little Rock Free Press	General	26x/yr	Area	20,000
The Times	General	1x/wk	Local	8,663

Note: Includes newspapers with circulations of 1,000 or more located in the city; n/a not available
Source: Burrelle's Media Directory, 1998 Edition

AM Radio Stations

Call Letters	Freq. (kHz)	Target Audience	Station Format	Music Format
KMTL	760	General	M	Christian
KGHT	880	General	M	Christian
KARN	920	General	N/S/T	n/a
KJBN	1050	Religious	M/T	Christian
KAAY	1090	Religious	M	Christian
KLRG	1150	General	M/N/S	Christian
KEZQ	1250	General	M	Adult Standards
KYXZ	1350	General	S/T	n/a
KITA	1440	Black	M	Christian

Note: Stations included broadcast in the Little Rock metro area; n/a not available
Station Format: E = Educational; M = Music; N = News; S = Sports; T = Talk
Source: Burrelle's Media Directory, 1998 Edition

FM Radio Stations

Call Letters	Freq. (mHz)	Target Audience	Station Format	Music Format
KABF	88.3	Black/Hisp	M/N/S/T	Alternative/Christian/Classic Rock/Country/Jazz/Oldies/R&B/Spanish/Urban Contemporary
KUAR	89.1	General	E/M/N	Big Band/Classical/Jazz
KLRE	90.5	General	M	Classical
KIPR	92.3	Black	M/N/S	Urban Contemporary
KKPT	94.1	General	M	Classic Rock
KSSN	95.7	General	M/N	Country
KURB	98.5	General	M	Adult Contemporary/Contemporary Top 40
KDDK	100.3	General	M/N	Country
KESR	102.1	General	M	Contemporary Top 40
KVLO	102.9	General	M	Adult Contemporary
KSYG	103.7	n/a	M/T	Christian
KOLL	104.9	General	M/N	Oldies
KMJX	105.1	General	M/N/S	AOR/Classic Rock
KMZX	106.3	Black	M/N/S	Adult Contemporary
KYTN	107.7	Religious	M/N/S	Adult Contemporary/Christian

Note: Stations included broadcast in the Little Rock metro area; n/a not available
Station Format: E = Educational; M = Music; N = News; S = Sports; T = Talk
Music Format: AOR = Album Oriented Rock; MOR = Middle-of-the-Road
Source: Burrelle's Media Directory, 1998 Edition

Television Stations

Name	Ch.	Affiliation	Type	Owner
KETS	2	PBS	Public	State of Arkansas
KARK	4	NBC	Commercial	Morris Network Inc.
KATV	7	ABC	Commercial	Allbritton Communications Company
KTHV	11	CBS	Commercial	Gannett Company Inc.
KLRT	16	Fox	Commercial	Clear Channel Communications
KVTN	25	n/a	Commercial	Agape Church Inc.
KASN	38	UPN	Commercial	MMC Television Corporation

Note: Stations included broadcast in the Little Rock metro area
Source: Burrelle's Media Directory, 1998 Edition

CLIMATE

Average and Extreme Temperatures

Temperature	Jan	Feb	Mar	Apr	May	Jun	Jul	Aug	Sep	Oct	Nov	Dec	Ann
Extreme High (°F)	83	85	91	95	98	105	112	108	103	97	86	80	112
Average High (°F)	50	54	63	73	81	89	92	91	85	75	62	53	73
Average Temp. (°F)	40	45	53	63	71	79	82	81	74	63	52	43	62
Average Low (°F)	30	34	42	51	60	68	72	70	63	51	41	34	51
Extreme Low (°F)	-4	-5	17	28	40	46	54	52	38	29	17	-1	-5

Note: Figures cover the years 1948-1990
Source: National Climatic Data Center, International Station Meteorological Climate Summary, 3/95

Average Precipitation/Snowfall/Humidity

Precip./Humidity	Jan	Feb	Mar	Apr	May	Jun	Jul	Aug	Sep	Oct	Nov	Dec	Ann
Avg. Precip. (in.)	4.1	4.2	4.9	5.2	5.4	3.6	3.5	3.2	3.8	3.5	4.8	4.5	50.7
Avg. Snowfall (in.)	3	2	1	Tr	0	0	0	0	0	0	Tr	1	5
Avg. Rel. Hum. 6am (%)	80	80	78	81	86	86	87	88	87	86	82	80	84
Avg. Rel. Hum. 3pm (%)	57	54	50	50	53	52	54	52	52	48	52	57	53

Note: Figures cover the years 1948-1990; Tr = Trace amounts (<0.05 in. of rain; <0.5 in. of snow)
Source: National Climatic Data Center, International Station Meteorological Climate Summary, 3/95

Weather Conditions

Temperature			Daytime Sky			Precipitation		
10°F & below	32°F & below	90°F & above	Clear	Partly cloudy	Cloudy	0.01 inch or more precip.	0.1 inch or more snow/ice	Thunder-storms
1	57	73	110	142	113	104	4	57

Note: Figures are average number of days per year and covers the years 1948-1990
Source: National Climatic Data Center, International Station Meteorological Climate Summary, 3/95

AIR & WATER QUALITY

Maximum Pollutant Concentrations

	Particulate Matter (ug/m³)	Carbon Monoxide (ppm)	Sulfur Dioxide (ppm)	Nitrogen Dioxide (ppm)	Ozone (ppm)	Lead (ug/m³)
MSA[1] Level	52	4	0.009	0.011	0.10	n/a
NAAQS[2]	150	9	0.140	0.053	0.12	1.50
Met NAAQS?	Yes	Yes	Yes	Yes	Yes	n/a

Note: (1) Metropolitan Statistical Area - see Appendix A for areas included; (2) National Ambient Air Quality Standards; ppm = parts per million; ug/m³ = micrograms per cubic meter; n/a not available
Source: EPA, National Air Quality and Emissions Trends Report, 1996

Pollutant Standards Index

In the Little Rock MSA (see Appendix A for areas included), the Pollutant Standards Index (PSI) exceeded 100 on 0 days in 1996. A PSI value greater than 100 indicates that air quality would be in the unhealthful range on that day. *EPA, National Air Quality and Emissions Trends Report, 1996*

Drinking Water

Water System Name	Pop. Served	Primary Water Source Type	Number of Violations in Fiscal Year 1997	Type of Violation/ Contaminants
Little Rock Muni Water Works	204,543	Surface	None	None

Note: Data as of January 16, 1998
Source: EPA, Office of Ground Water and Drinking Water, Safe Drinking Water Information System

Little Rock tap water is neutral, soft and fluoridated.
Editor & Publisher Market Guide, 1998

Madison, Wisconsin

Background

Madison was selected as the territorial capital in 1836 when it was only in the planning stages. Construction began in 1838 and despite repeated threats to move the capital elsewhere by the members of the legislature it has maintained its status. It was named for President James Madison in 1836 and later incorporated into a village in 1856. When Wisconsin attained statehood in 1848, the University of Wisconsin (one of the largest in the country) was established.

Most of the city, including its business center, is situated on an isthmus between Lake Mendota and Lake Minona in the southcentral part of the state. Two other lakes, Kengonsa and Waubesa lie to the south.

By ordinance, the city's skyline is dominated by the capitol dome, which weighs 2,500 tons.

Madison serves as the trade center of a rich agricultural and dairy region. Food processing is a major industry. Batteries, dairy equipment, medical supplies and machine tools are produced there as well.

Madison has the typical continental climate of interior North America with a large annual temperature range and frequent short period temperature changes. The range of extreme temperatures is from about 110 to -40 degrees. The city lies in the path of the frequent cyclones and anticyclones which move eastward over this area during fall, winter and spring. The most frequent air masses are of polar origin. Occasional influxes of arctic air affect this area during the winter months. Summers are pleasant, with only occasional periods of extreme heat or high humidity.

General Rankings and Evaluative Comments

- Madison was ranked #7 out of 300 cities by *Money's* 1997 "Survey of the Best Places to Live." Criteria used: health services, crime, economy, housing, education, transportation, weather, leisure and the arts. The city was ranked #1 in 1996 and #16 in 1995. *Money, July 1997; Money, September 1996; Money, September 1995*

  "Welcome to a place where the average winter temperature is a teeth-chattering 20 degrees Fahrenheit, yet bicycles outnumber cars by a ratio of 3 to 2. Where the public exchange of ideas is so cherished that the city built a pulpit at the end of a busy downtown street for speeches and rallies. Where it's so safe that the governor's residence in this sophisticated state capital is not up on a hill behind a forbidding fence but is just another house on a lovely block.

  ...High-tech companies keep the economy bubbling....The number of such firms has jumped 28% to 345 since 1991....

  The area's topnotch health care is nothing to sneeze at either. The University of Wisconsin Hospital and Clinics is renowned for doctors in its cancer, cardiology and gynecology departments. Most people speak highly about their managed-care plans too.

  Madison's best trait, though, may be its healthy mix of people and diversions. Walk along State Street's pedestrian mall and you'll see retirees, college kids and boomers in business suits winding their way among the street vendors, coffee shops and New Age stores. You can also find 24 kinds of ethnic restaurants scattered throughout this surprisingly diverse city.

  ....Housing costs are relatively high, particularly property taxes....But many Madisonians concede that's a price worth paying for the great schools and parks." *Money, July 1997*

- *Ladies Home Journal* ranked America's 200 largest cities based on the qualities women care about most. Madison ranked 1 out of 200. Criteria: low crime rate, good public schools, well-paying jobs, quality health and child care, the presence of women in government, proportion of women-owned businesses, size of the wage gap with men, local economy, divorce rates, the ratio of single men to single women, whether there are laws that require at least the same number of public toilets for women as men, and the probability of good hair days. *Ladies Home Journal, November 1997*

- Madison is among the 10 healthiest cities for women. Rank: 1 out of 10. Criteria: 1) number of doctors, psychologists and dietitians; 2) quality of hospital gynecology departments; 3) number of working mothers; 4) rate of violent crimes; 5) cleanliness of air and water; 6) number of fitness opportunities; 7) quality of public schools. *American Health, January/February 1997*

- Madison was ranked #6 out of 219 cities in terms of children's health, safety, and economic well-being. Criteria: total population, percent population change, birth rate, child immunization rate, infant mortality rate, percent low birth weight infants, percent of births to teens, physician-to-population ratio, student-to-teacher ratio, dropout rate, unemployment rate, median family income, percent of children in poverty, violent and property crime rates, number of juvenile arrests for violent crimes as a percent of the total crime index, number of days with pollution standard index (PSI) over 100, pounds toxic releases per 1,000 people and number of superfund sites. *Zero Population Growth, Children's Environmental Index 1997*

- Madison appeared on *New Mobility's* list of "10 Disability Friendly Cities". Rank: 9 out of 10. Criteria: affordable and accessible housing, transportation, quality medical care, personal assistance services and strong advocacy.

  "Answer: Weather, weather and weather. Question: What are three reasons not to live in Madison...? But once you get past that, this city is pretty nice....Wisconsin has relatively generous personal assistance Medicaid waiver programs. It would be even better but for financial strings running from the nursing home lobby to the Governor's mansion. The result: Medicaid waiver programs exist, but so do waiting lists. Access to Independence is the area's center for independent living.

...All the fixed-route buses are 100 percent accessible on weekends and holidays, and mostly accessible during the week, depending on what routes you use.

...all of Madison's numerous parks have accessible parking and paved pathways. Looking for a job? Oscar Mayer is here and has an open hiring policy." *New Mobility, December 1997*

- Madison appeared on the *Utne Reader's* list of "America's 10 Most Enlightened Towns". Criteria: access to alternative health care, lively media, sense of local culture, diverse spiritual opportunities, good urban design, progressive local politics, commitment to racial equality, tolerance for gays and lesbians, and decent conditions for working-class citizens. *Utne Reader, May/June 1997*

- Madison is among the 20 most livable cities for gay men and lesbians. The list was divided between 10 cities you might expect and 10 surprises. Madison was on the cities you wouldn't expect list. Rank: 5 out of 10. Criteria: legal protection from antigay discrimination, an annual gay pride celebration, a community center, gay bookstores and publications, and an array of organizations, religious groups, and health care facilities that cater to the needs of the local gay community. *The Advocate, June 1997*

- Madison was chosen as one of "America's 10 Best Bike Towns". Rank: 4 out of 10.

  "The best bike town in the Midwest, Madison has fantastic road riding, thanks to a web of quiet backroads built to transport dairy products from farm to market. In town, commuters enjoy 110 miles of bike routes. Madison also has been awarded more than $4 million in ISTEA grants for bike projects...requires bicycle parking at new developments...and has a dizzying assortment of weekly rides, bike clubs, bike shops, races and centuries and is home to several bike companies, including Trek." *Bicycling, August 1997*

- Promega Corp., headquartered in Madison, is among the "100 Best Companies for Working Mothers." Criteria: pay compared with competition, opportunities for women to advance, support for child care, flexible work schedules and family-friendly benefits. *Working Mother, October 1997*

- According to *Working Mother,* "Governor Tommy Thompson's welfare reform effort, 'Wisconsin Works,' included sweeping changes in the state's child care rules and funding. On the positive side, state funding is increasing by $36 million this year alone, which means all families on the waiting list for child care subsidies have now received them. In 1996-97, the state pumped $89 million in new state money into child care. By 1998, the number of children receiving aid will zoom from the current 17,000 to 60,000. This is a remarkable achievement.

  The state also gave a big one-time boost to efforts to increase supply and quality to the tune of $5 million. That money will translate into more staff for licensing, improved resource and referral services and more grants for caregiver training.

  At the same time, however, Wisconsin has created a new class of providers, known as 'provision' caregivers. These providers will not be required to have any training and the state will reimburse them at half the rate it pays those who are certified and have credentials in early education. Many advocates are worried that these policies—paying caregivers less and lowering training standards—could hurt the quality of child care in Wisconsin. (Wisconsin is among the 10 best states for child care.)" *Working Mother, July/August 1997*

Business Environment

STATE ECONOMY

State Economic Profile

"Wisconsin's economy in general, and manufacturing and wholesale trade in particular, continue to lag the nation....

Slow population growth is taking a serious toll on Wisconsin's labor market. Wisconsin is experiencing its tightest labor market since the late 1970's. Just as in other parts of the Midwest, skilled workers, such as machinists, are in short supply. Also, acute shortages are being felt in many entry-level distribution and retail trade jobs. The more industrialized southeastern MSAs of Wisconsin face tighter labor markets than the rest of Wisconsin. Slower household growth will erode demand for residential construction, eventually stifling the strong job growth that has characterized the construction industry of late.

Wisconsin is making a concerted effort to lighten the residential property tax burden, because differences in Wisconsin's and Minnesota's tax systems encourage people to locate their businesses in Wisconsin and commute from Minnesota. Another popular approach to economic development that Wisconsin is now employing is the use of enterprise development zones.

The outlook for Wisconsin is for moderate growth. Positive demographic trends will support service growth and retail and residential construction over the longer term....Wisconsin will be an average performer through the forecast." *National Association of Realtors, Economic Profiles: The Fifty States, July 1997*

IMPORTS/EXPORTS

Total Export Sales

Area	1993 ($000)	1994 ($000)	1995 ($000)	1996 ($000)	% Chg. 1993-96	% Chg. 1995-96
MSA[1]	357,688	417,083	497,462	522,408	46.1	5.0
U.S.	464,858,354	512,415,609	583,030,524	622,827,063	34.0	6.8

Note: (1) Metropolitan Statistical Area - see Appendix A for areas included
Source: U.S. Department of Commerce, International Trade Association, Metropolitan Area Exports: An Export Performance Report on Over 250 U.S. Cities, October 1997

Imports/Exports by Port

Type	Cargo Value			Share of U.S. Total	
	1995 (US$mil.)	1996 (US$mil.)	% Change 1995-1996	1995 (%)	1996 (%)
Imports	0	0	0	0	0
Exports	0	0	0	0	0

Source: Global Trade Information Services, WaterBorne Trade Atlas 1997

CITY FINANCES

City Government Finances

Component	FY92 ($000)	FY92 (per capita $)
Revenue	169,564	869.39
Expenditure	177,805	911.64
Debt Outstanding	136,760	701.19
Cash & Securities	158,687	813.62

Source: U.S. Bureau of the Census, City Government Finances: 1991-92

City Government Revenue by Source

Source	FY92 ($000)	FY92 (per capita $)	FY92 (%)
From Federal Government	7,581	38.87	4.5
From State Governments	47,559	243.84	28.0
From Local Governments	2,410	12.36	1.4
Property Taxes	53,793	275.81	31.7
General Sales Taxes	3	0.02	0.0
Selective Sales Taxes	2,630	13.48	1.6
Income Taxes	0	0.00	0.0
Current Charges	19,659	100.80	11.6
Utility/Liquor Store	14,382	73.74	8.5
Employee Retirement[1]	0	0.00	0.0
Other	21,547	110.48	12.7

Note: (1) Excludes "city contributions," classified as "nonrevenue," intragovernmental transfers.
Source: U.S. Bureau of the Census, City Government Finances: 1991-92

City Government Expenditures by Function

Function	FY92 ($000)	FY92 (per capita $)	FY92 (%)
Educational Services	5,754	29.50	3.2
Employee Retirement[1]	0	0.00	0.0
Environment/Housing	51,246	262.75	28.8
Government Administration	8,209	42.09	4.6
Interest on General Debt	7,409	37.99	4.2
Public Safety	45,252	232.02	25.5
Social Services	6,339	32.50	3.6
Transportation	20,435	104.77	11.5
Utility/Liquor Store	31,062	159.26	17.5
Other	2,099	10.76	1.2

Note: (1) Payments to beneficiaries including withdrawal of contributions.
Source: U.S. Bureau of the Census, City Government Finances: 1991-92

Municipal Bond Ratings

Area	Moody's	S & P
Madison	Aaa	n/a

Note: n/a not available; n/r not rated
Source: Moody's Bond Record, 2/98; Statistical Abstract of the U.S., 1997; Governing Magazine, 9/97, 3/98

POPULATION

Population Growth

Area	1980	1990	% Chg. 1980-90	July 1996 Estimate	% Chg. 1990-96
City	170,616	191,262	12.1	197,630	3.3
MSA[1]	323,545	367,085	13.5	395,366	7.7
U.S.	226,545,805	248,765,170	9.8	265,179,411	6.6

Note: (1) Metropolitan Statistical Area - see Appendix A for areas included
Source: 1980/1990 Census of Housing and Population, Summary Tape File 3C; Census Bureau Population Estimates

Population Characteristics

| Race | City | | | | | MSA[1] | |
| | 1980 | | 1990 | | % Chg. 1980-90 | 1990 | |
	Population	%	Population	%		Population	%
White	161,333	94.6	173,690	90.8	7.7	344,682	93.9
Black	4,557	2.7	7,925	4.1	73.9	10,414	2.8
Amer Indian/Esk/Aleut	454	0.3	778	0.4	71.4	1,326	0.4
Asian/Pacific Islander	3,176	1.9	7,406	3.9	133.2	8,582	2.3
Other	1,096	0.6	1,463	0.8	33.5	2,081	0.6
Hispanic Origin[2]	2,451	1.4	3,614	1.9	47.5	5,204	1.4

Note: (1) Metropolitan Statistical Area - see Appendix A for areas included;
(2) people of Hispanic origin can be of any race
Source: 1980/1990 Census of Housing and Population, Summary Tape File 3C

Ancestry

Area	German	Irish	English	Italian	U.S.	French	Polish	Dutch
City	44.2	16.7	12.9	3.7	1.4	3.9	5.1	2.4
MSA[1]	49.3	16.5	12.9	3.1	1.5	3.9	4.7	2.3
U.S.	23.3	15.6	13.1	5.9	5.3	4.2	3.8	2.5

Note: Figures are percentages and include persons that reported multiple ancestry (eg. if a person reported being Irish and Italian, they were included in both columns); (1) Metropolitan Statistical Area - see Appendix A for areas included
Source: 1990 Census of Population and Housing, Summary Tape File 3C

Age

| Area | Median Age (Years) | Age Distribution (%) | | | | | | |
		Under 5	Under 18	18-24	25-44	45-64	65+	80+
City	29.3	6.2	18.5	22.2	35.5	14.6	9.2	2.3
MSA[1]	30.7	7.0	22.7	15.7	36.3	16.0	9.2	2.3
U.S.	32.9	7.3	25.6	10.5	32.6	18.7	12.5	2.8

Note: (1) Metropolitan Statistical Area - see Appendix A for areas included
Source: 1990 Census of Population and Housing, Summary Tape File 3C

Male/Female Ratio

Area	Number of males per 100 females (all ages)	Number of males per 100 females (18 years old+)
City	96.5	92.9
MSA[1]	97.4	94.4
U.S.	95.0	91.9

Note: (1) Metropolitan Statistical Area - see Appendix A for areas included
Source: 1990 Census of Population, General Population Characteristics

INCOME

Per Capita/Median/Average Income

Area	Per Capita ($)	Median Household ($)	Average Household ($)
City	15,143	29,420	36,977
MSA[1]	15,542	32,703	39,589
U.S.	14,420	30,056	38,453

Note: all figures are for 1989; (1) Metropolitan Statistical Area - see Appendix A for areas included
Source: 1990 Census of Population and Housing, Summary Tape File 3C

Household Income Distribution by Race

Income ($)	City (%)					U.S. (%)				
	Total	White	Black	Other	Hisp.[1]	Total	White	Black	Other	Hisp.[1]
Less than 5,000	5.8	4.9	12.1	22.2	8.7	6.2	4.8	15.2	8.6	8.8
5,000 - 9,999	9.2	8.7	17.0	14.4	6.4	9.3	8.6	14.2	9.9	11.1
10,000 - 14,999	9.1	8.8	11.5	13.8	10.8	8.8	8.5	11.0	9.8	11.0
15,000 - 24,999	18.0	17.9	20.9	16.7	26.7	17.5	17.3	18.9	18.5	20.5
25,000 - 34,999	16.5	16.8	15.5	11.6	20.0	15.8	16.1	14.2	15.4	16.4
35,000 - 49,999	18.1	18.7	13.6	9.5	10.5	17.9	18.6	13.3	16.1	16.0
50,000 - 74,999	14.7	15.3	7.3	7.0	11.6	15.0	15.8	9.3	13.4	11.1
75,000 - 99,999	4.8	5.1	1.5	2.7	3.2	5.1	5.5	2.6	4.7	3.1
100,000+	3.7	3.9	0.7	1.9	2.0	4.4	4.8	1.3	3.7	1.9

Note: all figures are for 1989; (1) people of Hispanic origin can be of any race
Source: 1990 Census of Population and Housing, Summary Tape File 3C

Effective Buying Income

Area	Per Capita ($)	Median Household ($)	Average Household ($)
City	18,060	35,715	44,921
MSA[1]	19,162	41,369	49,101
U.S.	15,444	33,201	41,849

Note: data as of 1/1/97; (1) Metropolitan Statistical Area - see Appendix A for areas included
Source: Standard Rate & Data Service, Newspaper Advertising Source, 2/98

Effective Household Buying Income Distribution

Area	% of Households Earning						
	$10,000 -$19,999	$20,000 -$34,999	$35,000 -$49,999	$50,000 -$74,999	$75,000 -$99,000	$100,000 -$124,999	$125,000 and up
City	15.1	23.2	17.8	19.9	7.9	2.7	2.6
MSA[1]	12.4	21.5	19.1	24.1	9.2	3.1	3.1
U.S.	16.5	23.4	18.3	18.2	6.4	2.1	2.4

Note: data as of 1/1/97; (1) Metropolitan Statistical Area - see Appendix A for areas included
Source: Standard Rate & Data Service, Newspaper Advertising Source, 2/98

Poverty Rates by Race and Age

Area	Total (%)	By Race (%)				By Age (%)		
		White	Black	Other	Hisp.[2]	Under 5 years old	Under 18 years old	65 years and over
City	16.1	13.8	35.2	42.2	22.9	15.7	13.2	4.8
MSA[1]	10.5	8.9	35.0	37.6	21.3	10.6	8.8	5.0
U.S.	13.1	9.8	29.5	23.1	25.3	20.1	18.3	12.8

Note: figures show the percent of people living below the poverty line in 1989. The average poverty
threshold was $12,674 for a family of four in 1989; (1) Metropolitan Statistical Area - see Appendix A
for areas included; (2) people of Hispanic origin can be of any race
Source: 1990 Census of Population and Housing, Summary Tape File 3C

EMPLOYMENT

Labor Force and Employment

Area	Civilian Labor Force			Workers Employed		
	Dec. '95	Dec. '96	% Chg.	Dec. '95	Dec. '96	% Chg.
City	131,512	132,730	0.9	129,633	130,800	0.9
MSA[1]	260,593	262,982	0.9	256,981	259,295	0.9
U.S.	134,583,000	136,742,000	1.6	127,903,000	130,785,000	2.3

Note: Data is not seasonally adjusted and covers workers 16 years of age and older;
(1) Metropolitan Statistical Area - see Appendix A for areas included
Source: Bureau of Labor Statistics, http://stats.bls.gov

Unemployment Rate

Area	1997											
	Jan.	Feb.	Mar.	Apr.	May	Jun.	Jul.	Aug.	Sep.	Oct.	Nov.	Dec.
City	1.9	2.0	2.0	1.8	1.8	2.1	2.0	1.7	1.7	1.5	1.6	1.5
MSA[1]	2.0	2.0	2.0	1.7	1.5	1.8	1.7	1.5	1.5	1.3	1.4	1.4
U.S.	5.9	5.7	5.5	4.8	4.7	5.2	5.0	4.8	4.7	4.4	4.3	4.4

Note: Data is not seasonally adjusted and covers workers 16 years of age and older; All figures are percentages; (1) Metropolitan Statistical Area - see Appendix A for areas included
Source: Bureau of Labor Statistics, http://stats.bls.gov

Employment by Industry

Sector	MSA[1]		U.S.
	Number of Employees	Percent of Total	Percent of Total
Services	68,300	25.1	29.0
Retail Trade	47,800	17.6	18.5
Government	70,800	26.1	16.1
Manufacturing	29,600	10.9	15.0
Finance/Insurance/Real Estate	21,600	8.0	5.7
Wholesale Trade	11,800	4.3	5.4
Transportation/Public Utilities	9,600	3.5	5.3
Construction/Mining	12,100	4.5	5.0

Note: Figures cover non-farm employment as of 12/97 and are not seasonally adjusted; (1) Metropolitan Statistical Area - see Appendix A for areas included
Source: Bureau of Labor Statistics, http://stats.bls.gov

Employment by Occupation

Occupation Category	City (%)	MSA[1] (%)	U.S. (%)
White Collar	71.1	67.3	58.1
Executive/Admin./Management	13.3	13.6	12.3
Professional	22.0	18.5	14.1
Technical & Related Support	7.0	5.9	3.7
Sales	11.0	10.9	11.8
Administrative Support/Clerical	17.8	18.3	16.3
Blue Collar	13.4	17.5	26.2
Precision Production/Craft/Repair	5.5	7.7	11.3
Machine Operators/Assem./Insp.	3.4	4.3	6.8
Transportation/Material Movers	2.3	2.8	4.1
Cleaners/Helpers/Laborers	2.1	2.6	3.9
Services	14.6	13.0	13.2
Farming/Forestry/Fishing	0.9	2.2	2.5

Note: figures cover employed persons 16 years old and over; (1) Metropolitan Statistical Area - see Appendix A for areas included
Source: 1990 Census of Population and Housing, Summary Tape File 3C

Occupational Employment Projections: 1994 - 2005

Occupations Expected to have the Largest Job Growth (ranked by numerical growth)	Fast-Growing Occupations (ranked by percent growth)
1. Waiters & waitresses	1. Computer engineers
2. General managers & top executives	2. Systems analysts
3. Cashiers	3. Electronic pagination systems workers
4. Salespersons, retail	4. Personal and home care aides
5. Janitors/cleaners/maids, ex. priv. hshld.	5. Manicurists
6. Truck drivers, heavy & light	6. Credit authorizers
7. Systems analysts	7. Computer scientists
8. Teachers, secondary school	8. Pressers, hand
9. Marketing & sales, supervisors	9. Geologists/geophysicists/oceanographers
10. Registered nurses	10. Home health aides

Projections cover Wisconsin.
Source: U.S. Department of Labor, Employment and Training Administration, America's Labor Market Information System (ALMIS)

Average Wages

Occupation	Wage	Occupation	Wage
Professional/Technical/Clerical	$/Week	**Health/Protective Services**	$/Week
Accountants III	-	Corrections Officers	-
Attorneys III	-	Firefighters	-
Budget Analysts III	-	Nurses, Licensed Practical II	-
Buyers/Contracting Specialists II	-	Nurses, Registered II	-
Clerks, Accounting III	421	Nursing Assistants II	-
Clerks, General III	414	Police Officers I	-
Computer Operators II	431	**Hourly Workers**	$/Hour
Computer Programmers II	600	Forklift Operators	10.27
Drafters II	456	General Maintenance Workers	9.35
Engineering Technicians III	-	Guards I	7.03
Engineering Technicians, Civil III	-	Janitors	6.75
Engineers III	-	Maintenance Electricians	14.70
Key Entry Operators I	311	Maintenance Electronics Techs II	-
Personnel Assistants III	-	Maintenance Machinists	-
Personnel Specialists III	-	Maintenance Mechanics, Machinery	13.80
Secretaries III	500	Material Handling Laborers	8.68
Switchboard Operator-Receptionist	313	Motor Vehicle Mechanics	14.27
Systems Analysts II	807	Shipping/Receiving Clerks	10.69
Systems Analysts Supervisor/Mgr II	-	Tool and Die Makers	-
Tax Collectors II	-	Truckdrivers, Tractor Trailer	-
Word Processors II	418	Warehouse Specialists	11.63

Note: Wage data includes full-time workers only for 3/94 and cover the Metropolitan Statistical Area (see Appendix A for areas included). Dashes indicate that data was not available.
Source: Bureau of Labor Statistics, Occupational Compensation Survey

TAXES

Major State and Local Tax Rates

State Corp. Income (%)	State Personal Income (%)	Residential Property (effective rate per $100)	Sales & Use State (%)	Local (%)	State Gasoline (cents/ gallon)	State Cigarette (cents/ 20-pack)
7.9[a]	4.9 - 6.93	n/a	5.0	0.5	24.8	59

Note: Personal/corporate income tax rates as of 1/97. Sales, gasoline and cigarette tax rates as of 1/98; (a) Plus a surtax set annually by the Dept. of Revenue to finance a special recycling fund
Source: Federation of Tax Administrators, www.taxadmin.org; Washington D.C. Department of Finance and Revenue, Tax Rates and Tax Burdens in the District of Columbia: A Nationwide Comparison, June 1997; Chamber of Commerce

Total Taxes Per Capita and as a Percent of Income

Area	Per Capita Income ($)	Per Capita Taxes ($)			Taxes as Pct. of Income (%)		
		Total	Federal	State/Local	Total	Federal	State/Local
Wisconsin	25,105	9,165	5,825	3,340	36.5	23.2	13.3
U.S.	26,187	9,205	6,127	3,078	35.2	23.4	11.8

Note: Figures are for 1997
Source: Tax Foundation, Web Site, www.taxfoundation.org

Estimated Tax Burden

Area	State Income	Local Income	Property	Sales	Total
Madison	3,664	0	4,950	468	9,082

Note: The numbers are estimates of taxes paid by a married couple with two kids and annual earnings of $65,000. Sales tax estimates assume they spend average amounts on food, clothing, household goods and gasoline. Property tax estimates assume they live in a $225,000 home.
Source: Kiplinger's Personal Finance Magazine, June 1997

COMMERCIAL REAL ESTATE

Data not available at time of publication.

COMMERCIAL UTILITIES

Typical Monthly Electric Bills

Area	Commercial Service ($/month)		Industrial Service ($/month)	
	12 kW demand 1,500 kWh	100 kW demand 30,000 kWh	1,000 kW demand 400,000 kWh	20,000 kW demand 10,000,000 kWh
City	109	1,894	20,047	459,170
U.S.	162	2,360	25,590	545,677

Note: Based on rates in effect July 1, 1997
Source: Edison Electric Institute, Typical Residential, Commercial and Industrial Bills, Summer 1997

TRANSPORTATION

Transportation Statistics

Avg. travel time to work (min.)	16.9
Interstate highways	I-90; I-94
Bus lines	
In-city	Madison Metro Transit
Inter-city	8
Passenger air service	
Airport	Dane County Municipal Airport
Airlines	22
Aircraft departures	11,225 (1995)
Enplaned passengers	492,706 (1995)
Rail service	Amtrak Thruway Motorcoach Connection
Motor freight carriers	40
Major waterways/ports	None

Source: OAG, Business Travel Planner, Summer 1997; Editor & Publisher Market Guide, 1998; FAA Airport Activity Statistics, 1996; Amtrak National Time Table, Northeast Timetable, Fall/Winter 1997-98; 1990 Census of Population and Housing, STF 3C; Chamber of Commerce/Economic Development 1997; Jane's Urban Transport Systems 1997-98; Transit Fact Book 1997

Means of Transportation to Work

Area	Car/Truck/Van		Public Transportation			Bicycle	Walked	Other Means	Worked at Home
	Drove Alone	Car-pooled	Bus	Subway	Railroad				
City	61.2	11.6	7.4	0.0	0.0	3.3	12.7	1.0	2.7
MSA[1]	68.5	12.5	4.4	0.0	0.0	1.9	8.2	0.8	3.6
U.S.	73.2	13.4	3.0	1.5	0.5	0.4	3.9	1.2	3.0

Note: figures shown are percentages and only include workers 16 years old and over;
(1) Metropolitan Statistical Area - see Appendix A for areas included
Source: 1990 Census of Population and Housing, Summary Tape File 3C

BUSINESSES

Major Business Headquarters

Company Name	1997 Rankings	
	Fortune 500	Forbes 500
American Family Ins. Group	403	-

Note: Companies listed are located in the city; Dashes indicate no ranking
Fortune 500: companies that produce a 10-K are ranked 1 - 500 based on 1996 revenue
Forbes 500: private companies are ranked 1 - 500 based on 1996 revenue
Source: Forbes 12/1/97; Fortune 4/28/97

HOTELS & MOTELS

Hotels/Motels

Area	Hotels/ Motels	Rooms	Luxury-Level Hotels/Motels		Average Minimum Rates ($)		
			♦♦♦♦	♦♦♦♦♦	♦♦	♦♦♦	♦♦♦♦
City	30	3,372	0	0	62	80	n/a
Airport	8	709	0	0	n/a	n/a	n/a
Suburbs	1	153	0	0	n/a	n/a	n/a
Total	39	4,234	0	0	n/a	n/a	n/a

Note: n/a not available; Classifications range from one diamond (budget properties with basic amenities) to five diamond (luxury properties with the finest service, rooms and facilities).
Source: OAG, Business Travel Planner, Summer 1997

CONVENTION CENTERS

Major Convention Centers

Center Name	Meeting Rooms	Exhibit Space (sf)
Dane County Expo Center	7	91,000
Madison Civic Center	n/a	n/a
University of Wisconsin Extension Conference Centers	34	n/a

Note: n/a not available
Source: Trade Shows Worldwide 1997

Living Environment

COST OF LIVING

Cost of Living Index

Composite Index	Housing	Utilities	Groceries	Health Care	Trans-portation	Misc. Goods/ Services
110.1	125.0	90.6	99.5	107.6	104.8	109.1

Note: U.S. = 100
Source: ACCRA, Cost of Living Index, 3rd Quarter 1997

HOUSING

Median Home Prices and Housing Affordability

Area	Median Price[2] 3rd Qtr. 1997 ($)	HOI[3] 3rd Qtr. 1997	Afford-ability Rank[4]
MSA[1]	n/a	n/a	n/a
U.S.	127,000	63.7	–

Note: (1) Metropolitan Statistical Area - see Appendix A for areas included; (2) U.S. figures calculated from the sales of 625,000 new and existing homes in 195 markets; (3) Housing Opportunity Index - percent of homes sold that were within the reach of the median income household at the prevailing mortgage interest rate; (4) Rank is from 1-195 with 1 being most affordable; n/a not available
Source: National Association of Home Builders, Housing Opportunity Index, 3rd Quarter 1997

Average New Home Price

Area	Price ($)
City	165,900
U.S.	135,710

Note: Figures are based on a new home with 1,800 sq. ft. of living area on an 8,000 sq. ft. lot.
Source: ACCRA, Cost of Living Index, 3rd Quarter 1997

Average Apartment Rent

Area	Rent ($/mth)
City	743
U.S.	569

Note: Figures are based on an unfurnished two bedroom, 1-1/2 or 2 bath apartment, approximately 950 sq. ft. in size, excluding all utilities except water
Source: ACCRA, Cost of Living Index, 3rd Quarter 1997

RESIDENTIAL UTILITIES

Average Residential Utility Costs

Area	All Electric ($/mth)	Part Electric ($/mth)	Other Energy ($/mth)	Phone ($/mth)
City	–	46.59	46.26	17.65
U.S.	109.40	55.25	43.64	19.48

Source: ACCRA, Cost of Living Index, 3rd Quarter 1997

HEALTH CARE

Average Health Care Costs

Area	Hospital ($/day)	Doctor ($/visit)	Dentist ($/visit)
City	314.75	59.60	62.20
U.S.	392.91	48.76	60.84

Note: Hospital - based on a semi-private room. Doctor - based on a general practitioner's routine exam of an established patient. Dentist - based on adult teeth cleaning and periodic oral exam.
Source: ACCRA, Cost of Living Index, 3rd Quarter 1997

Distribution of Office-Based Physicians

Area	Family/Gen. Practitioners	Specialists		
		Medical	Surgical	Other
MSA[1]	152	371	231	340

Note: Data as of 12/31/96; (1) Metropolitan Statistical Area - see Appendix A for areas included
Source: American Medical Assn., Physician Characteristics & Distribution in the U.S., 1997-1998

Hospitals

Madison has 4 general medical and surgical hospitals, 1 psychiatric. *AHA Guide to the Healthcare Field 1997-98*

According to *U.S. News and World Report,* Madison has 1 of the best hospitals in the U.S.: **University of Wisconsin Hospital & Clinics**, noted for AIDS, cancer, endocrinology, gastroenterology, geriatrics, gynecology, neurology, ophthalmology, otolaryngology, pulmonology, rheumatology;   *U.S. News and World Report, "America's Best Hospitals", 7/28/97*

EDUCATION

Public School District Statistics

District Name	Num. Sch.	Enroll.	Classroom Teachers[1]	Pupils per Teacher	Minority Pupils (%)	Current Exp.[2] ($/pupil)
Madison Metropolitan Sch Dist	51	25,046	n/a	n/a	28.4	7,199

Note: Data covers the 1995-1996 school year unless otherwise noted; (1) Excludes teachers reported as working in school district offices rather than in schools; (2) Based on 1993-94 enrollment collected by the Census Bureau, not the enrollment figure shown in column 3; SD = School District; ISD = Independent School District; n/a not available
Source: National Center for Education Statistics, Common Core of Data Survey; Bureau of the Census

Educational Quality

School District	Education Quotient[1]	Graduate Outcome[2]	Community Index[3]	Resource Index[4]
Madison Metropolitan	144.0	146.0	141.0	146.0

Note: Nearly 1,000 secondary school districts were rated in terms of educational quality. The scores range from a low of 50 to a high of 150; (1) Average of the Graduate Outcome, Community and Resource indexes; (2) Based on graduation rates and college board scores (SAT/ACT); (3) Based on the surrounding community's average level of education and the area's average income level; (4) Based on teacher salaries, per-pupil expenditures and student-teacher ratios.
Source: Expansion Management, Ratings Issue 1997

Educational Attainment by Race

Area	High School Graduate (%)					Bachelor's Degree (%)				
	Total	White	Black	Other	Hisp.[2]	Total	White	Black	Other	Hisp.[2]
City	90.6	91.0	80.6	89.3	87.2	42.0	41.7	24.8	62.8	48.4
MSA[1]	88.9	89.2	80.1	87.0	82.9	34.2	33.8	24.0	57.6	41.5
U.S.	75.2	77.9	63.1	60.4	49.8	20.3	21.5	11.4	19.4	9.2

Note: figures shown cover persons 25 years old and over; (1) Metropolitan Statistical Area - see Appendix A for areas included; (2) people of Hispanic origin can be of any race
Source: 1990 Census of Population and Housing, Summary Tape File 3C

School Enrollment by Type

Area	Preprimary				Elementary/High School			
	Public		Private		Public		Private	
	Enrollment	%	Enrollment	%	Enrollment	%	Enrollment	%
City	2,039	54.5	1,705	45.5	19,043	90.4	2,023	9.6
MSA[1]	4,454	59.1	3,077	40.9	47,805	92.0	4,184	8.0
U.S.	2,679,029	59.5	1,824,256	40.5	38,379,689	90.2	4,187,099	9.8

Note: figures shown cover persons 3 years old and over;
(1) Metropolitan Statistical Area - see Appendix A for areas included
Source: 1990 Census of Population and Housing, Summary Tape File 3C

School Enrollment by Race

Area	Preprimary (%)				Elementary/High School (%)			
	White	Black	Other	Hisp.[1]	White	Black	Other	Hisp.[1]
City	84.8	7.7	7.5	3.0	84.7	9.1	6.3	2.3
MSA[2]	89.7	5.0	5.2	2.3	91.3	5.0	3.8	2.1
U.S.	80.4	12.5	7.1	7.8	74.1	15.6	10.3	12.5

Note: figures shown cover persons 3 years old and over; (1) people of Hispanic origin can be of any race; (2) Metropolitan Statistical Area - see Appendix A for areas included
Source: 1990 Census of Population and Housing, Summary Tape File 3C

SAT/ACT Scores

Area/District	1997 SAT				1997 ACT	
	Percent of Graduates Tested (%)	Average Math Score	Average Verbal Score	Average Combined Score	Percent of Graduates Tested (%)	Average Composite Score
Madison SD	23	631	616	1,247	63	24.5
State	7	590	579	1,169	64	22.3
U.S.	42	511	505	1,016	36	21.0

Note: Math and verbal SAT scores are out of a possible 800; ACT scores are out of a possible 36
Caution: Comparing or ranking states/cities on the basis of SAT/ACT scores alone is invalid and strongly discouraged by the The College Board and The American College Testing Program as students who take the tests are self-selected and do not represent the entire student population.
Source: Madison Metropolitan School District, 1997; American College Testing Program, 1997, College Board, 1997

Classroom Teacher Salaries in Public Schools

District	B.A. Degree		M.A. Degree		Ph.D. Degree	
	Min. ($)	Max ($)	Min. ($)	Max. ($)	Min. ($)	Max. ($)
Madison	24,938	42,395	27,432	44,888	31,173	52,370
Average[1]	26,120	39,270	28,175	44,667	31,643	49,825

Note: Salaries are for 1996-1997; (1) Based on all school districts covered; n/a not available
Source: American Federation of Teachers (unpublished data)

Higher Education

Two-Year Colleges		Four-Year Colleges		Medical Schools	Law Schools	Voc/Tech
Public	Private	Public	Private			
1	2	1	1	1	1	8

Source: College Blue Book, Occupational Education 1997; Medical School Admission Requirements, 1998-99; Peterson's Guide to Two-Year Colleges, 1997; Peterson's Guide to Four-Year Colleges, 1997; Barron's Guide to Law Schools 1997

MAJOR EMPLOYERS

Major Employers

American Family Mutual Insurance

Wisconsin Physicians Service Insurance

Madison Gas & Electric

Madison-Kipp Corp. (aluminum die-casting)

Meriter Hospital

University of Wisconsin Hospital & Clinics

Webcrafters (book printing)

CUNA Mutual Insurance

Dean Health Systems

Madison Newspapers

Marshall Erdman & Associates (general contractors)

Oscar Mayer Foods

WPL Holdings (electric services)

Wisconsin Power & Light

Note: companies listed are located in the city
Source: Dun's Business Rankings 1997; Ward's Business Directory, 1997

PUBLIC SAFETY

Crime Rate

Area	All Crimes	Violent Crimes				Property Crimes		
		Murder	Forcible Rape	Robbery	Aggrav. Assault	Burglary	Larceny -Theft	Motor Vehicle Theft
City	4,603.9	0.5	38.0	151.3	200.9	703.0	3,185.7	324.4
Suburbs[1]	3,565.5	0.5	14.6	15.1	164.5	435.6	2,816.4	118.6
MSA[2]	4,092.8	0.5	26.5	84.3	183.0	571.4	3,004.0	223.1
U.S.	5,078.9	7.4	36.1	202.4	388.2	943.0	2,975.9	525.9

Note: Crime rate is the number of crimes per 100,000 pop.; (1) defined as all areas within the MSA but located outside the central city; (2) Metropolitan Statistical Area - see Appendix A for areas incl.
Source: FBI Uniform Crime Reports 1996

RECREATION

Culture and Recreation

Museums	Symphony Orchestras	Opera Companies	Dance Companies	Professional Theatres	Zoos	Pro Sports Teams
6	1	1	1	2	1	0

Source: International Directory of the Performing Arts, 1996; Official Museum Directory, 1998; Chamber of Commerce/Economic Development 1997

Library System

The Madison Public Library has seven branches, holdings of 630,157 volumes and a budget of $7,097,794 (1996). *American Library Directory, 1997-1998*

MEDIA

Newspapers

Name	Type	Freq.	Distribution	Circulation
Badger Herald	n/a	5x/wk	Campus	community & alumni
The Capital Times	General	6x/wk	Area	22,000
Daily Cardinal	n/a	5x/wk	Campus & community	10,000
Isthmus	General	1x/wk	Local	60,000
The Madison Times	Black	1x/wk	Local	7,000
Wisconsin State Journal	n/a	7x/wk	Area	86,000

Note: Includes newspapers with circulations of 1,000 or more located in the city; n/a not available
Source: Burrelle's Media Directory, 1998 Edition

AM Radio Stations

Call Letters	Freq. (kHz)	Target Audience	Station Format	Music Format
WLBL	930	General	E/M/N/T	n/a
WHA	970	n/a	E/T	n/a
WTSO	1070	n/a	M	Oldies
WIBA	1310	General	N/T	n/a
WTDY	1480	General	N/T	n/a
WHIT	1550	General	S	n/a

Note: Stations included broadcast in the Madison metro area; n/a not available
Station Format: E = Educational; M = Music; N = News; S = Sports; T = Talk
Source: Burrelle's Media Directory, 1998 Edition

FM Radio Stations

Call Letters	Freq. (mHz)	Target Audience	Station Format	Music Format
WERN	88.7	n/a	E/M/T	Classical
WPNE	89.3	n/a	E/M	Classical
WORT	89.9	General	M/N/T	Alternative/Big Band/Classic Rock/Classical/Country/Christian/Jazz/Oldies/R&B/Spanish
WHLA	90.3	n/a	E/T	n/a
WHBM	90.3	General	E/T	n/a
WHHI	91.3	n/a	E/T	n/a
WMAD	92.1	n/a	M	Alternative
WJJO	94.1	General	M/N/S	AOR
WOLX	94.9	General	M/N	Oldies
WMLI	96.3	General	M/N/S	Easy Listening
WMGN	98.1	General	M	Adult Contemporary/Jazz
WIBA	101.5	General	M	Classic Rock
WNWC	102.5	Religious	M/N/S	Christian
WZEE	104.1	n/a	M	Contemporary Top 40
WMMM	105.5	General	M/N/S	Alternative
WWQM	106.3	General	M	Country

Note: Stations included broadcast in the Madison metro area; n/a not available
Station Format: E = Educational; M = Music; N = News; S = Sports; T = Talk
Music Format: AOR = Album Oriented Rock; MOR = Middle-of-the-Road
Source: Burrelle's Media Directory, 1998 Edition

Television Stations

Name	Ch.	Affiliation	Type	Owner
WISC	3	CBS	Commercial	Evening Telegram Co.
WMTV	15	NBC	Commercial	Bursett Broadcasting
WHRM	20	PBS	Public	State of Wisconsin Education Communications Board
WHA	21	PBS	Public	University of Wisconsin Board of Regents
WKOW	27	ABC	Commercial	Shockley Communications Corp.
WHWC	28	PBS	Public	State of Wisconsin Education Communications Board
WHLA	31	PBS	Public	State of Wisconsin Education Communications Board
WLEF	36	PBS	Public	State of Wisconsin Education Communications Board
WPNE	38	PBS	Public	State of Wisconsin Education Communications Board
WMSN	47	Fox	Commercial	Sullivan Broadcasting

Note: Stations included broadcast in the Madison metro area
Source: Burrelle's Media Directory, 1998 Edition

CLIMATE

Average and Extreme Temperatures

Temperature	Jan	Feb	Mar	Apr	May	Jun	Jul	Aug	Sep	Oct	Nov	Dec	Ann
Extreme High (°F)	56	61	82	94	93	101	104	102	99	90	76	62	104
Average High (°F)	26	30	42	58	70	79	84	81	72	61	44	30	57
Average Temp. (°F)	17	21	32	46	57	67	72	69	61	50	36	23	46
Average Low (°F)	8	12	22	35	45	54	59	57	49	38	27	14	35
Extreme Low (°F)	-37	-28	-29	0	19	31	36	35	25	13	-8	-25	-37

Note: Figures cover the years 1948-1990
Source: National Climatic Data Center, International Station Meteorological Climate Summary, 3/95

Average Precipitation/Snowfall/Humidity

Precip./Humidity	Jan	Feb	Mar	Apr	May	Jun	Jul	Aug	Sep	Oct	Nov	Dec	Ann
Avg. Precip. (in.)	1.1	1.1	2.1	2.9	3.2	3.8	3.9	3.9	3.0	2.3	2.0	1.7	31.1
Avg. Snowfall (in.)	10	7	9	2	Tr	0	0	0	Tr	Tr	4	11	42
Avg. Rel. Hum. 6am (%)	78	80	81	80	79	81	85	89	90	85	84	82	83
Avg. Rel. Hum. 3pm (%)	66	63	59	50	50	51	53	55	55	54	64	69	57

Note: Figures cover the years 1948-1990; Tr = Trace amounts (<0.05 in. of rain; <0.5 in. of snow)
Source: National Climatic Data Center, International Station Meteorological Climate Summary, 3/95

Weather Conditions

Temperature			Daytime Sky			Precipitation		
5°F & below	32°F & below	90°F & above	Clear	Partly cloudy	Cloudy	0.01 inch or more precip.	0.1 inch or more snow/ice	Thunder-storms
35	161	14	88	119	158	118	38	40

Note: Figures are average number of days per year and covers the years 1948-1990
Source: National Climatic Data Center, International Station Meteorological Climate Summary, 3/95

AIR & WATER QUALITY

Maximum Pollutant Concentrations

	Particulate Matter (ug/m^3)	Carbon Monoxide (ppm)	Sulfur Dioxide (ppm)	Nitrogen Dioxide (ppm)	Ozone (ppm)	Lead (ug/m^3)
MSA[1] Level	44	4	0.010	n/a	0.09	n/a
NAAQS[2]	150	9	0.140	0.053	0.12	1.50
Met NAAQS?	Yes	Yes	Yes	n/a	Yes	n/a

Note: (1) Metropolitan Statistical Area - see Appendix A for areas included; (2) National Ambient Air Quality Standards; ppm = parts per million; ug/m^3 = micrograms per cubic meter; n/a not available
Source: EPA, National Air Quality and Emissions Trends Report, 1996

Pollutant Standards Index

Data not available. *EPA, National Air Quality and Emissions Trends Report, 1996*

Drinking Water

Water System Name	Pop. Served	Primary Water Source Type	Number of Violations in Fiscal Year 1997	Type of Violation/ Contaminants
Madison Water Utility	191,262	Ground	None	None

Note: Data as of January 16, 1998
Source: EPA, Office of Ground Water and Drinking Water, Safe Drinking Water Information System

Madison tap water is alkaline, hard and fluoridated.
Editor & Publisher Market Guide, 1998

Milwaukee, Wisconsin

Background

Many people associate the city of Milwaukee with beer. Perhaps due to the television show, *Laverne and Shirley*, wherein the show's main characters worked in a brewery, or to the large influx of German immigrants during the 1840's, who left an indelible mark upon the city.

Milwaukee originally began as a trading post for French fur traders. Its favorable location on the western shore of Lake Michigan, as well as at the confluence of the Milwaukee, Menomonee, and Kinnickinnic Rivers made the site a natural meeting place. In 1818, Solomon Laurent Juneau, a son-in-law of a French fur trader, became Milwaukee's first founder and permanent white settler.

During the 1840's, Milwaukee saw a wave of German immigrants hit its shores. Many of these exiles were unsuccessful revolutionaries in the overthrow of German monarchies. Despite their lack of success back home, these immigrants managed to impart a considerable influence in the new country. These influences include areas such as politics—the city has had three Socialist mayors—the economy— Pabst and Schlitz Breweries made their home in Milwaukee—and culture—the Goethe House is a cultural resource center located in the central library of the Milwaukee Public Library System.

Today, Milwaukee is much more than just a German-dominated city. It includes many nationalities such as Irish, Serbian, Scandinavian, Polish, and Italian. On October 18, 1996 Milwaukee opened its 17.3 million dollar Museum Center, featuring a new museum of science and technology and natural history and the first IMAX theater in Wisconsin. Also, its economy no longer has just beer on its mind. Milwaukee is large in the areas of meat packing, farm equipment, education, fabricated metal, and river trade. But after a hard day's work in one of these industries, you may just want to reach for an ice cold beer.

Milwaukee is in a region where the weather is quite changeable. Arctic air masses from Canada bring the coldest winter temperatures, zero degrees or lower. Summer temperatures reach into the 90's but rarely exceed 100 degrees.

General Rankings and Evaluative Comments

- Milwaukee was ranked #175 out of 300 cities by *Money's* 1997 "Survey of the Best Places to Live." Criteria used: health services, crime, economy, housing, education, transportation, weather, leisure and the arts. The city was ranked #177 in 1996 and #123 in 1995.
  Money, July 1997; Money, September 1996; Money, September 1995

- *Ladies Home Journal* ranked America's 200 largest cities based on the qualities women care about most. Milwaukee ranked 78 out of 200. Criteria: low crime rate, good public schools, well-paying jobs, quality health and child care, the presence of women in government, proportion of women-owned businesses, size of the wage gap with men, local economy, divorce rates, the ratio of single men to single women, whether there are laws that require at least the same number of public toilets for women as men, and the probability of good hair days. *Ladies Home Journal, November 1997*

- Milwaukee was ranked #175 out of 219 cities in terms of children's health, safety, and economic well-being. Criteria: total population, percent population change, birth rate, child immunization rate, infant mortality rate, percent low birth weight infants, percent of births to teens, physician-to-population ratio, student-to-teacher ratio, dropout rate, unemployment rate, median family income, percent of children in poverty, violent and property crime rates, number of juvenile arrests for violent crimes as a percent of the total crime index, number of days with pollution standard index (PSI) over 100, pounds toxic releases per 1,000 people and number of superfund sites. *Zero Population Growth, Children's Environmental Index 1997*

- *Yahoo! Internet Life* selected "America's 100 Most Wired Cities & Towns". 50 cities were large and 50 cities were small. Milwaukee ranked 32 out of 50 large cities. Criteria: Internet users per capita, number of networked computers, number of registered domain names, Internet backbone traffic, and the per-capita number of Web sites devoted to each city. *Yahoo! Internet Life, March 1998*

- Milwaukee appeared on *Sales & Marketing Management's* list of the 20 hottest domestic markets to do business in. Rank: 17 out of 20. America's 320 Metropolitan Statistical Areas were ranked based on the market's potential to buy products in certain industries like high-tech, manufacturing, office equipment and business services, as well as population and household income growth. The study had nine criteria in all.

  "Milwaukee is one of the nation's leading manufacturing markets—it ranks third in the percentage (22%) of its workforce in manufacturing. Several downtown renovation and construction projects (a high-tech museum, a performing arts center) were recently completed, adding 3,000 jobs and more than $30 million to the city's economy." *Sales & Marketing Management, January 1998*

- Harley-Davidson, headquartered in Milwaukee, is among the "100 Best Companies to Work for in America." Criteria: trust in management, pride in work/company, camaraderie, company responses to the Hewitt People Practices Inventory, and employee responses to their Great Place to Work survey. The companies also had to be at least 10 years old and have a minimum of 500 employees. *Fortune, January 12, 1998*

- Marquette Medical Systems Inc., headquartered in Milwaukee, is among the "100 Best Companies for Working Mothers." Criteria: pay compared with competition, opportunities for women to advance, support for child care, flexible work schedules and family-friendly benefits. *Working Mother, October 1997*

- According to *Working Mother*, "Governor Tommy Thompson's welfare reform effort, 'Wisconsin Works,' included sweeping changes in the state's child care rules and funding. On the positive side, state funding is increasing by $36 million this year alone, which means all families on the waiting list for child care subsidies have now received them. In 1996-97, the state pumped $89 million in new state money into child care. By 1998, the number of children receiving aid will zoom from the current 17,000 to 60,000. This is a remarkable achievement.

  The state also gave a big one-time boost to efforts to increase supply and quality to the tune of $5 million. That money will translate into more staff for licensing, improved resource and referral services and more grants for caregiver training.

At the same time, however, Wisconsin has created a new class of providers, known as 'provision' caregivers. These providers will not be required to have any training and the state will reimburse them at half the rate it pays those who are certified and have credentials in early education. Many advocates are worried that these policies—paying caregivers less and lowering training standards—could hurt the quality of child care in Wisconsin. (Wisconsin is among the 10 best states for child care.)'' *Working Mother, July/August 1997*

Business Environment

STATE ECONOMY

State Economic Profile

"Wisconsin's economy in general, and manufacturing and wholesale trade in particular, continue to lag the nation....

Slow population growth is taking a serious toll on Wisconsin's labor market. Wisconsin is experiencing its tightest labor market since the late 1970's. Just as in other parts of the Midwest, skilled workers, such as machinists, are in short supply. Also, acute shortages are being felt in many entry-level distribution and retail trade jobs. The more industrialized southeastern MSAs of Wisconsin face tighter labor markets than the rest of Wisconsin. Slower household growth will erode demand for residential construction, eventually stifling the strong job growth that has characterized the construction industry of late.

Wisconsin is making a concerted effort to lighten the residential property tax burden, because differences in Wisconsin's and Minnesota's tax systems encourage people to locate their businesses in Wisconsin and commute from Minnesota. Another popular approach to economic development that Wisconsin is now employing is the use of enterprise development zones.

The outlook for Wisconsin is for moderate growth. Positive demographic trends will support service growth and retail and residential construction over the longer term....Wisconsin will be an average performer through the forecast." *National Association of Realtors, Economic Profiles: The Fifty States, July 1997*

IMPORTS/EXPORTS

Total Export Sales

Area	1993 ($000)	1994 ($000)	1995 ($000)	1996 ($000)	% Chg. 1993-96	% Chg. 1995-96
MSA[1]	2,337,305	2,913,545	3,506,904	3,717,211	59.0	6.0
U.S.	464,858,354	512,415,609	583,030,524	622,827,063	34.0	6.8

Note: (1) Metropolitan Statistical Area - see Appendix A for areas included
Source: U.S. Department of Commerce, International Trade Association, Metropolitan Area Exports: An Export Performance Report on Over 250 U.S. Cities, October 1997

Imports/Exports by Port

Type	Cargo Value			Share of U.S. Total	
	1995 (US$mil.)	1996 (US$mil.)	% Change 1995-1996	1995 (%)	1996 (%)
Imports	120	110	-7.54	0.03	0.03
Exports	87	40	-53.69	0.04	0.02

Source: Global Trade Information Services, WaterBorne Trade Atlas 1997

CITY FINANCES

City Government Finances

Component	FY94 ($000)	FY94 (per capita $)
Revenue	895,259	1,484.10
Expenditure	761,126	1,261.75
Debt Outstanding	559,363	927.28
Cash & Securities	2,406,458	3,989.27

Source: U.S. Bureau of the Census, City Government Finances: 1993-94

City Government Revenue by Source

Source	FY94 ($000)	FY94 (per capita $)	FY94 (%)
From Federal Government	59,792	99.12	6.7
From State Governments	277,946	460.76	31.0
From Local Governments	958	1.59	0.1
Property Taxes	157,585	261.23	17.6
General Sales Taxes	0	0.00	0.0
Selective Sales Taxes	5,175	8.58	0.6
Income Taxes	0	0.00	0.0
Current Charges	83,021	137.63	9.3
Utility/Liquor Store	47,425	78.62	5.3
Employee Retirement[1]	207,087	343.30	23.1
Other	56,270	93.28	6.3

Note: (1) Excludes "city contributions," classified as "nonrevenue," intragovernmental transfers.
Source: U.S. Bureau of the Census, City Government Finances: 1993-94

City Government Expenditures by Function

Function	FY94 ($000)	FY94 (per capita $)	FY94 (%)
Educational Services	21,764	36.08	2.9
Employee Retirement[1]	86,583	143.53	11.4
Environment/Housing	190,029	315.02	25.0
Government Administration	48,523	80.44	6.4
Interest on General Debt	35,057	58.12	4.6
Public Safety	213,156	353.36	28.0
Social Services	14,273	23.66	1.9
Transportation	55,920	92.70	7.3
Utility/Liquor Store	30,296	50.22	4.0
Other	65,525	108.62	8.6

Note: (1) Payments to beneficiaries including withdrawal of contributions.
Source: U.S. Bureau of the Census, City Government Finances: 1993-94

Municipal Bond Ratings

Area	Moody's	S & P
Milwaukee	Aa1	AA+

Note: n/a not available; n/r not rated
Source: Moody's Bond Record, 2/98; Statistical Abstract of the U.S., 1997;
Governing Magazine, 9/97, 3/98

POPULATION

Population Growth

Area	1980	1990	% Chg. 1980-90	July 1996 Estimate	% Chg. 1990-96
City	636,212	628,088	-1.3	590,503	-6.0
MSA[1]	1,397,143	1,432,149	2.5	1,457,655	1.8
U.S.	226,545,805	248,765,170	9.8	265,179,411	6.6

Note: (1) Metropolitan Statistical Area - see Appendix A for areas included
Source: 1980/1990 Census of Housing and Population, Summary Tape File 3C;
Census Bureau Population Estimates

Population Characteristics

Race	City				% Chg. 1980-90	MSA[1]	
	1980		1990			1990	
	Population	%	Population	%		Population	%
White	468,064	73.6	397,827	63.3	-15.0	1,184,263	82.7
Black	147,055	23.1	191,567	30.5	30.3	197,144	13.8
Amer Indian/Esk/Aleut	5,348	0.8	6,016	1.0	12.5	8,138	0.6
Asian/Pacific Islander	4,451	0.7	11,831	1.9	165.8	18,384	1.3
Other	11,294	1.8	20,847	3.3	84.6	24,220	1.7
Hispanic Origin[2]	26,111	4.1	37,420	6.0	43.3	48,276	3.4

Note: (1) Metropolitan Statistical Area - see Appendix A for areas included;
(2) people of Hispanic origin can be of any race
Source: 1980/1990 Census of Housing and Population, Summary Tape File 3C

Ancestry

Area	German	Irish	English	Italian	U.S.	French	Polish	Dutch
City	33.7	8.4	4.1	3.5	1.0	3.1	14.3	1.0
MSA[1]	48.4	11.4	6.7	4.3	1.1	3.9	15.0	1.6
U.S.	23.3	15.6	13.1	5.9	5.3	4.2	3.8	2.5

Note: Figures are percentages and include persons that reported multiple ancestry (eg. if a person reported being Irish and Italian, they were included in both columns); (1) Metropolitan Statistical Area - see Appendix A for areas included
Source: 1990 Census of Population and Housing, Summary Tape File 3C

Age

Area	Median Age (Years)	Age Distribution (%)						
		Under 5	Under 18	18-24	25-44	45-64	65+	80+
City	30.3	8.6	27.5	12.0	32.6	15.5	12.4	3.1
MSA[1]	32.7	7.7	26.3	9.9	32.9	18.4	12.5	3.0
U.S.	32.9	7.3	25.6	10.5	32.6	18.7	12.5	2.8

Note: (1) Metropolitan Statistical Area - see Appendix A for areas included
Source: 1990 Census of Population and Housing, Summary Tape File 3C

Male/Female Ratio

Area	Number of males per 100 females (all ages)	Number of males per 100 females (18 years old+)
City	89.6	84.8
MSA[1]	92.9	88.8
U.S.	95.0	91.9

Note: (1) Metropolitan Statistical Area - see Appendix A for areas included
Source: 1990 Census of Population, General Population Characteristics

INCOME

Per Capita/Median/Average Income

Area	Per Capita ($)	Median Household ($)	Average Household ($)
City	11,106	23,627	28,415
MSA[1]	14,785	32,316	38,958
U.S.	14,420	30,056	38,453

Note: all figures are for 1989; (1) Metropolitan Statistical Area - see Appendix A for areas included
Source: 1990 Census of Population and Housing, Summary Tape File 3C

Household Income Distribution by Race

Income ($)	City (%)					U.S. (%)				
	Total	White	Black	Other	Hisp.[1]	Total	White	Black	Other	Hisp.[1]
Less than 5,000	6.3	4.1	12.0	10.2	10.1	6.2	4.8	15.2	8.6	8.8
5,000 - 9,999	14.9	11.4	24.1	20.1	19.0	9.3	8.6	14.2	9.9	11.1
10,000 - 14,999	11.2	10.6	12.5	13.2	11.8	8.8	8.5	11.0	9.8	11.0
15,000 - 24,999	20.0	20.4	18.8	19.7	18.9	17.5	17.3	18.9	18.5	20.5
25,000 - 34,999	16.6	18.1	12.4	15.7	15.5	15.8	16.1	14.2	15.4	16.4
35,000 - 49,999	17.5	19.9	11.3	13.7	16.5	17.9	18.6	13.3	16.1	16.0
50,000 - 74,999	10.6	12.0	7.3	5.8	6.4	15.0	15.8	9.3	13.4	11.1
75,000 - 99,999	2.1	2.4	1.2	1.1	1.2	5.1	5.5	2.6	4.7	3.1
100,000+	1.0	1.2	0.4	0.5	0.5	4.4	4.8	1.3	3.7	1.9

Note: all figures are for 1989; (1) people of Hispanic origin can be of any race
Source: 1990 Census of Population and Housing, Summary Tape File 3C

Effective Buying Income

Area	Per Capita ($)	Median Household ($)	Average Household ($)
City	12,791	27,645	33,288
MSA[1]	17,074	38,746	45,403
U.S.	15,444	33,201	41,849

Note: data as of 1/1/97; (1) Metropolitan Statistical Area - see Appendix A for areas included
Source: Standard Rate & Data Service, Newspaper Advertising Source, 2/98

Effective Household Buying Income Distribution

Area	% of Households Earning						
	$10,000 -$19,999	$20,000 -$34,999	$35,000 -$49,999	$50,000 -$74,999	$75,000 -$99,000	$100,000 -$124,999	$125,000 and up
City	21.0	24.9	18.3	15.5	3.5	0.7	0.5
MSA[1]	14.5	21.4	19.7	22.9	7.8	2.2	2.4
U.S.	16.5	23.4	18.3	18.2	6.4	2.1	2.4

Note: data as of 1/1/97; (1) Metropolitan Statistical Area - see Appendix A for areas included
Source: Standard Rate & Data Service, Newspaper Advertising Source, 2/98

Poverty Rates by Race and Age

Area	Total (%)	By Race (%)				By Age (%)		
		White	Black	Other	Hisp.[2]	Under 5 years old	Under 18 years old	65 years and over
City	22.2	10.8	41.9	40.2	35.5	41.5	37.8	10.0
MSA[1]	11.6	5.8	41.3	32.8	30.3	22.5	19.4	7.1
U.S.	13.1	9.8	29.5	23.1	25.3	20.1	18.3	12.8

Note: figures show the percent of people living below the poverty line in 1989. The average poverty
threshold was $12,674 for a family of four in 1989; (1) Metropolitan Statistical Area - see Appendix A
for areas included; (2) people of Hispanic origin can be of any race
Source: 1990 Census of Population and Housing, Summary Tape File 3C

EMPLOYMENT

Labor Force and Employment

Area	Civilian Labor Force			Workers Employed		
	Dec. '95	Dec. '96	% Chg.	Dec. '95	Dec. '96	% Chg.
City	303,317	304,693	0.5	290,767	292,703	0.7
MSA[1]	808,675	812,953	0.5	786,315	791,550	0.7
U.S.	134,583,000	136,742,000	1.6	127,903,000	130,785,000	2.3

Note: Data is not seasonally adjusted and covers workers 16 years of age and older;
(1) Metropolitan Statistical Area - see Appendix A for areas included
Source: Bureau of Labor Statistics, http://stats.bls.gov

Unemployment Rate

Area	1997											
	Jan.	Feb.	Mar.	Apr.	May	Jun.	Jul.	Aug.	Sep.	Oct.	Nov.	Dec.
City	5.5	5.7	5.0	4.9	5.2	5.9	6.2	5.6	5.4	4.8	4.6	3.9
MSA[1]	3.6	3.7	3.5	3.3	3.5	3.9	4.0	3.6	3.5	3.1	3.0	2.6
U.S.	5.9	5.7	5.5	4.8	4.7	5.2	5.0	4.8	4.7	4.4	4.3	4.4

Note: Data is not seasonally adjusted and covers workers 16 years of age and older; All figures are percentages; (1) Metropolitan Statistical Area - see Appendix A for areas included
Source: Bureau of Labor Statistics, http://stats.bls.gov

Employment by Industry

Sector	MSA[1]		U.S.
	Number of Employees	Percent of Total	Percent of Total
Services	262,300	30.9	29.0
Retail Trade	134,400	15.9	18.5
Government	92,000	10.9	16.1
Manufacturing	178,500	21.1	15.0
Finance/Insurance/Real Estate	58,500	6.9	5.7
Wholesale Trade	50,700	6.0	5.4
Transportation/Public Utilities	40,400	4.8	5.3
Construction/Mining	31,100	3.7	5.0

Note: Figures cover non-farm employment as of 12/97 and are not seasonally adjusted; (1) Metropolitan Statistical Area - see Appendix A for areas included
Source: Bureau of Labor Statistics, http://stats.bls.gov

Employment by Occupation

Occupation Category	City (%)	MSA[1] (%)	U.S. (%)
White Collar	53.9	59.7	58.1
Executive/Admin./Management	9.2	12.3	12.3
Professional	12.1	14.3	14.1
Technical & Related Support	3.5	3.6	3.7
Sales	10.3	12.0	11.8
Administrative Support/Clerical	18.8	17.5	16.3
Blue Collar	29.1	26.9	26.2
Precision Production/Craft/Repair	10.2	11.2	11.3
Machine Operators/Assem./Insp.	10.2	8.6	6.8
Transportation/Material Movers	4.3	3.6	4.1
Cleaners/Helpers/Laborers	4.4	3.5	3.9
Services	16.4	12.5	13.2
Farming/Forestry/Fishing	0.6	0.8	2.5

Note: figures cover employed persons 16 years old and over; (1) Metropolitan Statistical Area - see Appendix A for areas included
Source: 1990 Census of Population and Housing, Summary Tape File 3C

Occupational Employment Projections: 1994 - 2005

Occupations Expected to have the Largest Job Growth (ranked by numerical growth)	Fast-Growing Occupations (ranked by percent growth)
1. Waiters & waitresses	1. Computer engineers
2. General managers & top executives	2. Systems analysts
3. Cashiers	3. Electronic pagination systems workers
4. Salespersons, retail	4. Personal and home care aides
5. Janitors/cleaners/maids, ex. priv. hshld.	5. Manicurists
6. Truck drivers, heavy & light	6. Credit authorizers
7. Systems analysts	7. Computer scientists
8. Teachers, secondary school	8. Pressers, hand
9. Marketing & sales, supervisors	9. Geologists/geophysicists/oceanographers
10. Registered nurses	10. Home health aides

Projections cover Wisconsin.
Source: U.S. Department of Labor, Employment and Training Administration, America's Labor Market Information System (ALMIS)

Average Wages

Occupation	Wage	Occupation	Wage
Professional/Technical/Clerical	$/Week	**Health/Protective Services**	$/Week
Accountants III	811	Corrections Officers	528
Attorneys III	1,339	Firefighters	739
Budget Analysts III	-	Nurses, Licensed Practical II	-
Buyers/Contracting Specialists II	681	Nurses, Registered II	-
Clerks, Accounting III	446	Nursing Assistants II	-
Clerks, General III	424	Police Officers I	743
Computer Operators II	460	**Hourly Workers**	$/Hour
Computer Programmers II	662	Forklift Operators	13.87
Drafters II	-	General Maintenance Workers	11.35
Engineering Technicians III	647	Guards I	7.30
Engineering Technicians, Civil III	716	Janitors	8.32
Engineers III	988	Maintenance Electricians	20.27
Key Entry Operators I	-	Maintenance Electronics Techs II	18.25
Personnel Assistants III	557	Maintenance Machinists	-
Personnel Specialists III	820	Maintenance Mechanics, Machinery	17.72
Secretaries III	542	Material Handling Laborers	9.56
Switchboard Operator-Receptionist	367	Motor Vehicle Mechanics	16.54
Systems Analysts II	940	Shipping/Receiving Clerks	11.67
Systems Analysts Supervisor/Mgr II	-	Tool and Die Makers	19.61
Tax Collectors II	-	Truckdrivers, Tractor Trailer	16.94
Word Processors II	516	Warehouse Specialists	-

Note: Wage data includes full-time workers only for 9/96 and cover the Metropolitan Statistical Area (see Appendix A for areas included). Dashes indicate that data was not available.
Source: Bureau of Labor Statistics, Occupational Compensation Survey, 2/97

TAXES

Major State and Local Tax Rates

State Corp. Income (%)	State Personal Income (%)	Residential Property (effective rate per $100)	Sales & Use State (%)	Sales & Use Local (%)	State Gasoline (cents/ gallon)	State Cigarette (cents/ 20-pack)
7.9[a]	4.9 - 6.93	3.32	5.0	0.5	24.8	59

Note: Personal/corporate income tax rates as of 1/97. Sales, gasoline and cigarette tax rates as of 1/98; (a) Plus a surtax set annually by the Dept. of Revenue to finance a special recycling fund
Source: Federation of Tax Administrators, www.taxadmin.org; Washington D.C. Department of Finance and Revenue, Tax Rates and Tax Burdens in the District of Columbia: A Nationwide Comparison, June 1997; Chamber of Commerce

Total Taxes Per Capita and as a Percent of Income

Area	Per Capita Income ($)	Per Capita Taxes ($)			Taxes as Pct. of Income (%)		
		Total	Federal	State/Local	Total	Federal	State/Local
Wisconsin	25,105	9,165	5,825	3,340	36.5	23.2	13.3
U.S.	26,187	9,205	6,127	3,078	35.2	23.4	11.8

Note: Figures are for 1997
Source: Tax Foundation, Web Site, www.taxfoundation.org

Estimated Tax Burden

Area	State Income	Local Income	Property	Sales	Total
Milwaukee	3,664	0	5,850	468	9,982

Note: The numbers are estimates of taxes paid by a married couple with two kids and annual earnings of $65,000. Sales tax estimates assume they spend average amounts on food, clothing, household goods and gasoline. Property tax estimates assume they live in a $225,000 home.
Source: Kiplinger's Personal Finance Magazine, June 1997

COMMERCIAL REAL ESTATE

Office Market

Class/Location	Total Space (sq. ft.)	Vacant Space (sq. ft.)	Vac. Rate (%)	Under Constr. (sq. ft.)	Net Absorp. (sq. ft.)	Rental Rates ($/sq.ft./yr.)
Ciass A						
CBD	4,409,560	385,572	8.7	n/a	11,288	18.00-25.00
Outside CBD	7,273,550	363,677	5.0	n/a	199,843	15.00-23.00
Class B						
CBD	8,820,440	1,499,474	17.0	n/a	105,846	15.00-20.00
Outside CBD	4,849,034	533,393	11.0	n/a	310,251	10.00-16.00

Note: Data as of 10/97 and covers Milwaukee; CBD = Central Business District; n/a not available;
Source: Society of Industrial and Office Realtors, 1998 Comparative Statistics of Industrial and Office Real Estate Markets

"Office development and redevelopment are heavily dependent on local government tax incentive programs. Without them, nothing will take place. Backfilling is beginning. Regional developer Opus is redeveloping the campus of the former St. Charles School. Construction financing has become both more abundant and more reasonable, but it is only available with significant pre-leasing, at least 30 to 50 percent. Much of the new leasing is still a game of musical chairs. Even then, the western Interstate 94 Corridor is the only location where new office construction is taking place. With replacement costs still higher than sales prices, speculative building is not a threat. Foreign investors have not yet ventured into Milwaukee."
Society of Industrial and Office Realtors, 1998 Comparative Statistics of Industrial and Office Real Estate Markets

Industrial Market

Location	Total Space (sq. ft.)	Vacant Space (sq. ft.)	Vac. Rate (%)	Under Constr. (sq. ft.)	Net Absorp. (sq. ft.)	Lease ($/sq.ft./yr.)
Central City	n/a	n/a	n/a	n/a	n/a	n/a
Suburban	201,000,000	7,035,000	3.5	250,000	1,540,000	2.50-6.50

Note: Data as of 10/97 and covers Milwaukee; n/a not available
Source: Society of Industrial and Office Realtors, 1998 Comparative Statistics of Industrial and Office Real Estate Markets

"Speculative construction is expected to decline during 1998 with about 250,000 sq. ft. of flex space built on scattered sites in the four county area. Construction of warehousing and distribution facilities is anticipated to increase sightly during 1998 with most of the activity in the build-to-suit market. Following the retreat in 1997, net absorption should pick up during 1998 but not reach the high levels of 1996. Absorption of warehousing and distribution space is expected to rise about six to ten percent with smaller increases in manufacturing and

High-Tech/R&D space. With absorption running ahead of new construction again during 1998 vacancy rates will fall further. Very low vacancy rates are expected to lead to increases in lease and sale prices during 1998." *Society of Industrial and Office Realtors, 1998 Comparative Statistics of Industrial and Office Real Estate Markets*

COMMERCIAL UTILITIES

Typical Monthly Electric Bills

Area	Commercial Service ($/month)		Industrial Service ($/month)	
	12 kW demand 1,500 kWh	100 kW demand 30,000 kWh	1,000 kW demand 400,000 kWh	20,000 kW demand 10,000,000 kWh
City	102	1,765	17,774	393,505
U.S.	162	2,360	25,590	545,677

Note: Based on rates in effect July 1, 1997
Source: Edison Electric Institute, Typical Residential, Commercial and Industrial Bills, Summer 1997

TRANSPORTATION

Transportation Statistics

Avg. travel time to work (min.)	20.1
Interstate highways	I-43; I-94
Bus lines	
In-city	Milwaukee County TS, 491 vehicles
Inter-city	5
Passenger air service	
Airport	General Mitchell International
Airlines	17
Aircraft departures	43,810 (1995)
Enplaned passengers	2,322,427 (1995)
Rail service	Amtrak
Motor freight carriers	500
Major waterways/ports	Port of Milwaukee; Lake Michigan; Milwaukee River

Source: OAG, Business Travel Planner, Summer 1997; Editor & Publisher Market Guide, 1998; FAA Airport Activity Statistics, 1996; Amtrak National Time Table, Northeast Timetable, Fall/Winter 1997-98; 1990 Census of Population and Housing, STF 3C; Chamber of Commerce/Economic Development 1997; Jane's Urban Transport Systems 1997-98; Transit Fact Book 1997

Means of Transportation to Work

Area	Car/Truck/Van		Public Transportation			Bicycle	Walked	Other Means	Worked at Home
	Drove Alone	Car-pooled	Bus	Subway	Railroad				
City	67.2	13.2	10.8	0.0	0.0	0.3	6.0	0.8	1.6
MSA[1]	76.7	11.0	5.1	0.0	0.0	0.3	4.0	0.6	2.2
U.S.	73.2	13.4	3.0	1.5	0.5	0.4	3.9	1.2	3.0

Note: figures shown are percentages and only include workers 16 years old and over;
(1) Metropolitan Statistical Area - see Appendix A for areas included
Source: 1990 Census of Population and Housing, Summary Tape File 3C

BUSINESSES

Major Business Headquarters

Company Name	1997 Rankings	
	Fortune 500	Forbes 500
Grede Foundries	-	452
Johnson Controls	143	-
Journal Communications	-	336
Manpower	239	-
Northwestern Mutual Life Ins.	111	-

Note: Companies listed are located in the city; Dashes indicate no ranking
Fortune 500: companies that produce a 10-K are ranked 1 - 500 based on 1996 revenue
Forbes 500: private companies are ranked 1 - 500 based on 1996 revenue
Source: Forbes 12/1/97; Fortune 4/28/97

Women-Owned Businesses: Number, Employment, Sales and Share

Area	Women-Owned Businesses in 1996				Share of Women-Owned Businesses in 1996	
	Number	Employment	Sales ($000)	Rank[2]	Percent (%)	Rank[3]
MSA[1]	35,100	90,800	10,698,800	41	36.0	32

Note: (1) Metropolitan Statistical Area - see Appendix A for areas included; (2) Calculated on an averaging of number of businesses, employment and sales and ranges from 1 to 50 where 1 is best; (3) Ranges from 1 to 50 where 1 is best
Source: The National Foundation for Women Business Owners, 1996 Facts on Women-Owned Businesses: Trends in the Top 50 Metropolitan Areas, March 26, 1997

Women-Owned Businesses: Growth

Area	Growth in Women-Owned Businesses (% change from 1987 to 1996)				Relative Growth in the Number of Women-Owned and All Businesses (% change from 1987 to 1996)			
	Num.	Empl.	Sales	Rank[2]	Women-Owned	All Firms	Absolute Difference	Relative Difference
MSA[1]	67.2	146.1	174.8	47	67.2	47.1	20.1	1.4:1

Note: (1) Metropolitan Statistical Area - see Appendix A for areas included; (2) Calculated on an averaging of the percent growth of number of businesses, employment and sales and ranges from 1 to 50 where 1 is best
Source: The National Foundation for Women Business Owners, 1996 Facts on Women-Owned Businesses: Trends in the Top 50 Metropolitan Areas, March 26, 1997

Minority Business Opportunity

Milwaukee is home to one company which is on the Black Enterprise Industrial/Service 100 list (largest based on gross sales): V&J Foods Inc. (Burger King franchisee). Criteria: 1) operational in previous calendar year; 2) at least 51% black-owned; 3) manufactures/owns the product it sells or provides industrial or consumer services. Brokerages, real estate firms and firms that provide professional services are not eligible. *Black Enterprise, July 1997*

One of the 500 largest Hispanic-owned companies in the U.S. are located in Milwaukee. *Hispanic Business, June 1997*

Small Business Opportunity

Milwaukee was included among *Entrepreneur* magazines listing of the "20 Best Cities for Small Business." It was ranked #13 among large metro areas. Criteria: risk of failure, business performance, economic growth, affordability and state attitude towards business. *Entrepreneur, 10/97*

According to *Forbes*, Milwaukee is home to one of America's 200 best small companies: Strattec Security. Criteria: companies must be publicly traded, U.S.-based corporations with latest 12-month sales of between $5 and $350 million. Earnings must be at least $1 million for the 12-month period. Limited partnerships, REITs and closed-end mutual funds were not considered. Banks, S&Ls and electric utilities were not included. *Forbes, November 3, 1997*

HOTELS & MOTELS

Hotels/Motels

Area	Hotels/ Motels	Rooms	Luxury-Level Hotels/Motels		Average Minimum Rates ($)		
			♦♦♦♦	♦♦♦♦♦	♦♦	♦♦♦	♦♦♦♦
City	18	3,213	3	0	61	83	161
Airport	13	1,928	0	0	n/a	n/a	n/a
Suburbs	35	4,262	0	0	n/a	n/a	n/a
Total	66	9,403	3	0	n/a	n/a	n/a

Note: n/a not available; Classifications range from one diamond (budget properties with basic amenities) to five diamond (luxury properties with the finest service, rooms and facilities).
Source: OAG, Business Travel Planner, Summer 1997

CONVENTION CENTERS

Major Convention Centers

Center Name	Meeting Rooms	Exhibit Space (sf)
Hyatt Regency Milwaukee	19	16,052
Wisconsin Center	42	250,000
Performing Arts Center	8	9,552

Source: Trade Shows Worldwide 1997

Living Environment

COST OF LIVING

Cost of Living Index

Composite Index	Housing	Utilities	Groceries	Health Care	Trans-portation	Misc. Goods/ Services
103.9	124.0	81.6	101.9	102.2	101.7	94.0

Note: U.S. = 100; Figures are for the Metropolitan Statistical Area - see Appendix A for areas included
Source: ACCRA, Cost of Living Index, 3rd Quarter 1997

HOUSING

Median Home Prices and Housing Affordability

Area	Median Price[2] 3rd Qtr. 1997 ($)	HOI[3] 3rd Qtr. 1997	Afford-ability Rank[4]
MSA[1]	117,000	60.3	145
U.S.	127,000	63.7	–

Note: (1) Metropolitan Statistical Area - see Appendix A for areas included; (2) U.S. figures calculated from the sales of 625,000 new and existing homes in 195 markets; (3) Housing Opportunity Index - percent of homes sold that were within the reach of the median income household at the prevailing mortgage interest rate; (4) Rank is from 1-195 with 1 being most affordable
Source: National Association of Home Builders, Housing Opportunity Index, 3rd Quarter 1997

It is projected that the median price of existing single-family homes in the metro area will increase by 7.9% in 1998. Nationwide, home prices are projected to increase 6.6%.
Kiplinger's Personal Finance Magazine, January 1998

Average New Home Price

Area	Price ($)
MSA[1]	168,700
U.S.	135,710

Note: Figures are based on a new home with 1,800 sq. ft. of living area on an 8,000 sq. ft. lot; (1) Metropolitan Statistical Area - see Appendix A for areas included
Source: ACCRA, Cost of Living Index, 3rd Quarter 1997

Average Apartment Rent

Area	Rent ($/mth)
MSA[1]	684
U.S.	569

Note: Figures are based on an unfurnished two bedroom, 1-1/2 or 2 bath apartment, approximately 950 sq. ft. in size, excluding all utilities except water; (1) Metropolitan Statistical Area - see Appendix A for areas included
Source: ACCRA, Cost of Living Index, 3rd Quarter 1997

RESIDENTIAL UTILITIES

Average Residential Utility Costs

Area	All Electric ($/mth)	Part Electric ($/mth)	Other Energy ($/mth)	Phone ($/mth)
MSA[1]	–	41.09	42.46	15.90
U.S.	109.40	55.25	43.64	19.48

Note: (1) (1) Metropolitan Statistical Area - see Appendix A for areas included
Source: ACCRA, Cost of Living Index, 3rd Quarter 1997

HEALTH CARE

Average Health Care Costs

Area	Hospital ($/day)	Doctor ($/visit)	Dentist ($/visit)
MSA[1]	386.10	54.40	59.00
U.S.	392.91	48.76	60.84

Note: Hospital - based on a semi-private room. Doctor - based on a general practitioner's routine exam of an established patient. Dentist - based on adult teeth cleaning and periodic oral exam; (1) Metropolitan Statistical Area - see Appendix A for areas included
Source: ACCRA, Cost of Living Index, 3rd Quarter 1997

Distribution of Office-Based Physicians

Area	Family/Gen. Practitioners	Specialists Medical	Surgical	Other
MSA[1]	373	1,033	738	928

Note: Data as of 12/31/96; (1) Metropolitan Statistical Area - see Appendix A for areas included
Source: American Medical Assn., Physician Characteristics & Distribution in the U.S., 1997-1998

Hospitals

Milwaukee has 11 general medical and surgical hospitals, 3 psychiatric, 1 rehabilitation, 1 alcoholism and other chemical dependency, 1 children's general. *AHA Guide to the Healthcare Field 1997-98*

EDUCATION

Public School District Statistics

District Name	Num. Sch.	Enroll.	Classroom Teachers[1]	Pupils per Teacher	Minority Pupils (%)	Current Exp.[2] ($/pupil)
Fox Point J2 Sch Dist	2	935	65	14.4	n/a	n/a
Glendale-River Hills Sch Dist	3	1,257	81	15.5	n/a	n/a
Maple Dale-Indian Hill Sch Dis	2	637	45	14.2	n/a	n/a
Milwaukee Sch Dist	155	98,378	n/a	n/a	76.4	6,978

Note: Data covers the 1995-1996 school year unless otherwise noted; (1) Excludes teachers reported as working in school district offices rather than in schools; (2) Based on 1993-94 enrollment collected by the Census Bureau, not the enrollment figure shown in column 3; SD = School District; ISD = Independent School District; n/a not available
Source: National Center for Education Statistics, Common Core of Data Survey; Bureau of the Census

Educational Quality

School District	Education Quotient[1]	Graduate Outcome[2]	Community Index[3]	Resource Index[4]
Milwaukee	95.0	59.0	81.0	146.0

Note: Nearly 1,000 secondary school districts were rated in terms of educational quality. The scores range from a low of 50 to a high of 150; (1) Average of the Graduate Outcome, Community and Resource indexes; (2) Based on graduation rates and college board scores (SAT/ACT); (3) Based on the surrounding community's average level of education and the area's average income level; (4) Based on teacher salaries, per-pupil expenditures and student-teacher ratios.
Source: Expansion Management, Ratings Issue 1997

Educational Attainment by Race

Area	High School Graduate (%) Total	White	Black	Other	Hisp.[2]	Bachelor's Degree (%) Total	White	Black	Other	Hisp.[2]
City	71.5	76.3	60.2	54.0	46.9	14.8	17.6	6.9	13.2	6.2
MSA[1]	79.7	82.5	60.7	60.5	51.7	21.3	23.0	7.6	19.4	8.5
U.S.	75.2	77.9	63.1	60.4	49.8	20.3	21.5	11.4	19.4	9.2

Note: figures shown cover persons 25 years old and over; (1) Metropolitan Statistical Area - see Appendix A for areas included; (2) people of Hispanic origin can be of any race
Source: 1990 Census of Population and Housing, Summary Tape File 3C

School Enrollment by Type

Area	Preprimary				Elementary/High School			
	Public		Private		Public		Private	
	Enrollment	%	Enrollment	%	Enrollment	%	Enrollment	%
City	6,616	66.3	3,359	33.7	92,372	80.6	22,277	19.4
MSA[1]	15,931	56.8	12,092	43.2	204,342	81.5	46,314	18.5
U.S.	2,679,029	59.5	1,824,256	40.5	38,379,689	90.2	4,187,099	9.8

Note: figures shown cover persons 3 years old and over;
(1) Metropolitan Statistical Area - see Appendix A for areas included
Source: 1990 Census of Population and Housing, Summary Tape File 3C

School Enrollment by Race

Area	Preprimary (%)				Elementary/High School (%)			
	White	Black	Other	Hisp.[1]	White	Black	Other	Hisp.[1]
City	54.3	38.4	7.3	7.2	43.2	47.0	9.8	10.0
MSA[2]	82.1	14.0	3.9	3.9	72.3	22.0	5.6	5.7
U.S.	80.4	12.5	7.1	7.8	74.1	15.6	10.3	12.5

Note: figures shown cover persons 3 years old and over; (1) people of Hispanic origin can be of any race; (2) Metropolitan Statistical Area - see Appendix A for areas included
Source: 1990 Census of Population and Housing, Summary Tape File 3C

SAT/ACT Scores

Area/District	1997 SAT				1997 ACT	
	Percent of Graduates Tested (%)	Average Math Score	Average Verbal Score	Average Combined Score	Percent of Graduates Tested (%)	Average Composite Score
Milwaukee PS	7	516	518	1,034	50	18.9
State	7	590	579	1,169	64	22.3
U.S.	42	511	505	1,016	36	21.0

Note: Math and verbal SAT scores are out of a possible 800; ACT scores are out of a possible 36
Caution: Comparing or ranking states/cities on the basis of SAT/ACT scores alone is invalid and strongly discouraged by the The College Board and The American College Testing Program as students who take the tests are self-selected and do not represent the entire student population.
Source: Milwaukee Public Schools, Division of Curriculum & Instruction, 1997; American College Testing Program, 1997; College Board, 1997

Classroom Teacher Salaries in Public Schools

District	B.A. Degree		M.A. Degree		Ph.D. Degree	
	Min. ($)	Max ($)	Min. ($)	Max. ($)	Min. ($)	Max. ($)
Milwaukee	24,684	42,820	27,893	48,660	31,361	54,001
Average[1]	26,120	39,270	28,175	44,667	31,643	49,825

Note: Salaries are for 1996-1997; (1) Based on all school districts covered
Source: American Federation of Teachers (unpublished data)

Higher Education

Two-Year Colleges		Four-Year Colleges		Medical Schools	Law Schools	Voc/ Tech
Public	Private	Public	Private			
1	1	1	8	1	1	19

Source: College Blue Book, Occupational Education 1997; Medical School Admission Requirements, 1998-99; Peterson's Guide to Two-Year Colleges, 1997; Peterson's Guide to Four-Year Colleges, 1997; Barron's Guide to Law Schools 1997

MAJOR EMPLOYERS

Major Employers

Allen-Bradley Co. (electronic equipment)	Briggs & Stratton Corp. (internal combustion engines)
Columbia Health System	Firstar Bank
Fleet Mortgage Corp.	Froedtert Memorial Lutheran Hospital
Harnischfeger Corp. (construction machinery)	Journal/Sentinel
Master Lock Co.	Miller Brewing
Northwestern Mutual Life	St. Francis Hospital
St. Joseph's Hospital of the Franciscan Sisters	St. Luke's Medical Center
Time Insurance	West Allis Memorial Hospital
Children's Health Systems of Wisconsin	Falk Corp. (speed changers)
Wicor (natural gas)	

Note: companies listed are located in the city
Source: Dun's Business Rankings 1997; Ward's Business Directory, 1997

PUBLIC SAFETY

Crime Rate

Area	All Crimes	Violent Crimes				Property Crimes		
		Murder	Forcible Rape	Robbery	Aggrav. Assault	Burglary	Larceny -Theft	Motor Vehicle Theft
City	7,912.6	20.7	44.8	534.7	352.4	1,215.4	4,137.5	1,607.1
Suburbs[1]	3,189.9	1.0	9.6	41.7	66.1	378.7	2,489.6	203.3
MSA[2]	5,206.8	9.4	24.7	252.2	188.4	736.0	3,193.4	802.8
U.S.	5,078.9	7.4	36.1	202.4	388.2	943.0	2,975.9	525.9

Note: Crime rate is the number of crimes per 100,000 pop.; (1) defined as all areas within the MSA but located outside the central city; (2) Metropolitan Statistical Area - see Appendix A for areas incl.
Source: FBI Uniform Crime Reports 1996

RECREATION

Culture and Recreation

Museums	Symphony Orchestras	Opera Companies	Dance Companies	Professional Theatres	Zoos	Pro Sports Teams
11	2	2	3	6	1	2

Source: International Directory of the Performing Arts, 1996; Official Museum Directory, 1998; Chamber of Commerce/Economic Development 1997

Library System

The Milwaukee Public Library has 12 branches, holdings of 2,121,280 volumes and a budget of $19,508,502 (1994). *American Library Directory, 1997-1998*

MEDIA

Newspapers

Name	Type	Freq.	Distribution	Circulation
Catholic Herald	Religious	1x/wk	Area	27,400
City Edition	General	1x/wk	Local	35,000
The Irish American Post	n/a	6x/yr	National	10,000
Milwaukee Community Journal	Black	2x/wk	Local	62,000
Milwaukee Courier	Black	1x/wk	Local	15,000
Milwaukee Journal-Sentinel	n/a	7x/wk	Area	320,000
Milwaukee Spanish Tribune	Hispanic	1x/mo	Area	10,500
The Milwaukee Times	Black	1x/wk	Local	15,000
Shepherd Express	General	1x/wk	Area	58,000
The Spanish Times	Hispanic	1x/wk	Area	20,000
The Weekend	Black	1x/wk	Local	22,000

Note: Includes newspapers with circulations of 10,000 or more located in the city; n/a not available
Source: Burrelle's Media Directory, 1998 Edition

AM Radio Stations

Call Letters	Freq. (kHz)	Target Audience	Station Format	Music Format
WTMJ	620	General	N/S/T	n/a
WVCY	690	Religious	n/a	n/a
WMUR	750	n/a	M/T	Alternative/Urban Contemporary
WNOV	860	n/a	M	Christian/R&B
WOKY	920	General	M/N	Adult Standards/Big Band/MOR
WISN	1130	Men	N/S/T	n/a
WEMP	1250	General	M	Oldies
WJYI	1340	General	M	Christian
WGLB	1560	General	M/N/S/T	Adult Contemporary/Jazz

Note: Stations included broadcast in the Milwaukee metro area; n/a not available
Station Format: E = Educational; M = Music; N = News; S = Sports; T = Talk
Music Format: AOR = Album Oriented Rock; MOR = Middle-of-the-Road
Source: Burrelle's Media Directory, 1998 Edition

FM Radio Stations

Call Letters	Freq. (mHz)	Target Audience	Station Format	Music Format
WMWK	88.1	n/a	E/M/N/T	Christian
WUWM	89.7	General	M/N	Alternative
WHAD	90.7	n/a	E/T	n/a
WMSE	91.7	Black/Hisp	M	Alternative/Big Band/R&B/Spanish/Urban Contemporary
WJZI	93.3	General	M	AOR
WKTI	94.5	General	M	Adult Contemporary
WZTR	95.7	General	M	Oldies
WKLH	96.5	General	M/N/S	Classic Rock
WLTQ	97.3	General	M	Adult Contemporary
WFMR	98.3	General	M/N	Classical
WVCX	98.9	General	M/N/T	Christian
WMYX	99.1	General	M	Adult Contemporary
WKKV	100.7	General	M	Urban Contemporary
KVCX	101.5	General	E/M/N/T	Christian
WLUM	102.1	General	M/N/S	Alternative
WLZR	102.9	n/a	M/N	AOR
WAMG	103.7	General	M/N	Adult Contemporary
WMIL	106.1	General	M/N	Country
WFMI	106.9	General	M/N	Adult Contemporary/Jazz
WVCY	107.7	General	E/M/N/S/T	Christian

Note: Stations included broadcast in the Milwaukee metro area; n/a not available
Station Format: E = Educational; M = Music; N = News; S = Sports; T = Talk
Music Format: AOR = Album Oriented Rock; MOR = Middle-of-the-Road
Source: Burrelle's Media Directory, 1998 Edition

Television Stations

Name	Ch.	Affiliation	Type	Owner
WTMJ	4	NBC	Commercial	Journal Communications Inc.
WITI	6	Fox	Commercial	Fox Television Stations Inc.
WMVS	10	PBS	Public	Milwaukee Area Technical College
WISN	12	ABC	Commercial	Hearst Argyle TV Inc.
WVTV	18	WB	Commercial	Glencairn Ltd.
WCGV	24	UPN	Commercial	Sinclair Broadcast Group
WVCY	30	n/a	Non-Commercial	VCY/America Inc.
WMVT	36	PBS	Public	Milwaukee Area Technical College
WJJA	49	n/a	Commercial	TV 49 Inc.
WDJT	58	CBS	Commercial	Weigel Broadcasting Company

Note: Stations included broadcast in the Milwaukee metro area
Source: Burrelle's Media Directory, 1998 Edition

CLIMATE

Average and Extreme Temperatures

Temperature	Jan	Feb	Mar	Apr	May	Jun	Jul	Aug	Sep	Oct	Nov	Dec	Ann
Extreme High (°F)	60	65	82	91	92	101	101	103	98	89	77	63	103
Average High (°F)	27	31	40	54	65	76	80	79	71	60	45	32	55
Average Temp. (°F)	20	24	33	45	55	66	71	70	62	51	38	25	47
Average Low (°F)	12	16	26	36	45	55	62	61	53	42	30	18	38
Extreme Low (°F)	-26	-19	-10	12	21	36	40	44	28	18	-5	-20	-26

Note: Figures cover the years 1948-1990
Source: National Climatic Data Center, International Station Meteorological Climate Summary, 3/95

Average Precipitation/Snowfall/Humidity

Precip./Humidity	Jan	Feb	Mar	Apr	May	Jun	Jul	Aug	Sep	Oct	Nov	Dec	Ann
Avg. Precip. (in.)	1.6	1.4	2.6	3.3	2.9	3.4	3.6	3.4	2.9	2.3	2.3	2.2	32.0
Avg. Snowfall (in.)	13	10	9	2	Tr	0	0	0	0	Tr	3	11	49
Avg. Rel. Hum. 6am (%)	76	77	78	78	77	79	82	86	86	82	80	80	80
Avg. Rel. Hum. 3pm (%)	68	66	64	58	58	58	59	62	61	61	66	70	63

Note: Figures cover the years 1948-1990; Tr = Trace amounts (<0.05 in. of rain; <0.5 in. of snow)
Source: National Climatic Data Center, International Station Meteorological Climate Summary, 3/95

Weather Conditions

Temperature			Daytime Sky			Precipitation		
5°F & below	32°F & below	90°F & above	Clear	Partly cloudy	Cloudy	0.01 inch or more precip.	0.1 inch or more snow/ice	Thunder-storms
22	141	10	90	118	157	126	38	35

Note: Figures are average number of days per year and covers the years 1948-1990
Source: National Climatic Data Center, International Station Meteorological Climate Summary, 3/95

AIR & WATER QUALITY

Maximum Pollutant Concentrations

	Particulate Matter (ug/m³)	Carbon Monoxide (ppm)	Sulfur Dioxide (ppm)	Nitrogen Dioxide (ppm)	Ozone (ppm)	Lead (ug/m³)
MSA[1] Level	69	3	0.028	0.021	0.12	0.03
NAAQS[2]	150	9	0.140	0.053	0.12	1.50
Met NAAQS?	Yes	Yes	Yes	Yes	Yes	Yes

Note: (1) Metropolitan Statistical Area - see Appendix A for areas included; (2) National Ambient Air Quality Standards; ppm = parts per million; ug/m³ = micrograms per cubic meter; n/a not available
Source: EPA, National Air Quality and Emissions Trends Report, 1996

Pollutant Standards Index

In the Milwaukee MSA (see Appendix A for areas included), the Pollutant Standards Index (PSI) exceeded 100 on 1 day in 1996. A PSI value greater than 100 indicates that air quality would be in the unhealthful range on that day. *EPA, National Air Quality and Emissions Trends Report, 1996*

Drinking Water

Water System Name	Pop. Served	Primary Water Source Type	Number of Violations in Fiscal Year 1997	Type of Violation/ Contaminants
Milwaukee Waterworks	682,332	Surface	None	None

Note: Data as of January 16, 1998
Source: EPA, Office of Ground Water and Drinking Water, Safe Drinking Water Information System

Milwaukee tap water is alkaline, medium hard and fluoridated.
Editor & Publisher Market Guide, 1998

Minneapolis, Minnesota

Background

If one were forced to describe the city of Minneapolis in sound bites, the two most likely words might be, "modern" and "progressive". Indeed, for a city that could theoretically scare many people due to its reputation of brutal winters alone, Minneapolis nevertheless attracts excellence in the fields of the performing arts, the visual arts, education, finance, advertising, and several manufacturing firms.

The area saw its first white man, a French Franciscan priest by the name of Father Louis Hennepin, in 1680. In 1819, Fort Snelling was established to protect fur traders from the Sioux and Chippewa Tribe's. In 1848, two towns, St. Anthony, later to be called St. Paul, and Minneapolis, grew simultaneously, thus forming the metropolitan area known today as the Twin Cities. A tide of Swedish, German, and Norwegian immigrants came in the late 19th century, giving the city a decidedly Scandinavian flavor.

Minneapolis's traditional industries were that of lumber and flour milling. The existence of corporations such as General Mills, Cargill, and Pillsbury suggests that flour milling remains a strong economic sector. However, since the 1950's, Minneapolis had entered its "brain industry" phase, wherein electronics, computers, and other related science industries play a vital role in the city's economy.

These businesses contribute significant funds to the arts. Programs such as The Five Percent Club, and institutions such as The Guthrie Theatre and the Walker Arts Center are allowed to continue on a financially unburdened path, providing entertaining and thought-provoking works to the public.

Minneapolis is located at the confluence of the Mississippi and Minnesota Rivers. Numerous lakes mark the surrounding region. The city itself has 22 lakes within the park system. The climate is predominantly continental, i.e., seasonal temperature variations are quite large. Temperatures range from less than -30 degrees to over 100 degrees.

Blizzards, freezing rain, tornadoes, wind and hail storms do occur. Due to the spring snow melt or excessive rain, floods do occur along the Mississippi River.

General Rankings and Evaluative Comments

■ Minneapolis was ranked #118 out of 300 cities by *Money's* 1997 "Survey of the Best Places to Live." Criteria used: health services, crime, economy, housing, education, transportation, weather, leisure and the arts. The city was ranked #87 in 1996 and #46 in 1995.
Money, July 1997; Money, September 1996; Money, September 1995

■ *Ladies Home Journal* ranked America's 200 largest cities based on the qualities women care about most. Minneapolis ranked 4 out of 200. Criteria: low crime rate, good public schools, well-paying jobs, quality health and child care, the presence of women in government, proportion of women-owned businesses, size of the wage gap with men, local economy, divorce rates, the ratio of single men to single women, whether there are laws that require at least the same number of public toilets for women as men, and the probability of good hair days. *Ladies Home Journal, November 1997*

■ Minneapolis was ranked #122 out of 219 cities in terms of children's health, safety, and economic well-being. Criteria: total population, percent population change, birth rate, child immunization rate, infant mortality rate, percent low birth weight infants, percent of births to teens, physician-to-population ratio, student-to-teacher ratio, dropout rate, unemployment rate, median family income, percent of children in poverty, violent and property crime rates, number of juvenile arrests for violent crimes as a percent of the total crime index, number of days with pollution standard index (PSI) over 100, pounds toxic releases per 1,000 people and number of superfund sites. *Zero Population Growth, Children's Environmental Index 1997*

■ Minneapolis is among the 20 most livable cities for gay men and lesbians. The list was divided between 10 cities you might expect and 10 surprises. Minneapolis was on the cities you wouldn't expect list. Rank: 1 out of 10. Criteria: legal protection from antigay discrimination, an annual gay pride celebration, a community center, gay bookstores and publications, and an array of organizations, religious groups, and health care facilities that cater to the needs of the local gay community. *The Advocate, June 1997*

■ *Conde Nast Traveler* polled 37,000 readers in terms of travel satisfaction. Cities were ranked based on the following criteria: people/friendliness, environment/ambiance, cultural enrichment, restaurants and fun/energy. Minneapolis appeared in the top thirty, ranking number 16, with an overall rating of 65.8 out of 100 based on all the criteria. The cities were also ranked in each category separately. Minneapolis appeared in the top 10 based on people/friendliness, ranking number 5 with a rating of 76.8 out of 100. Minneapolis appeared in the top 10 based on cultural enrichment, ranking number 10 with a rating of 63.8 out of 100. *Conde Nast Traveler, Readers' Choice Poll 1997*

■ *Yahoo! Internet Life* selected "America's 100 Most Wired Cities & Towns". 50 cities were large and 50 cities were small. Minneapolis ranked 6 out of 50 large cities. Criteria: Internet users per capita, number of networked computers, number of registered domain names, Internet backbone traffic, and the per-capita number of Web sites devoted to each city. Minneapolis was highlighted as having the most networked computers per person. *Yahoo! Internet Life, March 1998*

■ Minneapolis appeared on *Sales & Marketing Management's* list of the 20 hottest domestic markets to do business in. Rank: 13 out of 20. America's 320 Metropolitan Statistical Areas were ranked based on the market's potential to buy products in certain industries like high-tech, manufacturing, office equipment and business services, as well as population and household income growth. The study had nine criteria in all.

"With more than 1,300 technology-focused firms, this market has one of the largest concentration of high-tech business in the nation. A wide mix of industries—plus representation of big and small companies—makes the Twin Cities a market that any company should consider." *Sales & Marketing Management, January 1998*

■ Medtronic (implantable medical devices), General Mills, Apogee (installs windows, windshields, curtain walls) and Tennant (manufactures industrial floor sweepers and scrubbers), headquartered in Minneapolis, are among the "100 Best Companies to Work for in America." Criteria: trust in management, pride in work/company, camaraderie, company responses to the Hewitt People Practices Inventory, and employee responses to their Great Place to Work survey. The companies also had to be at least 10 years old and have a minimum of 500 employees. *Fortune, January 12, 1998*

■ Dayton Hudson Corp., headquartered in Minneapolis, is among the "100 Best Companies for Working Mothers." Criteria: pay compared with competition, opportunities for women to advance, support for child care, flexible work schedules and family-friendly benefits. *Working Mother, October 1997*

■ According to *Working Mother,* "Last spring Minnesota's legislature approved a major package of laws that granted more than $200 million to child care. This translates into 13,000 more families getting help paying for child care this year. State lawmakers also designated funds to expand resource and referral services to help families find care, and approved Governor Arne Carlson's proposal to give $1 million in new state money to train and recruit caregivers to meet the new demand.

Minnesota had several other important initiatives pass this year. One new law significantly boosts caregiver training across the state by funding scholarships for caregivers to get on-the-job training. Another new law gives grants for nontraditional care—such as programs for kids with special needs and care during weekends and other off hours. (Minnesota was among the top 10 states for child care.)" *Working Mother, July/August 1997*

Business Environment

STATE ECONOMY

State Economic Profile

"Minnesota is experiencing swift and broad-based growth across all major industries. Construction employment growth has been strong all year as a result of steady residential construction, and an infusion of commercial projects. Finance, insurance and real estate have shown strength throughout the year, bolstered by surging home sales, expansion of large depository institutions, and financial services employers....

Minnesota's commercial and industrial property tax burden is roughly twice that of Wisconsin's, and over twice that of South Dakota's. While the tax differential is not new, it has slowly escalated through the last two decades, constraining job creation.

There are now six Minnesota casinos that maintain labor forces of over 1,000 workers. The newest trend among these casinos is the addition of accompanying hotel/resort complexes. Minnesota's casinos differ from the riverboat casinos in Kansas City and St. Louis in that Minnesota caters mostly to instate gamblers, especially from Minneapolis, while the riverboat casinos are tourist-oriented and bring in out-of-state money. Therefore, Minnesota casinos act to redistribute money from the Twin Cities to elsewhere in the state, but do not add to state income.

The Minnesota health services industry is a leader in consolidation and reform. Several large health alliances and hospital systems now figure among Minnesota's top employers. As a result of consolidation, employment growth has been below the nation's during the past six years. Going forward, consolidation will continue unabated.

Minnesota is and will continue to be a strong Plains performer through the forecast horizon. Minnesota's economy is driven by its industrial center, the Minneapolis-St. Paul metropolitan area, which has been experiencing a prolonged period of growth. As a result of this expansion, labor shortages, space shortages, and high costs of doing business in Minneapolis-St. Paul all present downside risks to economic growth." *National Association of Realtors, Economic Profiles: The Fifty States, July 1997*

IMPORTS/EXPORTS

Total Export Sales

Area	1993 ($000)	1994 ($000)	1995 ($000)	1996 ($000)	% Chg. 1993-96	% Chg. 1995-96
MSA[1]	9,003,818	8,863,531	11,071,822	12,383,979	37.5	11.9
U.S.	464,858,354	512,415,609	583,030,524	622,827,063	34.0	6.8

Note: (1) Metropolitan Statistical Area - see Appendix A for areas included
Source: U.S. Department of Commerce, International Trade Association, Metropolitan Area Exports: An Export Performance Report on Over 250 U.S. Cities, October 1997

Imports/Exports by Port

Type	Cargo Value			Share of U.S. Total	
	1995 (US$mil.)	1996 (US$mil.)	% Change 1995-1996	1995 (%)	1996 (%)
Imports	0	0	0	0	0
Exports	0	0	0	0	0

Source: Global Trade Information Services, WaterBorne Trade Atlas 1997

CITY FINANCES

City Government Finances

Component	FY92 ($000)	FY92 (per capita $)
Revenue	750,435	2,059.56
Expenditure	795,166	2,182.32
Debt Outstanding	2,289,852	6,284.47
Cash & Securities	2,801,340	7,688.24

Source: U.S. Bureau of the Census, City Government Finances: 1991-92

City Government Revenue by Source

Source	FY92 ($000)	FY92 (per capita $)	FY92 (%)
From Federal Government	26,097	71.62	3.5
From State Governments	128,988	354.01	17.2
From Local Governments	14,917	40.94	2.0
Property Taxes	142,488	391.06	19.0
General Sales Taxes	0	0.00	0.0
Selective Sales Taxes	38,349	105.25	5.1
Income Taxes	0	0.00	0.0
Current Charges	95,360	261.71	12.7
Utility/Liquor Store	23,179	63.61	3.1
Employee Retirement[1]	107,562	295.20	14.3
Other	173,495	476.15	23.1

Note: (1) Excludes "city contributions," classified as "nonrevenue," intragovernmental transfers.
Source: U.S. Bureau of the Census, City Government Finances: 1991-92

City Government Expenditures by Function

Function	FY92 ($000)	FY92 (per capita $)	FY92 (%)
Educational Services	16,937	46.48	2.1
Employee Retirement[1]	29,689	81.48	3.7
Environment/Housing	253,725	696.34	31.9
Government Administration	30,151	82.75	3.8
Interest on General Debt	163,903	449.83	20.6
Public Safety	97,663	268.03	12.3
Social Services	9,948	27.30	1.3
Transportation	115,239	316.27	14.5
Utility/Liquor Store	29,311	80.44	3.7
Other	48,600	133.38	6.1

Note: (1) Payments to beneficiaries including withdrawal of contributions.
Source: U.S. Bureau of the Census, City Government Finances: 1991-92

Municipal Bond Ratings

Area	Moody's	S & P
Minneapolis	Aaa	AAA

Note: n/a not available; n/r not rated
Source: Moody's Bond Record, 2/98; Statistical Abstract of the U.S., 1997;
Governing Magazine, 9/97, 3/98

POPULATION

Population Growth

Area	1980	1990	% Chg. 1980-90	July 1996 Estimate	% Chg. 1990-96
City	370,951	368,383	-0.7	358,785	-2.6
MSA[1]	2,137,133	2,464,124	15.3	2,765,116	12.2
U.S.	226,545,805	248,765,170	9.8	265,179,411	6.6

Note: (1) Metropolitan Statistical Area - see Appendix A for areas included
Source: 1980/1990 Census of Housing and Population, Summary Tape File 3C;
Census Bureau Population Estimates

Population Characteristics

Race	City				% Chg. 1980-90	MSA[1]	
	1980		1990			1990	
	Population	%	Population	%		Population	%
White	325,415	87.7	289,246	78.5	-11.1	2,272,798	92.2
Black	28,469	7.7	48,032	13.0	68.7	89,359	3.6
Amer Indian/Esk/Aleut	9,198	2.5	12,213	3.3	32.8	23,338	0.9
Asian/Pacific Islander	5,358	1.4	15,809	4.3	195.1	64,944	2.6
Other	2,511	0.7	3,083	0.8	22.8	13,685	0.6
Hispanic Origin[2]	4,684	1.3	7,309	2.0	56.0	33,835	1.4

Note: (1) Metropolitan Statistical Area - see Appendix A for areas included;
(2) people of Hispanic origin can be of any race
Source: 1980/1990 Census of Housing and Population, Summary Tape File 3C

Ancestry

Area	German	Irish	English	Italian	U.S.	French	Polish	Dutch
City	30.2	13.3	8.5	2.1	1.2	4.8	5.2	1.5
MSA[1]	43.8	15.2	9.2	2.5	1.2	6.1	5.8	2.0
U.S.	23.3	15.6	13.1	5.9	5.3	4.2	3.8	2.5

Note: Figures are percentages and include persons that reported multiple ancestry (eg. if a person reported being Irish and Italian, they were included in both columns); (1) Metropolitan Statistical Area - see Appendix A for areas included
Source: 1990 Census of Population and Housing, Summary Tape File 3C

Age

Area	Median Age (Years)	Age Distribution (%)						
		Under 5	Under 18	18-24	25-44	45-64	65+	80+
City	31.5	7.3	20.6	13.3	39.2	14.1	12.9	3.9
MSA[1]	31.6	8.1	26.3	10.0	36.8	17.1	9.9	2.5
U.S.	32.9	7.3	25.6	10.5	32.6	18.7	12.5	2.8

Note: (1) Metropolitan Statistical Area - see Appendix A for areas included
Source: 1990 Census of Population and Housing, Summary Tape File 3C

Male/Female Ratio

Area	Number of males per 100 females (all ages)	Number of males per 100 females (18 years old+)
City	94.1	92.2
MSA[1]	95.5	92.6
U.S.	95.0	91.9

Note: (1) Metropolitan Statistical Area - see Appendix A for areas included
Source: 1990 Census of Population, General Population Characteristics

INCOME

Per Capita/Median/Average Income

Area	Per Capita ($)	Median Household ($)	Average Household ($)
City	14,830	25,324	33,245
MSA[1]	16,842	36,565	43,942
U.S.	14,420	30,056	38,453

Note: all figures are for 1989; (1) Metropolitan Statistical Area - see Appendix A for areas included
Source: 1990 Census of Population and Housing, Summary Tape File 3C

Household Income Distribution by Race

Income ($)	City (%)					U.S. (%)				
	Total	White	Black	Other	Hisp.[1]	Total	White	Black	Other	Hisp.[1]
Less than 5,000	6.3	4.7	13.3	17.3	7.1	6.2	4.8	15.2	8.6	8.8
5,000 - 9,999	12.7	11.1	21.8	21.0	12.1	9.3	8.6	14.2	9.9	11.1
10,000 - 14,999	10.6	10.1	13.0	14.9	12.4	8.8	8.5	11.0	9.8	11.0
15,000 - 24,999	19.8	20.0	19.3	17.8	26.5	17.5	17.3	18.9	18.5	20.5
25,000 - 34,999	15.8	16.4	12.9	11.4	15.0	15.8	16.1	14.2	15.4	16.4
35,000 - 49,999	16.2	17.2	11.0	10.3	14.2	17.9	18.6	13.3	16.1	16.0
50,000 - 74,999	11.9	12.9	6.6	5.2	7.7	15.0	15.8	9.3	13.4	11.1
75,000 - 99,999	3.6	3.9	1.4	1.5	3.3	5.1	5.5	2.6	4.7	3.1
100,000+	3.2	3.7	0.7	0.6	1.7	4.4	4.8	1.3	3.7	1.9

Note: all figures are for 1989; (1) people of Hispanic origin can be of any race
Source: 1990 Census of Population and Housing, Summary Tape File 3C

Effective Buying Income

Area	Per Capita ($)	Median Household ($)	Average Household ($)
City	16,584	29,198	38,076
MSA[1]	18,341	41,838	48,729
U.S.	15,444	33,201	41,849

Note: data as of 1/1/97; (1) Metropolitan Statistical Area - see Appendix A for areas included
Source: Standard Rate & Data Service, Newspaper Advertising Source, 2/98

Effective Household Buying Income Distribution

Area	% of Households Earning						
	$10,000 -$19,999	$20,000 -$34,999	$35,000 -$49,999	$50,000 -$74,999	$75,000 -$99,000	$100,000 -$124,999	$125,000 and up
City	19.7	24.5	17.1	15.8	4.9	1.8	1.8
MSA[1]	12.0	21.1	20.7	24.5	8.6	2.8	2.9
U.S.	16.5	23.4	18.3	18.2	6.4	2.1	2.4

Note: data as of 1/1/97; (1) Metropolitan Statistical Area - see Appendix A for areas included
Source: Standard Rate & Data Service, Newspaper Advertising Source, 2/98

Poverty Rates by Race and Age

Area	Total (%)	By Race (%)				By Age (%)		
		White	Black	Other	Hisp.[2]	Under 5 years old	Under 18 years old	65 years and over
City	18.5	11.7	40.5	47.4	28.9	33.1	30.6	11.0
MSA[1]	8.1	5.9	37.0	32.7	19.1	13.2	11.2	8.2
U.S.	13.1	9.8	29.5	23.1	25.3	20.1	18.3	12.8

Note: figures show the percent of people living below the poverty line in 1989. The average poverty threshold was $12,674 for a family of four in 1989; (1) Metropolitan Statistical Area - see Appendix A for areas included; (2) people of Hispanic origin can be of any race
Source: 1990 Census of Population and Housing, Summary Tape File 3C

EMPLOYMENT

Labor Force and Employment

Area	Civilian Labor Force			Workers Employed		
	Dec. '95	Dec. '96	% Chg.	Dec. '95	Dec. '96	% Chg.
City	204,784	210,251	2.7	198,486	205,500	3.5
MSA[1]	1,615,254	1,658,390	2.7	1,572,977	1,627,030	3.4
U.S.	134,583,000	136,742,000	1.6	127,903,000	130,785,000	2.3

Note: Data is not seasonally adjusted and covers workers 16 years of age and older;
(1) Metropolitan Statistical Area - see Appendix A for areas included
Source: Bureau of Labor Statistics, http://stats.bls.gov

Unemployment Rate

Area	1997											
	Jan.	Feb.	Mar.	Apr.	May	Jun.	Jul.	Aug.	Sep.	Oct.	Nov.	Dec.
City	3.2	2.7	2.7	2.8	2.8	3.7	3.2	3.4	4.0	3.5	2.7	2.3
MSA[1]	3.0	2.6	2.5	2.5	2.1	2.9	2.3	2.4	2.8	2.5	2.0	1.9
U.S.	5.9	5.7	5.5	4.8	4.7	5.2	5.0	4.8	4.7	4.4	4.3	4.4

Note: Data is not seasonally adjusted and covers workers 16 years of age and older; All figures are percentages; (1) Metropolitan Statistical Area - see Appendix A for areas included
Source: Bureau of Labor Statistics, http://stats.bls.gov

Employment by Industry

Sector	MSA[1]		U.S.
	Number of Employees	Percent of Total	Percent of Total
Services	482,400	29.2	29.0
Retail Trade	299,500	18.1	18.5
Government	227,000	13.7	16.1
Manufacturing	275,700	16.7	15.0
Finance/Insurance/Real Estate	116,900	7.1	5.7
Wholesale Trade	103,800	6.3	5.4
Transportation/Public Utilities	90,200	5.5	5.3
Construction/Mining	500	0.0	5.0

Note: Figures cover non-farm employment as of 12/97 and are not seasonally adjusted; (1) Metropolitan Statistical Area - see Appendix A for areas included
Source: Bureau of Labor Statistics, http://stats.bls.gov

Employment by Occupation

Occupation Category	City (%)	MSA[1] (%)	U.S. (%)
White Collar	65.7	65.0	58.1
Executive/Admin./Management	12.9	14.2	12.3
Professional	18.9	15.3	14.1
Technical & Related Support	4.6	4.6	3.7
Sales	11.1	12.7	11.8
Administrative Support/Clerical	18.2	18.3	16.3
Blue Collar	18.1	21.6	26.2
Precision Production/Craft/Repair	6.3	9.4	11.3
Machine Operators/Assem./Insp.	5.5	6.0	6.8
Transportation/Material Movers	3.0	3.2	4.1
Cleaners/Helpers/Laborers	3.1	3.1	3.9
Services	15.7	12.3	13.2
Farming/Forestry/Fishing	0.6	1.1	2.5

Note: figures cover employed persons 16 years old and over; (1) Metropolitan Statistical Area - see Appendix A for areas included
Source: 1990 Census of Population and Housing, Summary Tape File 3C

Occupational Employment Projections: 1994 - 2005

Occupations Expected to have the Largest Job Growth (ranked by numerical growth)	Fast-Growing Occupations[1] (ranked by percent growth)
1. Salespersons, retail	1. All other computer scientists
2. Computer systems analysts	2. Manicurists
3. General managers & top executives	3. Computer systems analysts
4. All other profess., paraprofess., tech.	4. Occupational therapy assistants
5. Cashiers	5. Electronic pagination systems workers
6. All other helper, laborer, mover	6. Physical therapy assistants and aides
7. Janitors/cleaners/maids, ex. priv. hshld.	7. Personal and home care aides
8. All other computer scientists	8. All other assemblers, fabricators
9. Waiters & waitresses	9. Computer engineers
10. Receptionists and information clerks	10. Home health aides

Projections cover Anoka, Carver, Dakota, Hennepin, Ramsey, Scott and Washington Counties.
Note: (1) Excludes occupations with less than 50 employees in 1994
Source: Minnesota Department of Economic Security, Twin Cities Area Employment Outlook by Occupation, 1994-2005

Average Wages

Occupation	Wage	Occupation	Wage
Professional/Technical/Clerical	$/Week	**Health/Protective Services**	$/Week
Accountants III	812	Corrections Officers	-
Attorneys III	1,338	Firefighters	763
Budget Analysts III	-	Nurses, Licensed Practical II	-
Buyers/Contracting Specialists II	656	Nurses, Registered II	-
Clerks, Accounting III	461	Nursing Assistants II	-
Clerks, General III	439	Police Officers I	775
Computer Operators II	-	**Hourly Workers**	$/Hour
Computer Programmers II	652	Forklift Operators	13.20
Drafters II	538	General Maintenance Workers	11.30
Engineering Technicians III	623	Guards I	7.60
Engineering Technicians, Civil III	705	Janitors	8.34
Engineers III	946	Maintenance Electricians	20.92
Key Entry Operators I	354	Maintenance Electronics Techs II	-
Personnel Assistants III	517	Maintenance Machinists	18.50
Personnel Specialists III	768	Maintenance Mechanics, Machinery	16.50
Secretaries III	535	Material Handling Laborers	-
Switchboard Operator-Receptionist	382	Motor Vehicle Mechanics	16.77
Systems Analysts II	958	Shipping/Receiving Clerks	-
Systems Analysts Supervisor/Mgr II	1,364	Tool and Die Makers	18.16
Tax Collectors II	650	Truckdrivers, Tractor Trailer	15.23
Word Processors II	-	Warehouse Specialists	15.69

Note: Wage data includes full-time workers only for 2/96 and cover the Metropolitan Statistical Area (see Appendix A for areas included). Dashes indicate that data was not available.
Source: Bureau of Labor Statistics, Occupational Compensation Survey, 8/96

TAXES

Major State and Local Tax Rates

State Corp. Income (%)	State Personal Income (%)	Residential Property (effective rate per $100)	Sales & Use		State Gasoline (cents/ gallon)	State Cigarette (cents/ 20-pack)
			State (%)	Local (%)		
9.8[a]	6.0 - 8.5	1.34	6.5	0.5	20	48

Note: Personal/corporate income tax rates as of 1/97. Sales, gasoline and cigarette tax rates as of 1/98; (a) 5.8% alternative minimum tax rate
Source: Federation of Tax Administrators, www.taxadmin.org; Washington D.C. Department of Finance and Revenue, Tax Rates and Tax Burdens in the District of Columbia: A Nationwide Comparison, June 1997; Chamber of Commerce

Total Taxes Per Capita and as a Percent of Income

Area	Per Capita Income ($)	Per Capita Taxes ($)			Taxes as Pct. of Income (%)		
		Total	Federal	State/Local	Total	Federal	State/Local
Minnesota	27,512	9,997	6,358	3,638	36.3	23.1	13.2
U.S.	26,187	9,205	6,127	3,078	35.2	23.4	11.8

Note: Figures are for 1997
Source: Tax Foundation, Web Site, www.taxfoundation.org

COMMERCIAL REAL ESTATE

Office Market

Class/Location	Total Space (sq. ft.)	Vacant Space (sq. ft.)	Vac. Rate (%)	Under Constr. (sq. ft.)	Net Absorp. (sq. ft.)	Rental Rates ($/sq.ft./yr.)
Class A						
CBD	11,165,605	459,037	4.1	0	-2,533,952	16.00-34.00
Outside CBD	5,400,004	189,459	3.5	468,000	-927,207	20.00-31.00
Class B						
CBD	10,881,145	974,941	9.0	0	4,200,791	13.00-24.00
Outside CBD	19,567,231	1,464,762	7.5	40,000	1,030,971	13.00-22.00

Note: Data as of 10/97 and covers Minneapolis/St. Paul; CBD = Central Business District; n/a not available;
Source: Society of Industrial and Office Realtors, 1998 Comparative Statistics of Industrial and Office Real Estate Markets

"Speculative office development is taking place in the southwest suburban area where absorption has historically been the highest. Officing at home, hoteling, and flexible hours will continue as firms try to reduce occupancy. This will not affect the state of the market as absorption and construction are predicted to rise up to 15 percent. Commercial real estate taxes are expected to be reduced by approximately 6 percent, which has been long in the waiting. The large financial services industry adds to the economic stability as First Bank and Norwest Corp, two of the nation's powerhouses, continue to acquire and hire, shielding the area from industry downsizing. Finding skilled employees will continue to be a challenge in 1998, but the outlook is positive." *Society of Industrial and Office Realtors, 1998 Comparative Statistics of Industrial and Office Real Estate Markets*

Industrial Market

Location	Total Space (sq. ft.)	Vacant Space (sq. ft.)	Vac. Rate (%)	Under Constr. (sq. ft.)	Net Absorp. (sq. ft.)	Net Lease ($/sq.ft./yr.)
Central City	78,247,000	2,335,298	3.0	250,000	3,779,862	3.50-4.50
Suburban	121,325,000	6,508,820	5.4	3,500,000	4,627,500	3.75-4.50

Note: Data as of 10/97 and covers Minneapolis-St. Paul; n/a not available
Source: Society of Industrial and Office Realtors, 1998 Comparative Statistics of Industrial and Office Real Estate Markets

"The industrial property tax in Minnesota is about twice that of neighboring states, resulting in a trend of businesses heading across the state border. Fortunately, with an economy as diverse as Minneapolis, new migrants will continue to be attracted to this metropolitan area. Despite the risk of a tight labor market and high business costs, employment growth is expected to regain its strength in the long-term. As the available supply of industrial space dwindles, construction is expected to continue at a rate of at least six percent for warehouse/distribution, manufacturing, and High-Tech/R&D space. Lease prices will increase up to five percent for all industrial property types. Manufacturing sales prices are expected to grow by at least six percent. Market trends are moving toward distribution centers and office warehouses with higher ceiling heights." *Society of Industrial and Office Realtors, 1998 Comparative Statistics of Industrial and Office Real Estate Markets*

Retail Market

Shopping Center Inventory (sq. ft.)	Shopping Center Construction (sq. ft.)	Construction as a Percent of Inventory (%)	Torto Wheaton Rent Index[1] ($/sq. ft.)
39,152,000	677,000	1.7	10.31

Note: Data as of 1997 and covers the Metropolitan Statistical Area - see Appendix A for areas included; (1) Index is based on a model that predicts what the average rent should be for leases with certain characteristics, in certain locations during certain years.
Source: National Association of Realtors, 1997-1998 Market Conditions Report

"Estimated at 2.81 million, Minneapolis' population has grown an average of 1.5% annually over the past two years, compared to 0.9% for the nation. Real personal income growth has been strong recently, which has helped push the area's retail rent index up 27% over the past three years. However, rents remain below the Midwest average of $12.30. Minneapolis, of course, is home to the 4.2 million square foot Mall of America, which boasts a multitude of bars and restaurants, a 14 screen megaplex, an indoor amusement park and an aquarium. The mall typifies a trend in several areas, where entertainment is being used to attract customers to retail centers." *National Association of Realtors, 1997-1998 Market Conditions Report*

COMMERCIAL UTILITIES

Typical Monthly Electric Bills

Area	Commercial Service ($/month)		Industrial Service ($/month)	
	12 kW demand 1,500 kWh	100 kW demand 30,000 kWh	1,000 kW demand 400,000 kWh	20,000 kW demand 10,000,000 kWh
City	122	1,948	21,281	473,746
U.S.	162	2,360	25,590	545,677

Note: Based on rates in effect July 1, 1997
Source: Edison Electric Institute, Typical Residential, Commercial and Industrial Bills, Summer 1997

TRANSPORTATION

Transportation Statistics

Avg. travel time to work (min.)	19.6
Interstate highways	I-35; I-94
Bus lines	
In-city	Metropolitan Council, 981 vehicles
Inter-city	3
Passenger air service	
Airport	Minneapolis-St. Paul International
Airlines	35
Aircraft departures	150,399 (1995)
Enplaned passengers	11,835,783 (1995)
Rail service	Amtrak; light rail proposed
Motor freight carriers	150
Major waterways/ports	Port of Minneapolis

Source: OAG, Business Travel Planner, Summer 1997; Editor & Publisher Market Guide, 1998; FAA Airport Activity Statistics, 1996; Amtrak National Time Table, Northeast Timetable, Fall/Winter 1997-98; 1990 Census of Population and Housing, STF 3C; Chamber of Commerce/Economic Development 1997; Jane's Urban Transport Systems 1997-98; Transit Fact Book 1997

A survey of 90,000 airline passengers during the first half of 1997 ranked most of the largest airports in the U.S. Minneapolis-St. Paul International ranked number 14 out of 36. Criteria: cleanliness, quality of restaurants, attractiveness, speed of baggage delivery, ease of reaching gates, available ground transportation, ease of following signs and closeness of parking. *Plog Research Inc., First Half 1997*

Means of Transportation to Work

Area	Car/Truck/Van		Public Transportation			Bicycle	Walked	Other Means	Worked at Home
	Drove Alone	Car-pooled	Bus	Subway	Railroad				
City	60.3	10.5	15.7	0.0	0.0	1.6	7.8	0.9	3.1
MSA[1]	76.0	11.2	5.2	0.0	0.0	0.4	3.2	0.6	3.4
U.S.	73.2	13.4	3.0	1.5	0.5	0.4	3.9	1.2	3.0

Note: figures shown are percentages and only include workers 16 years old and over;
(1) Metropolitan Statistical Area - see Appendix A for areas included
Source: 1990 Census of Population and Housing, Summary Tape File 3C

BUSINESSES

Major Business Headquarters

Company Name	1997 Rankings	
	Fortune 500	Forbes 500
Cargill	-	1
Carlson Cos	-	103
Cowles Media	-	420
Dayton Hudson	27	-
First Bank System	355	-
GFI America	-	460
General Mills	264	-
Genmar Holdings	-	340
Holiday Cos	-	140
Honeywell	195	-
Kraus-Anderson	-	448
Lutheran Brotherhood	483	-
MA Mortenson	-	265
Nash Finch	404	-
Northern States Power	489	-
Norwest	165	-

Note: Companies listed are located in the city; Dashes indicate no ranking
Fortune 500: companies that produce a 10-K are ranked 1 - 500 based on 1996 revenue
Forbes 500: private companies are ranked 1 - 500 based on 1996 revenue
Source: Forbes 12/1/97; Fortune 4/28/97

Fast-Growing Businesses

According to *Inc.*, Minneapolis is home to two of America's 100 fastest-growing private companies: Dynamic Data Solutions and Select Comfort Corp.. Criteria for inclusion: must be an independent, privately-held, U.S. corporation, proprietorship or partnership; sales of at least $200,000 in 1993; five-year operating/sales history; increase in 1997 sales over 1996 sales; holding companies, regulated banks, and utilities were excluded. *Inc. 500, 1997*

Minneapolis is home to one of *Business Week's* "hot growth" companies: Ault. Criteria: sales and earnings, return on capital and stock price. *Business Week, 5/26/97*

According to Deloitte & Touche LLP, Minneapolis is home to one of America's 100 fastest-growing high-technology companies: Spine-Tech Inc. Companies are ranked by percentage growth in revenue over a five-year period. Criteria for inclusion: must be a U.S. company developing and/or providing technology products or services; company must have been in business for five years with 1992 revenues of at least $50,000. *Deloitte & Touche LLP, January 7, 1998*

Minneapolis was ranked #9 out of 24 (#1 is best) in terms of the best-performing local stocks in 1996 according to the Money/Norby Cities Index. The index measures stocks of companies that have headquarters in 24 metro areas. *Money, 2/7/97*

Women-Owned Businesses: Number, Employment, Sales and Share

Area	Women-Owned Businesses in 1996				Share of Women-Owned Businesses in 1996	
	Number	Employment	Sales ($000)	Rank[2]	Percent (%)	Rank[3]
MSA[1]	104,300	237,100	30,926,700	12	37.3	20

Note: (1) Metropolitan Statistical Area - see Appendix A for areas included; (2) Calculated on an averaging of number of businesses, employment and sales and ranges from 1 to 50 where 1 is best; (3) Ranges from 1 to 50 where 1 is best
Source: The National Foundation for Women Business Owners, 1996 Facts on Women-Owned Businesses: Trends in the Top 50 Metropolitan Areas, March 26, 1997

Women-Owned Businesses: Growth

Area	Growth in Women-Owned Businesses (% change from 1987 to 1996)				Relative Growth in the Number of Women-Owned and All Businesses (% change from 1987 to 1996)			
	Num.	Empl.	Sales	Rank[2]	Women-Owned	All Firms	Absolute Difference	Relative Difference
MSA[1]	78.0	155.6	262.3	29	78.0	62.6	15.4	1.2:1

Note: (1) Metropolitan Statistical Area - see Appendix A for areas included; (2) Calculated on an averaging of the percent growth of number of businesses, employment and sales and ranges from 1 to 50 where 1 is best
Source: The National Foundation for Women Business Owners, 1996 Facts on Women-Owned Businesses: Trends in the Top 50 Metropolitan Areas, March 26, 1997

Minority Business Opportunity

One of the 500 largest Hispanic-owned companies in the U.S. are located in Minneapolis. *Hispanic Business, June 1997*

Small Business Opportunity

Minneapolis was included among *Entrepreneur* magazines listing of the "20 Best Cities for Small Business." It was ranked #7 among large metro areas. Criteria: risk of failure, business performance, economic growth, affordability and state attitude towards business. *Entrepreneur, 10/97*

According to *Forbes*, Minneapolis is home to four of America's 200 best small companies: EW Blanch Holdings, Dura Automotive Systems, Game Financial, Techne. Criteria: companies must be publicly traded, U.S.-based corporations with latest 12-month sales of between $5 and $350 million. Earnings must be at least $1 million for the 12-month period. Limited partnerships, REITs and closed-end mutual funds were not considered. Banks, S&Ls and electric utilities were not included. *Forbes, November 3, 1997*

HOTELS & MOTELS

Hotels/Motels

Area	Hotels/ Motels	Rooms	Luxury-Level Hotels/Motels		Average Minimum Rates ($)		
			♦♦♦♦	♦♦♦♦♦	♦♦	♦♦♦	♦♦♦♦
City	26	5,701	2	0	n/a	n/a	n/a
Airport	34	7,179	0	0	n/a	n/a	n/a
Suburbs	54	5,718	0	0	n/a	n/a	n/a
Total	114	18,598	2	0	n/a	n/a	n/a

Note: n/a not available; Classifications range from one diamond (budget properties with basic amenities) to five diamond (luxury properties with the finest service, rooms and facilities).
Source: OAG, Business Travel Planner, Summer 1997

CONVENTION CENTERS

Major Convention Centers

Center Name	Meeting Rooms	Exhibit Space (sf)
Minneapolis Convention Center	56	280,000
Earle Brown Heritage Center	10	13,000

Source: Trade Shows Worldwide 1997

Living Environment

COST OF LIVING

Cost of Living Index

Composite Index	Housing	Utilities	Groceries	Health Care	Trans- portation	Misc. Goods/ Services
102.9	98.1	100.4	99.6	126.6	114.3	101.7

Note: U.S. = 100
Source: ACCRA, Cost of Living Index, 3rd Quarter 1997

HOUSING

Median Home Prices and Housing Affordability

Area	Median Price[2] 3rd Qtr. 1997 ($)	HOI[3] 3rd Qtr. 1997	Afford- ability Rank[4]
MSA[1]	118,000	79.4	26
U.S.	127,000	63.7	–

Note: (1) Metropolitan Statistical Area - see Appendix A for areas included; (2) U.S. figures calculated from the sales of 625,000 new and existing homes in 195 markets; (3) Housing Opportunity Index - percent of homes sold that were within the reach of the median income household at the prevailing mortgage interest rate; (4) Rank is from 1-195 with 1 being most affordable
Source: National Association of Home Builders, Housing Opportunity Index, 3rd Quarter 1997

It is projected that the median price of existing single-family homes in the metro area will increase by 8.2% in 1998. Nationwide, home prices are projected to increase 6.6%.
Kiplinger's Personal Finance Magazine, January 1998

Average New Home Price

Area	Price ($)
City	127,725
U.S.	135,710

Note: Figures are based on a new home with 1,800 sq. ft. of living area on an 8,000 sq. ft. lot.
Source: ACCRA, Cost of Living Index, 3rd Quarter 1997

Average Apartment Rent

Area	Rent ($/mth)
City	613
U.S.	569

Note: Figures are based on an unfurnished two bedroom, 1-1/2 or 2 bath apartment, approximately 950 sq. ft. in size, excluding all utilities except water
Source: ACCRA, Cost of Living Index, 3rd Quarter 1997

RESIDENTIAL UTILITIES

Average Residential Utility Costs

Area	All Electric ($/mth)	Part Electric ($/mth)	Other Energy ($/mth)	Phone ($/mth)
City	–	49.92	50.77	22.28
U.S.	109.40	55.25	43.64	19.48

Source: ACCRA, Cost of Living Index, 3rd Quarter 1997

HEALTH CARE

Average Health Care Costs

Area	Hospital ($/day)	Doctor ($/visit)	Dentist ($/visit)
City	672.00	56.55	72.60
U.S.	392.91	48.76	60.84

Note: Hospital - based on a semi-private room. Doctor - based on a general practitioner's routine exam of an established patient. Dentist - based on adult teeth cleaning and periodic oral exam.
Source: ACCRA, Cost of Living Index, 3rd Quarter 1997

Distribution of Office-Based Physicians

Area	Family/Gen. Practitioners	Specialists		
		Medical	Surgical	Other
MSA[1]	1,026	1,490	1,112	1,246

Note: Data as of 12/31/96; (1) Metropolitan Statistical Area - see Appendix A for areas included
Source: American Medical Assn., Physician Characteristics & Distribution in the U.S., 1997-1998

Hospitals

Minneapolis has 6 general medical and surgical hospitals, 1 children's general, 2 children's other specialty. *AHA Guide to the Healthcare Field 1997-98*

According to *U.S. News and World Report,* Minneapolis has 2 of the best hospitals in the U.S.: **University of Minnesota Hospital and Clinic**, noted for cancer, endocrinology, geriatrics, gynecology, neurology, orthopedics, otolaryngology; **Hennepin County Medical Center**, noted for orthopedics; *U.S. News and World Report, "America's Best Hospitals", 7/28/97*

EDUCATION

Public School District Statistics

District Name	Num. Sch.	Enroll.	Classroom Teachers[1]	Pupils per Teacher	Minority Pupils (%)	Current Exp.[2] ($/pupil)
Cedar Riverside Community Sch	1	73	3	24.3	n/a	n/a
Frederick Douglass Math/Sci	1	51	n/a	n/a	n/a	n/a
Minneapolis	144	46,612	n/a	n/a	63.4	7,223
New Visions Charter School	1	138	n/a	n/a	n/a	n/a
Skills For Tomorrow Chart Sch	1	58	n/a	n/a	n/a	n/a

Note: Data covers the 1995-1996 school year unless otherwise noted; (1) Excludes teachers reported as working in school district offices rather than in schools; (2) Based on 1993-94 enrollment collected by the Census Bureau, not the enrollment figure shown in column 3; SD = School District; ISD = Independent School District; n/a not available
Source: National Center for Education Statistics, Common Core of Data Survey; Bureau of the Census

Educational Quality

School District	Education Quotient[1]	Graduate Outcome[2]	Community Index[3]	Resource Index[4]
Minneapolis	124.0	94.0	140.0	139.0

Note: Nearly 1,000 secondary school districts were rated in terms of educational quality. The scores range from a low of 50 to a high of 150; (1) Average of the Graduate Outcome, Community and Resource indexes; (2) Based on graduation rates and college board scores (SAT/ACT); (3) Based on the surrounding community's average level of education and the area's average income level; (4) Based on teacher salaries, per-pupil expenditures and student-teacher ratios.
Source: Expansion Management, Ratings Issue 1997

Educational Attainment by Race

Area	High School Graduate (%)					Bachelor's Degree (%)				
	Total	White	Black	Other	Hisp.[2]	Total	White	Black	Other	Hisp.[2]
City	82.6	84.9	71.9	66.3	73.1	30.3	32.8	13.8	21.4	23.8
MSA[1]	87.2	88.0	76.2	70.7	76.7	27.1	27.5	17.3	25.2	19.9
U.S.	75.2	77.9	63.1	60.4	49.8	20.3	21.5	11.4	19.4	9.2

Note: figures shown cover persons 25 years old and over; (1) Metropolitan Statistical Area - see Appendix A for areas included; (2) people of Hispanic origin can be of any race
Source: 1990 Census of Population and Housing, Summary Tape File 3C

School Enrollment by Type

Area	Preprimary				Elementary/High School			
	Public		Private		Public		Private	
	Enrollment	%	Enrollment	%	Enrollment	%	Enrollment	%
City	3,848	59.9	2,577	40.1	38,107	84.8	6,823	15.2
MSA[1]	35,492	63.1	20,730	36.9	359,955	89.1	44,235	10.9
U.S.	2,679,029	59.5	1,824,256	40.5	38,379,689	90.2	4,187,099	9.8

Note: figures shown cover persons 3 years old and over;
(1) Metropolitan Statistical Area - see Appendix A for areas included
Source: 1990 Census of Population and Housing, Summary Tape File 3C

School Enrollment by Race

Area	Preprimary (%)				Elementary/High School (%)			
	White	Black	Other	Hisp.[1]	White	Black	Other	Hisp.[1]
City	69.2	19.0	11.8	3.1	56.8	26.2	16.9	3.4
MSA[2]	90.7	4.3	5.0	1.9	87.8	5.3	6.9	2.1
U.S.	80.4	12.5	7.1	7.8	74.1	15.6	10.3	12.5

Note: figures shown cover persons 3 years old and over; (1) people of Hispanic origin can be of any race; (2) Metropolitan Statistical Area - see Appendix A for areas included
Source: 1990 Census of Population and Housing, Summary Tape File 3C

SAT/ACT Scores

Area/District	1996 SAT				1996 ACT	
	Percent of Graduates Tested (%)	Average Math Score	Average Verbal Score	Average Combined Score	Percent of Graduates Tested (%)	Average Composite Score
Minneapolis PS	18	571	566	1,137	46	21.1
State	9	593	582	1,175	59	22.1
U.S.	41	508	505	1,013	35	20.9

Note: Math and verbal SAT scores are out of a possible 800; ACT scores are out of a possible 36
Caution: Comparing or ranking states/cities on the basis of SAT/ACT scores alone is invalid and strongly discouraged by the The College Board and The American College Testing Program as students who take the tests are self-selected and do not represent the entire student population. 1996 SAT scores cannot be compared to previous years due to recentering.
Source: Minneapolis School District, Research, Evaluation & Assessment, 1996; American College Testing Program, 1996; College Board, 1996

Classroom Teacher Salaries in Public Schools

District	B.A. Degree		M.A. Degree		Ph.D. Degree	
	Min. ($)	Max ($)	Min. ($)	Max. ($)	Min. ($)	Max. ($)
Minneapolis	25,410	38,186	27,589	47,939	31,395	55,474
Average[1]	26,120	39,270	28,175	44,667	31,643	49,825

Note: Salaries are for 1996-1997; (1) Based on all school districts covered; n/a not available
Source: American Federation of Teachers (unpublished data)

Higher Education

Two-Year Colleges		Four-Year Colleges		Medical Schools	Law Schools	Voc/Tech
Public	Private	Public	Private			
2	3	1	3	1	1	12

Source: College Blue Book, Occupational Education 1997; Medical School Admission Requirements, 1998-99; Peterson's Guide to Two-Year Colleges, 1997; Peterson's Guide to Four-Year Colleges, 1997; Barron's Guide to Law Schools 1997

Major Employers

American Express Financial Corp.
Ceridian Corp. (navigation instruments)
Fairview Hospital
Honeywell
Methodist Hospital
Northern States Power Co.
Onan Corp. (motors)
Reliastar Financial Corp.
American Yearbook Co. (publishing)

Carlson Companies (management consulting)
Children's Health Care
General Mills
Medtronic Inc. (electromedical apparatus)
North Memorial Health Care
Norwest Nova (mortgage bankers)
Pillsbury Co.
Riscomp Industries (help supply services)

Note: companies listed are located in the city
Source: Dun's Business Rankings 1997; Ward's Business Directory, 1997

Crime Rate

Area	All Crimes	Violent Crimes				Property Crimes		
		Murder	Forcible Rape	Robbery	Aggrav. Assault	Burglary	Larceny -Theft	Motor Vehicle Theft
City	11,290.5	23.0	142.7	896.6	820.5	2,123.4	5,721.9	1,562.5
Suburbs[1]	4,443.7	1.7	39.1	75.3	137.7	671.4	3,170.2	348.2
MSA[2]	5,346.1	4.5	52.8	183.6	227.7	862.8	3,506.5	508.3
U.S.	5,078.9	7.4	36.1	202.4	388.2	943.0	2,975.9	525.9

Note: Crime rate is the number of crimes per 100,000 pop.; (1) defined as all areas within the MSA but located outside the central city; (2) Metropolitan Statistical Area - see Appendix A for areas incl.
Source: FBI Uniform Crime Reports 1996

Culture and Recreation

Museums	Symphony Orchestras	Opera Companies	Dance Companies	Professional Theatres	Zoos	Pro Sports Teams
8	2	1	3	6	1	3

Source: International Directory of the Performing Arts, 1996; Official Museum Directory, 1998; Chamber of Commerce/Economic Development 1997

Library System

The Minneapolis Public Library has 14 branches, holdings of 2,088,309 volumes and a budget of $16,652,865 (1995). *American Library Directory, 1997-1998*

MEDIA

Newspapers

Name	Type	Freq.	Distribution	Circulation
American Jewish World	Religious	1x/wk	Regional	7,000
Apple Valley-Rosemount-Sun-Current	n/a	1x/wk	Local	13,741
Brooklyn Park Sun Post	n/a	1x/wk	Local	17,667
Burnsville-Lakeville Sun Current	n/a	1x/wk	Local	14,488
City Pages	General	1x/wk	Local	103,000
Crystal-Robbinsdale Sun Post	n/a	1x/wk	Local	11,683
Eagan Sun-Current	n/a	1x/wk	Local	14,860
East Calhoun News	n/a	1x/mo	Local	5,500
Eden Prairie Sun Current	General	1x/wk	Local	14,525
Edina Sun-Current	General	1x/wk	Local	16,630
Excelsior-Shorewood Sun Sailor	General	1x/wk	Local	14,538
Finance & Commerce	General	5x/wk	National	1,100
Hopkins Sun Sailor	n/a	1x/wk	Local	14,565
Insight News	n/a	3x/wk	Local	35,000
Minneapolis Spokesman	Black	1x/wk	Local	16,000
The Minnesota Daily	n/a	5x/wk	Campus	30,000
Saint Paul Recorder	Black	1x/wk	Local	10,000
Skyway News	General	1x/wk	Area	55,000
The Southwest Journal	General	2x/mo	Local	40,000
Star Tribune	General	7x/wk	Area	387,300
The Whittier Globe	n/a	1x/mo	Local	10,000

Note: Includes newspapers with circulations of 1,000 or more located in the city; n/a not available
Source: Burrelle's Media Directory, 1998 Edition

AM Radio Stations

Call Letters	Freq. (kHz)	Target Audience	Station Format	Music Format
KTCJ	690	General	M/N/S	Alternative
KUOM	770	General	M/N/S	Alternative
WCCO	830	General	N/T	n/a
KSGS	950	Black	M	R&B
WCTS	1030	General	M	Christian
KFAN	1130	n/a	N/S/T	n/a
WWTC	1280	n/a	M	n/a
WMNN	1330	General	N	n/a
KDIZ	1440	General	M	AOR
KLBB	1470	n/a	M/N/S	Big Band/Oldies
KSTP	1500	General	T	n/a

Note: Stations included broadcast in the Minneapolis metro area; n/a not available
Station Format: E = Educational; M = Music; N = News; S = Sports; T = Talk
Music Format: AOR = Album Oriented Rock; MOR = Middle-of-the-Road
Source: Burrelle's Media Directory, 1998 Edition

FM Radio Stations

Call Letters	Freq. (mHz)	Target Audience	Station Format	Music Format
KBEM	88.5	General	M/N	Jazz
WCAL	89.3	General	E/M	Classical
KMOJ	89.9	General	M/N/S	Urban Contemporary
KFAI	90.3	Alternative	M/N/S	Adult Contemporary/AOR/Alternative/Christian/Country/Jazz/Oldies/R&B/Spanish/Urban Contemporary
WMCN	91.7	General	M	Alternative
KQRS	92.5	General	M	AOR/Classic Rock
KEGE	93.7	General	M	Alternative
KSTP	94.5	General	M	Adult Contemporary
KTCZ	97.1	General	M	AOR/Adult Contemporary/Alternative/Classic Rock
KDWB	101.3	General	M	Adult Contemporary
KEEY	102.1	General	M	Country
WLTE	102.9	General	M	Adult Contemporary
KMJZ	104.1	General	M	Adult Contemporary/Jazz
KXXU	105.3	General	M	AOR/Adult Contemporary
KDXL	106.5	General	M/N/S	AOR
KQQL	107.9	n/a	M	Oldies

Note: Stations included broadcast in the Minneapolis metro area; n/a not available
Station Format: E = Educational; M = Music; N = News; S = Sports; T = Talk
Music Format: AOR = Album Oriented Rock; MOR = Middle-of-the-Road
Source: Burrelle's Media Directory, 1998 Edition

Television Stations

Name	Ch.	Affiliation	Type	Owner
WCCO	4	CBS	Commercial	Westinghouse Broadcasting Company
KMSP	9	UPN	Commercial	United Television Inc.
KARE	11	NBC	Commercial	Gannett Company Inc.
WFTC	29	Fox	Commercial	Clear Channel Television

Note: Stations included broadcast in the Minneapolis metro area
Source: Burrelle's Media Directory, 1998 Edition

CLIMATE

Average and Extreme Temperatures

Temperature	Jan	Feb	Mar	Apr	May	Jun	Jul	Aug	Sep	Oct	Nov	Dec	Ann
Extreme High (°F)	57	60	83	95	96	102	105	101	98	89	74	63	105
Average High (°F)	21	27	38	56	69	79	84	81	71	59	41	26	54
Average Temp. (°F)	12	18	30	46	59	69	74	71	61	50	33	19	45
Average Low (°F)	3	9	21	36	48	58	63	61	50	39	25	11	35
Extreme Low (°F)	-34	-28	-32	2	18	37	43	39	26	15	-17	-29	-34

Note: Figures cover the years 1948-1990
Source: National Climatic Data Center, International Station Meteorological Climate Summary, 3/95

Average Precipitation/Snowfall/Humidity

Precip./Humidity	Jan	Feb	Mar	Apr	May	Jun	Jul	Aug	Sep	Oct	Nov	Dec	Ann
Avg. Precip. (in.)	0.8	0.8	1.9	2.2	3.1	4.0	3.8	3.6	2.5	1.9	1.4	1.0	27.1
Avg. Snowfall (in.)	11	9	12	3	Tr	0	0	0	Tr	Tr	7	10	52
Avg. Rel. Hum. 6am (%)	75	76	77	75	75	79	81	84	85	81	80	79	79
Avg. Rel. Hum. 3pm (%)	64	62	58	48	47	50	50	52	53	52	62	68	55

Note: Figures cover the years 1948-1990; Tr = Trace amounts (<0.05 in. of rain; <0.5 in. of snow)
Source: National Climatic Data Center, International Station Meteorological Climate Summary, 3/95

Weather Conditions

	Temperature			Daytime Sky			Precipitation	
5°F & below	32°F & below	90°F & above	Clear	Partly cloudy	Cloudy	0.01 inch or more precip.	0.1 inch or more snow/ice	Thunder-storms
45	156	16	93	125	147	113	41	37

Note: Figures are average number of days per year and covers the years 1948-1990
Source: National Climatic Data Center, International Station Meteorological Climate Summary, 3/95

AIR & WATER QUALITY

Maximum Pollutant Concentrations

	Particulate Matter (ug/m^3)	Carbon Monoxide (ppm)	Sulfur Dioxide (ppm)	Nitrogen Dioxide (ppm)	Ozone (ppm)	Lead (ug/m^3)
MSA[1] Level	91	7	0.041	0.027	0.09	0.01
NAAQS[2]	150	9	0.140	0.053	0.12	1.50
Met NAAQS?	Yes	Yes	Yes	Yes	Yes	Yes

Note: (1) Metropolitan Statistical Area - see Appendix A for areas included; (2) National Ambient Air Quality Standards; ppm = parts per million; ug/m^3 = micrograms per cubic meter; n/a not available
Source: EPA, National Air Quality and Emissions Trends Report, 1996

Pollutant Standards Index

In the Minneapolis MSA (see Appendix A for areas included), the Pollutant Standards Index (PSI) exceeded 100 on 1 day in 1996. A PSI value greater than 100 indicates that air quality would be in the unhealthful range on that day. *EPA, National Air Quality and Emissions Trends Report, 1996*

Drinking Water

Water System Name	Pop. Served	Primary Water Source Type	Number of Violations in Fiscal Year 1997	Type of Violation/ Contaminants
Minneapolis	473,073	Surface	None	None

Note: Data as of January 16, 1998
Source: EPA, Office of Ground Water and Drinking Water, Safe Drinking Water Information System

Minneapolis tap water is alkaline, soft and fluoridated..
Editor & Publisher Market Guide, 1998

Oklahoma City, Oklahoma

Background

The 1992 film Far and Away, directed by Ron Howard, shows Tom Cruise charging away on his horse to claim land in the Oklahoma Territory. That dramatic scene depicted a true event from the great Oklahoma Land Run of 1889. A pistol was fired from the Oklahoma Station house of the Santa Fe railroad and 10,000 homesteaders raced away to stake land claims in central Oklahoma territory. Overnight Oklahoma City, "OKC" as the locals like to call their town, had been founded.

The new town grew quickly along the tracks of the Santa Fe railroad. Soon it became a distribution center for the territory's crops and livestock. Today the city still functions as a major transportation center for the state's farm produce and huge livestock industry. By 1910 the city had become the state capital, which also furthered growth. But in 1928 growth went through the ceiling when oil was discovered within the Oklahoma City limits. Oil forever changed the economic face of Oklahoma City from one colored by livestock and feed to livestock, feed and oil.

After World War II, Oklahoma City, like many other cities, entered industry, most notably aircraft and aircraft related industries. The Tinker Air Force Base and the Federal Aviation Administration's Mike Monroney Aeronautical Center has made Oklahoma City one of the nations leading aviation centers. The city's industry includes executive aircraft, petroleum products, electronic equipment, and oil field machinery.

The area has a lot to offer those who like a Western lifestyle. The town is the home of the National Cowboy Hall of Fame and Western Heritage Center, while the Oklahoma State Museum of History has an outstanding collection of Native American artifacts. Each September the State Fair is held in Oklahoma City and each January, the International Finals Rodeo is held at the State Fair Park. If swinging a bat is more your style than trying to stay on a bronco, you can visit the National Softball Hall of Fame and Museum.

Don't be fooled however by what some might consider the city's "simple" tastes. Oklahoma City is sophisticated enough to hire the famous architect I.M. Pei to redesign its downtown area. Taking inspiration from the Tivoli Gardens of Copenhagen, the downtown now boasts of the Myriad Gardens, a 12-acre recreational park with gardens, an amphitheater, and the seven-story Crystal Bridge Tropical Conservatory.

On April 19, 1995 Oklahoma City became the site of the deadliest terrorist incident ever to occur in the United States. On that day a truck bomb destroyed part of the Alfred P. Murrah Federal Building in the downtown area, leaving 168 people dead and more than 500 injured. In the face of such tragedy, the world marveled at the way in which Oklahoma City and the State of Oklahoma carried itself with dignity and generosity. The people's response to and support for each other became known as the "Oklahoma Standard." Oklahoma and its principal city has always been a place where people care for their own. Today the Oklahoma City Memorial Foundation continues in its pledge to build a fitting memorial for those people whose lives were ended and for those whose lives were forever changed on April 19, 1995.

The weather is changeable. There are pronounced daily and seasonal temperature changes and considerable variation in seasonal and annual precipitation. Summers are long and usually hot. Winters are comparatively mild and short.

General Rankings and Evaluative Comments

■ Oklahoma City was ranked #222 out of 300 cities by *Money's* 1997 "Survey of the Best Places to Live." Criteria used: health services, crime, economy, housing, education, transportation, weather, leisure and the arts. The city was ranked #185 in 1996 and #216 in 1995. *Money, July 1997; Money, September 1996; Money, September 1995*

■ *Ladies Home Journal* ranked America's 200 largest cities based on the qualities women care about most. Oklahoma City ranked 115 out of 200. Criteria: low crime rate, good public schools, well-paying jobs, quality health and child care, the presence of women in government, proportion of women-owned businesses, size of the wage gap with men, local economy, divorce rates, the ratio of single men to single women, whether there are laws that require at least the same number of public toilets for women as men, and the probability of good hair days. *Ladies Home Journal, November 1997*

■ Oklahoma City was ranked #152 out of 219 cities in terms of children's health, safety, and economic well-being. Criteria: total population, percent population change, birth rate, child immunization rate, infant mortality rate, percent low birth weight infants, percent of births to teens, physician-to-population ratio, student-to-teacher ratio, dropout rate, unemployment rate, median family income, percent of children in poverty, violent and property crime rates, number of juvenile arrests for violent crimes as a percent of the total crime index, number of days with pollution standard index (PSI) over 100, pounds toxic releases per 1,000 people and number of superfund sites. *Zero Population Growth, Children's Environmental Index 1997*

■ *Yahoo! Internet Life* selected "America's 100 Most Wired Cities & Towns". 50 cities were large and 50 cities were small. Oklahoma City ranked 50 out of 50 large cities. Criteria: Internet users per capita, number of networked computers, number of registered domain names, Internet backbone traffic, and the per-capita number of Web sites devoted to each city. *Yahoo! Internet Life, March 1998*

■ According to *Working Mother,* "Oklahoma's Governor Frank Keating and state lawmakers have done little to expand or improve child care options for their constituents this year. State child care officials have promoted some measures, however, which could eventually improve the quality of care and help parents find care. Hearings were held this winter on the need to expand the state's resource and referral agencies: At the moment, the state has only three R&Rs, and they cover only half the state. Oklahoma is now planning to use federal funds to add six more R&Rs.

School-age care got a modest boost: The state hired two consultants to work with local communities to develop before- and after-school programs. This is a baby step, but it deserves recognition." *Working Mother, July/August 1997*

Business Environment

STATE ECONOMY

State Economic Profile

"All segments of the Oklahoma economy are booming....

Much of the reason for Oklahoma's success is due to its low business costs, which are reduced even further by generous incentive packages. Oklahoma's competitive advantage is further enhanced by the Quality Jobs program, which provides tax incentives for ten years for qualifying companies—those whose primary markets are outside of the state.

The energy industry remains one of the most important industries in the state. For example, mining accounts for 2.3% of the state's employment and 3.7% of output, whereas nationally, mining's share of employment is 0.5% and its share of output is only 1.1%. Moreover, Oklahoma has a much larger share of its employment in both chemicals and allied products and in petroleum and coal products. The recent drop in oil prices, though aiding profit margins at refiners and chemical manufacturers, will have a net negative impact on the state.

Oklahoma's economy shows no signs of weakness. The largest impediment to growth is a dearth of available workers. As the national economy softens, slack will materialize in the labor force. This is important since Oklahoma's low business costs and generous business incentives will continue to attract jobs. With an increasingly diverse economy, which is no longer at the mercy of one industry, Oklahoma's near-term prospects are also particularly strong. While weak consumer balance sheets and the absence of a significant high-tech base continue to throw a slight damper on the state's prospects. Oklahoma is well placed for above-average growth in both the short and long term." *National Association of Realtors, Economic Profiles: The Fifty States, July 1997*

IMPORTS/EXPORTS

Total Export Sales

Area	1993 ($000)	1994 ($000)	1995 ($000)	1996 ($000)	% Chg. 1993-96	% Chg. 1995-96
MSA[1]	478,853	488,563	485,803	483,903	1.1	-0.4
U.S.	464,858,354	512,415,609	583,030,524	622,827,063	34.0	6.8

Note: (1) Metropolitan Statistical Area - see Appendix A for areas included
Source: U.S. Department of Commerce, International Trade Association, Metropolitan Area Exports: An Export Performance Report on Over 250 U.S. Cities, October 1997

Imports/Exports by Port

Type	Cargo Value 1995 (US$mil.)	1996 (US$mil.)	% Change 1995-1996	Share of U.S. Total 1995 (%)	1996 (%)
Imports	0	0	0	0	0
Exports	0	0	0	0	0

Source: Global Trade Information Services, WaterBorne Trade Atlas 1997

CITY FINANCES

City Government Finances

Component	FY92 ($000)	FY92 (per capita $)
Revenue	407,225	896.71
Expenditure	416,887	917.98
Debt Outstanding	571,114	1,257.59
Cash & Securities	525,031	1,156.11

Source: U.S. Bureau of the Census, City Government Finances: 1991-92

City Government Revenue by Source

Source	FY92 ($000)	FY92 (per capita $)	FY92 (%)
From Federal Government	10,141	22.33	2.5
From State Governments	8,383	18.46	2.1
From Local Governments	111	0.24	0.0
Property Taxes	26,600	58.57	6.5
General Sales Taxes	136,863	301.37	33.6
Selective Sales Taxes	24,195	53.28	5.9
Income Taxes	0	0.00	0.0
Current Charges	97,264	214.17	23.9
Utility/Liquor Store	38,170	84.05	9.4
Employee Retirement[1]	14,290	31.47	3.5
Other	51,208	112.76	12.6

Note: (1) Excludes "city contributions," classified as "nonrevenue," intragovernmental transfers.
Source: U.S. Bureau of the Census, City Government Finances: 1991-92

City Government Expenditures by Function

Function	FY92 ($000)	FY92 (per capita $)	FY92 (%)
Educational Services	0	0.00	0.0
Employee Retirement[1]	5,999	13.21	1.4
Environment/Housing	95,817	210.99	23.0
Government Administration	15,699	34.57	3.8
Interest on General Debt	26,096	57.46	6.3
Public Safety	118,585	261.12	28.4
Social Services	1,125	2.48	0.3
Transportation	77,538	170.74	18.6
Utility/Liquor Store	49,109	108.14	11.8
Other	26,919	59.28	6.5

Note: (1) Payments to beneficiaries including withdrawal of contributions.
Source: U.S. Bureau of the Census, City Government Finances: 1991-92

Municipal Bond Ratings

Area	Moody's	S & P
Oklahoma City	Aa2	AA

Note: n/a not available; n/r not rated
Source: Moody's Bond Record, 2/98; Statistical Abstract of the U.S., 1997; Governing Magazine, 9/97, 3/98

POPULATION

Population Growth

Area	1980	1990	% Chg. 1980-90	July 1996 Estimate	% Chg. 1990-96
City	403,243	444,730	10.3	469,852	5.6
MSA[1]	860,969	958,839	11.4	1,026,657	7.1
U.S.	226,545,805	248,765,170	9.8	265,179,411	6.6

Note: (1) Metropolitan Statistical Area - see Appendix A for areas included
Source: 1980/1990 Census of Housing and Population, Summary Tape File 3C; Census Bureau Population Estimates

Population Characteristics

Race	City 1980 Population	%	City 1990 Population	%	% Chg. 1980-90	MSA[1] 1990 Population	%
White	323,665	80.3	333,108	74.9	2.9	779,187	81.3
Black	58,550	14.5	70,887	15.9	21.1	100,587	10.5
Amer Indian/Esk/Aleut	11,199	2.8	19,099	4.3	70.5	46,111	4.8
Asian/Pacific Islander	4,610	1.1	10,182	2.3	120.9	16,867	1.8
Other	5,219	1.3	11,454	2.6	119.5	16,087	1.7
Hispanic Origin[2]	11,295	2.8	21,148	4.8	87.2	32,851	3.4

Note: (1) Metropolitan Statistical Area - see Appendix A for areas included;
(2) people of Hispanic origin can be of any race
Source: 1980/1990 Census of Housing and Population, Summary Tape File 3C

Ancestry

Area	German	Irish	English	Italian	U.S.	French	Polish	Dutch
City	21.9	18.8	14.2	1.6	6.4	3.8	1.1	3.9
MSA[1]	24.0	20.3	15.1	1.6	7.0	4.1	1.2	4.2
U.S.	23.3	15.6	13.1	5.9	5.3	4.2	3.8	2.5

Note: Figures are percentages and include persons that reported multiple ancestry (eg. if a person reported being Irish and Italian, they were included in both columns); (1) Metropolitan Statistical Area - see Appendix A for areas included
Source: 1990 Census of Population and Housing, Summary Tape File 3C

Age

Area	Median Age (Years)	Age Distribution (%) Under 5	Under 18	18-24	25-44	45-64	65+	80+
City	32.3	7.7	25.9	9.9	33.8	18.6	11.8	2.6
MSA[1]	31.9	7.4	26.5	10.8	33.3	18.4	11.0	2.5
U.S.	32.9	7.3	25.6	10.5	32.6	18.7	12.5	2.8

Note: (1) Metropolitan Statistical Area - see Appendix A for areas included
Source: 1990 Census of Population and Housing, Summary Tape File 3C

Male/Female Ratio

Area	Number of males per 100 females (all ages)	Number of males per 100 females (18 years old+)
City	93.3	89.5
MSA[1]	95.0	91.3
U.S.	95.0	91.9

Note: (1) Metropolitan Statistical Area - see Appendix A for areas included
Source: 1990 Census of Population, General Population Characteristics

INCOME

Per Capita/Median/Average Income

Area	Per Capita ($)	Median Household ($)	Average Household ($)
City	13,528	25,741	33,258
MSA[1]	13,269	26,883	34,117
U.S.	14,420	30,056	38,453

Note: all figures are for 1989; (1) Metropolitan Statistical Area - see Appendix A for areas included
Source: 1990 Census of Population and Housing, Summary Tape File 3C

Household Income Distribution by Race

Income ($)	City (%)					U.S. (%)				
	Total	White	Black	Other	Hisp.[1]	Total	White	Black	Other	Hisp.[1]
Less than 5,000	6.9	5.4	13.7	10.6	6.8	6.2	4.8	15.2	8.6	8.8
5,000 - 9,999	10.6	9.4	16.9	11.1	14.7	9.3	8.6	14.2	9.9	11.1
10,000 - 14,999	10.4	10.0	12.2	12.3	14.5	8.8	8.5	11.0	9.8	11.0
15,000 - 24,999	20.7	20.4	21.0	23.6	26.2	17.5	17.3	18.9	18.5	20.5
25,000 - 34,999	16.9	17.2	15.3	16.2	17.1	15.8	16.1	14.2	15.4	16.4
35,000 - 49,999	16.1	17.0	11.9	13.9	12.3	17.9	18.6	13.3	16.1	16.0
50,000 - 74,999	12.3	13.5	7.3	9.2	5.7	15.0	15.8	9.3	13.4	11.1
75,000 - 99,999	3.3	3.8	1.2	2.1	1.2	5.1	5.5	2.6	4.7	3.1
100,000+	2.8	3.4	0.5	1.1	1.5	4.4	4.8	1.3	3.7	1.9

Note: all figures are for 1989; (1) people of Hispanic origin can be of any race
Source: 1990 Census of Population and Housing, Summary Tape File 3C

Effective Buying Income

Area	Per Capita ($)	Median Household ($)	Average Household ($)
City	14,310	27,900	35,878
MSA[1]	14,773	30,781	38,771
U.S.	15,444	33,201	41,849

Note: data as of 1/1/97; (1) Metropolitan Statistical Area - see Appendix A for areas included
Source: Standard Rate & Data Service, Newspaper Advertising Source, 2/98

Effective Household Buying Income Distribution

Area	% of Households Earning						
	$10,000 -$19,999	$20,000 -$34,999	$35,000 -$49,999	$50,000 -$74,999	$75,000 -$99,000	$100,000 -$124,999	$125,000 and up
City	20.0	26.3	17.2	14.7	4.1	1.3	1.6
MSA[1]	17.9	25.4	18.2	16.8	5.3	1.5	1.7
U.S.	16.5	23.4	18.3	18.2	6.4	2.1	2.4

Note: data as of 1/1/97; (1) Metropolitan Statistical Area - see Appendix A for areas included
Source: Standard Rate & Data Service, Newspaper Advertising Source, 2/98

Poverty Rates by Race and Age

Area	Total (%)	By Race (%)				By Age (%)		
		White	Black	Other	Hisp.[2]	Under 5 years old	Under 18 years old	65 years and over
City	15.9	11.2	32.4	25.6	30.7	27.4	22.9	13.1
MSA[1]	13.9	10.8	30.8	24.1	26.6	22.8	18.6	13.1
U.S.	13.1	9.8	29.5	23.1	25.3	20.1	18.3	12.8

Note: figures show the percent of people living below the poverty line in 1989. The average poverty threshold was $12,674 for a family of four in 1989; (1) Metropolitan Statistical Area - see Appendix A for areas included; (2) people of Hispanic origin can be of any race
Source: 1990 Census of Population and Housing, Summary Tape File 3C

EMPLOYMENT

Labor Force and Employment

Area	Civilian Labor Force			Workers Employed		
	Dec. '95	Dec. '96	% Chg.	Dec. '95	Dec. '96	% Chg.
City	240,757	242,717	0.8	232,794	235,344	1.1
MSA[1]	520,768	525,249	0.9	505,201	510,735	1.1
U.S.	134,583,000	136,742,000	1.6	127,903,000	130,785,000	2.3

Note: Data is not seasonally adjusted and covers workers 16 years of age and older;
(1) Metropolitan Statistical Area - see Appendix A for areas included
Source: Bureau of Labor Statistics, http://stats.bls.gov

Oklahoma City, Oklahoma   267

Unemployment Rate

Area	1997											
	Jan.	Feb.	Mar.	Apr.	May	Jun.	Jul.	Aug.	Sep.	Oct.	Nov.	Dec.
City	3.9	3.4	3.0	2.8	3.1	3.2	2.9	3.2	3.5	3.5	3.1	3.0
MSA[1]	3.5	3.1	2.8	2.6	2.8	2.9	2.8	2.9	3.1	3.2	2.9	2.8
U.S.	5.9	5.7	5.5	4.8	4.7	5.2	5.0	4.8	4.7	4.4	4.3	4.4

Note: Data is not seasonally adjusted and covers workers 16 years of age and older; All figures are percentages; (1) Metropolitan Statistical Area - see Appendix A for areas included
Source: Bureau of Labor Statistics, http://stats.bls.gov

Employment by Industry

Sector	MSA[1]		U.S.
	Number of Employees	Percent of Total	Percent of Total
Services	148,400	29.0	29.0
Retail Trade	98,700	19.3	18.5
Government	103,700	20.3	16.1
Manufacturing	55,400	10.8	15.0
Finance/Insurance/Real Estate	29,800	5.8	5.7
Wholesale Trade	24,600	4.8	5.4
Transportation/Public Utilities	24,900	4.9	5.3
Construction	18,100	3.5	4.5
Mining	7,500	1.5	0.5

Note: Figures cover non-farm employment as of 12/97 and are not seasonally adjusted;
(1) Metropolitan Statistical Area - see Appendix A for areas included
Source: Bureau of Labor Statistics, http://stats.bls.gov

Employment by Occupation

Occupation Category	City (%)	MSA[1] (%)	U.S. (%)
White Collar	61.7	60.9	58.1
Executive/Admin./Management	12.9	12.7	12.3
Professional	13.4	13.9	14.1
Technical & Related Support	4.4	4.2	3.7
Sales	13.6	12.7	11.8
Administrative Support/Clerical	17.5	17.4	16.3
Blue Collar	23.2	23.8	26.2
Precision Production/Craft/Repair	10.0	10.8	11.3
Machine Operators/Assem./Insp.	5.8	5.6	6.8
Transportation/Material Movers	3.8	4.0	4.1
Cleaners/Helpers/Laborers	3.6	3.4	3.9
Services	13.9	13.7	13.2
Farming/Forestry/Fishing	1.2	1.5	2.5

Note: figures cover employed persons 16 years old and over;
(1) Metropolitan Statistical Area - see Appendix A for areas included
Source: 1990 Census of Population and Housing, Summary Tape File 3C

Occupational Employment Projections: 1994 - 2005

Occupations Expected to have the Largest Job Growth (ranked by numerical growth)	Fast-Growing Occupations (ranked by percent growth)
1. Waiters & waitresses	1. Occupational therapy assistants
2. Nursing aides/orderlies/attendants	2. Ushers/lobby attendants/ticket takers
3. Registered nurses	3. Electronic pagination systems workers
4. General managers & top executives	4. Computer engineers
5. Janitors/cleaners/maids, ex. priv. hshld.	5. Computer scientists
6. Child care workers, private household	6. Amusement and recreation attendants
7. Teachers, secondary school	7. Occupational therapists
8. Cashiers	8. Home health aides
9. Licensed practical nurses	9. Human services workers
10. Secretaries, except legal & medical	10. Physical therapy assistants and aides

Projections cover Oklahoma.
Source: U.S. Department of Labor, Employment and Training Administration, America's Labor Market Information System (ALMIS)

Average Wages

Occupation	Wage	Occupation	Wage
Professional/Technical/Clerical	$/Week	**Health/Protective Services**	$/Week
Accountants III	-	Corrections Officers	-
Attorneys III	-	Firefighters	-
Budget Analysts III	-	Nurses, Licensed Practical II	-
Buyers/Contracting Specialists II	-	Nurses, Registered II	-
Clerks, Accounting III	432	Nursing Assistants II	-
Clerks, General III	472	Police Officers I	-
Computer Operators II	409	**Hourly Workers**	$/Hour
Computer Programmers II	586	Forklift Operators	10.53
Drafters II	433	General Maintenance Workers	9.84
Engineering Technicians III	626	Guards I	6.40
Engineering Technicians, Civil III	-	Janitors	6.39
Engineers III	-	Maintenance Electricians	-
Key Entry Operators I	290	Maintenance Electronics Techs II	18.91
Personnel Assistants III	-	Maintenance Machinists	19.04
Personnel Specialists III	-	Maintenance Mechanics, Machinery	15.20
Secretaries III	534	Material Handling Laborers	6.58
Switchboard Operator-Receptionist	300	Motor Vehicle Mechanics	13.41
Systems Analysts II	907	Shipping/Receiving Clerks	7.97
Systems Analysts Supervisor/Mgr II	-	Tool and Die Makers	19.52
Tax Collectors II	-	Truckdrivers, Tractor Trailer	13.51
Word Processors II	-	Warehouse Specialists	-

Note: Wage data includes full-time workers only for 7/96 and cover the Metropolitan Statistical Area (see Appendix A for areas included). Dashes indicate that data was not available.
Source: Bureau of Labor Statistics, Occupational Compensation Survey, 11/96

TAXES

Major State and Local Tax Rates

State Corp. Income (%)	State Personal Income (%)	Residential Property (effective rate per $100)	Sales & Use		State Gasoline (cents/ gallon)	State Cigarette (cents/ 20-pack)
			State (%)	Local (%)		
6.0	0.5 - 7.0[a]	1.10	4.5	3.875	17[b]	23

Note: Personal/corporate income tax rates as of 1/97. Sales, gasoline and cigarette tax rates as of 1/98; (a) Range is for persons not deducting federal income tax. Separate schedules, with rates ranging from 0.5% to 10%, apply to taxpayers deducting federal income taxes; (b) Rate is comprised of 16 cents excise and 1 cent motor carrier tax
Source: Federation of Tax Administrators, www.taxadmin.org; Washington D.C. Department of Finance and Revenue, Tax Rates and Tax Burdens in the District of Columbia: A Nationwide Comparison, June 1997; Chamber of Commerce

Total Taxes Per Capita and as a Percent of Income

Area	Per Capita Income ($)	Per Capita Taxes ($)			Taxes as Pct. of Income (%)		
		Total	Federal	State/Local	Total	Federal	State/Local
Oklahoma	20,775	6,835	4,630	2,206	32.9	22.3	10.6
U.S.	26,187	9,205	6,127	3,078	35.2	23.4	11.8

Note: Figures are for 1997
Source: Tax Foundation, Web Site, www.taxfoundation.org

Estimated Tax Burden

Area	State Income	Local Income	Property	Sales	Total
Oklahoma City	2,556	0	2,025	1,284	5,865

Note: The numbers are estimates of taxes paid by a married couple with two kids and annual earnings of $65,000. Sales tax estimates assume they spend average amounts on food, clothing, household goods and gasoline. Property tax estimates assume they live in a $225,000 home.
Source: Kiplinger's Personal Finance Magazine, June 1997

COMMERCIAL REAL ESTATE

Office Market

Class/Location	Total Space (sq. ft.)	Vacant Space (sq. ft.)	Vac. Rate (%)	Under Constr. (sq. ft.)	Net Absorp. (sq. ft.)	Rental Rates ($/sq.ft./yr.)
Class A						
CBD	3,442,640	688,528	20.0	n/a	-19,328	10.00-14.00
Outside CBD	5,096,331	305,780	6.0	n/a	-375,496	10.00-19.00
Class B						
CBD	1,903,988	730,945	38.4	n/a	-160,581	8.00-10.00
Outside CBD	3,397,554	370,481	10.9	n/a	356,810	9.50-12.00

Note: Data as of 10/97 and covers the Oklahoma City metro area; CBD = Central Business District; n/a not available;
Source: Society of Industrial and Office Realtors, 1998 Comparative Statistics of Industrial and Office Real Estate Markets

"SIOR's local reporter is optimistic for 1998. Rental rates are projected to appreciate by up to 10 percent in 1998. Any future gains would be accrued on top of the $0.75 to $1.50 per square foot average growth recognized in all categories in 1997. Suburban sales prices are expected to rise by another 10 - 15%, which was actually the case in prime properties last year. Pro-business policies, low wages, and population growth will continue to attract new firms and enhance the environment for expansions of existing firms. New state policies and actions include the reduction of unemployment insurance by 25%, provision of a 20% tax investment credit for small businesses and initiation of the Major Workers Compensation Reform."
Society of Industrial and Office Realtors, 1998 Comparative Statistics of Industrial and Office Real Estate Markets

Industrial Market

Location	Total Space (sq. ft.)	Vacant Space (sq. ft.)	Vac. Rate (%)	Under Constr. (sq. ft.)	Net Absorp. (sq. ft.)	Lease ($/sq.ft./yr.)
Central City	n/a	n/a	n/a	n/a	n/a	n/a
Suburban	69,000,000	3,000,000	4.3	1,900,000	3,000,000	2.00-6.50

Note: Data as of 10/97 and covers Oklahoma City; n/a not available
Source: Society of Industrial and Office Realtors, 1998 Comparative Statistics of Industrial and Office Real Estate Markets

"Almost two million sq. ft. are currently under construction. In addition, a moderate amount of new speculative construction should occur in 1998. Development will be concentrated in the Memorial Road and Southwest industrial areas. Lease and sales prices are expected to increase, although shrinking supply has not put pressure on prices yet. Economic growth should be generated through competitive business incentives, high-tech educational efforts and public projects including the $280 million Metropolitan Area Projects, now underway with a new baseball park and 20,000-seat arena. Warehouse and distribution properties should benefit the most by accelerated absorption. Forecasts of annual employment anticipate growth at close to two percent through the next century." *Society of Industrial and Office Realtors, 1998 Comparative Statistics of Industrial and Office Real Estate Markets*

Retail Market

Shopping Center Inventory (sq. ft.)	Shopping Center Construction (sq. ft.)	Construction as a Percent of Inventory (%)	Torto Wheaton Rent Index[1] ($/sq. ft.)
23,933,000	252,000	1.1	9.06

Note: Data as of 1997 and covers the Metropolitan Statistical Area - see Appendix A for areas included; (1) Index is based on a model that predicts what the average rent should be for leases with certain characteristics, in certain locations during certain years.
Source: National Association of Realtors, 1997-1998 Market Conditions Report

"During the 1990s, Oklahoma City worked diligently to diversify its economy. Increased diversity has contributed to strong payroll growth in recent years. However, relatively low wage rates are a burden on the retail trade sector. The area's retail rent index has steadily increased over the last two years, edging up 3.4% in 1996 and 4.0% in 1997. Rents still remain well below the South's average of $13.79 per square foot. Oklahoma City's retail market is expected to remain stable in the near future, with upward rent movement. America On-Line and Southwest Airlines have announced plans that will bring an estimated 2,100 jobs to the area." *National Association of Realtors, 1997-1998 Market Conditions Report*

COMMERCIAL UTILITIES

Typical Monthly Electric Bills

Area	Commercial Service ($/month)		Industrial Service ($/month)	
	12 kW demand 1,500 kWh	100 kW demand 30,000 kWh	1,000 kW demand 400,000 kWh	20,000 kW demand 10,000,000 kWh
City	164	2,358	24,216	358,571
U.S.	162	2,360	25,590	545,677

Note: Based on rates in effect July 1, 1997
Source: Edison Electric Institute, Typical Residential, Commercial and Industrial Bills, Summer 1997

TRANSPORTATION

Transportation Statistics

Avg. travel time to work (min.)	19.3
Interstate highways	None
Bus lines	
In-city	Metro Transit, 76 vehicles
Inter-city	2
Passenger air service	
Airport	Will Rogers World Airport
Airlines	8
Aircraft departures	28,850 (1955)
Enplaned passengers	1,648,494 (1995)
Rail service	No Amtrak Service
Motor freight carriers	32 regular routes; 170+ irregular
Major waterways/ports	None

Source: OAG, Business Travel Planner, Summer 1997; Editor & Publisher Market Guide, 1998; FAA Airport Activity Statistics, 1996; Amtrak National Time Table, Northeast Timetable, Fall/Winter 1997-98; 1990 Census of Population and Housing, STF 3C; Chamber of Commerce/Economic Development 1997; Jane's Urban Transport Systems 1997-98; Transit Fact Book 1997

Means of Transportation to Work

Area	Car/Truck/Van		Public Transportation			Bicycle	Walked	Other Means	Worked at Home
	Drove Alone	Car-pooled	Bus	Subway	Railroad				
City	80.8	12.8	0.8	0.0	0.0	0.1	2.0	1.2	2.3
MSA[1]	80.3	13.3	0.5	0.0	0.0	0.2	2.1	1.0	2.5
U.S.	73.2	13.4	3.0	1.5	0.5	0.4	3.9	1.2	3.0

Note: figures shown are percentages and only include workers 16 years old and over;
(1) Metropolitan Statistical Area - see Appendix A for areas included
Source: 1990 Census of Population and Housing, Summary Tape File 3C

BUSINESSES

Major Business Headquarters

Company Name	1997 Rankings	
	Fortune 500	Forbes 500
Fleming	69	-

Note: Companies listed are located in the city; Dashes indicate no ranking
Fortune 500: companies that produce a 10-K are ranked 1 - 500 based on 1996 revenue
Forbes 500: private companies are ranked 1 - 500 based on 1996 revenue
Source: Forbes 12/1/97; Fortune 4/28/97

Fast-Growing Businesses

According to *Inc.*, Oklahoma City is home to one of America's 100 fastest-growing private companies: Accord Human Resources. Criteria for inclusion: must be an independent, privately-held, U.S. corporation, proprietorship or partnership; sales of at least $200,000 in 1993; five-year operating/sales history; increase in 1997 sales over 1996 sales; holding companies, regulated banks, and utilities were excluded. *Inc. 500, 1997*

Women-Owned Businesses: Number, Employment, Sales and Share

Area	Women-Owned Businesses in 1996				Share of Women-Owned Businesses in 1996	
	Number	Employment	Sales ($000)	Rank[2]	Percent (%)	Rank[3]
MSA[1]	35,900	63,600	7,064,900	49	37.6	19

Note: (1) Metropolitan Statistical Area - see Appendix A for areas included; (2) Calculated on an averaging of number of businesses, employment and sales and ranges from 1 to 50 where 1 is best; (3) Ranges from 1 to 50 where 1 is best
Source: The National Foundation for Women Business Owners, 1996 Facts on Women-Owned Businesses: Trends in the Top 50 Metropolitan Areas, March 26, 1997

Women-Owned Businesses: Growth

Area	Growth in Women-Owned Businesses (% change from 1987 to 1996)				Relative Growth in the Number of Women-Owned and All Businesses (% change from 1987 to 1996)			
	Num.	Empl.	Sales	Rank[2]	Women-Owned	All Firms	Absolute Difference	Relative Difference
MSA[1]	55.7	166.7	231.2	42	55.7	25.3	30.4	2.2:1

Note: (1) Metropolitan Statistical Area - see Appendix A for areas included; (2) Calculated on an averaging of the percent growth of number of businesses, employment and sales and ranges from 1 to 50 where 1 is best
Source: The National Foundation for Women Business Owners, 1996 Facts on Women-Owned Businesses: Trends in the Top 50 Metropolitan Areas, March 26, 1997

Minority Business Opportunity

Oklahoma City is home to one company which is on the Black Enterprise Auto Dealer 100 list (largest based on gross sales): Southwest Ford Sales Inc. (Ford). Criteria: 1) operational in previous calendar year; 2) at least 51% black-owned. *Black Enterprise, June 1997*

One of the 500 largest Hispanic-owned companies in the U.S. are located in Oklahoma City. *Hispanic Business, June 1997*

Small Business Opportunity

According to *Forbes*, Oklahoma City is home to one of America's 200 best small companies: Sonic. Criteria: companies must be publicly traded, U.S.-based corporations with latest 12-month sales of between $5 and $350 million. Earnings must be at least $1 million for the 12-month period. Limited partnerships, REITs and closed-end mutual funds were not considered. Banks, S&Ls and electric utilities were not included. *Forbes, November 3, 1997*

HOTELS & MOTELS

Hotels/Motels

Area	Hotels/ Motels	Rooms	Luxury-Level Hotels/Motels		Average Minimum Rates ($)		
			♦♦♦♦	♦♦♦♦♦	♦♦	♦♦♦	♦♦♦♦
City	25	4,110	1	0	52	98	129
Airport	17	2,768	0	0	n/a	n/a	n/a
Suburbs	16	1,495	0	0	n/a	n/a	n/a
Total	58	8,373	1	0	n/a	n/a	n/a

Note: n/a not available; Classifications range from one diamond (budget properties with basic amenities) to five diamond (luxury properties with the finest service, rooms and facilities).
Source: OAG, Business Travel Planner, Summer 1997

CONVENTION CENTERS

Major Convention Centers

Center Name	Meeting Rooms	Exhibit Space (sf)
Civic Center Music Hall	4	3,500
Myriad Convention Center	24	275,000
State Fair Parks of Oklahoma	n/a	900,000
Will Rogers Center	1	6,000

Note: n/a not available
Source: Trade Shows Worldwide 1997

Living Environment

COST OF LIVING

Cost of Living Index

Composite Index	Housing	Utilities	Groceries	Health Care	Trans- portation	Misc. Goods/ Services
90.9	80.0	95.3	88.5	90.0	95.2	99.3

Note: U.S. = 100
Source: ACCRA, Cost of Living Index, 3rd Quarter 1997

HOUSING

Median Home Prices and Housing Affordability

Area	Median Price[2] 3rd Qtr. 1997 ($)	HOI[3] 3rd Qtr. 1997	Afford- ability Rank[4]
MSA[1]	82,000	77.4	36
U.S.	127,000	63.7	–

Note: (1) Metropolitan Statistical Area - see Appendix A for areas included; (2) U.S. figures calculated from the sales of 625,000 new and existing homes in 195 markets; (3) Housing Opportunity Index - percent of homes sold that were within the reach of the median income household at the prevailing mortgage interest rate; (4) Rank is from 1-195 with 1 being most affordable
Source: National Association of Home Builders, Housing Opportunity Index, 3rd Quarter 1997

It is projected that the median price of existing single-family homes in the metro area will increase by 1.4% in 1998. Nationwide, home prices are projected to increase 6.6%.
Kiplinger's Personal Finance Magazine, January 1998

Average New Home Price

Area	Price ($)
City	103,795
U.S.	135,710

Note: Figures are based on a new home with 1,800 sq. ft. of living area on an 8,000 sq. ft. lot.
Source: ACCRA, Cost of Living Index, 3rd Quarter 1997

Average Apartment Rent

Area	Rent ($/mth)
City	521
U.S.	569

Note: Figures are based on an unfurnished two bedroom, 1-1/2 or 2 bath apartment, approximately 950 sq. ft. in size, excluding all utilities except water
Source: ACCRA, Cost of Living Index, 3rd Quarter 1997

RESIDENTIAL UTILITIES

Average Residential Utility Costs

Area	All Electric ($/mth)	Part Electric ($/mth)	Other Energy ($/mth)	Phone ($/mth)
City	–	59.99	35.96	20.58
U.S.	109.40	55.25	43.64	19.48

Source: ACCRA, Cost of Living Index, 3rd Quarter 1997

HEALTH CARE

Average Health Care Costs

Area	Hospital ($/day)	Doctor ($/visit)	Dentist ($/visit)
City	279.10	42.14	61.40
U.S.	392.91	48.76	60.84

Note: Hospital - based on a semi-private room. Doctor - based on a general practitioner's routine exam of an established patient. Dentist - based on adult teeth cleaning and periodic oral exam.
Source: ACCRA, Cost of Living Index, 3rd Quarter 1997

Distribution of Office-Based Physicians

| Area | Family/Gen. Practitioners | Specialists | | |
		Medical	Surgical	Other
MSA[1]	244	533	470	535

Note: Data as of 12/31/96; (1) Metropolitan Statistical Area - see Appendix A for areas included
Source: American Medical Assn., Physician Characteristics & Distribution in the U.S., 1997-1998

Hospitals

Oklahoma City has 9 general medical and surgical hospitals, 1 psychiatric, 1 rehabilitation, 2 orthopedic. *AHA Guide to the Healthcare Field 1997-98*

Columbia Presbyterian Hospital is among the 100 best-run hospitals in the U.S. *Modern Healthcare, January 5, 1998*

EDUCATION

Public School District Statistics

District Name	Num. Sch.	Enroll.	Classroom Teachers[1]	Pupils per Teacher	Minority Pupils (%)	Current Exp.[2] ($/pupil)
Crooked Oak	4	853	56	15.2	n/a	n/a
Crutcho	1	395	25	15.8	n/a	n/a
Millwood	3	1,119	60	18.6	n/a	n/a
Oklahoma City	86	39,829	2,402	16.6	62.0	4,395
Putnam City	27	19,035	1,151	16.5	n/a	n/a
Western Heights	6	2,945	194	15.2	n/a	n/a

Note: Data covers the 1995-1996 school year unless otherwise noted; (1) Excludes teachers reported as working in school district offices rather than in schools; (2) Based on 1993-94 enrollment collected by the Census Bureau, not the enrollment figure shown in column 3; SD = School District; ISD = Independent School District; n/a not available
Source: National Center for Education Statistics, Common Core of Data Survey; Bureau of the Census

Educational Quality

School District	Education Quotient[1]	Graduate Outcome[2]	Community Index[3]	Resource Index[4]
Oklahoma City	72.0	55.0	99.0	61.0

Note: Nearly 1,000 secondary school districts were rated in terms of educational quality. The scores range from a low of 50 to a high of 150; (1) Average of the Graduate Outcome, Community and Resource indexes; (2) Based on graduation rates and college board scores (SAT/ACT); (3) Based on the surrounding community's average level of education and the area's average income level; (4) Based on teacher salaries, per-pupil expenditures and student-teacher ratios.
Source: Expansion Management, Ratings Issue 1997

Educational Attainment by Race

| Area | High School Graduate (%) | | | | | Bachelor's Degree (%) | | | | |
	Total	White	Black	Other	Hisp.[2]	Total	White	Black	Other	Hisp.[2]
City	78.2	80.8	72.6	61.9	47.5	21.6	23.7	12.9	14.9	10.3
MSA[1]	79.2	80.6	74.5	68.5	55.3	21.6	22.7	14.2	17.7	11.1
U.S.	75.2	77.9	63.1	60.4	49.8	20.3	21.5	11.4	19.4	9.2

Note: figures shown cover persons 25 years old and over; (1) Metropolitan Statistical Area - see Appendix A for areas included; (2) people of Hispanic origin can be of any race
Source: 1990 Census of Population and Housing, Summary Tape File 3C

School Enrollment by Type

Area	Preprimary				Elementary/High School			
	Public		Private		Public		Private	
	Enrollment	%	Enrollment	%	Enrollment	%	Enrollment	%
City	4,639	60.5	3,033	39.5	66,351	90.3	7,166	9.7
MSA[1]	10,338	60.2	6,849	39.8	156,353	92.8	12,146	7.2
U.S.	2,679,029	59.5	1,824,256	40.5	38,379,689	90.2	4,187,099	9.8

Note: figures shown cover persons 3 years old and over;
(1) Metropolitan Statistical Area - see Appendix A for areas included
Source: 1990 Census of Population and Housing, Summary Tape File 3C

School Enrollment by Race

Area	Preprimary (%)				Elementary/High School (%)			
	White	Black	Other	Hisp.[1]	White	Black	Other	Hisp.[1]
City	72.4	18.2	9.4	5.7	65.7	21.8	12.5	7.3
MSA[2]	79.1	12.1	8.8	4.3	75.6	13.7	10.7	4.9
U.S.	80.4	12.5	7.1	7.8	74.1	15.6	10.3	12.5

Note: figures shown cover persons 3 years old and over; (1) people of Hispanic origin can be of any race; (2) Metropolitan Statistical Area - see Appendix A for areas included
Source: 1990 Census of Population and Housing, Summary Tape File 3C

SAT/ACT Scores

Area/District	1995 SAT				1995 ACT	
	Percent of Graduates Tested (%)	Average Math Score	Average Verbal Score	Average Combined Score	Percent of Graduates Tested (%)	Average Composite Score
Oklahoma City	n/a	496	467	963	n/a	n/a
State	9	536	491	1,027	65	20.3
U.S.	41	482	428	910	37	20.8

Note: Math and verbal SAT scores are out of a possible 800; ACT scores are out of a possible 36
Caution: Comparing or ranking states/cities on the basis of SAT/ACT scores alone is invalid and strongly discouraged by the The College Board and The American College Testing Program as students who take the tests are self-selected and do not represent the entire student population.
Source: Oklahoma City Public Schools, Planning, Research & Evaluation Department; American College Testing Program, 1995; College Board, 1995

Classroom Teacher Salaries in Public Schools

District	B.A. Degree		M.A. Degree		Ph.D. Degree	
	Min. ($)	Max ($)	Min. ($)	Max. ($)	Min. ($)	Max. ($)
Oklahoma City	23,170	32,100	24,200	34,050	25,225	35,200
Average[1]	26,120	39,270	28,175	44,667	31,643	49,825

Note: Salaries are for 1996-1997; (1) Based on all school districts covered; n/a not available
Source: American Federation of Teachers (unpublished data)

Higher Education

Two-Year Colleges		Four-Year Colleges		Medical Schools	Law Schools	Voc/ Tech
Public	Private	Public	Private			
2	0	1	3	1	1	13

Source: College Blue Book, Occupational Education 1997; Medical School Admission Requirements, 1998-99; Peterson's Guide to Two-Year Colleges, 1997; Peterson's Guide to Four-Year Colleges, 1997; Barron's Guide to Law Schools 1997

MAJOR EMPLOYERS

Major Employers

Southwest Medical Center of Oklahoma	Baptist Medical Center of Oklahoma
St. Anthony Health Care Corp.	Mercy Health Center
Unit Parts (electrical equip.)	Kerr-McGee (chemicals)
Deaconess Hospital	Oklahoma Publishing
CMI Corp. (construction machinery)	Midwest City Memorial Hospital
American Fidelity Corp. (insurance)	Hob-Lob Limited Partnership (hobby & toy shops)

Note: companies listed are located in the city
Source: Dun's Business Rankings 1997; Ward's Business Directory, 1997

PUBLIC SAFETY

Crime Rate

Area	All Crimes	Violent Crimes				Property Crimes		
		Murder	Forcible Rape	Robbery	Aggrav. Assault	Burglary	Larceny -Theft	Motor Vehicle Theft
City	12,158.5	14.3	101.6	314.7	699.7	2,276.3	7,656.4	1,095.5
Suburbs[1]	4,925.5	3.6	37.9	69.8	236.7	1,082.1	3,157.7	337.7
MSA[2]	8,252.3	8.5	67.2	182.5	449.6	1,631.4	5,226.9	686.3
U.S.	5,078.9	7.4	36.1	202.4	388.2	943.0	2,975.9	525.9

Note: Crime rate is the number of crimes per 100,000 pop.; (1) defined as all areas within the MSA but located outside the central city; (2) Metropolitan Statistical Area - see Appendix A for areas incl.
Source: FBI Uniform Crime Reports 1996

RECREATION

Culture and Recreation

Museums	Symphony Orchestras	Opera Companies	Dance Companies	Professional Theatres	Zoos	Pro Sports Teams
12	1	1	1	1	1	0

Source: International Directory of the Performing Arts, 1996; Official Museum Directory, 1998; Chamber of Commerce/Economic Development 1997

Library System

The Metropolitan Library System in Oklahoma County has 12 branches, holdings of 785,590 volumes and a budget of $10,766,409 (1995-1996). *American Library Directory, 1997-1998*

MEDIA

Newspapers

Name	Type	Freq.	Distribution	Circulation
Baptist Messenger	Religious	1x/wk	State	100,000
Black Chronicle	Black	1x/wk	Local	29,803
The Capitol Hill Beacon	n/a	1x/wk	Local	1,400
The Daily Oklahoman	General	7x/wk	Local	227,894
El Nacional	Hispanic	2x/mo	Local	10,750
Friday	General	1x/wk	Local	22,000
Metro Buyer's Guide	General	1x/wk	Local	350,000
Oklahoma Gazette	General	1x/wk	Area	46,100
Oklahoma Journal Record	n/a	5x/wk	Area	4,100
Tinker Take Off	n/a	1x/wk	Local	28,600

Note: Includes newspapers with circulations of 1,000 or more located in the city; n/a not available
Source: Burrelle's Media Directory, 1998 Edition

AM Radio Stations

Call Letters	Freq. (kHz)	Target Audience	Station Format	Music Format
KQCV	800	Religious	T	n/a
KBYE	890	Religious	M	Christian
WKY	930	General	M/T	Christian
KTOK	1000	General	N/S/T	n/a
KVSP	1140	Black	M/N/T	R&B/Urban Contemporary
KTLV	1220	Black	M	Christian
KXXY	1340	Black/Hisp	M/S/T	R&B/Spanish
KZUE	1460	Hispanic	E/M/N/S/T	Spanish
KOMA	1520	General	M	Oldies

Note: Stations included broadcast in the Oklahoma City metro area; n/a not available
Station Format: E = Educational; M = Music; N = News; S = Sports; T = Talk
Source: Burrelle's Media Directory, 1998 Edition

FM Radio Stations

Call Letters	Freq. (mHz)	Target Audience	Station Format	Music Format
KOCC	88.9	General	M/S	Adult Contemporary/Christian/Country
KCSC	90.1	General	M/N	Classical
KOKF	90.9	General	M	Alternative/Christian/Urban Contemporary
KOMA	92.5	n/a	M/N/S	Oldies
KNRX	94.7	General	M	Alternative
KXXY	96.1	General	M/N	Country
KTNT	97.9	General	M	Adult Contemporary
KYIS	98.9	n/a	M/N/S	Adult Contemporary
KATT	100.5	General	M	AOR
KTST	101.9	General	M	Country
KJYO	102.7	General	M	Contemporary Top 40
KMGL	104.1	General	M	Adult Contemporary
KNTL	104.9	Religious	T	n/a
KRXO	107.7	n/a	M	Classic Rock

Note: Stations included broadcast in the Oklahoma City metro area; n/a not available
Station Format: E = Educational; M = Music; N = News; S = Sports; T = Talk
Music Format: AOR = Album Oriented Rock; MOR = Middle-of-the-Road
Source: Burrelle's Media Directory, 1998 Edition

Television Stations

Name	Ch.	Affiliation	Type	Owner
KOET	3	PBS	Public	Oklahoma Educational Television Authority
KFOR	4	NBC	Commercial	New York Times Company
KOCO	5	ABC	Commercial	Argyle Television Inc.
KWTV	9	CBS	Commercial	Griffin Television Inc.
KWET	12	PBS	Public	Oklahoma Educational TV Authority
KETA	13	PBS	Public	Oklahoma Educational Television Authority
KTBO	14	TBN	Commercial	Trinity Broadcasting
KOKH	25	Fox	Commercial	Heritage Media Corp.
KOCB	34	UPN	Commercial	Superior Communications Group Inc.
KTLC	43	PBS	Public	Oklahoma Educational TV Authority
KSBI	52	n/a	Commercial	Locke Supply Company

Note: Stations included broadcast in the Oklahoma City metro area
Source: Burrelle's Media Directory, 1998 Edition

CLIMATE

Average and Extreme Temperatures

Temperature	Jan	Feb	Mar	Apr	May	Jun	Jul	Aug	Sep	Oct	Nov	Dec	Ann
Extreme High (°F)	80	84	93	100	104	105	109	110	104	96	87	86	110
Average High (°F)	47	52	61	72	79	87	93	92	84	74	60	50	71
Average Temp. (°F)	36	41	50	60	69	77	82	81	73	62	49	40	60
Average Low (°F)	26	30	38	49	58	66	71	70	62	51	38	29	49
Extreme Low (°F)	-4	-3	1	20	32	47	53	51	36	22	11	-8	-8

Note: Figures cover the years 1948-1990
Source: National Climatic Data Center, International Station Meteorological Climate Summary, 3/95

Average Precipitation/Snowfall/Humidity

Precip./Humidity	Jan	Feb	Mar	Apr	May	Jun	Jul	Aug	Sep	Oct	Nov	Dec	Ann
Avg. Precip. (in.)	1.2	1.5	2.5	2.8	5.6	4.4	2.8	2.5	3.5	3.1	1.6	1.3	32.8
Avg. Snowfall (in.)	3	3	2	Tr	0	0	0	0	0	Tr	1	2	10
Avg. Rel. Hum. 6am (%)	78	78	76	77	84	84	81	81	82	79	78	77	80
Avg. Rel. Hum. 3pm (%)	53	52	47	46	52	51	46	44	47	46	48	52	49

Note: Figures cover the years 1948-1990; Tr = Trace amounts (<0.05 in. of rain; <0.5 in. of snow)
Source: National Climatic Data Center, International Station Meteorological Climate Summary, 3/95

Weather Conditions

Temperature			Daytime Sky			Precipitation		
10°F & below	32°F & below	90°F & above	Clear	Partly cloudy	Cloudy	0.01 inch or more precip.	0.1 inch or more snow/ice	Thunder-storms
5	79	70	124	131	110	80	8	50

Note: Figures are average number of days per year and covers the years 1948-1990
Source: National Climatic Data Center, International Station Meteorological Climate Summary, 3/95

AIR & WATER QUALITY

Maximum Pollutant Concentrations

	Particulate Matter (ug/m³)	Carbon Monoxide (ppm)	Sulfur Dioxide (ppm)	Nitrogen Dioxide (ppm)	Ozone (ppm)	Lead (ug/m³)
MSA[1] Level	56	8	0.005	0.014	0.10	0.01
NAAQS[2]	150	9	0.140	0.053	0.12	1.50
Met NAAQS?	Yes	Yes	Yes	Yes	Yes	Yes

Note: (1) Metropolitan Statistical Area - see Appendix A for areas included; (2) National Ambient Air Quality Standards; ppm = parts per million; ug/m³ = micrograms per cubic meter; n/a not available
Source: EPA, National Air Quality and Emissions Trends Report, 1996

Pollutant Standards Index

In the Oklahoma City MSA (see Appendix A for areas included), the Pollutant Standards Index (PSI) exceeded 100 on 1 day in 1996. A PSI value greater than 100 indicates that air quality would be in the unhealthful range on that day. *EPA, National Air Quality and Emissions Trends Report, 1996*

Drinking Water

Water System Name	Pop. Served	Primary Water Source Type	Number of Violations in Fiscal Year 1997	Type of Violation/ Contaminants
Oklahoma City Draper	276,000	Surface	None	None
Oklahoma City Hefner	276,000	Surface	None	None

Note: Data as of January 16, 1998
Source: EPA, Office of Ground Water and Drinking Water, Safe Drinking Water Information System

Oklahoma City tap water is alkaline, soft and fluoridated.
Editor & Publisher Market Guide, 1998

Saint Louis, Missouri

Background

St. Louis, "Gateway To The West", has experienced a series of ups and down throughout its history. Fortunately today, the city is on an upswing.

St. Louis began as an inland river trading post for French settlers from New Orleans. Founder Pierre Laclède had been granted exclusive rights by the Louisiana government to trade with the tribes of the region. The site that he chose to name after Louis XV of France was a land rich with wildlife. This wildlife, which included raccoon, beaver, muskrat, otter, and bear made for an active fur trade. In 1827, John Jacob Astor started a very profitable fur business called the American Fur Company.

After the Civil War, St. Louis experienced an industrial and cultural boom. The city expanded in industries such as iron, steel, leather, and food; and became a center for Hegelian thought, thanks to the large influx of German immigrants who flavored the identity of St. Louis in many ways.

Events such as World War I, the Depression, and Prohibition contributed to St. Louis's economic decline. Worse still, economic problems persisted during the 1950's, 60's, and 70's. Since the 1980's, however, St. Louis has been on the upswing. Institutions and corporations such as the Federal Reserve Bank for the 8th District, Washington University, St. Louis University, Anheuser Busch, McDonnell Douglas, General Dynamics, Ralston Purina, and a number of automobile manufacturing plants such as Ford, General Motors, and Chrysler give St. Louis a strong and diversified economic base. Over the past several years, St. Louis which has been called the "Silicon Valley of the Midwest" has become home to over 1,200 high-tech companies and more than $2 billion investment, generating 150,000 jobs. World Trade 4/97

Saint Louis, situated at the confluence of the Missouri and Mississippi Rivers is near the geographical center of the United States. It experiences the four seasons without the hardship of prolonged periods of extreme heat or high humidity. Winters are brisk, stimulating, and seldom severe. Thunderstorms which occur between 40-50 days a year are generally not severe. Tornadoes, on the other hand, have caused a great deal of damage and loss of life in the area.

General Rankings and Evaluative Comments

- Saint Louis was ranked #268 out of 300 cities by *Money's* 1997 "Survey of the Best Places to Live." Criteria used: health services, crime, economy, housing, education, transportation, weather, leisure and the arts. The city was ranked #247 in 1996 and #248 in 1995. *Money, July 1997; Money, September 1996; Money, September 1995*

- *Ladies Home Journal* ranked America's 200 largest cities based on the qualities women care about most. Saint Louis ranked 129 out of 200. Criteria: low crime rate, good public schools, well-paying jobs, quality health and child care, the presence of women in government, proportion of women-owned businesses, size of the wage gap with men, local economy, divorce rates, the ratio of single men to single women, whether there are laws that require at least the same number of public toilets for women as men, and the probability of good hair days. *Ladies Home Journal, November 1997*

- Saint Louis is among "The Best Places to Raise a Family". Rank: 34 out of 301 metro areas. Criteria: low crime rate, low drug and alcohol abuse, good public schools, high-quality health care, a clean environment, affordable cost of living and strong economic growth. *Reader's Digest, April 1997*

- Saint Louis was ranked #216 out of 219 cities in terms of children's health, safety, and economic well-being. Criteria: total population, percent population change, birth rate, child immunization rate, infant mortality rate, percent low birth weight infants, percent of births to teens, physician-to-population ratio, student-to-teacher ratio, dropout rate, unemployment rate, median family income, percent of children in poverty, violent and property crime rates, number of juvenile arrests for violent crimes as a percent of the total crime index, number of days with pollution standard index (PSI) over 100, pounds toxic releases per 1,000 people and number of superfund sites. *Zero Population Growth, Children's Environmental Index 1997*

- Saint Louis is among the 20 most livable cities for gay men and lesbians. The list was divided between 10 cities you might expect and 10 surprises. Saint Louis was on the cities you wouldn't expect list. Rank: 10 out of 10. Criteria: legal protection from antigay discrimination, an annual gay pride celebration, a community center, gay bookstores and publications, and an array of organizations, religious groups, and health care facilities that cater to the needs of the local gay community. *The Advocate, June 1997*

- *Conde Nast Traveler* polled 37,000 readers in terms of travel satisfaction. Cities were ranked based on the following criteria: people/friendliness, environment/ambiance, cultural enrichment, restaurants and fun/energy. Saint Louis appeared in the top thirty, ranking number 29, with an overall rating of 54.3 out of 100 based on all the criteria. *Conde Nast Traveler, Readers' Choice Poll 1997*

- *Yahoo! Internet Life* selected "America's 100 Most Wired Cities & Towns". 50 cities were large and 50 cities were small. Saint Louis ranked 15 out of 50 large cities. Criteria: Internet users per capita, number of networked computers, number of registered domain names, Internet backbone traffic, and the per-capita number of Web sites devoted to each city. *Yahoo! Internet Life, March 1998*

- A.G. Edwards (brokerage), headquartered in Saint Louis, is among the "100 Best Companies to Work for in America." Criteria: trust in management, pride in work/company, camaraderie, company responses to the Hewitt People Practices Inventory, and employee responses to their Great Place to Work survey. The companies also had to be at least 10 years old and have a minimum of 500 employees. *Fortune, January 12, 1998*

- According to *Working Mother*, "More and more school-age programs in Missouri are earning state accreditation, under a grants program developed three years ago by the state department of education. Happily, the Missouri Center for Accreditation reports it is now swamped with applications for accreditation, which means school-age programs are meeting higher standards. These new rules are not the same as those required for NAEYC accreditation, but they are far better than having no standards at all.

Advocates here managed to beat back a bill in the state legislature that would have hurt many family child care providers by requiring them to be in compliance with all local business zoning laws—a problem that plagues many child care providers across the county.

Child care programs in religious institutions are now subject to inspection, and state officials have asked for funding to hire more inspectors to visit these centers.'' *Working Mother, July/August 1997*

Business Environment

STATE ECONOMY

State Economic Profile

"...The housing industry improved upon its performance in 1993, but fell well short of the number of permits issued during the industry's peak in 1994.

Missouri's largest employer, McDonnell Douglas Corp. is attempting to merge with Boeing. The combined companies promise as much as $1 billion in savings per year, making job cuts in Missouri likely. Since McDonnell Douglas is more active in defense contracting than Boeing, much of the St. Louis manufacturing workforce and facilities will likely remain intact, while cutbacks are more likely at commercial aircraft facilities.

Bank mergers will begin to have a dampening effect on the state's economy..., Mercantile bank purchased Mark Twain Bancshares and Roosevelt Financial Group, while NationsBank purchased Boatmen's Banchsares. There will be considerable branch consolidation.

TWA continues to look like a bigger risk to the Missouri economy as time goes on. Already on shaky financial footing, TWA has yet to recover from the fallout of the Flight 800 explosion....

Missouri's economy will recover as the year goes on and will eventually shadow the national economy through the forecast. St. Louis will continue to be a drag on Missouri's growth, but faster growing Kansas City, Columbia, and Springfield will help pick up the slack. Sizable exposure to a few large employers is a downside risk in the overall outlook. Moderate population growth will keep Missouri on track to be an average performer through the forecast." *National Association of Realtors, Economic Profiles: The Fifty States, July 1997*

IMPORTS/EXPORTS

Total Export Sales

Area	1993 ($000)	1994 ($000)	1995 ($000)	1996 ($000)	% Chg. 1993-96	% Chg. 1995-96
MSA[1]	3,399,997	3,673,337	3,997,678	4,497,447	32.3	12.5
U.S.	464,858,354	512,415,609	583,030,524	622,827,063	34.0	6.8

Note: (1) Metropolitan Statistical Area - see Appendix A for areas included
Source: U.S. Department of Commerce, International Trade Association, Metropolitan Area Exports: An Export Performance Report on Over 250 U.S. Cities, October 1997

Imports/Exports by Port

Type	Cargo Value 1995 (US$mil.)	1996 (US$mil.)	% Change 1995-1996	Share of U.S. Total 1995 (%)	1996 (%)
Imports	0	1	344.79	0.00	0.00
Exports	0	0	0.00	0.00	0.00

Source: Global Trade Information Services, WaterBorne Trade Atlas 1997

CITY FINANCES

City Government Finances

Component	FY92 ($000)	FY92 (per capita $)
Revenue	604,356	1,569.78
Expenditure	603,267	1,566.95
Debt Outstanding	766,899	1,991.97
Cash & Securities	1,446,300	3,756.67

Source: U.S. Bureau of the Census, City Government Finances: 1991-92

City Government Revenue by Source

Source	FY92 ($000)	FY92 (per capita $)	FY92 (%)
From Federal Government	32,477	84.36	5.4
From State Governments	37,849	98.31	6.3
From Local Governments	3,567	9.27	0.6
Property Taxes	36,894	95.83	6.1
General Sales Taxes	50,526	131.24	8.4
Selective Sales Taxes	58,460	151.85	9.7
Income Taxes	113,908	295.87	18.8
Current Charges	93,024	241.62	15.4
Utility/Liquor Store	30,186	78.41	5.0
Employee Retirement[1]	79,684	206.97	13.2
Other	67,781	176.06	11.2

Note: (1) Excludes "city contributions," classified as "nonrevenue," intragovernmental transfers.
Source: U.S. Bureau of the Census, City Government Finances: 1991-92

City Government Expenditures by Function

Function	FY92 ($000)	FY92 (per capita $)	FY92 (%)
Educational Services	3,359	8.72	0.6
Employee Retirement[1]	58,053	150.79	9.6
Environment/Housing	60,517	157.19	10.0
Government Administration	44,187	114.77	7.3
Interest on General Debt	66,304	172.22	11.0
Public Safety	139,776	363.06	23.2
Social Services	34,602	89.88	5.7
Transportation	128,168	332.91	21.2
Utility/Liquor Store	28,223	73.31	4.7
Other	40,078	104.10	6.6

Note: (1) Payments to beneficiaries including withdrawal of contributions.
Source: U.S. Bureau of the Census, City Government Finances: 1991-92

Municipal Bond Ratings

Area	Moody's	S & P
Saint Louis	Baa1	A-

Note: n/a not available; n/r not rated
Source: Moody's Bond Record, 2/98; Statistical Abstract of the U.S., 1997;
Governing Magazine, 9/97, 3/98

POPULATION

Population Growth

Area	1980	1990	% Chg. 1980-90	July 1996 Estimate	% Chg. 1990-96
City	453,085	396,685	-12.4	351,565	-11.4
MSA[1]	2,376,998	2,444,099	2.8	2,548,238	4.3
U.S.	226,545,805	248,765,170	9.8	265,179,411	6.6

Note: (1) Metropolitan Statistical Area - see Appendix A for areas included
Source: 1980/1990 Census of Housing and Population, Summary Tape File 3C;
Census Bureau Population Estimates

Population Characteristics

Race	City				% Chg. 1980-90	MSA[1]	
	1980		1990			1990	
	Population	%	Population	%		Population	%
White	242,988	53.6	202,276	51.0	-16.8	1,986,599	81.3
Black	206,170	45.5	187,995	47.4	-8.8	422,234	17.3
Amer Indian/Esk/Aleut	679	0.1	1,331	0.3	96.0	5,726	0.2
Asian/Pacific Islander	2,214	0.5	3,566	0.9	61.1	22,808	0.9
Other	1,034	0.2	1,517	0.4	46.7	6,732	0.3
Hispanic Origin[2]	5,531	1.2	4,850	1.2	-12.3	25,036	1.0

Note: (1) Metropolitan Statistical Area - see Appendix A for areas included;
(2) people of Hispanic origin can be of any race
Source: 1980/1990 Census of Housing and Population, Summary Tape File 3C

Ancestry

Area	German	Irish	English	Italian	U.S.	French	Polish	Dutch
City	23.6	13.1	6.0	4.3	2.9	3.7	2.1	1.1
MSA[1]	41.2	19.3	12.2	4.6	3.7	6.1	3.0	2.0
U.S.	23.3	15.6	13.1	5.9	5.3	4.2	3.8	2.5

Note: Figures are percentages and include persons that reported multiple ancestry (eg. if a person reported being Irish and Italian, they were included in both columns); (1) Metropolitan Statistical Area - see Appendix A for areas included
Source: 1990 Census of Population and Housing, Summary Tape File 3C

Age

Area	Median Age (Years)	Age Distribution (%)						
		Under 5	Under 18	18-24	25-44	45-64	65+	80+
City	32.7	8.0	25.2	10.3	31.2	16.6	16.7	4.7
MSA[1]	33.1	7.5	26.2	9.4	32.7	18.9	12.8	3.1
U.S.	32.9	7.3	25.6	10.5	32.6	18.7	12.5	2.8

Note: (1) Metropolitan Statistical Area - see Appendix A for areas included
Source: 1990 Census of Population and Housing, Summary Tape File 3C

Male/Female Ratio

Area	Number of males per 100 females (all ages)	Number of males per 100 females (18 years old+)
City	83.6	78.1
MSA[1]	91.6	87.3
U.S.	95.0	91.9

Note: (1) Metropolitan Statistical Area - see Appendix A for areas included
Source: 1990 Census of Population, General Population Characteristics

INCOME

Per Capita/Median/Average Income

Area	Per Capita ($)	Median Household ($)	Average Household ($)
City	10,798	19,458	25,605
MSA[1]	14,917	31,774	39,114
U.S.	14,420	30,056	38,453

Note: all figures are for 1989; (1) Metropolitan Statistical Area - see Appendix A for areas included
Source: 1990 Census of Population and Housing, Summary Tape File 3C

Household Income Distribution by Race

Income ($)	City (%)					U.S. (%)				
	Total	White	Black	Other	Hisp.[1]	Total	White	Black	Other	Hisp.[1]
Less than 5,000	12.5	6.9	20.6	15.7	8.9	6.2	4.8	15.2	8.6	8.8
5,000 - 9,999	15.3	13.3	18.3	14.6	11.5	9.3	8.6	14.2	9.9	11.1
10,000 - 14,999	12.3	11.3	13.9	9.3	12.4	8.8	8.5	11.0	9.8	11.0
15,000 - 24,999	20.7	21.9	19.0	19.1	25.0	17.5	17.3	18.9	18.5	20.5
25,000 - 34,999	14.8	16.8	11.8	18.3	16.6	15.8	16.1	14.2	15.4	16.4
35,000 - 49,999	12.6	14.9	9.2	13.5	12.0	17.9	18.6	13.3	16.1	16.0
50,000 - 74,999	8.4	10.5	5.4	5.9	8.4	15.0	15.8	9.3	13.4	11.1
75,000 - 99,999	2.0	2.7	1.0	2.3	3.0	5.1	5.5	2.6	4.7	3.1
100,000+	1.3	1.8	0.7	1.4	2.1	4.4	4.8	1.3	3.7	1.9

Note: all figures are for 1989; (1) people of Hispanic origin can be of any race
Source: 1990 Census of Population and Housing, Summary Tape File 3C

Effective Buying Income

Area	Per Capita ($)	Median Household ($)	Average Household ($)
City	13,029	23,855	31,315
MSA[1]	17,353	38,436	45,932
U.S.	15,444	33,201	41,849

Note: data as of 1/1/97; (1) Metropolitan Statistical Area - see Appendix A for areas included
Source: Standard Rate & Data Service, Newspaper Advertising Source, 2/98

Effective Household Buying Income Distribution

Area	% of Households Earning						
	$10,000 -$19,999	$20,000 -$34,999	$35,000 -$49,999	$50,000 -$74,999	$75,000 -$99,000	$100,000 -$124,999	$125,000 and up
City	21.8	24.2	14.8	12.2	3.8	1.0	1.0
MSA[1]	13.9	21.4	19.5	21.6	8.3	2.6	2.7
U.S.	16.5	23.4	18.3	18.2	6.4	2.1	2.4

Note: data as of 1/1/97; (1) Metropolitan Statistical Area - see Appendix A for areas included
Source: Standard Rate & Data Service, Newspaper Advertising Source, 2/98

Poverty Rates by Race and Age

Area	Total (%)	By Race (%)				By Age (%)		
		White	Black	Other	Hisp.[2]	Under 5 years old	Under 18 years old	65 years and over
City	24.6	12.6	37.4	26.0	23.5	41.4	39.7	18.7
MSA[1]	10.8	6.3	31.3	14.7	13.1	17.6	15.9	10.3
U.S.	13.1	9.8	29.5	23.1	25.3	20.1	18.3	12.8

Note: figures show the percent of people living below the poverty line in 1989. The average poverty threshold was $12,674 for a family of four in 1989; (1) Metropolitan Statistical Area - see Appendix A for areas included; (2) people of Hispanic origin can be of any race
Source: 1990 Census of Population and Housing, Summary Tape File 3C

EMPLOYMENT

Labor Force and Employment

Area	Civilian Labor Force			Workers Employed		
	Dec. '95	Dec. '96	% Chg.	Dec. '95	Dec. '96	% Chg.
City	175,321	170,036	-3.0	162,212	159,081	-1.9
MSA[1]	1,382,326	1,356,484	-1.9	1,323,456	1,303,910	-1.5
U.S.	134,583,000	136,742,000	1.6	127,903,000	130,785,000	2.3

Note: Data is not seasonally adjusted and covers workers 16 years of age and older;
(1) Metropolitan Statistical Area - see Appendix A for areas included
Source: Bureau of Labor Statistics, http://stats.bls.gov

Unemployment Rate

Area	1997											
	Jan.	Feb.	Mar.	Apr.	May	Jun.	Jul.	Aug.	Sep.	Oct.	Nov.	Dec.
City	6.6	6.8	6.7	6.9	6.9	6.9	6.4	7.1	6.3	6.8	6.4	6.4
MSA[1]	4.6	4.3	4.0	3.9	3.7	4.0	4.3	3.9	3.7	3.6	3.6	3.9
U.S.	5.9	5.7	5.5	4.8	4.7	5.2	5.0	4.8	4.7	4.4	4.3	4.4

Note: Data is not seasonally adjusted and covers workers 16 years of age and older; All figures are percentages; (1) Metropolitan Statistical Area - see Appendix A for areas included
Source: Bureau of Labor Statistics, http://stats.bls.gov

Employment by Industry

Sector	MSA[1]		U.S.
	Number of Employees	Percent of Total	Percent of Total
Services	409,300	31.2	29.0
Retail Trade	245,200	18.7	18.5
Government	157,800	12.0	16.1
Manufacturing	197,800	15.1	15.0
Finance/Insurance/Real Estate	80,400	6.1	5.7
Wholesale Trade	72,200	5.5	5.4
Transportation/Public Utilities	83,000	6.3	5.3
Construction/Mining	66,900	5.1	5.0

Note: Figures cover non-farm employment as of 12/97 and are not seasonally adjusted;
(1) Metropolitan Statistical Area - see Appendix A for areas included
Source: Bureau of Labor Statistics, http://stats.bls.gov

Employment by Occupation

Occupation Category	City (%)	MSA[1] (%)	U.S. (%)
White Collar	55.9	61.6	58.1
Executive/Admin./Management	9.7	12.7	12.3
Professional	13.6	14.8	14.1
Technical & Related Support	4.0	4.0	3.7
Sales	9.6	12.2	11.8
Administrative Support/Clerical	19.0	17.8	16.3
Blue Collar	23.3	24.1	26.2
Precision Production/Craft/Repair	7.7	10.5	11.3
Machine Operators/Assem./Insp.	7.2	6.0	6.8
Transportation/Material Movers	3.8	3.8	4.1
Cleaners/Helpers/Laborers	4.6	3.8	3.9
Services	20.1	13.3	13.2
Farming/Forestry/Fishing	0.7	1.1	2.5

Note: figures cover employed persons 16 years old and over;
(1) Metropolitan Statistical Area - see Appendix A for areas included
Source: 1990 Census of Population and Housing, Summary Tape File 3C

Occupational Employment Projections: 1994 - 2005

Occupations Expected to have the Largest Job Growth (ranked by numerical growth)	Fast-Growing Occupations[1] (ranked by percent growth)
1. Waiters & waitresses	1. Computer engineers
2. General managers & top executives	2. Electronic pagination systems workers
3. Teachers, secondary school	3. Occupational therapists
4. Salespersons, retail	4. Machine assemblers
5. Janitors/cleaners/maids, ex. priv. hshld.	5. Home health aides
6. Registered nurses	6. Occupational therapy assistants
7. Food service and lodging managers	7. Systems analysts
8. Systems analysts	8. Database administrators
9. Cashiers	9. Physical therapists
10. Marketing & sales, supervisors	10. Manicurists

Projections cover the St. Louis MSA - see Appendix A for areas included.
Note: (1) Excludes occupations with employment less than 100 in 1994
Source: Missouri Dept. of Labor and Industrial Relations, St. Louis Employment Outlook, Projections to 2005 for Industries and Occupations

Average Wages

Occupation	Wage	Occupation	Wage
Professional/Technical/Clerical	$/Week	**Health/Protective Services**	$/Week
Accountants III	760	Corrections Officers	477
Attorneys III	1,254	Firefighters	-
Budget Analysts III	760	Nurses, Licensed Practical II	-
Buyers/Contracting Specialists II	619	Nurses, Registered II	-
Clerks, Accounting III	428	Nursing Assistants II	-
Clerks, General III	388	Police Officers I	610
Computer Operators II	418	**Hourly Workers**	$/Hour
Computer Programmers II	601	Forklift Operators	13.74
Drafters II	500	General Maintenance Workers	9.86
Engineering Technicians III	562	Guards I	-
Engineering Technicians, Civil III	579	Janitors	6.72
Engineers III	859	Maintenance Electricians	20.51
Key Entry Operators I	323	Maintenance Electronics Techs II	18.02
Personnel Assistants III	495	Maintenance Machinists	19.69
Personnel Specialists III	731	Maintenance Mechanics, Machinery	17.38
Secretaries III	532	Material Handling Laborers	-
Switchboard Operator-Receptionist	322	Motor Vehicle Mechanics	17.32
Systems Analysts II	-	Shipping/Receiving Clerks	11.04
Systems Analysts Supervisor/Mgr II	1,426	Tool and Die Makers	21.07
Tax Collectors II	-	Truckdrivers, Tractor Trailer	17.31
Word Processors II	413	Warehouse Specialists	-

Note: Wage data includes full-time workers only for 3/96 and cover the Metropolitan Statistical Area (see Appendix A for areas included). Dashes indicate that data was not available.
Source: Bureau of Labor Statistics, Occupational Compensation Survey, 9/96

TAXES

Major State and Local Tax Rates

State Corp. Income (%)	State Personal Income (%)	Residential Property (effective rate per $100)	Sales & Use		State Gasoline (cents/ gallon)	State Cigarette (cents/ 20-pack)
			State (%)	Local (%)		
6.25	1.5 - 6.0	n/a	4.225	2.625	17.05[a]	17[b]

Note: Personal/corporate income tax rates as of 1/97. Sales, gasoline and cigarette tax rates as of 1/98; (a) Rate is comprised of 17 cents excise and 0.05 cents motor carrier tax; (b) Counties and cities may impose an additional tax of 4 - 7 cents per pack
Source: Federation of Tax Administrators, www.taxadmin.org; Washington D.C. Department of Finance and Revenue, Tax Rates and Tax Burdens in the District of Columbia: A Nationwide Comparison, June 1997; Chamber of Commerce

Total Taxes Per Capita and as a Percent of Income

Area	Per Capita Income ($)	Per Capita Taxes ($)			Taxes as Pct. of Income (%)		
		Total	Federal	State/Local	Total	Federal	State/Local
Missouri	24,554	8,421	5,674	2,747	34.3	23.1	11.2
U.S.	26,187	9,205	6,127	3,078	35.2	23.4	11.8

Note: Figures are for 1997
Source: Tax Foundation, Web Site, www.taxfoundation.org

COMMERCIAL REAL ESTATE

Office Market

Class/Location	Total Space (sq. ft.)	Vacant Space (sq. ft.)	Vac. Rate (%)	Under Constr. (sq. ft.)	Net Absorp. (sq. ft.)	Rental Rates ($/sq.ft./yr.)
Class A						
CBD	5,409,623	508,644	9.4	0	97,974	13.00-23.00
Outside CBD	9,183,767	326,534	3.6	649,000	596,544	10.00-25.00
Class B						
CBD	5,868,016	1,149,043	19.6	0	267,591	6.00-22.00
Outside CBD	13,585,236	1,197,342	8.8	0	606,292	9.00-25.00

Note: Data as of 10/97 and covers Saint Louis; CBD = Central Business District; n/a not available;
Source: Society of Industrial and Office Realtors, 1998 Comparative Statistics of Industrial and Office Real Estate Markets

"Plans for 600,000 sq. ft. of speculative new construction are on the boards, most of it in suburban west St. Louis. Much more build-to-suit activity is underway as Class 'B' suburban buildings lease up. Tight suburban conditions should help downtown. Sales of Class 'A' buildings in the CBD could increase by 1-5%, the same rate anticipated for Class 'B' suburban product. Going forward, economists expect metropolitan growth to slow somewhat. Manufacturing job losses, banking mergers, declining gaming revenues, and a deteriorating outlook for TWA may all contribute to a slow economy. But, unemployment in St. Louis is only 3.8%, and these glum forecasts are certainly not reflected in the 1998 office market outlook." *Society of Industrial and Office Realtors, 1998 Comparative Statistics of Industrial and Office Real Estate Markets*

Industrial Market

Location	Total Space (sq. ft.)	Vacant Space (sq. ft.)	Vac. Rate (%)	Under Constr. (sq. ft.)	Net Absorp. (sq. ft.)	Gross Lease ($/sq.ft./yr.)
Central City	88,750,000	3,500,000	3.9	300,000	807,000	2.25-4.50
Suburban	117,585,000	2,500,000	2.1	2,500,000	3,130,000	3.75-6.50

Note: Data as of 10/97 and covers St. Louis; n/a not available
Source: Society of Industrial and Office Realtors, 1998 Comparative Statistics of Industrial and Office Real Estate Markets

"With lease prices, sales prices, and absorption up and vacancy rates down, SIOR's reporters see continuing expansion in this marketplace. A moderate to substantial shortage of smaller industrial properties and an eagerness from REITs and other national players will prompt regional players with ready financing to satisfy these needs. On the user side, Saint Louis should continue to grow from both internal growth of existing tenants and new locations for the area. Economists point to factors in the economy-manufacturing losses, poor gaming revenues, bank downsizing, and the inability of TWA to regain its former footing-that could stanch growth. SIOR's local experts counter that these are old stories, affecting many other regions and the nation as a whole. In any case Saint Louis' industrial market continues to flourish." *Society of Industrial and Office Realtors, 1998 Comparative Statistics of Industrial and Office Real Estate Markets*

Retail Market

Shopping Center Inventory (sq. ft.)	Shopping Center Construction (sq. ft.)	Construction as a Percent of Inventory (%)	Torto Wheaton Rent Index[1] ($/sq. ft.)
44,816,000	707,000	1.6	13.50

Note: Data as of 1997 and covers the Metropolitan Statistical Area - see Appendix A for areas included; (1) Index is based on a model that predicts what the average rent should be for leases with certain characteristics, in certain locations during certain years.
Source: National Association of Realtors, 1997-1998 Market Conditions Report

"In spite of slow population and income growth and a general strike at the McDonnell Douglas plant in 1996, St. Louis' retail market has fared relatively well. The area's rent index rose 9.2% in 1997 after a 2.9% drop in 1996. Rents remain above the Midwest average of $12.27 per square foot. A large amount of retail space was vacated in 1996 due to the closing of Central Hardware, the Schnucks/National Markets merger and the reorganization of Phar-Mor. Much of that space has since been absorbed by retailers such as Value City, Baby Superstores, Ace Hardware and Bed, Bath & Beyond. The St. Louis retail market is expected to remain stable over the next three years." *National Association of Realtors, 1997-1998 Market Conditions Report*

COMMERCIAL UTILITIES

Typical Monthly Electric Bills

Area	Commercial Service ($/month)		Industrial Service ($/month)	
	12 kW demand 1,500 kWh	100 kW demand 30,000 kWh	1,000 kW demand 400,000 kWh	20,000 kW demand 10,000,000 kWh
City	143	2,863	30,572	651,344
U.S.	162	2,360	25,590	545,677

Note: Based on rates in effect July 1, 1997
Source: Edison Electric Institute, Typical Residential, Commercial and Industrial Bills, Summer 1997

TRANSPORTATION

Transportation Statistics

Avg. travel time to work (min.)	22.0
Interstate highways	I-44; I-55; I-64; I-70
Bus lines	
In-city	Bi-State Transit System, 688 vehicles
Inter-city	2
Passenger air service	
Airport	Lambert-St. Louis International
Airlines	15
Aircraft departures	227,300 (1955)
Enplaned passengers	12,736,160 (1995)
Rail service	Amtrak; MetroLink; Light Rail
Motor freight carriers	350
Major waterways/ports	Mississippi River; Port of St. Louis

Source: OAG, Business Travel Planner, Summer 1997; Editor & Publisher Market Guide, 1998; FAA Airport Activity Statistics, 1996; Amtrak National Time Table, Northeast Timetable, Fall/Winter 1997-98; 1990 Census of Population and Housing, STF 3C; Chamber of Commerce/Economic Development 1997; Jane's Urban Transport Systems 1997-98; Transit Fact Book 1997

A survey of 90,000 airline passengers during the first half of 1997 ranked most of the largest airports in the U.S. Lambert-St. Louis International ranked number 25 out of 36. Criteria: cleanliness, quality of restaurants, attractiveness, speed of baggage delivery, ease of reaching gates, available ground transportation, ease of following signs and closeness of parking. *Plog Research Inc., First Half 1997*

Means of Transportation to Work

Area	Car/Truck/Van		Public Transportation			Bicycle	Walked	Other Means	Worked at Home
	Drove Alone	Car-pooled	Bus	Subway	Railroad				
City	66.5	14.1	11.8	0.0	0.0	0.3	4.6	1.1	1.7
MSA[1]	79.7	12.0	2.8	0.0	0.0	0.1	2.1	0.7	2.4
U.S.	73.2	13.4	3.0	1.5	0.5	0.4	3.9	1.2	3.0

Note: figures shown are percentages and only include workers 16 years old and over;
(1) Metropolitan Statistical Area - see Appendix A for areas included
Source: 1990 Census of Population and Housing, Summary Tape File 3C

BUSINESSES

Major Business Headquarters

Company Name	1997 Rankings	
	Fortune 500	Forbes 500
Alberici	-	378
Anheuser-Busch	127	-
Clark USA	-	29
Emerson Electric	120	-
Enterprise Rent-A-Car	-	38
General American Life Insurance	479	-
Graybar Electric	453	43
Jefferson Smurfit	397	-
May Department Stores	103	-
McCarthy	-	168
Monsanto	159	-
Purina Mills	-	147
Ralston Purina	236	-
Schnuck Markets	-	95
Trans World Airlines	383	-

Note: Companies listed are located in the city; Dashes indicate no ranking
Fortune 500: companies that produce a 10-K are ranked 1 - 500 based on 1996 revenue
Forbes 500: private companies are ranked 1 - 500 based on 1996 revenue
Source: Forbes 12/1/97; Fortune 4/28/97

Fast-Growing Businesses

According to *Fortune*, Saint Louis is home to one of America's 100 fastest-growing companies: Zoltek. Companies were ranked based on three years' earnings-per-share growth using least squares analysis to smooth out distortions. Criteria for inclusion: public companies with sales of least $50 million. Companies that lost money in the most recent quarter, or ended in the red for the past four quarters as a whole, were not eligible. Limited partnerships and REITs were also not considered. *Fortune, 9/29/97*

According to Deloitte & Touche LLP, Saint Louis is home to two of America's 100 fastest-growing high-technology companies: CBC Distribution & Marketing Inc. and Lasersight Inc. Companies are ranked by percentage growth in revenue over a five-year period. Criteria for inclusion: must be a U.S. company developing and/or providing technology products or services; company must have been in business for five years with 1992 revenues of at least $50,000. *Deloitte & Touche LLP, January 7, 1998*

Saint Louis was ranked #16 out of 24 (#1 is best) in terms of the best-performing local stocks in 1996 according to the Money/Norby Cities Index. The index measures stocks of companies that have headquarters in 24 metro areas. *Money, 2/7/97*

Women-Owned Businesses: Number, Employment, Sales and Share

Area	Women-Owned Businesses in 1996				Share of Women-Owned Businesses in 1996	
	Number	Employment	Sales ($000)	Rank[2]	Percent (%)	Rank[3]
MSA[1]	69,200	165,600	18,832,900	23	36.6	27

Note: (1) Metropolitan Statistical Area - see Appendix A for areas included; (2) Calculated on an averaging of number of businesses, employment and sales and ranges from 1 to 50 where 1 is best; (3) Ranges from 1 to 50 where 1 is best
Source: The National Foundation for Women Business Owners, 1996 Facts on Women-Owned Businesses: Trends in the Top 50 Metropolitan Areas, March 26, 1997

Women-Owned Businesses: Growth

Area	Growth in Women-Owned Businesses (% change from 1987 to 1996)				Relative Growth in the Number of Women-Owned and All Businesses (% change from 1987 to 1996)			
	Num.	Empl.	Sales	Rank[2]	Women-Owned	All Firms	Absolute Difference	Relative Difference
MSA[1]	62.9	178.2	255.8	36	62.9	44.8	18.1	1.4:1

Note: (1) Metropolitan Statistical Area - see Appendix A for areas included; (2) Calculated on an averaging of the percent growth of number of businesses, employment and sales and ranges from 1 to 50 where 1 is best
Source: The National Foundation for Women Business Owners, 1996 Facts on Women-Owned Businesses: Trends in the Top 50 Metropolitan Areas, March 26, 1997

Minority Business Opportunity

Saint Louis is home to one company which is on the Black Enterprise Auto Dealer 100 list (largest based on gross sales): Accent Motors Inc. (Ford). Criteria: 1) operational in previous calendar year; 2) at least 51% black-owned. *Black Enterprise, June 1997*

Two of the 500 largest Hispanic-owned companies in the U.S. are located in Saint Louis. *Hispanic Business, June 1997*

Saint Louis is home to one company which is on the Hispanic Business Fastest-Growing 100 list (greatest sales growth from 1992 to 1996): ASTEC Inc. (aerospace and environmental engineering svcs.) *Hispanic Business, July/August 1997*

Small Business Opportunity

Saint Louis was included among *Entrepreneur* magazines listing of the "20 Best Cities for Small Business." It was ranked #2 among large metro areas. Criteria: risk of failure, business performance, economic growth, affordability and state attitude towards business. *Entrepreneur, 10/97*

According to *Forbes*, Saint Louis is home to one of America's 200 best small companies: RehabCare Group. Criteria: companies must be publicly traded, U.S.-based corporations with latest 12-month sales of between $5 and $350 million. Earnings must be at least $1 million for the 12-month period. Limited partnerships, REITs and closed-end mutual funds were not considered. Banks, S&Ls and electric utilities were not included. *Forbes, November 3, 1997*

HOTELS & MOTELS

Hotels/Motels

Area	Hotels/ Motels	Rooms	Luxury-Level Hotels/Motels		Average Minimum Rates ($)		
			♦♦♦♦	♦♦♦♦♦	♦♦	♦♦♦	♦♦♦♦
City	32	7,036	1	0	83	124	n/a
Airport	23	4,689	0	0	n/a	n/a	n/a
Suburbs	55	6,344	1	0	n/a	n/a	n/a
Total	110	18,069	2	0	n/a	n/a	n/a

Note: n/a not available; Classifications range from one diamond (budget properties with basic amenities) to five diamond (luxury properties with the finest service, rooms and facilities).
Source: OAG, Business Travel Planner, Summer 1997

CONVENTION CENTERS

Major Convention Centers

Center Name	Meeting Rooms	Exhibit Space (sf)
Adam's Mark St. Louis	43	40,679
Cervantes Convention Center at America's Center	67	340,000
Frontenac Hilton	22	22,000
Henry VII Hotel	n/a	21,090
Hyatt Regency St. Louis at Union Station	24	24,300
Innsbrook Estates Executive Conference Center	9	n/a
Marriott's Pavillion Hotel	22	18,017
Regal Riverfront Hotel	24	30,855
The Ritz-Carlton, St. Louis	12	19,146
St. Louis Airport Marriott	n/a	14,980
St. Louis Arena	n/a	18,896
St. Louis Executive Conference Ctr. at America's Center	3	20,000
St. Louis Soccer Park & Convention Center	3	2,784

Note: n/a not available
Source: Trade Shows Worldwide 1997

Living Environment

COST OF LIVING

Cost of Living Index

Composite Index	Housing	Utilities	Groceries	Health Care	Trans-portation	Misc. Goods/Services
98.0	96.7	95.2	101.3	111.1	99.4	95.3

Note: U.S. = 100; Figures are for the Metropolitan Statistical Area - see Appendix A for areas included
Source: ACCRA, Cost of Living Index, 3rd Quarter 1997

HOUSING

Median Home Prices and Housing Affordability

Area	Median Price[2] 3rd Qtr. 1997 ($)	HOI[3] 3rd Qtr. 1997	Afford-ability Rank[4]
MSA[1]	109,000	72.4	75
U.S.	127,000	63.7	–

Note: (1) Metropolitan Statistical Area - see Appendix A for areas included; (2) U.S. figures calculated from the sales of 625,000 new and existing homes in 195 markets; (3) Housing Opportunity Index - percent of homes sold that were within the reach of the median income household at the prevailing mortgage interest rate; (4) Rank is from 1-195 with 1 being most affordable
Source: National Association of Home Builders, Housing Opportunity Index, 3rd Quarter 1997

It is projected that the median price of existing single-family homes in the metro area will decrease by -1.3% in 1998. Nationwide, home prices are projected to increase 6.6%.
Kiplinger's Personal Finance Magazine, January 1998

Average New Home Price

Area	Price ($)
MSA[1]	126,325
U.S.	135,710

Note: Figures are based on a new home with 1,800 sq. ft. of living area on an 8,000 sq. ft. lot;
(1) Metropolitan Statistical Area - see Appendix A for areas included
Source: ACCRA, Cost of Living Index, 3rd Quarter 1997

Average Apartment Rent

Area	Rent ($/mth)
MSA[1]	649
U.S.	569

Note: Figures are based on an unfurnished two bedroom, 1-1/2 or 2 bath apartment, approximately 950 sq. ft. in size, excluding all utilities except water; (1) Metropolitan Statistical Area - see Appendix A for areas included
Source: ACCRA, Cost of Living Index, 3rd Quarter 1997

RESIDENTIAL UTILITIES

Average Residential Utility Costs

Area	All Electric ($/mth)	Part Electric ($/mth)	Other Energy ($/mth)	Phone ($/mth)
MSA[1]	–	58.91	37.72	19.69
U.S.	109.40	55.25	43.64	19.48

Note: (1) (1) Metropolitan Statistical Area - see Appendix A for areas included
Source: ACCRA, Cost of Living Index, 3rd Quarter 1997

HEALTH CARE

Average Health Care Costs

Area	Hospital ($/day)	Doctor ($/visit)	Dentist ($/visit)
MSA[1]	471.00	56.80	62.70
U.S.	392.91	48.76	60.84

Note: Hospital - based on a semi-private room. Doctor - based on a general practitioner's routine exam of an established patient. Dentist - based on adult teeth cleaning and periodic oral exam; (1) Metropolitan Statistical Area - see Appendix A for areas included
Source: ACCRA, Cost of Living Index, 3rd Quarter 1997

Distribution of Office-Based Physicians

Area	Family/Gen. Practitioners	Specialists		
		Medical	Surgical	Other
MSA[1]	316	1,770	1,270	1,246

Note: Data as of 12/31/96; (1) Metropolitan Statistical Area - see Appendix A for areas included
Source: American Medical Assn., Physician Characteristics & Distribution in the U.S., 1997-1998

Hospitals

Saint Louis has 17 general medical and surgical hospitals, 2 psychiatric, 1 rehabilitation, 2 children's general, 1 children's other specialty. *AHA Guide to the Healthcare Field 1997-98*

According to *U.S. News and World Report,* Saint Louis has 3 of the best hospitals in the U.S.: **Barnes-Jewish Hospital**, noted for AIDS, cancer, cardiology, endocrinology, gastroenterology, geriatrics, gynecology, neurology, ophthalmology, orthopedics, otolaryngology, pulmonology, rheumatology, urology; **St. Louis University Hospital**, noted for cardiology, gastroenterology, geriatrics, orthopedics; **St. Louis Children's Hospital**, noted for pediatrics; *U.S. News and World Report, "America's Best Hospitals", 7/28/97*

EDUCATION

Public School District Statistics

District Name	Num. Sch.	Enroll.	Classroom Teachers[1]	Pupils per Teacher	Minority Pupils (%)	Current Exp.[2] ($/pupil)
Affton 101	4	2,563	149	17.2	n/a	n/a
Bayless	4	1,471	77	19.1	n/a	n/a
Hancock Place	2	1,579	86	18.4	n/a	n/a
Ladue School District	6	3,356	245	13.7	n/a	n/a
Lindbergh R-VIII	7	5,227	312	16.8	n/a	n/a
Mehlville R-IX	16	12,010	621	19.3	n/a	n/a
Normandy	13	5,968	313	19.1	n/a	n/a
Ritenour	9	6,582	340	19.4	n/a	n/a
Riverview Gardens	11	5,646	304	18.6	n/a	n/a
Spec. Sch. Dst. St. Louis Co.	14	6,398	1,651	3.9	n/a	n/a
St. Louis City	109	41,720	3,152	13.2	81.5	7,298
Wellston	4	660	62	10.6	n/a	n/a

Note: Data covers the 1995-1996 school year unless otherwise noted; (1) Excludes teachers reported as working in school district offices rather than in schools; (2) Based on 1993-94 enrollment collected by the Census Bureau, not the enrollment figure shown in column 3; SD = School District; ISD = Independent School District; n/a not available
Source: National Center for Education Statistics, Common Core of Data Survey; Bureau of the Census

Educational Quality

School District	Education Quotient[1]	Graduate Outcome[2]	Community Index[3]	Resource Index[4]
Saint Louis City	85.0	57.0	53.0	146.0

Note: Nearly 1,000 secondary school districts were rated in terms of educational quality. The scores range from a low of 50 to a high of 150; (1) Average of the Graduate Outcome, Community and Resource indexes; (2) Based on graduation rates and college board scores (SAT/ACT); (3) Based on the surrounding community's average level of education and the area's average income level; (4) Based on teacher salaries, per-pupil expenditures and student-teacher ratios.
Source: Expansion Management, Ratings Issue 1997

Educational Attainment by Race

Area	High School Graduate (%)					Bachelor's Degree (%)				
	Total	White	Black	Other	Hisp.[2]	Total	White	Black	Other	Hisp.[2]
City	62.8	67.4	56.3	66.8	61.9	15.3	20.2	8.0	32.1	18.8
MSA[1]	76.0	78.1	64.1	79.9	75.2	20.7	22.1	11.4	40.5	24.3
U.S.	75.2	77.9	63.1	60.4	49.8	20.3	21.5	11.4	19.4	9.2

Note: figures shown cover persons 25 years old and over; (1) Metropolitan Statistical Area - see Appendix A for areas included; (2) people of Hispanic origin can be of any race
Source: 1990 Census of Population and Housing, Summary Tape File 3C

School Enrollment by Type

Area	Preprimary				Elementary/High School			
	Public		Private		Public		Private	
	Enrollment	%	Enrollment	%	Enrollment	%	Enrollment	%
City	4,198	56.7	3,211	43.3	49,177	77.4	14,389	22.6
MSA[1]	26,907	50.2	26,648	49.8	337,304	80.6	81,322	19.4
U.S.	2,679,029	59.5	1,824,256	40.5	38,379,689	90.2	4,187,099	9.8

Note: figures shown cover persons 3 years old and over;
(1) Metropolitan Statistical Area - see Appendix A for areas included
Source: 1990 Census of Population and Housing, Summary Tape File 3C

School Enrollment by Race

Area	Preprimary (%)				Elementary/High School (%)			
	White	Black	Other	Hisp.[1]	White	Black	Other	Hisp.[1]
City	44.4	53.6	2.0	1.2	33.2	65.2	1.6	1.4
MSA[2]	81.3	16.9	1.8	1.2	74.9	23.3	1.8	1.3
U.S.	80.4	12.5	7.1	7.8	74.1	15.6	10.3	12.5

Note: figures shown cover persons 3 years old and over; (1) people of Hispanic origin can be of any race; (2) Metropolitan Statistical Area - see Appendix A for areas included
Source: 1990 Census of Population and Housing, Summary Tape File 3C

SAT/ACT Scores

Area/District	1997 SAT				1997 ACT	
	Percent of Graduates Tested (%)	Average Math Score	Average Verbal Score	Average Combined Score	Percent of Graduates Tested (%)	Average Composite Score
St. Louis	14	461	474	935	46	18.2
State	9	568	567	1,135	64	21.5
U.S.	42	511	505	1,016	36	21.0

Note: Math and verbal SAT scores are out of a possible 800; ACT scores are out of a possible 36
Caution: Comparing or ranking states/cities on the basis of SAT/ACT scores alone is invalid and strongly discouraged by the The College Board and The American College Testing Program as students who take the tests are self-selected and do not represent the entire student population.
Source: St. Louis Public Schools, Division of Evaluation & Research, 1997; American College Testing Program, 1997; College Board, 1997

Classroom Teacher Salaries in Public Schools

District	B.A. Degree		M.A. Degree		Ph.D. Degree	
	Min. ($)	Max. ($)	Min. ($)	Max. ($)	Min. ($)	Max. ($)
Saint Louis	24,551	41,284	25,331	42,857	28,153	46,037
Average[1]	26,120	39,270	28,175	44,667	31,643	49,825

Note: Salaries are for 1996-1997; (1) Based on all school districts covered; n/a not available
Source: American Federation of Teachers (unpublished data)

Higher Education

Two-Year Colleges		Four-Year Colleges		Medical Schools	Law Schools	Voc/ Tech
Public	Private	Public	Private			
2	1	2	10	2	2	20

Source: College Blue Book, Occupational Education 1997; Medical School Admission Requirements, 1998-99; Peterson's Guide to Two-Year Colleges, 1997; Peterson's Guide to Four-Year Colleges, 1997; Barron's Guide to Law Schools 1997

MAJOR EMPLOYERS

Major Employers

AG Edwards & Sons (security brokers)
May Department Stores
CH Management Services
Deaconess Health Services Corp.
Missouri Baptist Medical Center
St. Louis University
Southwestern Bell Telephone
St. Louis Children's Hospital
Anheuser-Busch

BJC Health System
Boatmen's Bancshares
Citicorp Mortgage
Edison Brothers Stores (clothing)
McDonnell Douglas Corp.
Ralston Purina
St. John's Mercy Medical Center
Union Electric Co.

Note: companies listed are located in the city
Source: Dun's Business Rankings 1997; Ward's Business Directory, 1997

PUBLIC SAFETY

Crime Rate

Area	All Crimes	Violent Crimes				Property Crimes		
		Murder	Forcible Rape	Robbery	Aggrav. Assault	Burglary	Larceny -Theft	Motor Vehicle Theft
City	15,128.8	44.4	71.9	1,092.4	1,519.1	2,643.3	7,814.1	1,943.6
Suburbs[1]	n/a	n/a	n/a	n/a	n/a	n/a	n/a	n/a
MSA[2]	n/a	n/a	n/a	n/a	n/a	n/a	n/a	n/a
U.S.	5,078.9	7.4	36.1	202.4	388.2	943.0	2,975.9	525.9

Note: Crime rate is the number of crimes per 100,000 pop.; (1) defined as all areas within the MSA but located outside the central city; (2) Metropolitan Statistical Area - see Appendix A for areas incl.
Source: FBI Uniform Crime Reports 1996

RECREATION

Culture and Recreation

Museums	Symphony Orchestras	Opera Companies	Dance Companies	Professional Theatres	Zoos	Pro Sports Teams
22	3	1	3	3	1	3

Source: International Directory of the Performing Arts, 1996; Official Museum Directory, 1998; Chamber of Commerce/Economic Development 1997

Library System

The St. Louis County Library has 17 branches, holdings of 2,314,267 volumes and a budget of $20,295,000 (1996). The St. Louis Public Library has 15 branches, holdings of 1,740,000 volumes and a budget of $n/a. Note: n/a means not available. *American Library Directory, 1997-1998*

MEDIA

Newspapers

Name	Type	Freq.	Distribution	Circulation
Central West End Journal	General	1x/wk	Local	6,849
Chesterfield Journal	General	2x/wk	Local	15,220
Citizen Journal	General	2x/wk	Local	22,550
County Star Journal	n/a	2x/wk	Local	39,536
Jewish Light	Religious	1x/wk	Local	15,000
Maryland Heights/Bridgeton Journal	n/a	2x/wk	Local	12,536
Mid-County Journal	n/a	2x/wk	Local	14,312
North County Journal East	n/a	2x/wk	Local	93,167
North County Journal West	n/a	2x/wk	Local	49,484
North Side Journal	n/a	1x/wk	Local	46,625
Noticias	n/a	1x/mo	Local	5,000
Oakville-Mehlville Journal	n/a	2x/wk	Local	19,975
Press Journal	General	2x/wk	Local	35,000
The Riverfront Times	General	1x/wk	Local	100,000
Saint Louis American	Black	1x/wk	Area	65,500
Saint Louis Argus	Black	1x/wk	Area	44,000
Saint Louis Daily Record	n/a	5x/wk	Local	1,000
Saint Louis Post-Dispatch	n/a	7x/wk	Area	338,793
Saint Louis Review	Religious	1x/wk	Local	87,000
Saint Louis Sentinel	Black	1x/wk	Local	25,000
South City Journal	n/a	1x/wk	Local	23,215
South County Journal	General	2x/wk	Local	24,145
South Side Journal	General	2x/wk	Local	38,500
Southwest City Journal	General	2x/wk	Local	27,325
Southwest County Journal	n/a	2x/wk	Local	29,258
Webster-Kirkwood Journal	General	2x/wk	Local	27,000
West County Journal	General	2x/wk	Local	28,844

Note: Includes newspapers with circulations of 1,000 or more located in the city; n/a not available
Source: Burrelle's Media Directory, 1998 Edition

AM Radio Stations

Call Letters	Freq. (kHz)	Target Audience	Station Format	Music Format
KSD	550	General	N/T	n/a
KFNS	590	n/a	N/S/T	n/a
KSTL	690	Religious	M	Christian
WEW	770	General	M/T	Adult Standards/Big Band/Jazz/Oldies/R&B
KFUO	850	General	M/T	Christian
WGNU	920	General	N/S/T	n/a
KMOX	1120	General	N/S/T	n/a
KGLX	1220	General	M/N	Jazz
WIBV	1260	General	N/S/T	n/a
KSIV	1320	Religious	N	n/a
WRTH	1430	n/a	M/N/S	Easy Listening
KATZ	1600	General	M	Christian

Note: Stations included broadcast in the Saint Louis metro area; n/a not available
Station Format: E = Educational; M = Music; N = News; S = Sports; T = Talk
Source: Burrelle's Media Directory, 1998 Edition

FM Radio Stations

Call Letters	Freq. (mHz)	Target Audience	Station Format	Music Format
KDHX	88.1	General	M/N/T	Alter./Country/Jazz/R&B/Spanish Urban Contemp.
KCFV	89.5	General	E/M/N/S	Jazz/Urban Contemporary
KRHS	90.1	General	M	AOR
KWUR	90.3	General	M/S/T	Alternative
KWMU	90.7	General	E/M/N/S/T	Classical/Jazz
WIL	92.3	General	M/N/S	Country
KSD	93.7	General	M	AOR/Classic Rock
KSHE	94.7	n/a	M/N/S	AOR
KIHT	96.3	General	M/N	Oldies
KXOK	97.1	Black	M/T	Adult Contemp./Jazz/Oldies/R&B/Urban Contemp.
KYKY	98.1	General	M	Adult Contemporary
KFUO	99.1	General	M/N	Classical
KATZ	100.3	n/a	M	Adult Contemporary/Urban Contemporary
WVRV	101.1	General	M	Adult Contemporary
KEZK	102.5	n/a	M	Adult Contemporary
KLOU	103.3	General	M	Oldies
WALC	104.1	n/a	M	Adult Contemporary/Contemporary Top 40
WCBW	104.9	Religious	M/T	Adult Contemporary
KPNT	105.7	General	M	Alternative
WKKX	106.5	General	M	Country
KMJM	107.7	Black	M/N/S	Urban Contemporary

Note: Stations included broadcast in the Saint Louis metro area; n/a not available
Station Format: E = Educational; M = Music; N = News; S = Sports; T = Talk
Music Format: AOR = Album Oriented Rock; MOR = Middle-of-the-Road
Source: Burrelle's Media Directory, 1998 Edition

Television Stations

Name	Ch.	Affiliation	Type	Owner
KTVI	2	Fox	Commercial	New World Communications
KMOV	4	CBS	Commercial	Viacom International Inc.
KSDK	5	NBC	Commercial	Gannett Company Inc.
KETC	9	PBS	Public	St. Louis Regional Educ. TV Commission
KPLR	11	WB	Commercial	Koplar Communications, Inc.
KNLC	24	CBN	Commercial	New Life Evangelistic Center Inc.
KDNL	30	ABC	Commercial	Sinclair Broadcast Group
WHSL	46	HSN	Commercial	Roberts Broadcasting Company

Note: Stations included broadcast in the Saint Louis metro area
Source: Burrelle's Media Directory, 1998 Edition

CLIMATE

Average and Extreme Temperatures

Temperature	Jan	Feb	Mar	Apr	May	Jun	Jul	Aug	Sep	Oct	Nov	Dec	Ann
Extreme High (°F)	77	83	89	93	98	105	115	107	104	94	85	76	115
Average High (°F)	39	43	54	67	76	85	89	87	80	69	54	42	66
Average Temp. (°F)	30	34	44	56	66	75	79	78	70	59	45	34	56
Average Low (°F)	21	25	34	46	55	65	69	67	59	48	36	26	46
Extreme Low (°F)	-18	-10	-5	22	31	43	51	47	36	23	1	-16	-18

Note: Figures cover the years 1945-1990
Source: National Climatic Data Center, International Station Meteorological Climate Summary, 3/95

Average Precipitation/Snowfall/Humidity

Precip./Humidity	Jan	Feb	Mar	Apr	May	Jun	Jul	Aug	Sep	Oct	Nov	Dec	Ann
Avg. Precip. (in.)	1.9	2.2	3.4	3.4	3.8	4.0	3.8	2.9	2.9	2.8	3.0	2.6	36.8
Avg. Snowfall (in.)	6	4	4	Tr	0	0	0	0	0	Tr	1	4	20
Avg. Rel. Hum. 6am (%)	80	81	80	78	81	82	84	86	87	83	81	81	82
Avg. Rel. Hum. 3pm (%)	62	59	54	49	51	51	51	52	50	50	56	63	54

Note: Figures cover the years 1945-1990; Tr = Trace amounts (<0.05 in. of rain; <0.5 in. of snow)
Source: National Climatic Data Center, International Station Meteorological Climate Summary, 3/95

Weather Conditions

Temperature			Daytime Sky			Precipitation		
10°F & below	32°F & below	90°F & above	Clear	Partly cloudy	Cloudy	0.01 inch or more precip.	0.1 inch or more snow/ice	Thunder-storms
13	100	43	97	138	130	109	14	46

Note: Figures are average number of days per year and covers the years 1945-1990
Source: National Climatic Data Center, International Station Meteorological Climate Summary, 3/95

AIR & WATER QUALITY

Maximum Pollutant Concentrations

	Particulate Matter (ug/m^3)	Carbon Monoxide (ppm)	Sulfur Dioxide (ppm)	Nitrogen Dioxide (ppm)	Ozone (ppm)	Lead (ug/m^3)
MSA[1] Level	107	6	0.102	0.025	0.13	0.03
NAAQS[2]	150	9	0.140	0.053	0.12	1.50
Met NAAQS?	Yes	Yes	Yes	Yes	No	Yes

Note: (1) Metropolitan Statistical Area - see Appendix A for areas included; (2) National Ambient Air Quality Standards; ppm = parts per million; ug/m^3 = micrograms per cubic meter; n/a not available
Source: EPA, National Air Quality and Emissions Trends Report, 1996

Pollutant Standards Index

In the Saint Louis MSA (see Appendix A for areas included), the Pollutant Standards Index (PSI) exceeded 100 on 4 days in 1996. A PSI value greater than 100 indicates that air quality would be in the unhealthful range on that day. *EPA, National Air Quality and Emissions Trends Report, 1996*

Drinking Water

Water System Name	Pop. Served	Primary Water Source Type	Number of Violations in Fiscal Year 1997	Type of Violation/ Contaminants
St. Louis City	437,500	Surface	None	None

Note: Data as of January 16, 1998
Source: EPA, Office of Ground Water and Drinking Water, Safe Drinking Water Information System

Saint Louis tap water is alkaline, moderately hard and fluoridated.
Editor & Publisher Market Guide, 1998

Saint Paul, Minnesota

Background

St. Paul, the state capitol, is the older of Minnesota's Twin Cities. Whereas Minneapolis is characterized by glass and steel skyscrapers, St. Paul is characterized by brick-and-stone mansions.

The Louisiana Purchase of 1803 brought land west of the Mississippi River under U.S. jurisdiction. Lt. Zebulon M. Pike was commissioned in 1805 to explore the area. He bought land at the confluence of the Mississippi and Minnesota rivers, intending it for the site of a military post. Instead, he became the incidental landlord to a host of squatters.

In 1819, Col. Henry Leavenworth built an army post at nearby Mendota. The Fort was moved across the river by Col. Josiah Snelling in the following year, and was named Fort Anthony. Catholic and Protestant missionaries flocked to the area to educate the local white settlers as well as the Native American tribes. However, the missionaries were viewed as squatters by the federal government. The group moved not far away from Fort Anthony, which had been renamed Fort Snelling, and established a settlement called Pig's Eye. Pig's Eye was named after their leader, Pierre "Pig's Eye" Parrant. In the following year, Father Lucian Galtier built a log chapel at the site, and dedicated it to St. Paul. Later, settlers decided to opt for St. Paul instead of Pig's Eye as the name of their settlement.

St. Paul enjoyed prosperity during the early 1800's as a steamboat terminus and fur trading site. In the modern era, although Minneapolis is seen as the more progressive of the two, St. Paul commands respect for its industry and culture. The city carves a competitive niche in computers, guidance systems, textiles, apparels, household appliances, paper, graphic arts, printing, publishing, beer brewing, and lumber. Also, St. Paul is home to fine learning and cultural institutions such as the College of St. Catherine and St. Thomas, Hamline University, University of Minnesota, the St. Paul Arts and Science Center, and the St. Paul Opera Association.

The climate is predominantly continental, i.e., seasonal temperature variations are quite large. Temperatures range from less than -30 degrees to over 100 degrees.

Blizzards, freezing rain, tornadoes, wind and hail storms do occur. Due to spring snow melt or excessive rain, floods are not uncommon along the Mississippi River. The flood problem at St. Paul is complicated because high water on the Minnesota River creates a greater flood potential. St. Paul, like Minnesota, lies on the confluence of the Missouri and Mississippi Rivers.

General Rankings and Evaluative Comments

- Saint Paul was ranked #118 out of 300 cities by *Money's* 1997 "Survey of the Best Places to Live." Criteria used: health services, crime, economy, housing, education, transportation, weather, leisure and the arts. The city was ranked #87 in 1996 and #46 in 1995. *Money, July 1997; Money, September 1996; Money, September 1995*

- *Ladies Home Journal* ranked America's 200 largest cities based on the qualities women care about most. Saint Paul ranked 12 out of 200. Criteria: low crime rate, good public schools, well-paying jobs, quality health and child care, the presence of women in government, proportion of women-owned businesses, size of the wage gap with men, local economy, divorce rates, the ratio of single men to single women, whether there are laws that require at least the same number of public toilets for women as men, and the probability of good hair days. *Ladies Home Journal, November 1997*

- Saint Paul was ranked #67 out of 219 cities in terms of children's health, safety, and economic well-being. Criteria: total population, percent population change, birth rate, child immunization rate, infant mortality rate, percent low birth weight infants, percent of births to teens, physician-to-population ratio, student-to-teacher ratio, dropout rate, unemployment rate, median family income, percent of children in poverty, violent and property crime rates, number of juvenile arrests for violent crimes as a percent of the total crime index, number of days with pollution standard index (PSI) over 100, pounds toxic releases per 1,000 people and number of superfund sites. *Zero Population Growth, Children's Environmental Index 1997*

- Saint Paul appeared on *Sales & Marketing Management's* list of the 20 hottest domestic markets to do business in. Rank: 13 out of 20. America's 320 Metropolitan Statistical Areas were ranked based on the market's potential to buy products in certain industries like high-tech, manufacturing, office equipment and business services, as well as population and household income growth. The study had nine criteria in all.

  "With more than 1,300 technology-focused firms, this market has one of the largest concentration of high-tech business in the nation. A wide mix of industries—plus representation of big and small companies—makes the Twin Cities a market that any company should consider." *Sales & Marketing Management, January 1998*

- Minnesota Mining & Manufacturing, St. Paul Companies (insurance), and H.B. Fuller (adhesives, sealants, specialty chemicals), headquartered in Saint Paul, are among the "100 Best Companies to Work for in America." Criteria: trust in management, pride in work/company, camaraderie, company responses to the Hewitt People Practices Inventory, and employee responses to their Great Place to Work survey. The companies also had to be at least 10 years old and have a minimum of 500 employees. *Fortune, January 12, 1998*

- 3M and The St. Paul Companies, headquartered in Saint Paul, are among the "100 Best Companies for Working Mothers." Criteria: pay compared with competition, opportunities for women to advance, support for child care, flexible work schedules and family-friendly benefits. *Working Mother, October 1997*

- According to *Working Mother,* "Last spring Minnesota's legislature approved a major package of laws that granted more than $200 million to child care. This translates into 13,000 more families getting help paying for child care this year. State lawmakers also designated funds to expand resource and referral services to help families find care, and approved Governor Arne Carlson's proposal to give $1 million in new state money to train and recruit caregivers to meet the new demand.

  Minnesota had several other important initiatives pass this year. One new law significantly boosts caregiver training across the state by funding scholarships for caregivers to get on-the-job training. Another new law gives grants for nontraditional care—such as programs for kids with special needs and care during weekends and other off hours. (Minnesota was among the top 10 states for child care.)" *Working Mother, July/August 1997*

Business Environment

STATE ECONOMY

State Economic Profile

"Minnesota is experiencing swift and broad-based growth across all major industries. Construction employment growth has been strong all year as a result of steady residential construction, and an infusion of commercial projects. Finance, insurance and real estate have shown strength throughout the year, bolstered by surging home sales, expansion of large depository institutions, and financial services employers....

Minnesota's commercial and industrial property tax burden is roughly twice that of Wisconsin's, and over twice that of South Dakota's. While the tax differential is not new, it has slowly escalated through the last two decades, constraining job creation.

There are now six Minnesota casinos that maintain labor forces of over 1,000 workers. The newest trend among these casinos is the addition of accompanying hotel/resort complexes. Minnesota's casinos differ from the riverboat casinos in Kansas City and St. Louis in that Minnesota caters mostly to instate gamblers, especially from Minneapolis, while the riverboat casinos are tourist-oriented and bring in out-of-state money. Therefore, Minnesota casinos act to redistribute money from the Twin Cities to elsewhere in the state, but do not add to state income.

The Minnesota health services industry is a leader in consolidation and reform. Several large health alliances and hospital systems now figure among Minnesota's top employers. As a result of consolidation, employment growth has been below the nation's during the past six years. Going forward, consolidation will continue unabated.

Minnesota is and will continue to be a strong Plains performer through the forecast horizon. Minnesota's economy is driven by its industrial center, the Minneapolis-St. Paul metropolitan area, which has been experiencing a prolonged period of growth. As a result of this expansion, labor shortages, space shortages, and high costs of doing business in Minneapolis-St. Paul all present downside risks to economic growth." *National Association of Realtors, Economic Profiles: The Fifty States, July 1997*

IMPORTS/EXPORTS

Total Export Sales

Area	1993 ($000)	1994 ($000)	1995 ($000)	1996 ($000)	% Chg. 1993-96	% Chg. 1995-96
MSA[1]	n/a	n/a	n/a	n/a	n/a	n/a
U.S.	464,858,354	512,415,609	583,030,524	622,827,063	34.0	6.8

Note: (1) Metropolitan Statistical Area - see Appendix A for areas included
Source: U.S. Department of Commerce, International Trade Association, Metropolitan Area Exports: An Export Performance Report on Over 250 U.S. Cities, October 1997

Imports/Exports by Port

Type	Cargo Value			Share of U.S. Total	
	1995 (US$mil.)	1996 (US$mil.)	% Change 1995-1996	1995 (%)	1996 (%)
Imports	0	0	0	0	0
Exports	0	0	0	0	0

Source: Global Trade Information Services, WaterBorne Trade Atlas 1997

CITY FINANCES

City Government Finances

Component	FY92 ($000)	FY92 (per capita $)
Revenue	373,320	1,389.12
Expenditure	483,910	1,800.63
Debt Outstanding	935,997	3,482.84
Cash & Securities	1,021,013	3,799.19

Source: U.S. Bureau of the Census, City Government Finances: 1991-92

City Government Revenue by Source

Source	FY92 ($000)	FY92 (per capita $)	FY92 (%)
From Federal Government	31,118	115.79	8.3
From State Governments	38,141	141.92	10.2
From Local Governments	8,753	32.57	2.3
Property Taxes	71,343	265.47	19.1
General Sales Taxes	0	0.00	0.0
Selective Sales Taxes	16,463	61.26	4.4
Income Taxes	0	0.00	0.0
Current Charges	76,863	286.01	20.6
Utility/Liquor Store	23,447	87.25	6.3
Employee Retirement[1]	12,178	45.31	3.3
Other	95,014	353.55	25.5

Note: (1) Excludes "city contributions," classified as "nonrevenue," intragovernmental transfers.
Source: U.S. Bureau of the Census, City Government Finances: 1991-92

City Government Expenditures by Function

Function	FY92 ($000)	FY92 (per capita $)	FY92 (%)
Educational Services	9,372	34.87	1.9
Employee Retirement[1]	14,829	55.18	3.1
Environment/Housing	142,905	531.75	29.5
Government Administration	20,824	77.49	4.3
Interest on General Debt	87,544	325.75	18.1
Public Safety	70,995	264.17	14.7
Social Services	9,159	34.08	1.9
Transportation	46,637	173.54	9.6
Utility/Liquor Store	44,015	163.78	9.1
Other	37,630	140.02	7.8

Note: (1) Payments to beneficiaries including withdrawal of contributions.
Source: U.S. Bureau of the Census, City Government Finances: 1991-92

Municipal Bond Ratings

Area	Moody's	S & P
Saint Paul	Aa2	AA+

Note: n/a not available; n/r not rated
Source: Moody's Bond Record, 2/98; Statistical Abstract of the U.S., 1997;
Governing Magazine, 9/97, 3/98

POPULATION

Population Growth

Area	1980	1990	% Chg. 1980-90	July 1996 Estimate	% Chg. 1990-96
City	270,230	272,235	0.7	259,606	-4.6
MSA[1]	2,137,133	2,464,124	15.3	n/a	n/a
U.S.	226,545,805	248,765,170	9.8	265,179,411	6.6

Note: (1) Metropolitan Statistical Area - see Appendix A for areas included
Source: 1980/1990 Census of Housing and Population, Summary Tape File 3C;
Census Bureau Population Estimates

Population Characteristics

Race	City 1980 Population	%	City 1990 Population	%	% Chg. 1980-90	MSA[1] 1990 Population	%
White	245,795	91.0	224,302	82.4	-8.7	2,272,798	92.2
Black	13,018	4.8	20,330	7.5	56.2	89,359	3.6
Amer Indian/Esk/Aleut	2,558	0.9	3,400	1.2	32.9	23,338	0.9
Asian/Pacific Islander	5,345	2.0	18,998	7.0	255.4	64,944	2.6
Other	3,514	1.3	5,205	1.9	48.1	13,685	0.6
Hispanic Origin[2]	7,864	2.9	10,318	3.8	31.2	33,835	1.4

Note: (1) Metropolitan Statistical Area - see Appendix A for areas included;
(2) people of Hispanic origin can be of any race
Source: 1980/1990 Census of Housing and Population, Summary Tape File 3C

Ancestry

Area	German	Irish	English	Italian	U.S.	French	Polish	Dutch
City	38.7	17.1	7.4	3.4	1.0	5.6	5.4	1.4
MSA[1]	43.8	15.2	9.2	2.5	1.2	6.1	5.8	2.0
U.S.	23.3	15.6	13.1	5.9	5.3	4.2	3.8	2.5

Note: Figures are percentages and include persons that reported multiple ancestry (eg. if a person reported being Irish and Italian, they were included in both columns); (1) Metropolitan Statistical Area - see Appendix A for areas included
Source: 1990 Census of Population and Housing, Summary Tape File 3C

Age

Area	Median Age (Years)	Age Distribution (%) Under 5	Under 18	18-24	25-44	45-64	65+	80+
City	31.2	8.4	24.5	12.2	35.0	14.5	13.8	3.8
MSA[1]	31.6	8.1	26.3	10.0	36.8	17.1	9.9	2.5
U.S.	32.9	7.3	25.6	10.5	32.6	18.7	12.5	2.8

Note: (1) Metropolitan Statistical Area - see Appendix A for areas included
Source: 1990 Census of Population and Housing, Summary Tape File 3C

Male/Female Ratio

Area	Number of males per 100 females (all ages)	Number of males per 100 females (18 years old+)
City	88.8	85.2
MSA[1]	95.5	92.6
U.S.	95.0	91.9

Note: (1) Metropolitan Statistical Area - see Appendix A for areas included
Source: 1990 Census of Population, General Population Characteristics

INCOME

Per Capita/Median/Average Income

Area	Per Capita ($)	Median Household ($)	Average Household ($)
City	13,727	26,498	33,259
MSA[1]	16,842	36,565	43,942
U.S.	14,420	30,056	38,453

Note: all figures are for 1989; (1) Metropolitan Statistical Area - see Appendix A for areas included
Source: 1990 Census of Population and Housing, Summary Tape File 3C

Household Income Distribution by Race

Income ($)	City (%)					U.S. (%)				
	Total	White	Black	Other	Hisp.[1]	Total	White	Black	Other	Hisp.[1]
Less than 5,000	5.3	4.4	11.8	12.0	8.4	6.2	4.8	15.2	8.6	8.8
5,000 - 9,999	12.4	11.3	21.7	19.8	12.1	9.3	8.6	14.2	9.9	11.1
10,000 - 14,999	9.7	9.2	10.0	16.9	12.0	8.8	8.5	11.0	9.8	11.0
15,000 - 24,999	19.8	19.5	21.9	20.6	20.1	17.5	17.3	18.9	18.5	20.5
25,000 - 34,999	16.5	17.1	12.6	11.2	14.1	15.8	16.1	14.2	15.4	16.4
35,000 - 49,999	17.7	18.5	12.0	11.0	18.7	17.9	18.6	13.3	16.1	16.0
50,000 - 74,999	12.6	13.3	7.8	6.9	11.8	15.0	15.8	9.3	13.4	11.1
75,000 - 99,999	3.6	3.9	1.2	1.3	2.7	5.1	5.5	2.6	4.7	3.1
100,000+	2.5	2.7	1.0	0.3	0.2	4.4	4.8	1.3	3.7	1.9

Note: all figures are for 1989; (1) people of Hispanic origin can be of any race
Source: 1990 Census of Population and Housing, Summary Tape File 3C

Effective Buying Income

Area	Per Capita ($)	Median Household ($)	Average Household ($)
City	15,367	30,562	37,865
MSA[1]	18,341	41,838	48,729
U.S.	15,444	33,201	41,849

Note: data as of 1/1/97; (1) Metropolitan Statistical Area - see Appendix A for areas included
Source: Standard Rate & Data Service, Newspaper Advertising Source, 2/98

Effective Household Buying Income Distribution

Area	% of Households Earning						
	$10,000 -$19,999	$20,000 -$34,999	$35,000 -$49,999	$50,000 -$74,999	$75,000 -$99,000	$100,000 -$124,999	$125,000 and up
City	18.4	25.0	18.8	16.7	5.1	1.3	1.5
MSA[1]	12.0	21.1	20.7	24.5	8.6	2.8	2.9
U.S.	16.5	23.4	18.3	18.2	6.4	2.1	2.4

Note: data as of 1/1/97; (1) Metropolitan Statistical Area - see Appendix A for areas included
Source: Standard Rate & Data Service, Newspaper Advertising Source, 2/98

Poverty Rates by Race and Age

Area	Total (%)	By Race (%)				By Age (%)		
		White	Black	Other	Hisp.[2]	Under 5 years old	Under 18 years old	65 years and over
City	16.7	10.2	39.2	52.3	25.6	30.6	26.9	10.7
MSA[1]	8.1	5.9	37.0	32.7	19.1	13.2	11.2	8.2
U.S.	13.1	9.8	29.5	23.1	25.3	20.1	18.3	12.8

Note: figures show the percent of people living below the poverty line in 1989. The average poverty threshold was $12,674 for a family of four in 1989; (1) Metropolitan Statistical Area - see Appendix A for areas included; (2) people of Hispanic origin can be of any race
Source: 1990 Census of Population and Housing, Summary Tape File 3C

EMPLOYMENT

Labor Force and Employment

Area	Civilian Labor Force			Workers Employed		
	Dec. '95	Dec. '96	% Chg.	Dec. '95	Dec. '96	% Chg.
City	141,218	145,162	2.8	137,003	141,844	3.5
MSA[1]	1,615,254	1,658,390	2.7	1,572,977	1,627,030	3.4
U.S.	134,583,000	136,742,000	1.6	127,903,000	130,785,000	2.3

Note: Data is not seasonally adjusted and covers workers 16 years of age and older;
(1) Metropolitan Statistical Area - see Appendix A for areas included
Source: Bureau of Labor Statistics, http://stats.bls.gov

Unemployment Rate

Area	1997											
	Jan.	Feb.	Mar.	Apr.	May	Jun.	Jul.	Aug.	Sep.	Oct.	Nov.	Dec.
City	3.4	2.9	2.8	3.0	2.8	4.0	3.2	3.3	4.0	3.4	2.6	2.3
MSA[1]	3.0	2.6	2.5	2.5	2.1	2.9	2.3	2.4	2.8	2.5	2.0	1.9
U.S.	5.9	5.7	5.5	4.8	4.7	5.2	5.0	4.8	4.7	4.4	4.3	4.4

Note: Data is not seasonally adjusted and covers workers 16 years of age and older; All figures are percentages; (1) Metropolitan Statistical Area - see Appendix A for areas included
Source: Bureau of Labor Statistics, http://stats.bls.gov

Employment by Industry

Sector	MSA[1]		U.S.
	Number of Employees	Percent of Total	Percent of Total
Services	482,400	29.2	29.0
Retail Trade	299,500	18.1	18.5
Government	227,000	13.7	16.1
Manufacturing	275,700	16.7	15.0
Finance/Insurance/Real Estate	116,900	7.1	5.7
Wholesale Trade	103,800	6.3	5.4
Transportation/Public Utilities	90,200	5.5	5.3
Construction/Mining	500	0.0	5.0

Note: Figures cover non-farm employment as of 12/97 and are not seasonally adjusted; (1) Metropolitan Statistical Area - see Appendix A for areas included
Source: Bureau of Labor Statistics, http://stats.bls.gov

Employment by Occupation

Occupation Category	City (%)	MSA[1] (%)	U.S. (%)
White Collar	63.4	65.0	58.1
Executive/Admin./Management	11.6	14.2	12.3
Professional	17.3	15.3	14.1
Technical & Related Support	4.7	4.6	3.7
Sales	10.6	12.7	11.8
Administrative Support/Clerical	19.3	18.3	16.3
Blue Collar	20.5	21.6	26.2
Precision Production/Craft/Repair	7.2	9.4	11.3
Machine Operators/Assem./Insp.	6.4	6.0	6.8
Transportation/Material Movers	3.5	3.2	4.1
Cleaners/Helpers/Laborers	3.4	3.1	3.9
Services	15.3	12.3	13.2
Farming/Forestry/Fishing	0.7	1.1	2.5

Note: figures cover employed persons 16 years old and over; (1) Metropolitan Statistical Area - see Appendix A for areas included
Source: 1990 Census of Population and Housing, Summary Tape File 3C

Occupational Employment Projections: 1994 - 2005

Occupations Expected to have the Largest Job Growth (ranked by numerical growth)	Fast-Growing Occupations[1] (ranked by percent growth)
1. Salespersons, retail	1. All other computer scientists
2. Computer systems analysts	2. Manicurists
3. General managers & top executives	3. Computer systems analysts
4. All other profess., paraprofess., tech.	4. Occupational therapy assistants
5. Cashiers	5. Electronic pagination systems workers
6. All other helper, laborer, mover	6. Physical therapy assistants and aides
7. Janitors/cleaners/maids, ex. priv. hshld.	7. Personal and home care aides
8. All other computer scientists	8. All other assemblers, fabricators
9. Waiters & waitresses	9. Computer engineers
10. Receptionists and information clerks	10. Home health aides

Projections cover Anoka, Carver, Dakota, Hennepin, Ramsey, Scott and Washington Counties.
Note: (1) Excludes occupations with less than 50 employees in 1994
Source: Minnesota Department of Economic Security, Twin Cities Area Employment Outlook by Occupation, 1994-2005

Average Wages

Occupation	Wage	Occupation	Wage
Professional/Technical/Clerical	$/Week	**Health/Protective Services**	$/Week
Accountants III	812	Corrections Officers	-
Attorneys III	1,338	Firefighters	763
Budget Analysts III	-	Nurses, Licensed Practical II	-
Buyers/Contracting Specialists II	656	Nurses, Registered II	-
Clerks, Accounting III	461	Nursing Assistants II	-
Clerks, General III	439	Police Officers I	775
Computer Operators II	-	**Hourly Workers**	$/Hour
Computer Programmers II	652	Forklift Operators	13.20
Drafters II	538	General Maintenance Workers	11.30
Engineering Technicians III	623	Guards I	7.60
Engineering Technicians, Civil III	705	Janitors	8.34
Engineers III	946	Maintenance Electricians	20.92
Key Entry Operators I	354	Maintenance Electronics Techs II	-
Personnel Assistants III	517	Maintenance Machinists	18.50
Personnel Specialists III	768	Maintenance Mechanics, Machinery	16.50
Secretaries III	535	Material Handling Laborers	-
Switchboard Operator-Receptionist	382	Motor Vehicle Mechanics	16.77
Systems Analysts II	958	Shipping/Receiving Clerks	-
Systems Analysts Supervisor/Mgr II	1,364	Tool and Die Makers	18.16
Tax Collectors II	650	Truckdrivers, Tractor Trailer	15.23
Word Processors II	-	Warehouse Specialists	15.69

Note: Wage data includes full-time workers only for 2/96 and cover the Metropolitan Statistical Area (see Appendix A for areas included). Dashes indicate that data was not available.
Source: Bureau of Labor Statistics, Occupational Compensation Survey, 8/96

TAXES

Major State and Local Tax Rates

State Corp. Income (%)	State Personal Income (%)	Residential Property (effective rate per $100)	Sales & Use		State Gasoline (cents/ gallon)	State Cigarette (cents/ 20-pack)
			State (%)	Local (%)		
9.8[a]	6.0 - 8.5	n/a	6.5	0.5	20	48

Note: Personal/corporate income tax rates as of 1/97. Sales, gasoline and cigarette tax rates as of 1/98; (a) 5.8% alternative minimum tax rate
Source: Federation of Tax Administrators, www.taxadmin.org; Washington D.C. Department of Finance and Revenue, Tax Rates and Tax Burdens in the District of Columbia: A Nationwide Comparison, June 1997; Chamber of Commerce

Total Taxes Per Capita and as a Percent of Income

Area	Per Capita Income ($)	Per Capita Taxes ($)			Taxes as Pct. of Income (%)		
		Total	Federal	State/Local	Total	Federal	State/Local
Minnesota	27,512	9,997	6,358	3,638	36.3	23.1	13.2
U.S.	26,187	9,205	6,127	3,078	35.2	23.4	11.8

Note: Figures are for 1997
Source: Tax Foundation, Web Site, www.taxfoundation.org

Estimated Tax Burden

Area	State Income	Local Income	Property	Sales	Total
Saint Paul	3,069	0	4,950	595	8,614

Note: The numbers are estimates of taxes paid by a married couple with two kids and annual earnings of $65,000. Sales tax estimates assume they spend average amounts on food, clothing, household goods and gasoline. Property tax estimates assume they live in a $225,000 home.
Source: Kiplinger's Personal Finance Magazine, June 1997

COMMERCIAL REAL ESTATE

Office Market

Class/Location	Total Space (sq. ft.)	Vacant Space (sq. ft.)	Vac. Rate (%)	Under Constr. (sq. ft.)	Net Absorp. (sq. ft.)	Rental Rates ($/sq.ft./yr.)
Class A						
CBD	11,165,605	459,037	4.1	0	-2,533,952	16.00-34.00
Outside CBD	5,400,004	189,459	3.5	468,000	-927,207	20.00-31.00
Class B						
CBD	10,881,145	974,941	9.0	0	4,200,791	13.00-24.00
Outside CBD	19,567,231	1,464,762	7.5	40,000	1,030,971	13.00-22.00

Note: Data as of 10/97 and covers Minneapolis/St. Paul; CBD = Central Business District; n/a not available;
Source: Society of Industrial and Office Realtors, 1998 Comparative Statistics of Industrial and Office Real Estate Markets

"Speculative office development is taking place in the southwest suburban area where absorption has historically been the highest. Officing at home, hoteling, and flexible hours will continue as firms try to reduce occupancy. This will not affect the state of the market as absorption and construction are predicted to rise up to 15 percent. Commercial real estate taxes are expected to be reduced by approximately 6 percent, which has been long in the waiting. The large financial services industry adds to the economic stability as First Bank and Norwest Corp, two of the nation's powerhouses, continue to acquire and hire, shielding the area from industry downsizing. Finding skilled employees will continue to be a challenge in 1998, but the outlook is positive." Society of Industrial and Office Realtors, 1998 Comparative Statistics of Industrial and Office Real Estate Markets

Industrial Market

Location	Total Space (sq. ft.)	Vacant Space (sq. ft.)	Vac. Rate (%)	Under Constr. (sq. ft.)	Net Absorp. (sq. ft.)	Net Lease ($/sq.ft./yr.)
Central City	78,247,000	2,335,298	3.0	250,000	3,779,862	3.50-4.50
Suburban	121,325,000	6,508,820	5.4	3,500,000	4,627,500	3.75-4.50

Note: Data as of 10/97 and covers Minneapolis-St. Paul; n/a not available
Source: Society of Industrial and Office Realtors, 1998 Comparative Statistics of Industrial and Office Real Estate Markets

"The industrial property tax in Minnesota is about twice that of neighboring states, resulting in a trend of businesses heading across the state border. Fortunately, with an economy as diverse as Minneapolis, new migrants will continue to be attracted to this metropolitan area. Despite the risk of a tight labor market and high business costs, employment growth is expected to regain its strength in the long-term. As the available supply of industrial space dwindles, construction is expected to continue at a rate of at least six percent for warehouse/distribution, manufacturing, and High-Tech/R&D space. Lease prices will increase up to five percent for all industrial property types. Manufacturing sales prices are expected to grow by at least six percent. Market trends are moving toward distribution centers and office warehouses with higher ceiling heights." *Society of Industrial and Office Realtors, 1998 Comparative Statistics of Industrial and Office Real Estate Markets*

Retail Market

Shopping Center Inventory (sq. ft.)	Shopping Center Construction (sq. ft.)	Construction as a Percent of Inventory (%)	Torto Wheaton Rent Index[1] ($/sq. ft.)
39,152,000	677,000	1.7	10.31

Note: Data as of 1997 and covers the Metropolitan Statistical Area - see Appendix A for areas included; (1) Index is based on a model that predicts what the average rent should be for leases with certain characteristics, in certain locations during certain years.
Source: National Association of Realtors, 1997-1998 Market Conditions Report

"Estimated at 2.81 million, Minneapolis' population has grown an average of 1.5% annually over the past two years, compared to 0.9% for the nation. Real personal income growth has been strong recently, which has helped push the area's retail rent index up 27% over the past three years. However, rents remain below the Midwest average of $12.30. Minneapolis, of course, is home to the 4.2 million square foot Mall of America, which boasts a multitude of bars and restaurants, a 14 screen megaplex, an indoor amusement park and an aquarium. The mall typifies a trend in several areas, where entertainment is being used to attract customers to retail centers." *National Association of Realtors, 1997-1998 Market Conditions Report*

COMMERCIAL UTILITIES

Typical Monthly Electric Bills

Area	Commercial Service ($/month)		Industrial Service ($/month)	
	12 kW demand 1,500 kWh	100 kW demand 30,000 kWh	1,000 kW demand 400,000 kWh	20,000 kW demand 10,000,000 kWh
City	122	1,948	21,281	473,746
U.S.	162	2,360	25,590	545,677

Note: Based on rates in effect July 1, 1997
Source: Edison Electric Institute, Typical Residential, Commercial and Industrial Bills, Summer 1997

TRANSPORTATION

Transportation Statistics

Avg. travel time to work (min.)	18.7
Interstate highways	I-35; I-94
Bus lines	
In-city	Metropolitan Council, 981 vehicles
Inter-city	2
Passenger air service	
Airport	Minneapolis-St. Paul International
Airlines	18
Aircraft departures	150,399 (1995)
Enplaned passengers	11,835,783 (1995)
Rail service	Amtrak
Motor freight carriers	100
Major waterways/ports	Port of St. Paul

Source: OAG, Business Travel Planner, Summer 1997; Editor & Publisher Market Guide, 1998; FAA Airport Activity Statistics, 1996; Amtrak National Time Table, Northeast Timetable, Fall/Winter 1997-98; 1990 Census of Population and Housing, STF 3C; Chamber of Commerce/Economic Development 1997; Jane's Urban Transport Systems 1997-98; Transit Fact Book 1997

A survey of 90,000 airline passengers during the first half of 1997 ranked most of the largest airports in the U.S. Minneapolis-St. Paul International ranked number 14 out of 36. Criteria: cleanliness, quality of restaurants, attractiveness, speed of baggage delivery, ease of reaching gates, available ground transportation, ease of following signs and closeness of parking. *Plog Research Inc., First Half 1997*

Means of Transportation to Work

Area	Car/Truck/Van		Public Transportation			Bicycle	Walked	Other Means	Worked at Home
	Drove Alone	Car-pooled	Bus	Subway	Railroad				
City	67.1	12.4	10.3	0.0	0.0	0.5	6.4	0.7	2.6
MSA[1]	76.0	11.2	5.2	0.0	0.0	0.4	3.2	0.6	3.4
U.S.	73.2	13.4	3.0	1.5	0.5	0.4	3.9	1.2	3.0

Note: figures shown are percentages and only include workers 16 years old and over;
(1) Metropolitan Statistical Area - see Appendix A for areas included
Source: 1990 Census of Population and Housing, Summary Tape File 3C

BUSINESSES

Major Business Headquarters

Company Name	1997 Rankings	
	Fortune 500	Forbes 500
API Group	-	407
Johnson Bros. Wholesale Liquor	-	419
Minnesota Mining & Mfg.	81	-
Northwest Airlines	147	-
Saint Paul Companies	238	-

Note: Companies listed are located in the city; Dashes indicate no ranking
Fortune 500: companies that produce a 10-K are ranked 1 - 500 based on 1996 revenue
Forbes 500: private companies are ranked 1 - 500 based on 1996 revenue
Source: Forbes 12/1/97; Fortune 4/28/97

Fast-Growing Businesses

Saint Paul was ranked #9 out of 24 (#1 is best) in terms of the best-performing local stocks in 1996 according to the Money/Norby Cities Index. The index measures stocks of companies that have headquarters in 24 metro areas. *Money, 2/7/97*

Small Business Opportunity

Saint Paul was included among *Entrepreneur* magazines listing of the ''20 Best Cities for Small Business.'' It was ranked #7 among large metro areas. Criteria: risk of failure, business performance, economic growth, affordability and state attitude towards business. *Entrepreneur, 10/97*

According to *Forbes*, Saint Paul is home to one of America's 200 best small companies: Empi. Criteria: companies must be publicly traded, U.S.-based corporations with latest 12-month sales of between $5 and $350 million. Earnings must be at least $1 million for the 12-month period. Limited partnerships, REITs and closed-end mutual funds were not considered. Banks, S&Ls and electric utilities were not included. *Forbes, November 3, 1997*

HOTELS & MOTELS

Hotels/Motels

Area	Hotels/ Motels	Rooms	Luxury-Level Hotels/Motels		Average Minimum Rates ($)		
			◆◆◆◆	◆◆◆◆◆	◆◆	◆◆◆	◆◆◆◆
City	12	2,411	0	0	70	114	n/a
Airport	2	25	0	0	n/a	n/a	n/a
Suburbs	25	2,051	0	0	n/a	n/a	n/a
Total	39	4,487	0	0	n/a	n/a	n/a

Note: n/a not available; Classifications range from one diamond (budget properties with basic amenities) to five diamond (luxury properties with the finest service, rooms and facilities).
Source: OAG, Business Travel Planner, Summer 1997

CONVENTION CENTERS

Major Convention Centers

Center Name	Meeting Rooms	Exhibit Space (sf)
Earle Brown Continuing Education Center	9	13,000
St. Paul Civic Center	21	180,000

Source: Trade Shows Worldwide 1997

Living Environment

COST OF LIVING

Cost of Living Index

Composite Index	Housing	Utilities	Groceries	Health Care	Trans-portation	Misc. Goods/ Services
101.5	97.0	96.2	100.4	126.0	107.0	101.3

Note: U.S. = 100
Source: ACCRA, Cost of Living Index, 3rd Quarter 1997

HOUSING

Median Home Prices and Housing Affordability

Area	Median Price[2] 3rd Qtr. 1997 ($)	HOI[3] 3rd Qtr. 1997	Afford-ability Rank[4]
MSA[1]	118,000	79.4	26
U.S.	127,000	63.7	–

Note: (1) Metropolitan Statistical Area - see Appendix A for areas included; (2) U.S. figures calculated from the sales of 625,000 new and existing homes in 195 markets; (3) Housing Opportunity Index - percent of homes sold that were within the reach of the median income household at the prevailing mortgage interest rate; (4) Rank is from 1-195 with 1 being most affordable
Source: National Association of Home Builders, Housing Opportunity Index, 3rd Quarter 1997

It is projected that the median price of existing single-family homes in the metro area will increase by 8.2% in 1998. Nationwide, home prices are projected to increase 6.6%.
Kiplinger's Personal Finance Magazine, January 1998

Average New Home Price

Area	Price ($)
City	125,263
U.S.	135,710

Note: Figures are based on a new home with 1,800 sq. ft. of living area on an 8,000 sq. ft. lot.
Source: ACCRA, Cost of Living Index, 3rd Quarter 1997

Average Apartment Rent

Area	Rent ($/mth)
City	614
U.S.	569

Note: Figures are based on an unfurnished two bedroom, 1-1/2 or 2 bath apartment, approximately 950 sq. ft. in size, excluding all utilities except water
Source: ACCRA, Cost of Living Index, 3rd Quarter 1997

RESIDENTIAL UTILITIES

Average Residential Utility Costs

Area	All Electric ($/mth)	Part Electric ($/mth)	Other Energy ($/mth)	Phone ($/mth)
City	–	46.23	50.82	20.63
U.S.	109.40	55.25	43.64	19.48

Source: ACCRA, Cost of Living Index, 3rd Quarter 1997

HEALTH CARE

Average Health Care Costs

Area	Hospital ($/day)	Doctor ($/visit)	Dentist ($/visit)
City	708.20	55.00	71.60
U.S.	392.91	48.76	60.84

Note: Hospital - based on a semi-private room. Doctor - based on a general practitioner's routine exam of an established patient. Dentist - based on adult teeth cleaning and periodic oral exam.
Source: ACCRA, Cost of Living Index, 3rd Quarter 1997

Distribution of Office-Based Physicians

| Area | Family/Gen. Practitioners | Specialists | | |
		Medical	Surgical	Other
MSA[1]	1,026	1,490	1,112	1,246

Note: Data as of 12/31/96; (1) Metropolitan Statistical Area - see Appendix A for areas included
Source: American Medical Assn., Physician Characteristics & Distribution in the U.S., 1997-1998

Hospitals

Saint Paul has 4 general medical and surgical hospitals, 1 other specialty, 1 children's general, 1 children's other specialty. *AHA Guide to the Healthcare Field 1997-98*

EDUCATION

Public School District Statistics

District Name	Num. Sch.	Enroll.	Classroom Teachers[1]	Pupils per Teacher	Minority Pupils (%)	Current Exp.[2] ($/pupil)
City Academy	1	51	n/a	n/a	n/a	n/a
Community of Peace Academy	1	161	n/a	n/a	n/a	n/a
Metro Deaf Charter School	1	32	6	5.3	n/a	n/a
Mounds View	22	12,148	n/a	n/a	n/a	n/a
Right Step Academy	1	107	n/a	n/a	n/a	n/a
St. Paul	142	42,520	n/a	n/a	54.1	6,170

Note: Data covers the 1995-1996 school year unless otherwise noted; (1) Excludes teachers reported as working in school district offices rather than in schools; (2) Based on 1993-94 enrollment collected by the Census Bureau, not the enrollment figure shown in column 3; SD = School District; ISD = Independent School District; n/a not available
Source: National Center for Education Statistics, Common Core of Data Survey; Bureau of the Census

Educational Quality

School District	Education Quotient[1]	Graduate Outcome[2]	Community Index[3]	Resource Index[4]
Saint Paul	114.0	79.0	130.0	134.0

Note: Nearly 1,000 secondary school districts were rated in terms of educational quality. The scores range from a low of 50 to a high of 150; (1) Average of the Graduate Outcome, Community and Resource indexes; (2) Based on graduation rates and college board scores (SAT/ACT); (3) Based on the surrounding community's average level of education and the area's average income level; (4) Based on teacher salaries, per-pupil expenditures and student-teacher ratios.
Source: Expansion Management, Ratings Issue 1997

Educational Attainment by Race

| Area | High School Graduate (%) | | | | | Bachelor's Degree (%) | | | | |
	Total	White	Black	Other	Hisp.[2]	Total	White	Black	Other	Hisp.[2]
City	81.1	83.3	76.4	54.7	67.4	26.5	28.0	14.8	16.0	14.8
MSA[1]	87.2	88.0	76.2	70.7	76.7	27.1	27.5	17.3	25.2	19.9
U.S.	75.2	77.9	63.1	60.4	49.8	20.3	21.5	11.4	19.4	9.2

Note: figures shown cover persons 25 years old and over; (1) Metropolitan Statistical Area - see Appendix A for areas included; (2) people of Hispanic origin can be of any race
Source: 1990 Census of Population and Housing, Summary Tape File 3C

School Enrollment by Type

| Area | Preprimary | | | | Elementary/High School | | | |
| | Public | | Private | | Public | | Private | |
	Enrollment	%	Enrollment	%	Enrollment	%	Enrollment	%
City	2,919	54.4	2,445	45.6	32,325	80.7	7,728	19.3
MSA[1]	35,492	63.1	20,730	36.9	359,955	89.1	44,235	10.9
U.S.	2,679,029	59.5	1,824,256	40.5	38,379,689	90.2	4,187,099	9.8

Note: figures shown cover persons 3 years old and over;
(1) Metropolitan Statistical Area - see Appendix A for areas included
Source: 1990 Census of Population and Housing, Summary Tape File 3C

School Enrollment by Race

Area	Preprimary (%)				Elementary/High School (%)			
	White	Black	Other	Hisp.[1]	White	Black	Other	Hisp.[1]
City	78.9	9.6	11.5	5.6	67.4	11.9	20.7	6.2
MSA[2]	90.7	4.3	5.0	1.9	87.8	5.3	6.9	2.1
U.S.	80.4	12.5	7.1	7.8	74.1	15.6	10.3	12.5

Note: figures shown cover persons 3 years old and over; (1) people of Hispanic origin can be of any race; (2) Metropolitan Statistical Area - see Appendix A for areas included
Source: 1990 Census of Population and Housing, Summary Tape File 3C

SAT/ACT Scores

Area/District	1997 SAT				1997 ACT	
	Percent of Graduates Tested (%)	Average Math Score	Average Verbal Score	Average Combined Score	Percent of Graduates Tested (%)	Average Composite Score
St. Paul	n/a	n/a	n/a	n/a	45	20.7
State	9	592	582	1,174	60	22.1
U.S.	42	511	505	1,016	36	21.0

Note: Math and verbal SAT scores are out of a possible 800; ACT scores are out of a possible 36
Caution: Comparing or ranking states/cities on the basis of SAT/ACT scores alone is invalid and strongly discouraged by the The College Board and The American College Testing Program as students who take the tests are self-selected and do not represent the entire student population.
Source: St. Paul Public Schools, Evaluation, Information & Student Services, 1997; American College Testing Program, 1997; College Board, 1997

Classroom Teacher Salaries in Public Schools

District	B.A. Degree		M.A. Degree		Ph.D. Degree	
	Min. ($)	Max. ($)	Min. ($)	Max. ($)	Min. ($)	Max. ($)
Saint Paul	26,500	40,054	27,918	49,106	31,949	55,864
Average[1]	26,120	39,270	28,175	44,667	31,643	49,825

Note: Salaries are for 1996-1997; (1) Based on all school districts covered; n/a not available
Source: American Federation of Teachers (unpublished data)

Higher Education

Two-Year Colleges		Four-Year Colleges		Medical Schools	Law Schools	Voc/ Tech
Public	Private	Public	Private			
1	0	1	9	0	2	5

Source: College Blue Book, Occupational Education 1997; Medical School Admission Requirements, 1998-99; Peterson's Guide to Two-Year Colleges, 1997; Peterson's Guide to Four-Year Colleges, 1997; Barron's Guide to Law Schools 1997

MAJOR EMPLOYERS

Major Employers

American Security Corp.	St. Paul Ramsey Medical Center
Blue Cross & Blue Shield of Minnesota	Cardiac Pacemakers
Healtheast Midway Hospital	Control Data Systems
FBS Information Services Corp.	Marsden Building Maintenance
Minnesota Mining & Manufacturing	Minnesota Mutual Life Insurance
Northwest Airlines	Northwest Publications
St. Paul Companies (insurance)	St. Paul Fire & Marine Insurance
West Publishing	Cray Research (computers)

Note: companies listed are located in the city
Source: Dun's Business Rankings 1997; Ward's Business Directory, 1997

PUBLIC SAFETY

Crime Rate

Area	All Crimes	Violent Crimes				Property Crimes		
		Murder	Forcible Rape	Robbery	Aggrav. Assault	Burglary	Larceny -Theft	Motor Vehicle Theft
City	7,745.8	9.7	87.5	327.4	487.1	1,544.0	4,303.9	986.2
Suburbs[1]	5,087.1	3.9	49.0	168.0	199.7	789.3	3,420.4	456.7
MSA[2]	5,346.1	4.5	52.8	183.6	227.7	862.8	3,506.5	508.3
U.S.	5,078.9	7.4	36.1	202.4	388.2	943.0	2,975.9	525.9

Note: Crime rate is the number of crimes per 100,000 pop.; (1) defined as all areas within the MSA but located outside the central city; (2) Metropolitan Statistical Area - see Appendix A for areas incl.
Source: FBI Uniform Crime Reports 1996

RECREATION

Culture and Recreation

Museums	Symphony Orchestras	Opera Companies	Dance Companies	Professional Theatres	Zoos	Pro Sports Teams
5	1	1	1	2	1	0

Source: International Directory of the Performing Arts, 1996; Official Museum Directory, 1998; Chamber of Commerce/Economic Development 1997

Library System

The St. Paul Public Library has 13 branches, holdings of 828,152 volumes and a budget of $7,839,401 (1995). *American Library Directory, 1997-1998*

MEDIA

Newspapers

Name	Type	Freq.	Distribution	Circulation
Asian Pages	Asian	2x/mo	Regional	35,000
The Catholic Spirit	Religious	1x/wk	Local	30,000
East Side Review	General	1x/wk	Local	19,305
Grand Gazette	General	1x/mo	Local	22,400
Highland Villager	General	2x/mo	Local	45,400
La Prensa de Minnesota	Hispanic	1x/wk	Local	12,000
Lillie Suburban Shopping Review	General	1x/wk	Local	23,767
Maplewood Review	General	1x/wk	Local	1,166
Minnesota Women's Press	General	26x/yr	Local	40,000
Park Bugle	General	1x/mo	Local	11,600
Ramsey County Review	General	1x/wk	Local	1,550
Roseville Review	General	1x/wk	Local	16,315
Saint Anthony Bulletin	General	1x/wk	Local	2,503
Saint Paul Pioneer Press	General	7x/wk	Area	212,648
The Saint Paul Voice	General	1x/mo	Local	15,000
South-West Review	General	1x/wk	Local	24,505
The Wanderer	Religious	1x/wk	Local	37,000
Woodbury South Maplewood Review	General	1x/wk	Local	12,911

Note: Includes newspapers with circulations of 1,000 or more located in the city; Source: Burrelle's Media Directory, 1998 Edition

AM Radio Stations

Call Letters	Freq. (kHz)	Target Audience	Station Format	Music Format
WMIN	740	General	M/N/S/T	Adult Standards/Spanish
KTIS	900	General	M/N/S	Christian
KSGS	950	Black	M	R&B
WWTC	1280	n/a	M	n/a
KLBB	1470	n/a	M/N/S	Big Band/Oldies
KSTP	1500	General	T	n/a

Note: Stations included broadcast in the Saint Paul metro area; n/a not available
Station Format: E = Educational; M = Music; N = News; S = Sports; T = Talk
Source: Burrelle's Media Directory, 1998 Edition

FM Radio Stations

Call Letters	Freq. (mHz)	Target Audience	Station Format	Music Format
KNOW	91.1	n/a	N	n/a
KRSU	91.3	n/a	M/N	Classical
WMCN	91.7	General	M	Alternative
KNOF	95.3	General	M/N/S	Christian
KTCZ	97.1	General	M	AOR/Adult Contemporary/Alternative/Classic Rock
KTIS	98.5	General	M/N/S	Christian
KSJN	99.5	General	M/S	Classical/Jazz
KDWB	101.3	General	M	Adult Contemporary

Note: Stations included broadcast in the Saint Paul metro area; n/a not available
Station Format: E = Educational; M = Music; N = News; S = Sports; T = Talk
Music Format: AOR = Album Oriented Rock; MOR = Middle-of-the-Road
Source: Burrelle's Media Directory, 1998 Edition

Television Stations

Name	Ch.	Affiliation	Type	Owner
KTCA	2	PBS	Public	Twin Cities Public Television, Inc.
KSTP	5	ABC	Commercial	Hubbard Broadcasting Inc.
KTCI	17	PBS	Public	Twin Cities Public Television, Inc.
KLGT	23	WB	Commercial	Lakeland Group Television Inc.

Note: Stations included broadcast in the Saint Paul metro area
Source: Burrelle's Media Directory, 1998 Edition

CLIMATE

Average and Extreme Temperatures

Temperature	Jan	Feb	Mar	Apr	May	Jun	Jul	Aug	Sep	Oct	Nov	Dec	Ann
Extreme High (°F)	57	60	83	95	96	102	105	101	98	89	74	63	105
Average High (°F)	21	27	38	56	69	79	84	81	71	59	41	26	54
Average Temp. (°F)	12	18	30	46	59	69	74	71	61	50	33	19	45
Average Low (°F)	3	9	21	36	48	58	63	61	50	39	25	11	35
Extreme Low (°F)	-34	-28	-32	2	18	37	43	39	26	15	-17	-29	-34

Note: Figures cover the years 1948-1990
Source: National Climatic Data Center, International Station Meteorological Climate Summary, 3/95

Average Precipitation/Snowfall/Humidity

Precip./Humidity	Jan	Feb	Mar	Apr	May	Jun	Jul	Aug	Sep	Oct	Nov	Dec	Ann
Avg. Precip. (in.)	0.8	0.8	1.9	2.2	3.1	4.0	3.8	3.6	2.5	1.9	1.4	1.0	27.1
Avg. Snowfall (in.)	11	9	12	3	Tr	0	0	0	Tr	Tr	7	10	52
Avg. Rel. Hum. 6am (%)	75	76	77	75	75	79	81	84	85	81	80	79	79
Avg. Rel. Hum. 3pm (%)	64	62	58	48	47	50	50	52	53	52	62	68	55

Note: Figures cover the years 1948-1990; Tr = Trace amounts (<0.05 in. of rain; <0.5 in. of snow)
Source: National Climatic Data Center, International Station Meteorological Climate Summary, 3/95

Weather Conditions

Temperature			Daytime Sky			Precipitation		
5°F & below	32°F & below	90°F & above	Clear	Partly cloudy	Cloudy	0.01 inch or more precip.	0.1 inch or more snow/ice	Thunder-storms
45	156	16	93	125	147	113	41	37

Note: Figures are average number of days per year and covers the years 1948-1990
Source: National Climatic Data Center, International Station Meteorological Climate Summary, 3/95

AIR & WATER QUALITY

Maximum Pollutant Concentrations

	Particulate Matter (ug/m^3)	Carbon Monoxide (ppm)	Sulfur Dioxide (ppm)	Nitrogen Dioxide (ppm)	Ozone (ppm)	Lead (ug/m^3)
MSA[1] Level	91	7	0.041	0.027	0.09	0.01
NAAQS[2]	150	9	0.140	0.053	0.12	1.50
Met NAAQS?	Yes	Yes	Yes	Yes	Yes	Yes

Note: (1) Metropolitan Statistical Area - see Appendix A for areas included; (2) National Ambient Air Quality Standards; ppm = parts per million; ug/m^3 = micrograms per cubic meter; n/a not available
Source: EPA, National Air Quality and Emissions Trends Report, 1996

Pollutant Standards Index

In the Saint Paul MSA (see Appendix A for areas included), the Pollutant Standards Index (PSI) exceeded 100 on 1 day in 1996. A PSI value greater than 100 indicates that air quality would be in the unhealthful range on that day. *EPA, National Air Quality and Emissions Trends Report, 1996*

Drinking Water

Water System Name	Pop. Served	Primary Water Source Type	Number of Violations in Fiscal Year 1997	Type of Violation/ Contaminants
Saint Paul	385,000	Surface	None	None

Note: Data as of January 16, 1998
Source: EPA, Office of Ground Water and Drinking Water, Safe Drinking Water Information System

Saint Paul tap water is alkaline, soft and fluoridated.
Editor & Publisher Market Guide, 1998

Sioux Falls, South Dakota

Background

Sioux Falls is located in the Big Sioux River Valley in southeast South Dakota. It was named for the falls of the Big Sioux River which winds through the city.

The city was founded prior to the Civil War by settlers who were attracted by the nearby stone quarries and the possibility of harnessing the river for water power. Many Scottish, English and Norwegians migrated to the area and used their skills as stonecutters.

The first settlement was temporarily abandoned during the Lakota tribal uprising in 1862. In 1865 resettlement began when the site was made a military post. The community was subsequently incorporated as a village in 1877 and as a city in 1883.

Sioux Falls is the trading center of a large agricultural and stock-raising area, and a major distribution point for farm machinery, automobiles and trucks. It is also a regional center for retail, tourism, marketing, banking, and medical care.

The climate is of the continental type. There are frequent weather changes from day to day or week to week as the area is visited by differing air masses. Temperatures fluctuate frequently as cold air masses move in very rapidly. During the late fall and winter, cold fronts accompanied by strong, gusty winds can cause temperatures to drop by 20-30 degrees in a 24-hour period.

Summer nights are comfortable with temperatures below 70 degrees. One or two heavy snows may fall each winter with 8-12 inches in 24 hours. Thunderstorms are frequent during the late spring and summer. There is occasional flooding in the lower areas along the Big Sioux River.

General Rankings and Evaluative Comments

- Sioux Falls was ranked #80 out of 300 cities by *Money's* 1997 "Survey of the Best Places to Live." Criteria used: health services, crime, economy, housing, education, transportation, weather, leisure and the arts. The city was ranked #49 in 1996 and #18 in 1995. *Money, July 1997; Money, September 1996; Money, September 1995*

- *Ladies Home Journal* ranked America's 200 largest cities based on the qualities women care about most. Sioux Falls ranked 67 out of 200. Criteria: low crime rate, good public schools, well-paying jobs, quality health and child care, the presence of women in government, proportion of women-owned businesses, size of the wage gap with men, local economy, divorce rates, the ratio of single men to single women, whether there are laws that require at least the same number of public toilets for women as men, and the probability of good hair days. *Ladies Home Journal, November 1997*

- Sioux Falls was ranked #10 out of 219 cities in terms of children's health, safety, and economic well-being. Criteria: total population, percent population change, birth rate, child immunization rate, infant mortality rate, percent low birth weight infants, percent of births to teens, physician-to-population ratio, student-to-teacher ratio, dropout rate, unemployment rate, median family income, percent of children in poverty, violent and property crime rates, number of juvenile arrests for violent crimes as a percent of the total crime index, number of days with pollution standard index (PSI) over 100, pounds toxic releases per 1,000 people and number of superfund sites. *Zero Population Growth, Children's Environmental Index 1997*

- Sioux Falls appeared on *New Mobility's* list of "10 Disability Friendly Cities". Rank: 4 out of 10. Criteria: affordable and accessible housing, transportation, quality medical care, personal assistance services and strong advocacy.

  "For exuberant citizen loyalty, no place ranks higher than Sioux Falls....Although the older sections of the city are not very accessible, the new areas are. The mainline transit system is 100 percent accessible, and the paratransit system is sufficient. As usual, accessible, affordable housing is scarce. Some help with personal assistance exists; Medicaid's waiver program serves about 40 people statewide. There are two major hospitals with full support services.

  Recreation opportunities include such outdoorsy activities as fishing and camping, the fully accessible state parks, fairgrounds and convention center, and South Dakota's largest shopping mall for competitive shoppers....

  It's a quality-of-life thing. This is a clean city with high employment, minimal crime and strong advocacy." *New Mobility, December 1997*

- According to *Working Mother,* "Child care advocates hope that Loila Hunking, the state's new child care services coordinator, will take action to improve child care in South Dakota. To date, neither Governor William Janklow or state lawmakers have made it a priority. In n interview earlier this year, Hunking said she hopes to involve both business leaders and educators in efforts to upgrade the quality of care. Many advocates hope her great enthusiasm to create new caregiver training programs will effect their implementation." *Working Mother, July/August 1997*

Business Environment

STATE ECONOMY

State Economic Profile

"South Dakota's economy, which has been expanding at a blistering pace for the last several years, is starting to slow. The state's job growth is at 0.5%. However, South Dakota's income growth is still above average, and its unemployment rate remains very low at 2.7%.

South Dakota's housing market is flourishing. Last year, an all-time high 5,100 permits were issued for residential construction, with strong house price appreciation and existing home resale activity. Weak household growth will eventually cause the market to slow; however, strong income growth will continue to support housing activity in the near term.

From 1991 to 1995 South Dakota experienced average population growth of 0.8%, however, the state's population growth has been steadily declining since 1993, and currently stands at 0.4%. Net migration has turned negative in the state, after being positive for the previous five years.

Despite showing signs of weakness toward the end of last year, South Dakota's economy continues to exhibit solid growth, and its growth will remain strong as firms continue to relocate to the state due to its low cost of doing business and favorable tax provisions. An expanding tourism industry and a booming construction industry will also benefit the state, although weakening prospects for South Dakota's farm economy will restrain short-term growth. Still, South Dakota's economy will perform slightly better than average through the forecast horizon." *National Association of Realtors, Economic Profiles: The Fifty States, July 1997*

IMPORTS/EXPORTS

Total Export Sales

Area	1993 ($000)	1994 ($000)	1995 ($000)	1996 ($000)	% Chg. 1993-96	% Chg. 1995-96
MSA[1]	n/a	n/a	n/a	n/a	n/a	n/a
U.S.	464,858,354	512,415,609	583,030,524	622,827,063	34.0	6.8

Note: (1) Metropolitan Statistical Area - see Appendix A for areas included
Source: U.S. Department of Commerce, International Trade Association, Metropolitan Area Exports: An Export Performance Report on Over 250 U.S. Cities, October 1997

Imports/Exports by Port

Type	Cargo Value			Share of U.S. Total	
	1995 (US$mil.)	1996 (US$mil.)	% Change 1995-1996	1995 (%)	1996 (%)
Imports	0	0	0	0	0
Exports	0	0	0	0	0

Source: Global Trade Information Services, WaterBorne Trade Atlas 1997

CITY FINANCES

City Government Finances

Component	FY92 ($000)	FY92 (per capita $)
Revenue	98,274	925.71
Expenditure	87,585	825.02
Debt Outstanding	69,415	653.87
Cash & Securities	162,438	1,530.11

Source: U.S. Bureau of the Census, City Government Finances: 1991-92

City Government Revenue by Source

Source	FY92 ($000)	FY92 (per capita $)	FY92 (%)
From Federal Government	3,457	32.56	3.5
From State Governments	2,381	22.43	2.4
From Local Governments	11	0.10	0.0
Property Taxes	13,112	123.51	13.3
General Sales Taxes	28,270	266.29	28.8
Selective Sales Taxes	303	2.85	0.3
Income Taxes	0	0.00	0.0
Current Charges	16,012	150.83	16.3
Utility/Liquor Store	12,368	116.50	12.6
Employee Retirement[1]	8,030	75.64	8.2
Other	14,330	134.98	14.6

Note: (1) Excludes "city contributions," classified as "nonrevenue," intragovernmental transfers.
Source: U.S. Bureau of the Census, City Government Finances: 1991-92

City Government Expenditures by Function

Function	FY92 ($000)	FY92 (per capita $)	FY92 (%)
Educational Services	1,938	18.26	2.2
Employee Retirement[1]	2,979	28.06	3.4
Environment/Housing	15,505	146.05	17.7
Government Administration	2,859	26.93	3.3
Interest on General Debt	1,886	17.77	2.2
Public Safety	17,207	162.08	19.6
Social Services	2,087	19.66	2.4
Transportation	19,185	180.72	21.9
Utility/Liquor Store	14,158	133.36	16.2
Other	9,781	92.13	11.2

Note: (1) Payments to beneficiaries including withdrawal of contributions.
Source: U.S. Bureau of the Census, City Government Finances: 1991-92

Municipal Bond Ratings

Area	Moody's	S & P
Sioux Falls	Aa1	n/a

Note: n/a not available; n/r not rated
Source: Moody's Bond Record, 2/98; Statistical Abstract of the U.S., 1997; Governing Magazine, 9/97, 3/98

POPULATION

Population Growth

Area	1980	1990	% Chg. 1980-90	July 1996 Estimate	% Chg. 1990-96
City	81,341	100,814	23.9	113,223	12.3
MSA[1]	n/a	123,809	n/a	156,598	26.5
U.S.	226,545,805	248,765,170	9.8	265,179,411	6.6

Note: (1) Metropolitan Statistical Area - see Appendix A for areas included
Source: 1980/1990 Census of Housing and Population, Summary Tape File 3C; Census Bureau Population Estimates

Population Characteristics

Race	City 1980 Population	%	City 1990 Population	%	% Chg. 1980-90	MSA[1] 1990 Population	%
White	79,581	97.8	97,583	96.8	22.6	120,490	97.3
Black	275	0.3	751	0.7	173.1	781	0.6
Amer Indian/Esk/Aleut	959	1.2	1,427	1.4	48.8	1,484	1.2
Asian/Pacific Islander	401	0.5	801	0.8	99.8	812	0.7
Other	125	0.2	252	0.2	101.6	242	0.2
Hispanic Origin[2]	350	0.4	666	0.7	90.3	680	0.5

Note: (1) Metropolitan Statistical Area - see Appendix A for areas included;
(2) people of Hispanic origin can be of any race
Source: 1980/1990 Census of Housing and Population, Summary Tape File 3C

Ancestry

Area	German	Irish	English	Italian	U.S.	French	Polish	Dutch
City	52.9	14.8	10.5	1.0	1.7	3.7	1.3	7.1
MSA[1]	53.6	14.3	10.0	1.0	1.7	3.5	1.3	7.8
U.S.	23.3	15.6	13.1	5.9	5.3	4.2	3.8	2.5

Note: Figures are percentages and include persons that reported multiple ancestry (eg. if a person reported being Irish and Italian, they were included in both columns); (1) Metropolitan Statistical Area - see Appendix A for areas included
Source: 1990 Census of Population and Housing, Summary Tape File 3C

Age

Area	Median Age (Years)	Age Distribution (%) Under 5	Under 18	18-24	25-44	45-64	65+	80+
City	31.3	7.9	25.9	11.4	34.8	16.3	11.7	3.0
MSA[1]	31.4	7.9	27.1	10.5	34.4	16.4	11.6	3.0
U.S.	32.9	7.3	25.6	10.5	32.6	18.7	12.5	2.8

Note: (1) Metropolitan Statistical Area - see Appendix A for areas included
Source: 1990 Census of Population and Housing, Summary Tape File 3C

Male/Female Ratio

Area	Number of males per 100 females (all ages)	Number of males per 100 females (18 years old+)
City	91.1	87.4
MSA[1]	92.8	89.5
U.S.	95.0	91.9

Note: (1) Metropolitan Statistical Area - see Appendix A for areas included
Source: 1990 Census of Population, General Population Characteristics

INCOME

Per Capita/Median/Average Income

Area	Per Capita ($)	Median Household ($)	Average Household ($)
City	13,677	27,286	34,023
MSA[1]	13,345	27,764	34,116
U.S.	14,420	30,056	38,453

Note: all figures are for 1989; (1) Metropolitan Statistical Area - see Appendix A for areas included
Source: 1990 Census of Population and Housing, Summary Tape File 3C

Household Income Distribution by Race

Income ($)	City (%)					U.S. (%)				
	Total	White	Black	Other	Hisp.[1]	Total	White	Black	Other	Hisp.[1]
Less than 5,000	5.4	5.0	15.3	22.2	14.0	6.2	4.8	15.2	8.6	8.8
5,000 - 9,999	8.3	8.1	12.5	24.2	11.9	9.3	8.6	14.2	9.9	11.1
10,000 - 14,999	9.8	9.7	21.3	11.0	9.1	8.8	8.5	11.0	9.8	11.0
15,000 - 24,999	21.5	21.6	19.4	17.5	27.3	17.5	17.3	18.9	18.5	20.5
25,000 - 34,999	19.2	19.4	20.8	9.6	4.9	15.8	16.1	14.2	15.4	16.4
35,000 - 49,999	19.3	19.5	4.2	11.8	14.7	17.9	18.6	13.3	16.1	16.0
50,000 - 74,999	11.2	11.3	6.5	3.7	18.2	15.0	15.8	9.3	13.4	11.1
75,000 - 99,999	2.6	2.7	0.0	0.0	0.0	5.1	5.5	2.6	4.7	3.1
100,000+	2.7	2.8	0.0	0.0	0.0	4.4	4.8	1.3	3.7	1.9

Note: all figures are for 1989; (1) people of Hispanic origin can be of any race
Source: 1990 Census of Population and Housing, Summary Tape File 3C

Effective Buying Income

Area	Per Capita ($)	Median Household ($)	Average Household ($)
City	19,120	38,680	48,250
MSA[1]	19,128	40,760	49,939
U.S.	15,444	33,201	41,849

Note: data as of 1/1/97; (1) Metropolitan Statistical Area - see Appendix A for areas included
Source: Standard Rate & Data Service, Newspaper Advertising Source, 2/98

Effective Household Buying Income Distribution

Area	% of Households Earning						
	$10,000 -$19,999	$20,000 -$34,999	$35,000 -$49,999	$50,000 -$74,999	$75,000 -$99,000	$100,000 -$124,999	$125,000 and up
City	13.3	23.1	20.4	21.1	8.0	2.5	3.1
MSA[1]	12.6	21.7	19.9	22.9	8.7	3.0	3.4
U.S.	16.5	23.4	18.3	18.2	6.4	2.1	2.4

Note: data as of 1/1/97; (1) Metropolitan Statistical Area - see Appendix A for areas included
Source: Standard Rate & Data Service, Newspaper Advertising Source, 2/98

Poverty Rates by Race and Age

Area	Total (%)	By Race (%)				By Age (%)		
		White	Black	Other	Hisp.[2]	Under 5 years old	Under 18 years old	65 years and over
City	8.5	7.6	30.4	40.5	25.2	11.4	9.6	9.5
MSA[1]	8.0	7.3	31.2	39.9	24.9	10.2	8.8	10.3
U.S.	13.1	9.8	29.5	23.1	25.3	20.1	18.3	12.8

Note: figures show the percent of people living below the poverty line in 1989. The average poverty threshold was $12,674 for a family of four in 1989; (1) Metropolitan Statistical Area - see Appendix A for areas included; (2) people of Hispanic origin can be of any race
Source: 1990 Census of Population and Housing, Summary Tape File 3C

EMPLOYMENT

Labor Force and Employment

Area	Civilian Labor Force			Workers Employed		
	Dec. '95	Dec. '96	% Chg.	Dec. '95	Dec. '96	% Chg.
City	68,714	71,175	3.6	67,161	69,915	4.1
MSA[1]	93,356	96,724	3.6	91,368	95,114	4.1
U.S.	134,583,000	136,742,000	1.6	127,903,000	130,785,000	2.3

Note: Data is not seasonally adjusted and covers workers 16 years of age and older;
(1) Metropolitan Statistical Area - see Appendix A for areas included
Source: Bureau of Labor Statistics, http://stats.bls.gov

Unemployment Rate

Area	1997											
	Jan.	Feb.	Mar.	Apr.	May	Jun.	Jul.	Aug.	Sep.	Oct.	Nov.	Dec.
City	2.8	2.4	2.4	1.8	1.7	1.8	1.6	1.7	1.6	1.4	1.6	1.8
MSA[1]	2.6	2.3	2.3	1.7	1.6	1.7	1.5	1.6	1.5	1.4	1.6	1.7
U.S.	5.9	5.7	5.5	4.8	4.7	5.2	5.0	4.8	4.7	4.4	4.3	4.4

Note: Data is not seasonally adjusted and covers workers 16 years of age and older; All figures are percentages; (1) Metropolitan Statistical Area - see Appendix A for areas included
Source: Bureau of Labor Statistics, http://stats.bls.gov

Employment by Industry

Sector	MSA[1]		U.S.
	Number of Employees	Percent of Total	Percent of Total
Services	30,400	29.1	29.0
Retail Trade	19,900	19.1	18.5
Government	10,100	9.7	16.1
Manufacturing	14,400	13.8	15.0
Finance/Insurance/Real Estate	12,200	11.7	5.7
Wholesale Trade	6,700	6.4	5.4
Transportation/Public Utilities	6,400	6.1	5.3
Construction/Mining	4,300	4.1	5.0

Note: Figures cover non-farm employment as of 12/97 and are not seasonally adjusted;
(1) Metropolitan Statistical Area - see Appendix A for areas included
Source: Bureau of Labor Statistics, http://stats.bls.gov

Employment by Occupation

Occupation Category	City (%)	MSA[1] (%)	U.S. (%)
White Collar	62.8	60.6	58.1
Executive/Admin./Management	12.0	11.5	12.3
Professional	13.4	13.0	14.1
Technical & Related Support	3.5	3.4	3.7
Sales	14.3	13.6	11.8
Administrative Support/Clerical	19.5	19.2	16.3
Blue Collar	22.3	23.4	26.2
Precision Production/Craft/Repair	9.4	10.0	11.3
Machine Operators/Assem./Insp.	5.3	5.3	6.8
Transportation/Material Movers	3.6	4.0	4.1
Cleaners/Helpers/Laborers	4.1	4.1	3.9
Services	13.9	14.0	13.2
Farming/Forestry/Fishing	1.0	2.1	2.5

Note: figures cover employed persons 16 years old and over;
(1) Metropolitan Statistical Area - see Appendix A for areas included
Source: 1990 Census of Population and Housing, Summary Tape File 3C

Occupational Employment Projections: 1994 - 2005

Occupations Expected to have the Largest Job Growth (ranked by numerical growth)	Fast-Growing Occupations (ranked by percent growth)
1. Cashiers	1. Electronic pagination systems workers
2. Salespersons, retail	2. Computer engineers
3. Waiters & waitresses	3. Human services workers
4. Janitors/cleaners/maids, ex. priv. hshld.	4. Systems analysts
5. Marketing & sales, supervisors	5. Numerical control machine tool oper.
6. Registered nurses	6. Occupational therapists
7. Truck drivers, heavy & light	7. Surgical technologists
8. Food preparation workers	8. Medical assistants
9. Nursing aides/orderlies/attendants	9. Personal and home care aides
10. Adjustment clerks	10. Machine assemblers

Projections cover South Dakota.
Source: South Dakota Department of Labor, Labor Market Information Center

Average Wages

Occupation	Wage	Occupation	Wage
Professional/Technical/Clerical	$/Week	**Health/Protective Services**	$/Week
Accountants III	-	Corrections Officers	-
Attorneys III	-	Firefighters	-
Budget Analysts III	-	Nurses, Licensed Practical II	-
Buyers/Contracting Specialists II	-	Nurses, Registered II	-
Clerks, Accounting III	383	Nursing Assistants II	-
Clerks, General III	361	Police Officers I	-
Computer Operators II	362	**Hourly Workers**	$/Hour
Computer Programmers II	548	Forklift Operators	9.59
Drafters II	411	General Maintenance Workers	8.32
Engineering Technicians III	558	Guards I	-
Engineering Technicians, Civil III	-	Janitors	6.79
Engineers III	-	Maintenance Electricians	14.53
Key Entry Operators I	294	Maintenance Electronics Techs II	11.77
Personnel Assistants III	-	Maintenance Machinists	-
Personnel Specialists III	-	Maintenance Mechanics, Machinery	12.60
Secretaries III	440	Material Handling Laborers	8.91
Switchboard Operator-Receptionist	300	Motor Vehicle Mechanics	11.95
Systems Analysts II	-	Shipping/Receiving Clerks	8.46
Systems Analysts Supervisor/Mgr II	-	Tool and Die Makers	15.32
Tax Collectors II	-	Truckdrivers, Tractor Trailer	-
Word Processors II	-	Warehouse Specialists	8.87

Note: Wage data includes full-time workers only for 5/95 and cover South Dakota. Dashes indicate that data was not available.
Source: Bureau of Labor Statistics, Occupational Compensation Survey

TAXES

Major State and Local Tax Rates

State Corp. Income (%)	State Personal Income (%)	Residential Property (effective rate per $100)	Sales & Use		State Gasoline (cents/ gallon)	State Cigarette (cents/ 20-pack)
			State (%)	Local (%)		
None	None	2.23	4.0	2.0	21[a]	33

Note: Personal/corporate income tax rates as of 1/97. Sales, gasoline and cigarette tax rates as of 1/98; (a) Does not include a 1 cent local option tax
Source: Federation of Tax Administrators, www.taxadmin.org; Washington D.C. Department of Finance and Revenue, Tax Rates and Tax Burdens in the District of Columbia: A Nationwide Comparison, June 1997; Chamber of Commerce

Total Taxes Per Capita and as a Percent of Income

Area	Per Capita Income ($)	Per Capita Taxes ($)			Taxes as Pct. of Income (%)		
		Total	Federal	State/Local	Total	Federal	State/Local
South Dakota	22,516	7,371	4,976	2,396	32.7	22.1	10.6
U.S.	26,187	9,205	6,127	3,078	35.2	23.4	11.8

Note: Figures are for 1997
Source: Tax Foundation, Web Site, www.taxfoundation.org

Estimated Tax Burden

Area	State Income	Local Income	Property	Sales	Total
Sioux Falls	0	0	4,050	822	4,872

Note: The numbers are estimates of taxes paid by a married couple with two kids and annual earnings of $65,000. Sales tax estimates assume they spend average amounts on food, clothing, household goods and gasoline. Property tax estimates assume they live in a $225,000 home.
Source: Kiplinger's Personal Finance Magazine, June 1997

COMMERCIAL REAL ESTATE

Office Market

Class/Location	Total Space (sq. ft.)	Vacant Space (sq. ft.)	Vac. Rate (%)	Under Constr. (sq. ft.)	Net Absorp. (sq. ft.)	Rental Rates ($/sq.ft./yr.)
Class A						
CBD	823,600	115,750	14.1	0	-15,050	14.50-18.50
Outside CBD	228,450	21,222	9.3	23,650	36,585	14.00-16.50
Class B						
CBD	473,000	82,600	17.5	0	-11,000	11.00-13.50
Outside CBD	246,800	19,856	8.0	9,800	28,499	11.00-13.50

Note: Data as of 10/97 and covers Sioux Falls; CBD = Central Business District; n/a not available; Source: Society of Industrial and Office Realtors, 1998 Comparative Statistics of Industrial and Office Real Estate Markets

"No new speculative development is expected in Sioux Falls for 1998. The market will be digesting 1997's deliveries. Approximately 80,000 sq. ft. of new space is anticipated for 1998. Absorption is expected to catch up with the pace of development. Next year rental rates will go back to 1996 rates. Regionally the upper midwest economy is very strong. Locally, there is concern about the tightening labor force as we continue to see less than two percent unemployment in Sioux Falls. However, the low cost of living, ample job opportunities, and well-perceived quality of life is drawing migrants to the area at about 1,500 net migrants per year." *Society of Industrial and Office Realtors, 1998 Comparative Statistics of Industrial and Office Real Estate Markets*

COMMERCIAL UTILITIES

Typical Monthly Electric Bills

Area	Commercial Service ($/month)		Industrial Service ($/month)	
	12 kW demand 1,500 kWh	100 kW demand 30,000 kWh	1,000 kW demand 400,000 kWh	20,000 kW demand 10,000,000 kWh
City	110	1,876	20,449	458,215
U.S.	162	2,360	25,590	545,677

Note: Based on rates in effect July 1, 1997
Source: Edison Electric Institute, Typical Residential, Commercial and Industrial Bills, Summer 1997

TRANSPORTATION

Transportation Statistics

Avg. travel time to work (min.)	14.1
Interstate highways	I-29; I-90
Bus lines	
In-city	Sioux Falls Transit
Inter-city	2
Passenger air service	
Airport	Sioux Falls Regional Airport; Joe Foss Field
Airlines	4
Aircraft departures	n/a
Enplaned passengers	n/a
Rail service	No Amtrak service
Motor freight carriers	50
Major waterways/ports	None

Source: OAG, Business Travel Planner, Summer 1997; Editor & Publisher Market Guide, 1998; FAA Airport Activity Statistics, 1996; Amtrak National Time Table, Northeast Timetable, Fall/Winter 1997-98; 1990 Census of Population and Housing, STF 3C; Chamber of Commerce/Economic Development 1997; Jane's Urban Transport Systems 1997-98; Transit Fact Book 1997

Means of Transportation to Work

Area	Car/Truck/Van		Public Transportation			Bicycle	Walked	Other Means	Worked at Home
	Drove Alone	Car-pooled	Bus	Subway	Railroad				
City	82.3	9.3	0.5	0.0	0.0	0.2	4.1	0.9	2.5
MSA[1]	81.4	9.6	0.4	0.0	0.0	0.2	4.2	0.8	3.4
U.S.	73.2	13.4	3.0	1.5	0.5	0.4	3.9	1.2	3.0

Note: figures shown are percentages and only include workers 16 years old and over; (1) Metropolitan Statistical Area - see Appendix A for areas included
Source: 1990 Census of Population and Housing, Summary Tape File 3C

BUSINESSES

Major Business Headquarters

Company Name	1997 Rankings	
	Fortune 500	Forbes 500

No companies listed.

Note: Companies listed are located in the city; Dashes indicate no ranking
Fortune 500: companies that produce a 10-K are ranked 1 - 500 based on 1996 revenue
Forbes 500: private companies are ranked 1 - 500 based on 1996 revenue
Source: Forbes 12/1/97; Fortune 4/28/97

HOTELS & MOTELS

Hotels/Motels

Area	Hotels/ Motels	Rooms	Luxury-Level Hotels/Motels		Average Minimum Rates ($)		
			◆◆◆◆	◆◆◆◆◆	◆◆	◆◆◆	◆◆◆◆
City	20	1,743	0	0	56	67	n/a
Airport	7	637	0	0	n/a	n/a	n/a
Total	27	2,380	0	0	n/a	n/a	n/a

Note: n/a not available; Classifications range from one diamond (budget properties with basic amenities) to five diamond (luxury properties with the finest service, rooms and facilities).
Source: OAG, Business Travel Planner, Summer 1997

CONVENTION CENTERS

Major Convention Centers

Center Name	Meeting Rooms	Exhibit Space (sf)
Sioux Falls Arena	4	30,000
Sioux Falls Coliseum and Recreation Center	4	19,000

Source: Trade Shows Worldwide 1997

Living Environment

COST OF LIVING

Cost of Living Index

Composite Index	Housing	Utilities	Groceries	Health Care	Trans-portation	Misc. Goods/Services
96.3	90.7	94.0	99.5	101.9	101.1	97.6

Note: U.S. = 100
Source: ACCRA, Cost of Living Index, 3rd Quarter 1997

HOUSING

Median Home Prices and Housing Affordability

Area	Median Price[2] 3rd Qtr. 1997 ($)	HOI[3] 3rd Qtr. 1997	Afford-ability Rank[4]
MSA[1]	n/a	n/a	n/a
U.S.	127,000	63.7	–

Note: (1) Metropolitan Statistical Area - see Appendix A for areas included; (2) U.S. figures calculated from the sales of 625,000 new and existing homes in 195 markets; (3) Housing Opportunity Index - percent of homes sold that were within the reach of the median income household at the prevailing mortgage interest rate; (4) Rank is from 1-195 with 1 being most affordable; n/a not available
Source: National Association of Home Builders, Housing Opportunity Index, 3rd Quarter 1997

It is projected that the median price of existing single-family homes in the metro area will increase by 10.8% in 1998. Nationwide, home prices are projected to increase 6.6%.
Kiplinger's Personal Finance Magazine, January 1998

Average New Home Price

Area	Price ($)
City	119,310
U.S.	135,710

Note: Figures are based on a new home with 1,800 sq. ft. of living area on an 8,000 sq. ft. lot.
Source: ACCRA, Cost of Living Index, 3rd Quarter 1997

Average Apartment Rent

Area	Rent ($/mth)
City	602
U.S.	569

Note: Figures are based on an unfurnished two bedroom, 1-1/2 or 2 bath apartment, approximately 950 sq. ft. in size, excluding all utilities except water
Source: ACCRA, Cost of Living Index, 3rd Quarter 1997

RESIDENTIAL UTILITIES

Average Residential Utility Costs

Area	All Electric ($/mth)	Part Electric ($/mth)	Other Energy ($/mth)	Phone ($/mth)
City	–	47.11	45.34	22.98
U.S.	109.40	55.25	43.64	19.48

Source: ACCRA, Cost of Living Index, 3rd Quarter 1997

HEALTH CARE

Average Health Care Costs

Area	Hospital ($/day)	Doctor ($/visit)	Dentist ($/visit)
City	401.00	56.38	55.75
U.S.	392.91	48.76	60.84

Note: Hospital - based on a semi-private room. Doctor - based on a general practitioner's routine exam of an established patient. Dentist - based on adult teeth cleaning and periodic oral exam.
Source: ACCRA, Cost of Living Index, 3rd Quarter 1997

Distribution of Office-Based Physicians

Area	Family/Gen. Practitioners	Specialists		
		Medical	Surgical	Other
MSA[1]	68	128	100	106

Note: Data as of 12/31/96; (1) Metropolitan Statistical Area - see Appendix A for areas included
Source: American Medical Assn., Physician Characteristics & Distribution in the U.S., 1997-1998

Hospitals

Sioux Falls has 3 general medical and surgical hospitals, 1 psychiatric, 1 children's other specialty. *AHA Guide to the Healthcare Field 1997-98*

EDUCATION

Public School District Statistics

District Name	Num. Sch.	Enroll.	Classroom Teachers[1]	Pupils per Teacher	Minority Pupils (%)	Current Exp.[2] ($/pupil)
East Dakota Educational Co-Op	3	124	n/a	n/a	n/a	n/a
Sd School For The Deaf	1	82	26	3.2	n/a	n/a
Sioux Falls 49-5	37	18,303	1,076	17.0	n/a	n/a

Note: Data covers the 1995-1996 school year unless otherwise noted; (1) Excludes teachers reported as working in school district offices rather than in schools; (2) Based on 1993-94 enrollment collected by the Census Bureau, not the enrollment figure shown in column 3; SD = School District; ISD = Independent School District; n/a not available
Source: National Center for Education Statistics, Common Core of Data Survey; Bureau of the Census

Educational Quality

School District	Education Quotient[1]	Graduate Outcome[2]	Community Index[3]	Resource Index[4]
Sioux Falls	105.0	132.0	126.0	56.0

Note: Nearly 1,000 secondary school districts were rated in terms of educational quality. The scores range from a low of 50 to a high of 150; (1) Average of the Graduate Outcome, Community and Resource indexes; (2) Based on graduation rates and college board scores (SAT/ACT); (3) Based on the surrounding community's average level of education and the area's average income level; (4) Based on teacher salaries, per-pupil expenditures and student-teacher ratios.
Source: Expansion Management, Ratings Issue 1997

Educational Attainment by Race

Area	High School Graduate (%)					Bachelor's Degree (%)				
	Total	White	Black	Other	Hisp.[2]	Total	White	Black	Other	Hisp.[2]
City	83.4	83.8	50.3	68.1	55.4	22.9	23.1	12.1	13.1	15.3
MSA[1]	83.1	83.5	53.4	67.7	57.4	21.3	21.4	11.3	12.7	12.8
U.S.	75.2	77.9	63.1	60.4	49.8	20.3	21.5	11.4	19.4	9.2

Note: figures shown cover persons 25 years old and over; (1) Metropolitan Statistical Area - see Appendix A for areas included; (2) people of Hispanic origin can be of any race
Source: 1990 Census of Population and Housing, Summary Tape File 3C

School Enrollment by Type

Area	Preprimary				Elementary/High School			
	Public		Private		Public		Private	
	Enrollment	%	Enrollment	%	Enrollment	%	Enrollment	%
City	1,407	65.7	735	34.3	13,903	87.0	2,076	13.0
MSA[1]	1,625	65.9	841	34.1	18,697	89.0	2,316	11.0
U.S.	2,679,029	59.5	1,824,256	40.5	38,379,689	90.2	4,187,099	9.8

Note: figures shown cover persons 3 years old and over;
(1) Metropolitan Statistical Area - see Appendix A for areas included
Source: 1990 Census of Population and Housing, Summary Tape File 3C

School Enrollment by Race

Area	Preprimary (%)				Elementary/High School (%)			
	White	Black	Other	Hisp.[1]	White	Black	Other	Hisp.[1]
City	95.7	2.4	2.0	1.4	94.9	1.4	3.7	1.1
MSA[2]	96.3	2.1	1.7	1.2	95.9	1.1	3.0	0.8
U.S.	80.4	12.5	7.1	7.8	74.1	15.6	10.3	12.5

Note: figures shown cover persons 3 years old and over; (1) people of Hispanic origin can be of any race; (2) Metropolitan Statistical Area - see Appendix A for areas included
Source: 1990 Census of Population and Housing, Summary Tape File 3C

SAT/ACT Scores

Area/District	1997 SAT				1997 ACT	
	Percent of Graduates Tested (%)	Average Math Score	Average Verbal Score	Average Combined Score	Percent of Graduates Tested (%)	Average Composite Score
Sioux Falls SD	n/a	n/a	n/a	n/a	66	22.0
State	4	570	574	1,144	68	21.3
U.S.	42	511	505	1,016	36	21.0

Note: Math and verbal SAT scores are out of a possible 800; ACT scores are out of a possible 36
Caution: Comparing or ranking states/cities on the basis of SAT/ACT scores alone is invalid and strongly discouraged by the The College Board and The American College Testing Program as students who take the tests are self-selected and do not represent the entire student population.
Source: Sioux Falls School District, Office of Instructional Support, 1997; American College Testing Program, 1997; College Board, 1997

Classroom Teacher Salaries in Public Schools

District	B.A. Degree		M.A. Degree		Ph.D. Degree	
	Min. ($)	Max ($)	Min. ($)	Max. ($)	Min. ($)	Max. ($)
Sioux Falls	20,804	25,797	24,757	36,640	30,750	46,815
Average[1]	26,120	39,270	28,175	44,667	31,643	49,825

Note: Salaries are for 1996-1997; (1) Based on all school districts covered
Source: American Federation of Teachers (unpublished data)

Higher Education

Two-Year Colleges		Four-Year Colleges		Medical Schools	Law Schools	Voc/ Tech
Public	Private	Public	Private			
1	2	0	3	0	0	5

Source: College Blue Book, Occupational Education 1997; Medical School Admission Requirements, 1998-99; Peterson's Guide to Two-Year Colleges, 1997; Peterson's Guide to Four-Year Colleges, 1997; Barron's Guide to Law Schools 1997

MAJOR EMPLOYERS

Major Employers

First National Bank in Sioux Falls
Children's Care Hospital & School
Electronic Systems
Midland National Life Insurance
Presentation Sisters (health services)
Sencore Inc. (measuring instruments)
Sioux Valley Hospital Association
First Bank of South Dakota

Central Plains Clinic
Citibank South Dakota
Balance Systems (metal doors)
Orion Enterprises (frozen food)
Raven Industries (mens clothing)
Sioux Falls Newspapers
Star-Mark (wood kitchen cabinets)

Note: companies listed are located in the city
Source: Dun's Business Rankings 1997; Ward's Business Directory, 1997

PUBLIC SAFETY

Crime Rate

Area	All Crimes	Violent Crimes				Property Crimes		
		Murder	Forcible Rape	Robbery	Aggrav. Assault	Burglary	Larceny -Theft	Motor Vehicle Theft
City	4,828.2	0.9	73.9	58.6	293.1	779.1	3,434.0	188.5
Suburbs[1]	2,516.8	0.0	84.8	4.2	120.9	659.4	1,547.8	99.7
MSA[2]	4,138.4	0.6	77.2	42.4	241.7	743.4	2,871.2	162.0
U.S.	5,078.9	7.4	36.1	202.4	388.2	943.0	2,975.9	525.9

Note: Crime rate is the number of crimes per 100,000 pop.; (1) defined as all areas within the MSA but located outside the central city; (2) Metropolitan Statistical Area - see Appendix A for areas incl.
Source: FBI Uniform Crime Reports 1996

RECREATION

Culture and Recreation

Museums	Symphony Orchestras	Opera Companies	Dance Companies	Professional Theatres	Zoos	Pro Sports Teams
5	1	0	1	1	1	0

Source: International Directory of the Performing Arts, 1996; Official Museum Directory, 1998; Chamber of Commerce/Economic Development 1997

Library System

The Siouxland Libraries has 10 branches, holdings of 332,217 volumes and a budget of $2,798,361 (1995). *American Library Directory, 1997-1998*

MEDIA

Newspapers

Name	Type	Freq.	Distribution	Circulation
Argus Leader	n/a	7x/wk	Area	52,000
Tempest	General	2x/mo	Local	10,000

Note: Includes newspapers with circulations of 500 or more located in the city; n/a not available
Source: Burrelle's Media Directory, 1998 Edition

AM Radio Stations

Call Letters	Freq. (kHz)	Target Audience	Station Format	Music Format
KXRB	1000	General	M/N/S	Country
KSOO	1140	General	M/N/S/T	Adult Standards
KWSN	1230	General	N/T	n/a
KNWC	1270	General	M/N/S	Christian
KELO	1320	General	M/N	Adult Contemporary/Contemporary Top 40/Oldies
KCGN	1520	General	M/S/T	Christian

Note: Stations included broadcast in the Sioux Falls metro area; n/a not available
Station Format: E = Educational; M = Music; N = News; S = Sports; T = Talk
Source: Burrelle's Media Directory, 1998 Edition

FM Radio Stations

Call Letters	Freq. (mHz)	Target Audience	Station Format	Music Format
KRSD	88.1	n/a	M	Classical
KAUR	89.1	n/a	M/N/S	AOR/Alternative/Jazz
KCSD	90.9	n/a	M/N/S	n/a
KELO	92.5	n/a	M	Adult Contemporary
KCFS	94.5	Alternative	M/N/S	Alternative/Christian
KNWC	96.5	General	M/N/S	n/a
KMXC	97.3	General	M	Adult Contemporary/Contemporary Top 40
KTWB	101.9	General	M	Country
KRRO	103.7	General	M	AOR
KKLS	104.7	General	M	Oldies

Note: Stations included broadcast in the Sioux Falls metro area; n/a not available
Station Format: E = Educational; M = Music; N = News; S = Sports; T = Talk
Music Format: AOR = Album Oriented Rock; MOR = Middle-of-the-Road
Source: Burrelle's Media Directory, 1998 Edition

Television Stations

Name	Ch.	Affiliation	Type	Owner
KDLO	3	CBS	Commercial	Young Broadcasting Inc.
KPRY	4	ABC	Commercial	Ray Com Media Inc.
KDLT	5	NBC	Commercial	Red River Broadcast Corporation
KPLO	6	CBS	Commercial	Young Broadcasting
KELO	11	CBS	Commercial	Young Broadcasting Inc.
KSFY	13	ABC	Commercial	Raycom Media Inc.
KTTW	17	Fox	Commercial	Independent Communications Inc.

Note: Stations included broadcast in the Sioux Falls metro area
Source: Burrelle's Media Directory, 1998 Edition

CLIMATE

Average and Extreme Temperatures

Temperature	Jan	Feb	Mar	Apr	May	Jun	Jul	Aug	Sep	Oct	Nov	Dec	Ann
Extreme High (°F)	66	70	88	94	104	110	110	109	104	94	76	62	110
Average High (°F)	25	30	41	59	71	80	86	84	74	62	43	29	57
Average Temp. (°F)	15	20	32	47	59	69	75	72	62	50	33	20	46
Average Low (°F)	5	10	22	35	47	57	62	60	49	38	23	10	35
Extreme Low (°F)	-36	-31	-23	4	17	33	38	34	22	9	-17	-28	-36

Note: Figures cover the years 1932-1990
Source: National Climatic Data Center, International Station Meteorological Climate Summary, 3/95

Average Precipitation/Snowfall/Humidity

Precip./Humidity	Jan	Feb	Mar	Apr	May	Jun	Jul	Aug	Sep	Oct	Nov	Dec	Ann
Avg. Precip. (in.)	0.6	0.8	1.6	2.4	3.3	3.9	2.8	3.2	2.8	1.5	1.0	0.7	24.6
Avg. Snowfall (in.)	7	8	9	2	Tr	0	0	0	Tr	Tr	5	7	38
Avg. Rel. Hum. 6am (%)	n/a	n/a	n/a	n/a	n/a	n/a	n/a	n/a	n/a	n/a	n/a	n/a	n/a
Avg. Rel. Hum. 3pm (%)	n/a	n/a	n/a	n/a	n/a	n/a	n/a	n/a	n/a	n/a	n/a	n/a	n/a

Note: Figures cover the years 1932-1990; Tr = Trace amounts (<0.05 in. of rain; <0.5 in. of snow)
Source: National Climatic Data Center, International Station Meteorological Climate Summary, 3/95

Weather Conditions

Temperature			Daytime Sky			Precipitation		
5°F & below	32°F & below	90°F & above	Clear	Partly cloudy	Cloudy	0.01 inch or more precip.	0.1 inch or more snow/ice	Thunder-storms
n/a	n/a	n/a	95	136	134	n/a	n/a	n/a

Note: Figures are average number of days per year and covers the years 1932-1990
Source: National Climatic Data Center, International Station Meteorological Climate Summary, 3/95

AIR & WATER QUALITY

Maximum Pollutant Concentrations

	Particulate Matter (ug/m³)	Carbon Monoxide (ppm)	Sulfur Dioxide (ppm)	Nitrogen Dioxide (ppm)	Ozone (ppm)	Lead (ug/m³)
MSA[1] Level	53	n/a	n/a	n/a	n/a	n/a
NAAQS[2]	150	9	0.140	0.053	0.12	1.50
Met NAAQS?	Yes	n/a	n/a	n/a	n/a	n/a

Note: (1) Metropolitan Statistical Area - see Appendix A for areas included; (2) National Ambient Air Quality Standards; ppm = parts per million; ug/m³ = micrograms per cubic meter; n/a not available
Source: EPA, National Air Quality and Emissions Trends Report, 1996

Pollutant Standards Index

Data not available. *EPA, National Air Quality and Emissions Trends Report, 1996*

Drinking Water

Water System Name	Pop. Served	Primary Water Source Type	Number of Violations in Fiscal Year 1997	Type of Violation/ Contaminants
Sioux Falls	100,814	Surface	None	None

Note: Data as of January 16, 1998
Source: EPA, Office of Ground Water and Drinking Water, Safe Drinking Water Information System

Sioux Falls tap water is alkaline, hard and fluoridated.
Editor & Publisher Market Guide, 1998

Springfield, Missouri

Background

At the edge of the Ozark Mountains, Springfield is the gateway to the scenic White River region in the Ozarks. The entire metro area consists of comparatively flat or very gently rolling tableland.

Settled in 1827, it was incorporated as a town in 1838 and as a city in 1847. Throughout the Civil War, its location made it a military target for both Confederate and Union armies. On August 10, 1861 the Confederates took the city only to be permanently driven out a year later. Union forces held the area until the end of the war.

Today, Springfield is the center of a food-processing area. Major economic activities include shipping, wholesaling, meat-packing and dairy-product processing. As a regional agribusiness center, the Southwest Regional Stockyards is the sixth largest feeder cattle operation in the United States. The city also manufactures boats, auto trailers, railroad equipment, fabricated metals, prepressed concrete, paper products, chemical products, furniture and clothing among others.

The city enjoys a plateau climate which is characterized by mild temperatures, low humidity and plenty of sunshine. The air is remarkably free from industrial smoke and most fogs.

General Rankings and Evaluative Comments

- Springfield was ranked #103 out of 300 cities by *Money's* 1997 "Survey of the Best Places to Live." Criteria used: health services, crime, economy, housing, education, transportation, weather, leisure and the arts. The city was ranked #61 in 1996 and #76 in 1995. *Money, July 1997; Money, September 1996; Money, September 1995*

- *Ladies Home Journal* ranked America's 200 largest cities based on the qualities women care about most. Springfield ranked 111 out of 200. Criteria: low crime rate, good public schools, well-paying jobs, quality health and child care, the presence of women in government, proportion of women-owned businesses, size of the wage gap with men, local economy, divorce rates, the ratio of single men to single women, whether there are laws that require at least the same number of public toilets for women as men, and the probability of good hair days. *Ladies Home Journal, November 1997*

- Springfield was ranked #89 out of 219 cities in terms of children's health, safety, and economic well-being. Criteria: total population, percent population change, birth rate, child immunization rate, infant mortality rate, percent low birth weight infants, percent of births to teens, physician-to-population ratio, student-to-teacher ratio, dropout rate, unemployment rate, median family income, percent of children in poverty, violent and property crime rates, number of juvenile arrests for violent crimes as a percent of the total crime index, number of days with pollution standard index (PSI) over 100, pounds toxic releases per 1,000 people and number of superfund sites. *Zero Population Growth, Children's Environmental Index 1997*

- According to *Working Mother*, "More and more school-age programs in Missouri are earning state accreditation, under a grants program developed three years ago by the state department of education. Happily, the Missouri Center for Accreditation reports it is now swamped with applications for accreditation, which means school-age programs are meeting higher standards. These new rules are not the same as those required for NAEYC accreditation, but they are far better than having no standards at all.

  Advocates here managed to beat back a bill in the state legislature that would have hurt many family child care providers by requiring them to be in compliance with all local business zoning laws—a problem that plagues many child care providers across the county.

  Child care programs in religious institutions are now subject to inspection, and state officials have asked for funding to hire more inspectors to visit these centers." *Working Mother, July/August 1997*

Business Environment

STATE ECONOMY

State Economic Profile

"...The housing industry improved upon its performance in 1993, but fell well short of the number of permits issued during the industry's peak in 1994.

Missouri's largest employer, McDonnell Douglas Corp. is attempting to merge with Boeing. The combined companies promise as much as $1 billion in savings per year, making job cuts in Missouri likely. Since McDonnell Douglas is more active in defense contracting than Boeing, much of the St. Louis manufacturing workforce and facilities will likely remain intact, while cutbacks are more likely at commercial aircraft facilities.

Bank mergers will begin to have a dampening effect on the state's economy..., Mercantile bank purchased Mark Twain Bancshares and Roosevelt Financial Group, while NationsBank purchased Boatmen's Banchsares. There will be considerable branch consolidation.

TWA continues to look like a bigger risk to the Missouri economy as time goes on. Already on shaky financial footing, TWA has yet to recover from the fallout of the Flight 800 explosion....

Missouri's economy will recover as the year goes on and will eventually shadow the national economy through the forecast. St. Louis will continue to be a drag on Missouri's growth, but faster growing Kansas City, Columbia, and Springfield will help pick up the slack. Sizable exposure to a few large employers is a downside risk in the overall outlook. Moderate population growth will keep Missouri on track to be an average performer through the forecast." *National Association of Realtors, Economic Profiles: The Fifty States, July 1997*

IMPORTS/EXPORTS

Total Export Sales

Area	1993 ($000)	1994 ($000)	1995 ($000)	1996 ($000)	% Chg. 1993-96	% Chg. 1995-96
MSA[1]	81,121	103,823	120,178	120,349	48.4	0.1
U.S.	464,858,354	512,415,609	583,030,524	622,827,063	34.0	6.8

Note: (1) Metropolitan Statistical Area - see Appendix A for areas included
Source: U.S. Department of Commerce, International Trade Association, Metropolitan Area Exports: An Export Performance Report on Over 250 U.S. Cities, October 1997

Imports/Exports by Port

Type	Cargo Value			Share of U.S. Total	
	1995 (US$mil.)	1996 (US$mil.)	% Change 1995-1996	1995 (%)	1996 (%)
Imports	0	0	0	0	0
Exports	0	0	0	0	0

Source: Global Trade Information Services, WaterBorne Trade Atlas 1997

CITY FINANCES

City Government Finances

Component	FY92 ($000)	FY92 (per capita $)
Revenue	280,916	1,964.65
Expenditure	257,462	1,800.62
Debt Outstanding	296,583	2,074.22
Cash & Securities	286,736	2,005.36

Source: U.S. Bureau of the Census, City Government Finances: 1991-92

City Government Revenue by Source

Source	FY92 ($000)	FY92 (per capita $)	FY92 (%)
From Federal Government	5,152	36.03	1.8
From State Governments	13,849	96.86	4.9
From Local Governments	1,626	11.37	0.6
Property Taxes	6,026	42.14	2.1
General Sales Taxes	24,453	171.02	8.7
Selective Sales Taxes	8,094	56.61	2.9
Income Taxes	0	0.00	0.0
Current Charges	26,986	188.73	9.6
Utility/Liquor Store	161,235	1,127.64	57.4
Employee Retirement[1]	5,845	40.88	2.1
Other	27,650	193.38	9.8

Note: (1) Excludes "city contributions," classified as "nonrevenue," intragovernmental transfers.
Source: U.S. Bureau of the Census, City Government Finances: 1991-92

City Government Expenditures by Function

Function	FY92 ($000)	FY92 (per capita $)	FY92 (%)
Educational Services	0	0.00	0.0
Employee Retirement[1]	2,860	20.00	1.1
Environment/Housing	41,076	287.27	16.0
Government Administration	6,001	41.97	2.3
Interest on General Debt	7,594	53.11	2.9
Public Safety	22,240	155.54	8.6
Social Services	8,007	56.00	3.1
Transportation	27,998	195.81	10.9
Utility/Liquor Store	139,730	977.24	54.3
Other	1,956	13.68	0.8

Note: (1) Payments to beneficiaries including withdrawal of contributions.
Source: U.S. Bureau of the Census, City Government Finances: 1991-92

Municipal Bond Ratings

Area	Moody's	S & P
Springfield	n/r	n/a

Note: n/a not available; n/r not rated
Source: Moody's Bond Record, 2/98; Statistical Abstract of the U.S., 1997; Governing Magazine, 9/97, 3/98

POPULATION

Population Growth

Area	1980	1990	% Chg. 1980-90	July 1996 Estimate	% Chg. 1990-96
City	133,116	140,494	5.5	143,407	2.1
MSA[1]	207,704	240,593	15.8	296,345	23.2
U.S.	226,545,805	248,765,170	9.8	265,179,411	6.6

Note: (1) Metropolitan Statistical Area - see Appendix A for areas included
Source: 1980/1990 Census of Housing and Population, Summary Tape File 3C; Census Bureau Population Estimates

Population Characteristics

Race	City				% Chg.	MSA[1]	
	1980		1990		1980-90	1990	
	Population	%	Population	%		Population	%
White	128,478	96.5	134,286	95.6	4.5	233,078	96.9
Black	2,900	2.2	3,373	2.4	16.3	3,626	1.5
Amer Indian/Esk/Aleut	733	0.6	1,116	0.8	52.3	1,816	0.8
Asian/Pacific Islander	686	0.5	1,328	0.9	93.6	1,578	0.7
Other	319	0.2	391	0.3	22.6	495	0.2
Hispanic Origin[2]	1,088	0.8	1,240	0.9	14.0	2,001	0.8

Note: (1) Metropolitan Statistical Area - see Appendix A for areas included;
(2) people of Hispanic origin can be of any race
Source: 1980/1990 Census of Housing and Population, Summary Tape File 3C

Ancestry

Area	German	Irish	English	Italian	U.S.	French	Polish	Dutch
City	30.7	21.6	20.3	2.0	5.9	5.0	1.3	4.0
MSA[1]	31.4	22.0	20.1	2.0	6.5	4.9	1.2	4.0
U.S.	23.3	15.6	13.1	5.9	5.3	4.2	3.8	2.5

Note: Figures are percentages and include persons that reported multiple ancestry (eg. if a person reported being Irish and Italian, they were included in both columns); (1) Metropolitan Statistical Area - see Appendix A for areas included
Source: 1990 Census of Population and Housing, Summary Tape File 3C

Age

Area	Median Age (Years)	Age Distribution (%)						
		Under 5	Under 18	18-24	25-44	45-64	65+	80+
City	31.7	6.2	20.6	17.8	29.3	17.1	15.2	4.2
MSA[1]	32.5	6.5	23.8	13.8	31.0	18.3	13.1	3.3
U.S.	32.9	7.3	25.6	10.5	32.6	18.7	12.5	2.8

Note: (1) Metropolitan Statistical Area - see Appendix A for areas included
Source: 1990 Census of Population and Housing, Summary Tape File 3C

Male/Female Ratio

Area	Number of males per 100 females (all ages)	Number of males per 100 females (18 years old+)
City	89.4	85.7
MSA[1]	92.2	88.4
U.S.	95.0	91.9

Note: (1) Metropolitan Statistical Area - see Appendix A for areas included
Source: 1990 Census of Population, General Population Characteristics

INCOME

Per Capita/Median/Average Income

Area	Per Capita ($)	Median Household ($)	Average Household ($)
City	11,878	21,577	28,471
MSA[1]	12,250	24,546	31,107
U.S.	14,420	30,056	38,453

Note: all figures are for 1989; (1) Metropolitan Statistical Area - see Appendix A for areas included
Source: 1990 Census of Population and Housing, Summary Tape File 3C

Household Income Distribution by Race

Income ($)	City (%)					U.S. (%)				
	Total	White	Black	Other	Hisp.[1]	Total	White	Black	Other	Hisp.[1]
Less than 5,000	8.3	8.2	10.0	15.8	8.5	6.2	4.8	15.2	8.6	8.8
5,000 - 9,999	13.1	13.0	16.9	17.6	17.9	9.3	8.6	14.2	9.9	11.1
10,000 - 14,999	12.9	12.9	17.4	12.0	17.6	8.8	8.5	11.0	9.8	11.0
15,000 - 24,999	22.8	22.9	26.1	14.8	21.2	17.5	17.3	18.9	18.5	20.5
25,000 - 34,999	17.1	17.1	16.0	16.0	18.5	15.8	16.1	14.2	15.4	16.4
35,000 - 49,999	13.7	13.9	6.4	11.9	8.5	17.9	18.6	13.3	16.1	16.0
50,000 - 74,999	7.9	8.0	5.4	8.0	5.8	15.0	15.8	9.3	13.4	11.1
75,000 - 99,999	1.8	1.9	1.0	0.0	0.0	5.1	5.5	2.6	4.7	3.1
100,000+	2.3	2.3	0.8	4.0	2.0	4.4	4.8	1.3	3.7	1.9

Note: all figures are for 1989; (1) people of Hispanic origin can be of any race
Source: 1990 Census of Population and Housing, Summary Tape File 3C

Effective Buying Income

Area	Per Capita ($)	Median Household ($)	Average Household ($)
City	14,463	27,023	35,612
MSA[1]	14,732	30,485	38,454
U.S.	15,444	33,201	41,849

Note: data as of 1/1/97; (1) Metropolitan Statistical Area - see Appendix A for areas included
Source: Standard Rate & Data Service, Newspaper Advertising Source, 2/98

Effective Household Buying Income Distribution

Area	% of Households Earning						
	$10,000 -$19,999	$20,000 -$34,999	$35,000 -$49,999	$50,000 -$74,999	$75,000 -$99,000	$100,000 -$124,999	$125,000 and up
City	21.3	27.1	16.9	12.6	3.8	1.1	1.9
MSA[1]	18.7	26.1	18.9	15.4	4.8	1.3	2.0
U.S.	16.5	23.4	18.3	18.2	6.4	2.1	2.4

Note: data as of 1/1/97; (1) Metropolitan Statistical Area - see Appendix A for areas included
Source: Standard Rate & Data Service, Newspaper Advertising Source, 2/98

Poverty Rates by Race and Age

Area	Total (%)	By Race (%)				By Age (%)		
		White	Black	Other	Hisp.[2]	Under 5 years old	Under 18 years old	65 years and over
City	17.8	17.0	30.7	42.2	30.1	26.4	21.2	13.4
MSA[1]	13.5	13.0	28.4	34.3	20.0	20.4	15.4	13.8
U.S.	13.1	9.8	29.5	23.1	25.3	20.1	18.3	12.8

Note: figures show the percent of people living below the poverty line in 1989. The average poverty threshold was $12,674 for a family of four in 1989; (1) Metropolitan Statistical Area - see Appendix A for areas included; (2) people of Hispanic origin can be of any race
Source: 1990 Census of Population and Housing, Summary Tape File 3C

EMPLOYMENT

Labor Force and Employment

Area	Civilian Labor Force			Workers Employed		
	Dec. '95	Dec. '96	% Chg.	Dec. '95	Dec. '96	% Chg.
City	89,287	86,224	-3.4	85,902	83,484	-2.8
MSA[1]	173,763	167,604	-3.5	167,246	162,539	-2.8
U.S.	134,583,000	136,742,000	1.6	127,903,000	130,785,000	2.3

Note: Data is not seasonally adjusted and covers workers 16 years of age and older;
(1) Metropolitan Statistical Area - see Appendix A for areas included
Source: Bureau of Labor Statistics, http://stats.bls.gov

Unemployment Rate

Area	1997											
	Jan.	Feb.	Mar.	Apr.	May	Jun.	Jul.	Aug.	Sep.	Oct.	Nov.	Dec.
City	4.0	3.7	3.5	3.3	3.2	3.4	2.8	3.2	2.8	3.0	3.1	3.2
MSA[1]	4.2	3.9	3.5	3.3	3.1	3.3	2.7	3.0	2.5	2.7	2.9	3.0
U.S.	5.9	5.7	5.5	4.8	4.7	5.2	5.0	4.8	4.7	4.4	4.3	4.4

Note: Data is not seasonally adjusted and covers workers 16 years of age and older; All figures are percentages; (1) Metropolitan Statistical Area - see Appendix A for areas included
Source: Bureau of Labor Statistics, http://stats.bls.gov

Employment by Industry

Sector	MSA[1]		U.S.
	Number of Employees	Percent of Total	Percent of Total
Services	48,100	29.6	29.0
Retail Trade	33,500	20.6	18.5
Government	20,600	12.7	16.1
Manufacturing	24,000	14.8	15.0
Finance/Insurance/Real Estate	6,900	4.2	5.7
Wholesale Trade	12,400	7.6	5.4
Transportation/Public Utilities	10,500	6.5	5.3
Construction/Mining	6,400	3.9	5.0

Note: Figures cover non-farm employment as of 12/97 and are not seasonally adjusted;
(1) Metropolitan Statistical Area - see Appendix A for areas included
Source: Bureau of Labor Statistics, http://stats.bls.gov

Employment by Occupation

Occupation Category	City (%)	MSA[1] (%)	U.S. (%)
White Collar	58.6	56.7	58.1
Executive/Admin./Management	10.0	10.3	12.3
Professional	13.4	12.9	14.1
Technical & Related Support	3.6	3.4	3.7
Sales	15.3	14.5	11.8
Administrative Support/Clerical	16.3	15.6	16.3
Blue Collar	24.2	26.6	26.2
Precision Production/Craft/Repair	9.5	10.7	11.3
Machine Operators/Assem./Insp.	6.5	6.9	6.8
Transportation/Material Movers	4.1	4.8	4.1
Cleaners/Helpers/Laborers	4.1	4.3	3.9
Services	16.2	14.5	13.2
Farming/Forestry/Fishing	1.0	2.1	2.5

Note: figures cover employed persons 16 years old and over;
(1) Metropolitan Statistical Area - see Appendix A for areas included
Source: 1990 Census of Population and Housing, Summary Tape File 3C

Occupational Employment Projections: 1990 - 2000

Occupations Expected to have the Largest Job Growth (ranked by numerical growth)	Fast-Growing Occupations[1] (ranked by percent growth)
1. Salespersons, retail	1. Ushers/lobby attendants/ticket takers
2. Waiters & waitresses	2. Plastic molding/casting mach. oper.
3. General managers & top executives	3. Hotel desk clerks
4. Cashiers	4. Baggage porters & bellhops
5. Food preparation workers	5. Musicians
6. Janitors/cleaners/maids, ex. priv. hshld.	6. Music directors/singers & related occs.
7. Nursing aides/orderlies/attendants	7. Housekeeper supervisors, institutional
8. Maids/housekeepers	8. Maids/housekeepers
9. Food preparation, fast food	9. Producers/directors/actors/entertainers
10. Truck drivers, heavy	10. Hosts/hostesses, restaurant & lounge

Projections cover Polk, Dallas, Greene, Webster, Christian, Stone and Taney Counties.
Note: (1) Excludes occupations with employment less than 50 in 1990
Source: Missouri Department of Labor and Industrial Relations, Missouri Service Delivery Area 8, Employment Outlook, Projections to 2000

Average Wages

Occupation	Wage	Occupation	Wage
Professional/Technical/Clerical	$/Week	**Health/Protective Services**	$/Week
Accountants III	-	Corrections Officers	-
Attorneys III	-	Firefighters	-
Budget Analysts III	-	Nurses, Licensed Practical II	-
Buyers/Contracting Specialists II	-	Nurses, Registered II	-
Clerks, Accounting III	362	Nursing Assistants II	-
Clerks, General III	367	Police Officers I	-
Computer Operators II	363	**Hourly Workers**	$/Hour
Computer Programmers II	515	Forklift Operators	9.45
Drafters II	407	General Maintenance Workers	8.43
Engineering Technicians III	-	Guards I	5.12
Engineering Technicians, Civil III	-	Janitors	6.30
Engineers III	-	Maintenance Electricians	14.41
Key Entry Operators I	282	Maintenance Electronics Techs II	-
Personnel Assistants III	-	Maintenance Machinists	14.10
Personnel Specialists III	-	Maintenance Mechanics, Machinery	12.91
Secretaries III	487	Material Handling Laborers	10.12
Switchboard Operator-Receptionist	287	Motor Vehicle Mechanics	13.20
Systems Analysts II	803	Shipping/Receiving Clerks	9.00
Systems Analysts Supervisor/Mgr II	-	Tool and Die Makers	13.39
Tax Collectors II	-	Truckdrivers, Tractor Trailer	13.25
Word Processors II	-	Warehouse Specialists	10.27

Note: Wage data includes full-time workers only for 6/95 and cover southern Missouri. Dashes indicate that data was not available.
Source: Bureau of Labor Statistics, Occupational Compensation Survey

TAXES

Major State and Local Tax Rates

State Corp. Income (%)	State Personal Income (%)	Residential Property (effective rate per $100)	Sales & Use		State Gasoline (cents/ gallon)	State Cigarette (cents/ 20-pack)
			State (%)	Local (%)		
6.25	1.5 - 6.0	n/a	4.225	1.875	17.05[a]	17[b]

Note: Personal/corporate income tax rates as of 1/97. Sales, gasoline and cigarette tax rates as of 1/98; (a) Rate is comprised of 17 cents excise and 0.05 cents motor carrier tax; (b) Counties and cities may impose an additional tax of 4 - 7 cents per pack
Source: Federation of Tax Administrators, www.taxadmin.org; Washington D.C. Department of Finance and Revenue, Tax Rates and Tax Burdens in the District of Columbia: A Nationwide Comparison, June 1997; Chamber of Commerce

Total Taxes Per Capita and as a Percent of Income

Area	Per Capita Income ($)	Per Capita Taxes ($)			Taxes as Pct. of Income (%)		
		Total	Federal	State/Local	Total	Federal	State/Local
Missouri	24,554	8,421	5,674	2,747	34.3	23.1	11.2
U.S.	26,187	9,205	6,127	3,078	35.2	23.4	11.8

Note: Figures are for 1997
Source: Tax Foundation, Web Site, www.taxfoundation.org

COMMERCIAL REAL ESTATE

Data not available at time of publication.

COMMERCIAL UTILITIES

Typical Monthly Electric Bills

Area	Commercial Service ($/month)		Industrial Service ($/month)	
	12 kW demand 1,500 kWh	100 kW demand 30,000 kWh	1,000 kW demand 400,000 kWh	20,000 kW demand 10,000,000 kWh
City	n/a	n/a	n/a	n/a
U.S.	162	2,360	25,590	545,677

Note: Based on rates in effect July 1, 1997; n/a not available
Source: Edison Electric Institute, Typical Residential, Commercial and Industrial Bills, Summer 1997

TRANSPORTATION

Transportation Statistics

Avg. travel time to work (min.)	15.7
Interstate highways	I-44
Bus lines	
In-city	City Utilities
Inter-city	1
Passenger air service	
Airport	Springfield/Branson Regional Airport
Airlines	6
Aircraft departures	n/a
Enplaned passengers	n/a
Rail service	No Amtrak service
Motor freight carriers	22
Major waterways/ports	None

Source: OAG, Business Travel Planner, Summer 1997; Editor & Publisher Market Guide, 1998; FAA Airport Activity Statistics, 1996; Amtrak National Time Table, Northeast Timetable, Fall/Winter 1997-98; 1990 Census of Population and Housing, STF 3C; Chamber of Commerce/Economic Development 1997; Jane's Urban Transport Systems 1997-98; Transit Fact Book 1997

Means of Transportation to Work

Area	Car/Truck/Van		Public Transportation			Bicycle	Walked	Other Means	Worked at Home
	Drove Alone	Car-pooled	Bus	Subway	Railroad				
City	80.4	11.0	0.9	0.0	0.0	0.3	4.2	0.8	2.4
MSA[1]	81.5	10.9	0.6	0.0	0.0	0.2	2.9	0.7	3.2
U.S.	73.2	13.4	3.0	1.5	0.5	0.4	3.9	1.2	3.0

Note: figures shown are percentages and only include workers 16 years old and over;
(1) Metropolitan Statistical Area - see Appendix A for areas included
Source: 1990 Census of Population and Housing, Summary Tape File 3C

BUSINESSES

Major Business Headquarters

Company Name	1997 Rankings	
	Fortune 500	Forbes 500

No companies listed.

Note: Companies listed are located in the city; Dashes indicate no ranking
Fortune 500: companies that produce a 10-K are ranked 1 - 500 based on 1996 revenue
Forbes 500: private companies are ranked 1 - 500 based on 1996 revenue
Source: Forbes 12/1/97; Fortune 4/28/97

HOTELS & MOTELS

Hotels/Motels

Area	Hotels/ Motels	Rooms	Luxury-Level Hotels/Motels		Average Minimum Rates ($)		
			♦♦♦♦	♦♦♦♦♦	♦♦	♦♦♦	♦♦♦♦
City	24	2,775	0	0	n/a	n/a	n/a
Airport	1	6	0	0	n/a	n/a	n/a
Suburbs	2	398	0	0	n/a	n/a	n/a
Total	27	3,179	0	0	n/a	n/a	n/a

Note: n/a not available; Classifications range from one diamond (budget properties with basic amenities) to five diamond (luxury properties with the finest service, rooms and facilities).
Source: OAG, Business Travel Planner, Summer 1997

CONVENTION CENTERS

Major Convention Centers

Center Name	Meeting Rooms	Exhibit Space (sf)
University Plaza Trade Center	n/a	69,000
West Plains Civic Center	n/a	30,000
Hammons Student Center	3	35,000

Note: n/a not available
Source: Trade Shows Worldwide 1997

Living Environment

COST OF LIVING

Cost of Living Index

Composite Index	Housing	Utilities	Groceries	Health Care	Trans- portation	Misc. Goods/ Services
92.4	87.4	74.2	96.0	96.0	96.4	97.5

Note: U.S. = 100
Source: ACCRA, Cost of Living Index, 3rd Quarter 1997

HOUSING

Median Home Prices and Housing Affordability

Area	Median Price[2] 3rd Qtr. 1997 ($)	HOI[3] 3rd Qtr. 1997	Afford- ability Rank[4]
MSA[1]	n/a	n/a	n/a
U.S.	127,000	63.7	–

Note: (1) Metropolitan Statistical Area - see Appendix A for areas included; (2) U.S. figures calculated from the sales of 625,000 new and existing homes in 195 markets; (3) Housing Opportunity Index - percent of homes sold that were within the reach of the median income household at the prevailing mortgage interest rate; (4) Rank is from 1-195 with 1 being most affordable; n/a not available
Source: National Association of Home Builders, Housing Opportunity Index, 3rd Quarter 1997

Average New Home Price

Area	Price ($)
City	116,700
U.S.	135,710

Note: Figures are based on a new home with 1,800 sq. ft. of living area on an 8,000 sq. ft. lot.
Source: ACCRA, Cost of Living Index, 3rd Quarter 1997

Average Apartment Rent

Area	Rent ($/mth)
City	490
U.S.	569

Note: Figures are based on an unfurnished two bedroom, 1-1/2 or 2 bath apartment, approximately 950 sq. ft. in size, excluding all utilities except water
Source: ACCRA, Cost of Living Index, 3rd Quarter 1997

RESIDENTIAL UTILITIES

Average Residential Utility Costs

Area	All Electric ($/mth)	Part Electric ($/mth)	Other Energy ($/mth)	Phone ($/mth)
City	–	39.58	34.92	16.29
U.S.	109.40	55.25	43.64	19.48

Source: ACCRA, Cost of Living Index, 3rd Quarter 1997

HEALTH CARE

Average Health Care Costs

Area	Hospital ($/day)	Doctor ($/visit)	Dentist ($/visit)
City	385.00	47.89	56.66
U.S.	392.91	48.76	60.84

Note: Hospital - based on a semi-private room. Doctor - based on a general practitioner's routine exam of an established patient. Dentist - based on adult teeth cleaning and periodic oral exam.
Source: ACCRA, Cost of Living Index, 3rd Quarter 1997

Distribution of Office-Based Physicians

Area	Family/Gen. Practitioners	Specialists		
		Medical	Surgical	Other
MSA[1]	64	172	157	153

Note: Data as of 12/31/96; (1) Metropolitan Statistical Area - see Appendix A for areas included
Source: American Medical Assn., Physician Characteristics & Distribution in the U.S., 1997-1998

Hospitals

Springfield has 4 general medical and surgical hospitals, 1 psychiatric. *AHA Guide to the Healthcare Field 1997-98*

Cox Health Systems is among the 100 best-run hospitals in the U.S.
Modern Healthcare, January 5, 1998

EDUCATION

Public School District Statistics

District Name	Num. Sch.	Enroll.	Classroom Teachers[1]	Pupils per Teacher	Minority Pupils (%)	Current Exp.[2] ($/pupil)
Springfield R-XII	57	24,740	1,479	16.7	7.2	3,919

Note: Data covers the 1995-1996 school year unless otherwise noted; (1) Excludes teachers reported as working in school district offices rather than in schools; (2) Based on 1993-94 enrollment collected by the Census Bureau, not the enrollment figure shown in column 3; SD = School District; ISD = Independent School District; n/a not available
Source: National Center for Education Statistics, Common Core of Data Survey; Bureau of the Census

Educational Quality

School District	Education Quotient[1]	Graduate Outcome[2]	Community Index[3]	Resource Index[4]
Springfield	100.0	124.0	97.0	78.0

Note: Nearly 1,000 secondary school districts were rated in terms of educational quality. The scores range from a low of 50 to a high of 150; (1) Average of the Graduate Outcome, Community and Resource indexes; (2) Based on graduation rates and college board scores (SAT/ACT); (3) Based on the surrounding community's average level of education and the area's average income level; (4) Based on teacher salaries, per-pupil expenditures and student-teacher ratios.
Source: Expansion Management, Ratings Issue 1997

Educational Attainment by Race

Area	High School Graduate (%)					Bachelor's Degree (%)				
	Total	White	Black	Other	Hisp.[2]	Total	White	Black	Other	Hisp.[2]
City	77.0	77.3	70.6	68.9	77.0	20.7	20.9	12.4	20.1	27.6
MSA[1]	78.5	78.8	71.8	71.0	77.7	19.6	19.7	14.4	19.1	23.2
U.S.	75.2	77.9	63.1	60.4	49.8	20.3	21.5	11.4	19.4	9.2

Note: figures shown cover persons 25 years old and over; (1) Metropolitan Statistical Area - see Appendix A for areas included; (2) people of Hispanic origin can be of any race
Source: 1990 Census of Population and Housing, Summary Tape File 3C

School Enrollment by Type

Area	Preprimary				Elementary/High School			
	Public		Private		Public		Private	
	Enrollment	%	Enrollment	%	Enrollment	%	Enrollment	%
City	1,135	62.4	683	37.6	16,946	92.8	1,316	7.2
MSA[1]	2,229	61.2	1,415	38.8	35,278	93.9	2,297	6.1
U.S.	2,679,029	59.5	1,824,256	40.5	38,379,689	90.2	4,187,099	9.8

Note: figures shown cover persons 3 years old and over;
(1) Metropolitan Statistical Area - see Appendix A for areas included
Source: 1990 Census of Population and Housing, Summary Tape File 3C

School Enrollment by Race

Area	Preprimary (%)				Elementary/High School (%)			
	White	Black	Other	Hisp.[1]	White	Black	Other	Hisp.[1]
City	94.6	1.4	4.0	1.4	93.8	3.2	3.0	1.2
MSA[2]	96.5	0.9	2.6	1.1	96.1	1.8	2.0	1.0
U.S.	80.4	12.5	7.1	7.8	74.1	15.6	10.3	12.5

Note: figures shown cover persons 3 years old and over; (1) people of Hispanic origin can be of any race; (2) Metropolitan Statistical Area - see Appendix A for areas included
Source: 1990 Census of Population and Housing, Summary Tape File 3C

SAT/ACT Scores

Area/District	1997 SAT				1997 ACT	
	Percent of Graduates Tested (%)	Average Math Score	Average Verbal Score	Average Combined Score	Percent of Graduates Tested (%)	Average Composite Score
Springfield PS	7	605	611	1,216	66	22.4
State	9	568	567	1,135	64	21.5
U.S.	42	511	505	1,016	36	21.0

Note: Math and verbal SAT scores are out of a possible 800; ACT scores are out of a possible 36
Caution: Comparing or ranking states/cities on the basis of SAT/ACT scores alone is invalid and strongly discouraged by the The College Board and The American College Testing Program as students who take the tests are self-selected and do not represent the entire student population.
Source: Springfield Public Schools, Assistant Superintendent, Secondary Education, 1997; American College Testing Program, 1997; College Board, 1997

Classroom Teacher Salaries in Public Schools

District	B.A. Degree		M.A. Degree		Ph.D. Degree	
	Min. ($)	Max ($)	Min. ($)	Max. ($)	Min. ($)	Max. ($)
Springfield	21,772	29,972	23,024	35,736	25,905	38,638
Average[1]	26,120	39,270	28,175	44,667	31,643	49,825

Note: Salaries are for 1996-1997; (1) Based on all school districts covered
Source: American Federation of Teachers (unpublished data)

Higher Education

Two-Year Colleges		Four-Year Colleges		Medical Schools	Law Schools	Voc/ Tech
Public	Private	Public	Private			
0	1	1	5	0	0	7

Source: College Blue Book, Occupational Education 1997; Medical School Admission Requirements, 1998-99; Peterson's Guide to Two-Year Colleges, 1997; Peterson's Guide to Four-Year Colleges, 1997; Barron's Guide to Law Schools 1997

MAJOR EMPLOYERS

Major Employers

Bass Pro Shops (mail order)
Lester E Cox Medical Center
Paul Mueller Co. (fabricated metal products)
Springfield Remanufacturing Corp.
American National Property & Casualty
Ozark Automotive Distributors

Cox Alternative Care of the Ozarks
New Prime Inc. (trucking)
St. John's Regional Health Center
Indiana Western Express (trucking)
Trailiner Corp (trucking)

Note: companies listed are located in the city
Source: Dun's Business Rankings 1997; Ward's Business Directory, 1997

PUBLIC SAFETY

Crime Rate

Area	All Crimes	Violent Crimes				Property Crimes		
		Murder	Forcible Rape	Robbery	Aggrav. Assault	Burglary	Larceny -Theft	Motor Vehicle Theft
City	7,567.9	2.6	50.0	113.8	356.5	1,435.3	5,164.3	445.3
Suburbs[1]	1,814.4	0.0	17.1	13.0	117.6	453.9	1,082.1	130.6
MSA[2]	4,537.3	1.2	32.7	60.7	230.7	918.4	3,014.1	279.6
U.S.	5,078.9	7.4	36.1	202.4	388.2	943.0	2,975.9	525.9

Note: Crime rate is the number of crimes per 100,000 pop.; (1) defined as all areas within the MSA but located outside the central city; (2) Metropolitan Statistical Area - see Appendix A for areas incl.
Source: FBI Uniform Crime Reports 1996

RECREATION

Culture and Recreation

Museums	Symphony Orchestras	Opera Companies	Dance Companies	Professional Theatres	Zoos	Pro Sports Teams
5	1	1	1	1	1	0

Source: International Directory of the Performing Arts, 1996; Official Museum Directory, 1998; Chamber of Commerce/Economic Development 1997

Library System

The Springfield-Green County Library has seven branches, holdings of 464,750 volumes and a budget of $4,846,013 (1995-1996). *American Library Directory, 1997-1998*

MEDIA

Newspapers

Name	Type	Freq.	Distribution	Circulation
The News-Leader	n/a	7x/wk	Area	62,553

Note: Includes newspapers with circulations of 500 or more located in the city; n/a not available
Source: Burrelle's Media Directory, 1998 Edition

AM Radio Stations

Call Letters	Freq. (kHz)	Target Audience	Station Format	Music Format
KWTO	560	General	N/S/T	n/a
KTOZ	1060	General	M/N	n/a
KTTS	1260	General	M/N/S	Country
KGMY	1400	General	M/N	Adult Standards
KLFJ	1550	Religious	M/N/S	Christian

Note: Stations included broadcast in the Springfield metro area; n/a not available
Station Format: E = Educational; M = Music; N = News; S = Sports; T = Talk
Source: Burrelle's Media Directory, 1998 Edition

FM Radio Stations

Call Letters	Freq. (mHz)	Target Audience	Station Format	Music Format
KWFC	89.1	General	E/M/N/S	Christian
KSMU	91.1	General	E/M/N	n/a
KTTS	94.7	General	M/N/S	Country
KTOZ	95.5	General	M	Alternative
KXUS	97.3	General	M	Classic Rock
KWTO	98.7	General	M	Classic Rock
KADI	99.5	Religious	M/N/S	Christian
KGMY	100.5	General	M	Country
KTXR	101.3	General	M	Easy Listening
KGBX	105.9	General	M/N/S	Adult Contemporary

Note: Stations included broadcast in the Springfield metro area; n/a not available
Station Format: E = Educational; M = Music; N = News; S = Sports; T = Talk
Source: Burrelle's Media Directory, 1998 Edition

Television Stations

Name	Ch.	Affiliation	Type	Owner
KYTV	3	NBC	Commercial	Schurz Communications Inc.
KOLR	10	CBS	Commercial	Independent Broadcasting Company
KOZK	21	PBS	Public	Ozark Public Telecommunications Inc.
KDEB	27	Fox	Commercial	Petracom Broadcasting Inc.
KSPR	33	ABC	Commercial	Davis Goldfarb

Note: Stations included broadcast in the Springfield metro area
Source: Burrelle's Media Directory, 1998 Edition

CLIMATE

Average and Extreme Temperatures

Temperature	Jan	Feb	Mar	Apr	May	Jun	Jul	Aug	Sep	Oct	Nov	Dec	Ann
Extreme High (°F)	76	81	87	93	93	101	113	106	104	93	80	77	113
Average High (°F)	42	47	56	68	75	84	89	88	80	70	56	45	67
Average Temp. (°F)	32	37	45	56	65	74	78	77	69	59	46	36	56
Average Low (°F)	22	26	34	45	54	63	67	65	58	47	35	26	45
Extreme Low (°F)	-13	-17	-8	18	29	42	44	44	30	21	4	-16	-17

Note: Figures cover the years 1940-1990
Source: National Climatic Data Center, International Station Meteorological Climate Summary, 3/95

Average Precipitation/Snowfall/Humidity

Precip./Humidity	Jan	Feb	Mar	Apr	May	Jun	Jul	Aug	Sep	Oct	Nov	Dec	Ann
Avg. Precip. (in.)	1.8	2.2	3.5	4.2	4.8	5.0	3.4	3.3	4.3	3.6	3.2	2.8	42.0
Avg. Snowfall (in.)	5	4	4	Tr	Tr	0	0	0	0	Tr	2	3	18
Avg. Rel. Hum. 6am (%)	78	80	79	79	85	86	87	88	87	82	80	79	82
Avg. Rel. Hum. 3pm (%)	58	56	52	50	55	55	53	50	52	50	54	59	54

Note: Figures cover the years 1940-1990; Tr = Trace amounts (<0.05 in. of rain; <0.5 in. of snow)
Source: National Climatic Data Center, International Station Meteorological Climate Summary, 3/95

Weather Conditions

Temperature			Daytime Sky			Precipitation		
10°F & below	32°F & below	90°F & above	Clear	Partly cloudy	Cloudy	0.01 inch or more precip.	0.1 inch or more snow/ice	Thunder-storms
12	102	42	113	119	133	109	14	55

Note: Figures are average number of days per year and covers the years 1940-1990
Source: National Climatic Data Center, International Station Meteorological Climate Summary, 3/95

AIR & WATER QUALITY

Maximum Pollutant Concentrations

	Particulate Matter (ug/m^3)	Carbon Monoxide (ppm)	Sulfur Dioxide (ppm)	Nitrogen Dioxide (ppm)	Ozone (ppm)	Lead (ug/m^3)
MSA[1] Level	148	3	0.089	0.011	0.10	n/a
NAAQS[2]	150	9	0.140	0.053	0.12	1.50
Met NAAQS?	Yes	Yes	Yes	Yes	Yes	n/a

Note: (1) Metropolitan Statistical Area - see Appendix A for areas included; (2) National Ambient Air Quality Standards; ppm = parts per million; ug/m^3 = micrograms per cubic meter; n/a not available
Source: EPA, National Air Quality and Emissions Trends Report, 1996

Pollutant Standards Index

Data not available. *EPA, National Air Quality and Emissions Trends Report, 1996*

Drinking Water

Water System Name	Pop. Served	Primary Water Source Type	Number of Violations in Fiscal Year 1997	Type of Violation/ Contaminants
Springfield	149,237	Surface	None	None

Note: Data as of January 16, 1998
Source: EPA, Office of Ground Water and Drinking Water, Safe Drinking Water Information System

Springfield tap water is alkaline, hard and fluoridated.
Editor & Publisher Market Guide, 1998

Comparative Statistics

Population Growth: City

City	Population			% Change	
	1980	1990	1996[1]	1980-90	1990-96
Ann Arbor	107,960	109,592	108,758	1.5	-0.8
Chicago	3,005,072	2,783,726	2,721,547	-7.4	-2.2
Des Moines	191,003	193,187	193,422	1.1	0.1
Detroit	1,203,339	1,027,974	1,000,272	-14.6	-2.7
Evansville	130,496	126,272	123,456	-3.2	-2.2
Fort Wayne	172,196	173,072	184,783	0.5	6.8
Grand Rapids	181,843	189,126	188,242	4.0	-0.5
Green Bay	87,899	96,466	102,076	9.7	5.8
Indianapolis	700,807	731,321	746,737	4.4	2.1
Kansas City	448,159	435,141	441,259	-2.9	1.4
Little Rock	158,461	175,781	175,752	10.9	-0.0
Madison	170,616	191,262	197,630	12.1	3.3
Milwaukee	636,212	628,088	590,503	-1.3	-6.0
Minneapolis	370,951	368,383	358,785	-0.7	-2.6
Okla. City	403,243	444,730	469,852	10.3	5.6
St. Louis	453,085	396,685	351,565	-12.4	-11.4
St. Paul	270,230	272,235	259,606	0.7	-4.6
Sioux Falls	81,341	100,814	113,223	23.9	12.3
Springfield	133,116	140,494	143,407	5.5	2.1
U.S.	**226,545,805**	**248,765,170**	**265,179,411**	**9.8**	**6.6**

Note: (1) Census Bureau estimate as of 7/96
Source: 1980 Census; 1990 Census of Population and Housing, Summary Tape File 3C

Population Growth: Metro Area

MSA[1]	Population			% Change	
	1980	1990	1996[2]	1980-90	1990-96
Ann Arbor	264,740	282,937	529,898	6.9	87.3
Chicago	6,060,387	6,069,974	7,733,876	0.2	27.4
Des Moines	367,561	392,928	427,436	6.9	8.8
Detroit	4,488,072	4,382,299	4,318,145	-2.4	-1.5
Evansville	276,252	278,990	288,735	1.0	3.5
Fort Wayne	354,156	363,811	475,299	2.7	30.6
Grand Rapids	601,680	688,399	1,015,099	14.4	47.5
Green Bay	175,280	194,594	213,072	11.0	9.5
Indianapolis	1,166,575	1,249,822	1,492,297	7.1	19.4
Kansas City	1,433,458	1,566,280	1,690,343	9.3	7.9
Little Rock	474,464	513,117	548,352	8.1	6.9
Madison	323,545	367,085	395,366	13.5	7.7
Milwaukee	1,397,143	1,432,149	1,457,655	2.5	1.8
Minneapolis	2,137,133	2,464,124	2,765,116	15.3	12.2
Okla. City	860,969	958,839	1,026,657	11.4	7.1
St. Louis	2,376,998	2,444,099	2,548,238	2.8	4.3
Minneapolis	2,137,133	2,464,124	0	15.3	-100.0
Sioux Falls	(a)	123,809	156,598	(a)	26.5
Springfield	207,704	240,593	296,345	15.8	23.2
U.S.	**226,545,805**	**248,765,170**	**265,179,411**	**9.8**	**6.6**

Note: (1) Metropolitan Statistical Area - see Appendix A for areas included; (2) Census Bureau estimate as of 7/96; (a) Sioux Falls was not an MSA in 1980
Source: 1980 Census; 1990 Census of Population and Housing, Summary Tape File 3C

Population Characteristics: City

City	1990 Percent of Total (%)					
	White	Black	American Indian/ Esk./Aleut.	Asian/ Pacific Islander	Other	Hispanic Origin[1]
Ann Arbor	82.3	8.9	0.2	7.8	0.8	2.4
Chicago	45.5	39.0	0.2	3.7	11.5	19.2
Des Moines	89.3	7.1	0.4	2.3	1.0	2.4
Detroit	21.6	75.7	0.3	0.8	1.5	2.6
Evansville	89.5	9.5	0.2	0.6	0.2	0.4
Fort Wayne	80.3	16.7	0.4	1.0	1.6	2.5
Grand Rapids	76.7	18.6	0.8	1.0	2.9	4.5
Green Bay	94.4	0.6	2.3	2.4	0.4	1.1
Indianapolis	75.9	22.5	0.2	0.9	0.4	1.0
Kansas City	66.9	29.6	0.5	1.1	1.9	3.9
Little Rock	64.7	34.1	0.3	0.8	0.1	0.8
Madison	90.8	4.1	0.4	3.9	0.8	1.9
Milwaukee	63.3	30.5	1.0	1.9	3.3	6.0
Minneapolis	78.5	13.0	3.3	4.3	0.8	2.0
Okla. City	74.9	15.9	4.3	2.3	2.6	4.8
St. Louis	51.0	47.4	0.3	0.9	0.4	1.2
St. Paul	82.4	7.5	1.2	7.0	1.9	3.8
Sioux Falls	96.8	0.7	1.4	0.8	0.2	0.7
Springfield	95.6	2.4	0.8	0.9	0.3	0.9
U.S.	**80.3**	**12.0**	**0.8**	**2.9**	**3.9**	**8.8**

Note: (1) People of Hispanic origin can be of any race
Source: 1990 Census of Population and Housing, Summary Tape File 3C

Population Characteristics: Metro Area

MSA[1]	1990 Percent of Total (%)					
	White	Black	American Indian/ Esk./Aleut.	Asian/ Pacific Islander	Other	Hispanic Origin[2]
Ann Arbor	83.8	11.1	0.3	4.2	0.6	2.0
Chicago	67.6	21.9	0.2	3.8	6.5	11.8
Des Moines	93.9	3.7	0.3	1.5	0.7	1.8
Detroit	76.1	21.5	0.4	1.3	0.7	1.8
Evansville	93.5	5.8	0.2	0.5	0.1	0.4
Fort Wayne	89.8	8.3	0.3	0.7	0.9	1.7
Grand Rapids	90.8	5.9	0.5	1.1	1.7	3.1
Green Bay	96.0	0.5	1.8	1.3	0.3	0.8
Indianapolis	85.0	13.7	0.2	0.8	0.3	0.9
Kansas City	84.4	12.8	0.5	1.0	1.3	2.9
Little Rock	78.9	19.9	0.4	0.6	0.3	0.9
Madison	93.9	2.8	0.4	2.3	0.6	1.4
Milwaukee	82.7	13.8	0.6	1.3	1.7	3.4
Minneapolis	92.2	3.6	0.9	2.6	0.6	1.4
Okla. City	81.3	10.5	4.8	1.8	1.7	3.4
St. Louis	81.3	17.3	0.2	0.9	0.3	1.0
Minneapolis	92.2	3.6	0.9	2.6	0.6	1.4
Sioux Falls	97.3	0.6	1.2	0.7	0.2	0.5
Springfield	96.9	1.5	0.8	0.7	0.2	0.8
U.S.	**80.3**	**12.0**	**0.8**	**2.9**	**3.9**	**8.8**

Note: (1) Metropolitan Statistical Area - see Appendix A for areas included;
(2) People of Hispanic origin can be of any race
Source: 1990 Census of Population and Housing, Summary Tape File 3C

Age: City

City	Median Age (Years)	Age Distribution (%)						
		Under 5	Under 18	18-24	25-44	45-64	65+	80+
Ann Arbor	27.1	5.7	17.1	27.1	35.7	12.8	7.3	1.8
Chicago	31.1	7.7	26.0	11.3	33.3	17.7	11.8	2.5
Des Moines	32.2	7.8	24.2	11.9	33.3	17.2	13.3	3.4
Detroit	30.7	9.0	29.4	11.0	30.7	16.7	12.1	2.5
Evansville	34.5	6.9	23.0	10.3	30.9	18.7	17.1	4.2
Fort Wayne	31.5	8.0	26.4	10.9	33.1	16.2	13.4	3.4
Grand Rapids	29.8	9.4	27.6	12.5	32.9	14.0	13.0	3.8
Green Bay	31.3	8.1	25.9	11.2	34.3	16.0	12.7	3.2
Indianapolis	31.6	8.0	25.6	10.4	34.9	17.6	11.4	2.6
Kansas City	32.7	7.7	24.7	9.8	34.2	18.4	12.9	3.2
Little Rock	32.7	7.3	24.9	10.3	34.9	17.4	12.5	3.1
Madison	29.3	6.2	18.5	22.2	35.5	14.6	9.2	2.3
Milwaukee	30.3	8.6	27.5	12.0	32.6	15.5	12.4	3.1
Minneapolis	31.5	7.3	20.6	13.3	39.2	14.1	12.9	3.9
Okla. City	32.3	7.7	25.9	9.9	33.8	18.6	11.8	2.6
St. Louis	32.7	8.0	25.2	10.3	31.2	16.6	16.7	4.7
St. Paul	31.2	8.4	24.5	12.2	35.0	14.5	13.8	3.8
Sioux Falls	31.3	7.9	25.9	11.4	34.8	16.3	11.7	3.0
Springfield	31.7	6.2	20.6	17.8	29.3	17.1	15.2	4.2
U.S.	**32.9**	**7.3**	**25.6**	**10.5**	**32.6**	**18.7**	**12.5**	**2.8**

Source: 1990 Census of Population and Housing, Summary Tape File 3C

Age: Metro Area

MSA[1]	Median Age (Years)	Age Distribution (%)						
		Under 5	Under 18	18-24	25-44	45-64	65+	80+
Ann Arbor	29.2	6.7	21.5	19.4	36.1	15.5	7.5	1.7
Chicago	32.5	7.5	25.4	10.2	33.7	18.9	11.8	2.5
Des Moines	32.5	7.5	25.5	10.7	33.8	18.4	11.7	2.9
Detroit	33.0	7.6	26.1	9.8	33.0	19.2	11.8	2.4
Evansville	34.0	7.0	25.4	9.5	31.8	19.3	14.0	3.2
Fort Wayne	32.1	7.8	27.9	9.7	33.2	17.6	11.6	2.6
Grand Rapids	30.6	8.7	28.6	11.0	33.3	16.6	10.5	2.6
Green Bay	31.4	7.8	27.0	11.0	34.2	17.0	10.8	2.6
Indianapolis	32.3	7.7	26.4	9.8	34.4	18.4	11.1	2.5
Kansas City	32.9	7.7	26.4	9.1	34.2	18.7	11.6	2.8
Little Rock	32.2	7.3	26.5	10.5	33.4	18.2	11.3	2.6
Madison	30.7	7.0	22.7	15.7	36.3	16.0	9.2	2.3
Milwaukee	32.7	7.7	26.3	9.9	32.9	18.4	12.5	3.0
Minneapolis	31.6	8.1	26.3	10.0	36.8	17.1	9.9	2.5
Okla. City	31.9	7.4	26.5	10.8	33.3	18.4	11.0	2.5
St. Louis	33.1	7.5	26.2	9.4	32.7	18.9	12.8	3.1
Minneapolis	31.6	8.1	26.3	10.0	36.8	17.1	9.9	2.5
Sioux Falls	31.4	7.9	27.1	10.5	34.4	16.4	11.6	3.0
Springfield	32.5	6.5	23.8	13.8	31.0	18.3	13.1	3.3
U.S.	**32.9**	**7.3**	**25.6**	**10.5**	**32.6**	**18.7**	**12.5**	**2.8**

Note: (1) Metropolitan Statistical Area - see Appendix A for areas included
Source: 1990 Census of Population and Housing, Summary Tape File 3C

Male/Female Ratio: City

City	Number of males per 100 females (all ages)	Number of males per 100 females (18 years old+)
Ann Arbor	97.4	96.2
Chicago	91.8	88.4
Des Moines	89.0	85.0
Detroit	86.3	80.7
Evansville	86.6	82.2
Fort Wayne	91.2	86.3
Grand Rapids	90.2	85.6
Green Bay	91.8	87.4
Indianapolis	90.4	86.1
Kansas City	90.3	86.6
Little Rock	85.3	81.6
Madison	96.5	92.9
Milwaukee	89.6	84.8
Minneapolis	94.1	92.2
Okla. City	93.3	89.5
St. Louis	83.6	78.1
St. Paul	88.8	85.2
Sioux Falls	91.1	87.4
Springfield	89.4	85.7
U.S.	**95.0**	**91.9**

Source: 1990 Census of Population, General Population Characteristics

Male/Female Ratio: Metro Area

MSA[1]	Number of males per 100 females (all ages)	Number of males per 100 females (18 years old+)
Ann Arbor	97.3	95.8
Chicago	93.3	89.9
Des Moines	91.7	87.4
Detroit	92.7	88.9
Evansville	91.5	87.3
Fort Wayne	94.6	90.7
Grand Rapids	94.8	91.1
Green Bay	95.4	92.1
Indianapolis	92.4	88.4
Kansas City	93.5	89.9
Little Rock	92.0	88.2
Madison	97.4	94.4
Milwaukee	92.9	88.8
Minneapolis	95.5	92.6
Okla. City	95.0	91.3
St. Louis	91.6	87.3
Minneapolis	95.5	92.6
Sioux Falls	92.8	89.5
Springfield	92.2	88.4
U.S.	**95.0**	**91.9**

Note: (1) Metropolitan Statistical Area - see Appendix A for areas included
Source: 1990 Census of Population, General Population Characteristics

Educational Attainment by Race: City

City	High School Graduate (%)					Bachelor's Degree (%)				
	Total	White	Black	Other	Hisp.[1]	Total	White	Black	Other	Hisp.[1]
Ann Arbor	93.9	95.4	77.6	95.2	94.1	64.2	65.9	33.4	78.7	74.0
Chicago	66.0	72.2	63.1	49.2	40.8	19.5	26.6	10.5	15.5	6.6
Des Moines	81.0	82.4	70.7	58.2	61.7	18.9	19.6	10.8	13.6	10.5
Detroit	62.1	61.3	62.6	55.8	45.3	9.6	12.1	8.4	18.7	7.2
Evansville	72.4	73.3	61.3	73.6	61.4	14.6	15.1	7.0	34.0	13.9
Fort Wayne	77.1	79.6	64.4	61.4	60.0	15.7	17.1	6.9	15.3	7.2
Grand Rapids	76.4	80.0	63.8	46.9	41.0	20.8	23.7	7.7	10.7	8.2
Green Bay	80.9	81.8	78.8	54.5	53.0	16.7	17.0	25.9	4.7	6.2
Indianapolis	76.4	79.2	65.2	79.8	75.2	21.7	24.5	9.6	39.4	20.2
Kansas City	78.8	82.9	68.5	68.6	62.4	22.0	26.5	10.0	18.5	11.4
Little Rock	82.0	87.0	68.9	80.5	78.6	30.3	35.4	16.5	45.5	34.7
Madison	90.6	91.0	80.6	89.3	87.2	42.0	41.7	24.8	62.8	48.4
Milwaukee	71.5	76.3	60.2	54.0	46.9	14.8	17.6	6.9	13.2	6.2
Minneapolis	82.6	84.9	71.9	66.3	73.1	30.3	32.8	13.8	21.4	23.8
Okla. City	78.2	80.8	72.6	61.9	47.5	21.6	23.7	12.9	14.9	10.3
St. Louis	62.8	67.4	56.3	66.8	61.9	15.3	20.2	8.0	32.1	18.8
St. Paul	81.1	83.3	76.4	54.7	67.4	26.5	28.0	14.8	16.0	14.8
Sioux Falls	83.4	83.8	50.3	68.1	55.4	22.9	23.1	12.1	13.1	15.3
Springfield	77.0	77.3	70.6	68.9	77.0	20.7	20.9	12.4	20.1	27.6
U.S.	**75.2**	**77.9**	**63.1**	**60.4**	**49.8**	**20.3**	**21.5**	**11.4**	**19.4**	**9.2**

Note: Figures shown cover persons 25 years old and over; (1) people of Hispanic origin can be of any race
Source: 1990 Census of Population and Housing, Summary Tape File 3C

Educational Attainment by Race: Metro Area

MSA[1]	High School Graduate (%)					Bachelor's Degree (%)				
	Total	White	Black	Other	Hisp.[2]	Total	White	Black	Other	Hisp.[2]
Ann Arbor	87.2	88.5	74.3	92.1	82.0	41.9	43.0	21.5	67.0	44.9
Chicago	75.7	80.5	65.6	58.0	44.2	24.4	27.9	11.8	24.0	8.0
Des Moines	85.4	86.2	71.7	66.8	68.9	22.6	23.0	12.1	21.9	12.6
Detroit	75.7	78.5	64.4	73.2	62.9	17.7	19.2	9.9	34.1	13.1
Evansville	75.1	75.8	61.1	77.4	72.3	14.8	15.1	7.5	37.0	20.2
Fort Wayne	80.6	82.0	65.6	65.5	63.0	17.3	18.0	8.0	17.7	9.3
Grand Rapids	80.2	81.6	65.9	54.1	48.0	20.2	21.0	8.4	12.4	7.7
Green Bay	82.6	83.2	71.3	60.9	59.0	17.7	17.9	18.0	8.1	8.1
Indianapolis	78.6	80.4	65.6	79.9	76.3	21.1	22.4	9.9	37.9	21.6
Kansas City	82.3	84.2	70.3	71.8	67.3	23.4	24.9	11.7	22.0	13.3
Little Rock	76.6	79.0	64.8	74.8	76.0	20.4	21.8	13.1	24.7	19.3
Madison	88.9	89.2	80.1	87.0	82.9	34.2	33.8	24.0	57.6	41.5
Milwaukee	79.7	82.5	60.7	60.5	51.7	21.3	23.0	7.6	19.4	8.5
Minneapolis	87.2	88.0	76.2	70.7	76.7	27.1	27.5	17.3	25.2	19.9
Okla. City	79.2	80.6	74.5	68.5	55.3	21.6	22.7	14.2	17.7	11.1
St. Louis	76.0	78.1	64.1	79.9	75.2	20.7	22.1	11.4	40.5	24.3
Minneapolis	87.2	88.0	76.2	70.7	76.7	27.1	27.5	17.3	25.2	19.9
Sioux Falls	83.1	83.5	53.4	67.7	57.4	21.3	21.4	11.3	12.7	12.8
Springfield	78.5	78.8	71.8	71.0	77.7	19.6	19.7	14.4	19.1	23.2
U.S.	**75.2**	**77.9**	**63.1**	**60.4**	**49.8**	**20.3**	**21.5**	**11.4**	**19.4**	**9.2**

Note: Figures shown cover persons 25 years old and over; (1) Metropolitan Statistical Area - see Appendix A for areas included; (2) people of Hispanic origin can be of any race
Source: 1990 Census of Population and Housing, Summary Tape File 3C

Per Capita/Median/Average Income: City

City	Per Capita ($)	Median Household ($)	Average Household ($)
Ann Arbor	17,786	33,344	44,963
Chicago	12,899	26,301	34,682
Des Moines	13,710	26,703	33,199
Detroit	9,443	18,742	25,601
Evansville	12,564	22,936	29,445
Fort Wayne	12,726	26,344	31,336
Grand Rapids	12,070	26,809	32,106
Green Bay	12,969	26,770	32,080
Indianapolis	14,478	29,006	35,946
Kansas City	13,799	26,713	33,510
Little Rock	15,307	26,889	36,897
Madison	15,143	29,420	36,977
Milwaukee	11,106	23,627	28,415
Minneapolis	14,830	25,324	33,245
Okla. City	13,528	25,741	33,258
St. Louis	10,798	19,458	25,605
St. Paul	13,727	26,498	33,259
Sioux Falls	13,677	27,286	34,023
Springfield	11,878	21,577	28,471
U.S.	**14,420**	**30,056**	**38,453**

Note: Figures are for 1989
Source: 1990 Census of Population and Housing, Summary Tape File 3C

Per Capita/Median/Average Income: Metro Area

MSA[1]	Per Capita ($)	Median Household ($)	Average Household ($)
Ann Arbor	17,115	36,307	45,105
Chicago	16,447	35,265	44,583
Des Moines	14,972	31,182	37,958
Detroit	15,694	34,612	42,218
Evansville	13,265	27,229	33,710
Fort Wayne	14,287	31,689	37,952
Grand Rapids	14,370	33,515	39,827
Green Bay	13,906	31,303	36,923
Indianapolis	15,159	31,655	39,103
Kansas City	15,067	31,613	38,701
Little Rock	12,809	26,501	33,336
Madison	15,542	32,703	39,589
Milwaukee	14,785	32,316	38,958
Minneapolis	16,842	36,565	43,942
Okla. City	13,269	26,883	34,117
St. Louis	14,917	31,774	39,114
Minneapolis	16,842	36,565	43,942
Sioux Falls	13,345	27,764	34,116
Springfield	12,250	24,546	31,107
U.S.	**14,420**	**30,056**	**38,453**

Note: Figures are for 1989; (1) Metropolitan Statistical Area - see Appendix A for areas included
Source: 1990 Census of Population and Housing, Summary Tape File 3C

Household Income Distribution: City

City	\% of Households Earning								
	Less than $5,000	$5,000 -$9,999	$10,000 -$14,999	$15,000 -$24,999	$25,000 -$34,999	$35,000 -$49,999	$50,000 -$74,999	$75,000 -$99,999	$100,000 and up
Ann Arbor	5.6	7.9	8.4	15.7	14.6	15.3	17.3	7.5	7.8
Chicago	10.6	10.2	8.9	18.0	15.4	16.6	12.8	4.0	3.5
Des Moines	6.0	10.2	10.2	20.2	18.7	18.1	11.5	2.7	2.3
Detroit	16.1	16.2	10.9	16.5	13.0	13.6	9.7	2.8	1.2
Evansville	8.3	13.0	11.3	21.1	16.9	16.3	9.1	1.9	2.2
Fort Wayne	5.0	9.9	10.1	22.1	18.6	18.9	11.5	2.3	1.5
Grand Rapids	6.1	11.2	10.0	19.3	17.9	18.4	12.4	2.9	1.9
Green Bay	4.2	12.4	10.7	19.6	17.8	19.5	11.5	2.5	1.8
Indianapolis	5.9	8.6	9.0	19.1	17.0	18.8	14.4	4.0	3.2
Kansas City	8.4	9.5	9.5	19.2	16.8	17.3	12.9	3.5	2.9
Little Rock	7.1	9.7	10.1	19.3	16.0	15.6	13.7	4.1	4.4
Madison	5.8	9.2	9.1	18.0	16.5	18.1	14.7	4.8	3.7
Milwaukee	6.3	14.9	11.2	20.0	16.6	17.5	10.6	2.1	1.0
Minneapolis	6.3	12.7	10.6	19.8	15.8	16.2	11.9	3.6	3.2
Okla. City	6.9	10.6	10.4	20.7	16.9	16.1	12.3	3.3	2.8
St. Louis	12.5	15.3	12.3	20.7	14.8	12.6	8.4	2.0	1.3
St. Paul	5.3	12.4	9.7	19.8	16.5	17.7	12.6	3.6	2.5
Sioux Falls	5.4	8.3	9.8	21.5	19.2	19.3	11.2	2.6	2.7
Springfield	8.3	13.1	12.9	22.8	17.1	13.7	7.9	1.8	2.3
U.S.	**6.2**	**9.3**	**8.8**	**17.5**	**15.8**	**17.9**	**15.0**	**5.1**	**4.4**

Note: Figures are for 1989
Source: 1990 Census of Population and Housing, Summary Tape File 3C

Household Income Distribution: Metro Area

MSA[1]	\% of Households Earning								
	Less than $5,000	$5,000 -$9,999	$10,000 -$14,999	$15,000 -$24,999	$25,000 -$34,999	$35,000 -$49,999	$50,000 -$74,999	$75,000 -$99,999	$100,000 and up
Ann Arbor	4.7	6.7	7.4	14.9	14.5	17.9	19.7	7.7	6.6
Chicago	6.2	7.0	6.7	14.8	14.9	19.1	18.4	6.9	6.1
Des Moines	4.2	7.7	8.6	18.1	17.9	20.5	15.3	4.3	3.3
Detroit	6.3	8.6	7.3	14.2	14.1	18.7	18.7	7.1	5.1
Evansville	6.7	10.4	9.5	19.0	16.7	18.7	13.1	3.2	2.6
Fort Wayne	3.6	7.3	8.0	18.9	17.8	21.3	16.1	4.1	2.9
Grand Rapids	3.3	7.3	7.5	16.5	17.7	22.3	17.2	4.6	3.6
Green Bay	3.1	9.2	8.8	17.4	18.0	22.1	15.2	3.5	2.8
Indianapolis	4.7	7.5	8.2	18.0	16.7	19.7	16.5	4.9	3.8
Kansas City	5.3	7.6	8.1	17.4	16.9	19.5	16.4	4.9	3.8
Little Rock	7.2	9.5	10.0	20.3	17.0	17.5	12.6	3.1	2.8
Madison	4.0	7.3	7.9	17.2	16.8	20.8	17.0	5.1	3.9
Milwaukee	3.8	9.5	8.2	16.5	15.9	20.7	17.1	4.8	3.6
Minneapolis	3.1	7.0	6.5	15.1	15.7	21.5	19.7	6.3	5.1
Okla. City	6.6	9.9	9.9	20.0	17.2	17.3	13.0	3.5	2.7
St. Louis	5.6	8.2	8.2	16.8	16.1	19.6	16.7	5.0	4.0
Minneapolis	3.1	7.0	6.5	15.1	15.7	21.5	19.7	6.3	5.1
Sioux Falls	5.2	8.3	9.6	20.9	19.4	19.7	11.6	2.7	2.6
Springfield	6.9	11.1	11.5	21.5	18.1	16.3	9.9	2.3	2.5
U.S.	**6.2**	**9.3**	**8.8**	**17.5**	**15.8**	**17.9**	**15.0**	**5.1**	**4.4**

Note: Figures are for 1989; (1) Metropolitan Statistical Area - see Appendix A for areas included
Source: 1990 Census of Population and Housing, Summary Tape File 3C

Effective Buying Income: City

City	Per Capita ($)	Median Household ($)	Average Household ($)
Ann Arbor	20,402	39,335	53,055
Chicago	14,522	30,801	39,965
Des Moines	15,945	31,815	39,166
Detroit	10,494	21,282	28,758
Evansville	14,699	26,934	34,510
Fort Wayne	14,788	30,705	36,481
Grand Rapids	14,498	32,240	39,150
Green Bay	15,258	31,437	37,873
Indianapolis	16,864	34,180	41,684
Kansas City	15,668	31,151	38,554
Little Rock	19,056	34,656	46,227
Madison	18,060	35,715	44,921
Milwaukee	12,791	27,645	33,288
Minneapolis	16,584	29,198	38,076
Okla. City	14,310	27,900	35,878
St. Louis	13,029	23,855	31,315
St. Paul	15,367	30,562	37,865
Sioux Falls	19,120	38,680	48,250
Springfield	14,463	27,023	35,612
U.S.	**15,444**	**33,201**	**41,849**

Note: Data as of 1/1/97
Source: Standard Rate & Data Service, Newspaper Advertising Source, 2/98

Effective Buying Income: Metro Area

MSA[1]	Per Capita ($)	Median Household ($)	Average Household ($)
Ann Arbor	18,945	44,359	52,666
Chicago	19,019	43,449	53,209
Des Moines	17,860	38,151	45,650
Detroit	17,547	39,473	46,927
Evansville	15,956	33,145	40,460
Fort Wayne	16,451	37,274	43,762
Grand Rapids	16,479	38,944	45,860
Green Bay	16,720	38,117	44,484
Indianapolis	18,101	38,688	46,658
Kansas City	17,469	37,630	45,369
Little Rock	16,504	34,959	43,421
Madison	19,162	41,369	49,101
Milwaukee	17,074	38,746	45,403
Minneapolis	18,341	41,838	48,729
Okla. City	14,773	30,781	38,771
St. Louis	17,353	38,436	45,932
Minneapolis	18,341	41,838	48,729
Sioux Falls	19,128	40,760	49,939
Springfield	14,732	30,485	38,454
U.S.	**15,444**	**33,201**	**41,849**

Note: Data as of 1/1/97; (1) Metropolitan Statistical Area - see Appendix A for areas included
Source: Standard Rate & Data Service, Newspaper Advertising Source, 2/98

Effective Household Buying Income Distribution: City

City	% of Households Earning						
	$10,000 -$19,999	$20,000 -$34,999	$35,000 -$49,999	$50,000 -$74,999	$75,000 -$99,000	$100,000 -$124,999	$125,000 and up
Ann Arbor	14.3	20.0	15.4	19.6	10.5	4.6	5.2
Chicago	16.2	22.4	17.1	16.6	6.1	2.1	2.4
Des Moines	17.5	25.8	20.1	17.0	4.8	1.2	1.7
Detroit	20.6	20.1	14.5	12.2	3.8	1.0	0.5
Evansville	20.5	25.9	17.5	14.1	3.1	1.0	1.6
Fort Wayne	18.3	27.5	20.3	16.5	4.2	1.0	1.0
Grand Rapids	17.4	24.4	19.5	18.2	5.2	1.5	1.3
Green Bay	19.1	25.0	20.3	17.3	4.4	1.1	1.2
Indianapolis	15.8	24.2	19.0	19.0	6.6	2.0	2.1
Kansas City	17.0	24.2	18.2	17.0	5.5	1.7	1.8
Little Rock	15.8	23.1	16.7	18.3	7.8	2.8	3.8
Madison	15.1	23.2	17.8	19.9	7.9	2.7	2.6
Milwaukee	21.0	24.9	18.3	15.5	3.5	0.7	0.5
Minneapolis	19.7	24.5	17.1	15.8	4.9	1.8	1.8
Okla. City	20.0	26.3	17.2	14.7	4.1	1.3	1.6
St. Louis	21.8	24.2	14.8	12.2	3.8	1.0	1.0
St. Paul	18.4	25.0	18.8	16.7	5.1	1.3	1.5
Sioux Falls	13.3	23.1	20.4	21.1	8.0	2.5	3.1
Springfield	21.3	27.1	16.9	12.6	3.8	1.1	1.9
U.S.	**16.5**	**23.4**	**18.3**	**18.2**	**6.4**	**2.1**	**2.4**

Note: Data as of 1/1/97
Source: Standard Rate & Data Service, Newspaper Advertising Source, 2/98

Effective Household Buying Income Distribution: Metro Area

MSA[1]	% of Households Earning						
	$10,000 -$19,999	$20,000 -$34,999	$35,000 -$49,999	$50,000 -$74,999	$75,000 -$99,000	$100,000 -$124,999	$125,000 and up
Ann Arbor	11.7	19.0	17.9	24.1	11.5	4.2	3.8
Chicago	11.3	18.8	18.1	23.1	10.6	4.1	4.6
Des Moines	13.9	23.1	20.4	21.8	7.6	2.4	2.4
Detroit	13.5	19.1	17.7	22.0	9.6	3.2	3.0
Evansville	16.8	23.5	18.6	19.6	5.6	1.8	1.8
Fort Wayne	14.2	24.3	21.2	21.8	6.7	1.9	1.8
Grand Rapids	13.6	22.2	20.7	22.9	7.5	2.3	2.3
Green Bay	14.8	22.4	21.6	22.2	7.0	1.8	2.0
Indianapolis	13.8	22.3	18.9	21.9	8.7	2.7	2.7
Kansas City	13.9	22.7	19.6	21.1	7.9	2.5	2.6
Little Rock	15.2	23.6	18.4	19.4	7.3	2.3	2.5
Madison	12.4	21.5	19.1	24.1	9.2	3.1	3.1
Milwaukee	14.5	21.4	19.7	22.9	7.8	2.2	2.4
Minneapolis	12.0	21.1	20.7	24.5	8.6	2.8	2.9
Okla. City	17.9	25.4	18.2	16.8	5.3	1.5	1.7
St. Louis	13.9	21.4	19.5	21.6	8.3	2.6	2.7
Minneapolis	12.0	21.1	20.7	24.5	8.6	2.8	2.9
Sioux Falls	12.6	21.7	19.9	22.9	8.7	3.0	3.4
Springfield	18.7	26.1	18.9	15.4	4.8	1.3	2.0
U.S.	**16.5**	**23.4**	**18.3**	**18.2**	**6.4**	**2.1**	**2.4**

Note: Data as of 1/1/97; (1) Metropolitan Statistical Area - see Appendix A for areas included
Source: Standard Rate & Data Service, Newspaper Advertising Source, 2/98

Poverty Rates by Race and Age: City

City	Total (%)	By Race (%)				By Age (%)		
		White	Black	Other	Hisp.[1]	Under 5 years old	Under 18 years old	65 years and over
Ann Arbor	16.1	14.4	20.8	27.2	21.5	9.8	8.4	7.4
Chicago	21.6	11.0	33.2	23.7	24.2	35.6	33.9	15.9
Des Moines	12.9	11.0	30.8	23.5	18.3	21.8	19.3	9.1
Detroit	32.4	21.9	35.2	36.7	35.7	52.7	46.6	20.1
Evansville	14.6	12.1	37.4	21.8	15.7	25.5	21.7	12.5
Fort Wayne	11.5	8.4	25.8	16.4	11.9	18.6	16.5	9.0
Grand Rapids	16.1	10.8	33.8	31.1	33.3	24.6	23.2	10.0
Green Bay	13.4	11.1	17.4	56.7	34.2	25.1	19.2	9.9
Indianapolis	12.5	8.4	26.4	13.8	13.0	20.1	18.9	11.7
Kansas City	15.3	8.7	29.6	21.8	18.4	26.2	22.8	14.6
Little Rock	14.6	7.2	28.9	12.4	19.8	23.6	21.7	13.5
Madison	16.1	13.8	35.2	42.2	22.9	15.7	13.2	4.8
Milwaukee	22.2	10.8	41.9	40.2	35.5	41.5	37.8	10.0
Minneapolis	18.5	11.7	40.5	47.4	28.9	33.1	30.6	11.0
Okla. City	15.9	11.2	32.4	25.6	30.7	27.4	22.9	13.1
St. Louis	24.6	12.6	37.4	26.0	23.5	41.4	39.7	18.7
St. Paul	16.7	10.2	39.2	52.3	25.6	30.6	26.9	10.7
Sioux Falls	8.5	7.6	30.4	40.5	25.2	11.4	9.6	9.5
Springfield	17.8	17.0	30.7	42.2	30.1	26.4	21.2	13.4
U.S.	**13.1**	**9.8**	**29.5**	**23.1**	**25.3**	**20.1**	**18.3**	**12.8**

Note: Figures show the percent of people living below the poverty line in 1989. The average poverty threshold was $12,674 for a family of four in 1989; (1) People of Hispanic origin can be of any race
Source: 1990 Census of Population and Housing, Summary Tape File 3C

Poverty Rates by Race and Age: Metro Area

MSA[1]	Total (%)	By Race (%)				By Age (%)		
		White	Black	Other	Hisp.[2]	Under 5 years old	Under 18 years old	65 years and over
Ann Arbor	12.2	10.0	23.0	25.8	18.9	12.6	10.8	8.0
Chicago	12.4	5.8	30.0	18.4	20.7	19.9	19.1	10.5
Des Moines	8.8	7.7	29.6	19.9	14.3	14.4	11.7	8.5
Detroit	12.9	7.1	33.0	17.7	20.6	22.9	19.6	10.5
Evansville	11.4	9.8	36.6	14.8	16.8	18.3	15.0	12.4
Fort Wayne	7.6	5.8	24.9	15.7	10.6	12.3	10.0	8.3
Grand Rapids	8.3	6.4	31.4	20.0	22.9	12.5	10.7	8.1
Green Bay	9.2	7.8	14.6	47.9	27.1	16.7	12.1	8.5
Indianapolis	9.6	6.9	26.2	12.1	11.5	15.1	13.7	10.3
Kansas City	9.8	6.9	28.1	16.1	14.9	15.9	13.7	11.2
Little Rock	13.5	9.2	30.8	12.2	17.4	19.8	18.2	16.8
Madison	10.5	8.9	35.0	37.6	21.3	10.6	8.8	5.0
Milwaukee	11.6	5.8	41.3	32.8	30.3	22.5	19.4	7.1
Minneapolis	8.1	5.9	37.0	32.7	19.1	13.2	11.2	8.2
Okla. City	13.9	10.8	30.8	24.1	26.6	22.8	18.6	13.1
St. Louis	10.8	6.3	31.3	14.7	13.1	17.6	15.9	10.3
Minneapolis	8.1	5.9	37.0	32.7	19.1	13.2	11.2	8.2
Sioux Falls	8.0	7.3	31.2	39.9	24.9	10.2	8.8	10.3
Springfield	13.5	13.0	28.4	34.3	20.0	20.4	15.4	13.8
U.S.	**13.1**	**9.8**	**29.5**	**23.1**	**25.3**	**20.1**	**18.3**	**12.8**

Note: Figures show the percent of people living below the poverty line in 1989. The average poverty threshold was $12,674 for a family of four in 1989; (1) Metropolitan Statistical Area - see Appendix A for areas included; (2) People of Hispanic origin can be of any race
Source: 1990 Census of Population and Housing, Summary Tape File 3C

Major State and Local Tax Rates

City	State Corp. Income (%)	State Personal Income (%)	Residential Property (effective rate per $100)	Sales & Use State (%)	Sales & Use Local (%)	State Gasoline (cents/ gallon)	State Cigarette (cents/ 20-pack)
Ann Arbor	2.3[a]	4.4	n/a	6.0	None	19	75
Chicago	7.3[b]	3.0	1.79	6.25	2.5	19.3[c]	58[d]
Des Moines	6.0 - 12.0	0.4 - 9.98	2.95	5.0	None	20	36
Detroit	2.3[a]	4.4	2.76	6.0	None	19	75
Evansville	7.9[e]	3.4	n/a	5.0	None	15	15.5
Fort Wayne	7.9[e]	3.4	n/a	5.0	None	15	15.5
Grand Rapids	2.3[a]	4.4	n/a	6.0	None	19	75
Green Bay	7.9[f]	4.9 - 6.93	n/a	5.0	None	24.8	59
Indianapolis	7.9[e]	3.4	1.93	5.0	None	15	15.5
Kansas City	6.25	1.5 - 6.0	1.20	4.225	2.375	17.05[g]	17[h]
Little Rock	1.0 - 6.5	1.0 - 7.0[i]	1.25	4.625	1.5	18.7[j]	31.5
Madison	7.9[f]	4.9 - 6.93	n/a	5.0	0.5	24.8	59
Milwaukee	7.9[f]	4.9 - 6.93	3.32	5.0	0.5	24.8	59
Minneapolis	9.8[k]	6.0 - 8.5	1.34	6.5	0.5	20	48
Okla. City	6.0	0.5 - 7.0[l]	1.10	4.5	3.875	17[m]	23
Saint Louis	6.25	1.5 - 6.0	n/a	4.225	2.625	17.05[g]	17[h]
Saint Paul	9.8[k]	6.0 - 8.5	n/a	6.5	0.5	20	48
Sioux Falls	None	None	2.23	4.0	2.0	21[n]	33
Springfield	6.25	1.5 - 6.0	n/a	4.225	1.875	17.05[g]	17[h]

(a) Value added tax imposed on the sum of federal taxable income of the business, compensation paid to employees, dividends, interest, royalties paid and other items; (b) Includes a 2.5% personal property replacement tax; (c) Rate is comprised of 19 cents excise and 0.3 cent motor carrier tax. Carriers pay an additional surcharge of 6.3 cents. Rate does not include a 5 cent local option tax in Chicago.; (d) Counties and cities may impose an additional tax of 10 - 15 cents per pack; (e) Consists of 3.4% on income from sources within the state plus a 4.5% supplemental income tax; (f) Plus a surtax set annually by the Dept. of Revenue to finance a special recycling fund; (g) Rate is comprised of 17 cents excise and 0.05 cents motor carrier tax; (h) Counties and cities may impose an additional tax of 4 - 7 cents per pack; (i) A special tax table is available for low income taxpayers reducing their tax payments; (j) Rate is comprised of 18.5 cents excise plus 0.2 cent motor carrier tax; (k) 5.8% alternative minimum tax rate; (l) Range is for persons not deducting federal income tax. Separate schedules, with rates ranging from 0.5% to 10%, apply to taxpayers deducting federal income taxes; (m) Rate is comprised of 16 cents excise and 1 cent motor carrier tax; (n) Does not include a 1 cent local option tax
Source: Source: Federation of Tax Administrators, www.taxadmin.org; Washington D.C. Department of Finance and Revenue, Tax Rates and Tax Burdens in the District of Columbia: A Nationwide Comparison, June 1997; Chambers of Commerce

Employment by Industry

MSA[1]	Services	Retail	Gov't.	Manuf.	Finance/ Ins./R.E.	Whole- sale	Transp./ Utilities	Constr.	Mining
Ann Arbor	23.9	17.2	26.6	19.4	3.6	3.2	2.4	3.7	(a)
Chicago	31.0	16.6	11.9	16.1	7.7	6.6	6.2	3.9	0.0
Des Moines	28.6	18.6	12.6	9.3	14.0	7.8	5.0	4.0	(a)
Detroit	30.4	18.0	11.0	21.0	5.3	6.0	4.5	3.8	0.0
Evansville	28.1	20.1	9.2	20.6	4.9	5.5	4.5	6.1	0.8
Fort Wayne	22.7	18.6	10.2	27.6	5.5	5.9	4.7	4.8	(a)
Grand Rapids	25.8	18.5	9.9	27.7	4.0	6.4	3.4	4.2	(a)
Green Bay	24.5	18.6	11.8	20.9	7.0	5.1	7.3	4.8	(a)
Indianapolis	26.8	19.9	12.3	15.1	7.5	6.6	6.1	5.6	0.1
Kansas City	29.1	18.0	14.4	11.5	7.0	6.9	8.2	4.9	(a)
Little Rock	29.1	17.7	19.4	10.9	5.7	5.7	7.0	4.6	(a)
Madison	25.1	17.6	26.1	10.9	8.0	4.3	3.5	4.5	(a)
Milwaukee	30.9	15.9	10.9	21.1	6.9	6.0	4.8	3.7	(a)
Minneapolis	29.2	18.1	13.7	16.7	7.1	6.3	5.5	0.0	(a)
Okla. City	29.0	19.3	20.3	10.8	5.8	4.8	4.9	3.5	1.5
Sioux Falls	29.1	19.1	9.7	13.8	11.7	6.4	6.1	4.1	(a)
Springfield	29.6	20.6	12.7	14.8	4.2	7.6	6.5	3.9	(a)
St. Louis	31.2	18.7	12.0	15.1	6.1	5.5	6.3	5.1	(a)
St. Paul	29.2	18.1	13.7	16.7	7.1	6.3	5.5	0.0	(a)
U.S.	**29.0**	**18.5**	**16.1**	**15.0**	**5.7**	**5.4**	**5.3**	**4.5**	**0.5**

Note: Figures cover non-farm employment as of 12/97 and are not seasonally adjusted; (1) Metropolitan Statistical Area - see Appendix A for areas included; (a) Mining is included with construction
Source: Bureau of Labor Statistics, http://stats.bls.gov

Labor Force, Employment and Job Growth: City

Area	Civilian Labor Force			Workers Employed		
	Dec. '95	Dec. '96	% Chg.	Dec. '95	Dec. '96	% Chg.
Ann Arbor	64,579	65,522	1.5	63,445	64,638	1.9
Chicago	1,296,199	1,302,194	0.5	1,214,188	1,228,468	1.2
Des Moines	124,126	122,224	-1.5	119,030	118,815	-0.2
Detroit	381,698	383,793	0.5	350,392	359,642	2.6
Evansville	66,141	67,551	2.1	63,615	64,767	1.8
Fort Wayne	96,729	98,230	1.6	93,186	95,064	2.0
Grand Rapids	106,407	108,997	2.4	101,567	104,958	3.3
Green Bay	63,099	63,098	-0.0	60,850	60,859	0.0
Indianapolis	412,855	422,096	2.2	400,442	408,340	2.0
Kansas City	260,223	257,747	-1.0	247,614	247,479	-0.1
Little Rock	102,342	102,286	-0.1	98,638	98,814	0.2
Madison	131,512	132,730	0.9	129,633	130,800	0.9
Milwaukee	303,317	304,693	0.5	290,767	292,703	0.7
Minneapolis	204,784	210,251	2.7	198,486	205,500	3.5
Okla. City	240,757	242,717	0.8	232,794	235,344	1.1
Sioux Falls	68,714	71,175	3.6	67,161	69,915	4.1
Springfield	89,287	86,224	-3.4	85,902	83,484	-2.8
St. Louis	175,321	170,036	-3.0	162,212	159,081	-1.9
St. Paul	141,218	145,162	2.8	137,003	141,844	3.5
U.S.	**134,583,000**	**136,742,000**	**1.6**	**127,903,000**	**130,785,000**	**2.3**

Note: Data is not seasonally adjusted and covers workers 16 years of age and older
Source: Bureau of Labor Statistics, http://stats.bls.gov

Labor Force, Employment and Job Growth: Metro Area

Area	Civilian Labor Force			Workers Employed		
	Dec. '95	Dec. '96	% Chg.	Dec. '95	Dec. '96	% Chg.
Ann Arbor	282,399	285,916	1.2	275,064	280,236	1.9
Chicago	4,075,063	4,103,252	0.7	3,879,369	3,924,995	1.2
Des Moines	260,007	257,079	-1.1	251,932	251,475	-0.2
Detroit	2,172,045	2,211,680	1.8	2,088,728	2,143,873	2.6
Evansville	152,268	155,119	1.9	146,505	149,547	2.1
Fort Wayne	259,607	264,256	1.8	252,228	257,310	2.0
Grand Rapids	560,545	575,496	2.7	541,647	559,732	3.3
Green Bay	130,906	130,951	0.0	127,679	127,699	0.0
Indianapolis	809,267	826,621	2.1	788,116	803,660	2.0
Kansas City	953,956	962,004	0.8	916,305	930,387	1.5
Little Rock	297,598	297,812	0.1	286,356	286,868	0.2
Madison	260,593	262,982	0.9	256,981	259,295	0.9
Milwaukee	808,675	812,953	0.5	786,315	791,550	0.7
Minneapolis	1,615,254	1,658,390	2.7	1,572,977	1,627,030	3.4
Okla. City	520,768	525,249	0.9	505,201	510,735	1.1
Sioux Falls	93,356	96,724	3.6	91,368	95,114	4.1
Springfield	173,763	167,604	-3.5	167,246	162,539	-2.8
St. Louis	1,382,326	1,356,484	-1.9	1,323,456	1,303,910	-1.5
St. Paul	1,615,254	1,658,390	2.7	1,572,977	1,627,030	3.4
U.S.	**134,583,000**	**136,742,000**	**1.6**	**127,903,000**	**130,785,000**	**2.3**

Note: Data is not seasonally adjusted and covers workers 16 years of age and older;
(1) Metropolitan Statistical Area - see Appendix A for areas included
Source: Bureau of Labor Statistics, http://stats.bls.gov

Unemployment Rate: City

Area	1997											
	Jan.	Feb.	Mar.	Apr.	May	Jun.	Jul.	Aug.	Sep.	Oct.	Nov.	Dec.
Ann Arbor	2.3	2.0	1.9	1.9	1.6	2.0	2.1	1.5	1.6	1.5	1.5	1.3
Chicago	6.4	6.4	6.4	6.2	5.9	6.0	5.9	5.8	5.9	5.8	5.8	5.7
Des Moines	4.4	4.1	3.7	3.5	3.0	3.2	2.4	2.6	2.6	2.3	2.6	2.8
Detroit	9.7	8.3	8.0	7.8	7.1	8.4	10.1	6.9	7.6	6.6	6.5	6.3
Evansville	4.7	4.5	4.8	4.9	4.4	4.4	4.9	4.5	4.3	4.9	4.3	4.1
Fort Wayne	3.6	3.4	3.6	3.4	3.1	3.4	3.4	3.6	3.4	3.7	3.2	3.2
Grand Rapids	5.6	5.2	4.9	4.1	4.2	5.2	5.1	4.1	4.1	3.7	3.9	3.7
Green Bay	4.9	5.0	4.9	4.5	4.2	5.1	4.7	4.2	4.3	3.8	3.9	3.5
Indianapolis	2.9	2.8	3.0	3.1	2.9	3.0	2.9	3.0	3.1	3.4	3.0	3.3
Kansas City	4.5	4.5	4.2	5.2	4.3	4.5	4.2	4.4	4.6	4.2	4.0	4.0
Little Rock	3.7	3.9	3.7	3.3	3.4	4.2	4.4	4.3	3.8	3.4	3.0	3.4
Madison	1.9	2.0	2.0	1.8	1.8	2.1	2.0	1.7	1.7	1.5	1.6	1.5
Milwaukee	5.5	5.7	5.0	4.9	5.2	5.9	6.2	5.6	5.4	4.8	4.6	3.9
Minneapolis	3.2	2.7	2.7	2.8	2.8	3.7	3.2	3.4	4.0	3.5	2.7	2.3
Okla. City	3.9	3.4	3.0	2.8	3.1	3.2	2.9	3.2	3.5	3.5	3.1	3.0
Sioux Falls	2.8	2.4	2.4	1.8	1.7	1.8	1.6	1.7	1.6	1.4	1.6	1.8
Springfield	4.0	3.7	3.5	3.3	3.2	3.4	2.8	3.2	2.8	3.0	3.1	3.2
St. Louis	6.6	6.8	6.7	6.9	6.9	6.9	6.4	7.1	6.3	6.8	6.4	6.4
St. Paul	3.4	2.9	2.8	3.0	2.8	4.0	3.2	3.3	4.0	3.4	2.6	2.3
U.S.	**5.9**	**5.7**	**5.5**	**4.8**	**4.7**	**5.2**	**5.0**	**4.8**	**4.7**	**4.4**	**4.3**	**4.4**

Note: All figures are percentages, are not seasonally adjusted and covers workers 16 years of age and older
Source: Bureau of Labor Statistics, http://stats.bls.gov

Unemployment Rate: Metro Area

Area	1997											
	Jan.	Feb.	Mar.	Apr.	May	Jun.	Jul.	Aug.	Sep.	Oct.	Nov.	Dec.
Ann Arbor	3.6	3.1	2.9	2.7	2.2	2.6	3.1	2.1	2.2	1.9	2.0	2.0
Chicago	5.2	5.2	5.1	4.7	4.2	4.3	4.3	4.2	4.1	4.0	4.1	4.3
Des Moines	3.4	3.2	2.9	2.7	2.3	2.4	1.8	2.0	2.0	1.8	2.0	2.2
Detroit	4.9	4.3	4.1	3.8	3.4	4.0	4.9	3.3	3.6	3.2	3.2	3.1
Evansville	4.5	4.2	4.5	4.3	3.9	4.1	4.8	4.0	3.8	4.1	3.7	3.6
Fort Wayne	2.8	2.7	3.0	2.8	2.6	2.7	2.9	2.8	2.7	2.9	2.5	2.6
Grand Rapids	4.5	4.1	3.7	3.1	3.0	3.7	3.5	2.9	3.0	2.8	2.9	2.7
Green Bay	3.5	3.6	3.5	3.2	3.0	3.5	3.2	2.9	2.9	2.6	2.7	2.5
Indianapolis	2.6	2.6	2.7	2.6	2.5	2.6	2.6	2.6	2.6	2.9	2.6	2.8
Kansas City	4.0	3.9	3.6	4.1	3.5	3.6	3.4	3.4	3.6	3.4	3.3	3.3
Little Rock	4.1	4.3	4.0	3.4	3.4	4.1	4.4	4.2	3.8	3.5	3.3	3.7
Madison	2.0	2.0	2.0	1.7	1.5	1.8	1.7	1.5	1.5	1.3	1.4	1.4
Milwaukee	3.6	3.7	3.5	3.3	3.5	3.9	4.0	3.6	3.5	3.1	3.0	2.6
Minneapolis	3.0	2.6	2.5	2.5	2.1	2.9	2.3	2.4	2.8	2.5	2.0	1.9
Okla. City	3.5	3.1	2.8	2.6	2.8	2.9	2.8	2.9	3.1	3.2	2.9	2.8
Sioux Falls	2.6	2.3	2.3	1.7	1.6	1.7	1.5	1.6	1.5	1.4	1.6	1.7
Springfield	4.2	3.9	3.5	3.3	3.1	3.3	2.7	3.0	2.5	2.7	2.9	3.0
St. Louis	4.6	4.3	4.0	3.9	3.7	4.0	4.3	3.9	3.7	3.6	3.6	3.9
St. Paul	3.0	2.6	2.5	2.5	2.1	2.9	2.3	2.4	2.8	2.5	2.0	1.9
U.S.	**5.9**	**5.7**	**5.5**	**4.8**	**4.7**	**5.2**	**5.0**	**4.8**	**4.7**	**4.4**	**4.3**	**4.4**

Note: All figures are percentages, are not seasonally adjusted and covers workers 16 years of age and older
(1) Metropolitan Statistical Area - see Appendix A for areas included
Source: Bureau of Labor Statistics, http://stats.bls.gov

Average Wages: Selected Professional Occupations

MSA[1] (Month/Year)	Accountant III	Attorney III	Computer Program. II	Engineer III	Systems Analyst II	Systems Analyst Supv./Mgr. II
Ann Arbor (7/95)	-	-	-	-	878	-
Chicago (6/96)	781	1,281	681	987	969	1,504
Des Moines (6/95)	-	-	593	-	876	-
Detroit (1/96)	840	1,357	672	958	940	1,421
Evansville (8/94)	837	-	521	-	903	-
Fort Wayne (2/94)	-	-	633	-	823	-
Grand Rapids (5/95)	-	-	-	-	-	-
Green Bay (5/94)	-	-	569	-	823	-
Indianapolis (8/96)	785	1,385	606	908	918	-
Kansas City (9/96)	805	1,285	677	900	958	1,400
Little Rock (12/94)	649	1,022	473	-	741	-
Madison (3/94)	-	-	600	-	807	-
Milwaukee (9/96)	811	1,339	662	988	940	-
Minneapolis (2/96)	812	1,338	652	946	958	1,364
Okla. City (7/96)	-	-	586	-	907	-
Sioux Falls (5/95)	-	-	548	-	-	-
Springfield (6/95)	-	-	515	-	803	-
St. Louis (3/96)	760	1,254	601	859	-	1,426
St. Paul (2/96)	812	1,338	652	946	958	1,364

Notes: Figures are average weekly earnings; Dashes indicate that data was not available;
(1) Metropolitan Statistical Area - see Appendix A for areas included
Source: Bureau of Labor Statistics, Occupational Compensation Surveys

Average Wages: Selected Technical and Clerical Occupations

MSA[1] (Month/Year)	Accounting Clerk III	General Clerk II	Computer Operator II	Key Entry Operator I	Secretary III	Switchboard Operator/ Receptionist
Ann Arbor (7/95)	421	-	-	-	628	352
Chicago (6/96)	462	434	473	347	593	361
Des Moines (6/95)	404	335	421	276	507	344
Detroit (1/96)	475	433	470	349	620	-
Evansville (8/94)	351	337	356	258	530	292
Fort Wayne (2/94)	427	346	407	310	486	293
Grand Rapids (5/95)	463	388	-	-	600	330
Green Bay (5/94)	406	378	403	257	476	300
Indianapolis (8/96)	445	377	467	326	491	363
Kansas City (9/96)	436	381	430	312	538	353
Little Rock (12/94)	382	484	331	279	429	257
Madison (3/94)	421	414	431	311	500	313
Milwaukee (9/96)	446	424	460	-	542	367
Minneapolis (2/96)	461	439	-	354	535	382
Okla. City (7/96)	432	472	409	290	534	300
Sioux Falls (5/95)	383	361	362	294	440	300
Springfield (6/95)	362	367	363	282	487	287
St. Louis (3/96)	428	388	418	323	532	322
St. Paul (2/96)	461	439	-	354	535	382

Notes: Figures are average weekly earnings; Dashes indicate that data was not available;
(1) Metropolitan Statistical Area - see Appendix A for areas included
Source: Bureau of Labor Statistics, Occupational Compensation Surveys

Average Wages: Selected Health and Protective Service Occupations

MSA[1] (Month/Year)	Corrections Officer	Firefighter	Lic. Prac. Nurse II	Registered Nurse II	Nursing Assistant II	Police Officer I
Ann Arbor (7/95)	-	-	-	-	-	-
Chicago (6/96)	623	-	-	-	-	816
Des Moines (6/95)	-	-	-	-	-	-
Detroit (1/96)	618	672	-	-	-	698
Evansville (8/94)	378	542	418	588	297	519
Fort Wayne (2/94)	-	-	-	602	-	-
Grand Rapids (5/95)	-	-	-	672	-	-
Green Bay (5/94)	-	-	-	-	-	-
Indianapolis (8/96)	401	639	-	-	-	645
Kansas City (9/96)	424	605	-	-	-	616
Little Rock (12/94)	375	446	372	629	218	405
Madison (3/94)	-	-	-	-	-	-
Milwaukee (9/96)	528	739	-	-	-	743
Minneapolis (2/96)	-	763	-	-	-	775
Okla. City (7/96)	-	-	-	-	-	-
Sioux Falls (5/95)	-	-	-	-	-	-
Springfield (6/95)	-	-	-	-	-	-
St. Louis (3/96)	477	-	-	-	-	610
St. Paul (2/96)	-	763	-	-	-	775

Notes: Figures are average weekly earnings; Dashes indicate that data was not available;
(1) Metropolitan Statistical Area - see Appendix A for areas included
Source: Bureau of Labor Statistics, Occupational Compensation Surveys

Average Wages: Selected Maintenance, Material Movement and Custodial Occupations

MSA[1] (Month/Year)	General Maintenance	Guard I	Janitor	Maintenance Electrician	Motor Vehicle Mechanic	Truckdriver (Trac. Trail.)
Ann Arbor (7/95)	8.94	-	8.83	21.28	20.47	-
Chicago (6/96)	10.32	6.84	9.19	20.07	18.28	15.66
Des Moines (6/95)	10.19	5.90	6.39	16.41	14.10	13.27
Detroit (1/96)	11.24	6.75	9.21	21.24	17.80	15.42
Evansville (8/94)	8.76	-	6.67	14.89	11.55	15.33
Fort Wayne (2/94)	10.04	7.25	7.44	16.59	15.64	13.72
Grand Rapids (5/95)	9.47	5.94	7.92	18.22	17.65	14.74
Green Bay (5/94)	9.37	6.24	6.17	16.37	15.00	12.44
Indianapolis (8/96)	10.18	6.98	8.03	20.14	16.83	-
Kansas City (9/96)	9.27	6.56	7.68	19.67	-	14.95
Little Rock (12/94)	7.40	6.86	5.09	15.77	16.35	15.33
Madison (3/94)	9.35	7.03	6.75	14.70	14.27	-
Milwaukee (9/96)	11.35	7.30	8.32	20.27	16.54	16.94
Minneapolis (2/96)	11.30	7.60	8.34	20.92	16.77	15.23
Okla. City (7/96)	9.84	6.40	6.39	-	13.41	13.51
Sioux Falls (5/95)	8.32	-	6.79	14.53	11.95	-
Springfield (6/95)	8.43	5.12	6.30	14.41	13.20	13.25
St. Louis (3/96)	9.86	-	6.72	20.51	17.32	17.31
St. Paul (2/96)	11.30	7.60	8.34	20.92	16.77	15.23

Notes: Figures are average hourly earnings; Dashes indicate that data was not available;
(1) Metropolitan Statistical Area - see Appendix A for areas included
Source: Bureau of Labor Statistics, Occupational Compensation Surveys

Means of Transportation to Work: City

City	Car/Truck/Van		Public Transportation			Bicycle	Walked	Other Means	Worked at Home
	Drove Alone	Car-pooled	Bus	Subway	Railroad				
Ann Arbor	61.8	9.2	5.4	0.0	0.0	2.1	17.1	0.5	3.9
Chicago	46.3	14.8	19.3	7.9	1.5	0.3	6.4	1.7	1.7
Des Moines	74.4	15.1	3.5	0.0	0.0	0.2	3.6	0.7	2.5
Detroit	67.8	16.1	10.2	0.0	0.0	0.1	3.4	1.3	1.1
Evansville	80.7	11.3	1.6	0.0	0.0	0.4	3.7	0.7	1.6
Fort Wayne	79.9	12.1	2.0	0.0	0.0	0.3	3.1	0.7	1.8
Grand Rapids	76.8	11.7	3.2	0.0	0.0	0.3	4.3	1.0	2.7
Green Bay	80.4	9.7	2.1	0.0	0.0	0.5	4.8	0.6	2.0
Indianapolis	78.0	13.4	3.1	0.0	0.0	0.2	2.4	0.8	2.0
Kansas City	74.7	13.6	5.6	0.0	0.0	0.1	2.8	1.0	2.2
Little Rock	80.5	13.5	1.4	0.0	0.0	0.1	1.9	1.0	1.7
Madison	61.2	11.6	7.4	0.0	0.0	3.3	12.7	1.0	2.7
Milwaukee	67.2	13.2	10.8	0.0	0.0	0.3	6.0	0.8	1.6
Minneapolis	60.3	10.5	15.7	0.0	0.0	1.6	7.8	0.9	3.1
Okla. City	80.8	12.8	0.8	0.0	0.0	0.1	2.0	1.2	2.3
St. Louis	66.5	14.1	11.8	0.0	0.0	0.3	4.6	1.1	1.7
St. Paul	67.1	12.4	10.3	0.0	0.0	0.5	6.4	0.7	2.6
Sioux Falls	82.3	9.3	0.5	0.0	0.0	0.2	4.1	0.9	2.5
Springfield	80.4	11.0	0.9	0.0	0.0	0.3	4.2	0.8	2.4
U.S.	**73.2**	**13.4**	**3.0**	**1.5**	**0.5**	**0.4**	**3.9**	**1.2**	**3.0**

Note: Figures shown are percentages and only include workers 16 years old and over
Source: 1990 Census of Population and Housing, Summary Tape File 3C

Means of Transportation to Work: Metro Area

MSA[1]	Car/Truck/Van		Public Transportation			Bicycle	Walked	Other Means	Worked at Home
	Drove Alone	Car-pooled	Bus	Subway	Railroad				
Ann Arbor	73.5	9.6	2.9	0.0	0.0	1.0	9.2	0.5	3.2
Chicago	63.8	12.0	8.7	4.1	3.9	0.2	4.2	1.1	2.0
Des Moines	77.3	13.7	2.1	0.0	0.0	0.1	2.9	0.6	3.4
Detroit	83.4	10.1	2.2	0.0	0.0	0.1	1.9	0.6	1.6
Evansville	82.3	11.3	0.8	0.0	0.0	0.2	2.6	0.6	2.0
Fort Wayne	82.3	11.0	1.1	0.0	0.0	0.2	2.3	0.6	2.5
Grand Rapids	82.7	9.8	1.1	0.0	0.0	0.2	2.8	0.6	2.8
Green Bay	81.5	8.8	1.3	0.0	0.0	0.4	4.2	0.5	3.3
Indianapolis	79.7	12.9	1.9	0.0	0.0	0.1	2.2	0.7	2.4
Kansas City	79.9	12.5	2.0	0.0	0.0	0.1	1.9	0.8	2.8
Little Rock	79.8	14.4	0.8	0.0	0.0	0.1	1.9	1.0	2.0
Madison	68.5	12.5	4.4	0.0	0.0	1.9	8.2	0.8	3.6
Milwaukee	76.7	11.0	5.1	0.0	0.0	0.3	4.0	0.6	2.2
Minneapolis	76.0	11.2	5.2	0.0	0.0	0.4	3.2	0.6	3.4
Okla. City	80.3	13.3	0.5	0.0	0.0	0.2	2.1	1.0	2.5
St. Louis	79.7	12.0	2.8	0.0	0.0	0.1	2.1	0.7	2.4
Minneapolis	76.0	11.2	5.2	0.0	0.0	0.4	3.2	0.6	3.4
Sioux Falls	81.4	9.6	0.4	0.0	0.0	0.2	4.2	0.8	3.4
Springfield	81.5	10.9	0.6	0.0	0.0	0.2	2.9	0.7	3.2
U.S.	**73.2**	**13.4**	**3.0**	**1.5**	**0.5**	**0.4**	**3.9**	**1.2**	**3.0**

Note: Figures shown are percentages and only include workers 16 years old and over;
(1) Metropolitan Statistical Area - see Appendix A for areas included
Source: 1990 Census of Population and Housing, Summary Tape File 3C

Cost of Living Index

Area	Composite	Groceries	Health	Housing	Misc.	Transp.	Utilities
Ann Arbor[4]	113.5	105.8	118.0	123.9	108.4	125.3	97.0
Chicago	n/a	n/a	n/a	n/a	n/a	n/a	n/a
Des Moines	99.1	97.1	98.1	95.0	104.5	96.6	98.8
Detroit[5]	108.1	106.1	118.8	117.6	100.1	104.7	107.5
Evansville	97.5	102.8	91.6	97.8	97.6	96.3	91.5
Fort Wayne[2]	91.9	100.3	90.6	84.0	93.1	94.1	96.7
Grand Rapids[6]	107.8	107.3	104.5	112.7	107.9	105.9	95.3
Green Bay	98.2	95.4	105.2	100.6	98.9	99.6	85.4
Indianapolis	98.3	104.5	98.5	92.8	100.5	99.3	94.2
Kansas City[1]	95.8	96.2	103.3	90.4	101.6	97.5	81.9
Little Rock[3,5]	86.7	95.5	70.8	79.0	85.2	92.8	107.6
Madison	110.1	99.5	107.6	125.0	109.1	104.8	90.6
Milwaukee[1]	103.9	101.9	102.2	124.0	94.0	101.7	81.6
Minneapolis	102.9	99.6	126.6	98.1	101.7	114.3	100.4
Okla. City	90.9	88.5	90.0	80.0	99.3	95.2	95.3
Saint Louis[1]	98.0	101.3	111.1	96.7	95.3	99.4	95.2
Saint Paul	101.5	100.4	126.0	97.0	101.3	107.0	96.2
Sioux Falls	96.3	99.5	101.9	90.7	97.6	101.1	94.0
Springfield	92.4	96.0	96.0	87.4	97.5	96.4	74.2
U.S.	**100.0**	**100.0**	**100.0**	**100.0**	**100.0**	**100.0**	**100.0**

Note: n/a not available; (1) Metropolitan Statistical Area (MSA) - see Appendix A for areas included; (2) Ft. Wayne-Allen County; (3) Little Rock-North Little Rock; (4) 4th Quarter 1996; (5) 1st Quarter 1997; (6) 2nd Quarter 1997
Source: ACCRA, Cost of Living Index, 3rd Quarter 1997 unless otherwise noted

Median Home Prices and Housing Affordability

MSA[1]	Median Price[2] 3rd Qtr. 1997 ($)	HOI[3] 3rd Qtr. 1997	Affordability Rank[4]
Ann Arbor	146,000	57.5	159
Chicago	148,000	61.0	139
Des Moines	93,000	81.2	18
Detroit	120,000	62.8	132
Evansville	n/a	n/a	n/a
Fort Wayne	n/a	n/a	n/a
Grand Rapids	96,000	73.1	65
Green Bay	100,000	72.5	73
Indianapolis	125,000	68.9	100
Kansas City	98,000	83.3	11
Little Rock	100,000	67.9	106
Madison	n/a	n/a	n/a
Milwaukee	117,000	60.3	145
Minneapolis	118,000	79.4	26
Okla. City	82,000	77.4	36
St. Louis	109,000	72.4	75
St. Paul	118,000	79.4	26
Sioux Falls	n/a	n/a	n/a
Springfield	n/a	n/a	n/a
U.S.	**127,000**	**63.7**	–

Note: (1) Metropolitan Statistical Area - see Appendix A for areas included; (2) U.S. figures calculated from the sales of 625,000 new and existing homes in 195 markets; (3) Housing Opportunity Index - percent of homes sold that were within the reach of the median income household at the prevailing mortgage interest rate; (4) Rank is from 1-195 with 1 being most affordable; n/a not available
Source: National Association of Home Builders, Housing News Service, 3rd Quarter 1997

Average Home Prices

Area	Price ($)
Ann Arbor[4]	155,000
Chicago	n/a
Des Moines	128,280
Detroit[5]	163,000
Evansville	136,150
Fort Wayne[2]	110,240
Grand Rapids[6]	153,399
Green Bay	136,900
Indianapolis	124,111
Kansas City[1]	119,370
Little Rock[3,5]	109,000
Madison	165,900
Milwaukee[1]	168,700
Minneapolis	127,725
Okla. City	103,795
Saint Louis[1]	126,325
Saint Paul	125,263
Sioux Falls	119,310
Springfield	116,700
U.S.	**135,710**

Note: Figures are based on a new home with 1,800 sq. ft. of living area on an 8,000 sq. ft. lot; n/a not available;
(1) Metropolitan Statistical Area (MSA) - see Appendix A for areas included; (2) Ft. Wayne-Allen County; (3) Little
Rock-North Little Rock; (4) 4th Quarter 1996; (5) 1st Quarter 1997; (6) 2nd Quarter 1997
Source: ACCRA, Cost of Living Index, 3rd Quarter 1997 unless otherwise noted

Average Apartment Rent

Area	Rent ($/mth)
Ann Arbor[4]	807
Chicago	n/a
Des Moines	566
Detroit[5]	709
Evansville	440
Fort Wayne[2]	509
Grand Rapids[6]	586
Green Bay	536
Indianapolis	600
Kansas City[1]	578
Little Rock[3,5]	436
Madison	743
Milwaukee[1]	684
Minneapolis	613
Okla. City	521
Saint Louis[1]	649
Saint Paul	614
Sioux Falls	602
Springfield	490
U.S.	**569**

Note: Figures are based on an unfurnished two bedroom, 1-1/2 or 2 bath apartment, approximately 950 sq. ft. in size,
excluding all utilities except water; n/a not available; (1) Metropolitan Statistical Area (MSA) - see Appendix A for areas
included; (2) Ft. Wayne-Allen County; (3) Little Rock-North Little Rock; (4) 4th Quarter 1996; (5) 1st Quarter 1997; (6) 2nd
Quarter 1997
Source: ACCRA, Cost of Living Index, 3rd Quarter 1997 unless otherwise noted

Average Residential Utility Costs

Area	All Electric ($/mth)	Part Electric ($/mth)	Other Energy ($/mth)	Phone ($/mth)
Ann Arbor[4]	-	57.85	39.99	22.53
Chicago	n/a	n/a	n/a	n/a
Des Moines	-	55.49	45.34	19.76
Detroit[5]	-	67.10	48.70	16.82
Evansville	-	52.15	38.68	21.36
Fort Wayne[2]	-	45.80	49.22	23.83
Grand Rapids[6]	-	52.43	44.10	21.00
Green Bay	-	38.87	49.14	15.94
Indianapolis	-	48.01	47.39	19.66
Kansas City[1]	-	55.17	26.96	18.13
Little Rock[3,5]	-	71.03	39.19	23.63
Madison	-	46.59	46.26	17.65
Milwaukee[1]	-	41.09	42.46	15.90
Minneapolis	-	49.92	50.77	22.28
Okla. City	-	59.99	35.96	20.58
Saint Louis[1]	-	58.91	37.72	19.69
Saint Paul	-	46.23	50.82	20.63
Sioux Falls	-	47.11	45.34	22.98
Springfield	-	39.58	34.92	16.29
U.S.	**109.40**	**55.25**	**43.64**	**19.48**

Note: Dashes indicate data not applicable; n/a not available;
(1) Metropolitan Statistical Area (MSA) - see Appendix A for areas included; (2) Ft. Wayne-Allen County; (3) Little Rock-North Little Rock; (4) 4th Quarter 1996; (5) 1st Quarter 1997; (6) 2nd Quarter 1997
Source: ACCRA, Cost of Living Index, 3rd Quarter 1997 unless otherwise noted

Average Health Care Costs

Area	Hospital ($/day)	Doctor ($/visit)	Dentist ($/visit)
Ann Arbor[4]	535.00	48.80	71.00
Chicago	n/a	n/a	n/a
Des Moines	407.75	43.83	60.33
Detroit[5]	545.80	48.86	76.30
Evansville	374.67	44.20	54.20
Fort Wayne[2]	450.67	41.40	52.00
Grand Rapids[6]	414.00	52.25	60.20
Green Bay	343.67	56.10	65.60
Indianapolis	396.25	47.80	59.20
Kansas City[1]	505.49	48.71	57.75
Little Rock[3,5]	221.80	35.20	39.40
Madison	314.75	59.60	62.20
Milwaukee[1]	386.10	54.40	59.00
Minneapolis	672.00	56.55	72.60
Okla. City	279.10	42.14	61.40
Saint Louis[1]	471.00	56.80	62.70
Saint Paul	708.20	55.00	71.60
Sioux Falls	401.00	56.38	55.75
Springfield	385.00	47.89	56.66
U.S.	**392.91**	**48.76**	**60.84**

Note: n/a not available; Hospital - based on a semi-private room. Doctor - based on a general practitioner's routine exam of an established patient. Dentist - based on adult teeth cleaning and periodic oral exam; (1) Metropolitan Statistical Area (MSA) - see Appendix A for areas included; (2) Ft. Wayne-Allen County; (3) Little Rock-North Little Rock; (4) 4th Quarter 1996; (5) 1st Quarter 1997; (6) 2nd Quarter 1997
Source: ACCRA, Cost of Living Index, 3rd Quarter 1997 unless otherwise noted

Distribution of Office-Based Physicians

MSA[1]	General Practitioners	Specialists		
		Medical	Surgical	Other
Ann Arbor	111	499	320	520
Chicago	1,621	5,664	3,539	3,923
Des Moines	81	173	175	171
Detroit	574	2,508	1,690	1,727
Evansville	104	145	145	131
Fort Wayne	151	162	190	183
Grand Rapids	200	384	347	346
Green Bay	43	102	96	99
Indianapolis	455	939	752	845
Kansas City	169	511	427	360
Little Rock	190	404	356	411
Madison	152	371	231	340
Milwaukee	373	1,033	738	928
Minneapolis	1,026	1,490	1,112	1,246
Okla. City	244	533	470	535
St. Louis	316	1,770	1,270	1,246
St. Paul	1,026	1,490	1,112	1,246
Sioux Falls	68	128	100	106
Springfield	64	172	157	153

Note: Data as of 12/31/96; (1) Metropolitan Statistical Area - see Appendix A for areas included
Source: Physician Characteristics & Distribution in the U.S. 1997-98

Educational Quality

City	School District	Education Quotient[1]	Graduate Outcome[2]	Community Index[3]	Resource Index[4]
Ann Arbor	Ann Arbor	142.0	146.0	147.0	134.0
Chicago	City of Chicago	98.0	53.0	95.0	147.0
Des Moines	Des Moines	108.0	101.0	131.0	91.0
Detroit	Detroit	78.0	53.0	58.0	123.0
Evansville	Evansville-Vanderburgh	105.0	94.0	86.0	134.0
Fort Wayne	Fort Wayne	112.0	79.0	121.0	137.0
Grand Rapids	Grand Rapids	n/a	n/a	n/a	n/a
Green Bay	Green Bay	124.0	139.0	122.0	110.0
Indianapolis	Indianapolis	76.0	51.0	105.0	73.0
Kansas City	Kansas City	96.0	58.0	102.0	129.0
Little Rock	Little Rock	110.0	75.0	112.0	142.0
Madison	Madison Metropolitan	144.0	146.0	141.0	146.0
Milwaukee	Milwaukee	95.0	59.0	81.0	146.0
Minneapolis	Minneapolis	124.0	94.0	140.0	139.0
Okla. City	Okla. City	72.0	55.0	99.0	61.0
Saint Louis	Saint Louis City	85.0	57.0	53.0	146.0
Saint Paul	Saint Paul	114.0	79.0	130.0	134.0
Sioux Falls	Sioux Falls	105.0	132.0	126.0	56.0
Springfield	Springfield	100.0	124.0	97.0	78.0

Note: Nearly 1,000 secondary school districts were rated in terms of educational quality. The scores range from a low of 50 to a high of 150; (1) Average of the Graduate Outcome, Community and Resource indexes; (2) Based on graduation rates and college board scores (SAT/ACT); (3) Based on the surrounding community's average level of education and the area's average income level; (4) Based on teacher salaries, per-pupil expenditures and student-teacher ratios.
Source: Expansion Management, Ratings Issue 1997

School Enrollment by Type: City

City	Preprimary Public Enrollment	%	Private Enrollment	%	Elementary/High School Public Enrollment	%	Private Enrollment	%
Ann Arbor	1,151	55.4	928	44.6	9,948	88.5	1,299	11.5
Chicago	27,249	61.1	17,333	38.9	391,046	79.5	101,138	20.5
Des Moines	2,441	67.2	1,194	32.8	26,321	91.6	2,402	8.4
Detroit	13,196	72.4	5,027	27.6	180,245	87.3	26,179	12.7
Evansville	1,110	52.2	1,017	47.8	16,003	85.9	2,621	14.1
Fort Wayne	1,880	53.2	1,652	46.8	24,519	83.7	4,783	16.3
Grand Rapids	3,105	60.8	2,004	39.2	24,319	76.0	7,660	24.0
Green Bay	1,213	61.8	751	38.2	12,907	82.0	2,831	18.0
Indianapolis	6,699	51.1	6,414	48.9	101,922	87.2	14,951	12.8
Kansas City	4,496	55.5	3,601	44.5	57,590	85.6	9,712	14.4
Little Rock	1,427	40.4	2,108	59.6	22,873	79.7	5,818	20.3
Madison	2,039	54.5	1,705	45.5	19,043	90.4	2,023	9.6
Milwaukee	6,616	66.3	3,359	33.7	92,372	80.6	22,277	19.4
Minneapolis	3,848	59.9	2,577	40.1	38,107	84.8	6,823	15.2
Okla. City	4,639	60.5	3,033	39.5	66,351	90.3	7,166	9.7
St. Louis	4,198	56.7	3,211	43.3	49,177	77.4	14,389	22.6
St. Paul	2,919	54.4	2,445	45.6	32,325	80.7	7,728	19.3
Sioux Falls	1,407	65.7	735	34.3	13,903	87.0	2,076	13.0
Springfield	1,135	62.4	683	37.6	16,946	92.8	1,316	7.2
U.S.	2,679,029	59.5	1,824,256	40.5	38,379,689	90.2	4,187,099	9.8

Note: Figures shown cover persons 3 years old and over
Source: 1990 Census of Population and Housing, Summary Tape File 3C

School Enrollment by Type: Metro Area

MSA[1]	Preprimary Public Enrollment	%	Private Enrollment	%	Elementary/High School Public Enrollment	%	Private Enrollment	%
Ann Arbor	3,711	62.5	2,225	37.5	35,078	91.0	3,490	9.0
Chicago	70,174	57.4	52,166	42.6	837,481	82.5	178,237	17.5
Des Moines	5,840	67.4	2,829	32.6	59,903	93.4	4,230	6.6
Detroit	63,323	68.3	29,435	31.7	685,077	88.7	87,455	11.3
Evansville	2,844	55.3	2,299	44.7	41,082	86.9	6,197	13.1
Fort Wayne	4,397	54.1	3,726	45.9	56,218	84.7	10,137	15.3
Grand Rapids	12,129	66.4	6,136	33.6	103,726	81.8	23,081	18.2
Green Bay	2,488	59.7	1,679	40.3	27,918	81.3	6,414	18.7
Indianapolis	12,635	53.2	11,125	46.8	191,105	90.0	21,252	10.0
Kansas City	18,724	56.8	14,261	43.2	236,921	89.4	28,033	10.6
Little Rock	4,862	53.5	4,231	46.5	80,860	88.7	10,321	11.3
Madison	4,454	59.1	3,077	40.9	47,805	92.0	4,184	8.0
Milwaukee	15,931	56.8	12,092	43.2	204,342	81.5	46,314	18.5
Minneapolis	35,492	63.1	20,730	36.9	359,955	89.1	44,235	10.9
Okla. City	10,338	60.2	6,849	39.8	156,353	92.8	12,146	7.2
St. Louis	26,907	50.2	26,648	49.8	337,304	80.6	81,322	19.4
Minneapolis	35,492	63.1	20,730	36.9	359,955	89.1	44,235	10.9
Sioux Falls	1,625	65.9	841	34.1	18,697	89.0	2,316	11.0
Springfield	2,229	61.2	1,415	38.8	35,278	93.9	2,297	6.1
U.S.	2,679,029	59.5	1,824,256	40.5	38,379,689	90.2	4,187,099	9.8

Note: Figures shown cover persons 3 years old and over;
(1) Metropolitan Statistical Area - see Appendix A for areas included
Source: 1990 Census of Population and Housing, Summary Tape File 3C

School Enrollment by Race: City

City	Preprimary (%) White	Black	Other	Hisp.[1]	Elementary/High School (%) White	Black	Other	Hisp.[1]
Ann Arbor	82.9	9.4	7.7	3.6	72.4	17.0	10.6	2.5
Chicago	36.1	50.5	13.5	17.5	30.7	48.4	20.9	27.8
Des Moines	92.2	4.7	3.1	3.0	83.5	11.0	5.5	3.7
Detroit	18.1	78.5	3.4	3.5	13.5	83.3	3.1	3.3
Evansville	83.7	14.2	2.0	1.1	83.5	14.9	1.6	0.5
Fort Wayne	74.6	21.5	3.9	3.4	69.8	26.0	4.2	4.3
Grand Rapids	73.4	20.5	6.1	5.5	62.8	29.6	7.6	7.3
Green Bay	90.0	2.4	7.6	2.5	89.7	0.7	9.5	1.7
Indianapolis	76.0	22.5	1.5	1.2	67.8	30.4	1.8	1.3
Kansas City	65.3	31.4	3.3	4.2	55.4	40.0	4.6	5.5
Little Rock	65.5	34.1	0.4	1.0	45.6	53.0	1.4	0.6
Madison	84.8	7.7	7.5	3.0	84.7	9.1	6.3	2.3
Milwaukee	54.3	38.4	7.3	7.2	43.2	47.0	9.8	10.0
Minneapolis	69.2	19.0	11.8	3.1	56.8	26.2	16.9	3.4
Okla. City	72.4	18.2	9.4	5.7	65.7	21.8	12.5	7.3
St. Louis	44.4	53.6	2.0	1.2	33.2	65.2	1.6	1.4
St. Paul	78.9	9.6	11.5	5.6	67.4	11.9	20.7	6.2
Sioux Falls	95.7	2.4	2.0	1.4	94.9	1.4	3.7	1.1
Springfield	94.6	1.4	4.0	1.4	93.8	3.2	3.0	1.2
U.S.	**80.4**	**12.5**	**7.1**	**7.8**	**74.1**	**15.6**	**10.3**	**12.5**

Note: Figures shown cover persons 3 years old and over; (1) People of Hispanic origin can be of any race
Source: 1990 Census of Population and Housing, Summary Tape File 3C

School Enrollment by Race: Metro Area

MSA[1]	Preprimary (%) White	Black	Other	Hisp.[2]	Elementary/High School (%) White	Black	Other	Hisp.[2]
Ann Arbor	83.4	12.4	4.1	1.9	78.3	16.6	5.1	2.4
Chicago	68.6	23.0	8.4	9.4	56.2	29.0	14.8	17.5
Des Moines	95.8	2.2	2.1	1.7	91.2	5.3	3.5	2.7
Detroit	77.6	19.5	2.9	2.3	69.8	26.9	3.3	2.6
Evansville	90.8	7.7	1.5	0.9	91.1	7.8	1.2	0.5
Fort Wayne	88.1	9.6	2.3	2.4	85.5	11.9	2.6	2.7
Grand Rapids	89.6	6.5	3.9	2.6	86.5	8.4	5.1	4.5
Green Bay	93.4	1.2	5.4	1.2	93.7	0.7	5.6	1.1
Indianapolis	85.9	12.8	1.4	1.1	81.0	17.5	1.5	1.2
Kansas City	85.4	12.3	2.3	3.3	80.0	16.3	3.7	4.0
Little Rock	77.6	21.9	0.5	1.1	69.4	29.0	1.6	1.3
Madison	89.7	5.0	5.2	2.3	91.3	5.0	3.8	2.1
Milwaukee	82.1	14.0	3.9	3.9	72.3	22.0	5.6	5.7
Minneapolis	90.7	4.3	5.0	1.9	87.8	5.3	6.9	2.1
Okla. City	79.1	12.1	8.8	4.3	75.6	13.7	10.7	4.9
St. Louis	81.3	16.9	1.8	1.2	74.9	23.3	1.8	1.3
Minneapolis	90.7	4.3	5.0	1.9	87.8	5.3	6.9	2.1
Sioux Falls	96.3	2.1	1.7	1.2	95.9	1.1	3.0	0.8
Springfield	96.5	0.9	2.6	1.1	96.1	1.8	2.0	1.0
U.S.	**80.4**	**12.5**	**7.1**	**7.8**	**74.1**	**15.6**	**10.3**	**12.5**

Note: Figures shown cover persons 3 years old and over; (1) Metropolitan Statistical Area - see Appendix A for areas included; (2) People of Hispanic origin can be of any race
Source: 1990 Census of Population and Housing, Summary Tape File 3C

Crime Rate: City

City	All Crimes	Violent Crimes				Property Crimes		
		Murder	Forcible Rape	Robbery	Aggrav. Assault	Burglary	Larceny -Theft	Motor Vehicle Theft
Ann Arbor	4,271.5	0.9	33.7	102.8	234.7	731.3	2,986.2	181.9
Chicago	n/a	28.6	n/a	975.3	1,347.0	1,469.6	4,338.7	1,237.8
Des Moines	7,754.7	9.7	51.2	164.2	248.7	917.9	5,743.5	619.6
Detroit	11,991.2	42.7	111.6	948.2	1,216.0	2,144.2	4,109.9	3,418.6
Evansville	5,633.1	5.3	31.2	126.3	430.6	1,094.7	3,600.5	344.6
Fort Wayne	7,500.7	7.0	65.0	268.0	234.2	1,034.9	5,052.2	839.4
Grand Rapids	7,590.0	10.4	52.5	350.9	856.2	1,576.7	4,185.4	557.8
Green Bay	4,486.8	2.9	37.4	65.2	268.5	560.0	3,338.0	214.8
Indianapolis	4,877.0	14.7	54.5	334.4	550.5	1,002.9	2,166.3	753.7
Kansas City	11,661.8	23.2	91.9	642.4	1,223.7	1,995.0	6,271.0	1,414.6
Little Rock	11,496.8	15.9	90.8	457.9	943.7	1,850.1	7,250.0	888.4
Madison	4,603.9	0.5	38.0	151.3	200.9	703.0	3,185.7	324.4
Milwaukee	7,912.6	20.7	44.8	534.7	352.4	1,215.4	4,137.5	1,607.1
Minneapolis	11,290.5	23.0	142.7	896.6	820.5	2,123.4	5,721.9	1,562.5
Okla. City	12,158.5	14.3	101.6	314.7	699.7	2,276.3	7,656.4	1,095.5
St. Louis	15,128.8	44.4	71.9	1,092.4	1,519.1	2,643.3	7,814.1	1,943.6
St. Paul	7,745.8	9.7	87.5	327.4	487.1	1,544.0	4,303.9	986.2
Sioux Falls	4,828.2	0.9	73.9	58.6	293.1	779.1	3,434.0	188.5
Springfield	7,567.9	2.6	50.0	113.8	356.5	1,435.3	5,164.3	445.3
U.S.	**5,078.9**	**7.4**	**36.1**	**202.4**	**388.2**	**943.0**	**2,975.9**	**525.9**

Note: Crime rate is the number of crimes per 100,000 population; n/a not available;
Source: FBI Uniform Crime Reports 1996

Crime Rate: Suburbs

Suburbs[1]	All Crimes	Violent Crimes				Property Crimes		
		Murder	Forcible Rape	Robbery	Aggrav. Assault	Burglary	Larceny -Theft	Motor Vehicle Theft
Ann Arbor	4,109.9	2.2	52.5	78.1	228.3	709.9	2,690.7	348.3
Chicago	n/a	n/a	n/a	n/a	n/a	n/a	n/a	n/a
Des Moines	3,460.3	0.0	8.0	21.4	126.2	568.4	2,550.5	185.9
Detroit	4,314.4	2.7	33.4	80.1	267.2	601.8	2,795.9	533.4
Evansville	n/a	n/a	n/a	n/a	n/a	n/a	n/a	n/a
Fort Wayne	2,463.5	1.0	17.2	23.1	166.8	438.8	1,631.8	184.8
Grand Rapids	3,886.2	2.2	42.9	46.7	211.1	699.1	2,658.1	226.1
Green Bay	3,134.8	0.0	17.0	11.3	42.4	446.5	2,480.2	137.5
Indianapolis	5,974.8	4.8	41.3	125.4	304.8	960.7	4,007.0	530.9
Kansas City	n/a	n/a	n/a	n/a	n/a	n/a	n/a	n/a
Little Rock	5,150.1	7.9	59.6	122.6	288.2	955.3	3,370.8	345.6
Madison	3,565.5	0.5	14.6	15.1	164.5	435.6	2,816.4	118.6
Milwaukee	3,189.9	1.0	9.6	41.7	66.1	378.7	2,489.6	203.3
Minneapolis	4,443.7	1.7	39.1	75.3	137.7	671.4	3,170.2	348.2
Okla. City	4,925.5	3.6	37.9	69.8	236.7	1,082.1	3,157.7	337.7
St. Louis	n/a	n/a	n/a	n/a	n/a	n/a	n/a	n/a
St. Paul	5,087.1	3.9	49.0	168.0	199.7	789.3	3,420.4	456.7
Sioux Falls	2,516.8	0.0	84.8	4.2	120.9	659.4	1,547.8	99.7
Springfield	1,814.4	0.0	17.1	13.0	117.6	453.9	1,082.1	130.6
U.S.	**5,078.9**	**7.4**	**36.1**	**202.4**	**388.2**	**943.0**	**2,975.9**	**525.9**

Note: Crime rate is the number of crimes per 100,000 population; n/a not available; (1) Defined as all areas within the MSA but located outside the central city
Source: FBI Uniform Crime Reports 1996

Crime Rate: Metro Area

| MSA[1] | All Crimes | Violent Crimes | | | | Property Crimes | | |
		Murder	Forcible Rape	Robbery	Aggrav. Assault	Burglary	Larceny -Theft	Motor Vehicle Theft
Ann Arbor	4,144.3	1.9	48.5	83.3	229.6	714.4	2,753.5	312.9
Chicago	n/a	n/a	n/a	n/a	n/a	n/a	n/a	n/a
Des Moines	5,459.9	4.5	28.1	87.9	183.2	731.1	4,037.2	387.8
Detroit	6,081.7	11.9	51.4	280.0	485.6	956.9	3,098.4	1,197.6
Evansville	n/a	n/a	n/a	n/a	n/a	n/a	n/a	n/a
Fort Wayne	4,432.6	3.4	35.9	118.8	193.2	671.8	2,968.9	440.7
Grand Rapids	4,602.2	3.8	44.7	105.5	335.8	868.7	2,953.3	290.2
Green Bay	3,804.8	1.4	27.1	38.0	154.4	502.7	2,905.3	175.8
Indianapolis	5,400.0	10.0	48.2	234.8	433.4	982.8	3,043.2	647.6
Kansas City	n/a	n/a	n/a	n/a	n/a	n/a	n/a	n/a
Little Rock	7,257.4	10.5	69.9	234.0	505.9	1,252.4	4,658.9	525.8
Madison	4,092.8	0.5	26.5	84.3	183.0	571.4	3,004.0	223.1
Milwaukee	5,206.8	9.4	24.7	252.2	188.4	736.0	3,193.4	802.8
Minneapolis	5,346.1	4.5	52.8	183.6	227.7	862.8	3,506.5	508.3
Okla. City	8,252.3	8.5	67.2	182.5	449.6	1,631.4	5,226.9	686.3
St. Louis	n/a	n/a	n/a	n/a	n/a	n/a	n/a	n/a
St. Paul	5,346.1	4.5	52.8	183.6	227.7	862.8	3,506.5	508.3
Sioux Falls	4,138.4	0.6	77.2	42.4	241.7	743.4	2,871.2	162.0
Springfield	4,537.3	1.2	32.7	60.7	230.7	918.4	3,014.1	279.6
U.S.	**5,078.9**	**7.4**	**36.1**	**202.4**	**388.2**	**943.0**	**2,975.9**	**525.9**

Note: Crime rate is the number of crimes per 100,000 population; n/a not available;
(1) Metropolitan Statistical Area - see Appendix A for areas included
Source: FBI Uniform Crime Reports 1996

Temperature & Precipitation: Yearly Averages and Extremes

City	Extreme Low (°F)	Average Low (°F)	Average Temp. (°F)	Average High (°F)	Extreme High (°F)	Average Precip. (in.)	Average Snow (in.)
Ann Arbor	-21	39	49	58	104	32.4	41
Chicago	-27	40	49	59	104	35.4	39
Des Moines	-24	40	50	60	108	31.8	33
Detroit	-21	39	49	58	104	32.4	41
Evansville	-23	42	53	62	104	40.2	25
Fort Wayne	-22	40	50	60	106	35.9	33
Grand Rapids	-22	38	48	57	102	34.7	73
Green Bay	-31	34	44	54	99	28.3	46
Indianapolis	-23	42	53	62	104	40.2	25
Kansas City	-23	44	54	64	109	38.1	21
Little Rock	-5	51	62	73	112	50.7	5
Madison	-37	35	46	57	104	31.1	42
Milwaukee	-26	38	47	55	103	32.0	49
Minneapolis	-34	35	45	54	105	27.1	52
Okla. City	-8	49	60	71	110	32.8	10
Sioux Falls	-36	35	46	57	110	24.6	38
Springfield	-17	45	56	67	113	42.0	18
St. Louis	-18	46	56	66	115	36.8	20
St. Paul	-34	35	45	54	105	27.1	52

Note: Tr = Trace
Source: National Climatic Data Center, International Station Meteorological Climate Summary, 3/95

Weather Conditions

City	Temperature			Daytime Sky			Precipitation		
	10°F & below	32°F & below	90°F & above	Clear	Partly cloudy	Cloudy	.01 inch or more precip.	1.0 inch or more snow/ice	Thunder-storms
Ann Arbor	(a)	136	12	74	134	157	135	38	32
Chicago	(a)	132	17	83	136	146	125	31	38
Des Moines	(a)	137	26	99	129	137	106	25	46
Detroit	(a)	136	12	74	134	157	135	38	32
Evansville	19	119	19	83	128	154	127	24	43
Fort Wayne	(a)	131	16	75	140	150	131	31	39
Grand Rapids	(a)	146	11	67	119	179	142	57	34
Green Bay	(a)	163	7	86	125	154	120	40	33
Indianapolis	19	119	19	83	128	154	127	24	43
Kansas City	22	110	39	112	134	119	103	17	51
Little Rock	1	57	73	110	142	113	104	4	57
Madison	(a)	161	14	88	119	158	118	38	40
Milwaukee	(a)	141	10	90	118	157	126	38	35
Minneapolis	(a)	156	16	93	125	147	113	41	37
Okla. City	5	79	70	124	131	110	80	8	50
Sioux Falls	(a)	n/a	n/a	95	136	134	n/a	n/a	n/a
Springfield	12	102	42	113	119	133	109	14	55
St. Louis	13	100	43	97	138	130	109	14	46
St. Paul	(a)	156	16	93	125	147	113	41	37

Note: Figures are average number of days per year; (a) Figures for 10 degrees and below are not available; (b) Figures for 32 degrees and below are not available
Source: National Climatic Data Center, International Station Meteorological Climate Summary, 3/95

Air Quality

MSA[1]	PSI>100[2] (days)	Ozone (ppm)	Carbon Monoxide (ppm)	Sulfur Dioxide (ppm)	Nitrogen Dioxide (ppm)	PM10 (ug/m3)	Lead (ug/m3)
Ann Arbor	n/a	0.10	n/a	n/a	n/a	n/a	n/a
Chicago	4	0.13	5	0.032	0.032	122	0.06
Des Moines	n/a	0.08	4	n/a	n/a	130	n/a
Detroit	3	0.11	6	0.079	0.021	106	0.04
Evansville	n/a	0.12	4	0.097	0.017	59	n/a
Fort Wayne	n/a	0.11	3	0.010	0.007	80	0.02
Grand Rapids	4	0.13	3	0.011	0.009	71	0.01
Green Bay	n/a	0.11	n/a	0.011	n/a	n/a	n/a
Indianapolis	5	0.12	3	0.041	0.018	71	0.07
Kansas City	3	0.11	4	0.057	0.022	120	0.07
Little Rock	0	0.10	4	0.009	0.011	52	n/a
Madison	n/a	0.09	4	0.010	n/a	44	n/a
Milwaukee	1	0.12	3	0.028	0.021	69	0.03
Minneapolis	1	0.09	7	0.041	0.027	91	0.01
Okla. City	1	0.10	8	0.005	0.014	56	0.01
Saint Louis	4	0.13	6	0.102	0.025	107	0.03
Saint Paul	1	0.09	7	0.041	0.027	91	0.01
Sioux Falls	n/a	n/a	n/a	n/a	n/a	53	n/a
Springfield	n/a	0.10	3	0.089	0.011	148	n/a
NAAQS[3]	-	0.12	9	0.140	0.053	150	1.50

Note: (1) Metropolitan Statistical Area - see Appendix A for areas included; (2) Number of days the Pollutant Standards Index (PSI) exceeded 100 in 1996. A PSI value greater than 100 indicates that air quality would be in the unhealthful range on that day; (3) National Ambient Air Quality Standard; ppm = parts per million; ug/m^3 = micrograms per cubic meter; n/a not available
Source: EPA, National Air Quality and Emissions Trends Report, 1996

Water Quality

City	Tap Water
Ann Arbor	Alkaline, soft and fluoridated
Chicago	Alkaline (Lake Michigan); fluoridated
Des Moines	Alkaline, soft and fluoridated
Detroit	Alkaline, soft
Evansville	Alkaline, hard and fluoridated
Fort Wayne	Alkaline, hard and fluoridated
Grand Rapids	Alkaline, hard and fluoridated
Green Bay	Alkaline, hard and fluoridated and comes from Lake Michigan
Indianapolis	Alkaline, hard and fluoridated. Three separate systems with separate sources & purification plants
Kansas City	Neutral, soft and fluoridated
Little Rock	Neutral, soft and fluoridated
Madison	Alkaline, hard and fluoridated
Milwaukee	Alkaline, medium hard and fluoridated
Minneapolis	Alkaline, soft and fluoridated.
Okla. City	Alkaline, soft and fluoridated
Saint Louis	Alkaline, moderately hard and fluoridated
Saint Paul	Alkaline, soft and fluoridated
Sioux Falls	Alkaline, hard and fluoridated
Springfield	Alkaline, hard and fluoridated

Source: Editor & Publisher Market Guide 1998

Appendix A

Metropolitan Statistical Areas

Ann Arbor, MI

Includes Lenawee, Livingston and Washtenaw Counties (as of 6/30/93)

Includes Washtenaw County (prior to 6/30/93)

Chicago, IL

Includes Cook, DeKalb, DuPage, Grundy, Kane, Kendall, Lake, McHenry and Will Counties (as of 6/30/93)

Includes Cook, DuPage and McHenry Counties (prior to 6/30/93)

Des Moines, IA

Includes Dallas, Polk, and Warren Counties

Detroit, MI

Includes Lapeer, Macomb, Monroe, Oakland, St. Clair, and Wayne Counties

Evansville-Henderson, IN-KY

Includes Posey, Vanderburgh and Warren Counties, IN; Henderson County, KY

Ft. Wayne

Includes Adams, Allen, DeKalb, Huntington, Wells and Whitley Counties (as of 6/30/93)

Includes Allen, DeKalb and Whitley Counties (prior to 6/30/93)

Grand Rapids-Muskegon-Holland, MI

Includes Allegan, Kent, Muskegon and Ottawa Counties (as of 6/30/93)

Includes Kent and Ottawa Counties (prior to 6/30/93)

Green Bay, WI

Includes Brown County

Indianapolis, IN

Includes Boone, Hamilton, Hancock, Hendricks, Johnson, Madison, Marion, Morgan, and Shelby Counties (as of 6/30/93)

Includes Boone, Hamilton, Hancock, Hendricks, Johnson, Marion, Morgan, and Shelby Counties (prior to 6/30/93)

Kansas City, KS-MO

Includes Cass, Clay, Clinton, Jackson, Lafayette, Platte, and Ray Counties, MO; Johnson, Leavenworth, Miami, and Wyandotte Counties, KS (as of 6/30/93)

Includes Cass, Clay, Jackson, Lafayette, Platte, and Ray Counties, MO; Johnson, Leavenworth, Miami, and Wyandotte Counties, KS (prior to 6/30/93)

Little Rock-North Little Rock, AR

Includes Faulkner, Lonoke, Pulaski and Saline Counties

Madison, WI

Includes Dane County

Milwaukee-Waukesha, WI

Includes Milwaukee, Ozaukee, Washington, and Waukesha Counties

Minneapolis-St. Paul, MN-WI

Includes Anoka, Carver, Chisago, Dakota, Hennepin, Isanti, Ramsey, Scott, Sherburne, Washington, Wright and Pierce Counties, MN; St. Croix County, WI (as of 6/30/93)

Includes Anoka, Carver, Chisago, Dakota, Hennepin, Isanti, Ramsey, Scott, Washington, and Wright Counties, MN; St. Croix County, WI (prior to 6/30/93)

Oklahoma City, OK

Includes Canadian, Cleveland, Logan, McClain, Oklahoma and Pottawatomie Counties

St. Louis, MO-IL

Includes St. Louis and Sullivan Cities; Crawford (part), Franklin, Jefferson, Lincoln, St. Charles, St. Louis and Warren Counties, MO; Clinton, Jersey, Madison, Monroe, and St. Clair Counties, IL (as of 6/30/93)

Includes St. Louis and Sullivan Cities; Franklin, Jefferson, St. Charles and St. Louis Counties, MO; Clinton, Jersey, Madison, Monroe, and St. Clair Counties, IL (prior to 6/30/93)

St. Paul, MN

See Minneapolis-St. Paul, MN-WI

Sioux Falls, SD

Includes Lincoln and Minnehaha Counties (as of 6/30/93)

Includes Minnehaha County (prior to 6/30/93)

Springfield, MO

Includes Christian, Greene and Webster Counties (as of 6/30/93)

Includes Christian and Greene Counties (prior to 6/30/93)

Appendix B

Chambers of Commerce and Economic Development Organizations

Ann Arbor

Ann Arbor Area
Chamber of Commerce
425 S. Main, Suite 103
Ann Arbor, MI 48104
Phone: (313) 665-4433
Fax: (313) 665-4191

Chicago

Chicagoland Chamber of Commerce
One IBM Plaza #2800
Chicago, IL 60611
Phone: (312) 494-6700
Fax: (312) 494-0196

City of Chicago Department of
Planning and Development
City Hall, Room 1000
121 North La Salle Street
Chicago, IL 60602
Phone: (312) 744-0632
Fax: (312) 744-CITY

Des Moines

Greater Des Moines
Chamber of Commerce
601 Locust St., Suite 100
Des Moines, IA 50309
Phone: (515) 286-4950
Fax: (515) 286-4974

Detroit

Greater Detroit
Chamber of Commerce
600 W. Lafayette Blvd.
P.O. Box 33840
Detroit, MI 48232-0840
Phone: (313) 964-4000
Fax: (313) 964-0168

Evansville

Metro Evansville
Chamber of Commerce
100 N.W. Second St.
Suite 202
Evansville, IN 47708

Fort Wayne

City of Fort Wayne
Community & Econ. Dev. Div.
City-County Building
One Main Street
Ft. Wayne, IN 46802
Phone: (219) 427-1140

Greater Ft. Wayne
Chamber of Commerce
826 Ewing St.
Ft. Wayne, IN 46802-2182
Phone: (219) 424-1435
Fax: (219) 426-7232

Grand Rapids

Grand Rapids Area
Chamber of Commerce
111 Pearl St. NW
Grand Rapids, MI 49503-2831
Phone: (616) 771-0300
Fax: (616) 771-0318

Green Bay

Advance-Green Bay Area
Economic Development
835 Potts Ave.
Green Bay, WI 54304
Phone: (414) 496-9010

Green Bay Area
Chamber of Commerce
P.O. Box 1660
Green Bay, WI 54305
Phone: (414) 437-8704
Fax: (414) 496-6009

Indianapolis

Indianapolis Chamber of Commerce
320 N. Meridian St. #200
Indianapolis, IN 46204-1777
Phone: (317) 464-2200
Fax: (317) 464-2217

Indianapolis Economic
Development Corp.
320 N. Meridian St. #900
Indianapolis, IN 46204
Phone: (317) 236-6262
Fax: (317) 236-6275

Kansas City

Greater Kansas City
Chamber of Commerce
911 Main Street
Kansas City, MO 64105-2049
Phone: (816) 221-2424
Fax: (816) 221-7440

Kansas City Area Development Council
911 Main Street, Suite 2600
Kansas City, MO 64105-2049
Phone: (816) 221-2121
Fax: (816) 842-2865

Little Rock

Greater Little Rock
Chamber of Commerce
101 S. Spring St., Suite 200
Little Rock, AR 72201
Phone: (501) 374-4871
Fax: (501) 374-6018

Madison

Greater Madison
Chamber of Commerce
615 E. Washington Ave.
PO Box 71
Madison, WI 53701-0071
Phone: (608) 256-8348
Fax: (608) 256-0333

Milwaukee

City of Milwaukee
Dept. of City Development
Economic Development Division
809 N. Broadway
Milwaukee, WI 53202
Phone: (414) 286-5467
Fax: (414) 286-5840

Metropolitan Milwaukee
Association of Commerce
756 N. Milwaukee St.
Milwaukee, WI 53202
Phone: (414) 287-4100
Fax: (414) 271-7753

Minneapolis

Greater Minneapolis
Chamber of Commerce
81 S. Ninth St., Suite 200
Minneapolis, MN 55402
Phone: (612) 370-9132
Fax: (612) 370-9195

Minneapolis Community
Development Agency
105 5th Ave. S #200
Minneapolis, MN 55401

Minnepolis

Minnepolis City Planning Dept.
350 S. 5th St.
Room 210 City Hall
Minneapolis, MN 55415-1385

Oklahoma City

Greater Oklahoma City
Chamber of Commerce
123 Park Ave.
Oklahoma City, OK 73102
Phone: (405) 297-8900
Fax: (405) 297-8916

Saint Louis

Economic Council of
St. Louis County
121 S. Meramec #900
St. Louis, MO 63105

St. Louis Regional
Commerce & Growth Assn.
100 S. Fourth Street
Suite 500
St. Louis, MO 63102
Phone: (314) 231-5555
Fax: (314) 444-1122

Saint Paul

City of St. Paul
Dept. of Planning & Econ. Dev.
25 W. 4th
1300 City Hall Annex
St. Paul, MN 55102
Phone: (612) 266-6655
Fax: (612) 228-3261

Metro East Development Partnership
First National Bank Building, #N-205
332 Minnesota Street
St. Paul, MN 55101

Sioux Falls

Sioux Falls Area
Chamber of Commerce
200 N. Phillips Ave. #102
P.O. Box 1425
Sioux Falls, SD 57101-1425
Phone: (605) 336-1620
Fax: (605) 336-6499

Sioux Falls Development Foundation
P.O. Box 907
Sioux Falls, SD 57101
Phone: (605) 339-0103
Fax: (605) 339-0055

Springfield

City of Springfield
Dept. of Planning & Development
840 Boonville Avenue
Springfield, MO 65802
Phone: (417) 864-1031
Fax: (417) 864-1030

Springfield Area Chamber of Commerce
P.O. Box 1687
Springfield, MO 65801-1687
Phone: (417) 862-5567
Fax: (417) 862-1611

Appendix C

State Departments of Labor and Employment

Arkansas

Arkansas Dept. of Employ. Security
P.O. Box 2981
Little Rock, AR 72203-2981

Illinois

Illinois Dept. of Employment Security
Occupational Employment Statistics
401 S. State Street
Chicago, IL 60605

Indiana

Indiana Department of
Workforce Development
10 North Senate Avenue
Indianapolis, IN 46204

Iowa

Iowa Workforce Development
1000 East Grand Ave.
Des Moines, IA 50319-0209

Michigan

Michigan Employment
Security Commission
7310 Woodward Avenue
Detroit, MI 48202

Minnesota

Minnesota Department of
Economic Security
390 North Robert Street
St. Paul, MN 55101

Missouri

Missouri Department of Labor
& Industrial Relations
Division of Employment Security
PO Box 59
Jefferson City, MO 65104

Oklahoma

Oklahoma Employment
Security Commission
2401 North Lincoln
Oklahoma City, OK 73105

South Dakota

South Dakota Department of Labor
Labor Market Information Center
PO Box 4730
Aberdeen, SD 57402

Wisconsin

Wisconsin Department of Industry,
Labor & Human Relations
Bureau of Workforce Information
PO Box 7944
Madison, WI 53791